A Textbook of

Modern Macroeconomics

Theory, Policy and Practice

A Textbook of
Modern Macroeconomics
Theory, Policy and Practice

Second Edition

Lakshmi N. Dutta
Retired Professor of Economics
Ranchi University
Ranchi (Jharkhand)

I.K. International Pvt. Ltd.
NEW DELHI

Published by
I.K. International Pvt. Ltd.
4435-36/7, Ansari Road, Daryaganj
New Delhi-110002 (India)
E-mail: info@ikinternational.com
Website: www.ikbooks.com

ISBN 978-93-90620-89-0

Published by Krishan Makhijani for I.K. International Pvt. Ltd., 4435-36/7, Ansari Road, Daryaganj, New Delhi-110002 and Printed by Rekha Printers Pvt. Ltd., Okhla Industrial Area, Phase II, New Delhi–110 020.

Dedicated to

My parents

Late G.C. Dutta and Late Siddheshwari Dutta

Preface to the Second Edition

Enormous encouragement from the readers, my former colleagues as well as a constant inspiration from my publisher have prompted me to revise the first edition of my book. New developments in the world of macroeconomy over the past several years have been incorporated in the present edition in proper perspectives.

In the present edition, I have tried to put in place, in a large measure, the 'missing links', while at the same time, adding several new chapters to provide a complete macroeconomic framework.

As in the earlier edition, the present edition too contains enough illustrative examples on Indian macroeconomy.

In completing this edition, I have received valuable help from my son, Shubhendu in terms of solutions of knotty mathematical problems as well as other computational difficulties. My grandson, Ayanesh has also extended his helping hand, from time to time, towards preparing the typescript of this revised edition for which I am thankful to them.

Lakshmi N. Dutta

Preface to the First Edition

I took up writing this book at a time when the Great Recession (2008) had just set in the United States in the guise of 'sub-prime' crisis. The great fall of the ill-conceived notion of 'too big to fall' financial institutions in the United States spurred long debates and discussions among eminent economists of the United States and elsewhere regarding the efficacy of neo-liberal economic policies being pursued over much of the world economy. To me, it appeared that perhaps this would herald a beginning of rethinking of the current macroeconomic theories and policies. Predominantly, it is this thought that inspired me to write this book.

Since it has been written basically as a textbook, I don't claim to provide something 'new' in it. By and large, it is a review of major macroeconomic theories, supplemented by evidence principally from Indian economy as also from other economies of the world.

For past several years, there was also persistent demand from students pursuing economics courses at various levels for a good textbook on macroeconomics which would focus not only on theoretical aspects but also on applied aspects to help understand the working of Indian economy as well. Needless to say that most macroeconomics textbooks have been written in the context of western capitalist economies like Great Britain or US which do not often match the development environment of underdeveloped world. The present book is intended to fill this gap with ample evidence from Indian economic development.

The present book is the product of nearly four years of my post-retirement period. It is particularly significant in view of the fact that my post-retirement years have been full of jerks—the biggest jerk occurred when I suffered coronary heart problem followed by heart surgery. After recoupment, I was at a loss to find how to spend my spare time. Just at this time, precisely, the opportunity came and I finally took a decision to write this book. But as I could not put in sustained efforts, I managed to pool them whenever I could.

It is worth mentioning here that I used to teach Macroeconomics and Econometrics, besides other papers, to postgraduate classes. The class notes of the teaching days, needless to say, helped me a great deal in writing this book. The book is intended for the students of Economics (Honours), postgraduate Economics as well as students pursuing management courses.

Lakshmi N. Dutta

Acknowledgements

I would like to express my deepest sense of gratitude to my revered teacher, late Dr. R.N. Tripathy, who had time and again inspired me to write good books. Other colleagues who directly or indirectly helped my ideas to mature through various debates and discussions deserve my heartfelt thanks. The numerous students who interacted with me at various levels of my teaching career have always been a constant source of inspiration. In the completion of this book, my son, Shubhendu, has been an invaluable help in managing to obtain me all valuable and relevant materials, recently published books, journals and other materials—whenever required. He deserves special thanks for this. My debt goes to my wife, Arati, who helped me in looking after my health as also reminding me, from time to time, to finish my book at an early date. My grandson, Ayanesh, acted as 'interluder' amidst my writing as he entertained and refreshed my energy.

Lakshmi N. Dutta

Contents

PART-5
Post-Keynesian Macroeconomics

PART-6
Macro-theories of Consumption/Savings

PART-7
Economic Growth and Business Cycles

PART-8
Inflation and Phillips Curve

PART-9
International Macroeconomics

PART-10
Macroeconomic Policies

Introduction

1. MICROECONOMICS VS. MACROECONOMICS

Theoretical economics primarily falls into two broad fields, microeconomics and macroeconomics and it is often instructive to understand their broad contours. Just as we have, in ordinary parlance, the concepts of microscopic view as distinguished from macroscopic view, the former meaning a narrower view while the latter meaning a broader view of something, economics as a subject of study can also be looked at a smaller unit such as a household or a producing firm, a selling unit, a particular market and so on. On the other hand, it can be looked at from a larger, a more broad based unit such as the economy as a whole, the national or aggregate economy. Thus, while microeconomics is the study of parts, macroeconomics is the study of the whole. The whole is, of course, the sum total of the parts. In order to study the whole, however, one need not go into the details of the parts. Similarly, for studying the parts, one need not go deep into the whole. However, the studies of both are interrelated in the sense that before moving to the study of the whole we must have a workable knowledge of the parts.

Let us suppose, we intend to study the decision behaviour of a given household, how it decides to make purchases of a certain bundle of goods like various food items and services of various kinds, with a certain amount of money income and given a certain size of the household, our study pertains to the category of 'microeconomics'. Similarly, if our inquiry is centred around a production unit engaged in producing auto parts and tries to understand how he gets his finances managed, how he hires labour services, how he estimates his business profits and so on, the study is of the microeconomics category.

Similarly, if we take up a farm unit, an agricultural producer owning a particular size of farm, say 10 acres of land and tries to study his entire production cycle of crops grown during the whole year, how he disposes of his surplus produce and at what selling price, how he computes his farm profit, how much labour units he hires and from where he obtains credit, etc., we are again engaged in the study of microeconomics.

If we now change our perspective to understand the functioning of the entire economy, such as, how does the national income behave, why it is not growing rapidly enough, what is the status of investment and aggregate consumption in the national economy, why are prices rising so rapidly, why is the nation's income from abroad not satisfactory, we are in the domain of macroeconomics.

Then, every national economy has a national government who is responsible for its economic policy making for tackling its short-run and long-run problems. Such a government necessarily carries out the taxation and public expenditure functions for the broader socio-economic agenda. All these come under 'macroeconomics'. Thus, the division between microeconomics and macroeconomics is largely a matter of convenience but one approach feeds into the other for a complete understanding of the 'body economic' very like 'body politic'.

2. MAJOR CONCERNS, ISSUES AND MODEL BUILDING OF MACROECONOMICS

In the previous section, we broadly discussed what macroeconomics deals with and how it differs from microeconomics. In this section, we go somewhat deeper and dwell on major macroeconomic issues and concerns. At the same time, we attempt a broad framework within which these issues can be analysed and understood.

1. **Economic growth:** The first major issue with which macroeconomics is grappled is the long-run growth of the economy. Long-run growth can come through consistent rise in national output. Raising national output to the maximum potential level by utilising all productive resources is the basic of all macroeconomic issues. Every economy, therefore, must devise all possible means to achieve this goal. Economic growth, as some economists would think, is the issue in the very long run where supplies of productive resources are substantially increased through technological change as also by changes in the structure of demand. Population growth, and its patterns in the long run, happens to be one important component to account for such changes in the structure of demand.

   Strategies of economic growth may differ from developed to developing economies which are, initially, aspiring to climb the ladders of economic development. Hence, the time frame of the relative achievement of this goal will, most probably, differ. Also, the proximate determinant of development might also differ from country to country. But the aim of all groups of economies is basically the same, to achieve long-run economic growth. Economic growth necessarily carries with it consistent rise in the incomes of the people and the standard of living of the masses.
2. **Full employment/unemployment:** Intimately linked with the first concern is the maximisation of employment or to achieve a full employment goal. National economies and their governments must strive for providing adequate employment opportunities to their citizens for earning their respectful living. To put it otherwise, national economies must set the goal of reaching zero or near zero unemployment rate.

Unemployment gives rise to numerous socioeconomic and political issues which, in turn, creates various short term and long-term problems in the economic system. However, it has to be conceded that unemployment is the product of structural changes in the economy. Sometimes, cyclical factors such as economic downturn that accompany every capitalist economy are also responsible for generating unemployment. By constantly watching and monitoring the labour market and the employment / unemployment data, the macroeconomic policy makers have to devise appropriate policies to tackle fluctuations in output in a manner to reduce unemployment of workers in the economy.

3. **Business cycles:** As mentioned in the previous section, business cycles are yet another macroeconomic issue that plague economic as well as political policy makers. It is now widely accepted that business cycles (booms and recessions) are inescapable events in a capitalist economy. There are phases of uptrend in the economy when overall conditions are improving, business expectations are high and optimistic, market demand is high and so do employment, and incomes of the people.

   Similarly, there are downward phases in the economy when, due to one or several factors, businesses are sluggish, expectations are low and pessimistic and so incomes, output and employment continue to fall. Unemployment, is naturally on the rise. To understand the inherent causes of such cyclical behaviour of the economy as well as to devise appropriate macroeconomic policies to deal with is another concern of macroeconomics.

4. **Inflation/deflation:** Inflation, or the phenomenon of rise in the prices of commodities in the economy is another important concern of macroeconomics. Inflation adversely affects the cost of living of the people. Unjustified and abnormal inflation is a constant headache for economists and political policy makers. Macroeconomists need to be watchful about the trend in inflation that affects different groups of people differently in the society. At the same time, very low level of inflation that adversely affects production and profits in the economy has to be avoided. Deflation, or the falling price levels, is equally worrisome for macroeconomists. Therefore, macroeconomists' concern is to devise specific policies with regard to the maximum tolerable limit of inflation rate while keeping an eye on the minimum level below which inflation may not turn into deflation, the falling level of prices. It is widely believed that inflation is the result of excessive increase of money supply in the economy. This may be partially true. But macroeconomics is concerned with both the demand side as well as supply side factors of inflation both from the short run and long runs. Macroeconomists, naturally, need to devise appropriate policies to deal with inflation problem.

5. **Internal and external management of the economy:** To observe and oversee the internal health of the economy is also an important aspect of macroeconomic concern. The issue of internal management of the economy is linked with raising adequate resources in terms of taxes and other sources of revenue as well as their prudent spending for the overall progress of the economy and society. In fact, three important aspects are relevant in terms of overall health of the economy:
   - (i) **Fiscal management:** Government expenditures on various development and non-development items with an ultimate objective of social welfare is a vital area of fiscal policy. Similarly, formulating taxation policies and raising tax resources from individual and corporate incomes as well as commodities and services taxes are equally important concerns. For sound health of the economy, maintaining a reasonable balance is essential. Sometimes, governments set a certain target of fiscal deficit to achieve a reasonable balance.
   - (ii) **Monetary management:** Alongside fiscal management is also important the monetary management. This requires ensuring a well developed financial institutions (such as banks, insurance agencies and other non-bank institutions) so that the supply of money and financial resources (loanable funds) in the economy is sufficient to fulfil the demand for such resources (loanable funds). Macroeconomists' task is to monitor the functioning of these financial institutions with specific focus on the policies of the apex bank, the central bank of the country.
   - (iii) **External management of the economy:** Macroeconomics is equally concerned with the management of its external sector. By external sector we mean the country's trade and financial relationship with rest of other countries. Such relationships are broadly captured by what is referred to the balance of payments. Macroeconomists analyse various aspects of balance of payments including the external value of the national currency and even suggest ways to correct any imbalance that occurs on this front.

The formal model building:

An economic model building is a pretty abstract exercise by which dominant variables that influence the great events occurring in the economy can be captured so that future events can be predicted. This is essential, because every detail of the causes of any event cannot be explained most of which may be much less important than the dominant factors. Also, in economics, as in other social sciences, time perspective becomes important, because certain variables are important in the short period (or short run) while certain others assume importance only in the long period (or long run).

Macroeconomics requires such a model showing all the dominant variables interacting with each other at different time perspectives. We attempt such an exercise below:

Aggregate demand, aggregate supply and price level:

In macroeconomics, as in microeconomics, an economy-wide equilibrium model is needed. Such a model can be visualised in terms of aggregate demand and aggregate supply in relation to the average level of prices in the economy. The derivation of aggregate demand and aggregate supply is postponed for the time being for technical reasons. However, we will note that major variables that affect aggregate demand can be obtained from the expenditure components of GNP, the gross national product. These are identified as (a) consumption expenditures, (b) investment expenditures, (c) government expenditures and (d) net exports or, exports minus imports. The last component represents net foreign demand for domestic goods and services. The factors influencing aggregate supply are (a) supplies of productive resources and (b) technology. Supplies of productive resources include the availability of land, labour and capital while technology refers to a particular body of knowledge relating to production and distribution of goods and services available at a particular period of time. The behaviour of aggregate supply, clearly, depends on the time horizon we have. If we consider short period or, short run, spanning roughly five-six years,(although, economists disagree on exact time span of short or long runs), when there are enough possibilities of unused or unemployed productive resources, we can say that aggregate output will continue to respond to aggregate demand. How do these two forces, aggregate demand and aggregate supply, respond to general level of prices? The answer is that, at a given level of prices aggregate supply will be infinitely large. In Fig. 0.1, this may be depicted as a horizontal curve

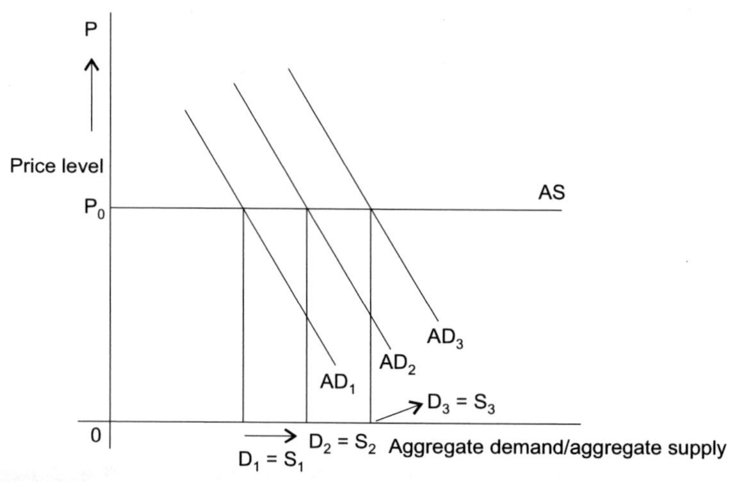

Figure 0.1 *Short run AD/AS model*

at a certain given price. The aggregate demand curve, however, will show up as downward sloping from left to right with respect to price level, thus suggesting that at higher level of aggregate prices, the aggregate demand will be less while at low level of prices, aggregate demand will be high. However, equilibrium of the economy will not be possible except at the point of intersection of the two curves (Fig. 0.1). In fact, this is one extreme case of our model. The model also suggests that shifting of aggregate demand curve to the right will result in higher output and real income without affecting the level of prices (or inflation).

The other extreme of our model is the case of full utilisation of all the productive resources and the economy operating at *potential* output level. This is, obviously, a full employment level where unemployment rate is limited to just the natural rate, i.e., unemployment that arises due to workers changing jobs from one place to another and searching for new jobs, better known as 'frictional unemployment.' In this case, the shape of the aggregate supply curve is vertical suggesting no further scope of expanding aggregate output. Here, all the policies intending to raise aggregate demand, just end up in raising the level of prices (inflation). This is the long-run situation (Fig. 0.2).

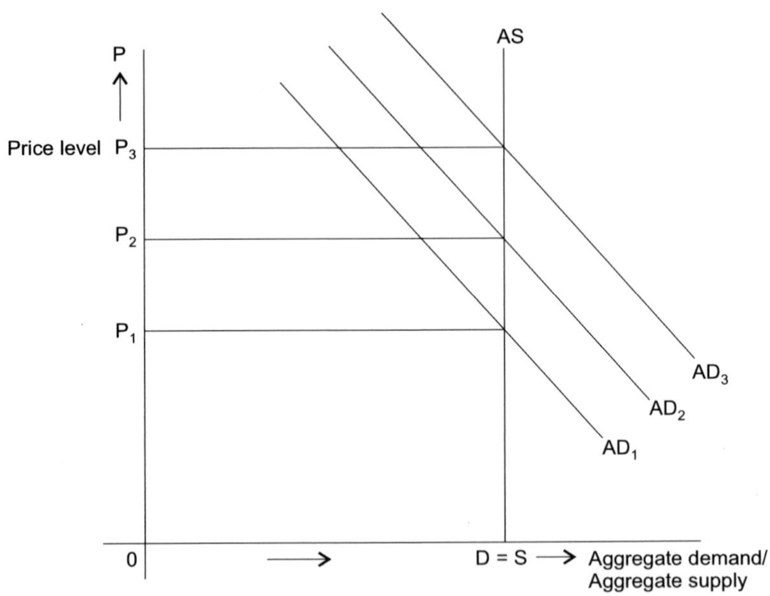

Figure 0.2 *Long-run AD/AS model*

All other macroeconomic models fall in between these two extreme cases and are, mostly, the medium-run or intermediate cases where both aggregate supply curve and aggregate demand curve behave normally-both responding to the level of prices. Different sub models can be created based on different sets of assumptions within these two limits (Fig. 0.3).

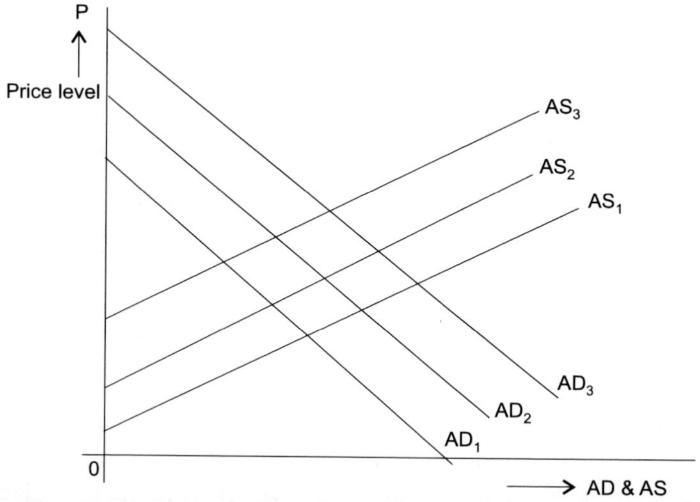

Figure 0.3 *Intermediate AD/ AS model*

It is worth mentioning here that the first model shown in Fig. (0.1) represents the Keynesian model of the short-run variety while the second one depicted by Fig. (0.2) represents the classical model of long-run variety.

If our time horizon is very long, spanning more than fifty years or so, our model suggests outright shifting of the vertical aggregate supply curve because, in the very long run, our focus is on growth of the economy whereby stock of aggregate supply of goods and services increase manifold (Fig. 0.4).

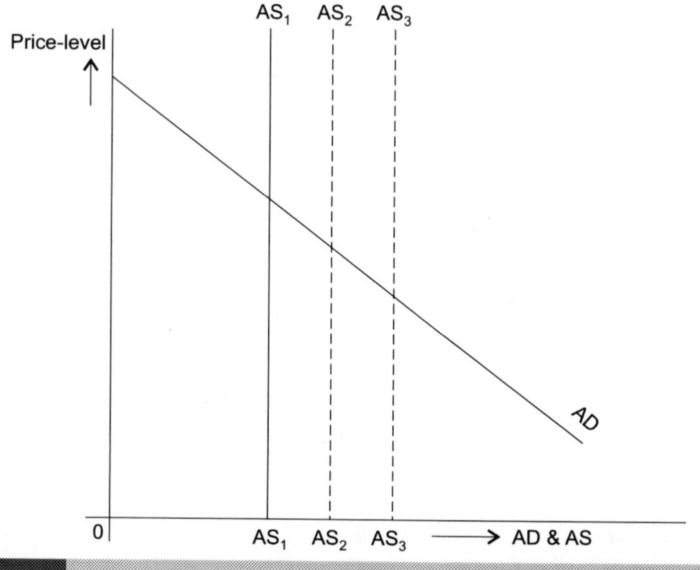

Figure 0.4 *Very long-run AD/AS model*

3 MICROFOUNDATION OF MACROECONOMICS

Most macroeconomic relationships originate from the micro level relationships that are found in human behaviour. For instance, consumption behaviour at the macro or the aggregate level can largely be observed in the micro or household level. In fact, aggregate consumption behaviour is nothing but reflection of the aggregated (or average) micro level or household level behaviour. Similarly, firm level production relationships when suitably aggregated, will produce macro level relationships, although there are methodological problems associated with any such aggregation process. Similar macro level relations in other areas can be observed in the micro, household, firm or industry levels as well. We can conclude, therefore, that macroeconomics has largely the microfoundation behind its structure. Also, just as there are certain basic assumptions which hold in the microeconomic relations (e.g. maximization of utility/profit for individual units) these are equally implied when dealing with macroeconomic relations.

However, there are certain exceptions. The government, for instance, has its own economic agenda on which it works. When government formulates certain policies and implements them, economic agents (individuals, firms, other businesses) have to make adjustments with their respective behaviours. For instance, in matters of taxation, if government imposes certain taxes on the citizens, they have to make suitable adjustments to their purchase or sales plans. However, this should not be understood as one way causation. If government is elected on democratic principles, its members represent the people of the country and hence represent also the wishes and aspirations of the people. The people, at the micro level can, therefore, influence the economic or other policies being pursued or intended to be pursued by the government indirectly through their elected representatives. Therefore, policy formulations as well as implementation at the macro level by the government also, to a large extent, reflect the micro level decisions of the people.

Interdependence of Micro- and Macroeconomics

In terms of pure theoretical analysis, it is obvious that a good number of macroeconomic relations are derived from their micro level relationships even though the process of derivations are sometimes complicated. When, at primary levels, household behaviour is derived on theoretical basis and expressed in some kind of suggested or approximate relationships between or among variables we obtain market behaviour. An example of this kind is, derivation from individual level or (household level) demand curve, to market demand curve (quantity demanded is negatively related to price, other things remaining the same). Now, market demands of all goods and services, if suitably aggregated will produce the aggregate demand curve which would apply to the entire economy. Similarly, aggregate supply curve for the economy can also be derived from individual, firm level supply curves. Certain disturbances or bottlenecks at the micro level will be reflected in the macro level relationships provided they are of relatively long duration nature. However, application of appropriate macroeconomic policies may correct such disturbances or imbalances at the macro level. It is possible, though, that incorrect or inadequate macro policies may not produce the desired results.

Change in the behaviour pattern of the individual members of the societies, most likely, produces change or shift in the existing macro relationships. For instance, if all producers, for some reason or other, collectively decide to supply lesser amounts of goods and services at the same old price level, the collective impact will be the shifting of the aggregate supply curve towards the left at the macro level. Similarly, if individual savers prefer to spend more on consumption and save less, aggregate savings (supply of loanable funds) will be reduced, thus shifting to the left the supply curve of loanable funds which will have the ultimate effect on the price of loanable funds (rate of interest going up). On the other hand, if government imposes, at the macro level, certain taxes or incurs useful public expenditures, the consumption expenditure will, most likely, be reduced or enhanced, as the case may be, at the micro level. Likewise, a new invention and its subsequent public use will have a far reaching effects on micro as well as macro levels– much to the social and economic benefits. Innovations, in any field in the same manner may percolate from macro to micro levels or go upwards from micro to macro levels.

The interdependence between macro and microeconomic relations can better be captured with the help of the following types of schematic pattern.

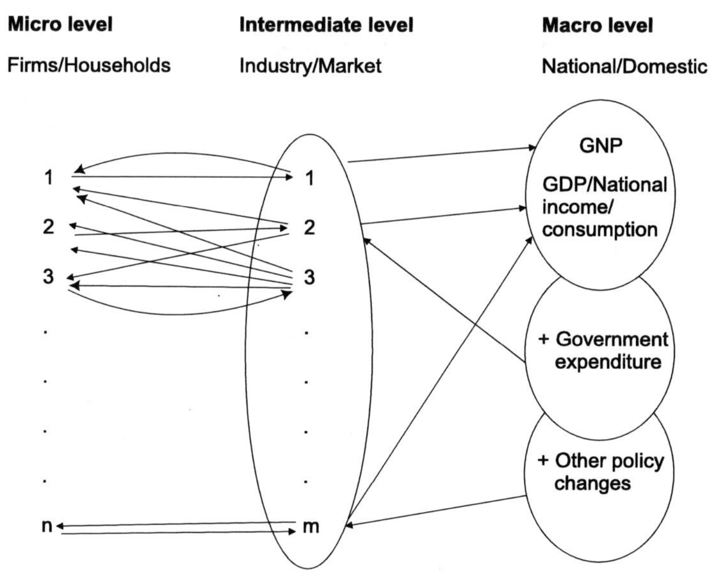

The above schematic shows two-way relationship as well as interdependence between macro and micro levels. Assuming the economy consists of 'n' number of producing firms and similar number of households who, respectively, take their individual decisions about how much to produce about certain good or service, how much resources to employ for the purpose and how to sell them to the market. Households would similarly decide how much to consume of a certain good or service, how much to spend on various goods and services and how to earn their incomes by selling their labour days or hours or using some other means of income or assets. These individual decisions on the part of firms or households find their expressions in the collective market or industry levels–industry levels for firms and market levels for household consumers. When all industry level or market level decisions are aggregated they find expressions in what is known as macro level aggregates such as GNP, GDP, NI, etc., and aggregate consumptions, savings or investment expenditures. This is how macro aggregates depend upon micro level behaviour. On the other hand, national governments and their designated authorities are concerned about these macro aggregates. Their concern is to run the government, conduct its different activities–economic, political, social, cultural, etc. based on their own predesigned policies. They arrange for adequate national resources particularly for growing population and for development purposes. They need to tax the individuals and business firms on their incomes. The government then form a certain policy on public expenditure and make changes in them whenever and however necessary. The effects of these policies percolate to the micro levels via their intermediate levels as shown in the schematic through arrows. Micro level agents then make suitable alterations/adjustments in the production and consumption behaviour. Similarly, if the country's central bank takes a decision to expand the supply of money and credit in order to meet the growing needs of the economic system, its effects will trickle down to the market as also to all micro level units including individuals who will find their income levels increased via different productive activities. These incomes will be translated into higher individual demand and ultimately higher aggregate demand. If individual supplies of goods and services fail to respond immediately or respond inadequately to demand stimuli, the aggregate supply rise will lag behind the aggregate demand rise and the result will be rise in the level of prices (or, inflation). This, in brief, illustrates how macro or aggregate level decisions in one direction get ultimately reflected in other micro variables but only through all related micro level channels.

PART-1

National Income Analysis

1

National Income Analysis

SECTION I: BASIC CONCEPTS

The basic purpose of this chapter is to provide an exposure to the readers the fundamental concept of national income and several other related concepts which, in some way or the other, run through the entire book. In fact, macroeconomics is concerned with the interrelationships among the aggregative concepts that we are going to discuss in this chapter. A proper understanding of national income analysis is, therefore, essential to grasp the rest of the topics of the book.

The chapter is divided essentially into two parts. Part one deals with the meaning and concepts of national income, national output and other aggregative concepts as well as their measurements and interrelationships with each other. The second part is concerned with circular flow of income.

As we have mentioned in the previous section, macroeconomics is the study of the aggregates. The most important aggregates, in this regard, are the 'National Income' or 'National Output' and Gross Domestic Product (GDP). However, there are a few other concepts which are related to these, such as, National Capital, Investment, Depreciation, Capital formation, Inventories, etc. We shall try to understand these concepts and their significance.

1.1 GROSS DOMESTIC PRODUCT (GDP)

We know that during a particular period of time (a year, for instance) a country's economic resources (land, including forests, water and other natural resources, all forms of capital, all means of transport and communication, together with labour force are constantly engaged in producing a series of goods and services which are "finally" consumed by the people of that country. The value of these finally produced goods and services which, of course, are produced within the national territory is known as the Gross Domestic Product (GDP).

1.2 NET DOMESTIC PRODUCT (NDP)

It has to be remembered, however, that the resources or factors which enter into production process are not all of such kinds that are used up fully and finished once for all. Some of these resources are such (for instance machines, farm and factory implements, etc.) that have longer life period than just one year. These resources, known as durable use factors of production, gradually depreciate in value by constant use year after year and finally become useless at the end of their life periods. Now, in order to compensate such year after year loss, a part of the Gross Domestic Product needs to be set aside which is known as cost on depreciation or 'depreciation allowance' or 'capital consumption'. When we deduct such depreciation cost/allowance from the GDP we obtain Net Domestic Product. Thus, GDP = NDP + Dep. All. Alternatively, NDP = GDP – Dep. All.

1.3 GDP/NDP AT FACTOR COST AND MARKET PRICE

When the question of valuing GDP or NDP arises, there are, basically, two methods of doing it:

(i) On the basis of factor costs

(ii) On the basis of market prices.

If GDP is measured at factor costs, i.e., on the basis of all costs of factors of production like rent of land, wages of labour, interest on capital (as well as depreciation cost of capital) and entrepreneurs' profit/remuneration, it is called GDP at factor cost. It includes all costs of the products before they enter the market. In fact, after the products leave their farm or factory gates, a few more costs are added. These are: (a) indirect taxes (such as excise duties, VAT). But sometimes government bears a part of the actual market price to help the consumers obtain them at lower than actual market price. This part is known as 'government subsidies'.

When measuring GDP at market prices, total of such subsidies needs to be deducted. Thus we can write:

GDP at market prices = GDP at factor costs + Indirect taxes – Subsidies

Again, each of the components of GDP can be evaluated either at current price-level or constant price-level. The difference between the two is explained below.

GDP at Current Price-Level

When evaluated at the price-level prevailing in the year for which GDP is measured, it is known as GDP at current price-level. It is also known as nominal GDP. For example, if we are concerned with GDP of India for the year, 2005-06 and all the items included in GDP are measured in terms of their prices prevailing in 2005-06, the money value of the GDP is the current-price or nominal GDP. Similarly, nominal GDP for any other accounting or fiscal year can be obtained.

GDP at Constant Price-Level

When some base year is chosen and GDPs of all different years are expressed in terms of price-level of all goods of the base year, then GDP so obtained is known as GDP at constant prices. The implication is that GDP values for different years change not in terms of their prices (since prices are held at the same level of the selected base year) but, if at all, in terms of quantities of goods and services produced. Since, actual quantities or volumes in GDP are more important for all practical purposes, such changes are real value changes. For this reason, such GDP measure is known as GDP in real terms or real GDP.

Now, the basic question is, given the GDPs in current prices, how can we convert them into GDPs in constant prices, i.e., at prices of some selected base period? There are basically two methods of doing this.

1. To select the base period/year (like 2000-01) and record the bundle of goods and services included in GDP along with their price-levels. For any period thereafter, like 2008-09 for instance, we keep the same bundle of goods and services (possibly with their changed quantities) and evaluate them at the prices of 2000-01, i.e., the base period. The new value of GDP will give GDP at constant prices (or, real GDP in the year 2008-09.
2. The second method is to calculate a number (or, ratio) known as "GDP deflator" and then divide the nominal GDP of a given year by this deflator. A deflator is defined as a number or coefficient that "deflates" or reduces the value of some other number. Usually, GDP deflator is expressed in terms of an 'index number' which can be obtained by the following method:

$$\text{GDP deflator} = \frac{\begin{array}{c}\text{Cost of purchase of a given bundle of}\\ \text{goods and services at current year's prices}\end{array}}{\begin{array}{c}\text{Cost of purchase of the same bundle of}\\ \text{goods and services at base year's prices}\end{array}} \times 100$$

Here, both the numerator and the denominator are expressed in terms of index numbers. But while the denominator is assigned the number 100 (since, it is the base year's cost of purchase and helps easy comparison), the numerator actually depends upon the price-movements of different goods and services that enter the GDP calculation.[1]

[1] In fact, the whole task of collection of relevant data and calculation of GDP is usually assigned to certain government organization/agency. For instance, in India, Central Statistical Organisation (CSO) has been given this responsibility.

Now, supposing the index number of the numerator is expressed as 130, then the GDP deflator = 130/100 or, in percentage term, i.e., $\frac{130}{100} \times 100 = 130$ for the current year. If we now divide GDP at current prices, by this ratio (130/100), we get the real GDP for the year 2008-09. Therefore, real GDP in 2008-09 will be calculated as:

$$\frac{\text{Nominal GDP in 2008-09}}{\frac{130}{100}} = \frac{\text{Nominal GDP in 2008-09} \times 100}{130}$$

This is equivalent to dividing the nominal GDP in 2008-09 by 1.3.

In the similar manner, real GDP for any period following or preceding the base year can be calculated with the help of GDP deflator thus obtained. It is obvious now that GDP deflator will change from year to year depending upon the price-level changes.[1] (For this reason, GDP deflator is also known as the best measure of inflation).

In Table 2.1, data on GDP at both current and constant prices are reproduced for Indian economy for a six-year period (2004-05 to 2009-10) which have a base period of 2004-05. We may mention here that both sets of data have already been prepared and published by India's CSO, using appropriate deflators, about which we have no knowledge. But, still, we can make use of these data to obtain "implicit" GDP deflators which we have done and presented in the last column of Table 1.1.

Table 1.1 *GDP at current prices and GDP at constant prices (India: 2008-09)*

Base year: 2004-05 = 100 *(At market price)* *(Amount in ₹ crores)*

Years 1	*At current prices* 2	*At constant prices* 3	*Implicit deflator* 4 = (2 ÷ 3) × 100
2004-05	3242209	3242209	100.0000
2005-06	3692485	3544348	104.1795
2006-07	4293672	3872974	110.8624
2007-08	4986426	4253184	117.2398
2008-09	5582623	4462967	125.0877
2009-10	6550271	4869317	134.5213

Source: CSO/http//:www.rbi.org.in

It is worth mentioning in this connection that almost all major macro aggregates are presented in two sets of values–one at constant prices and the other at current prices.

[1] Readers are advised to consult any book on statistics which explains the method of index number calculation.

1.4 GROSS NATIONAL PRODUCT (GNP)

Gross National Product is a broader concept. It includes, with GDP values, the values of products/incomes that are generated or earned abroad by domestic resources which go out of the country in search of earnings. For example, resources like labour, capital and entrepreneurship can, under liberalised rules through trade and investment connections, move out to other countries. Similarly, such resources can move in from other countries to work within the domestic economy. The net earnings from GNP, therefore, can be defined as the value of all final goods and services produced within the national territory with domestic resources + net resources income from abroad.

These resources, that is, earnings received minus the earnings paid, is added to the gross domestic product to give gross national product.

1.5 NET NATIONAL PRODUCT (NNP)

Just as we dealt with Net Domestic Product by deducting 'depreciation' or 'capital consumption' part from GDP, similarly, we can deduct the depreciation or capital consumption portion from GNP also to arrive at Net National Product (NNP). Needless to add that some of these depreciation costs originate in foreign countries where domestic capital resources of durable nature have moved. Hence, depreciation costs in both GDP and GNP will not be the same. Thus, we can write:

$$\text{NNP} = \text{GNP} - \text{Dep./Capital consumption}$$

1.6 NATIONAL INCOME (NI)

If the approach is from the point of view of factor incomes, viz., incomes earned by land, labour, capital and enterprise in the form of rent, wages, interest and profit and add them together, we obtain national income. Some of these incomes may be earned within the domestic economy or outside, if the factors of production work outside the economy. However, care has to be taken to see that just as factor incomes are earned outside the country, foreign factors of production, particularly labour and capital, may work inside the country so that their incomes may go out of the country. Therefore, only net incomes of the factors (i.e., incomes earned – incomes paid out) are added to the national income. It is clear, therefore, that if net incomes from abroad is positive (i.e., more incomes earned than incomes paid out) national income will be larger than domestic income. On the other hand, if net income from abroad is negative, national income will be less than the domestic income. We can write, thus,

$$\text{National Income (NI)} = \text{Domestic Factor Income} + \text{Net Factor Income from abroad.}$$

Essentially, there is little difference between the two aggregates: National Product and National Income. Only the approach of looking at the two is different. In fact, we can safely write

Net National Product (NNP) = National Income.

This will be immediately clear if we remember that GNP, like GDP, is the value of final goods and services produced during a specified period of time. Out of this, 'depreciation cost' or capital consumption is deducted so that what is left is called 'value-added total'. And we have already seen that GNP – Dep. = NNP. So NNP = Value-added total. This value-added total is then distributed among the factors of production. Thus, rent is paid for land use, wages and salaries are paid for all forms of labour including managerial remuneration, interest and dividend are paid for the use of capital and the rest is paid as profit of the entrepreneur including his organizational ability. Adding all these, therefore, gives the factor incomes total or 'national income'.

1.7 DISPOSABLE INCOME

Incomes earned by factors of production are not necessarily fully retained by them. A certain part of such incomes is generally paid out to government in the form of direct taxes (such as income tax, wealth tax and corporation/municipal tax). The rest, i.e., total earned income – direct taxes is defined as disposable income. However, such earnings include transfer payments by government. This is the part of the earnings which is 'spendible' and fit for expenditure on various goods and services. However, if the whole of this 'spendible' income is not spent, the balance is known as 'saving'. For such individuals who do not have to pay any of the above-mentioned taxes, the whole of the earning is equivalent to disposable income.

1.8 TRANSFER PAYMENTS

Transfer payments refer to a kind of payments which are not part of actual earnings of factors of production, but are gratuitous payments or for welfare reasons or simply as gestures of goodwill. For instance, 'pension' received by retired employees of the government, other social security benefits, charity contributions by various business classes or individuals to any voluntary institution or religious trusts, etc., are examples of transfer payments. Obviously, transfer payments are made without expectation of any return (or, quid-pro-quo). Transfer payments are not included in the calculation of national income.

1.9 PERSONAL INCOME

Personal income is defined as the earnings (after deductions on account of compulsory savings in the form of contribution to provident fund and other social security schemes) but before the direct taxes are paid. Therefore, the difference between 'disposable' and 'personal' incomes lies in whether direct taxes have been deducted from the net earnings or not. We can, accordingly write:

Disposable income = Gross earnings – Social security contributions
– Direct taxes + Transfer payments

Personal income = Gross earnings – Social security contributions

1.10 NATIONAL CAPITAL

National capital is the sum total of capital assets of the nation valued at a certain price-level on a specific point in time. Its main components are: (a) gross fixed capital assets and (b) inventories. Gross fixed assets are all assets of durable nature. This includes their regular depreciation costs. The nation, for instance possesses a variety of physical assets like railways, roads, dams, airports, factories, government buildings, other house property, waterways, defence equipment, etc., besides all privately owned assets. There are methods of valuing them and aggregating them–the task generally taken up by the designated government agency. However, if certain capital assets belong to foreign nationals or governments, working in domestic country, these are deducted from the total value. Similarly, if some capital asset belonging to the domestic government is kept abroad to work, their values are added.

Inventories are the stocks of raw materials and finished goods that the producers of the nation maintain during a certain time period. Such stocks are kept for the smooth operation of the production system. 'Capital' is a stock variable. The value of national capital needs to be stock variable. The value of material capital needs to be measured on a particular date of the year. For instance, stock of capital as on 31st March 2005 will have some meaning and not that during the year of 2005.

Investment: Any addition to the stock of capital after allowance is made for 'depreciation' or 'wear and tear' of the existing capital is termed *investment.* Therefore, it is *net addition* to capital stock. For instance, the capital stock as on 31st March 2000 valued at current prices is ₹ 10,000 crore and that it becomes ₹ 10,500 crore on 31st March, 2001. The addition to capital stock or investment during the one year period (1st April 2000 – 31st March, 2001) is, therefore, ₹ 500 crore. This is, however, defined as the 'gross investment' since this includes replacement investment—the investment that is needed to replace the old worn-out capital assets. When the amount is left out, the remaining is defined as net investment. It may be noted here that the concept of investment is a flow concept although capital and wealth are stock concepts. Gross investment is the same thing as 'gross fixed capital formation'.

Stocks and Flows

The two concepts, stocks and flows as mentioned above, need to be clarified further. Let us try to understand with an example. In a water reservoir the amount of water measured as at 6 a.m. of 1st May, 2003, stands at 10,000 litres. Since, water is constantly flowing in and flowing out of the reservoir, its stock is also changing depending upon how much is flowing in against how much flowing out. Hence, its stock can be measured only on a particular point in time as mentioned above. However, net flow of water (amount flowing in – amount flowing out) during a particular day (and time) can be measured as the difference of stocks at two different points in time. During this period, the water is a 'flow' variable very like the concept of capital vis-à-vis investment. Examples of flow concepts are: income, expenditure, savings, investments, imports, exports, etc., on the other hand, concepts like capital, wealth, money supply, foreign exchange reserves, consumer price index numbers, etc., are examples of stock variables.

1.11 RELATIONSHIP BETWEEN STOCK AND FLOW VARIABLES

Certain stock variables have their flow counterpart, while flow variables can be converted into stock variables. For instance, a certain stock of wealth (like house property or bonds) results in the flow of income over a period of time. Similarly, a certain stock of national capital at the beginning of a year results in investment in the subsequent period which is the flow counterpart. Similarly, a certain machine represents a stock variable but the services of the machine during a year for use is a flow variable. Likewise, investment activities together during a certain period of time might result in larger capital stock at certain other point in time.

1.12 MEASUREMENT/ESTIMATION OF NATIONAL PRODUCT/ NATIONAL INCOME

Measurement of national income is a very complicated method. There are several types of difficulties associated with the measurement. The task of measuring national income is assigned to an independent body equipped with sufficient knowledge and expertise. In India, Central Statistical Organisation (CSO) is mainly responsible for measuring the national income and other related statistics.

There are basically three methods of measurement of national income: (1) Product census method, (2) Income method and (3) Expenditure method. The product census method is also known as the 'value added method'.

1.12.1 Product Census (Value Added) Method

This method takes a complete census of all final products that are produced during a particular time period. Alternatively, at each stage of production, all the 'values added' are to be taken into account. Value added means value of the product minus input costs of production.

In fact, value of all final products includes all values added in the whole production process. Therefore, following either of the two methods, gives the correct estimation of national income (product) provided there are no foreign transactions for the time being. Clearly, there is the risk of 'double counting' in the estimation process unless sufficient care is taken not to erroneously include final products and some intermediate products or values added along with input costs.

In India, generally, the primary sector GDP (agricultural GDP along with its allied activities like forestry, logging, fishery animal husbandry and mining) as well as registered manufacturing is estimated by this method. Certain items need to be excluded while some others included while applying this method. For instance, inventories or unsold stocks of goods should be included. Every year, at the beginning, the nation inherits certain stocks of goods which remained unused in the previous year but which await their use in the current year. Similarly, at the end of the year, certain stocks are left out which means accumulation of new inventories. Such accumulated addition of inventories ought to be included in the product census method.

Some examples of value added method

1. Bread manufacturing

(a) Stage 1: Farmer grows wheat and adds value equal to ₹2000 per quintal.

(b) Stage 2: He sells this to flour manufacturer @ ₹ 2000 who in turn grinds wheat into flour and thereby adds some more value equal to ₹ 2100 and sells the same to bread manufacturer at this price. (₹ 2100).

(c) Stage 3: The bread manufacturer now adds further value by whatever process/processes the bread manufacturing requires and finally sells it to the consumers of bread for ₹ 2500. Thus, there are mainly 3 stages involved in this example, although some other stages might be involved.

Now the value added in this case can be calculated as follows:

Stage 1: ₹ 2000.

Stage 2: ₹ 2100 – ₹ 2000 = ₹ 100.

Stage 3: ₹ 2500 – ₹ 2100 = ₹ 400.

The total value added is therefore, ₹ 2000 + ₹ 100 + ₹ 400 = ₹ 2500 which is the value of the final product, i.e., bread.

2. Readymade Cotton Garment

(a) Stage 1: The cotton grower grows raw cotton on the field and adds value to it equivalent to ₹ 1000 per bale. He sells the cotton at this price to the stockist of cotton.

(b) Stage 2: The stockist adds further value to it by properly maintianing the bales of cotton in his warehouse. He sells the bale @ ₹ 1200 to the yarn manufacturer.

(c) Stage 3: Yarn manufacturer produces cotton yarn and thereby adds further value and sells it to the textile mill owner @ ₹ 1500.

(d) Stage 4: The textile mill owner, through various processes in his mill, produces cotton textile and thereby adds value. He sells the textile to the readymade garment manufacturer for ₹ 2000.

(e) Stage 5: Garment manufacturer in turn, produces readymade garment equivalent to ₹ 2500. This is the final value of the readymade garment after all the value additions.

Let us now calculate the separate value added at each stage of production:

Stage 1 ₹ 1000
Stage 2 ₹ 1200 – ₹ 1000 = ₹ 200.
Stage 3 ₹ 1500 – ₹ 1200 = ₹ 300.
Stage 4 ₹ 2000 – ₹ 1500 = ₹ 500.
Stage 5 ₹ 2500 – ₹ 2000 = ₹ 500.

The total amount of value added, therefore, is sum total of ₹ 1000 + ₹ 200 + ₹ 300 + ₹ 500 + ₹ 500 = ₹ 2500.

It is clear from the above example that at each stage of production of a certain final product, raw material costs enter into the value of the product besides other costs. Since, at the final stage of production these raw material costs are already included, we exclude them in estimating the value of the final product. In other words, if we include the cost of some or all these raw materials by mistakes or oversight, we would be committing an error known as error of 'double counting'. Now, just as value added can be estimated for a single final product, it can be estimated for all final products at the aggregate level – first by different industries or sectors and then aggregating them over the whole economy to get at the gross domestic product (GDP) at factor cost.

An important point to be noticed here is that in the value-added method only raw material costs of the current year's production are excluded but not those that are drawn from previous or any past year's production. These latter products, in fact, act as 'depreciation costs'. If we exclude these depreciation costs also, we actually get at the 'value added' or Net Domestic Product (NDP). Clearly, all factor payments are made out of this value-added total. Payments for rent, wages, interest, profit as well as depreciation costs are made out of gross value added excluding depreciation cost from this total, therefore, gives the sum total of factor payment viz., rent, wages, interest and profit, which is another way or method of measurement of GDP/GNP by income method.

1.12.2 Income Method

In the income method, incomes accruing in the form of rent, wages, interest and profits are to be added for all citizens of the country. Obviously, these are factor incomes, i.e., incomes as owners of factors of production. Estimation process of these factor incomes encounters certain problems. For those factors which are exchangeable in the market and have their market prices do not produce any problem. But those which are not actually exchanged; for instance, owned landed property like agricultural land or living houses, labourers working for their own occupations (self-employed workers), capital employed in own business enterprises and entrepreneurs organizing and undertaking risks for own organisation, pose the proper valuation problems. Normally, they are 'imputed' values for their output. But appropriate price for such valuation is a problem. There are several methods for different factor incomes which are often not satisfactory.

Secondly, certain types of income like 'transfer payments' by government must not be included in the income estimates. Transfer payments are not made for current production nor are they made against any return. Hence, they do not form part of the national income. Thirdly, incomes of the professionals like doctors, lawyers, other consultants and similar professionals are difficult to estimate since they often do not keep true records of their incomes. Even the fees charged from individual clients, often differ.

1.12.3 The Expenditure Method

This method estimates GNP by aggregating all expenditures made by residents of the country on consumption goods and investment goods. Similar expenditure by the government on purchases of goods and services of either consumption or investment category are added to form total expenditure. Thus, total expenditures are divided between: (a) private expenditures and (b) public expenditures. However, like the product census methods, expenditures on final goods and services only are included and those on intermediate goods are excluded. Also, expenditures at market prices are to be evaluated.

It may be mentioned here that whichever method is adopted, all lead to identical results. In other words:

$$\text{NNP} = NI = C + I + G$$

where, C = Private Consumption Expenditure, I = Private Investment Expenditure and G = Government Expenditure.

1.13 NATIONAL INCOME IDENTITIES IN A CLOSED ECONOMY

As we mentioned earlier, in the national income estimation, the results are the same even though methods are different. This will be amply clear when we decompose the different components of each method. On this basis, we give below some of the main identities in the national income calculation.

Consumption Expenditure (Private) + Investment Expenditure (Private)
= NNP at factor cost = National Income
= Consumption Expenditure + Savings (1.1)

Now from this accounting identity if consumption expenditure is subtracted from both sides we get

Investment Expenditure = Savings (1.2)

This means that an increase/decrease in savings is transmitted into an increase/decrease in investment. This can be understood otherwise also. We know that investment expenditures are composed of inventory accumulation and net investment. Any change in savings also means a change in consumption expenditure, i.e., increase in savings is equivalent to decrease in consumption expenditures and decrease in savings is equivalent to increase in consumption expenditures. Therefore, when savings increase consumption expenditures decrease which is reflected in the rise in inventory accumulation, i.e., increase in investment. Similar logic holds for a decrease in savings.

Now, the same identity gets changed when government sector is introduced. We have seen earlier that the government imposes indirect taxes on the citizens as also grants subsidies on certain goods and services. This makes all the difference between the NNP at factor cost and that at market price. We have noted this difference as:

NNP at market prices = NNP at factor cost + Indirect Taxes – Subsidies (1.3)

Now, NNP at factor cost includes all factor incomes including the profit incomes of the business sector/corporate sector. The profits of the business sector are divided into three parts: (a) dividends distributed among the shareholders, (b) undistributed profits retained by the corporates (retained profits) and (c) corporate profits tax.

Replacing these components in the NNP at factor costs, we get,

NNP at factor cost = Personal Income[1] + Undistributed/
Retained Profits + Corporate Profits Tax (1.4)

Secondly, the difference between 'personal income' and disposable income is made by the 'direct tax' payments to government on the one hand and 'transfer payments' to citizens on welfare and social security items. While the first part

[1] Personal income includes all factor incomes (rent, wages, interest and profits of un-incorporated business payments). Dividends of the shareholders are nothing but a part of their incomes.

is a deduction from personal income the latter are an addition to the personal income. This necessitates the following changes to be made:

Disposable Income = Personal Incomes – Direct Taxes
+ Government Transfer Payments (1.5)

The 'disposable income' part is divided into: (i) Consumption expenditure and (ii) Personal savings. Incorporating these changes, identity (1.3) can now be rewritten as:

NNP at market price = NNP at factor cost + Indirect Taxes – Subsidies
= Consumption Expenditure + Personal Savings
+ Direct Taxes on Personal Income
– Govt. Transfer Payments
+ Undistributed Corporate Profits
+ Corporate Profits Tax + Indirect Taxes
– Subsidies (1.6)

Since NNP at market price of (1.6) consists of the value of consumer goods sold, the value of capital stocks accumulated, the value of inventory accumulation and the government purchase of goods and services, (1.6) reduces to:

NNP at market price = Consumption Expenditure + Investment Expenditure + Government Expenditure on goods and services. (Since Investment Expenditure = Value of capital stocks accumulated + Value of inventory accumulated). (1.7)

Identity (1.6) and (1.7) have the same left-hand side. Therefore, equating the right-hand sides and re-arranging after cancelling consumption expenditure from both (1.6) & (1.7), we have:

Investment expenditure = Personal savings + Undistributed Corporate Profits + (Direct Taxes on Personal Income + Corporate Profit Tax + Indirect Taxes – Government Transfer Payments + Subsidies + Government Expenditure on goods and services) (1.8)

Identity (1.8) reduces further to:

Investment Expenditure = Private savings + Public savings (1.9)

Since, Personal savings + Undistributed Corporate Profits = Total private savings; while rest of the items, viz., direct taxes on both personal income, corporate profits tax, together with indirect taxes are sources of government's budgetary receipts. On the other hand, government transfer payments plus subsidies plus government expenditure on goods and services together, are government's budgetary expenditures. The differences between total budgetary receipts, and total budgetary expenditures is termed budget surplus or deficit as the difference is positive or negative. This is equivalent to public savings, positive or negative.

Identity (1.9) is highly significant for analytical purposes. If public savings part is negative, it implies some or all of the components of government expenditures are higher in value than the government receipts. Now if the government intends to fill this gap by borrowing from the market through issue of new bonds, this encroaches upon private savings, hence private investment is reduced. Thus, the identity is maintained in the accounting sense. Similarly, if the public savings is positive, arising out of budget surplus, the private savings component exceeds private investment. The budget surplus is used by the government for repaying old debts or building up the surplus for other purposes. However, the identity is again maintained by suitable adjustment in both sides of the identity.

1.14 NATIONAL INCOME IDENTITIES IN AN OPEN ECONOMY

In an open economy, i.e., the economy with international trade relations, the national income identity becomes more complex. It includes certain incomes while excludes certain others.

We have already seen in the beginning that National Income/Product is defined as the Net Domestic Product at market price plus Net Factor Income from abroad. Net Factor Income refers to the factor incomes earned abroad minus foreign factor incomes earned (sent abroad) within the country. Thus, we write the identity as:

NNP (at market prices) = NDP at market prices
+ Domestic Factor Earnings abroad
– Foreign Factor Earnings within the country (1.10)

Identity (1.6) gives us the equivalence of NNP at market prices in terms of Consumption Expenditure and other items. Now, in case of open economy, the Consumption Expenditure is divided into Consumption Expenditure on domestic goods and Consumption Expenditure on imported goods. Similarly, Disposable Income will now include incomes received (through remittances from abroad) but exclude similar income transfers abroad. This correction will be made in identity (1.10) above so that it now becomes:

NNP at market prices = Consumption Expenditure on domestic goods + Consumption Expenditure on imported goods + Personal savings
+ Transfers made abroad
– Transfer from abroad (1.11)

When the economy becomes open, the basic identity of the national income is changed to take account of the imports and exports of goods and services as well as other international transactions. The identity is formally written as:

$$Y = C + I + G + NX \tag{1.12}$$

where, NX = net exports, that is, exports minus imports $(X - M)$. NX may be either positive or negative depending on whether exports are greater than imports or the opposite. If the NX is negative we may call it the external deficit. Now, there is a relationship/link between internal deficit (budget deficit) and the external deficit which we seek to establish below.

The internal deficit is defined as $G - Ta + Tr$, where, G is government expenditures, Ta and Tr are, respectively, taxation and transfer payments. From equation (1.12), we proceed as follows:

$$NX = Y - (C + I + G) \tag{1.13}$$

Since, $Y = Yd + (Ta - Tr)$,

we can write, $NX = Yd + (Ta - Tr) - (C + I + G)$,

$$= (C + S) + (Ta - Tr) - (C + I + G) \tag{1.14}$$

where Yd is disposable income which is allocated between consumption and savings $(C + S)$. On the right-hand side of eqn. (1.14), positive C cancels the negative C so that we are left with:

$$NX = S - I - G + Ta - Tr = [S - I] - [G - T_a + T_r]$$

$$= (S - I) + Ta - (G + Tr) \tag{1.15}$$

Thus, external deficit, $(-NX)$ depends upon two parts, $(S - I)$ and the size of the internal deficit that is, $Ta - (G + Tr)$ which also is negative, because government expenditures including the transfers $(G + Tr)$ are greater than the taxation (Ta). Thus, it is clear that if the size of the internal deficit is larger/smaller, the external deficit will also be larger/smaller, given $S - I$. However, if domestic saving (S) is greater than domestic investment (I), in an open economy, the excess savings will be flying abroad in search of earnings (interest) and helping thereby to reduce the external deficit. On the other hand, if (I) is greater than (S), extra savings will be coming from abroad only to increase the size of the external deficit.

SECTION II: THE CIRCULAR FLOW MODEL

1.15 THE CIRCULAR FLOW OF INCOME

Income generated with the help of productive resources within the economy keep constantly flowing from one sector to another through expenditures on goods and services produced. Such flow of income takes place in a circular fashion. To understand this circular flow, we can start with the simplest type of unit known as 'household' and move to more complex units—'business sector' and 'government sector'.

1.15.1 The Household Sector

The household sector consists of persons or groups of persons who earn income and spend it on goods and services, which they usually get from business firms. The households generally produce labour and other factor services which they sell to the firms sector. They obtain wages for their labour services, which they spend on various goods and services produced by the firms. Thus, money income flows from households to firms in return for goods and services sold by the firms while money income flows from firms to households in return for the labour services purchased by the firms.

This simple circular relationship of income flow between households and business firms is illustrated in Fig. 1.1. Thus, households, who possess labour services, sell to the firms worth ₹ 10,000 – the money flows from firms to households worth the same ₹ 10,000. The households, in turn, spend this sum (₹ 10,000) on goods and services supplied by firms, so money flows back to business firms in return for goods and services.

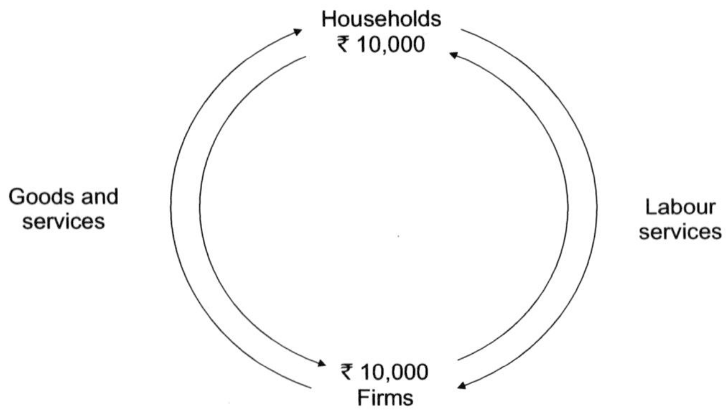

Figure 1.1 *Circular flow of income between households and business firms.*

Thus, total income generated in this process is equal to ₹ 10,000 (value of the produce by firms) which is totally spent on consumption items by the households. Therefore, we can write:

$$Y = C \tag{1.1}$$

where, Y is the total income (or, aggregate demand) and C is consumption expenditure.

Now, if we suppose that the households, instead of spending their entire income on consumption, save a part (say ₹ 1,000) and spend only the rest on purchase of goods and services from the firms, the circular flow diagram will look like the following:

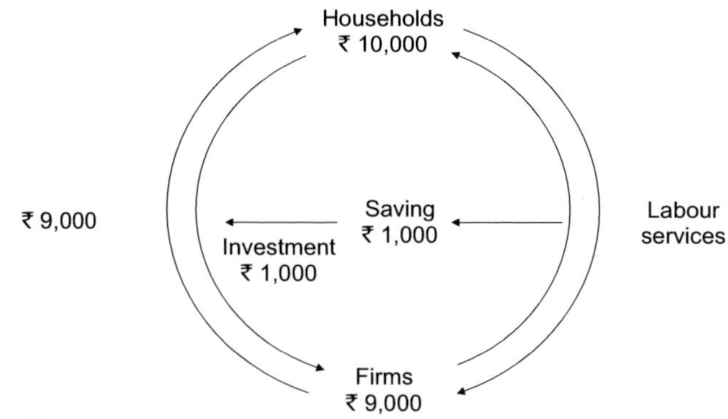

Figure 1.2 *Circular flow of income between consumption, saving and investment.*

Figure 1.2 shows that out of ₹ 10,000 received by the households they spend on consumption goods only ₹ 9,000 and save ₹ 1,000 – in various forms. This saving is likely to be channeled to investment in producing capital goods like machines, implements or new factories. Therefore, investment goods equal to ₹ 1,000 goes to the productive sector for the production activities (of real goods and services). Now, if savings is exactly equal to investment, the flow of income that was taken off the route is brought back in the form of investment, so that total income generated will be equal to ₹ 10,000. We can, therefore, write:

$$Y = C + I \tag{1.2}$$

where, $S = I$

where, Y = Aggregate income (or, aggregate demand),

C = Consumption expenditure,

I = Investment expenditure.

This is an equilibrium situation.

If, however, saving is not equal to investment (S π I) then $S > I$ creates a situation when Y (or, AD) falls and $S < I$ leads to Y (or, AD) being higher. It is, for this reason, said that S is a "withdrawal" from the circular flow of income while I is an "injection" to the circular flow of income.

If there is *government in existence*, it performs among other duties, at least two or three functions which have implications for circular flow of income. The first is imposition of "taxes" on citizens. The second is the "transfer payments" that it makes to various categories of citizens in various forms as we have discussed in Section I of this chapter. The third is the government purchase of various goods and services from the firms sector and the household sector. Of these three activities, the first–the taxes–are treated as "withdrawal" from the circular flow while the second and third are treated as "injections" into the system. Together with government functions, therefore, the circular flow diagram will look like that in Fig. 1.3.

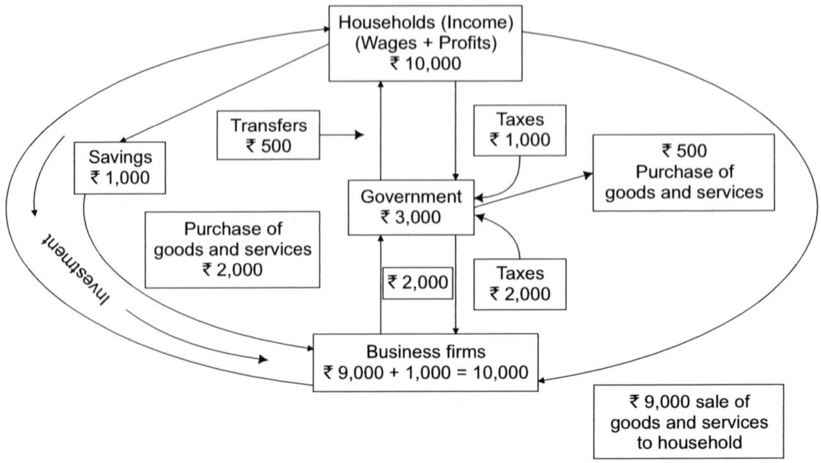

Figure 1.3 *Closed economy: Circular flow with government sector in a closed economy.*

Figure 1.3 shows that the households originally receive total factor income equal to ₹ 10,000. Out of this amount the sector has already saved ₹ 1,000. Therefore, the total amount it spends now on purchase of goods and services from the business sector is only ₹ 9,000. Assuming that the savings of ₹ 1,000 of the household returns to the business sector via the financial sector in the form of investment so that the business sector gets back ₹ 10,000. Now, the government comes into existence. It operates two prime functions–collects ₹ 3000 – ₹ 2,000 from the businesses and ₹ 1,000 from the households in the form of taxes. Thus, income with the businesses gets reduced to ₹ 8,000 while that of households gets reduced to ₹ 9,000. However, additionally, the government makes a transfer payment of ₹ 500 to the household and purchase goods and services (particularly, services) worth ₹ 500. With this the households get back the total of ₹ 10,000. However, it is assumed, in this example, that the government budget is exactly balanced, i.e., whatever amount it spends is entirely met by taxes. In practice, however, this is rarely the case. But this is just an example of simplified circular flow.

In terms of equation (1), we can make a modification as follows:

$$Y = C + I + G - T \tag{1.3}$$

where, $G = T$

Hence, there is no basic change in circular flow. If, however, $G > T$, it results in government deficit budget. The government will have to procure the amount of extra expenditure from within the circular flow. It may either impose new taxes/

increase the rate of taxes or reduce the expenditure. In other words, it can raise more tax revenue from the circular flow (households and businesses) or reduce its expenditure (purchase of goods and services, from the businesses and the household or reduce its transfer payments) or both. If, however, the government is unable to do so to the desired extent, it has the option to tap the investment flow going to the businesses by borrowing from the system. In that case, part of the investible fund is diverted to the government for its expenditure. There is another option left with the government, i.e., printing new currency notes for its expenditure in which case it will raise the money value of all goods and services. The goods and services worth ₹ 10,000 will now be simply more than ₹ 10,000, as will be all components of this amount.

The circular flow model is extended to include the external sector – the rest of the world. The main changes in this model are: (a) imports and (b) exports. While imports mean "withdrawal" from the circular flow, because part of the income goes out to the rest of the world in the shape of purchase of import goods and services, exports mean "injection" into the system in the form of sale (and hence, receipts) of goods and services from the rest of the world. The circular flow diagram will now look like Fig. 1.4.

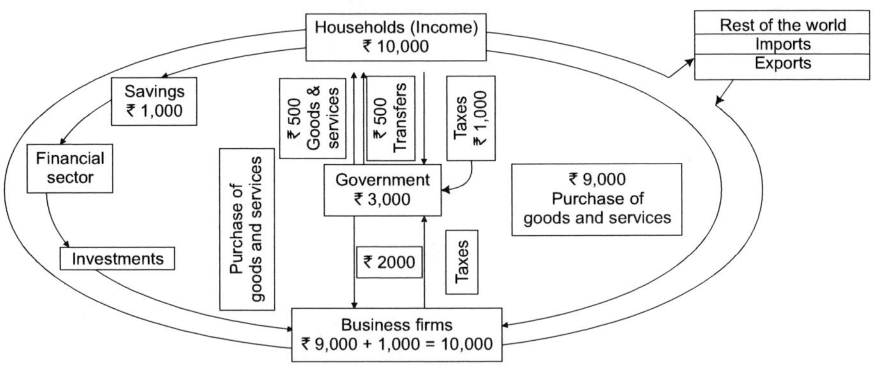

Figure 1.4 *Open economy: Circular flow model with government sector and imports and exports.*

There is another "withdrawal" or leakage from this circular flow – "imports", while there is another "injection" – exports. So, part of the ₹ 10,000 of income generated within the domestic economy will be going out to purchase imports while part of the rest of the world economy's income will flow back to the domestic economy for the sale of exports. If, for example, imports with ₹ 600 is purchased and exports worth ₹ 500 is sold to the rest of the world, there will be a net outflow of ₹ 100 from the circular flow. On the other hand, if exports worth ₹ 600 is sold while imports worth ₹ 500 is purchased, there will be net inflow of ₹ 100 to the circular flow. This will be the net change in the domestic income – either negative or positive. The income identity of (2) will now be changed as follows:

$$Y = C + I + G - T + (X - M) \tag{1.4}$$

where, X stands for exports and M stands for imports.

The schematic pattern of the circular flow of income as explained above is the summarized version of the working of the economy. Understanding of this schematic helps to grasp the further discussion on income generation and expenditure flow process and their determinants (i.e., factors which influence various components of the income and expenditure) to be followed in subsequent chapters. The "withdrawals" and "injections" from and to the circular flow of income can be summarized as follows:

"Withdrawals"	"Injections"
1. Savings (–)	Investments (+)
2. Taxes (–)	Subsidies, Transfers,
3. Imports (–)	Government Purchase of goods and services (+)
	Exports (+)

National income analysis in India (new method of calculation) of GVA

In January, 2015, the Central Statistical Office came out with a new set of data on GDP, termed GVA (Gross Value Added). The following are the major differences between the old method and the new method.

1. GVA is measured at market price of goods and services instead of factor costs. Thus, It includes product taxes but excludes product subsidies.
2. GVA is calculated at basic prices of goods and services. For a particular sector, for example, GVA is the sum of expenditures made in that sector when looked at from an expenditure angle. This means it is the sum total of compensation of employees (wages and salaries), operating surplus (OS), depreciation allowance (or, consumption of fixed capital) and mixed income (MI). Thus, GVA is the sum of payments made to labour, surplus of business entity (profit), the income of self-employed persons and depreciation allowances. (GDP at market prices = sum of GVA at basic prices + product taxes – product subsidies).

Basic prices are the amount receivable by the producer from the purchaser for a unit of goods or service produced as output minus any tax payable plus any subsidy receivable by the producer as a consequence of its production or sale. It needs to be mentioned here that production taxes are paid by the producer independent of quantity of production so that it is not per unit tax imposed on a commodity rather it is a general tax like land revenue or stamp duty. Similarly, production subsidies are general subsidies and not per unit subsidies. On the other hand, product taxes and product subsidies are paid or received on a per unit basis such as excise duty, sales tax/GST and food, fertiliser subsidies.

The question why CSO introduced these changes in the calculation of GDP is that it is intended to make India's national income accounting in conformity with global standards. Globally, the most accepted and followed national income accounting format is the System of National Accounting (SNA) prepared by the United Nations and ratified by the IMF, World Bank, OECD and European Commission (EC). The SNA describes a coherent, consistent and integrated set of measures in the context of internationally agreed concepts, definitions, classifications and accounting rules (SNA was launched in 1992 and later upgraded in 2008).

Besides the methodological change, as stated above, there have been two other changes in the estimation of new GDP series. One is the coverage of the data for different sectors of the economy and the other is the change in the base year from 2004-05 to 2011-12.

In the old series, for manufacturing and trading activities, the index of industrial production (IIP) or factory output used to be the main source of data. The problem with these data was that they counted only the number of units produced but failed to distinguish between more valuable and less valuable units in terms of market prices. Thus, the value addition aspect was ignored such as the value of a luxury car as distinguished from other cars. Secondly, earlier, organised industrial activity was based on IIP which used to be updated two years later upon getting fresh data from Annual Survey of Industries (ASI). The ASI data had limitations in so far as they recorded goods' value at the factory gate and that too for firms registered under the Factories Act.

The present data used for GVA are taken from the Corporate Affairs Ministry's MCA21 records which is a comprehensive balance sheet data of about 5 lakh firms. This change has enabled to expand the coverage of data as also to broaden the scope to include such activities as marketing of goods.

Similarly, in the case of labour input, a method of "effective labour input" was used by assigning different 'weights' to different categories of labour such as an owner, a hired professional or helper.

In agriculture, value addition has been taken care of by including the value of byproducts with the principal products.

In the case of the financial sector, the new series data is expanded by including stock brokers, stock exchanges, asset management companies, mutual funds, pension funds, etc.

In trade and commerce, the new series used NSSO's 2011-12 establishments survey data instead of 1999 survey data used in earlier survey. The old series data used extrapolated data from the 1999 survey.

There has, since, been controversy around the GDP estimates as also its growth rates using new methods of calculation. For instance, the new data series for 2012-13 and 2013-14 showing growth rates of 5.1% and 6.9% respectively, as against 4.7% and 5% in the old series have baffled the economists. Also, the economists were surprised at sectoral growth rate data. The manufacturing and financial sector, for instance, reported higher growth rate which was not reflected in data on factory output as well as bank credit. On the other hand, the trade sector showed significantly lower growth in terms of value addition. The CSO, at a later date, clarified its stand in terms of new sources of data for the trading sector and its expanded scope which did not show higher growth.

It may not be out of place to mention here that in recent times (later half of 2018-19), there has been controversy surrounding the authenticity of Indian national income statistics, particularly their growth rates. Critics have pointed out that there has been political and government interference in the publication of highly sensitive data and hence their reliability is at stake. Experts have even suggested setting up of an impartial body to examine this issue in detail. It has been lately reported that one such independent body is to be set up under the chairmanship of Pronab Sen, currently chairman, Statistical Commission of India.

Reference: Gourav Choudhary, Hindustan Times, January 30, 2016.

An illustrative example of GDP (from expenditure or, demand side) from Indian data is given in Table 1.2.

$$GDP/AD = C + I + G + (X - M)$$

Gross Domestic Product (At market prices)
Base year 2011-2012 (Rupees Crores)

Table 1.2

Year	Private final consumption expenditure (C)		Government final consumption expenditure (G)		Exports of goods and services (X)		Import of goods and services (M)		GDP at market prices	Gross capital formation (investment) (I)	
	% share	Current prices	% share	Current prices	% share	Current prices	% share	Current prices	Current prices	% share	Current prices
2019-20	60%	12262064	12%	2446579	18%	3745473	21%	4298950	20339849	30%	6034369
2018-19	59%	11254014	11%	2104235	20%	3766294	24%	4468166	18971237	32%	6013580
2017-18	59%	10090759	11%	1838117	19%	3211521	22%	3751389	17098304	31%	5269522
2016-17	59%	9126533	10%	1586658	19%	2948772	21%	3220591	15391669	30%	4644081
2015-16	59%	8126408	10%	1436171	20%	2728647	22%	3044923	13771874	32%	4423076
2014-15	58%	7247340	10%	1301762	23%	2863636	26%	3235962	12467959	34%	4272496
2013-14	58%	6475650	10%	1156509	25%	2856781	28%	3191811	11233522	34%	3822003
2012-13	56%	5614484	11%	1062404	25%	2439707	31%	3108428	9944013	38%	3813272
2011-12	56%	4910447	11%	968375	25%	2143931	31%	2715554	8736329	40%	3458749

2010-11	55%	4177954	11%	840373	22%	1710193	27%	2050182	7634472	40%	3037422
2009-10	56%	3562634	11%	729569	20%	1298780	26%	1647139	6366407	39%	2499248
2008-09	57%	3125246	11%	581108	24%	1328765	29%	1614040	5514152	38%	2118671
2007-08	56%	2731519	10%	483112	21%	1018907	25%	1219109	4898662	42%	2055028
2006-07	56%	2387270	10%	417059	21%	904872	24%	1040535	4254629	39%	1659242
2005-06	57%	2084067	10%	376511	20%	712087	22%	813466	3632125	37%	1359441
2004-05	58%	1859274	10%	331528	18%	569051	20%	625945	3186332	35%	1118290

Source: RBI

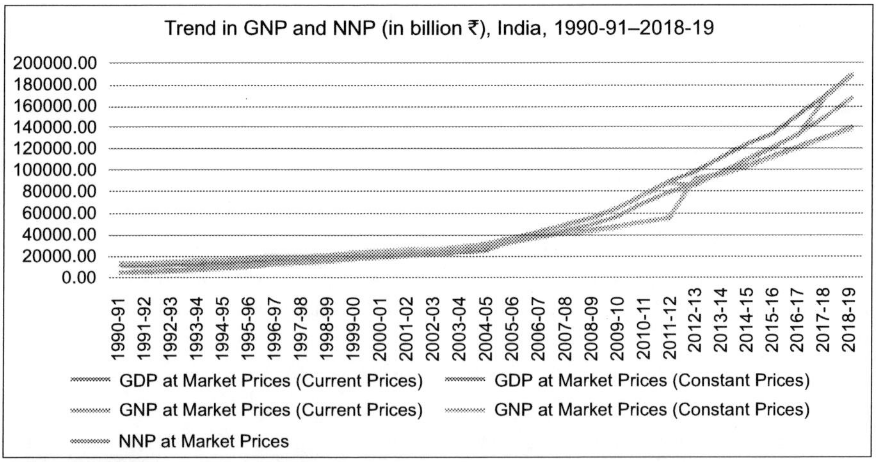

Figure 1.5 *Trends of GDP, GNP and NNP (at current and constant prices), India, 1990-91–2018-19.*

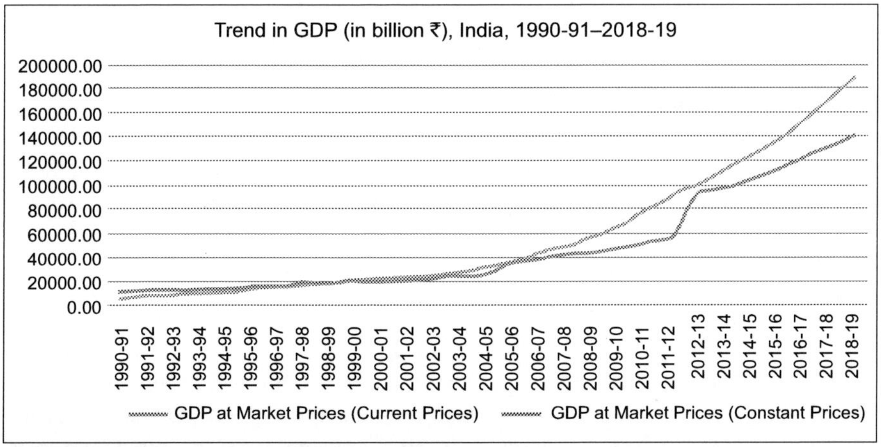

Figure 1.6 *Trends of GDP at current and constant prices.*

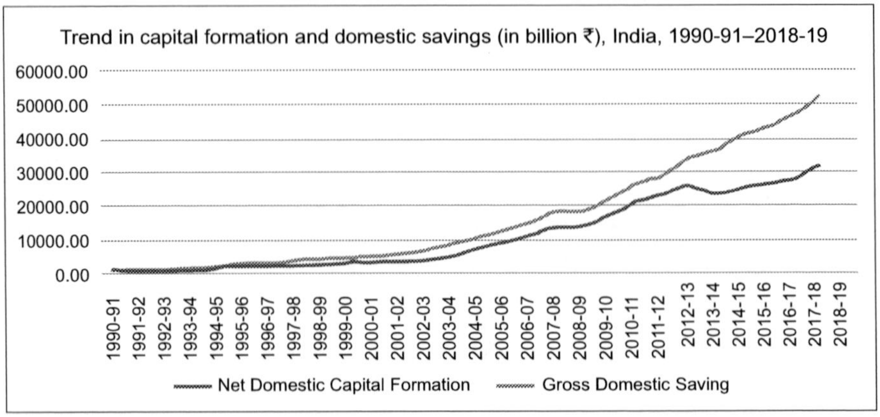

Figure 1.7 *Trends of domestic capital formation and savings.*

We have provided trends of certain categories of India's national income and related statistics for the period 1990-91 to 2018-19 in the three tables: Figures 1.5 to 1.7. A careful look at these tables suggests that, by and large, all the three aggregates, GDP, GNP and NNP have a tendency to rise very slowly particularly up to the year 2003-04. Thereafter, however, these are growing relatively at rapid rates. Secondly, the distinction between their values at current and constant prices (i.e., nominal values and real values) is rather blurred before 2003-04. This distinction is, however, clear enough thereafter so much so that the nominal GDP is rising faster than the real GDP. But real GDP between 2011-12 and 2013-14 is showing certain jerk-like increase to smoothen thereafter. The explanation lies mainly in the rising inflation rate after 2003-04 which is much more pronounced after 2009-10 till 2013-14.

Figure 1.7 reveals another dimension of the national economy, namely, the trends of savings and investment. Here, net domestic capital formation represents the investment. Between 1990-91 and 1997-98, there does not seem to be much divergence between savings and investment data suggesting that domestic savings were not rising enough to account for rising investment. But, after 2001-02, the domestic savings are rising faster than the investment. One more important thing to observe is the trend after 2012-13 particularly in investment figures which show a decelerating tendency.

SUMMARY

1. The concept of national income and related aggregative concepts are essential to understand the macroeconomic characteristics of an economy. National income and national output are just two sides of the same aggregate, looked at different angles. Concepts like Gross

Domestic Product and Gross National Product are the end results of all productive activities carried out during a specific period of time, except that GDP is the product generated within the national territory while GNP includes the net factor incomes from abroad.

2. All the major aggregates can be expressed in terms of "gross" and "net" values. While gross value is obtained without deducting the depreciation or capital consumption of fixed capital during the process of production, net value is obtained after deducting such costs.
3. Regarding the prices at which the NI or GDP, etc., are evaluated, there can be two ways to express them: one at current prices and the other at constant prices. The latter refers to certain base-period prices chosen at will. There is a method of converting the GNP/GDP, etc., at current prices to their constant prices by using a 'deflator' which is an index number of prices of all goods and services entering into their calculations.
4. Again, these concepts have two aspects – when they are produced with all factors of production like land, labour, capital and organisation which have their own costs. When only these factor costs are included, GNP/ GDP, etc., are expressed at factor costs. But besides these costs, when they enter into market, certain costs are added or some deducted also. Indirect taxes are added while subsidies, (a part of cost borne by the government) are deducted. Hence, finally they are expressed in terms of market prices.
5. There are three methods of estimating NI/GDP
   (a) the product census or value-added method
   (b) the income method, and
   (c) the expenditure method.

   There are different kinds of difficulties associated with evaluation process but some kind of solutions are also available.
6. There are certain 'identities' among these aggregative measures and their components based upon the relationships between income, expenditure and product.
7. Of the NI and other aggregates, some are flow concepts while others are stock concepts. Flow concepts have a time dimension – referring to a certain period of time while stock concepts refer to a certain specific point in time. Income and expenditure are examples of flow concepts while wealth, capital and money supply are examples of stock concepts. There is, however, a close relationship between stock and flow variables.
8. There is always a circular flow of income in the whole economy during a specified period of time. Income and expenditure flow from one sector

to the other and come back to the same sector in different forms. To understand this process, one may start from the simplest economic structure involving only households and firms, where all income receipts are assumedly expended. Then, sub-divisions of expenditure into savings and investments may be introduced and possibly a separate category of persons or organizations may be included. Then, the government sector may be introduced to perform functions like collection of taxes from different sectors and make public expenditure providing public goods and services to all sectors.

9. Finally, rest-of-the world or external sector may be introduced to allow income and expenditure flows from and to the domestic economy to and from all other economies with which trade and investment relations are established. Imports are goods obtained from abroad in exchange for part of NI sacrificed while exports are goods sent abroad in exchange for incomes received from abroad. The circular flow of income within the national economy is, thus, accordingly affected and the only difference between the two kinds of income flow is either added or subtracted from NI.
10. Looked at as a whole, certain flows are "withdrawals" from while certain others are "injections" into the circular flow. Savings, imports and taxes are "withdrawals" from the system, while investments, exports and government transfers (including subsidies) and government purchase of goods and services are "injections".
11. The NI accounting process is simply translating the incomes and expenditures in terms of debits and credits of respective amounts by sectors as is normally followed in preparing commercial accounting. There can be different sets of such accounts such as income and production accounts, and the rest-of-the world sector accounts.

EXERCISE

1. How does the concept of GNP differ from GDP? Explain the difference between GNP and NNP; GDP and NDP with suitable numerical examples.
2. Define disposable income. What is the difference between disposable income and personal income?
3. Given the following figures of nominal GDP and price index numbers for GDP at respective periods of time; calculate the real GDP for the same years.

Years	*Nominal GDP (in ₹ 000 crore)*	*Index Numbers*
2000-01	1925	100
2001-02	2098	105
2002-03	2261	110
2003-04	2538	115
2004-05	2878	120
2005-06	3389	124
2006-07	3952	132
2007-08	4851	144
2009-10	5285	144
2010-11	6133	160

4. Distinguish between investment and capital with suitable examples.
5. Define GDP 'deflator'. Explain that it is the best measure of inflation. How is GDP deflator used in calculating the 'real GDP?
6. Identify the important 'stock' and 'flow' variables in the national income analysis.
7. Explain in what respect the national income identify is modified in an open economy.
8. Construct a circular flow model of an economy involving households, firms and government.
9. Distinguish between GDP and GVA. What recent changes have been introduced in the calculation of India's GDP and why?
10. What is 'basic' price? What is the difference between GVA at market price and GVA at factor cost?

REFERENCES

1. Ackley, G. (1978), Macroeconomics: Theory and Policy, Macmillan, New York.
2. Mankiw, Gregory, N. (2006), Macroeconomics, 6th Edition, Worth Publishers.
3. Dornbush R., Fischer S. and Startz R. (2009), Macroeconomics, 9th Edition, McGraw Hill, USA.
4. Crouch, R.L. (1972), Macroeconomics, Harcourt Brace Jovanovitch.
5. Reserve Bank of India, www.rbi.org.in, Handbook of Statistics of Indian Economy.
6. Lipsey, R. (1969), An Introduction to Positive Economics, ELBS Edition.

PART-2

Product Market Analysis: Output, Employment and Income Determination

2

The Classical Theory: Employment and Output in the Long Run

2.1 BASIC POSTULATES OF CLASSICAL MACROECONOMICS

The classical macroeconomic structure is built upon the writings of famous classical economists like Adam Smith, David Ricardo, J.B. Say, T.R. Malthus, A.C. Pigou, to mention the greatest few. Their scattered writings, when put together, produce a systematic and coherent macroeconomic framework. To understand this framework, one needs to bear in mind the basic postulates/assumptions that classical economists built around their macroeconomic conclusions. These are, broadly, as under.

2.1.1 Full Employment

Classical economists believed that there will always be full employment (or, near full employment) in the economy – full employment not only of labour but also of other major resources such as land, capital and other factors of production. In case of labour, for instance, they held the view that all labour will normally find employment in a free enterprise capitalist economy with 'flexible labour market' (explained below). However, such full employment does not mean that temporary unemployment (i.e., unemployment for a temporarily short period) will not exist. But unemployment of relatively longer period or what Keynes later termed 'involuntary unemployment' is totally ruled out by the classicals. For instance, temporary unemployment may occur due to maladjustment between demand and supply of resources in a capitalist economy or frictions in the economy – workers changing jobs, locations, etc. – or change in the structure of the economy such as old industries shutting down and new ones coming up or unemployment that occurs during business cycles (recessions or depression).

Full employment will, then, occur only in the **long run**. So, long run perspective is implicit in all these postulates. The classicals generally ignore short run problems however serious they may be. In the long run, total demand for labour will always be equal to total supply of labour and total output (of goods and services) will be at its full potential level.

Lapses from full employment, classicals suggest, may be corrected by appropriate wage cut given sufficient flexibility in the wage system. Thus, classical economists viewed unemployment as a passing phase in the development of capitalist economy while full employment being a normal phenomenon.

2.1.2 Wage-Price Flexibility

Classical economists postulated that in the capitalist system, wages as also prices (including interest rates) are flexible and not rigid. This means that these rates are capable of moving upward and downward under normal pressures of demand and supply in their respective markets. In other words, the demand and supply curves are fairly responsive to prices and wages – or, to say the same thing, demand and supply curves are price-elastic (as also wage-elastic).

In the case of wage rate flexibility, it is argued that, this is always in the interest of both the employers and workers. Employers gain from wage rate reduction because this reduces their wage cost and hence increases their profit margin. They will, therefore, be tempted to employ more workers and thereby increase output. Workers will gain in terms of increased employment of labour force (though not in terms of wage rate or wage per worker). Wage rate rise, similarly, works in opposite direction. On the other hand, workers will respond by increasing their supply when wage rate is higher and decrease their supply when wage rate is lower. These outcomes are, in fact, based on explanations, at the micro level from both employer's and worker's normal decision behaviour. The implication is that in case of any deviations from equilibrium occurring anywhere in the economic system, wage price flexibility will ensure that such deviations will soon disappear and the economy will eventually return to the equilibrium position.

Two other implications need clarification in this context.

Wage rate here means "real wage rate" and not money wage rate. Any change in money wage rate is suitably adjusted by change in price level so that the impact of price level change on real wage rate is neutralized. To state it differently, money wage and price level move in the same direction and to the same extent to leave the real wages unaffected. In case both do not move in the same direction or to the same extent, this would mean real wage rate is either rising or falling.

The price system also needs to be flexible – sufficient to allow (a) to happen. Flexibility in wage price system is, thus, a precondition for bringing about equilibrium in both labour and commodity markets. Similarly, equilibrium in the entire economic system is established as well as maintained by the equality of savings and investments (discussed in Section 2.3) which is possible only when interest rate is flexible. Change in the rate of interest is required to give sufficient signal to both savers and investors to respond to the desired extent to help re-establish equilibrium.

2.1.3 Say's Law of Market

One of the significant propositions of classical macroeconomics is Say's law of market, succinctly expressed as: 'supply creates its own demand'[1]. This law tries to emphasize that supply of a particular product itself ensures that equivalent demand for it is created so that in the aggregate total demand is always equal to total supply. For instance, whenever a producer of a certain good comes to the market for sale it reflects that he is in need of some other good in exchange which the producer of that good provides. If all producers act in this fashion and bring all their surplus produce (after meeting their self consumption needs) to the market, all supplies (or, aggregate supply) will essentially be equal to all demands (or, aggregate demand). This means there will be no overproduction or underproduction of any good in the economy. It is possible, however, that supply of any particular good at a point of time may either be greater or less than its demand possibly due to the failure of the producer to correctly predict the actual requirement. But soon necessary correction is made through appropriate adjustment in its supply through re-allocation of his productive resources in the next period. For instance, producer of wheat might bring to the market an excess supply of wheat which is not fully in demand. This would be evident from the fact that he might have expected to get a certain quantity of sugar (for instance) in exchange for his wheat. But actually he ends up having less quantity of sugar. This means that commodity exchange rate for wheat is less while that of sugar is more than expected by their respective producers. The wheat producer, however, would be making suitable adjustment of his supply next time by re-allocating his resources to some other goods.

Another way of understanding Say's law is that the process of production itself produces equivalent demand for the product through factor payments – rent, wages, interest and profit which are factor incomes creating demands for various goods including the particular one in question. Thus, aggregating all factor incomes gives aggregate demand equal to aggregate supply. There is no scope for overproduction or unemployment. Different classical writers have interpreted Say's law in different ways but the essence is that all have endorsed this law as the cornerstone of classical macroeconomics. Keynes held the view that Say's law is the basis on which the entire classical theory stands: without it the theory breaks down.[2]

The underlying argument of Say's law seems plausible in a barter-type exchange economy. The critics have however, raised doubts if the law would be

---

[1] J.B. Say (1767-1832, A French economist who propounded this law).

[2] J.M Keynes, The General Theory of Employment, Interest and Money, MacMillan 1936, p. 19.

applicable in a more complex money economy where people exchange goods for money (income). Secondly, whether it is applicable in a situation where all money incomes are not necessarily fully expended but a part of it is saved and also if part of it is used in adding to the capital stock (by businesses or producers). To the question of its applicability in a money economy, Say's law is supported by the concurrently prevailing monetary theory – the Quantity Theory of Money. This theory asserts that the only purpose of money is to help all transactions – purchase-sale of goods and services in the economy, be it at household or business level. Thus, any addition to the supply of money in the economic system adds to the incomes of the people which is then totally spent on purchase of goods and services. Thus, any exchange, even if done for money is almost immediately used for purchase of other goods or services. The classical Quantity Theory of Money, therefore, ensures that Say's law does apply equally to money economy.

Regarding the second question, that is, in a still more complex economy where saving and investment (addition to capital stock) take place, it has been asserted that the then prevailing theory of saving and investment jointly determining the rate of interest largely supports and is consistent with Say's law. This latter theory has been advanced in terms of saving (desired or intended) being always equal to investment (desired or intended). If not, temporarily, an equilibrium between the two is brought about by the rate of interest (see Section 2.3). The classical theory of saving and investment, thus supports, rather than contradicts the Say's law of market.

2.1.4 Dichotomised Economy

Classicals assumed that the economy broadly consists of two sectors, viz., monetary sector (or, money economy) and real sector (or, real economy). While monetary sector comprises money market, real sector comprises labour and commodity markets. These two broad sectors, according to classicals, are independent, separable or decomposable in the sense that any change in the monetary sector has no effect on the real sector. Thus, the economy can be viewed as dichotomized between money and real economies (generally referred to as 'classical dichotomy'). What this postulate asserts is that there are two different price levels which are determined separately and independently in each of the two markets mentioned above. The price level determined in the monetary sector is known as absolute price level or nominal price level or simply 'level of prices'. On the other hand, the price level determined in the real sector is known as relative price level (price of one product in terms of other product). For understanding the underlying meaning of this classical dichotomy, we take an example. Let us suppose there are two goods: wheat and potato whose nominal prices are ₹ 10.00 per kg and ₹ 15.00 per kg respectively (or, their real price ratio is 1.5 units of wheat: 1 unit of potato). If, for some reason, the supply of money in the economy suddenly doubles, the prices of wheat and potato also double to ₹ 20 per kg and ₹ 30 per kg. But their relative price ratio remains the same, i.e., 1.5 units of wheat : 1 unit of potato. This is because the relative price level is something determined by factors such as, relative factor supplies of goods services and technology of production which are independent of the factors affecting the monetary sector.

Surprisingly, however, the reverse causation is not true, so that changes in the real sector do influence the monetary sector.

2.1.5 Absence of Money Illusion

According to this postulate, there is complete absence of money illusion in the economy. All groups of people in the economy – the workers, employers, savers, investors, etc., are completely free from money illusion. For instance, if workers are influenced by the money value (or, nominal value) of their wage rate and not by their real value (or real wage rate), we say workers are guided by the money illusion. If, instead, workers are only guided by real wage rate, they are said to be free from money illusion. Accordingly, if workers are willing to supply more working hours/days at higher real wages and not high money wages, we say there is no money illusion in the labour market. Similarly, if savers are guided by the real rate of interest (money rate of interest minus the rate of inflation) they are said to be not suffering from any money illusion. Also, another related assumption is that *money is neutral* – it does not affect any other price like interest rate. Needless to say that this particular assumption of the classicals also holds a key position and frees them from many complications which the later-day economists notably Keynes and his followers incorporated in their analytical framework.

2.2 THE CLASSICAL THEORY OF EMPLOYMENT AND OUTPUT

In the previous section, we examined the basic postulates of classical economics where we briefly discussed the postulate of full employment. In this section, we will try to understand the basic logic of the attainment of full employment in the classical system. Let us first look at the behaviour of the labour market in terms of demand for and supply of labour and their interaction in the determination of real wage rate from a purely microeconomic point of view. Figure 2.1 shows two curves, demand and supply curves of labour, the former falling downward from left to right and the latter rising upward to the right. Both these curves are responsible for the real wage rate (money wage rate deflated by the price level). The real wage rate and demand for labour are inversely related while real wage rate and supply of labour are directly related. Let us analyse these in somewhat more detail.

Let us suppose there is a pool of unemployed labour waiting to be employed. Labour is demanded by the producers of goods and services. When the wage rate is very high, they demand a small quantity of labour. But as the wage rate falls, they are tempted to hire larger quantities of labour because their wage cost falls and the profit margin rises. Hence, the demand for the labour curve is downward sloping from left to right. However, behind this curve lies the marginal productivity curve of labour which, again, is downward sloping. In fact, the marginal productivity curve represents the demand curve for labour which is directly derived from the total output curve. Total output curve is assumed to behave in a manner that with greater and greater employment of labour (as also other variable factors) it rises, eventually, at a slower rate, ultimately to reach a plateau (maximum height).

Given the marginal productivity curve of labour, employers would like to optimise the use of labour at a point where marginal productivity of labour is equal to the wage rate (real). If the marginal productivity of labour is falling, the real wage rate must fall too in order to tempt the employers to employ more and more labour. This tendency must go on so long as the real wage rate has a tendency to fall against existing unemployment. This requires that the real wage rate must be quite flexible, responding quickly to demand and supply pressures in the labour market. Also, it requires that the market be fully competitive from both sides, employers and labourers. While the employers must be ready to employ more labourers at lower wages, the labourers must be ready to accept lower wages. Figure 2.1 shows the behaviour of demand for labour curve (DL).

We now look at the supply behaviour of labour. Labourers offer their labour services against certain wages. These wages must have certain minimum levels below which the labourers will not be prepared to offer their services. In fact, there are two aspects to consider before the labourers: (a) marginal utility of income from work and (b) marginal disutility of work. In fact, no work is without pain and discomfort. But, so long as marginal utility of income from work is greater than its marginal disutility, labourers continue to offer their services. Only when the marginal disutility is greater than marginal utility, the labourers stop offering labour services to their employers. As the wage rate increases, the marginal utility is assumed to be in excess of marginal disutility; hence greater and greater labour supply at higher and higher wage rates. It is sometimes possible though that at a very high wage rate, the labourers would prefer leisure rather than work, hence they have a tendency to absent themselves from work. In such a situation, the labour supply curve, after a stage, turns backward to the left. Thus, the behaviour of both the demand and supply curves of labour follows rational maximising principles when they are applied at the micro level decision-making process.

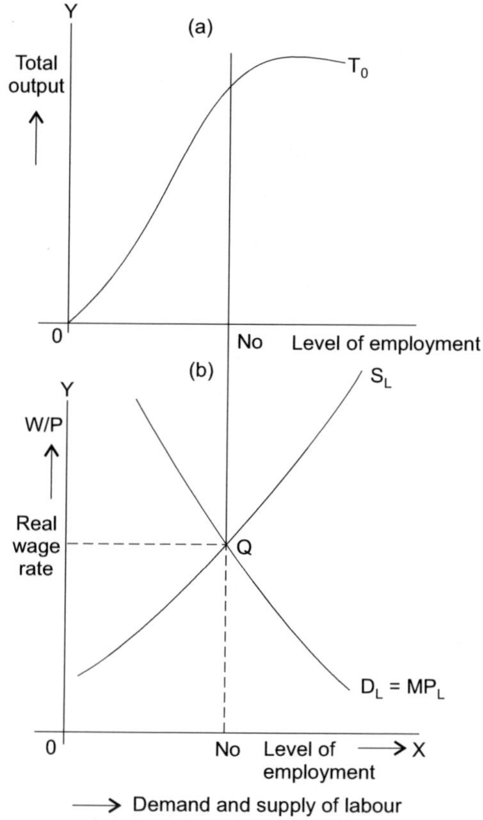

Figure 2.1 *Equilibrium in the labour market and full employment.*

Now, according to classical economists, when there is unemployment, employment can increase only when the real wage rate falls and the gap between the supply of labour and the demand for it is gradually narrowed. When the wage rate reaches a level where the total demand for labour is exactly equal to the total supply, the labour market is said to be in equilibrium and is the situation of full employment. This process is invariably linked to the increase in output. Total output will rise along with employment and will eventually attain its potential level at full employment.

This is a simple analysis of the labour market and the process of attainment of full employment with potential output in the economy. Now, the real wage rate, as we have mentioned above, has two components: money wage rate and price level. Classical economists seem to have focused attention to the general level of prices which have a bearing on the cost of living of the workers. So, the real wage rate would, most likely, fall when the money wage falls to a greater extent than the general price level. This is essentially a micro approach to the solution of unemployment. What the classical economists stress upon is that given sufficient time to the adjustment between demand-supply gap and flexibility of money wage as well as price level, full employment in the economy will be achieved provided all firms in the industry and all industries in the economy behave in the same manner. This will be possible only in the long run. However, in the short run, fluctuations in the labour market with demand supply mismatch may be observed. Thus, unemployment is a short-run phenomenon which may be addressed by allowing flexibility in the wage price system and is just a passing phase in the process of attainment of full employment in the capitalist economy. Figures 2.1 (a) and (b) explain the individual producer behaviour and labour market equilibrium.

We shall now try to take this simple logic to the macro level to see the implication of the employment theory. Supposing there is homogeneous labour–labour of the identical efficiency, and an aggregate production function behaving in the same manner as the one at the individual producer level. There is also a money wage rate at the macro level and an aggregate price level (may be thought of in terms of price index numbers). The ratio of this money wage rate and aggregate (average) price level would, therefore, represent the real wage rate at the macro level. When there is unemployment in the economy, the real wage rate (W/P) will have to decrease in order to effect increase in output and employment. Employers would cut money wages, real wages would fall, employment would rise, output would rise and the economy would move towards full employment and potential output (Yp). This is the initial change in the real sector of the economy. This change in the real sector will have some effect on the monetary sector 2. Since total output will now be higher, the price level must proportionately fall to equate the two sides of the quantity equation ($MV = PY$). A fall in the price level will mean a reduction in the money wage rate. But the fall in the price level will be smaller than the fall in money wage rate; so that there will be further fall in real wage rate and further rise in employment and output. Thus, the unemployment gap will gradually be filled and full employment reached at actual output being equal to potential output.

There remains some confusion between real sector and monetary sector changes. A change in the monetary sector does not have any effect on the real sector. By this postulate, an increase in the supply of money simply alters the money value of all prices without affecting their relative prices. This means that such an increase in money supply will simply raise the money value of GNP and also the money value of the wage rate. Thus, nominal GNP as well as money wage rate are to be increased without affecting either real GNP or real wage rate, since money wage rate and price level rise by the same proportion. Obviously, this will be the long-run effect of a rise in the supply of money after the economy has initially reached equilibrium which is shown by the quantity theory equation: $MV = PY$ (see chapter 7, Quantity Theory of Money).

Thus, the classical position seems to be clear: all fluctuations either in employment or output are short term and temporary in nature causing unemployment or less than potential output, but having attained equilibrium in the long run, any change in M leads to a proportionate change in P; it causes inflation.

What, then, causes unemployment in the short run? Classical economists assert that lack of flexibility in the wage-price system may be due to market imperfections. Once labour market imperfections are corrected and a perfectly competitive system is ensured in all other markets, full employment will automatically be restored.

A critical analysis: The classical employment theory seems to be unsatisfactory and confusing when it is sought to be applied at the macro level. Classical economists were, in fact, not so much concerned with macro level employment theory. They have merely extended the logic of profit maximising principle as applicable at the micro level individual producers to the macro level and vaguely reasoned that what is applicable at the micro level must be applicable at the macro level too. For one thing, imagining a macro level production function (total output curve as shown in Fig. 2.1) and its logical conclusions are often difficult to come by, let alone other implications of macro production theory.

In fact, the moment we come down to short run fluctuations in the labour market, we are sure to face formidable problems in the path to the attainment of full employment. For instance, wages and prices are not flexible in the short run and wages, in particular, tend to be sticky in character due to several reasons which we have discussed in chapter 3.

Most criticism of the classical employment theory has come from J.M. Keynes and his followers, the Keynesians. Keynes argued that rigidity in wages would force the labour market to remain at a stage where total supply of labour will be in excess of the total demand for labour and unemployment will persist. The classical dichotomy–the separation of real sector from the monetary sector–is useless and unrealistic since, in the real world, the monetary sector does impact the real sector by influencing several variables before affecting the general level of prices. In fact, much of the confusion surrounding money wages and real wages and falling real wages in the face of unemployment is due to this dichotomy. In any case, the wage price relationship in the classical employment theory is far from being clear.

When Keynes advanced this line of criticism against the classical employment theory, A.C. Pigou, one of the foremost classical economists argued vehemently that if unemployment persists, the best course would be to allow wage-price deflation (falling wages and prices) which would ultimately restore full employment. But Keynes' counter argument was that wage reduction at the micro level might be logical and plausible but when viewed from a macro perspective, this will lead to general wage cut in the economy and consequent fall in the aggregate demand. This will further cause unemployment in the economy. Classical economists, though, do not admit any deficiency in aggregate demand and contend that aggregate supply alone will ensure sufficiency of aggregate demand (Say's law). Pigou, however, provided another line of reasoning in favour of full employment even if wage price deflation would lead to fall in aggregate demand. This was the wealth effect of a fall in the price level. Thus, when the price level falls, the value of the consumer's (as also community's) wealth rises giving extra purchasing power in the hands of the consumers. This would presumably raise aggregate demand as also output and employment. The wealth effect (which was later known as real balance effect), no doubt has some favourable effect on aggregate demand and hence employment and output, but whether the effects would be enough to solve the existing unemployment problem is doubtful. Secondly, people keep their wealth in different forms such as money, bonds or houses. When there is a fall in the general price level, the value of money might be up, but other forms of wealth might experience different impacts. For instance, there is a general tendency of the rate of interest to fall along with price level. In the case of bonds, their prices increase if the rate of interest falls, so that demand for bonds declines. Thus, investment demand might be hampered, which is a part of aggregate demand.

In spite of the above mentioned shortcomings of the classical employment theory, there have been attempts at reviving the theory and applying the underlying policy aspects to most capitalist economies of the world. These theories and policies are known as New Classical Economics although, side by side, another set of theories known as New Keynesian Economics, (refinements of Keynesian strands) are also going on, debating on different issues inherent in them.

2.3 EQUILIBRIUM IN THE GOODS MARKET: THE SAVING-INVESTMENT THEORY

In this section, we examine the equilibrium in the goods market as it is dealt in the classical system. Equilibrium in the goods market means total demand for goods is equal to the total supply of goods. The classical economists always prefer to view all variables in real terms. In fact, they think that the monetary sector or money economy is independent of the real sector or real economy. Equilibrium in the goods sector is also to be viewed in terms of real savings and real investments which, together with the real rate of interest, determine the equilibrium of the economy.

We may draw a cue from the Say's law of market hat aggregate demand is always equal to aggregate supply so that no overproduction or unemployment/underproduction takes place in the economy. However, if a part of the aggregate demand takes the route of 'exit' from the circular flow in the form of 'savings', (withdrawal from the circular flow) then there will be disequilibrium in the goods market. However, if the same savings are totally invested in the creation of capital goods which, in the process, creates additional demand, (injection), then the circular flow of income will be restored. Thus, the classical economists view that the entire "intended" savings of the community are equal to the total "intended" investments in equilibrium. But then we have to search for a mechanism which helps restore the equilibrium. The classical economists found that such an equilibrating mechanism is the 'rate of interest', albeit the real rate of interest. We can state, using symbols, thus: $S = S(r)$, with $S'(r) > 0$ and $I = I(r)$ with $I'(r) < 0$ and the equilibrium condition: $S = I$.

Let us examine, now, the behaviour of saving and investment in response to the real rate of interest.

At the outset, it ought to be remembered that the theory of saving and investment explains the determination of the rate of interest, which in classical economists' view, is real phenomenon in the sense that interest rate is determined by real factors. While productivity of capital is the main factor behind the behaviour of investment, time preference is the factor behind the behaviour of savings. Both these factors are real factors and are not influenced by monetary factors. Further, interest rate acts as a mechanism for bringing about equality between volumes of investment and savings. Let us elaborate these factors in some detail.

The meaning of investment is addition to capital stock. If, at any point in time (say at the end of a year), the capital stock valued is rupees ₹ 500 crore and at any other point in time (say at the end of next year), the capital stock is valued at ₹ 550 crore, then this addition of ₹ 50 crore in one year period is investment. The value must, however, be at constant price level so that ₹ 50 crore must, necessarily be the addition to physical capital stock in real terms.

Now the classical economists believe that such investment takes place in the economy mainly because capital is more productive. Now, the acquisition of new capital asset, such as purchasing a new machine involves costs – costs in terms of interest for borrowed fund from savers. But, as more and more investment is taken up, the marginal productivity of capital declines just as the marginal productivity of labour or any other factor declines with its increasing volume. Therefore, any rational entrepreneur would be interested in acquiring more capital assets (investment) so long as the marginal productivity of an additional capital is higher than the interest cost. Hence, investment is higher at lower rate of interest; or, to say in other words, investment is a decreasing function of the rate of interest.

On the other hand, the savers or the lenders of investible funds are guided primarily by the propensity to prefer present consumption to future consumption. People postpone present consumption (save) only to consume it at some future date. But why should they go for such postponement for the future unless they are induced to do so for a return in terms of interest payment for the time period they forgo consumption? Secondly, why should, even if they save, go for higher amount of saving unless the rate of return is higher? Thus, the volume of saving goes on increasing with higher rate of interest; or, to say the same thing, saving is an increasing function of the rate of interest. Now, in the market for borrowers and lenders for investible funds, there will be one particular rate of interest at which the volume of investment will be equal to the volume of saving. This is the equilibrium rate of interest. At any other interest rate, either the savings will exceed investment or investment will exceed savings. In case savings exceed investment, the extra savings will not be in demand by investors because this will be only at a higher than the equilibrium rate of interest at which additional investment will not be profitable (or, productive); so, the rate of interest will be a bit down and savers will now be induced to save less. On the other hand, if volume of investment is in excess of savings, which occurs at lower than equilibrium rate of interest, competition among borrowers of investible fund for limited amount available will push up the rate of interest and will ultimately be equal to the equilibrium rate. This is how the volume of savings and investment are brought into equality by the equilibrating mechanism – the rate of interest. It is needless to comment here that this theory like any other classical theory presupposes that there is fairly enough flexibility in the rate of interest to allow the equilibrium to take place. In terms of diagram the theory can be represented as shown in Fig. 2.2.

Figure 2.2 depicts two curves, savings (S) and investment (I) – the first upward rising with rate of interest and the second, downward falling with rate of interest. The equilibrium rate of interest is established at point E, where the total volume of savings is exactly equal to the total volume of investment (S_0, I_0) at the corresponding rate of interest, r_0. At r_1 rate of interest ($r_1 > r_0$), the volume of saving is greater than the volume of investment by the amount *AB*. Similarly, at r_2 rate of interest, volume of savings is less than the volume of investment by *CD* amount. This disequilibrium point will, however, automatically restore equilibrium through appropriate changes in the rate of interest by competitive forces of demand and supply of saving and investment. Thus, in equilibrium, $S = I$.

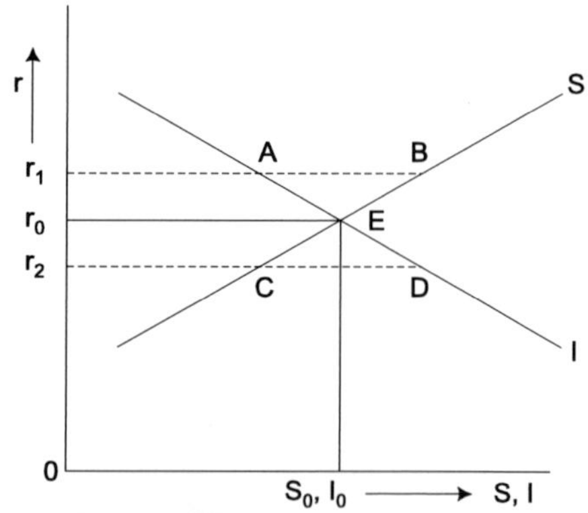

Figure 2.2 *Savings and investment behaviour in response to the rate of interest.*

2.4 WAGE-PRICE RELATIONSHIP AND FULL EMPLOYMENT

In this section, we examine the relationship between wages and prices in the classical system that would ensure full employment. We refer to Fig. 2.1(b), given below, which shows the equilibrium condition in the labour market in terms of total demand for labour being equal to the total supply of labour. The real wage rate W/P, in this situation, is $(W/P)_0$. In other words, the labour market clears only at $(W/P)_0$ real wage rate; hence this is the full employment equilibrium. This is because employers optimize their resources in order to maximize their profits at the output level of *Yp*- the potential output and at $(W/P)_0$ wage rate. According to classical, this situation is easily attainable the capitalist system given sufficient flexibility of wages and prices.

It should be mentioned here that this presupposes the existence of full competition in the labour market which means that the employers compete among themselves for hiring labour.

Assuming for the time being that all labourers are homogeneous and wages paid to them are standardized wages paid in terms of money, i.e., money wages (W). This is because, normally all employers pay their workers in terms of money wages. But how do they get at the real wages then? In other words, what is the relevant price level to be chosen? Since workers generally consider the average price level (taking all important items that enter their cost of living, may be, including the price of the product of the firm in which they are presently employed), the real wage rate is evaluated as money wage rate divided by the average price level. Alternatively, money wage rate can be taken, for simplicity, the economy-wide money wages since we are assuming homogeneized labour force. Now we suppose there is unemployment in the labour market so that there is excess supply of labour over the total demand for labour and the real wage rate is well above the equilibrium wage rate $(W/P)_0$. The actual output is also below the potential level of *Yp*. Now, if there is flexibility of wage rate, the employers will be induced to hire more labourers only when (W/P) falls from the present level. Also, the unemployed labourers are prepared to accept lower wage rate rather than remaining unemployed. This would, most likely, happen given the type of competition we have assumed in the labour market. However, falling (W/P) implies any of the following possibilities:

(a) Money wage rate falls but price level remains the same;

(b) Both money wage rate and the price level fall but the money wage rate falls to a greater extent than that of the price level;

(c) Money wages remain unchanged but price level rises.

Of the above three possibilities, classical economists assumed the wage-price deflation as the likely scenario reflecting the decline in the real wage rate, i.e., the possibility (*b*). Therefore, so long as the real wage rate continues to fall, the employers would be ready to hire more and more labourers and thereby increase output beyond the present level until the entire unemployed labour force is absorbed and they reach the potential output level of *Yp*. This is essentially a short run phenomenon when such fluctuations in output and employment take place amidst unemployment of labour as well as other unused resources. But in the long run, full employment is bound to be restored.

Some unanswered questions, however, remain to be solved.

Firstly, any reduction in money wage rate is always accompanied by the corresponding decline in the price level; at least this is what the quantity theory conclusions suggest. Not only this, reduction of money wages by a certain percentage leads to the same percentage decline in price level. If this is the implication of the classical theory, then, in any case, real wage rate remains at the same level and there is no chance of further increase in employment so that unemployment is most likely to persist.

However, one possible situation seems relevant, although remotely. If, at the individual employer's level (micro level), lowering of the price of the product is initiated as a result of lower money wage rate, then, at the macro level, this is likely to result in lower average price level. This, in turn, implies that transaction demand for money is lower ($Md = mPoY$). Since, in equilibrium, total demand for money is equal to its total supply, this further implies that supply of money must have been proportionately decreased causing decline in the average price-level.

In any case, the exact relationship between money wage rate and price level is far from being clear in the classical theory of employment.

2.4.1 Critical Evaluation

In spite of many shortcomings and simplistic assumptions of the classical macroeconomic system and Keynesian revolution in the post-1930s, the 1970s and period thereafter has witnessed a kind of revival of classical system. The new classical macroeconomics has focussed on further refinements of the basic classical tenets and popularization of policy tools based on these tenets. The rise of supply side economics with its root is Say's law, market fundamentalism of the capitalist economy with minimum government intervention in the functioning of the economic system and rising importance of monetary policy vis-a-vis fiscal policy are some of the recent developments in the macroeconomics field with their application in most of the western capitalist economies and gradual policy changes in emerging economies of the world. The most important drawback of the classical/new classical economic policies being pursued in most of western capitalist world based on free enterprise and market economy rules is the failure of predicting correctly the occurrence of 'crises'. Business cycles do occur in spite of tall claims by the authors belonging to this group which virtually jeopardize the functioning of the capitalist system.

SUMMARY

1. Classical macroeconomics is based on a set of postulates/assumptions such as long period, Say's law of market, full employment, flexibility of wages and prices, neutrality of money, absence of money illusion and dichotomy between real and monetary sectors. If these postulates are accepted, classical macroeconomics produces a neat systematic and logical theory to explain the working of the economy.
2. Long period is the key assumption which allow economic agents to sufficiently adjust and revise their decisions and attain the new level of equilibrium. Even though they do consider changes occurring during short period, but such changes are not important for the classicals.
3. Say's law of market and full employment are somewhat inseparable in the sense that Say's law implies, on the one hand, that there is no possibility of overproduction or unemployment of resources while on the other it also implies that supply and hence production will be carried on to the level of full employment. The law argues that there may be temporary maladjustment between demand and supply of a certain product and hence temporary unemployment but in the aggregate, all demands will ultimately be equal to all supplies. Say's law, it has been argued, applies not only to a barter-type economy which is obvious from its original presentation, but also to a money economy when money and labour services, instead of goods, are exchanged and also where savings and investments take place.
4. Classicals hold the view that wages and prices are flexible, capable of changing in both directions whenever needed. Hence, demand and supply curves of labour are not inelastic in shape. Flexibility of wages is easily transmitted into flexible prices and vice versa.
5. Dichotomy between real and monetary sectors implies that real sector and monetary sector are separable or decomposable such that changes in monetary sector changes only the nominal variables but not the real variables such as relative prices, real wages, employment, output, etc. However, the converse is not true; that is, changes in real sector surely have impacts on the monetary sector.

   The classical quantity theory of money tries to establish that money supply and price level (general price level) have a direct and proportional relationship while the velocity of money is constant. The theory lends support to the major elements such as Say's law, full employment and dichotomized economy.
6. The classical theory of saving and investment is a real theory. It states that saving is an increasing function while investment is a decreasing function of the rate of interest and both functions mutually determine

the equilibrium rate of interest. If, either saving or investment deviate from equilibrium, the rate of interest changes bring them into equality. However, both saving and investment are determined by factors such as people's time – preference in case of saving and productivity of capital in case of investments.

EXERCISE

1. Discuss Say's law, supply creates its own demand and examine its relevance in the modern system of exchange economy.
2. What do you understand by classical dichotomy? Illustrate with example.
3. Examine the classical employment theory. How far is it relevant to macroeconomic logic?

REFERENCES

1. Gardner Ackley, Macroeconomics: Theory and Policy, MacMillan 1978.
2. Don Patinkin, Money, Interest and Prices, 2nd Edition, Harper & Row, 1965.
3. R.L. Crouch, Macroeconomics, Harcourt Brace Jovanovitch, 1972.
4. Joseph A Schumpeter, History of Economic Analysis, Oxford University Press, 1954.
5. William J. Baumol, Economic Theory and Operations Analysis, Prentice-Hall of India, 1966.
6. Edward Shapiro (ed.), Macroeconomics: Selected Readings, Harcourt Brace Jovanovitch, 1970.

3

The Keynesian Theory: Employment and Output Determination in the Short Run

3.1 REJECTION OF MAJOR POSTULATES OF THE CLASSICS

3.1.1 Underemployment Equilibrium

Keynes put forward the idea that full employment was never a normal phenomenon in the capitalist economy. On the contrary, unemployment was the normal feature and full employment was just accidental. It (full employment) is a passing phase in the development of capitalist economy. Classicals held the view that some percentage of unemployment would always be there in the economy, but these are largely 'voluntary' in character; and if not, they arise due to "temporary" mismatch between location-wise availability of jobs and job-seekers or lack of labour mobility among skills and occupations (frictional or structural unemployment). Keynes departed from this view by characterizing unemployment as "involuntary" – people seeking employment but not able to get.

With a view to explaining his theory of employment, Keynes provided the theory of 'effective demand'. This theory was just the opposite of the classical dictum of Say's law – supply creating its own demand. Thus, for the first time the entire argument was reversed in terms of 'demand creating its own supply'. Keynes developed the concept of underemployment equilibrium – suggesting that economy may well reach equilibrium (aggregate demand = aggregate supply) even before full employment.

3.1.2 Short-Period Analysis

The assumption of '*long period*' was discarded by Keynes. To him for all practical purposes, short period is the most relevant time consideration. Keynes said, 'in the long run we are all dead'. In fact, changes occurring during short period have significant policy implications and if left to automatic forces, may lead to disastrous consequences. Keynes' analysis, therefore, attaches greater importance to 'short period' as against classicals' 'long period' assumption.

3.1.3 Wage-Price Rigidity

Keynes did not agree with the classical view that wages and prices are flexible. As far as wages are concerned, they are, in reality, not sufficiently flexible to allow the full employment to happen in the classical sense. In fact, employers are constrained to bring down wages at will, neither are the workers ready to accept the wage reduction whenever desired by their employers. So, wages are "sticky" downward suggesting that wage reductions are more difficult than wage increases. This is due not only to demand-supply situation of the labour market but also due to unionized labour, minimum wage legislation by the government and other socio-political considerations. If such is the reality, the structure of labour demand and labour supply curves will be different from those postulated by the classicals. In particular, the labour demand curve will be relatively inelastic while the labour supply curve will be partly more elastic (even perfectly elastic in case labourers are strongly unionized) and partly inelastic when all members of the union are employed. Thus, to Keynes, wages are, generally, 'rigid' in character and not flexible as assumed by the classicals.

Similarly, in the economy, most prices are also not flexible due to imperfect information system, existence of administered prices or some other political factors. It may be pointed out here that classical economists advocated for a free and perfectly competitive market structure devoid of government intervention which, of course, was more of an idealized situation than the real-world ground reality.

3.1.4 Role of Money

Regarding the role of money in the economy, Keynes extended the classical position in a significant way insofar as the money acts not only as a medium of exchange (fulfilling transaction demand) but also as a 'store of value' (fulfilling the asset demand). Money, according to Keynes, can be 'held' or stored as an asset; hence it acts as a link between 'present' and the 'future'. Thus, in the Keynesian formulation, we have two components of demand for money, viz., transaction demand and asset demand for money. The role of money, as we shall see later in the chapter, plays much more influencing part in the determination of 'effective demand' and hence the level of employment, output, income and interest rate. In this formulation, therefore, we can imagine two distinct categories of money: "money sitting" referring to its role as a store of value; and "money on the wings", referring to its role as a medium of transaction.

3.1.5 Irrelevance of the Dichotomy Assumption

The classical dichotomy assumption naturally lost its relevance in the Keynesian theory. Keynes believed that real and monetary sectors are not separable and, in fact, changes in monetary sector do influence the variables in the real sector such as real output and employment through real income and expenditure or 'aggregate demand'. Even though Keynes himself did not work out the process of integrating of monetary and real sectors which was the major contribution of later Keynesians (Hicks, Hansen Patinkin and others), one certainly finds obvious links between monetary sector changes and aggregate demand influencing real output and employment.

3.1.6 Existence of Money Illusion

Keynes challenged the classical assertion of absence of money illusion in all major markets by emphasising that money illusion is very much the reality since people are apt to be affected by this notion. For instance, labour supply is a function of money wage rate. If money wages increase, workers surely are tempted to increase labour days/hours even though real wages do not increase. Similarly, labour demand function is also affected by money wages since the employers have to make payment of wages in money terms. Other markets such as capital and land, and, of course, prices attached to them (interest and rent) too suffer from money illusion.

In the same manner, money is 'not neutral' in the Keynesian framework as against the assumption of the classicals. In other words, changes in money supply do not leave other prices such as rate of interest, unaffected.

3.1.7 Interest Rate – A Monetary Phenomenon

Lastly, the rate of interest, according to Keynes is a *monetary* phenomenon and not a real phenomenon as assumed by classicals. Rate of interest is determined by demand for and supply of money and not by real factors like capital productivity and people's time preference (or, investment and saving in real terms).

Thus, Keynes virtually demolished almost all underlying postulates of classical macroeconomics. In doing so, however, he continued to repose trust on at least some of the fundamental tenets of his predecessors – the classicals, to which group he himself belonged in the early years of his career.

3.2 KEYNESIAN THEORY OF EFFECTIVE DEMAND

3.2.1 The Concepts of 'Potential Output'

The potential output of an economy may be defined as the level of output that the economy is capable of producing at full employment of its resources without causing inflation or deflation. In other words, it is the full capacity utilisation level of output of an economy. Potential output is not observable. Instead, it can be estimated on the basis of the existing potential of the economy. It may be expressed in terms of the level of real output or the rate of growth of output. For instance, in the case of Indian economy, various government agencies (CSO, RBI), international organisations (IMF, World Bank), and independent economists have been estimating the potential output as well as the potential growth rate from time to time. There is no doubt the estimation of potential output for an economy is an extremely complicated exercise.

As against potential output, there is the concept of actual output, the output (or, the rate of growth of output) the economy actually experiences during a certain period of time. If the actual output is equal or exceeds the potential output level, there is every chance that the economy experiences inflationary conditions. On the other hand, if the actual output is less than the potential output, it indicates unemployment of resources including labour. It also suggests that the prospects of further non-inflationary growth in the economy exist. The difference between actual output and potential output is known as the output gap (AO – PO = OG).

As we have already noted earlier, Keynes' theory starts with the basic idea that employment and output in the economy are 'demand determined'. The concept of 'effective demand' was advanced by Keynes in the context of employment determination at the macro level. In order to understand the concept of effective demand we have to visualize two prices operating in the economy, viz., aggregate demand price and aggregate supply price. The aggregate demand price refers to the level of price (aggregate or average) at which goods and services are *actually* sold, i.e., the producers actually receive the price by selling their goods and services. In other words, this is the price which the consumers are prepared to pay for purchasing goods and services. On the other hand, aggregate supply price is the *minimum* price necessary for producers to carry on production of such goods and services. Below this minimum price no producer would be willing to carry production. Now, in the short run, as long as the aggregate demand price is greater than the aggregate supply price, all producers will experience profits which would motivate them to increase output and employment. Only when the aggregate demand price is just equal to the aggregate supply price the producers find themselves in a state of indifference or 'equilibrium'. If this point is exceeded, i.e., if aggregate supply price is greater than the aggregate demand price so that producers are not able to receive their expected minimum price, they would rather be rethinking about continuing output and employment. The point of equilibrium or equality between aggregate demand and aggregate supply prices has been defined as the 'effective demand'.

Relevant to the idea of aggregate demand and aggregate supply prices are associated two curves: aggregate demand curve and aggregate supply curve. While both the curves appear as upward rising from left to right, the former (aggregate demand curve) lies above the latter (aggregate supply curve). Also, while *AD* curve increases at a decreasing rate, the *AS* curve increases with an increasing rate and the gap between the two gradually reduces until both become equal (Fig. 3.1). The aggregate supply and demand functions (*AD* & *AS*) can also be looked upon as aggregate sale proceeds from the producers' point of view or aggregate expenditure made by the community over the total amount of goods and services produced. The equilibrium in the economy and equilibrium level of employment occurs at point *E* where *AD* = *AS* with equilibrium level of employment of *OY*. However, *OY* is not necessarily the full employment level even though economy is at equilibrium. This is what Keynes defined as *underemployment equilibrium*. In fact, the total available supply of labour is OY_1 – more than *OY* by YY_1 suggesting the magnitude of involuntary unemployment.

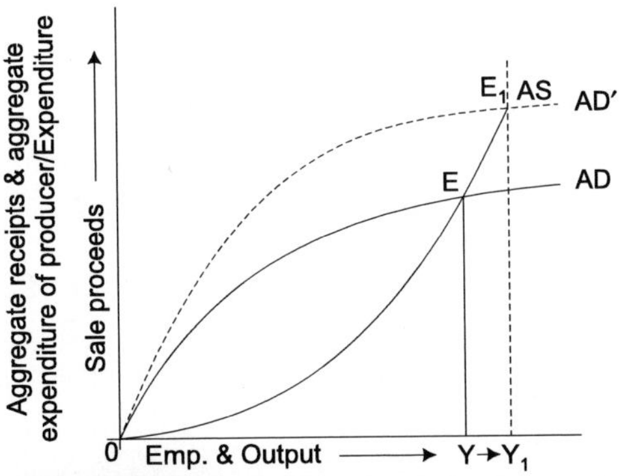

Figure 3.1 *Effective demand: The interaction between aggregate demand and aggregate supply.*

Why does such a situation of underemployment equilibrium develop in the economy? Clearly, Keynes visualizes that the extent of aggregate demand (or, aggregate expenditures) falls short of the producers' expectations (or, aggregate supply or their minimum supply prices necessary to continue output and absorb the unemployed labour force. Clearly, the prescription suggested is to increase the level of aggregate demand. In terms of Fig. 3.1, it would possibly happen when the entire *AD* function shifts upward so much that *AD* intersects *AS* beyond *E* and employment increases so much to allow the producers to produce at the 'potential level', Y_1, as shown in Fig. 3.1 by shifted *AD* curve (*AD′*) and the ultimate equilibrium point of E_1. Thus, in terms of Keynesian analysis, economy may achieve 'equilibrium' but not necessarily at full employment output. It is a coincidence if that happens but the normal situation is that of underemployment equilibrium with potential output greater than the actual output.

Professor P.A. Samuelson, one of the greatest followers of Keynes has provided a new explanation of Keynesian underemployment equilibrium in terms of aggregate demand and aggregate supply (*AD* – *AS*) framework. Figure 3.2 illustrates this.

While general price level is shown along the vertical axis, aggregate demand and aggregate supply curves are shown along the horizontal axis. (The *AD* curve can be derived from the aggregate sales proceeds and the total sale units by dividing the former by the latter which gives the per unit price). The *AS* curve is upward rising from left to right and becomes vertical at the full employment level or where actual output is equal to potential output. However, the *AD* curve is downward sloping, intersects the *AS* curve much before the point of full employment suggesting underemployment equilibrium. Thus, underemployment equilibrium is explained in terms of insufficiency of aggregate demand. Only when the *AD* curve goes up higher and intersects with the aggregate supply curve at the vertical point, the full employment will be achieved.

The figure suggests clear policy implication, for raising aggregate demand, additional private consumption demand or additional private investment demand needs to be stepped up, but short of these, public (or government) investment demand has to be raised sufficiently so that the *AD* curve cuts the *AS* curve on the vertical part as shown in Fig. 3.2. Beyond this point, however, additional demand will result in inflation without a rise in output or employment.

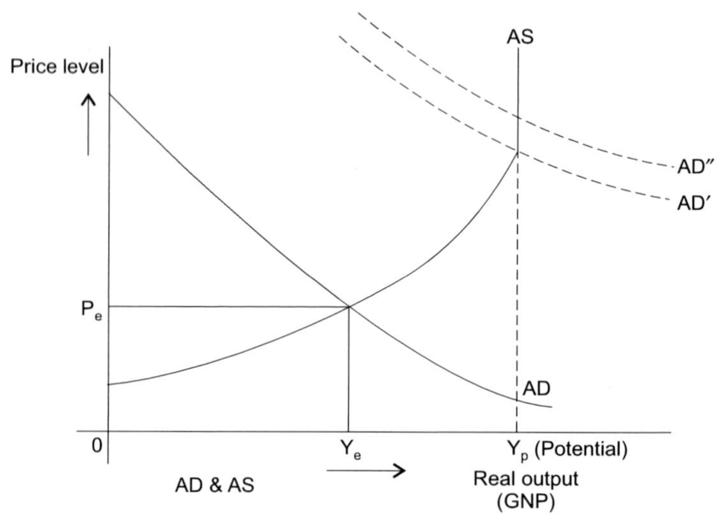

Figure 3.2 *Keynes' underemployment equilibrium in AD/AS framework*

However, the critics say that the model seems to be self contradictory. For, there is a dilemma between general equilibrium and labour market equilibrium. If there is labour market disequilibrium, there cannot be general equilibrium in the economy when all the markets are in equilibrium.

Keynes' 'Paradox of Thrift'

One of the key elements in Keynes' theory of employment is the paradox of thrift which is expressed in the dictum, 'saving is a private virtue but public vice'. The message it gives is that normally, individuals treat saving as a boon because it helps them in financially difficult times. However, if the community as a whole decides to save their incomes, it will result in lower aggregate demand and hence lower aggregate expenditure and more unemployment. This is particularly important during recessionary phases or depression in the economy when the community requires to make more and more expenditures to reverse the course of the cyclical phase. "Under conditions of unemployment, the attempt to save may result in not more saving" Samuelson declared. Keynes, of course, said practically the same thing, not more eloquently thus: "The more virtuous we are, the more determinedly thrifty, the more obstinately orthodox in our national and personal finance, the more our incomes will have to fall" (*General Theory of Employment, Interest and Money*, Macmillan, London, 1936).

Paradox of thrift is shown in Fig. 3.3. In the Keynesian cross model, the increased community thrift (savings) results in a leftward shift of the savings curve which intersects the Keynesian investment curve thus resulting in less equilibrium income.

However, the critics have said that Keynes was confused between 'saving' and 'hoarding', the latter term meaning totally idle part of income either kept in lockers or left languishing uninvested without any active use. In fact, saving is a potential source of economic growth. The rate of saving is an important element of growth theory as has been demonstrated in various growth models.

In conclusion, we may say that while saving/thrift is unwelcome during depression/recession, it is of great value during a more normal period of time since more saving means more investment and more investment means more economic growth.

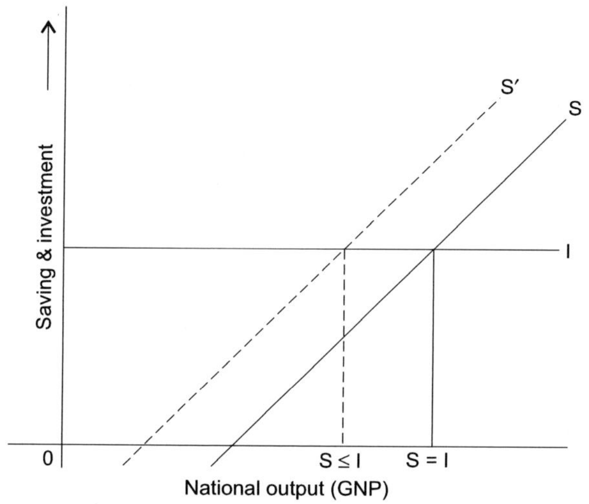

Figure 3.3 *Paradox of thrift.*

Now the question is: why are wages sticky or inflexible as argued by Keynes? This can be explained using demand and supply curves of labour as shown in Fig. 3.4. The demand and supply curves of labour are drawn against the money wage rate instead of the real wage rate because Keynes held the view that workers are generally guided by money wages they are paid by their employers. At the same time they suffer very much from money illusion.

As shown in the figure, the labour market does not clear as the two curves do not intersect at the equilibrium point. This is because the money wage rate is inflexible due to certain structural factors like unionised labour force and minimum wage legislations even if there is unemployment in the labour market. This is why unemployment persists.

In the later years, new Keynesian economists discovered two other factors of the persistence of unemployment: these are (a) inelasticity of the investment demand function and (b) liquidity trap. Regarding (a), it is argued that the investment demand function is no doubt a decreasing function of the rate of interest, but it is relatively inelastic in nature. Keynes originally thought that investment sentiment is 'fickle', meaning it is unpredictable. In fact, investment demand by the entrepreneurial class depends on several factors principally the expectations of the investors about the future outlook of business besides the cost of capital, that is, the rate of interest. However, the new Keynesians later relented on this but still maintained that it is inelastic, not so much responsive to interest rate.

Regarding (b), the new Keynesians argue that when the economy suffers from recession, depression or slowdown so that demand for goods and services in the economy is slackening, demand for money becomes highly elastic so that at very low rate of interest, the demand for bonds (by the investing class) is low. If we look at the current economic scenario around the developed world suffering from slow growth despite persistent attempts to spur growth by conventional policies, this fact will be clear.

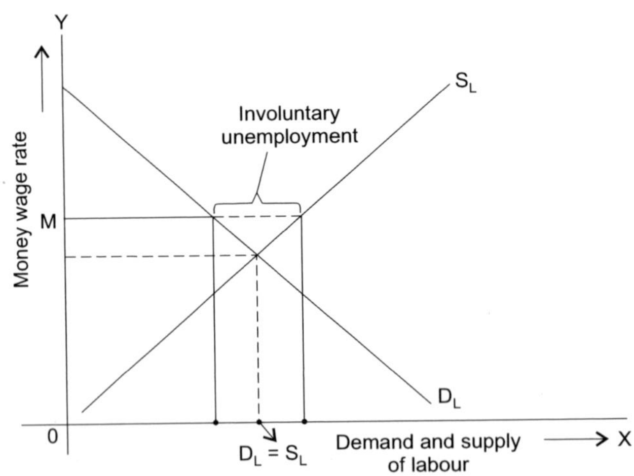

Figure 3.4 *Sticky wages and unemployment.*

3.3 KEYNES VS. CLASSICAL DEBATE ON UNEMPLOYMENT

There was a long debate between the classical economists and Keynes and the Keynesians on the subject of unemployment. Specifically, they argued on how unemployment arises in the economy and under what conditions does unemployment persist and how unemployment is tackled. These are some of the questions on which the classical and Keynesian economists have debated over long periods and, in fact, are still debating. We review, below, the main debating points on unemployment.

- Classical economists were of the view that unemployment simply does not occur in a free enterprise capitalist economy given the basic postulates of flexible wages and prices. In particular, wages are capable of changing easily without hindrance in both ways. This implies that the labour market needs to be flexible. Similarly, prices, including the interest rate, are assumed to be flexible too. Such flexibility would, according to classics, ensure attainment of full employment. However, classics concede that unemployment of some kind, for a temporary period, may occur. People changing their jobs in search of better jobs or at better locations may remain unemployed for a certain period. This is quite natural in a capitalist economy. But unemployment for a longer period or permanent unemployment cannot be visualised. Keynes, however, would not agree with this condition of the economy. The real-world situation is far more complex. In particular, wages are inflexible (or rigid) downward. This means it may be easy to raise wages upwards but is difficult to reduce downwards. They are, in fact," sticky" in character. In the face of unemployment, labour supply does not respond to labour demand even at higher wages and there remains excess supply of labour in the labour market. Secondly, according to Keynes, "involuntary" unemployment will always be there (people seeking employment but are unable to get).
- Classical economists, notably AC Pigou, was of the view that in the short period, unemployment, even of involuntary type, might occur in the economy. But if perfect competition is allowed to prevail and wage price flexibility is ensured in the market, the unemployment will no longer be there. This might necessitate wage deflation as a policy by cutting wages as well as the prices and thereby reducing the real wage rate. This would raise the demand for labour at the employer's end and thus increase employment until full employment is reached. Keynes and the Keynesians would, however, argue that even if wage reduction is granted, after a point, it will meet the resistance of labour unions who will not allow the wage rate to fall below a certain level. Secondly, there will be minimum wage legislation in place in most situations. The

wage rate therefore does not come down sufficiently to clear the labour market, that is, demand for labour is not equated to its supply.

- Classical economist Pigou offered another powerful defence against the Keynesian argument of lack of adequate aggregate demand causing unemployment. This was his wealth effect argument. Price deflation (falling price level) increases the real value of assets such as physical goods, houses, bonds as also money. This would raise the purchasing power in the hands of the consumers, thus pushing up aggregate demand. Critics, however, point out that the price deflation method is not an effective channel of restoring full employment. Firstly, even if wealth effects may have some favourable impact on consumption, it may prove to be insufficient for full employment. Secondly, most of the community's assets consist of money and bonds. Now if the price level falls, the rate of interest too has a tendency to fall. Since, the price of bonds as assets rises (due to falling rate of interest), the investors would not be interested in buying bonds since they become costly now. So, investment demand, which is one of the key components of aggregate demand, will be discouraged. Perhaps, for this reason, Keynesians later advanced the "inelastic investment demand function" as an obstacle to the attainment of full employment.
- Classics asserted that unemployment is a passing phase in the development of the capitalist economy and not a permanent feature, but Keynes argued that full employment is a passing phase and unemployment is rather a permanent feature of the capitalist economy.
- Unemployment, to Keynes, is the product of deficiency in the aggregate demand which, in turn, is related to potential output. Classics, however, rely on " Say's law" and argue that aggregate supply itself would guarantee sufficiency of aggregate demand. Hence, deficiency of aggregate demand poses no problem for the classics. In fact, short run fluctuations in the economy which Keynes addressed so brilliantly to highlight the unemployment problem in a free enterprise capitalist economy, are likened to the 'tempest' in the ocean which would subside with time when the storm would peter out. Classics are thus concerned with only the level of the sea but do not try to gauge the undercurrent beneath the sea level.
- At the root of the debate lies 'the long run' versus 'short run' perspectives of the classics' and Keynes. While classics would subscribe to the long-run view and ignore largely the short-run problems of unemployment and underemployment arguing that the economy would self-correct without any government intervention, albeit in the long run. Keynes' suggestive reply to long versus short run debate was that "in the long run we are all dead". To quote Keynes, "...... but this long run is a

misleading guide to current affairs. In the long run, we are all dead. Economists set themselves too easy, too useless a task if in tempestuous seasons they can only tell us that when the storm is long past, the ocean is flat again" (*The Collected Writings of John Maynard Keynes*, vol. 15, Macmillan, London)

- The classical economists viewed the equilibrium in the labour market as arising out of the optimising behaviour of the producer at the micro level and assumed that the same would be applicable also at the macro level. Hence, there is no possibility of disequilibrium in the labour market causing unemployment at the macro level. Unemployment is, therefore, inconsistent with producer rationality (or, profit maximisation). Keynes, however, differed from this view and argued that what may be true at the micro level may not be true at the macro level. For instance, saving is a private virtue at the micro level. But if everyone begins saving, at the macro level, the result becomes disastrous, since there will be very little spending or demand at the aggregate. This is Keynes' famous 'paradox of thrift' (discussed at page 54).

3.4 TYPES OF UNEMPLOYMENT: FRICTIONAL, STRUCTURAL, CYCLICAL AND TECHNOLOGICAL

Unemployment, it is needless to say, is the biggest problem of the capitalist economy. However, it has different variants which appear at different circumstances. We discuss below four of these variants, namely, frictional structural, cyclical and technological unemployment.

Frictional unemployment: This type of unemployment takes place when the workers change jobs in search of new or better jobs. Workers sometimes are not satisfied with their present jobs due to unfavourable work conditions, lower wages, locational hazards or some other reasons. In the process of searching and waiting for new jobs, workers remain unemployed. This is frictional unemployment. Needless to say that those workers who are either entering the labour market for the first time or re-entering it after some kind of training but remain unemployed in the meanwhile also represent the category of frictionally unemployed. Such type of unemployment is quite natural in any economy and society. However, in a full employment or near full employment situation such unemployment is widely prevalent. This also means that workers have the necessary skills to negotiate with.

In advanced economies frictional unemployment composes not more than 5% of the labour force. For this reason, policy makers in those countries often define full employment as being less than 5% unemployment. This is also known as the natural rate of unemployment.

Structural unemployment: This is the type of unemployment existing in the economy due to certain structural rigidities in the labour market resulting in the prevalence of higher than equilibrium wage rate. Obviously, in such a situation, the supply of labour is greater than the demand for it. This is the unemployment that Keynes termed as "involuntary unemployment", workers seek jobs but are unable to get them.

There can be various types of structural rigidities such as 'sticky' or 'rigid' wage rate, particularly in the downward direction due to unionised labour pressure or existence of minimum wage legislations which together make the labour market inflexible. In fact, in terms of demand-supply diagram of labour, one can argue that Minimum Wages Act makes the labour supply curve look like a horizontal one starting at the point of minimum wage rate and having intersected the demand curve for labour, goes vertically upward. But the labour market does not make it clear while the wage rate remains higher than the equilibrium wage rate.

Geographical immobility of the labour market due to several factors such as language barriers, cultural and environmental barriers or lack of sufficient living spaces also act as rigidities in the labour market. Instances in recent history in the European Union, particularly in the Eurozone countries illustrate how the above mentioned rigidities in the labour market in relatively debt ridden countries like Greece, Spain and Portugal prevented their movement to other countries of Europe and caused unemployment along with high wage rate in those countries.

Structural rigidities in the labour market may also occur if there is technological change in the production technology resulting in complete mismatch between the demand for labour and the availability or supply of labour. We discuss separately below the technological unemployment due to the special nature of this problem even though it is a part of the broader concept of structural unemployment.

Cyclical unemployment: Unemployment which is associated with cyclical fluctuations or business cycles like recession/slowdown or even depression in the economy is known as cyclical unemployment. Business cycles are an inescapable feature of capitalist economy. There is a strong correlation between output growth and employment growth. During the entire downward phase of the business cycle, output growth slows and even becomes negative which implies that unemployment grows in the economy. This kind of unemployment is cyclical unemployment. Needless to say that when there is a revival in the economy after the bad times are gone, there is growth in output and employment and hence reduction in unemployment.

In the advanced countries of the west, there have occurred several recessions during the eighties and nineties besides the longest recession of 2008-09 in the US and several European countries which had impacted other Asian countries as well including India. However, the Great Depression of 1929-30 was the worst kind of economic depression of the 20th century when aggregate demand fell dramatically resulting in fall in economic output, income, prices and employment of the affected nations even as unemployment rates had risen above 25% in advanced countries. Most cyclical unemployment occurs due to demand deficiency but sometimes supply shocks (which are mainly negative), are also responsible for recessions or downward movement of the cyclical fluctuations. In India, during the first and second quarters of 2019, there is much discussion in the policy circles of slowdown taking place in the economy, growth rate slipping to 4.5%, the lowest ever, along with job losses in several sectors like automobiles, consumer goods and marginal, small, medium enterprises (MSMEs).

It may be mentioned here that adoption of appropriate anti-cyclical policy measures can cure unemployment and usher in economic revival.

Technological unemployment: Technological unemployment refers to the loss of jobs due to technological advancement in many areas of human lives which are traditionally performed manually. The invention of machines of various kinds from time to time over the whole span of human history has caused this kind of unemployment. In fact, technological unemployment is a part of the broader concept of structural unemployment described above since it further complicates the structure of the labour market.

With scientific inventions constantly taking place ever since the Industrial Revolution in Europe in the 18th century (taking into account only the recent history), labour has been displaced and rendered unemployed. In the textile industry, the invention of the power loom replaced the handloom long back in our country and thereby killed our most important traditional sector of employment.

In the agricultural sector, machine power has been in use in a labour abundant country like India and elsewhere ever since the 1960s (tractors, power tillers, reapers, etc.) which are all examples of technological unemployment.

In recent times, automation, robots, artificial intelligence, machine learning and digitisation are examples of newer technological changes which the industries are increasingly using for raising worker productivity–doing jobs faster and more efficiently but labour displacing at the same time.

The broader question involving technological unemployment centres around the possibility of creating enough alternative jobs not only for new entrants with new skills but also for absorbing the displaced ones through training and retraining them. Whether these outcomes are going to happen in the future shall be anxiously awaited and examined for human welfare. Several international organisations including the World Bank, however, expressed concern over the technological unemployment in future.

In his recent book entitled, *Shaping the Fourth Industrial Revolution*, World Economic Forum, 2018, Klaus Schwab, Founder and Executive Chairman, World Economic Forum, reminds of the challenges of the potential impact on employment thus: " a wide range of jobs are at risk of automation, far greater than in previous revolutions and rapid scaling means the job losses could accumulate quickly. Meanwhile, the rate of job creation in industries at the technological frontier is slower today than in previous decades. Jobs being created in new industries demand technical and non-cognitive skills posing challenges for less skilled workers. In advanced economies, the majority of new jobs consist of independent contracting, part time, temporary or "gig economy" activities which tend to lack the statutory protections and social benefits of full time work. In the US, for example, 94% of new jobs created between 2005 and 2015 are in alternative forms of work, lacking social protection, labour rights or even meaningful control on the part of workers. Fourth Industrial Revolution technologies, therefore, appear to be undermining humans' choice and ability to apply their skills and interests to meaningful work and may lead to generations of workers living precarious and fragmented lives ..."

Seasonal unemployment: There is also another type of unemployment–seasonal unemployment, mostly observed in agriculture and the rural sector of an economy. There are busy and slack seasons in agriculture such as sowing and transplantation and harvesting seasons as busy while the remaining periods of the year are slack seasons. What is characteristic of the seasonal unemployment is that during the slack period, the agricultural workers are rendered unemployed or partially unemployed (since, during slack seasons also, certain types of jobs associated with busy season agricultural pursuits, arranging for different tools and implements, their repair works, storage of harvested grains, etc., have to be performed by the farmers). Seasonal unemployment, however, is gradually disappearing in recent times due to various kinds of rural employment schemes being undertaken by various governments.

3.5 UNEMPLOYMENT MEASUREMENT IN INDIA

Before we attempt to measure employment/unemployment in an economy, it is important to understand certain concepts like labour force, work force, working age population, etc.

Labour force constitutes that part of the population which is available for doing some jobs for earning income. Usually, the proportion of the population falling within the age-group (15-59) years, is known as the working age population. Out of this population, those who offer themselves for jobs, constitute the 'labour force'. Obviously, a certain percentage of the working age population, will be students studying in higher classes in schools and colleges while others (females in particular) might be 'homemakers', not opting for earning jobs. However, this age-group limitation of labour force does not mean that some people outside the group do not work for paid jobs. For instance, in underdeveloped countries, above 59 years of age as also below 15 years boys and girls are found working for paid works (child labour). However, the internationally accepted definition of labour force is those belonging to the 15-59 age group1[1]. Now, out of this labour force, some members are able to find employment (jobs for earning income), while others may not. Those who find employment/jobs, are called 'employed' and those who fail to find any job are called 'unemployed'. Those employed may also be called 'workforce' or 'workers'. Those unemployed are in search of jobs and mostly get themselves registered in the Employment Exchanges.

Those who are employed fall within the wage employment or self-employment groups.

The measurement of employment/unemployment depends on the yardstick or yardsticks applied for this purpose. Then the ratio of the number of employed or unemployed people out of the total number of the labour force (employed + unemployed), expressed in percentage terms are known as rate of employment or rate of unemployment at a certain point in time (the survey date). In fact, such measurements are usually based on surveys conducted in any country from time to time. In India, for example, such surveys are conducted by the NSSO (National Sample Survey Organization). In advanced countries like the US, such surveys are carried out on a regular basis.

In India, NSSO surveys categorise three groups of the employed / unemployed which are as follows:

1. usual/principal status,
2. weekly status, and
3. daily status.

The usual or principal status employed persons are those who find themselves employed or unemployed for the maximum number of days during the year preceding the survey (generally, more than 50%).

Those belonging to the second category, are persons employed or unemployed at least for a day during the previous week preceding the survey.

Within the third category are included those who find or do not find employment on the day preceding the day of survey.

Counting the number as well as the percentage of employed or unemployed persons of all categories as mentioned above provide a measure of rates of employment or unemployment as well as underemployment (employment below full time).

An example will clarify the method of measurement of employment/ unemployment based on Indian NSSO survey done in 2011-12.

India's labour force was between 440 million and 484 million in 2011-12 the lower number indicating people who looked for work every day (unemployment on daily basis) while the higher number points to those who joined the workforce

1. In developed countries like the U.S., U.K., and other Western countries, this age-group extends to 15-64 years.

(employed at some point in the year). Out of 440 million, 416 million were found to be employed at the time of the survey indicating that about 24 million were unemployed on a daily basis. We can get the figures in percentage terms as well such as (24/440)*100 = 6% which is the unemployment rate. Similarly, (416/440)*100 = 94% is the employment rate.

Recently, the NSSO has also published the annual Periodic Labour Force Survey (PLFS), 2017-18 and 2020-21 which have thrown up valuable data relating to employment/unemployment situation in India.

However, the above measurement does not reflect regular employment/unemployment status which contrasts with advanced economies data on employment being regular wage/salary employment. In fact, in India, only 18% of the working people were found to be on regular wage/salary employment–the rest being casual (30%) as well as self employment (52%).

It is worth mentioning that jobless or unemployment data on more accurate daily, weekly and monthly basis is being reportedly compiled by other private agencies notably Centre for Monitoring Indian Economy (CMIE), which is expected to complement, to a large extent, the Government of India and the RBI which are interested in forecasting growth rate of the economy along with monetary policy as well as unemployment rates in future. This will be in keeping with the present-day needs for the fast changing economic scenario of the country as well as the world.

SUMMARY

1. Keynes rejected almost all the underlying postulates of the classical economists and held the view that in the real-world situation, underemployment equilibrium rather than full employment equilibrium prevails. Full employment is just a passing phase and not a normal phenomenon in the economic system. This is because the underlying conditions required for full employment are, by and large, absent. For instance, there are rigidities in the labour market which do not allow the flexibility of labour market to exit the wages, in particular, are, very often, sticky in character.
2. According to Keynes' analysis, 'demand creates its own supply rather than 'supply creates its own demand'. Thus, aggregate demand plays a crucial role in the employment and output determination of the economy. If the aggregate demand is insufficient, the economy will not move forward enough to absorb the available stock of labour force so that there will be unemployment as well as underemployment in the economy. There will be more job seekers than jobs available.
3. Keynes termed such unemployment as "involuntary unemployment'. In a situation of underemployment equilibrium, the only solution is raising

of aggregate demand schedule through more and more government investment or government purchases of goods and services.

4. On the question of unemployment prevalence, there has been a long debate among classical economists and Keynes. The classics have argued that correcting the market imperfections in the economy, particularly, in the labour market and ensuring flexibility in the wage price system would automatically ensure full employment. Similarly, in the face of deficient aggregate demand, if the general price level is lowered, there will be rise in the real value of assets which will raise the overall aggregate demand. Keynes' argument was that in actual practice, prevalence of labour unions and minimum wage legislations will not allow the full flexibility in the wage-price system neither will the asset price raise (real balance effect) be able to raise aggregate demand sufficient to remove unemployment.
5. In the real-world situation, there are various categories of unemployment, viz, frictional, structural, cyclical and technological each create a variety of market imperfections. While frictional unemployment occurs due to workers changing their jobs either due to better pay or better locations and which according to classics quite natural in the capitalist economy and hence does not pose any problem, the structural unemployment arises due to the existence of structural rigidities like labour unions or minimum wage legislations or, obstacles in the labour movements in the labour market. Cyclical unemployment is the result of business cycles (recessions and depressions) while the technological unemployment is due to the technological changes in the production and distribution spheres.
6. Keynes reversed the argument of the classical economists by stating that instead of supply creating its own demand, it is the demand which creates its own supply. Keynes provided the most important theory of aggregate demand which determines the level of employment and output. The economy, in the face of unemployment, can reach an equilibrium position – known as underemployment equilibrium. However, unemployment in a capitalist economy can nevertheless persist due to the shortage of aggregate demand which, in turn, depends upon a variety of reasons.
7. There are basically two components of aggregate demand: private consumption demand (*C*) and private investment demand (*I*). These two demands together determine the level of aggregate income and employment. However, private consumption demand (or, expenditure) varies directly with income but any increase in income is generally followed by increase in consumption demand but by less than the increase in income. This is expressed as marginal propensity to consume (MPC) being less than one.
8. Investment demand (expenditures) adds to the consumption demand to enhance aggregate income and employment. Investment demand may,

either be taken as autonomous (or, fixed constant amount) or 'induced'. In the latter case, investment expenditure, too, varies directly with income.

In case, $C + I$ taken together, fail to generate enough aggregate income to absorb the available aggregate supply, government expenditure (G) needs to be added with C and I to enhance income and employment and for attaining equilibrium – though not necessarily at full potential output level.

9. A given increase in autonomous investment (or, any other autonomous components) and the resulting increase in income are linked by the concept of 'multiplier' which is defined as $\Delta Y/\Delta I$. Given a certain value of MPC, multiplier value is easily calculated since multiplier is proved to be equal to 1/(1 – MPC). Multiplier process works through various rounds of income changes in different time periods.
10. When the Keynesian model is extended to incorporate essential government functions through fiscal policy such as government expenditures and taxation, the process of income generation takes different routes. Consequently, for different functions, the related multiplier effects also differ. In some cases, the value of the multiplier increases while in some other cases, it decreases.

EXERCISE

1. What is involuntary unemployment? How does it differ from 'voluntary unemployment' of the classics? Give some examples.
2. Why does involuntary unemployment persist in the economy? Explain.
3. Discuss the main points of disagreement between Keynes and the classics on unemployment. Explain how wage rigidity causes unemployment.
4. Explain price deflation method proposed by Prof. A. C. Pigou as a solution of unemployment.
5. Distinguish clearly between frictional and structural unemployment with some examples.
6. Explain and illustrate the problem of technological unemployment.

REFERENCES

1. Ackley, G. (1978), Macroeconomics: Theory and Policy, Macmillan, New York.
2. Hansen, A.H. (1953), A Guide to Keynes, McGraw Hill.
3. Mankiw, Gregory, N. (2006), Macroeconomics, 6th Edition, Worth Publishers.
4. Keynes, J.M. (1936), General Theory of Employment, Interest and Money, Macmillan, London.
5. Samuelson, P.A. William D. Nordhaus, (2021), (adapted by Sudip Choudhury) Macroeconomics, McGraw Hill, 20th Edition.
6. Samuelson, P.A. (2019), Economics (SIE), 20th Edition.

4

Keynesian Theory of Income Determination

4.1 COMPONENTS OF AGGREGATE DEMAND

As we have seen in chapter 1 (National Income Analysis) that, looked at from the demand/expenditure side, aggregate demand can be broadly classified into (a) aggregate private consumption demand, (b) aggregate private investment demand (c) aggregate government demand (in terms of purchases of goods and services) and (d) the net foreign demand (exports minus imports or net exports). In the Keynesian income determination model also, we have the same broad classification/components of aggregate demand. Of the four components, mentioned above, first two, i.e., private consumption demand and private investment demand are the demand generated in the private sector of the domestic economy. The government purchases of goods and services forms the third demand component in the government sector. The fourth component is generated in the external sector of the economy, i.e., rest of the world economy with which the domestic economy has trade relations in forms of export of goods and services and import of goods and services.

In the present chapter on Keynesian income determination model, we shall take up, one by one, each component of aggregate demand and analyse their behaviour and impact in the income generation process.

4.2 KEYNESIAN MODEL OF INCOME DETERMINATION

As we have seen in the previous section, aggregate demand is the key factor determining the level of employment which, in turn, determines aggregate real output or aggregate real income. Real output and real income are synonymous (and, in fact equal) and the level of employment is positively related to the level of real income. The basic question in the Keynesian analysis of income determination is: what constitutes 'aggregate demand' and in what manner it influences aggregate income in the economy.

There are several models of income determination depending upon whether we take the simple case of the economic structure where only private investment decisions matter most or we allow more complex structure with government sector playing a dominant investment decision-role or still more complex structure incorporating international trade and business in the income determination process. We begin with the simple Keynesian model with private consumption and private investment expenditures as the two components of aggregate demand.

4.2.1 The Simple Keynesian Model

Let us suppose the aggregate demand is composed of (a) what the community as a whole (individuals as well as businesses) decides to purchase the whole set of consumption goods – the food articles, clothings, medicines, housing, education (materials and services) transportation etc. and (b) what the community decides to purchase or make expenditures on adding to their stock of capital – purchasing new machines/implements, building new factories, farmhouses, improving irrigation system, planting new trees, purchasing tractors, farm animals, etc.

These two sets of aggregate demand or aggregate expenditures can be categorized as (a) consumption expenditure (C) and investment expenditures (I) which, in turn, determine the level of real output of all goods and services to be produced or real income created. So, on the one hand, aggregate real expenditures (or, demands) are made while, on the other, aggregate real incomes or output are produced. Now, if the economy is to be in equilibrium (or, in balance), the two sides of aggregate expenditure and aggregate income must be equal. Using symbols and stated in simple equation this can be expressed as:

$$Y = C + I \tag{4.1}$$

where, Y is aggregate real income, C is total consumption expenditure and I is the total investment expenditure. Thus, aggregate demand consisting of C and I together will determine how much total output is to be produced. If either C or I or both increase so will increase the total output and employment. Conversely, if any one of C or I decreases, both the levels of output and employment will fall.

Now C has a *behavioural* aspect which means that aggregate consumption expenditure depends upon disposable income of the community in a certain manner. This is as much true of the individual households as the community as a whole. The precise relationship between consumption expenditure and disposable income might differ from individual to individual but, on the average, as disposable income increases, consumption expenditure also increases although not by the same proportion as disposable income. In fact, the latter increases by somewhat less than the former. This is Keynes' very famous 'psychological law of consumption' or the 'propensity to consume' or, what in the current use is referred to as *consumption function*.

For simplicity, we may assume the consumption function to be '*linear*' in form suggesting a constant positive relationship between consumption expenditure and disposable income.[1] In terms of simple algebraic equation, the consumption function can be expressed as

$$C = a + bY \tag{4.2}$$

where, C is consumption expenditure, Y is disposable income, and a and b are the two constant (or, coefficient) terms. While a signifies the level of consumption expenditure even when Y is zero, b signifies the 'increment in consumption expenditure' due to small increment in disposable income and is defined as the 'marginal propensity to consume' (MPC or $\Delta C/\Delta Y$). Its numerical value is generally less than one (although positive) due to generally observable behaviour of the community as consumer. For every increase in income, people do not generally spend the whole of it on consumption items but save a part of it. Hence, we may write $0 < b < 1$. The significance of the constant a is better understood if we imagine a situation when consumers have necessarily to spend on consumption items (even when their disposable income is zero) by drawing upon their past savings, disposing of their assets or borrowing from their friends and relatives. Hence, the value of a, will generally be positive[2]. Regarding I, the investment expenditure, it can be assumed, at least for the present simple model, that it is 'exogenous' or 'autonomous' in kind. This means that investment expenditure is independent of the level of income. Whatever investment expenditures are made by the private business community is for carrying on or maintaining current level of production or the business and government together might have made certain investments at earlier periods which are cumulatively existing in the economy. We can, therefore, treat I as fixed at a certain level, $\bar{I}$.

Now, eqn. (4.1) along with eqn. (4.2) can be written as:

$$Y = a + bY + \bar{I} \tag{4.3}$$

Equation (4.3) now can be solved for Y as follows:

$$Y - bY = a + \bar{I}$$

$$\Rightarrow \quad Y(1 - b) = a + \bar{I}$$

$$\Rightarrow \quad Y = \frac{a + \bar{I}}{(1 - b)}$$

$$\Rightarrow \quad Y = \frac{1}{(1 - b)}\{a + \bar{I}\} \tag{4.4}$$

Equation (4.4) states that equilibrium level of income, Y, depends on the exogenously given investment, $\bar{I}$, provided the parameter values of a and b are

[1] Disposable income is defined as gross income minus the direct tax payments to govt. In case we exclude govt. from our model, disposable income is equivalent to gross income.

[2] The value of a being negative means 'dissaving' which finds its reflection in the corresponding savings function, discussed later, while a being zero is only a theoretical possibility.

known and given. Thus, we can say that for a certain level of exogenous (or, autonomous) investment, Y is determined by (1) marginal propensity to consume b and (2) autonomous part of consumption expenditure a[1] such that greater the value of a or b or both, higher will be the equilibrium level of income, Y. Similarly, if autonomous investment, $\bar{I}$, is raised, for some reason or other, other parameters remaining constant, the equilibrium level of income will also be higher. Conversely, if any of the parameter values mentioned above, is lower, equilibrium income will be lower. We are not considering the combined effects of the parameters but can, easily, be analysed by assuming changing values in opposite directions.

The equilibrium income deter-mination model as presented in algebraic form can be shown graphically as well as depicted in Fig. 4.1. On the horizontal axis of Fig. 4.1 is shown real income (or, output) level, Y, while on the vertical axis are shown magnitudes of two variables, C and I. A line forming 45° angle is drawn with Y-axis, every point of which indicates equal values on both sides of Y and X axes. A straight line (linear) C curve has been drawn representing eqn. (4.2) i.e., $C = a + bY$. Obviously, b is the slope of the curve and a is the positive intercept (distance between starting point and the origin). Since b represents marginal propensity to consume (MPC), its value is generally positive but less than one ($0 < b < 1$) for behavioural reasons mentioned above.

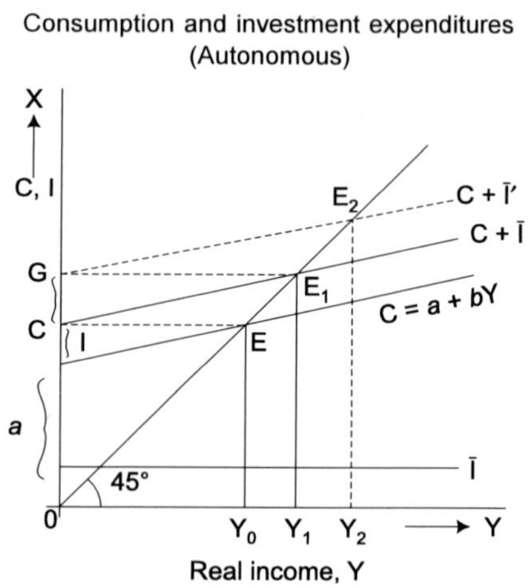

Figure 4.1 *Income determination with consumption and autonomous investment expenditures.*

The level of autonomous investment, $\bar{I}$, has been drawn as horizontal straight line parallel to Y-axis and the same has been added with C curve as parallel to it to represent $C + \bar{I}$ curve. It is clear from Fig. 4.1 that in the absence of autonomous investment, $\bar{I}$, equilibrium income, Y_0 is determined at point E where total consumption expenditure OC is exactly equal to OY_0, the real income. At E, therefore, C alone determines income. When we have $\bar{I}$ curve added with C curve the equilibrium income is reached at E_1, where total of $C + \bar{I}$, i.e., OG is just equal to OY_1. Obviously, the level of equilibrium income is higher at Y_1. It

[1] a, the intercept term of the consumption function can also be called the autonomous level of consumption.

is also clear from Fig. 4.1 that if autonomous investment level is raised higher so that $\bar{I}$ is now shifted to $\bar{I}'$, the equilibrium income will also be raised from Y_1 to Y_2.

Within the consumption function, of the two parameters, *a* and *b*, *b* assumes greater significance than *a*; because, for several reasons (which we shall discuss later in Chapter 13 on Aggregate Consumption/Saving Behaviour), *a* remains relatively stable. Let us analyse, then how, *b* affects the determination of equilibrium income.

In Fig. 4.2 we have drawn two consumption curves *C* and *C′* with *C′* having a greater slope than *C*. We write the respective equations of *C* and *C′* as $C = a + b_1Y$ and $C' = a + b_2Y$. Obviously $b_2 > b_1$. In other words, MPC of *C′* is greater than that of *C*. We have now two different equilibrium income levels, Y_1 and Y_2 corresponding to equilibrium points E_1 and E_2. Since $Y_2 > Y_1$, we conclude that with higher MPC, equilibrium income is higher. This can be easily verified by the coefficient $(1/1 - b)$ in eqn. (4.4).

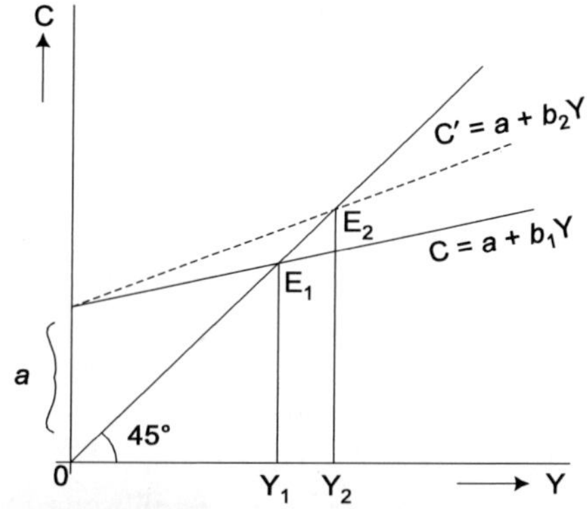

Figure 4.2 *Income determination with increase in consumption expenditure.*

If the value of *b* increases, the value of the coefficient will be higher[1]. We can conclude the above discussion by stating that equilibrium income in a simple Keynesian model depends on $\bar{I}$, *a* and *b* – the autonomous investment expenditure and the parameters of the consumption function, respectively.

The consumption function: $C = a + bY$ has its obverse (or, complement) the savings function which can be derived, first mathematically, and then diagrammatically as follows:

Since savings can be defined as the residual part of the income not spent on consumption, we write

$$S = Y - C, \quad \text{where, } S \text{ is savings}$$

we substitute it in eqn. (4.4) to obtain,

$$S = Y - a - bY$$

$$\Rightarrow \qquad S = -a + (1 - b)\,Y \qquad (4.5)$$

The *S* function in eqn. (4.5) has intercept of – *a*, i.e., the negative of the intercept in the consumption function and slope equal to 1 minus the slope of the

[1] The coefficient $(1/1 - b)$ is also known as 'multiplier'. There are different variants of 'multiplier' of which this is one which we may call either 'consumption multiplier' or 'investment multiplier'.

consumption function. For instance, if MPC or $b = 0.8$, MPS or $1 - b = 0.2$ (MPS = Marginal propensity to save). So, if consumption function is known, we can graphically also draw the corresponding savings function as we have done in Fig. 4.3.

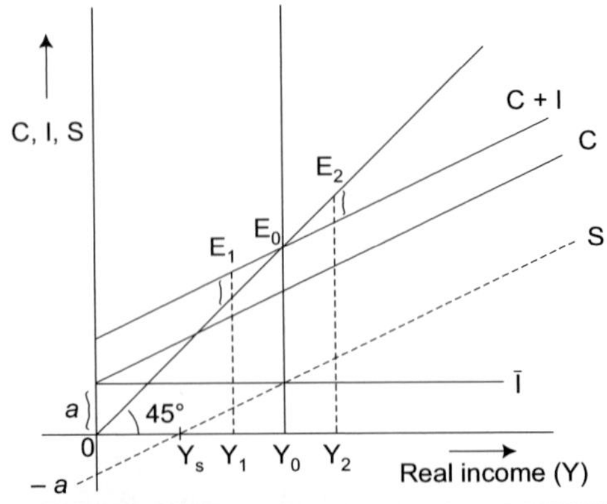

Figure 4.3 *Income determination with consumption investment and savings.*

In Fig. 4.3, *a*, the intercept coefficient of savings function represents the magnitude of 'dissaving'. The positive saving, in fact, starts after certain 'threshold' income level, *Ys*, is achieved. It can be verified from the figure that the same level of equilibrium income, Y_1, will be attained in terms of savings function as well, when $\bar{I} = S$, i.e., the autonomous investment is equal to intended level of savings. Thus, there are two ways of looking at equilibrium income: (i) $Y = C + I$ and (ii) $S = I$.

The determination of equilibrium income implies that total spending in the economy, $C + I$ is just enough to encourage producers to produce total output, OY_0. To state the same thing, the community intends to save (or, not spend on consumption) just enough which the business sector would like to purchase (or, convert into) investment goods.

Situations of disequilibrium can be identified when either the total expenditure falls short of or exceeds the equilibrium income. For instance, at point E_1 on $C + I$ curve, (Fig. 4.3) the aggregate demand is more than the real income (and output). The higher aggregate demand would induce producers to produce more and raise real income. This process will continue until it settles at E_0 where aggregate demand is just equal to aggregate real income Y_0. Similarly, if aggregate demand falls short of the equilibrium income, Y_0, let us say, at Y_2, further output will be discouraged and, in fact, present level of output will be curtailed resulting in unused productive resources thus reducing real income and this process in the backward direction will continue until point E_0 is reached.

In terms of saving-investment equality also, the disequilibrium situations can be analysed as follows:

At Y_1 (or, E_1) investment is greater than saving so that the business community decides to invest more than what the savers have desired to save. This increases aggregate demand resulting in more output and real income and thus ultimately settling at Y_0 (or, E_0). Similarly, at Y_2 (or, E_2) savings exceed the volume of investment and the extra savings are not converted into investment. Aggregate demand falls thus leading to reduced real income. Subsequently, real income is settled at equilibrium level, Y_0.

It ought to be mentioned at this stage that point E_0 in Fig. 4.3 suggests equilibrium of the economy where aggregate demand is equal to aggregate supply since real income or output is the same as aggregate supply. However, this is, by no means, the full employment equilibrium. In most likely situation, this is what Keynes has described as 'underemployment' or unemployment equilibrium. In terms of Keynesian analysis, therefore, economy may be in equilibrium even at less than full employment level. Full employment, in fact, results when the economy operates at the point of 'potential' output which is defined as the maximum output capable to be produced with all the potential of the economy in terms of land, labour, capital and technology. If potential output is expressed as Y_p, it would be clear from the above discussion that if, for some reason, aggregate demand, $C + I$ falls short of what is required for potential output, the actual income and employment levels will always be short of full employment level and unemployment of the involuntary type will result. It is also clear from eqn. (4.3) that, given the behaviour of consumption function, output and employment can be increased by increased investment. In other words, more and more investment will result in higher and higher income and employment – the latter approaching Y_p, the full employment or potential output. The exact process of income propagation as a result of increased investment is captured by the coefficient of multiplier which indicates increase in income by several times the increase in investment. (This part has been taken up for discussion in the next Section 4.3.2).

4.2.2 The Logic of Multiplier and Income Propagation

In the Keynesian theory of income determination, the concept of multiplier is central to the process of income generation. As one shot increase in autonomous investment or, for that matter, in any of the autonomous components – a, $\overline{I}$, $\overline{G}$ increases income by several times to increase in any one of these autonomous components. Also, the value of the multiplier (as we have seen above) depends on the marginal propensity to consume (MPC). For the present, we will concentrate our analysis on the increase in investment and its resulting impact on total increase in income. Thus, if ΔY stands for total increase in income, and ΔI, the one shot increase in investment, the ratio $\Delta Y/\Delta I$ is defined as 'multiplier'. Since, there can be several such multipliers, we define it here as "investment (or, income) multiplier". The basic question we seek to investigate here is how this ratio is obtained and why it is equal to the reciprocal of (1 – MPC). Secondly, what is the process of income propagation in several of the time periods – in other words, what is the 'dynamics' of multiplier?

There are several ways in which the above enquiries can be addressed. Using diagram, the multiplier formula can be derived as follows: Two curves, $(C + I)$

and $(C + I) + \Delta I$ have been drawn parallelly over the 45° line. Corresponding to these two curves, two equilibrium income levels, Y_1 and Y_2 are shown on the horizontal axis. As we have stated above, the investment multiplier is the simple ratio, $\frac{\Delta Y}{\Delta I}$, i.e., the increase in income and increase in investment. In the figure (Fig. 4.4), this is shown as MN/QW. Now, since $QW = QN - WN$, by substitution, we can write:

$$\frac{MN}{QN - WN} = \frac{MN}{MN - WN}$$

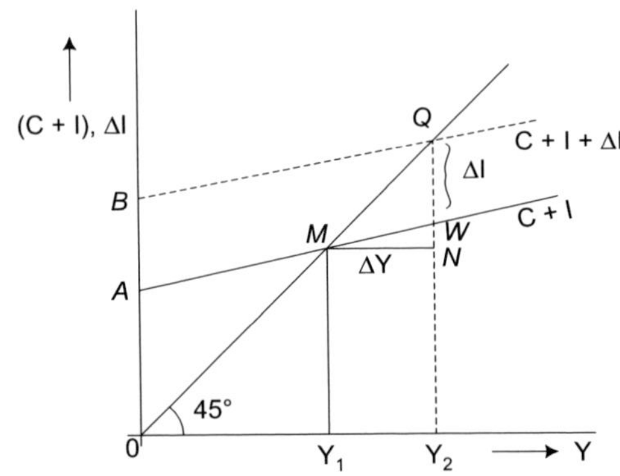

Figure 4.4 *Keynesian multiplier measured in figure*

(since $QN = MN$, both being equal distances from 45° line).

Now, dividing both the numerator and the denominator by MN we get,

$$\frac{\frac{MN}{MN}}{\frac{(MN - WN)}{MN}} = \frac{1}{\frac{MN}{MN} - \frac{WN}{MN}}$$

$$\Rightarrow \qquad \frac{1}{1 - \frac{WN}{MN}}$$

We further know that WN/MN measures the slope of the C-curve between two discrete points and is, therefore, the marginal propensity to consume (MPC). Hence, we conclude,

$$\frac{\Delta Y}{\Delta I} = \frac{1}{1 - \text{MPC}}.$$

By using simple logic and basic definition of MPC, with some mathematical notations, we can arrive at the above-mentioned result thus:

Let there be a certain increase in income, ΔY. Since, in our present model, we have only two main sources of increase in income, viz., a certain increase in consumption expenditure and a certain increase in autonomous investment, we can write:

$$\Delta Y = \Delta C + \Delta I \ldots \tag{4.6}$$

Dividing through by ΔY, we obtain,

$$\frac{\Delta Y}{\Delta Y} = \frac{\Delta C}{\Delta Y} + \frac{\Delta I}{\Delta Y}$$

$$\Rightarrow \quad 1 = \text{MPC} + \frac{\Delta I}{\Delta Y}$$

$$\Rightarrow \quad \frac{\Delta I}{\Delta Y} = 1 - \text{MPC}$$

$$\Rightarrow \quad \frac{1}{\frac{\Delta I}{\Delta Y}} = \frac{1}{1 - \text{MPC}}$$

$$\Rightarrow \quad \frac{\Delta Y}{\Delta I} = \frac{1}{1 - \text{MPC}} = \text{Multiplier.} \tag{4.7}$$

Intuitively also, multiplier formula can be derived when we bear in mind the process of income propagation in several rounds.

Supposing investment expenditure initially increases by ΔI. Those employed in the investment project (either new or old) will experience increase in their incomes by the same amount of ΔI. This is the first round increase in income. In the next round, however, the income recipients of the first round will not fully spend their incomes, but by the fraction equal to the MPC so that in the second round income will increase by MPC times ΔI. This will enhance incomes of those who are employed in all such production sectors on whose products the income will be spent. In the third round, these new recipients of income will spend by only MPC times (MPC ΔI). In the fourth round, by the similar process, income will increase by MPC $(\text{MPC})^2 \Delta I = (\text{MPC})^3 \Delta I$ times. This process continues until the increment in income becomes smaller and approaches a level almost insignificant so that it can be approximated to zero. For instance, let us assume there are 1, 2, …, n rounds of effects of ΔI. The increase in income in all these rounds can be expressed as follows:

(For simplicity of expression, we symbolise MPC by 'b').

Eqn. (4A)

$$\underset{\text{1st round}}{\Delta Y = \Delta I} + \underset{\text{2nd round}}{b\Delta I} + \underset{\text{3rd round}}{b^2\Delta I} + \underset{\text{4th round}}{b^3\Delta I} + \ldots + \underset{n\text{th round}}{b^{n-1}\Delta I} \tag{4A}$$

Now, multiplying eqn. (4A) by b, we get,

Eqn. (4B)

$$b\Delta Y = b\Delta I + b^2\Delta I + b^3\Delta I + b^4\Delta I + \ldots + b^n\Delta I \tag{4B}$$

Now, subtracting (4B) from (4A), we obtain:

Eqn. (4C)

$$\Delta Y - b\Delta Y = \Delta I - b\Delta I + b\Delta I - b^2\Delta I + b^2\Delta I - b^3\Delta I + b^3\Delta I - \ldots - b^{n-1}\Delta I + b^{n-1}\Delta I - b^n\Delta I$$

$\Rightarrow$ $(1 - b)\Delta Y = \Delta I - b^n\Delta I$ (4C) (since all other terms cancel out)

Since, b is a fraction (e.g., 0.8, 0.7, etc., i.e., < 1) as higher and higher powers are raised over b, its value will tend towards zero, i.e.,

$$b^n \to 0$$

Hence, $b^n\Delta I$ can be ignored.

Thus,

$$\Delta Y(1 - \text{MPC}) = \Delta I$$

$$\Rightarrow \quad \Delta Y = \frac{\Delta I}{1 - \text{MPC}}$$

$$\Rightarrow \quad \frac{\Delta Y}{\Delta I} = \frac{1}{1 - \text{MPC}}; \text{ hence multiplier} = \frac{1}{1 - \text{mpc}} = \frac{1}{\text{mps}}$$

where, mpc is marginal propensity to consume and mps = marginal propensity to save.

4.2.3 The 'Dynamics' of Multiplier Analysis

The above discussion clearly suggests that the whole income generation process of a given increase in investment involves time-lags. For full working of the multiplier, it is equally important to understand the 'dynamic' process – the whole time path through which the process works. Assuming there are n periods of time – time denoted by t such that t takes the values $t - 1$, t, $t + 1$, $t + 2$, …, $t + n$. The first term $(t - 1)$, therefore, indicates the previous one period. For simplicity, different periods may be taken to be different years. Accordingly, corresponding incomes generated in these different periods are denoted by Y_{t-1}, Y_t, $Y_t + 1$, …, Y_{t+n}. Figure 4.5 illustrates the dynamic process by showing period-wise income changes on Y-axis while plotting the different time periods on X-axis. Assuming an initial increase in investment, ΔI, takes place in period $t - 1$. This results in rise in income of the equal amount of ΔI in the next period – t; so that Y_t is the increased income in period t. This

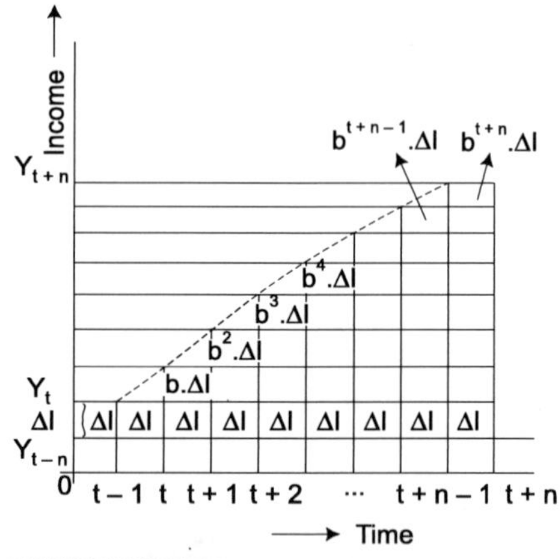

Figure 4.5 *Dynamics of multiplier.*

income is partially re-spent equal to the amount $b\Delta I$ in the next period, i.e., $t + 1$; so that total income in period $t + 1$ is equal to $Y_t + 1 = \Delta I + b\Delta I$. Similarly, in period $t + 2$, the increased income ($b\Delta I$) is, again, re-spent on various goods and services by the amount $b^2\Delta I$ so that, in this period the total income generated is $Y_t + 2 = (\Delta I + b\Delta I + b^2\Delta I)$. This process continues till the end of period $t + n$ when income increases by $b^n\Delta I$. Thus, the total income increases by the amount: $\Delta I + b\Delta I + b^2\Delta I + \ldots + b^{t+n-1}\,\Delta I$. This is shown by the area of the last vertical rectangle raised over the time period $(t + n - 1)$. The interesting point to note here is that each subsequent rectangle in different periods showing income increases, gets smaller and smaller in area. Here, it must be noted that ΔI in the initial period is a 'permanent' injection of investment expenditures which continues over the whole time periods. The rest of the expenditures in all subsequent periods are secondary expenditures that are encouraged or induced by subsequent increases in income.

4.2.4 Importance of Multiplier

The concept of multiplier plays a very significant role in the policy making of both the government and the business corporates. On theoretical level, it has occupied a central position not only in the Keynesian literature but also in the entire post-Keynesian analysis. Since the concept is now more general and applies to various fields such as foreign trade, money supply, employment, consumption etc., multiplier is an integral part of economic analysis.

The understanding of the implications of this concept helps understand the ups and downs in the economy – particularly during the business cycles. The boom period, for example, characterized by higher and higher rates of investment is aided by the 'multiplier' process of income and employment generation. An associated concept – the 'accelerator' combined with multiplier becomes the strong driver of economic growth at a much higher rate during the upswing of the business cycle. Similarly, when the economy experiences the downswing or recessionary phase, the concept of multiplier still plays its part in slowing down the economy by somewhat greater pace when the investment expenditures are cut by a certain percentage.

In the operation of the fiscal policy of the government – either expansionary or contractionary – multiplier plays a significant role. For instance, in the case of increased government expenditure, experts can estimate the multiplied effects on income generation as also associated employment growth in the economy so that further policy follow-up can be taken up. Thus, government expenditures, particularly when they are stepped up during reecessionary phase, help to smoothen the cyclical fluctuations in the economy. The current global recession beginning in 2008 and the subsequent government expenditures by US and other governments of the world bear the testimony of the role of multiplier as a policy tool since the expected rise in output and employment must have been estimated by the government agencies. Public works policies such as expenditures on public health, education, roads, railway bridges, etc., help increase income growth to a greater extent due to higher multiplied effects on such projects.

4.2.5 Limitations of Multiplier Application

The application of multiplier is constrained by various leakages from the circular flow of income and expenditure of the economy. Also, the working of multiplier process depends upon certain assumptions. When these assumptions are not fulfilled or fulfilled partially, the process of income generation is hindered and the full impact of it is not realized.

The leakages, mentioned above, may be in the form of higher savings of the society due to income increase. This, in fact, lowers the value of MPC in subsequent periods by raising the rate of savings of the economy. Of course, in a sense, this is the violation of the basic assumption of multiplier (MPC remaining constant).

Another kind of leakage may take place when the rate of taxation in the economy is raised. Since taxes also act as withdrawal from the circular flow, it lowers the disposable incomes of the citizens which ultimately impact upon the income propagation of the multiplier.

In case the economy is an open one with international trade and investment then a rise in imports and fall in exports act as obstacles to the full operation of multiplier. In fact, as we have seen later in this chapter, the existence of foreign trade multiplier reduces the value of the multiplier. Apart from the above-mentioned leakages, the operation of multiplier is conditional upon sufficient availability of consumption goods in the economy so that regular consumption expenditures are sustained due to increase in autonomous expenditure. If there are 'supply rigidities' as often happens in the most underdeveloped economies, the multiplier process gets a setback. If supply responses are not flexible enough there may develop the different types of 'lags' in the working process of the multiplier.

Lastly, for working out the full circle of the multiplier, a concurrent flow of investment must take place in other related sectors of the economy so that the process does not stop in the midway.

It must, however, be remembered that just as multiplier works in the positive direction in enhancing income and employment manifold, it equally works in the negative or 'reverse' direction when there is sizeable cut in autonomous investment. However, in the reverse direction, although negative, the value of the multiplier may be smaller. This is possibly due to relatively small fall in consumption expenditure by the community as compared to their rise in the upward direction (see Chapter 13 on macro-behaviour of consumption saving).

4.3 INVESTMENT–THE SECOND COMPONENT OF AGGREGATE DEMAND

The Investment Function

The theory of investment is, perhaps one of the most complicated theories in macroeconomics. This is because there are a number of theories of investment behaviour. Also, there is a good amount of confusion between 'financial investment' and 'real investment'.

In the present section we attempt to give an overview of the real investment behaviour and examine the major determinants of the investment function.

The general confusion about real and financial investments arises from the fact that the latter are investments in financial instruments like 'bonds', 'shares' (equities), life insurance funds, different kinds of debt instruments, mutual funds etc. These are different channels through which supply of loanable funds (savings) are mobilized. Those who issue or sell these instruments (either government, business corporations or other financial institutions) have the ultimate objective of transforming them into real investment by using these funds for producing goods and services. However, financial instruments bought and sold in the secondary market simply represent the 'change of ownership' of such instruments.

Our concern in the present section is the 'real investment' and examining the reasons, factors and circumstances under which real investment takes place.

Meaning of Investment

Investment is the second important component of aggregate demand in the income determination model. We have, in earlier pages, examined the role of autonomous investment – the investment which is independent of income. However, investment too has a behavioural aspect which we seek to investigate in this section.

Investment is defined as the net addition to capital stock. There are two concepts '*gross investment*' and '*net investment*'. Let us suppose, K_0 stands for the stock of capital (valued at some constant price-level) at the end of the year 2001, and K_1 is the stock of capital (at the same price level) at the end of 2002, the difference between K_1 and K_0 $(K_1 - K_0)$ or, ΔK is the addition to the stock of capital. However, we must not forget that during the period of 2002, certain capital assets might have worn out or depreciated by use partially or wholly. The wholly worn-out capital assets need replacement by new ones while partially worn-out ones need maintenance. Thus, out of the total addition, ΔK, some are simply replacement of the old stock. Only the rest of the ΔK is the net addition to capital stock. ΔK is, then, defined as gross investment (I_g) and ΔK minus the replacement capital is defined as net investment (I_n), i.e., $I_n = I_g - D$, where D

stands for depreciation. Now, I_n may be positive, negative or zero. When $I_g > D$, I_n is positive, when $I_g = D$, I_n is zero and when $I_g < D$, I_n is negative. $I_g < D$ is possible when even worn-out capital is not replaced, may be due to continuously falling demand for output.

4.3.1 Behaviour of Investment – The Investment Function

There are basically two approaches to analyse the behaviour of investment function: (a) capital stock adjustment approach or demand-supply approach and (b) marginal efficiency of capital or Keynesian approach. Both approaches, however, by and large, lead to the same result. We prefer to begin with Keynesian approach and then deal with the capital-stock adjustment approach.

The Keynesian Approach

Keynes provided a theory of investment in terms of a rational decision from the point of view of an entrepreneur who intends to acquire a capital asset for investment purpose. An entrepreneur basically looks at two aspects before taking such a decision: (a) the initial cost of the capital asset, for instance, the price of a machine he intends to purchase; and (b) the expected return of the capital asset in terms of the income stream over the life-time of the capital. The entrepreneur then weighs these two aspects before coming to a decision whether to acquire the capital asset or not. Part (a), i.e., the initial cost of the capital is its purchase price. But part (b), i.e., the expected income stream over the life span of the capital asset has to be estimated and discounted at a certain rate to get at their 'present value'. Surely, there are problems relating to the estimation of the income stream (or, prospective yields) at different periods of time and also the choice of an appropriate rate of discount. Based upon popular perception, experience and technical conditions, an entrepreneur makes reasonable estimate of these income streams and rate of discount. Finally, the sum of these present values is compared with the initial cost of the capital. For being worthwhile purchasing it, the present value must exceed or equal the initial cost of the machine.

There exists a standard formula for obtaining 'present value' of a capital asset. Let us assume, $Q_1, Q_2, \ldots, Q_n$ are the expected incomes of a machine at time periods, 1, 2, ..., n and i is the rate of discount at which these future incomes are converted into their present values, then the present value of the machine is given by the following formula:

$$PV_m = \frac{Q_1}{1+i} + \frac{Q_2}{(1+i)^2} + \ldots + \frac{Q_n}{(1+i)^n} \tag{4.8}$$

where, PV_m is the discounted present value of the entire income stream[1]. This formula is basically derived from the future value (or, compound value) concept.

[1] In fact, $Q_1, Q_2, \ldots, Q_n$ are net expected incomes, i.e., expected incomes less all associated costs. Hence, PV_m is sometimes called Net Present Value (NPV_m)

Assuming that a certain sum of money, A_0, deposited in a bank with interest on it at i per cent annually becomes A_1 at the end of one year [A_0 (1 + i) = A_1], then we can say that its present value A_0 will be $A_1/(1 + i)$. Similarly, after two years, if the sum accumulated is A_2, its present value will be $\frac{A_2}{(1+i)^2}$, after three years, $\frac{A_3}{(1+i)^3}$ and so on.

PV_m, thus estimated, is then compared with the cost of the machine. If $PV_m \geq C$ (where C is the cost of the machine), then a rational entrepreneur would like to purchase the machine. In fact, this principle of rational investment decision applies to any investment project, before it is taken up.

We can now approach the problem slightly differently. We now seek to arrive at an appropriate rate of discount (which is not known), which just equates the cost and expected return, i.e., $PV_m = C$. In other words, we want to solve eqn. (4.8) for i so that

$$C = PV_m = \frac{Q_1}{(1+i)} + \frac{Q_2}{(1+i)^2} + \ldots + \frac{Q_n}{(1+i)^n}. \tag{4.9}$$

The value of i is, then, defined as the marginal efficiency of capital (MEC). This is also known as marginal efficiency of investment (MEI) or, internal rate of return (IRR).

As far as calculation of i is concerned, the easiest method is the 'trial and error' method, i.e., try assuming some rate of discount, calculate the PV_m, compare with C and depending upon the extent of difference, recalculate it on another value of i, and so on. This way we can get as near a value of PV_m with C as possible.

In the modern age, computer or even simple calculator can easily give the value of i. This value of MEC is then compared with the market rate of interest at which the fund for the machine might have been financed. If MEC $\geq$ market rate of interest, a rational decision for investment is suggested.

An example is given below:

A machine costs ₹ 1,00,000.00. The rate of interest that the purchaser of the machine has to bear is 10% per annum. The machine is expected to give the following net returns in five years, assuming that the life of the machine is 5 years and there is no scrap value of the machine. We can, therefore, write the following equation:

$$\text{₹ 1 lakh} = \frac{\text{₹ } 30{,}000}{(1+i)} + \frac{\text{₹ } 40{,}000}{(1+i)^2} + \frac{\text{₹ } 35{,}000}{(1+i)^3} + \frac{\text{₹ } 25{,}000}{(1+i)^4} + \frac{\text{₹ } 20{,}000}{(1+i)^5}.$$

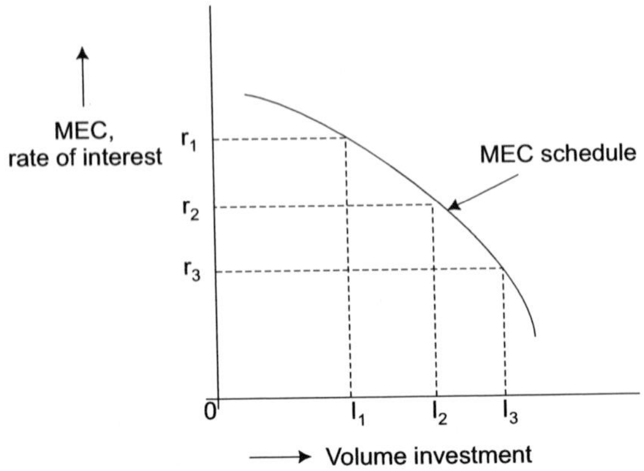

Figure 4.6 *Keynes' MEC, rate of interest and volume of investment.*

Assuming i = 10% (= 0.1), the return on the machine is worked out as ₹ 1,16,106. Hence, for return to be equal to the cost of the machine i must be more than 10%. Thus MEC > the rate of interest.

Now, as the volume of investment increases (more and more capital is acquired) MEC diminishes. For instance, if more and more new machines are used for production resulting in the increased volume of investment, the MEC of machine will decline. Generally, MEC declines at slower rate at the beginning, but gradually the decline will be sharper. This happens because, with rising volume of investment, the cost of capital increases on the one hand, while on the other, the prospective yield of new investment diminishes. In the short run, for instance, competition among firms for limited capital may bid up the rate of interest, while in the long run, prospective yield (or, net return) from new capital may decrease[1]. The relationship between MEC and volume of investment is shown in Fig. 4.6.

In the figure, MEC as well as rate of interest are shown on vertical axis while, volume of investment is shown on the horizontal axis. As we have seen above, in equilibrium, MEC and rate of interest are equal, hence each point on MEC curve shows the equilibrium situation. This suggests an inverse relationship between the rate of interest and the volume of investment.

The Keynesian approach to the theory of investment in terms of a falling MEC schedule, it has to be admitted, is an inadequate explanation of the theory of investment. In particular, equating MEC to the rate of interest poses a problem inasmuch as there are several rates of interest in the market – short term as well

[1] Entrepreneurs, very often, have a limited "pay-off" period of a certain capital asset even though real life of such capital may be slightly longer. This is, due mainly to discount for a number of uncertainties of the future.

as long term ones. The choice of an appropriate rate of interest is, therefore, a real problem. Secondly, from practical point of view, there may not actually exist any real value of MEC satisfying our eqn. (4.9). In such a situation, an imaginary value of MEC has to be equated to a real value of market rate of interest.

4.3.2 The Capital Stock Adjustment or Demand-Supply Approach

This approach looks at an 'optimum' or 'desired' stock of capital that entrepreneurs, at individual levels as also aggregative macro level, want to achieve or maintain. But at a certain point in time, in the short run, the actual stock of capital may diverge from the optimum. Very often, the actual capital stock may fall short of the optimum one. Investment, particularly the net investment, is looked upon as a process of actual stock of capital gradually adjusting to the optimum stock of capital. The optimum capital stock depends upon demand for capital goods and supply of capital goods. In fact, it is the equilibrium level of capital stock (demand = supply of capital goods). Since the demand for capital goods will have a demand price and supply of capital goods will have a supply price, the behaviour of each of these, i.e., demand function and supply function of capital need an explanation. As normally behaved, the demand function of capital is downward sloping with its price (as happens in the case of any other factor of production), while the supply function is upward sloping with price. What determines demand price of a certain capital good such as a machine? The demand price is the maximum price that a certain entrepreneur would be willing to pay for the capital good.

It depends on the net present value of the machine which, in turn, depends on the series of net yields of the machine discounted at a certain rate of interest. This can be understood by the NPV type equation discussed earlier. For reference, the equation is expressed as:

$$D_m = \text{NPV}_m = \frac{Q_1}{1+r} + \frac{Q_2}{(1+r)^2} + \ldots + \frac{Q_n}{(1+r)^n} \tag{4.10}$$

Here, D_m is the demand price of the machine since this is the maximum price that a purchaser of the machine is prepared to pay, with the difference that r here is the market rate of interest and not Keynes' MEC which, in the earlier equation, is unknown and needs to be estimated or calculated. Now, if the demand price of machine is lower, the entrepreneur would like to purchase more machines, since this will lead to optimum combination of capital with other factors. Hence, demand curve for capital goods (machine) is downward sloping from left to right with price. Aggregating for the economy as a whole, D_m curve, shown in Fig. 4.7(a), is the aggregate demand curve for capital. It is evident from eqn. (4.10) that for any lower value of r, the D_m curve will shift upward. Analogously, for any higher value of r, the D_m curve will shift downward.

The other aspect of the capital stock is its supply which comes from capital goods – producing industry. The supply behaviour of capital is normal – that is, upward sloping from left to right. This implies that more and more machines (for instance) are supplied at higher prices. The main reason behind upward sloping supply curve is the increasing marginal cost of producing new machines. The curve S_m in Fig. 4.7(b) is the supply curve of new machines. At each price of new machine, $P_{m'}$, $P_{m''}$, ... the number of machines supplied are, respectively, S_{m1}, S_{m2}, ... etc. Since new machines add to capital stock including the worn-out ones, these are equivalent to gross investment. Figure 4.7(c) shows the net investment function which decreases with rate of interest.

In Fig. 4.7(a), the short-run capital stock is fixed at $K\overline{K}$ level. The demand curve for capital is given by D_m, when rate of interest is r_1, so that the equilibrium

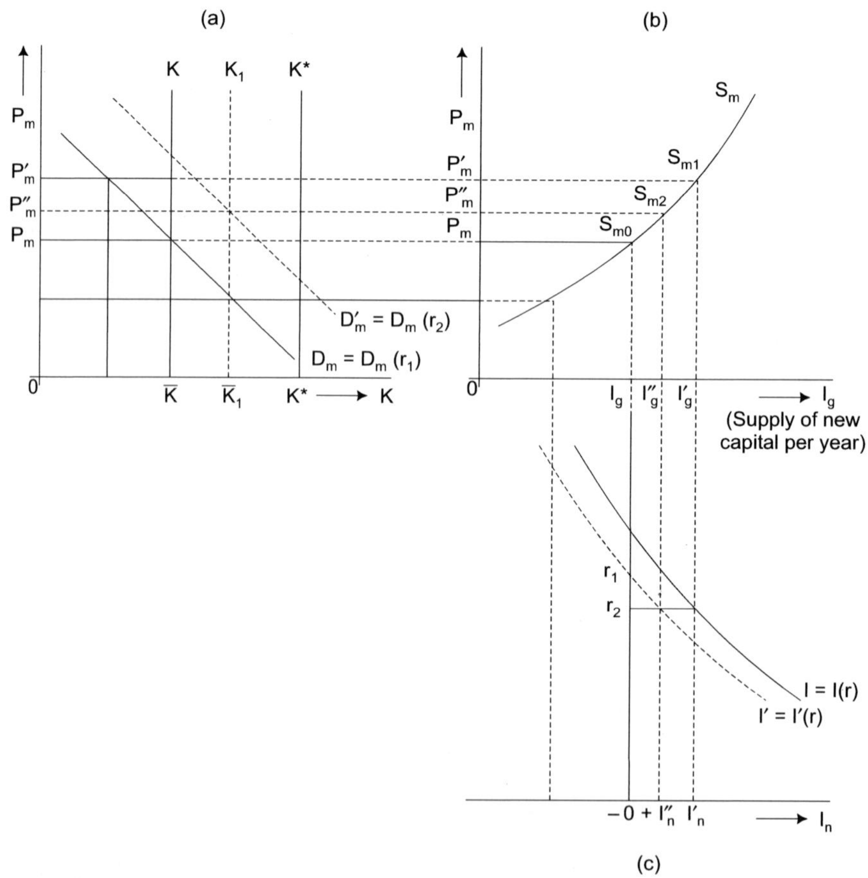

Figure 4.7(a, b & c) *Demand for capital and supply of capital.*

price of the machine is P_m. At this equilibrium price, the supply of the number of machines is OI_g or, gross investment per year (Fig. 4.7(b)). Hence, in Fig. 4.7(c) this is shown as net investment being zero. Now, if the rate of interest is lower at r_2 the demand curve for capital shifts up to D'_m showing excess demand for capital. This results in higher price of capital in the short run. The capital-producing industry finds itself in a profitable situation, so supply of capital is enhanced to OI'_g, giving the net investment equal to OI'_n as shown in Fig. 4.7(c). This is the rate at which the actual capital stock moves towards 'desired' or optimum capital stock. Figure 4.7(c) clearly gives the inverse relationship between rate of interest and net investment.

This is the first period process of adjustment and the rate of net investment of the individual firms. Once this process is completed, the stock of capital in existence increases from, let us say, $K\overline{K}$ to $K_1\overline{K}_1$. With demand curve being D'_m, now the equilibrium price of capital good, in the short run, is P''_m which is less than P'_m. This results in lower rate of supply of capital good as shown at point S_{m2} and I''_g along OI_g-axis in Fig. 4.7(b).

In Fig. 4.7(c), therefore, net investment is I''_n. With the rate of interest at r_2 this means that the entire I_n curve has shifted downwards. The rate of net investment is now OI'' instead of OI'. So, even though the net investment is higher, the rate of increase of net investment is lower. This process continues until the actual short-run capital stock of all firms is equal to the 'desired' level, K^*K^*.[1]

The argument can be extended to take account of the rise in the rate of interest (r_3) (not shown in the figure) in which case, the demand curve would shift leftward so that gross investment would be lesser than I_g and net investment would be *negative*, moving leftward (or, – 0).

4.3.3 Investment and the Level of Income

We have established above that investment is a decreasing function of the rate of interest. This result is obtained both in the neo-classical demand-supply (or, capital stock adjustment) approach as well as Keynesian marginal efficiency of capital approach. In the above analysis, however, we have assumed that level of income does not influence the investment function. Keynesian economists later argued that level of income should be taken as a parameter, i.e., assumed constant at a certain level. If the level of income changes this causes shift in the investment function. Higher level of income shifts the investment function to the right and lower level of income shifts the investment function to the left as shown in Fig. 4.8. Thus, when we recognize the role of change in income along with interest rate we write explicitly as:

---

[1] Most neo-Keynesian economists have argued for such rate of investment in terms of relatively inelastic investment function.

$$I = I(r, Y) \text{ with } I'(r) < 0$$

and $I'(Y) > 0$,

implying that investment is a decreasing function of the rate of interest and increasing function of the level of income (I' is the expression for the first derivative or slope of the investment function).

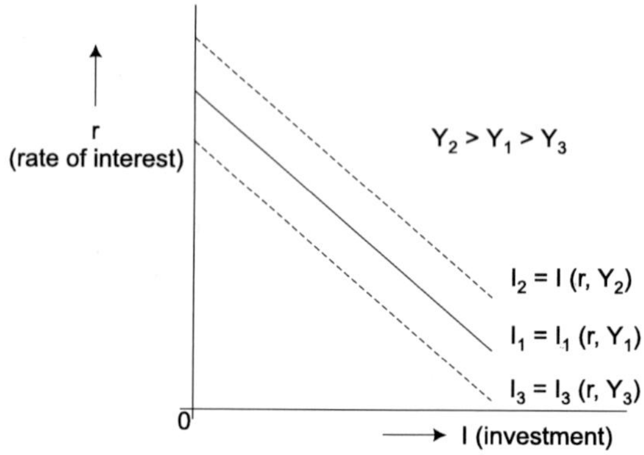

Figure 4.8 *Investment, rate of interest and the level of income.*

Investment and the change in the level of income, in fact, depend upon two factors: (a) the higher level of income, and hence demand, raises the businesses' *willingness* to invest in new and relatively risky capital projects because their *expectations* about future appear more favourable in terms of expected profits. So, rising demand leading to higher expectation acts as a motivating force behind rising investment. (b) At the same time, most businesses' *ability* to invest more in a new environment of higher expectation is higher so that they can take up higher investment. So, the businesses' (or, entrepreneurs') 'willingness' and 'ability' to invest are greatly influenced by the rising level of income.

4.3.4 Investment and Expectation

We have pointed out above that entrepreneurs' expectations have a crucial role to play in the investment function. Expectation, however, may be more optimistic or less optimistic depending upon how expectations are formed and how they are influenced by several factors. In fact, investment takes time. An entrepreneur who takes a decision to expand his productive capacity through investment has to wait for several years for his project to bear fruit in terms of net income or profit or growing market share. Much depends upon his 'foresight' about the growth in demand for his product as also the growth in competition. His foresight and guesswork about the actual outcome may turn out to be either 'correct' or 'incorrect'. For instance, if he decides to expand capacity but unfortunately the market does not expand according to expectation he is most likely to end up with unused plant and equipment whose fixed costs may be quite burdensome. On the other hand, if he under-guesses the expansion of demand while his competitors succeed in making right guesses and captures the market earlier, he may still be lagging behind his competitors.

There are other types of uncertainties which influence expectations. Government policy, for instance (industrial policy, monetary and fiscal policies) affects expectations either favourably or unfavourably and hence investment decisions by entrepreneurs are also accordingly influenced. Occasionally, mob psychology can predominate investment decisions and a feeling of pessimism about the future can snowball into a general cut in investment expenditure or a feeling of optimism can snowball into an investment boom based on expectations that later turn out to be false[1]. A good example of the latter is the recent global recession (2008-09).

4.3.5 Investment and the Rate of Change in Income: The Acceleration Principle

Investment is influenced as much by the *level* of income (GNP) as the *rate of change* in income. This unique relationship between investment and the change in income has been called the acceleration principle. Symbolically, we may write: $I = I\Delta Y)$, where, ΔY stands for change in income. The basic argument behind acceleration principle is as follows:

When the level of income (GNP) (and hence final demand) is constant, there is no need to expand productive capacity – the existing plant and machinery are adequate to take care of the output and income. Whatever investment is there, it is limited to replacement investment, that is due to depreciation of the existing plant and machinery. But if income is growing and the growth is sufficient to employ all the existing capacity, it will be necessary for firms to increase investment to expand the capacity of output. If GNP is constantly rising by, say, 10% annually, investment expenditures on expansion of productive capacity must be followed to sustain such growth of GNP. New plants and equipment have to be installed for this purpose. At the same time, the new investment expenditure that will be necessary may be several times more, initially, than the rise in income. A rupees one thousand crore increase in income (in real terms) may require more than just rupees one thousand crore increase in investment. This is because investment involves setting up of such machinery, equipment and fixed productive assets which have long life period and are expected to produce income during their whole life-span. Income that results from just one year from their existence, must be less in terms of value than the value of net investment.

It can be said, therefore, that new investment expenditure is certain multiple, B, of the change in income. This multiple, B, is called 'accelerator'. Symbolically, we can write:

[1] Richard G. Lipsey, An Introduction to Positive Economics, ELBS, Weidenfield and Nicholson, 1969, p. 617.

$$I_n = B\ \Delta Y \tag{4.11}$$

where, I_n stands for new investment, ΔY is change in income and B is accelerator (or accelerator coefficient). B can also be called capital-output ratio (the amount of capital per unit of output) which is assumed to be constant.[1]

The basic assumption of the principle of accelerator is that there is an optimum relation between the stock of capital (K^*) and the level of income, i.e., $K^* = BY$. In other words, for maintaining certain level of national output (income), a certain proportion of it is required to be kept as capital stock whose services are to be needed annually for keeping that output flowing. Now, supposing that at a certain period of time, t, the actual stock of capital (K) is just equal to the desired capital stock, i.e., the equilibrium situation holds, so that we can write:

$$K_t = BY_t$$

where, K_t is the actual capital stock in period t.

In the same vein, we can write that in period $t + 1$ also, $K_{t+1} = BY_{t+1}$. Now, subtracting the first expression from the second, we can write:

$$K_{t+1} - K_t = B(Y_{t+1} - Y_t) \tag{4.12}$$

Since, net investment I_n is defined as the change in capital stock between $t + 1$ and t periods of time, and change in income, ΔY as $Y_{t+1} - Y_t$, we can finally return to eqn. (4.11): $I_n = B\Delta Y$.

An example will perhaps clarify some of the hidden concepts in the acceleration principle:

Supposing $B = 4 : 1$. That is, for every additional annual output there are four units of the capital stock required. If the current rate of replacement investment (for maintaining the existing stock of capital) is 100 machines per year and additional 400 machines will be required for additional 100 units of additional income but if the rate at which actual stock of machines is taking place (net investment) is 50 per year, the gross investment in the next year will be 100 + 50 = 150 machines. In subsequent years, however, the number of new machines may either be more or less. In any case, as more machines are added, the gap between 'optimum' and 'actual' stock of capital is gradually reduced. Therefore net investment also depends on the rate at which such adjustment of the capital stock is made. On this basis, we can write, using symbols,

$$I_t = BY_t - \alpha K_t \tag{4.13}$$

where, α stands for the rate of adjustment between actual and optimum stock of capital.

---

[1] Constancy of capital-output ratio may result from the assumption of 'fixed-proportion input-output type of production function which states, for each level of output, a fixed proportion of productive factors (labour and capital, for instance) is used. Even in case of neo-classical smooth continuous production function with assumption of constant returns to scale and factor prices and product price remaining constant the constancy of capital-output ratio holds. But latter will be a long-run possibility.

Now, instead of looking at net investment as the change in capital stock between two discrete periods of time like, t and $t + 1$ or $t - 1$ or any such 'lagged' time periods, we look at it as 'time rate of change' of capital stock written in terms of time derivative, i.e., $I = dK/dt$, the investment function in eqn. (4.11) can be written as:

$$I_n = \beta \frac{dY}{dt} \tag{4.14}$$

Net investment, I_n, can now be interpreted as an increasing function of the rate of change in income over a period of time. If $dY/dt > 0$, $I_n > 0$, if $dY/dt = 0$, $I_n = 0$ and if $dY/dt < 0$, $I_n < 0$. This is also known as acceleration theory of investment.

SUMMARY

1. Investment refers to the 'real investment'. By real investment is meant the addition to existing capital stock in real terms, for instance, the number of machines used in production process.
2. There are two concepts relevant to real investment, gross investment and net investment. Gross investment includes replacement investment while net investment is gross investment minus replacement investment. Replacement investment is no new addition to capital stock but only the part of investment needed for worn-out capital assets.
3. Investment behaves with the rate of interest as a decreasing function, i.e., volumes of net investment increases with fall in the rate of interest. This behaviour is explained in terms of two approaches: Keynesian MEC approach and neo-classical capital stock adjustment approach.
4. Marginal Efficiency of Capital (MEC) is defined as the particular rate of discount which makes the cost of the capital good (supply price of a machine, for example) just equal to the net present value (NPV) of the series of expected incomes (prospective yields) of the capital good. MEC is also known as marginal efficiency of investment (MEI) or internal rate of return (IRR). An individual entrepreneur makes a rational decision regarding acquiring a certain capital asset on the criteria: MEC $\geq$ r, where r is the market rate of interest relevant to the purchase price of the capital asset.
5. With volumes of investment, MEC would generally fall. This gives a falling MEC schedule. In equilibrium (MEC = r), every point on the MEC curve gives a downward sloping investment curve (or, investment function).
6. This approach, however, overlooks the supply behaviour of the capital goods concerned. This has been taken care of by the demand-supply or

capital stock adjustment approach. While the demand for capital good is determined by the same principle of net present value (NPV) criterion based on a certain market rate of interest, the supply price of the capital asset is determined by the supply conditions in the capital-good producing industry. Generally, the supply curve of the capital good rises with its price due to rising marginal cost of production. The demand curve, however, is downward sloping with the price of capital (NPV). From, entrepreneurs' point of view there is always a gap between a certain 'desired' or 'optimum' capital stock and actual capital stock which they try to fill up as per requirement.

7. In the short run, the stock of capital remains fixed, giving a vertical supply of capital curve. With the existing demand for capital curve, there is an equilibrium price of capital good. Now, with fall in the rate of interest, the demand curve shifts to the right, showing greater demand for capital good at lower cost (interest rate). This raises the price of the capital good in the short run giving a higher short run profit to the capital good producing industry. The supply curve, being upward sloping, new supplies of capital goods flow and entrepreneurs begin to add to their stock of capital, i.e., net investment takes place. This process continues, with every fall in the rate of interest, until the full adjustment is complete, i.e., until the actual capital stock becomes equal to the desired (or, optimum) capital stock.
8. Apart from interest rate, investment function is influenced by the level of income also. Level of income, if viewed as a parameter, shifts the investment function to the right in case of rise and to the left in case of fall in the level of income.
9. Investment is equally influenced by the rate of change in income or final consumption in which case it leads to the acceleration principle such that a given change in income results in several times higher investment: this is also known as 'induced investment' effect.
10. See also summary of Chapter 3.

EXERCISE

1. How does consumption expenditures (c) determine the income determination process in the Keynesian model?
2. Define Marginal Propensity to Consume (MPC) and Marginal Propensity to Save (MPS) and derive the concept of investment multiplier.
3. What is 'dynamic multiplier'? Illustrate its behaviour in diagrammatic terms.
4. What is 'autonomous' consumption? How does it influence the income determination process?

5. Distinguish clearly among 'gross investment', 'net investment' and 'replacement investment'.
6. What do you understand by marginal efficiency of capital (MEC)? Examine its role in the investment decision of a firm.
7. How does 'expectation' determine the volume of private investment? Explain.
8. Define 'acceleration' principle. Examine its role in the private investment decision.
9. Explain and illustrate the process of income determination in a closed Keynesian model.

REFERENCES

1. W.J. Baumol, (1971), Economic Theory and Operations Analysis, Prentice-Hall.
2. Richard G. Lipsey, (1969), An Introduction to Positive Economics, ELBS, Weidenfield and Nicolson.
3. G. Ackley, (1978), Macroeconomics: Theory and Policy, Macmillan, New York.
4. R L Crouch, (1972). Macroeconomics: Harcourt Brace Jovanovitch.

5

Income Determination Model with Government

5.1 GOVERNMENT EXPENDITURES, TAXES AND TRANSFERS

Government, with its twin functions of public expenditures and taxation plays an essential role in the income determination process. By including these major budgetary functions, the basic Keynesian model can now be extended. Of the various budgetary functions, 'government expenditure' and taxation are decisive functions. Government expenditures include mainly: (a) direct purchase of goods and services by different government agencies or departments, (b) transfer payments such as pension and other social security expenditures, subsidies, providing 'public goods' in terms of defence, national security, public administration, deliverance of justice, public health, education, making provision for recreational parks, playgrounds, community services, etc., through its different departments. For this, the governments have to incur sizeable amount of expenditures either directly or purchase of goods and services indirectly. In most countries, certain departments like defence, railways, post and telegraph, ports and harbours are run directly by the governments. Besides this, in abnormal times like wars, national disasters such as floods, famines and earthquakes, governments have to make heavy expenditures. In most democracies of the world, holding of political elections involves sizeable amount of public expenditure. A large part of government expenditure is the result of political decision. In sum, broadly, these public or government expenditures (either of the developmental or non-developmental types) can be lumped together and symbolized as G.

The other important fiscal function of the government is to raise public revenue through taxes. While some taxes are levied on citizens' incomes and wealth and are known as direct taxes, a substantial part of taxes are imposed on commodities and services and are known as 'indirect taxes'. Although such indirect taxes are raised directly from sellers of commodities and services, they are ultimately passed on, partially or wholly, to the consumers.

Government expenditures (G), for several reasons explained above, can be taken as exogenously given and to be denoted by $\overline{G}$. However, taxes can be taken as depending principally on the level of GDP or GNP such that higher level of GNP yields higher amount of taxes. For simplicity, we can assume total taxes to be linearly related to GNP.

The aggregate demand, Y, can now be redefined as composing of (a) consumption expenditure (C), (b) investment expenditure (I) and (c) government expenditure (G) where, for the present model $I = \bar{I}$ and $G = \overline{G}$, i.e., these are largely exogenous in nature. In equational form, eqn. (4.1) can now be extended as:

$$Y = C + I + G \tag{5.1}$$

where, $I = \bar{I}$ and $G = \overline{G}$.

Also, we are now specifying a tax function as follows:

$$T_x = m + nY \tag{5.2}$$

where, n indicates the marginal tax rate with its value being positive but less than one, (the rate at which taxes increase as a result of rise in income) and m is the autonomous part of taxes which can be taken as 'negative'. This is because, taxes, in most cases are imposed on incomes above a certain minimum or threshold levels (also known as exemption limit). Until that minimum level is reached, taxes are zero, hence m, the intercept of tax function is negative[1].

Another component of government expenditure, viz., transfer payments is presumed to leave favourable effect on people receiving such payments from the government. These payments generally are made on people or community earning nil or marginal incomes. For instance, pensions or subsidies are made to those who have either ceased to earn or have very low and minimum incomes. However, as income levels increase, the rate of such transfer falls, so that we can think of a linear type 'transfer function' with a positive intercept and negative slope (Fig. 8.1) such as

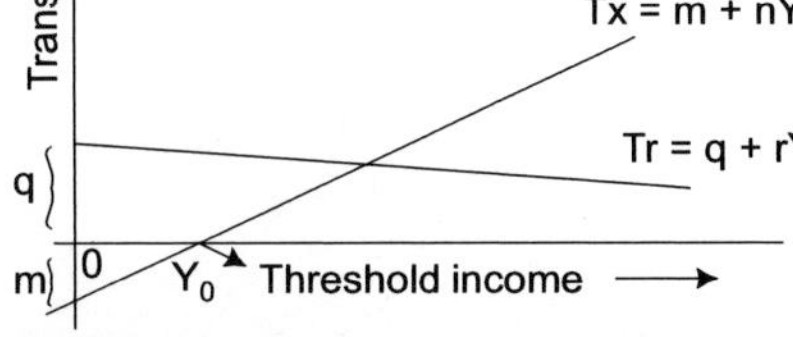

Figure 5.1 *Government expenditures with tax and transfers.*

$$Tr = q + rY, \tag{5.3}$$

where, Tr = amount of transfer payments by the govt., q is the intercept indicating the amount of transfer to zero income-earners, r is the marginal rate of transfer.

---

[1] The tax function will however, not be linear in case of progressive tax system. The curve showing tax function in that case will be convex from below (with gradually increasing slope) suggesting that the rate of tax increases with level of income. Here we have assumed a linear tax function to avoid complication. The value of n indicates the marginal tax rate, the rate at which taxes increase with level of taxable income.

The value of r is numerically less than one but negative in sign. This is because the amount of transfer gradually decreases with the level of income on the one hand and the transfer amount does not, generally, fully compensate for the whole of income loss. Y is the level of real income. Since Tr has favourable effect on Y and Tx has unfavourable effect on Y, we can combine them together to obtain a net tax function (by deducting the first from the second) as follows:

$$T = m + nY - q - rY = (m - q) + (n - r)Y. \tag{5.4}$$

where, $T = (Tx - Tr)$, $(m - q)$ is the net effect on the intercept (which obviously is negative with a greater value, since m is already negative) and $(n - r)$ is the net marginal rate of tax which will be almost the same as that of the tax function. We can, therefore, rewrite our net tax function as follows:

$$T = t_0 + t_1 Y \tag{5.5}$$

where, $t_0 = (m - q)$ and $t_1 = (n - r)$.

We are now in a position to introduce the concept of disposable income (DI) as the difference between the gross real income minus taxes (direct) plus the transfers or,

$$DI = Y - Tx + Tr.$$

$$= Y - T \quad (\text{since } T = Tx - Tr).$$

$$\Rightarrow \quad DI = Y - t_0 - t_1 Y$$

$$\Rightarrow \quad DI = -t_0 + (1 - t_1)Y \tag{5.6}$$

The consumption function, originally presented in eqn. 4.2 and Fig. 4.1, is now modified by substituting DI for Y as follows:

$$C = a + bDI$$

$$= a + b[-t_0 + (1 - t_1)Y]$$

$$\Rightarrow \quad C = a - bt_0 + b(1 - t_1)Y \tag{5.7}$$

which, by substitution in (5.1) yields,

$$Y = a - bt_0 + b(1 - t_1)Y + \bar{I} + \bar{G}$$

$$\Rightarrow \quad Y[1 - b(1 - t_1) = a - bt_0 + \bar{I} + \bar{G}$$

$$\Rightarrow \quad Y = \frac{1}{1 - b(1 - t_1)}\{a - bt_0 + \bar{I} + \bar{G}\} \tag{5.8}$$

Equation (5.8) gives the new equilibrium income when government operations such as government expenditure (along with transfer payments[1]) and taxation are pursued simultaneously. Equation (5.8) also gives a modified value of the multiplier which contains the coefficients of consumption function, b, as also the coefficient of the tax function, t_1. However, while b is negative (as in the original multiplier of eqn. (4.4)), $t_1 b$ is positive so that a smaller fraction is subtracted from unity in the denominator part giving a smaller value of the multiplier $(1/1 - b(1 - t_1))$.

[1] In a country like India, transfer payments play an important role since a substantial part is provided in the form of subsidies and other social welfare heads in government budgets.

The explanation of this smaller multiplier is simple. Inclusion of net tax function in the consumption function reduces the impact of it on income propagation because it takes away a certain part (or, withdraws) of income from the system. The other components of eqn. (5.8) can be analysed as follows:

An increase in the value of any of the autonomous components, viz., a, t_0, $\bar{I}$, $\bar{G}$ will have the effect of increasing income by the value of the multiplier. An increase in t_0, however, will have a combined effect with b, and hence income will increase but by less than the value of the multiplier. For instance, if the government decides to raise the exemption limit on income (increase in t_0), there will be a revenue loss to the government equal to the amount by which t_0 increases (of course, multiplied by tax rate). But this amount increases the disposable income of the previous tax payers and, assuming marginal propensity to consume (MPC) to be constant, total consumption expenditure will be higher and so will the equilibrium income.[1]

The diagrammatic representation of eqn. (5.8) is given in Fig. 5.2.

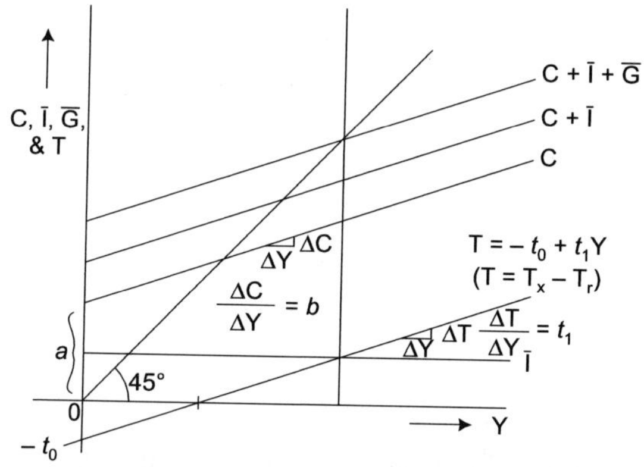

Figure 5.2 *Income determination process with government expenditures, transfer payments and taxation.*

We now take a few specific numerical examples to illustrate the income determination process:

Example 1 Let us suppose, an economy's autonomous investment is worth ₹ 10 thousand crore, the aggregate consumption function is represented by $C = 5 + 0.8Y$ (a = ₹ 5 thousand crore). In case of simple Keynesian model, the equilibrium income will be solved as:

$$Y = \frac{1}{1-b}\,[a + \bar{I}]$$

1 Readers should not get confused from the negative sign of bt_0 within the bracket of eqn. (5.8). Since t_0 originally is negative although in eqn. (5.7) we have written t_0 in the positive. Hence, ultimately bt_0 will have positive effect upon equilibrium income.

$$= \frac{1}{1 - 0.8} [5 + 10]$$

$$= \frac{1}{0.2} \times 15$$

$$= 5 \times 15 = ₹\ 75 \text{ thousand crore.}$$

Example 2 If in example 1, the autonomous investment increases to ₹ 15 thousand crore, while other parameters remaining the same, the new equilibrium income will be:

$$Y = \frac{1}{0.2} [5 + 15]$$

$$= 5 \times 20 = ₹\ 100 \text{ thousand crore.}$$

Example 3 If a, for some reason, increases to ₹ 7 thousand crore while $\bar{I} = 15$ thousand crore, Y will increase to:

$$Y = \frac{1}{0.2} [7 + 15]$$

$$= 5 \times 22$$

$$= ₹\ 110 \text{ thousand crore}$$

Example 4 If, in example 1, government decides to spend ₹ 10 thousand crore on building roads, the GNP will increase to:

$$Y = \frac{1}{1 - 0.8} [5 + 10 + 10]$$

$$= \frac{1}{0.2} \times 25 = 5 \times 25$$

$$= 125 \text{ thousand crore}$$

Example 5 Given a = ₹ 5 thousand crore, $b = 0.75$, t_0 = ₹ 8 thousand crore $t_1 = 0.2$, $\bar{I}$ = ₹ 10 thousand crore and $\overline{G}$ = ₹ 15 thousand crore, the equilibrium income will now be determined as follows:

Since, $$Y = \frac{1}{1 - b(1 - t_1)} \{a - bt_0 + \bar{I} + \overline{G}\}$$

Putting the respective values in the equation gives:

$$Y = \frac{1}{1 - 0.75\ (1 - 0.2)} \{5 - 0.75 \times 8 + 10 + 15\}$$

$$= \frac{1}{1 - 0.75\quad 0.8} \{5 - 6 + 25\}$$

$$= \frac{1}{0.4} \times 24 = 2.5 \times 24 = ₹\ 60 \text{ thousand crore.}$$

Example 6 If government decides to raise the marginal tax rate from 20% to 30% but increases government expenditure by 10% (from that given in example 5, the equilibrium income will be affected as follows:

Now, the values of the equation will be:

$$Y = \frac{1}{1 - 0.75\ (1 - 0.3)}\ \{5 - 0.75 \times 8 + 10 + 16.5\}$$

$$= \frac{1}{1 - 0.75\ (0.7)}\ \{5 - 6 + 26.5\}$$

$$= \frac{1}{1 - 0.525} \times 25.5$$

$$= \frac{1}{0.475} \times 25.5$$

$$= 2.105 \times 25.5 = ₹\ 53.6775 \text{ crore}$$

The above result shows that increase in marginal tax rate and increase in government expenditure by the same percentage, leads to fall in equilibrium income (in this case, by 6.3225 thousand crore of rupees).

Example 7 In the example 6, what will be the percentage increase in government expenditure needed to maintain equilibrium income at ₹ 60 thousand crore?

The relevant equation to be solved is:

$$60 = \frac{1}{1 - 0.75\ (1 - 0.3)}\ \{5 - 0.75 \times 8 + 10 + x\}$$

where, x is unknown government expenditure

$$= \frac{1}{0.475}\ \{5 - 6 + 10 + x\}$$

$$= 2.105 \times (9 + x)$$

$$\Rightarrow \quad 60 = 18.945 + 2.105x$$

$$\Rightarrow \quad 60 - 18.945 = 2.105x$$

$$\Rightarrow \quad 41.055 = 2.105x$$

$$\Rightarrow \quad x = \frac{41.055}{2.105} = 19.5$$

So the government expenditure will have to be increased from ₹ 15 thousand crore to ₹ 19.5 thousand crore, i.e., by ₹ 4.5 crore or by 30%.

Example 8 If the government announces increase in the exemption limit of personal income tax such that on government estimate, the tax collections will fall by ₹ 1 thousand crore, all other parameters remaining unchanged as in example 5, examine its impact on equilibrium income.

Referring to example 5, the value of t_0 will fall from ₹ 8 thousand crore to ₹ 7 thousand crore (fall by 1 thousand crore)

Now substituting this value in example 5, will give:

The equation in example 5 is:

$$Y = \frac{1}{1 - b(1 - t_1)}\ \{a - bt_0 + \bar{I} + \overline{G}\}$$

Replacing relevant values in the equation, we get,

$$Y = \frac{1}{1 - 0.75\ (1 - 0.2)} \{5 - 0.75 \times 7 + 10 + 15\}$$

$$= \frac{1}{0.4} \{5 - 5.25 + 25\}$$

$$= \frac{1}{0.4} \times 24.75$$

$$= 2.5 \times 24.75 = ₹\ 61.875 \text{ thousand crore}$$

i.e., an increase of ₹ 1.875 thousand crore.

Example 9 If the government intends to increase GNP by 5% from the level set in example 5, what will be the appropriate increase in government expenditure, given all other parameters?

The equilibrium GNP in example 5 is ₹ 60 thousand crore. An increase by 5% of 60 = 3 thousand crore of rupees. The required GNP level is thus 60 + 3 = ₹ 63 thousand crore. We substitute this value in the equation for equilibrium income, i.e.,

$$63 = \frac{1}{1 - 0\ .75\ (1 - 0.2)} \{5 - 0.75 \times 8 + 10 + x\}$$

where, x is unknown

$$\Rightarrow \quad 63 = \frac{1}{0.4} \{5 - 6 + 10 + x\}$$

$$= 2.5\ \{9 + x\}$$

$$\Rightarrow \quad 63 = 2.5x + 22.5$$

$$\Rightarrow \quad 2.5x = 63 - 22.5 = 40.5$$

$$\Rightarrow \quad x = \frac{40.5}{2.5} = 16.2$$

Thus, the increase in government expenditure required is 16.2 – 15 = 1.2 thousand crore of rupees.

Example 10 Given the parameters of example 5, what will be the amount of tax cut required for increase in GNP of 4%?

For an increase in GNP of 4%, i.e., 60 × 4% = 2.4, the total GNP will have to be 60 + 2.4 = ₹ 62.4 thousand crore. We have to solve the equation for unknown value of t_0. Thus, we write:

$$62.4 = \frac{1}{1 - 0.75\ (1 - 0.2)} \{5 - 0.75 \times t_0 + 10 + 15\}$$

$$\Rightarrow \quad 62.4 = \frac{1}{0.4} \{30 - 0.75\ t_0\}$$

$$= 2.5\ \{30 - 0.75\ t_0\}$$

$$= 75 - 1.875\ t_0$$

$$\Rightarrow \quad 1.875\ t_0 = 75 - 62.4$$

$$\Rightarrow \quad t_0 = \frac{12.6}{1.875} = 6.7$$

Thus, the difference in t_0 is 8 – 6.7 = 1.3.

Hence, the required tax-cut will be ₹ 1.3 thousand crore.

Example 11 The government of India announces to pay a total sum of ₹ 5000 crore to the unemployed youth of the country as unemployment allowance. Given the parameters of example 5, examine its impact on the GNP growth.

Payment of unemployment allowance is a kind of 'transfer payment' by the government. It has the same effect as tax-cut or decrease in the absolute value of t_0 by the amount of the allowance. Hence, the equation to be solved will be:

$$Y = \frac{1}{1 - b(1 - t_1)} \{5 - 0.75\ (8 - 5) + 10 + 15\}$$

$$= \frac{1}{1 - 0.75\ (1 - 0.2)} \{5 - 0.75 \times 3 + 25\}$$

$$= \frac{1}{0.4} \{30 - 2.25\}$$

$$= 2.5 \times 27.75$$

$$= 69.375$$

Hence, equilibrium income will increase from ₹ 60 thousand crore to 69.375 crore, i.e., by ₹ 9.375 thousand crore.

5.2 THE BALANCED BUDGET MULTIPLIER

The concept of balanced budget multiplier is associated with government's fiscal operations in a manner that the entire increase in government expenditure is financed through additional taxes. Thus, $\Delta G = \Delta T$ where ΔG and ΔT are, respectively, increase in government expenditure and increase in taxation. The government budget is therefore, 'balanced'. It can be easily established that even in such a situation, equilibrium income will increase – and increase by exactly the amount of additional government expenditure. The value of the multiplier, in this case will be one. To prove this result we proceed as follows:

We refer to eqn. 3.13 which is reproduced here:

$$Y = \frac{1}{1 - b(1 - t_1)} [a - bt_0 + \bar{I} + \bar{G}] \qquad (5.9)$$

It would be clear from eqn. (5.9) that an increase in government expenditure, ΔG, with no change in net taxes – either t_0 or t_1 – would raise income by the multiplier, 1/1 – b. Similarly, an increase in total taxes, ΔT, with no change in government expenditure would decrease income by the multiplier, $-b/1-b$.[1] Thus, the total change in equilibrium income ΔY, will be equal to

$$\Delta Y = \frac{1}{1-b}\Delta G - \frac{b}{1-b}\Delta T \tag{5.10}$$

Now, since $\Delta G = \Delta T$, by substitution in eqn. (5.10), we get

$$\Delta Y = \frac{1}{1-b}\Delta G - \frac{b}{1-b}\Delta G$$

which reduces to:

$$\Rightarrow \qquad \Delta Y = \frac{1-b}{1-b}\Delta G = \Delta G \tag{5.11}$$

Hence, the value of the balanced-budget multiplier $(1 - b)/(1 - b) = 1$. The equilibrium income Y increases by the amount of the increase in government expenditure.

This is an interesting conclusion for fiscal policy of the government. Even if the government balances its budget – the amount of expenditures just being equal to the amount of tax revenues, the total income will still be raised by the amount of expenditures. In fact, the logic of multiplier process is involved here, which we shall be taking up later for further analysis. In a crude manner, we can present here the application of multiplier logic as follows:

If ΔG is the increase in government expenditure and b is marginal propensity to consume (or, expenditure), increase in income, ΔY will be equal to ΔG in the first round of income generation, since all the increase in government expenditure will be reflected in additional income of the community. However, in the second and subsequent rounds, income will increase by b. ΔG, $b\,(b\Delta G) = b^2\Delta G$, $b^3\Delta G$ and so on. Adding up these for n rounds, we get the overall increase in income as

$$\Delta Y_G = \Delta G + b^2\Delta G + b^3\Delta G + \ldots + b^n\Delta G \tag{5.12}$$

However, equal amounts of taxes collected, ΔT will, by reducing the community's disposable income, will result in reduction in income in different periods by,

$$-\Delta Y_T = -(b\Delta T + b^2\Delta T + b^3\Delta T + \ldots + b^n\Delta T) \tag{5.13}$$

Thus, the net effect on income propagation will be the sum total of eqns. (5.9) and (5.10), i.e.,

$$\begin{aligned} \Delta Y_n &= \Delta Y_G - \Delta Y_T \\ &= \Delta G + b^2\Delta G + b^3\Delta G + \ldots + b^n\Delta G - b\Delta T \\ &\quad - b^2\Delta T - b^3\Delta T - \ldots - b^n\Delta T \\ &= \Delta G \end{aligned}$$

(since all other terms cancel out, given that $\Delta G = \Delta T$)

[1] This can be derived by taking $t_1 = 0$ and $t_0 = \Delta T$ and differentiating eqn. (5.6) with respect to ΔT.

So, the conclusion is that total income increases by the amount of increase in government expenditure in the case of balanced budget operation.

In terms of our eqn. (5.9) also, we can derive the balanced budget multiplier as follows:

$$Y = \frac{1}{1 - b(1 - t_1)} [a - bt_0 + \bar{I} + \bar{G}] \tag{5.14}$$

We first get the increase in Y by taking the first derivative of eqn. (5.14) with respect to G (G is not $\bar{G}$ now),

$$\frac{dY}{dG} = \frac{1}{1 - b(1 - t_1)}$$

and now, also get the first derivative of Y with respect to 't_0' (assuming that there has been increase in taxes simultaneously)

$$\frac{dY}{dt_0} = \frac{-b}{1 - b(1 - t_1)}$$

The net increase in equilibrium income will be affected by these two multipliers taken together. Adding them together gives,

$$\frac{1}{1 - b(1 - t_1)} - \frac{b}{1 - b + bt_1}$$

(we assume, however that there is no change in tax-rates, $bt_1 = 0$)

$$\Rightarrow \quad \frac{1}{1 - b} - \frac{b}{1 - b} = \frac{1 - b}{1 - b} = 1$$

Let us take an example. Referring to eqn. (5.9), let us initially assume the following values and find the equilibrium income.

$a = 10$, $b = 0.7$, $t_0 = 6$, $t_1 = 0.3$, $\bar{I} = 10$ and $\bar{G} = 15$,

The resulting value of Y will be:

$$Y = \frac{1}{1 - 0.7\,(1 - 0.3)} \{10 - 0.7 \times 6 + 10 + 15\}$$

$$= \frac{1}{1 - 0.7 \quad 0.7} \{10 - 4.2 + 10 + 15\}$$

$$= \frac{1}{1 - 0.49} \{30.8\}$$

$$= \frac{1}{0.51} \times 30.8$$

$= 1.96 \times 30.8 = 60.368$ (in thousand crore of rupees)

Let us now first increase G by ₹ 4 thousand crore and find out the new equilibrium income:

$$Y = \frac{1}{1 - 0.7\,(1 - 0.3)} [10 - 0.7 \times 6 + 10 + 19]$$

$$= \frac{1}{0.51}[10 - 4.2 + 29] = \frac{1}{0.51} \times 34.8$$

$$= 1.96 \times 34.8 = ₹\ 68.208 \text{ thousand crore}$$

In the next step we increase taxes (increase in t_0) by the same amount, i.e., ₹ 4 thousand crore and find out the new equilibrium income:

$$Y = \frac{1}{0.51}[10 - 0.7 \times 10 + 10 + 19]$$

$$= \frac{1}{0.51}[10 - 7 + 29] = \frac{1}{0.51} \times 32$$

$$= 1.96 \times 32 = ₹\ 62.72 \text{ thousand crore}$$

The net increase in equilibrium income is thus ₹ 62.72 thousand crore – ₹ 60.368 = ₹ 2.352 thousand crore. In fact, the value of the multiplier, in this case is less than one $\left(\frac{1}{0.51} - \frac{0.7}{0.51} = \frac{0.3}{0.51} = 0.59\right)$. This result renders the balanced budget multiplier theorem invalid.

The non-validity of this result is explained in terms of relatively larger shift of the net tax function – thus affecting negatively the net disposable income to a greater extent than the positive impact of government expenditure of a balanced budget particularly when the government already exists and operates simultaneously the expenditure and taxation functions. In fact, government's total tax collection exceeds the expected amount of tax by the balanced budget and the budget tends to become a surplus one. Therefore, it is suggestive that if the government intends to raise the amount of tax exactly equal to the amount of its expenditure ($\Delta T = \Delta G$), an appropriate value of t_0 ought to be determined with the help of tax function (flexible tax balanced budget case).

5.3 KEYNESIAN MODEL IN AN OPEN ECONOMY

When the economy is open, i.e., allows international trade (export and imports of goods and services) to take place, the process of income determination is further modified. In fact, imports and exports in an open economy become additional components influencing aggregate demand and therefore, the determination of equilibrium national income.

As far as imports are concerned it can be easily visualized that a country's (or economy's) level and growth of national income is largely responsible for the volume of imports required for the economy. For simplicity, therefore, imports can be assumed to be a function of the country's level of national income (GNP or Y) such as:

$$M = mY \tag{5.15}$$

where, M is the total value of imports, Y is national income and m is the constant proportion of national income.

On the other hand, exports depend largely upon other countries demand for goods and services (the countries where these goods and services are exported). Hence, exporting country (domestic country) has no control over the volume of exports and therefore, exports can be taken as exogenously determined. We denote this given volume of exports by $\overline{X}$ and can express the difference between exports and imports ($\overline{X} - M$) and call it the 'net exports'.[1]

We can now enlarge our original concept of aggregate demand to take account of the 'net exports' such as:

$$Y = C + I + G + (X - M) \tag{5.16}$$

where, we have assumed $I = \overline{I}$, $G = \overline{G}$ and $X = \overline{X}$ at certain levels.

Since $C = a + bDI$ and $DI = Y - T$, where $T = t_0 + t_1 Y$ making use of these relations or using our expanded consumption function (eqn. (5.5)), and substituting it in eqn. (5.16), we obtain,

$$Y = a - bt_0 + b(1 - t_1)\,Y + \overline{I} + \overline{G} + (\overline{X} - M)$$

$$\Rightarrow \quad Y = a - bt_0 + b(1 - t_1)\,Y + \overline{I} + \overline{G} + \overline{X} - mY$$

and solve for Y as

$$Y - b\,(1 - t_1)Y + mY = a - bt_0 + \overline{I} + \overline{G} + \overline{X}$$

$$\Rightarrow \quad Y[1 - b\,(1 - t_1) + m] = a - bt_0 + \overline{I} + \overline{G} + \overline{X}$$

$$\Rightarrow \quad Y = \frac{1}{1 - b(1 - t_1) + m}\,[a - bt_0 + \overline{I} + \overline{G} + \overline{X}] \tag{5.17}$$

Equation (5.17) gives a finally modified version of the multiplier $1/1 - b(1 - t_1) + m$. The value of this multiplier obviously is smaller compared to that in eqn. (5.6). The constant m here is also known as import coefficient which appears in the denominator and its value is positive but less than one.[2] Thus, in an open economy, the multiplier associated with GNP is further decreased. Equilibrium income is, therefore, further reduced to the extent of the import coefficient as compared to the closed economy. It is intuitively clear why the multiplier value is smaller. The aggregate income generated in an open economy is not wholly spent on purchase of domestic goods but a certain part of it is spent on the purchase of imported goods. This part of the diverted expenditure is, therefore, unable to create national output.

Graphically also, income determination process with imports and exports can be illustrated by introducing a new import function and an exogenous export as shown in Fig. 5.3.

In Fig. 5.3, we have obtained curve $C(Y) - m(Y)$ by subtracting import function $M = m(Y)$ from our basic consumption function $C(Y)$. Obviously, the difference between these two curves, although not shown separately here, represents the import function. Exports may be shown as a straight line parallel to the horizontal line (also not shown). Other exogenous functions (I, G) are

---

[1] In case of the value of imports exceeding the value of exports, $(X - M)$ will be negative.

[2] A country imports only a certain fraction of its own GDP in value terms, hence $0 < m < 1$.

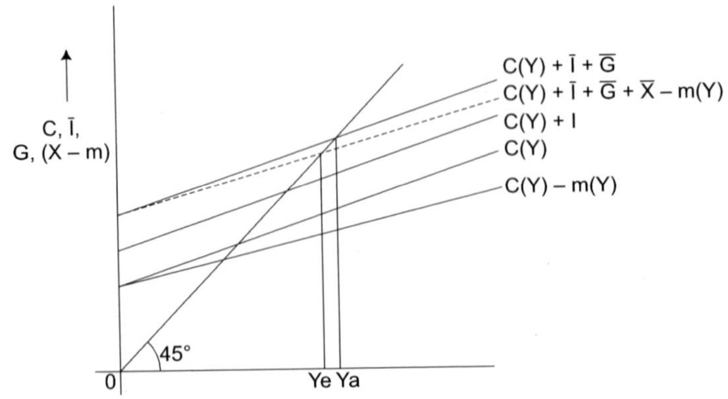

Figure 5.3 *Income determination model in open economy.*

shown parallel to the curve. The new and final aggregate demand function $C(Y) + \bar{I} + \bar{G} + \bar{X} - m(Y)$ has been drawn parallel to $C(Y) - m(Y)$ function. Thus, we have two equilibrium levels of income. *Ya* is the level of income in a closed economy model while *Ye* is the level of income in an open economy. Thus, with import function, the equilibrium level of income is reduced by *YaYe*. Here, we have assumed $[X - m(Y)]$ as negative implying imports exceeding the volume of exports. In the similar vein, we can imagine that if $X - m(Y)$ is positive (i.e., exports exceed imports) the new aggregate demand curve will be added up with $C + I + G$ curve and so the equilibrium income will further rise.[1]

It may be noted here that even though the new multiplier in eqn. (5.17) is smaller in magnitude, we have $\bar{X}$ as an additional exogenous factor, like $\bar{I}$ and $\bar{G}$, which positively influence the determination of equilibrium income. The following numerical example illustrates the net effect of $(X - M)$. Let us suppose we have the same values and parameters as in example 5. In addition, we have $m = 0.5$ and $\bar{X}$ = ₹ 6 thousand crore. Substituting these values in eqn. (5.17), we have

$$Y = \frac{1}{1 - 0.75\,(1 - 0.2) + 0.5}\,[5 - 0.7 \times 8 + 10 + 15 + 6]$$

$$= \frac{1}{1 - 0.75 \times 0.8 + 0.5}\,[5 - 6 + 25 + 6]$$

$$= \frac{1}{1 - 0.6 + 0.5}\,[30]$$

$$= \frac{1}{1 - 0.1} \times 30$$

$$= \frac{1}{0.9} \times 30 = \text{₹ } 33.33 \text{ thousand crore.}$$

Thus, the equilibrium income has decreased from ₹ 60 thousand crore to ₹ 33.33 thousand crore.

---

[1] We shall further examine the open economy model and its related problems in Chapter 16.

SUMMARY

1. Keynesian model of income determination with government assumes special importance since government's fiscal functions such as public expenditures and taxation play decisive role in income generation process.
2. Among various public expenditures, transfer payments—pensions, other social security payments, subsidies of various kinds—play special part in either raising incomes of the low income earners and unemployed youth and the retirees on preventing fall in incomes in economically difficult situations.
3. Providing 'public good' is perhaps the most important government's budgetary and fiscal function in terms of national security and defence, public administration, justice delivery, public health, recreational parks, playgrounds and other community services. These involve public expenditures which individually or collectively raise national income manifold.
4. The volume of transfer payments, however, varies with the level of national income such that at low level of national income this volume is relatively high, but as the level of income rises, the volume of transfer payments decreases.
5. Taxation is equally important function for the government for running the government, it needs revenues for which it imposes various kinds of taxes—income taxes on individuals and corporates/businesses as well as commodity taxes. The government may follow either progressive tax policy or proportional tax policy depending upon subjects/commodities on which taxes are imposed. The various government agencies are engaged in formulating and executing the tax policies.
6. Given the specific manner in which taxes and transfers are related to national income/GDP, the equilibrium income is easily solved by solving the relevant equation. In the main text, sufficient examples are available to illustrate the income determination in the basic Keynesian framework.
7. An interesting case of 'balanced budget multiplier' occurs when the national income/GDP is raised several times even when the government budget is balanced, i.e., the entire amount of government expenditures is financed by raising taxes ($\Delta G = \Delta T$)

EXERCISE

1. What do you understand by 'public good'? How does it differ from private good? Why are public goods so important in the context of public finance/government expenditure?
2. Examine the behaviour of 'transfer payments'. Why are transfer payments larger in relatively underdeveloped countries?
3. How does the 'net tax function' behave? Explain its intercept part as well as its slope.
4. Given the following data informations, obtain the equilibrium income for the economy. Consumption function is represented by the equation: $C = 10 + 0.75Y$ and the autonomous investment is ₹50,000 crore.
5. If the government decides to spend ₹50,000 crore on constructing railway tracks, the equilibrium GDP is likely to increase to ...
   (consumption function is the same → $C = 10 + 0.75Y$ and autonomous investment is ₹50,000 crore).

REFERENCES

1. G. Ackley, Macroeconomics: Theory and Policy, MacMillan 1978.
2. R.L. Crouch, Macroeconomics, Harcourt Brace Jovanovitch, 1972.
3. Gregory N. Mankiw, Macroeconomics, 6th Edition, Worth Publishers, 2006.
4. Gregory N. Mankiw, Principles of Macroeconomics, 5th Edition, South Western Cengage Learning, 2008.

PART-3

Money Market Analysis

6

Supply of Money and the Banking System

6.1 DEFINITION, EVOLUTION AND FUNCTION OF MONEY

6.1.1 A Brief Evolution of Money and the Problem of Defining Money

Money has evolved over a long period of time in history–from various kinds of commodities (barter system) to its present form of currency (notes and coins) and bank deposits used as means of exchange and settlement of debt obligations. Over this long evolution process 'convenience' (or avoidance of inconvenience) of human beings in society has played a decisive role. Whenever, inconvenience of a particular system came in the way, it was gradually replaced by another one. Hence, barter system gave way to the metallic money (gold, silver and other precious metals) in order to avoid the inconvenience of the double coincidence of wants and precise measurement of exchange value. When gold and other precious metals came to be used as means of payment, its durability rendered an important function in terms of store of value of money. For a pretty long time, precious metals served as money, although in its early stage, two problems were associated with it, viz., weighing large quantities of gold and caring if from one place to another for purposes of payment. Subsequently, keeping gold in large quantifies was a security problem. People tried to solve this problem by keeping their gold with goldsmiths who usually possessed large sized and relatively secure iron safes. Whenever payment to other persons would be required they would be taken to the goldsmith, get back their gold and payments made. This system was purely based on trust. At a later stage, other persons who got their payments from the same goldsmith too felt the need to keep their gold under safe custody. The goldsmith now did not need to part with the gold but issue, instead, 'receipts' to the depositors of gold except under special circumstances. Subsequently, these receipts used to serve as money for payments.[1]

[1] It may be pointed out here that the banking system in modern times had its antecedent in the goldsmith's practice of gold deposits and issuing receipts.

Under kingships in different countries of the world, gold coins, bearing the imprints of kings used to be circulated as money. In case of other precious metals, equivalent amount of gold used to be held as 'reserve'. Hence, all coins were fully backed by gold. In case of minting of coins, it was ensured that the intrinsic value of the metal was equal to the face-value of the coin. But while carrying gold coins in large quantities continued to be inconvenient and fraught with security problem, increasing use of these scarce resources caused the problem of supply which could be augmented only through new finds through gold mining.

By eighteenth century, most countries of the world were on 'gold standard'. For all international transactions, payments used to be made in terms of gold; hence gold continued to hold the prestigious position and country's richness used to be recognized by accumulation of gold.[1] As far as internal trade and payment was concerned paper money came into existence thus saving the scarce precious metals. But every paper money still used to be 100 per cent backed by gold reserves with 'promise to pay the bearer' the equivalent amount of gold on demand. Until mid-twentieth century all commercial banks were empowered to issue notes (paper money) fully backed by gold. For instance, until 1947, Bank of England served as a private institution, although having a link with the government, and issued notes backed by country's gold reserves.

In subsequent years, the problem of maintaining the convertibility of the paper money into gold gave birth to the system of 'fractionally backed paper money' under which instead of 100%, only a fraction was required to be maintained as gold reserve. The actual fraction of the paper currency to be maintained (in gold) used to depend on several factors including the country's accessibility to gold and the strength of the national currency concerned.

When the function of note-issue was completely taken over by the Central Bank of the country, the concept of 'fiat money' or 'legal tender' came into being. Now, all notes and coins used to bear the 'imprimatur of the State'. For instance, in U.K., the Bank of England, in USA, the Federal Reserve Bank and in India, Reserve Bank of India[2], started issuing currency notes and coins although coins of lower denominations were issued by the government itself. (Presently, the RBI issues all currencies bearing the seal and signature of the governor, RBI, while all coins upto the denomination of five rupees are issued by the ministry of finance, government of India[3].)

[1] Gold standard had, at least, one foolproof advantage. Inflation (or, deflation) had little chance of occurring among countries since the 'golden rule' of gold standard was 'to expand credit when gold comes in and to contract credit when gold goes out'. In other words, expansion and contraction of credit money (through banking system) were, as a matter of avowed policy, to be in line with expansion and contraction of gold via international trade. This would ensure automatic correction of inflationary situation in one country and deflationary situation in other country. However, gold standard broke down during the period between the first and the second world wars due mainly to problems associated with wars and their after effects.

[2] Reserve Bank of India was established in 1935 by the then British government.

[3] One and two rupee notes and coins and, recently, five rupee coins are issued by the Ministry of Finance, Government of India.

Development of the deposit money through the commercial banking system was the last leg in the evolution of money. Deposit money refers to the credit money created by the commercial banks. With the help of initial deposit money by the depositors, the commercial banks bring about multifold increase in total deposits through granting loans to the customers as well as making profitable investments. The deposit money creation reminds us of the old system of creating 'trust' by the goldsmiths based on their experience that all depositors of gold normally did not turn up at a time, to claim refund of their gold and so they could do with only a certain fraction of gold in their 'safes' and use the rest for any profitable business.

The commercial banks in modern times follow the similar practice with the exception that they keep a certain proportion of total deposits in liquid cash reserve (currency) and use the rest for lending and investment purposes. At the same time, commercial banks in most countries of the world, are overseen by their regulator, the Central Banks.

Deposit money is, today, created by the non-banking finance companies also who are empowered to accept deposits from the public and lend to willing borrowers.

The problem of giving a proper and precise definition of money stems from the fact that there are essentially two aspects relating to it: one is the legalistic aspect and the other is the functional aspect and both aspects do not often converge to definite entities. From purely legal point of view, all notes and coins (legal tender) bearing the seal and signature of either the Government of the Nation or its Central Bank are defined as money. However, from functional point of view, all papers (including notes and coins), bank deposits and a host of debt instruments which are capable of performing the major functions, such as general acceptability as means of exchange, measure of value, store of wealth and standard of fulfilling debt obligations ought be defined as money. From this broader point of view, all debt obligations "created" by a large number of non-banking financial institutions in the modern capitalist economy are also fit to be included within the category of money. It may be mentioned, in this connection, that in modern times, credit cards are being widely (although not so much in underdeveloped countries) used as mode of payment. Hence, they too qualify, to a large extent, as money. Some hold the view that credit cards can best be defined as "near money". But the fact is that the dividing line between 'money' and 'near money' is thin. However, one distinctive feature of money is its complete liquidity. So, money is the most liquid asset while near monies are relatively less liquid in character. It is precisely for this reason that a proper definition of money has become a difficult task.

6.1.2 Functions of Money

In the last section, we saw how the concept of money evolved over the years in history, from barter system to metallic money (gold and silver), to fiat money (paper money) and to bank money. On analysis, it would be clear that the process of evolution itself has been punctuated by the basic functions that money has been performing. These basic functions are: (1) serving as a unit of account, (2) as a medium of exchange and (3) as a store of value. Economists sometimes add the fourth function as the standard of deferred payment. We briefly describe each of these functions. At the same time, we try to understand some of the emerging concepts which are likened with money such as credit and debit cards and bitcoins (or, crypto currencies).

Unit of account: Money serves as accounting units for measuring the relative values of all goods and services the people in the society transact upon. Because money has the characteristic feature of being divided into smaller units, values of all goods and services can be easily measured in terms of money. If a person goes to a shopkeeper and asks him what price a certain piece of cloth is, he will answer 'so much of rupees' or 'so much dollars' or' so much euros' or something like that depending upon which country he is in. Similarly, if a certain worker is hired by a factory owner, his wages are negotiated on certain fixed money terms. If a borrower gets a certain amount of debt from a bank or any other creditor, the amount of debt is determined in terms of monetary units. Thus, almost all calculations are done in terms of money, no matter what the currency it may be. A country's national income, national debt, etc., are also measured in terms of monetary units.

Medium of exchange: This is perhaps the most important function of money, it acts as a medium through which all kinds of monetary transactions are carried out in the society and economy. As the barter system was replaced by the money economy, it proved to be a better medium for exchanging goods and services in the society. Money became the generally acceptable medium as such. Every individual, social organisation or financial institution will have to accept money in exchange for anything else. This is because money has the sanction of the State so that nobody can refuse to accept it in the process of transaction. As a medium of exchange, money circulates in the whole economy and in fact, a certain unit of money circulates several times due to its durability and convenience of handling as also carrying it from one place to another. It is worth mentioning here that exchanges are not necessarily done in cash money but in other more convenient modes of payment like bank cheque or modern digital payment systems.

Store of value: Money has yet another property of being stored due to its durability. In fact, its value can be stored for future use. If someone saves a certain amount of money in whatever form, the same can be used anytime in future. From this point of view, money serves as a 'link between the present and the future'. Most people have a tendency to store or save money out of their money income with a view to meeting their future needs. Had the money not possessed the store of value property, this could not have been possible. However, given that 'money today is more valuable than money tomorrow', there exists a system to incentivise the savers with some extra returns in the form of 'interest'. The store of value function of money enables its holder to take advantage of its extra earning capacity in case it is "saved" in proper form. It is this function of money that prompted economist JM Keynes to propound his very famous liquidity preference theory of interest (L_2 function of money).

As mentioned above, sometimes economists also recognise the fourth function of money, namely, the standard of deferred payment. In a kind of monetary transaction where a certain entity gets a certain amount of money from someone with a promise to pay it back sometime later, the payment is generally made in terms of money only because it is the appropriate standard of payment.

However, this function of money is somehow inherent in other functions mentioned above and so the main functions remain the first three discussed above.

We now try to examine if the modern digital payment tools like debit cards or credit cards can be called money. The most convenient yardstick to test this is whether these cards are generally accepted as transaction modes. On this, it can be said that in advanced countries, these are very much in vogue and so are accepted in general. But in underdeveloped and poor economies including India, payment through cards alongside cash transactions is prevalent. Secondly, in the rural areas of India and elsewhere with less literate population, cash transaction is the dominant mode. If debit or credit cards are widely used throughout the economy, they can certainly qualify as money.

The new digital or virtual currency (cryptocurrency), which is being talked about these days for being qualified as money has two basic drawbacks. First, it has no asset backing. It exists only in the imaginary world. Secondly, it has no sanction of the State or government of the land. Hence, cryptocurrency cannot be called money.

However, in recent time, several central banks, including India's Reserve Bank of India are mooting the idea of issuing 'digital currency' as a mode of payment and medium of exchange in view of increasingly greater digitization in the payments domain. However, in underdeveloped countries (including India) these are certain limitations to the idea to be implemented which, however, need to be addressed at the first place.

6.2 MEASURES OF MONEY SUPPLY

Supply of money is a 'stock' concept. So, any attempt to measure the supply of money means measuring it at a certain specific point of time – either on

31st December or 30th September of a certain year and so on. Secondly, as we have seen above, there is complexity in providing a precise definition of money. Hence, measurement of money supply is also complex and difficult. It is for this reason, any single measure of money supply is not able to capture full characteristic features of money.

In developed countries like U.K., U.S. and underdeveloped countries like India, various measures of money supply have been suggested which are broadly as follows:

M_1 : This is the first basic measure of money supply consisting of currency with the public and demand deposits with banks. Currency with the public refers to all notes and coins which are currently in circulation (with which transactions are continuously carried on) as also the part of the currency kept in the form of 'reserves' with the banking system. The demand deposits are those deposits of commercial banks which are withdrawable anytime during the business hours of banks. The savings deposits of the banks are treated at par with currency with the public. Instead of keeping cash with themselves, households prefer to keep them in banks' savings deposits. These carry negligible rate of interest and have certain restrictions on withdrawals. In the Indian context, however, M_1 includes certain other deposits of Reserve Bank of India, even though this part of deposits is not significantly larger. Thus, if we denote currency with the public by C and demand deposits with banks by D, we can write: $M_1 = C + D$.

The above measure of money supply is almost common in all countries of the world. However, this concept is 'narrow' in scope and hence is known as 'narrow money'.[1]

M_2 : This is another measure of money stock which includes, besides, M_1, some other savings deposits. In India, $M_2 = M_1$ + savings deposits of government post offices.

M_3 : This is the broad measure of money supply defined as M_1 + time deposits of banks. Time deposits refer to all those deposits which are kept for a certain specified period of time, normally not withdrawable before the period expires. However, in recent years, these deposits (except some) have been made withdrawable at a certain discount. In India, as also in some of the developed countries, M_3 represents 'aggregate monetary resources' or simply 'broad money'.

[1] In U.S., M_1 includes foreign demand balances at Federal Reserve Bank but excludes from demand deposits of commercial banks, domestic inter-bank and US Govt. demand deposits and cash items in the process of collection and Federal Reserve Float.

M_4 : This has been defined as M_3 + all post office deposits in India. Needless to add that Indian postal department accepts a number of deposits such as ordinary savings deposits and time deposits of different kinds. However, M_4 does not include deposits under National Savings Certificates (NSC).

The above-mentioned measures of monetary aggregates have been in vogue in India since 1970, following the recommendations of Second Working Group on Measures of Monetary Aggregates. However, in view of new developments since then, particularly during 1980s and 1990s in the sphere of creation of liquidity by the non-banking financial institutions, the Govt. of India appointed Third Working Group to study the monetary system and provide suitable new measures to capture adequately the overall liquidity in the Indian economy. The Working Group submitted its Report (Report of the Working Group on Money Supply: Analytics and Methodology of Compilation) in June, 1998 (Chairman, Y.V. Reddy). Since then, the above-mentioned measures have been modified and there are, now, four different measures on 'monetary aggregates', viz., M_0, M_1, M_2 and M_3 and three different 'liquidity aggregates' specified as L_1, L_2 and L_3 with changed methods of compilation. The new measures are as follows.

6.2.1 Monetary Aggregates

There are, now, two methods of compilation of monetary aggregates, **weekly compilation** and **fortnightly compilation**. Within the weekly compilation of M_0, only the 'reserve money' or 'monetary base' compiled from the balance sheet of RBI is estimated. This includes currency in circulation + commercial banks' deposits with RBI + other deposits with RBI.

Fortnightly Compilation

M_1 : Currency with the public + Demand Deposits with the banking system + Other deposits with RBI = Currency with the public + Current deposits with the banking system + Demand liabilities portion of savings deposits with the banking system + Other deposits with RBI.

M_2 : M_1 + Time liabilities portion of savings deposits of the banking system + Certificate of Deposits issued by banks + Term deposits (excluding FCNB (B) deposits) with a contractual maturity of upto and including one year with the banking system.

M_3 : M_2 + Term Deposits (excluding FCNR(B) Deposits) with a contractual maturity of over one year with the banking system + Call borrowings from Non-Depository Financial Corporations by the banking system.

6.2.2 Liquidity Aggregates

Monthly Compilation

L_1 : M_3 + All Deposits with the Post Office Savings Banks (excluding National Savings Certificate).

L_2 : L_1 + Term Deposits with Term Lending Institutions and Refinance Institutions (FIs) + Term Borrowings by FIs + Certificate of Deposits issued by FIs.

Quarterly Compilation

L_3 : L_2 + Public Deposits of Non-Banking Financial Companies.

Following the new measures of both the monetary aggregates and liquidity aggregates in India, it has been possible, to a large extent, to monitor the changes in the supply of money at different points in time and thereby bring desirable changes in the monetary policy of RBI.

6.3 CREDIT CREATION AND FRACTIONAL RESERVE SYSTEM

As has been mentioned in the previous pages, bank money or credit money plays an important part in the total supply of money in the economy. The process of credit creation by commercial banks is known as multiple expansion of credit through deposit multiplier. The process is explained below:

The two major functions of commercial banks are: (i) to accept deposits from the public and (ii) to advance loans to the customers. In the process of these two functions, the banks earn interest income since deposit rates of interest are, generally, lower than the lending rates. Now, depositors keep their deposits under various categories of deposits, some of which are withdrawable at will while others have certain limitations or restrictions on withdrawals. Since the depositors do not, normally, turn up for withdrawals all at a time during a single day of transaction (except in an abnormal situation of 'run' on bank or bank failure), the banks do not require to keep all their public deposits in cash all the time. Based on their experience of day-to-day transactions and certain statutory norms determined by the Central Bank of the country, they keep a certain proportion – only a fraction of total deposits in cash.[1] The banks may use rest of their deposits as loans to the needy customers. These loans, in fact, create credit through new deposits inasmuch as new accounts are opened in their names and withdrawal facilities by cheques are provided to them.

[1] In India, there are two types of reserve requirements: Statutory Liquidity Ratio (SLR) and Cash Reserve Ratio: (CRR). Under the former, commercial banks are required to keep with themselves a certain percentage of total deposits in liquid form such as cash, gold or approved government securities, while under the latter the commercial banks are required to keep a certain percentage of deposits with Reserve Bank of India.

Let us suppose, a loan-seeker comes to the bank and asks for loan for specific purpose/purposes. If he fulfils bank's required norms (e.g., appropriate securities and credit worthiness) the loan is normally granted. However, the loan amount is, generally, advanced through a new deposit account opened with the bank and amount credited to the customer's account with withdrawal facility by cheques.[1] The customer concerned, then, spends the amount of the loan for whatever purpose/purposes by drawing cheques to different parties for payment. These parties, in turn, will possibly deposit their cheques in their own accounts' lying in different banks. The cheques are subsequently cleared through central clearing system and appropriate entries are made in the balance sheets of all these banks (along with our original bank).

Now, looking at the banking system as a whole and assuming that most (rather all) payments are made by cheques, all income receivers from the loan amount, possibly in the next round, will make payments to different parties which will, at least, partly come back to our original bank in the form of 'deposits'.

In fact, the entire amount of loan comes back to the banking system, provided the public do not hold back a certain part of it in liquid cash. Now, again, keeping a certain necessary minimum in cash reserve, the bank(s) can advance the rest of the 'come-back' deposit to other prospective customers as loans. The same process is followed and thus, in the next round also, new deposits are created through credit in the banking system. This process goes on until the entire original amount of deposit is exhausted.

Let us illustrate the whole process with an example. Let us suppose Bank *A* starts operations by accepting deposit from the public equal to ₹ 1 lakh. This amount is known as primary deposit with the bank. This deposit amount becomes the liability of the bank to the public and is shown in its balance sheet as 'liability'. Supposing the bank follows a norm of maintaining 20% of the deposit in cash, the actual cash reserve with the bank will be ₹ 20 thousand only. The rest of the amount of deposit, i.e., ₹ 80 thousand, known as excess reserve, is used by the Bank as loans to the borrowers. Now Bank *A*'s balance sheet will show this amount of ₹ 80 thousand as also ₹ 20 thousand as 'assets' in its balance sheet. The bank may open a new deposit account in the borrower's name and ₹ 80, thousand is credited in the account. The borrower may withdraw his loan amount by issuing cheques to different parties who may or may not have their deposit accounts with Bank *A*. If some of them have their accounts, part of the loan amount will come back to Bank *A*. Others will, possibly, deposit their cheques to their own respective banks like banks *B*, *C* and so on. The moment part or whole of the loan amount is deposited in these banks, their respective balance sheets will show these entries as 'liabilities'. Thus, the entire amount of loan (₹ 80 thousand) becomes new deposits in the banking system. This completes the first round of deposit as also credit creation.

---

[1] The bank may, instead, make payment of the loan amount by issuing cheque in which case the customer deposits it with his own bank.

In the second round, the Bank A or all banks taken together where deposits have been created, will follow the same norm of setting apart 20% of ₹ 80 thousand as reserves and lend out the rest ₹ 64 thousand to new borrowers. Again the same process will be followed and ultimately the whole of ₹ 64 thousand will come back to the banking system in the form of new deposits through corresponding new credits. There will be changes in the balance sheets of all banks – one bank's liability becoming another bank's asset or one bank's asset becoming another bank's liability – but the net impact in the banking system as a whole will be zero.

In the third and subsequent rounds also, the same process goes on until the entire original deposit is exhausted in new credits. From the above, it is clear that the total amount of deposits created is ₹ 1 lakh + ₹ 80 thousand + ₹ 64 thousand + ... +. This can be written as:

$$
\begin{aligned}
TD &= ₹\ 1 \text{ lakh} + 1 \text{ lakh} \quad 80\% + (1 \text{ lakh} \quad 80\%) \quad 80\% + \ldots + \\
&= 1 \text{ lakh} + 1 \text{ lakh } (1 - 20\%) + 1 \text{ lakh } (1 - 20\%)\ (1 - 20\%) + \ldots + \\
&= 1 \text{ lakh} + 1 \text{ lakh } (1 - 0.2) + 1 \text{ lakh } (1 - 0.2)^2 + \ldots \\
&\quad + 1 \text{ lakh } (1 - 0.2)^n
\end{aligned}
$$

assuming there are n rounds of credit creation.

$$
\Rightarrow \quad TD = 1 \text{ lakh } [1 + (1 - 0.2) + (1 - 0.2)^2 + (1 - 0.2)^3 + \ldots + (1 - 0.2)^n] \tag{6.1}
$$

Eqn. (7.1) is a convergent geometric series whose sum is equal to:

$$
\begin{aligned}
TD &= 1 \text{ lakh} \left[\frac{1}{1 - (1 - 0.2)}\right] \\
&= 1 \text{ lakh} \left[\frac{1}{0.2}\right] = ₹\ 5 \text{ lakh}
\end{aligned}
$$

(TD = Total Deposits).

So, with only ₹ 1 lakh as primary deposit, total deposit creation (and hence, credit creation) is equivalent to ₹ 5 lakh. In other words, the deposit (or, credit) multiplier is 5.

In symbolic notation, if DI stands for initial deposit with the banking system, and rr stands for reserve requirement by banks (in percentage terms) then total credit created can be written as:

$$
C = \frac{DI}{rr} = DI\left[\frac{1}{rr}\right] \tag{6.2}
$$

where, $\frac{1}{rr}$ is the credit multiplier (Cm)[1]

[1] Readers should not be confused between deposit multiplier and credit multiplier. In fact, values of both the multipliers are the same even though total volumes of deposits and credit differ by the percentage of reserve requirement. In the above example, total volume of deposits is ₹ 5 lakh with initial deposit of ₹ 1 lakh while total volume of credit is ₹ 4 lakh with initial credit of ₹ 80 thousand.

Equation (7.2) clearly suggests that, given DI, Cm varies inversely with rr; i.e., lower the reserve requirement, higher will be the credit multiplier and higher the rr, lower will be the credit multiplier.[1]

The above process of credit creation by commercial banks assumes that there is no 'leakage' in the form of public preferring to keep a certain part of the credit money in cash for some reason or other. In other words, it is assumed that the entire credit money created comes back to the banking system. However, if this assumption is relaxed (and a part of it is held back in cash by the households) the process of credit expansion will be somewhat affected and the value of credit multiplier will be accordingly less.

Let us suppose, the public desires to hold a certain constant fraction, b of the credit money in cash ($1 > b > 0$). The total deposits and deposit multiplier, now will be equal to:

$$\frac{DI}{rr + b} = DI\left[\frac{1}{rr + b}\right] \qquad (6.3)$$

where, $\frac{1}{rr + b}$ is the deposit (or credit multiplier).

It may be pointed out here that the process of credit creation through deposit expansion is as much true of the banking system as non-banking financial institutions, which, like banks, accept public deposits and advance loans but unlike banks cannot transfer accounts from one depositor to another. But they can, certainly, engage themselves in creating manifold debt obligations as in the banking sector. It is, for this reason, credit money has become so much important for the development of the entire market for financial instruments.

It must be remembered, however, that the measure of credit multiplier is the 'potential' rather than 'actual' measure of commercial banks' ability to create credit. In fact, the actual measure of credit multiplier may fall short of its potentiality if there is shortage of demand for credit. The measure of credit multiplier, thus, is based on the assumption that there will be no shortage of credit takers ('supply creates its own demand' a traditionally classical type of assumption).

6.4 PROXIMATE DETERMINANTS OF MONEY SUPPLY

It has been assumed in the discussion of income determination model that the supply of money is exogenously determined – by the monetary authority of the country independently of any endogenous variables. But we shall soon see that this is a false notion. In fact, monetary authority (Central Bank) alone is not responsible for determination of money supply. There are, at least, two

[1] We shall examine later in chapter on Monetary Policy, how rr is used by the Central Bank as an instrument to control the expansion of credit by commercial banks.

behavioural aspects of the community with regard to money supply which are determined within the economic system. These are: (1) the behaviour of the public with regard to their preference for currency vis-à-vis bank deposits, i.e., currency-deposit ratio and (2) the behaviour of the banking system with regard to their preference for 'reserves' vis-à-vis deposits, i.e., reserve-deposit ratio. These two aspects of behaviour on the part of the public and the banks together influence the supply of money as decided ultimately by the monetary authority. No doubt, the Central Bank has a dominant role to play in deciding upon the supply of money but, in the process, it has to keep in mind the above-mentioned behavioural aspects. Before we examine these proximate determinants, let us try to understand the concepts of High Powered Money (H) and Money Multiplier (m).

High Powered Money (H): This consists of the 'reserve money' held by the commercial banks (vault cash) + currency in circulation with the public + reserves with the Central Bank. The sum total of these, in fact, provides the 'base' for the total money supply in the economy. That is why, it is also known as 'Base Money'. Writing R for total reserves and C for currency with the public, H can be expressed as:

$$H = C + R \tag{6.4}$$

where, R = Vault cash (Commercial banks' own statutory minimum reserves) + Banks' deposits with the Central Bank (Reserve Bank of India).

Now, let the behaviour relating to the currency (cash) and demand deposit of the public be denoted by C/DD. The ratio C/DD, thus reflects the public choice of apportioning their money holding between currency and deposit with banks. If, for example, out of a sum of ₹ 100, currency amount is 10%, i.e., ₹ 10, the deposit amount must be 90% or ₹ 90. C/DD is then 10 : 90 or, 1 : 9 (= 1/9). Similarly, let the commercial banks' choice between reserves and deposits be denoted by R/DD. Here, R must not fall below some statutorily determined minimum but the actual value of R may exceed this minimum. It depends upon banks' choice of what ratio would be appropriate for them.

Now, total supply of money (or, stock of money) as we have defined earlier (in the narrow sense) consists of C and DD, i.e.,

$$M = C + DD \tag{6.5}$$

We have also seen in eqn. (6.4) that high-powered money or base money (H) is equal to the sum of $C + R$, where H is exogenously determined by monetary authority. Let us suppose, the optimum relation between currency holding and demand deposit by the public is given by the equation:

$$C = \alpha\, DD$$

where, $1 > \alpha \geq 0$ (6.6)

(In a special case, the public may hold the entire money in cash so that the value of $\alpha = 1$).

Similarly, the optimum reserve-deposit ratio of banks is given by the relation:

$$R = \beta\ DD$$

where, $1 > \beta > 0$ (6.7)

Now, substituting the values of R and C (from eqns. 6.7 & 6.6) in eqn. (6.4), we get,

$$H = \alpha\ DD + \beta\ DD$$

$$\Rightarrow \quad H = (\alpha + \beta)\ DD$$

$$\Rightarrow \quad DD = \frac{1}{\alpha + \beta} H \tag{6.8}$$

Eqn. (7.8) shows that DD, an endogenous variable, varies directly with H and inversely with α and β. Thus, if α and β or both increase given base money, H, deposit money will decrease and conversely, if α or β or both decrease, deposit money will increase. Therefore, $\frac{1}{\alpha + \beta}$ may be called the deposit multiplier, given the value of base money. Again, substituting the values of DD obtained in eqn. (6.8) and of C in eqn. (6.6) into eqn. (6.5), we get:

$$M = \alpha\ DD + \frac{1}{\alpha + \beta} H$$

$$\Rightarrow \quad M = \frac{1 + \alpha}{\alpha + \beta} H \quad \text{(on simplification)} \tag{6.9}$$

Equation (6.9) shows the relationship between money supply, M (in the narrow sense) and high-powered money, H. The coefficient attached with this relationship, $\frac{1 + \alpha}{\alpha + \beta}$, is known as money multiplier. Simply put:

$$M = mH \tag{6.9a}$$

where, $$m = \left(\frac{1 + \alpha}{\alpha + \beta}\right)$$

or, $$m = \frac{M}{H} \tag{6.9b}$$

where, m is the money multiplier.

From the above analysis, it can be concluded that α, β and H that is, people's choice regarding currency and deposit (currency-deposit ratio), banks' choice regarding reserve and deposits (reserve-deposit ratio) along with the volume of high-powered money can be called the proximate determinants of money supply even though they are by no means the ultimate determinants. Therefore, as against the ordinarily held view, M, the money supply is not wholly a policy determined variable. It is partly an endogenous variable determined by the public choice (currency-deposit ratio) on the one hand and commercial banks' choice (reserve-deposit ratio) on the other.

However, the central bank can influence H by its monetary policy changes and thereby influence M, the money supply. For instance, it can enforce a higher or lower percentage of minimum reserves to be maintained by commercial banks. Similarly, it can raise or lower the cash reserve ratio (CRR) which the commercial banks need to keep with central bank.

In the above analysis we have taken into consideration the money supply in the narrow sense ($M_1 = C + DD$). However, when a broader concept of money supply, M_3, the above formulation is altered in the following manner:

$$M = C + DD + TD \tag{6.10}$$

where, TD = Time Deposits of Banks.

Now, assuming that banks maintain a certain optimum relationship between reserves and total deposits and the people maintain a certain optimum relation between their demand deposits and time deposits, we have the following new relationships:

$$TD = t\,DD \tag{6.11}$$

Equation (6.11) shows the optimum relation between time deposits, TD, and demand deposits DD on the part of the people. The optimum relation between reserves and total deposits of the banks is now expressed by the equation:

$$R = \beta\,(DD + TD) \tag{6.12}$$

$$= \beta\,(DD + t\,DD)$$

$$= \beta\,DD\,(1 + t) \tag{6.13}$$

Money supply in the broader sense, M_3, is expressed as:

$$M_3 = C + D \tag{6.14}$$

where, D = total deposits (demand + time deposits)

Now, by definition, $H = C + R$, from which we can write:

$$H = \alpha\,DD + \beta\,DD\,(1 + t) \tag{6.15}$$

Substituting from eqns. (6.6) and (6.13).

$$\Rightarrow \quad H = DD\,\{\alpha + \beta\,(1 + t)\}$$

$$\Rightarrow \quad DD = \left[\frac{1}{\alpha + \beta\,(1 + t)}\right] H \tag{6.16}$$

Now, from eqn. (7.10)

$$M_3 = C + DD + TD$$

$$= \alpha\,DD + DD + t\,DD$$

$$= DD\,(\alpha + 1 + t)$$

$$\Rightarrow \quad M_3 = \frac{\alpha + 1 + t}{\alpha + \beta\,(1 + t)} \cdot H \tag{6.17}$$

where, the coefficient, $\dfrac{\alpha + 1 + t}{\alpha + \beta\,(1 + t)}$ is the new money multiplier.

It appears that as compared to the old multiplier, the new multiplier is higher since t, a ratio is added with numerator while βt, both being ratios, is added to the denominator value. However, the new multiplier may be insignificantly higher depending upon the values of ratios t and β.

In the early part of this chapter, we explained the creation of credit money by the banking sector through the fractional reserve system. Fractional reserve system allows banks to maintain a certain optimum level of reserve-deposit ratio. Sometimes, this is dictated by the 'statutory minimum' by the Central Bank. Secondly, in the process of credit creation, a part of the created credit money may be leaked out and kept by the public in the form of cash. This, together with other cash holdings leads to certain currency-deposit ratio to be maintained by the public. We have mentioned earlier, that these ratios, besides the high-powered money, serve as proximate determinants of money supply. However, these are based upon certain assumptions:

1. The ratios are assumed to be independent of one another, i.e., one does not affect the other. However, the central bank, while attempting to control money supply through open-market operations such as sale of government securities and thus reducing the reserve base of commercial banks, may result in portfolio adjustment by the banks. This, in turn, may affect the currency-deposit ratio of the public which was assumed constant. At the same time, this is likely to affect the portfolios of non-banking financial institutions which too, are indulged in credit creation process like banks. Thus, whenever, the proximate determinants of money supply are themselves, interlinked, it is no longer so simple to identify them.
2. Secondly, the determinants are based on 'narrow' definition of money supply (initially). However, using a broader concept of money (M_3), by and large, fulfill the requirement of a fairly good guide to the level of money supply; although even here they fail to capture the debt obligations created by a large section of non-banking financial institutions which equally influence the creation of credit money in the economic system.

In any case, the ultimate determinant of money supply is the demand for credit which is directly linked with rise in the level of income and the expectation of people regarding future income growth. Thus, even if the banking sector experiences a flush of funds for credit, and adopt fairly liberal policy in advancing credit to the borrowers, this may not work short of genuine demand for credit. If borrowers with no genuine credit-worthiness are induced to avail of the credit facilitates and if the number of such borrowers multiplies, the banking system – indeed the entire financial system may land itself in trouble. The recent global financial crisis (2008-10) resulting in failure of giant-sized banks and insurance companies in U.S. is a fit case in point (See Chapter 16)

6.5 CONTROL OF MONEY SUPPLY BY CENTRAL BANK

Central banks all over the world, have certain powers which they can exercise in controlling or regulating the supply of money in the economy. We have already seen how the supply of high-powered money (H) can be directly influenced by central bank's policy of reserve requirements by commercial banks. In Indian context for instance, RBI changes the Cash Reserve Ratio (CRR) – the percentage of total deposits that all commercial banks have to keep with RBI. Besides, commercial banks have to keep with themselves a certain minimum percentage of their deposits in liquid form (cash and investment in govt. securities) known as Statutory Liquidity Ratio (SLR). These reserve requirements are meant to meet any eventuality of liquidity shortage on the part of the banks. Now, as we already know, commercial banks are able to "create" credit money only out of the residual reserve (after meeting for CRR and SLR). If CRR or SLR or both are raised, the commercial banks are left with less residual reserves to create credit money. On the other hand, if these ratios are lowered, banks' credit creating ability is enhanced and the total supply of money is, thereby, increased. However, it is left to the prudence of the Central Banks to "read" correctly the condition of the economy and devise the monetary policy accordingly. Apart from the above-mentioned policy mix, there is the overall interest rate policy of the Central Bank, known as bank rate which acts as a guide to all commercial banks' lending policy. In fact, bank rate is the traditional measure of credit control by the Central Bank, although as a short-term rate, it has lost its importance in recent years particularly since economic and banking sector reforms have been initiated in India in the past 1991 era. Bank rate is the relatively long-term rate of interest at which the Central Bank advances loans to commercial banks in need of emergency. Lowering bank rate means relatively cheaper funds available from Central Bank which the commercial banks can use in credit creating process. Earlier, any change in the bank rate implied that all commercial banks essentially had to respond by similar change in their lending and deposit rates. But during liberalization policy regime, now the commercial banks have been provided with sufficient autonomy with regard to interest rate policy. In practice, however, commercial banks continue to respond, by and large, to signals given by the central bank.

6.5.1 Open Market Operations

Purchase and sale of securities has been one of the powerful instruments of controlling credit by the central bank. If the central bank intends to limit credit creation, it sells bonds and securities held by it to the banks and financial institutions. This way, the excess liquidity in the market is siphoned off and goes to the central bank. Similarly, in case of credit crunch, the central bank purchases its own securities (as also other securities held by the banking sector) and releases liquidity to the market.

In recent years, India's RBI has been using the short-term policy instruments for regulating the supply of money and credit. Notable among them are: (a) Repo Rate ('Repo', for 'Repurchase') and (b) Reverse Repo Rate. Repo Rate is the rate of interest at which RBI buys securities (which include government securities) from the banking and financial sector (the money market) for a short period, generally not exceeding one month, and thereby releases funds to the economic system. The Reverse Repo Rate is the rate of interest at which RBI sells securities to the banking and financial sector and thereby reduces the excess liquidity. Repo and Reverse Repo are essentially short-term rates. The rate for Repo is generally higher than that of Reverse Repo. In other words, the RBI sells securities to the market at higher rate but purchases at lower rate.

Table 6.1 shows Repo and Reverse Repo Rates used by RBI in recent years. RBI presently makes a six-weekly (besides quarterly) review of the monetary situation and monitors the changes in the system through appropriate policy rate changes keeping in view the primary objectives of the monetary policy as also the government's priorities.

Table 6.1 *Repo and Reverse Repo Rates in India: March, 2004 – April, 2010*

Effective Dates	*Repo Rate (%)*	*Reverse Rate (%)*
March 3, '04	6.0	4.5
September 18, '04	6.0	4.5
October 2, '04	6.0	4.5
October 27, '04	6.0	4.75
April 29, '05	6.0	5.0
October 26, '05	6.25	5.25
January 24, '06	6.5	5.5
June 29, '06	6.5	5.75
October 31, '06	6.75	6.0
December 23, '06	7.0	6.0
January 6, '07	7.25	6.0
January 31, '07	7.5	6.0
March 3, '07	7.75	6.0
June 11, '08	8.0	6.0
June 23, '08	8.5	6.0
July 29, '08	9.0	6.0
October 20, '08	8.0	6.0
November 3, '08	7.5	6.0
December 6, '08	6.5	5.0
January 2, '09	5.5	4.0
March 5, '09	5.0	3.5
April 21, '09	4.75	3.25
March 19, '10	5.00	3.50
April 20, '10	5.25	3.75

Note: Recent monetary policy rates (repo & reverse) are given at p. 548 of chapter 19 on monetary policy.

An analysis of Table 6.1 can be made in the context of growth performance of Indian economy as also recent global financial crisis and prolonged recession. Indian economy exhibited a fairly satisfactory growth period prior to October 2008. There was virtually a boom period in the economy reflected in the continuously growing credit demand. The RBI responded by gradually raising repo and reverse repo rates possibly to avoid inflationary potential of the economy, but not hindering the growth process. Since, banks were experiencing, during this period, substantial deposit growth, they were facilitated with allowing them to park their excess funds with RBI with a higher reverse repo rate. However, it was indeed somewhat surprising that despite high demand for credit during the boom period, the RBI followed a cautious policy. Instead of lowering the policy rate, the apex bank either maintained the same rate or gradually but cautiously kept increasing the rate. RBI policy in this regard, has been criticized in some quarters, but the policy has been justified possibly to avoid 'overheating' type of situation.

Following October, 2008, when the global recession set in and the world financial system was crumbling starting in U.S. and gradually spreading to European and Asian economies including India, RBI responded with liberal policy by lowering both the short-term repo and reverse repo rates, reaching to a lowest level of 4.75% and 3.25%, respectively, in April 21, 2009. In early 2010, CRR also was increased showing a policy shift. On February 13, 2010, CRR was hiked from 5% to 5.5% followed by 5.75% on February 27, 2010. So, within one month, CRR was raised twice. The main cause of such a shift in policy was the rising inflation (around 9%), particularly food inflation which was hovering around 18-19%.

Whether such monetary policy change has been in the correct line may be a matter of debate, but the Central Bank as well as the government seems to be seized with the conflicting aims of controlling inflation on the one hand and attempting to bridge the fiscal deficit through public borrowing programme for the fiscal year 2010-11.[1] It may be remembered that earlier the Government had already announced substantial stimulus package in the budget 2009-10 and 2010-11 in terms of lower tax burden and raising government expenditure in order to fight recessionary tendency resulting in large fiscal deficit. Government's borrowing programme might have become difficult in case policy rates were hiked beyond a point resulting in rise in rate of interest. Thus, RBI is now facing a kind of dilemma – of balancing between fiscal management and inflation – growth management. This is, possibly, the cause of 'go-slow' approach of the RBI's monetary policy announcement.

[1] The Govt. intended to raise a hefty sum of ₹ 4.57 lakh crore through public borrowing to meet its target of fiscal deficit of 5.8% GDP in the fiscal year 2010-11.

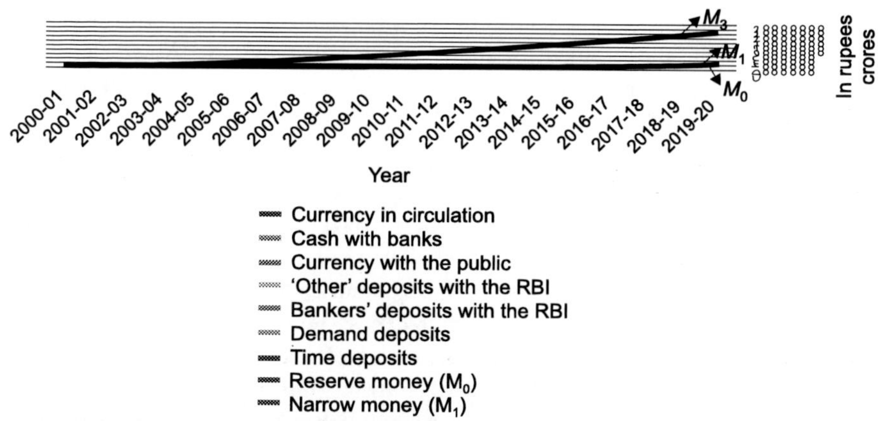

Figure 6.1 *Trends of major components of money stock (M_0, M_1 & M_3) in India.*

Money Multiplier in India, US and Eurozone countries: An illustration

From the formula of money multiplier (chapter 6, p. 121). it is clear that if people's preference for cash holding is lower (value of α is lower α being a fraction) the value of money multiplier will be higher. Similarly, if banks' preference for reserves (with the central bank) is higher (value of β is higher), the value of money multiplier will be lower.

According to a recent study by T. Kundu, "Money multiplier in India", reported in Mint/Bloomberg, December 3, 2015, money multiplier in India has gone up in recent years. Citing a comparative picture of India, U.S. and Eurozone countries, the report gives figures of money multiplier as 5.8 for India as against 3.01 for US and 6.61 for Eurozone. Further, between 31st January, 2002 and 31st October, 2015, money multiplier in India has increased due to a couple of reasons:

(1) the propensity of Indians to keep cash in hand (currency-deposit ratio) has been falling over the years due to higher level of literacy on the one hand and higher spread of banks and financial institutions on the other;

(2) the financial inclusion of greater percentage of population across all income groups of people has been expanding such that, between 2011 and 2014, account penetration as percent of population has gone up from 35.23% to 53.14% for all adult population while for the poorest 40%, the data show an improvement from 27% to 44% (World Bank Global Findex Database). However, the problem of dormant accounts is still associated with the problem of account penetration. In any case, this has resulted in the rise in the proportion of deposits with the commercial banks leading to rise in the value of money multiplier.

In more recent time, demonetisation of high value currency notes (of ₹ 1000 and ₹ 500) by the Government of India on 8th November, 2016 and the surge in bank deposits, following this decision, has further strengthened the case of money multiplier being on the higher side.

Contrarily, money multiplier in US and EU, as the above study shows, has decreased in recent years, particularly since the financial crisis of 2008 (in the US, it has decreased from 8.38% in 2002 to 3.01% in 2015 and in EU, from 11.15% to 6.61% during the same period). The main reason of this phenomenon, according to the study, is that banks in these countries have been reluctant to lend to the public and are rather holding their excess reserves with their respective central banks even at the cost of "negative rate of interest". This has happened despite several rounds of Quantitative Easing (QE), i.e., continuous bond purchases by the US Fed and European Central Bank with a view to fighting with long recession and low growth of those economies (US Fed. has, only recently, on 17th December, 2015, after a long 8 years since the financial crisis, raised interest rate by 0.25% followed by another few rate rises till mid-2018). Fed interest rate stands at 1.75% as on July 10, 2018

SUMMARY

1. In macroeconomic management, supply of money has a significant role to play. What constitutes the supply of money and how to define money have been crucial questions. From purely legal point of view, money is defined as all notes and coins or papers bearing the legal sanction of the state (legal tender). However, from functional point of view, besides the notes and coins, all such papers relating to 'debt obligations' which are capable of performing the function of 'medium of exchange', 'store of wealth', 'measure of value' and means of clearing debt obligations can be included within the category of money.
2. There are various measures of money supply prevalent in various countries of the world keeping in view the extent of liquidity covered. In India, for instance, until 1998, four measures of money supply – M_1, M_2, M_3 and M_4 were in vogue. Among the measures, M_1 – currency with the public and demand deposits with banks – was considered 'narrow money' or 'base money', while M_3 – currency with the public and demand deposits as well as time deposits with banks – was considered 'broad money' or 'aggregate monetary resources'. Other measures like M_2 and M_4 include, besides M_1, post-office savings deposits and all types of post office deposits, respectively.
3. Since 1998, following the Third Working Group's Recommendations (chairman-YV Reddy), two categories of measures, viz., monetary aggregates and liquidity aggregates have been separately brought under

use. Monetary measures are expressed as M_0, M_1, M_2 and M_3 while liquidity aggregates were symbolically measured as L_1, L_2 and L_3. Under these new measures, now, the monetary aggregates are compiled on weekly and fortnightly bases. Under liquidity aggregates, attempts have been made to capture the total liquidity in the monetary and financial system and measured on monthly and quarterly basis.

4. Credit money or bank money is created by the commercial banking system on the basis of fractional reserve system. The commercial banks keep a fraction of their total deposits in cash to meet the current requirement of depositor who do not normally turn up for withdrawal at a time. The banks advance the rest amount as loans to their customers. These loans, even if withdrawn in full from a particular bank, are spent for purposes for which they are taken and ultimately come back to the banking system in the form of deposits. In the next round, these deposits are advanced as loans after keeping the required reserves which again come back to the banking system. This way, in several rounds, multiple deposits and credits are created with the initial fixed amount of deposit. This, precisely, is the process of credit creation.
5. It is generally believed that money supply is exogenously determined by the central bank of the country. But, there are also certain proximate determinants of money supply which lie beyond the central banking authority. To that extent, money supply is endogenous in nature. At least, there are two behavioural factors which indirectly influence the money supply, viz., (a) reserve-deposit ratio of the banks and (b) the currency-deposit ratio of the public. These are, respectively, the choice variables of the banks and the public. If these choice variables are specified, it can be shown that money supply partly depends upon these ratios along with the 'base money' or high-powered money (H). The ultimate determinant of the money supply is, however, the 'demand' for credit which the central bank estimates from time to time. Thus, by and large, it can be concluded that the central bank enjoys the sole power of influencing the money supply in the economy. In either increasing or decreasing money supply, no doubt, it keeps in mind the overall monetary and other considerations.
6. By using various monetary policy tools, the central banks can control the supply of money and credit in the economy. It can affect the high-powered money by changing, in either direction, the reserve requirements of other commercial banks (e.g., CRR in case of India) banks' own reserves as required by norms set by the apex bank and other short-term rates such as repo and reserve repo rates operated through open market operations. The central bank can change the bench mark rate (bank rate) as a guide to all commercial banks regarding the lending and deposit rates.

EXERCISE

1. Explain why it is rather difficult to define money.
2. What are the new measures of money supply in India? How are they different from old measures?
3. Explain fractional reserve system of the modern banking system.
4. If the primary deposit of the banking system is ₹ 1000 and reserve requirement by banks is 15%, what is the amount of total deposits? Calculate the deposit multiplier in this case.
5. If the total deposit creation is ₹ 1,00,000 and the reserve requirement is 25%, what is the amount of initial (primary) deposit?
6. With primary deposit of ₹ 50,000 and the total deposit is ₹ 3,00,000, find out the reserve requirement in percentage.
7. Define high-powered money. Why is it called base money?
8. What do you understand by the proximate determinants of money supply?
9. Define the concept of broad money in the context of Indian economy.
10. Given the following values of α, β and t and the supply of broad money, M_3 in the economy, find out the value of high powered money, H.
    $\alpha = 0.2$, $\beta = 0.3$, $t = 0.1$, $M_3 =$ ₹ 20 thousand crore.
11. In ex. (10) values are as follows:
    $\alpha = 0.1$, $\beta = 0.2$, $t = 0.4$ and $H =$ ₹ 25 thousand crore,
    find the value of M_3.
12. Briefly explain how repo and reverse repo rates affect the money supply in the economy.

REFERENCES

1. Richard G. Lipsey, An Introduction to Positive Economics, ELBS & Weidenfeld and Nicolson, 1969.
2. Reserve Bank of India website http//:www.rbi.gov.in
3. Amit Bhaduri, Macroeconomics, Macmillan India, 1990.
4. Government of India, Economic Survey, 2003-04, 2004-05, 2010-11.

7

Theories of Demand for Money

7.1 CLASSICAL THEORY OF DEMAND FOR MONEY: THE QUANTITY THEORY APPROACH

7.1.1 The Quantity Theory of Money

Quantity theory of money occupies a central place in the classical macroeconomic discussions. In subsequent periods beyond the classical era, when the theory was revived in the hands of the Nobel laureate late Professor Milton Friedman, the quantity theory assumed a new dimension. We shall examine this in a subsequent chapter. In the present chapter, we begin with the original version of the theory.

Simply put, the quantity theory states that the quantity (or supply) of money determines the level of prices in the economy. Essentially, the quantity theory of money has two approaches: (a) transaction approach and (b) cash balance approach. The transaction approach, in turn, has two versions: the pure transaction (or Fisherian version) and aggregate income version. The pure transaction version is also known as "strict" quantity theory. It may be mentioned here that the income version of the quantity theory has become a more popular and convenient expression of the theory.

The Fisherian version of the quantity theory is expressed in terms of the following equation:

$$M\,V = P\,T \tag{7.1}$$

where, M = quantity of money used for purchase-sale of goods during a specified period of time, V = velocity of circulation of money, T is the total volume of transactions of all goods and P is the average price level. Equation (7.1) is an expression that simply equates two sides of the transaction (purchase and sale) of all goods in the economy with the help of money. The right side of the equation shows the total quantity of goods sold valued at their average price level while the left hand side shows the total amount of money required for goods bought. This seems to be an obvious fact and shows the equilibrium condition of the economy. The explanation of the various terms of the equation (*M*, *V*, *P* and *T* is as follows.

M, the supply of money, refers to the money in circulation (notes and coins) as also bank money (demand deposits). *M* is supposed to be exogenously given. At the time when the quantity theory was originally developed, *M* was supposed to constitute only the currency in circulation. However, when transactions by individuals and businesses included operations through banks, bank deposits or bank money was also included in *M*.

V, the velocity of circulation of *M*, stands for the average number of times money is used up in the process of transaction of goods during a specified period of time. This means that although the individual units of money such as individual notes or coins of different denominations may be used up a different number of times, *V* stands for their average number.

T refers to the total volume of goods transacted. It includes all goods, intermediate goods (goods used as inputs to industries) as well as the final goods. *P* is the average price level, that is, the prices of all goods taken at their average value.

Let us now go back to eqn. (7.1) and somewhat elaborate the inherent significance of the terms therein. The value of *T* is given and constant by the classical assumption of full employment where the output of goods reaches its potential level. Also, the total volume of *T* is at its maximum feasible level. In other words, full use of available technology and resources is assumed to have been made to produce the total volume of *T* (or the supply of goods) at full employment. *T* is also independent of *M* and *V*. Remembering the classical dichotomy postulate, the goods sector (or real sector) is independent of the monetary sector, *T*, which represents the total output of goods in the economy, is naturally independent of *M* and *V*. In fact, *T* is determined by the factor supplies and technology. *V* is a significant factor in the equation. It is the frequency with which units of money circulate within the economy. It is constant as also unrelated to either *M* or *T*. In fact, it is determined by the institutional and structural factors of the economy and society which we explain separately below.

The aggregate income (or national income) version of the quantity theory has gained popularity due to its relative simplicity and also for avoiding the problem of aggregation and measurement of a large number of physical goods as encountered in case of *T*. The national income version, instead can be stated as follows:

$$MV = PY \tag{7.2}$$

where, M = supply of money, V = income velocity of money, Y is the real national income and P is the average price level of Y. (P can also be defined as GNP deflator, a number or ratio used to obtain real GNP from nominal GNP.)

In eqn. (7.2), V is the average number of times M (or the units of money) is used for transaction of final goods and services only, that is, Y or GNP. Obviously, the value of V in eqn. (7.2) is less than the V in eqn. (7.1), since the volume of Y is less than T.

In the present formulation also, the earlier conclusions and implications of eqn. (7.1) hold, viz., the constancy of V and Y, both being at their maximum feasible levels. Also, both are independent of M and P for reasons explained in the context of eqn. (7.1). Hence, the ultimate conclusion, M and P are directly and proportionately related, equally holds true.

One significant implication of eqn. (7.2) that emerges is that now V the velocity can be expressed as a ratio of nominal GNP (PY) and money supply (M) so that the behaviour of V can be empirically verified with actual data of the economy. An illustration from Indian economy data is given in Appendix Table (7A) at page 163-165.

Determinants of velocity

We have already seen that classical quantity theory of money forms an important element of the classical macroeconomic structure. Here we reconsider the theory to examine in detail some of its important properties. The transaction version of the quantity theory ($MV = PT$), has one of its elements, V, the velocity of circulation of money–the average number of times (or, the frequency) a unit of money changes hands during a specified period of time. We have mentioned earlier that V depends upon institutional and structural factors of the economy. What are these institutional and structural factors?

Institutional factors: Institutional factors generally refer to the system of income-payment gap, that is, the time interval between receipt of income of a certain individual or business entity and its expenditure pattern. For instance, an individual unit may receive income once a month or once a week or any time interval depending on the prevailing system. On the other hand, he might be spending the income throughout the month or week. Both these income receiving and expenditure patterns depend on the payment systems of wages and salaries as well as settlement of bills in the society and the various needs and requirements of the individuals and businesses. If the system is largely on a weekly basis, then the velocity of circulation of units of money will be higher since each unit of money will be changing hands more frequently. On the other hand, if the system involves a greater interval of time, monthly or yearly, the velocity of circulation of money will be lower. Similarly, if most payments are made by cheques rather than cash, the velocity of money will be less. However, this, in no way, depends on the total quantity of money or the volume of transactions.

Structural factors: These factors refer to the structure of business organisations. For instance, the producing firms and other business organisations may be either more vertically integrated or less vertically (or, laterally) integrated. By vertical integration we mean that firms are so integrated that a single business entity manages several operating units within it which are themselves engaged in production processes based on the same raw materials. For instance, firms producing raw materials for certain goods combine also the processing, melting, fabricating activities, etc., under a single enterprise. Now, in such a vertically integrated organization, it may not be necessary to make separate and explicit payments for each operating unit since many payments are two-way transactions. Therefore, the velocity of money in such cases will be lower as compared to cases where industries are either not vertically integrated or less vertically integrated. In other words, velocity of money depends also on the degree of business integration. Such economic structure is, again, not related to either the total supply of money or the volume of transactions. Hence, V is said to be independent of T or M.

In the context of quantity theory, it is assumed that V is constant since the above mentioned institutional or structural factors normally remain constant over a fairly long period of time.

The quantity theory and the demand for money

The quantity theory of money, when looked at as an equation of exchange ($MV = PT$, or, $MV = PY$), is simply an "identity" which should hold true for all times. All goods and services valued at their average prices when transacted, must necessarily be equal to the total supply of money times its velocity. There does not seem to be any theory behind this. However, assuming V remains constant for a fairly long period, and Y being the total supply of goods and services being determined by the total productive resources in the economy and the level of technology which again are fixed at full employment, the quantity theory does provide a causal relationship between the quantity of money and the price level. The relationship is that the supply of money determines the price level in a direct and proportional manner. This means percentage increase/ decrease in the money supply leads to percentage increase/decrease in the price level. Since, percentage increase in the price level means the rate of inflation, the quantity theory provides us a theory of inflation.

However, there is another fundamentally different approach to look at it. It is the "demand for money" or, the "cash balances" that the individuals and the businesses "hold" rather than spend, an approach suggested by the classical/neo-classical economists (Marshall, Pigou, Robertson and Keynes) of the Cambridge school.

In fact, spending and holding of money are the two sides of the same coin. Still, holding of money or the demand for money represents a fundamentally different approach. It emphasises that the community always "desires" to hold a certain fraction of total national income in cash balances. This desired cash balance may differ from the one that the community "actually" holds. Let this desired cash balance be denoted by k. Now, holding cash balances and spending of cash are opposite of one another and hence k can be denoted as $1/V$ or V can be written as $1/k$. Instead of PT, if we substitute PY, Y representing the national income, and thus converting the equation as $MV = PY$, and substitute $1/k$ for V it gives us a theory of demand for money. In reformulated form, the demand for money function can now be written as:

$$Md = k\ P\ Y \tag{7.3}$$

where, Md is the demand for money, PY is the nominal (or money) national income and k is the fraction of nominal national income that the community desires to hold in cash balances. Equation (7.3) is the nominal demand function for money which states that nominal demand for money depends on (a) real GNP and (b) the level of prices.

The real demand function for money can be written by simply dividing eqn. (7.3) by P the price level, or by deflating it as shown in eqn. (7.4).

$$Md/P. = k\ Y. \tag{7.4}$$

Equation (7.4) tells us that the real demand for money depends upon real national income. If the real national income increases, so will increase the real demand for money. If M stands for the supply of money and if the supply of money is equal to demand for money (the equilibrium condition), we can write $Md = M$, so that (7.3) becomes:

$$M = k\ PY \tag{7.5}$$

It is to be remembered that the above equilibrium condition may not hold for ever. There might be disequilibrium if there is discrepancy between desired and actual cash balances of the community. For instance, if the supply of money is increased, the extra money goes to the community's actual cash balances which are higher than its desired cash balances. This prompts them to spend the extra cash on purchasing goods or services. But the fact that real national income (Y) is constant (because it is held at full employment level), it simply pushes up the price level, P. The increased price level of goods and services now requires the community to hold larger cash balances. This way, their actual cash balances become equal to the desired cash balances and the equilibrium is again restored.

Thus, the cash balance approach also leads to the same conclusion that the supply of money determines the level of prices in the economy. However, it is not clear through which channel, the disequilibrium takes place and the process through which the equilibrium is restored. The credit for discovering this channel goes to Knut Wicksell, a Swedish economist whose approach we examine separately below.

Wicksell's contribution to quantity theory of money

Knut Wicksell, a Swedish economist, having allegiance to classical economic thinking, made a significant contribution to the quantity theory of money by integrating the theory of savings and investment with the quantity theory. The quantity theory asserted that any increase in the quantity of money (supply), leads to the proportionate increase in the price level. However, classical quantity theory failed to spell out the exact channel through which this would happen by simply postulating the separation of monetary sector from the real sector. It goes to the credit of Wicksell who discovered this channel. Wicksell's view was that the increase in the supply of money would most likely result from the banking sector advancing credit to the investors who would approach them with their new investment project and asking for credit. The banking sector, in turn, would be willing to grant investment loans over and above its savings deposits. This way, the investment would exceed savings–thus shifting rightward the investment curve in the saving–investment plan shown in Fig. 7.1. This would push up the equilibrium rate of interest–the "natural rate of interest" in Wicksellian terminology. The higher investment demand and the consequent increase in the supply of money would raise the incomes of the people who would benefit from the investment project and ultimately raise the aggregate demand of the community.

The rise in aggregate demand will be reflected in the increased expenditures of the people and so the price level will increase. This is how, in the classical quantity theory scheme, increase in the quantity of money leads to the rise in the price level via the rise in aggregate demand. From this point of view, it can be said that Wicksell was a forerunner, and in fact, very near to Keynes' analysis of aggregate demand. Wicksell's analysis can be illustrated in Fig. 7.1.

Figure 7.1 shows savings and investment curves along with the rate of interest. The intersection of *SS* and *II* curves gives the equilibrium rate of interest equal to *Oro* (which is the natural rate of interest as well as the market rate of interest). So there is no divergence between "natural" and "market" rate of interest in this case. However, when *I* curve shifts up rightward due to the banking sector's credit advancement while the *SS* curve remains unaffected, the natural (equilibrium) rate of interest goes up (Or_1). This creates a divergence between the natural and the market rate of interest while the banking sector continues to advance loans at the old market rate of interest (or even a slightly higher rate since it does not have any idea of the natural rate of interest). Thus, ultimately, this divergence between the two rates of interest and its fallout on investment project and aggregate demand and additional income which is expended on goods and services leads to rise in the price level. This process of rising prices would continue until this interest rate divergence disappears and both the rates are once again equal.

Wicksell's analysis of classical quantity theory provides a new explanation and interpretation which helps to integrate Quantity Theory with the Saving Investment Theory. The analysis also adequately helps to understand the process of inflation that develops when money and credit supply by the banks to the entrepreneurial class takes place in the economy by creating excess demand. (We have discussed this aspect of inflation in chapter 17 on Inflation.)

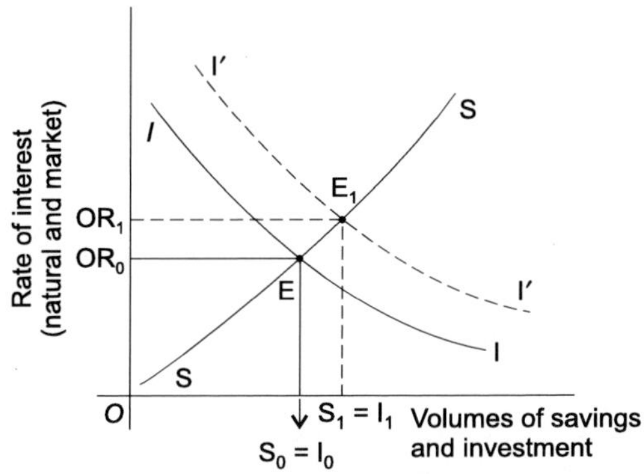

Figure 7.1 *Saving-investment in relation to natural/market rate of interest.*

7.2 KEYNESIAN THEORY OF DEMAND FOR MONEY

In the present section, we will discuss the Keynesian theory of demand for money, the turning point in the thinking of money as an "asset" besides money as a medium of exchange as was hitherto supposed to be.

Keynes brought to the focus the role of interest rate as a determinant of the demand for money. Keynes specified that there are, in fact, three motives behind the individuals' as well as the community's desire for keeping money in cash. These motives are: (a) transaction motive, (b) precautionary motive and (c) speculative motive. Accordingly, the demand for money arising out of these motives are called, respectively, the transaction demand, precautionary demand and speculative demand for money. We explain below each of these motives.

(a) Transaction demand for money: Individuals and businesses always require a certain amount of money in cash for carrying out their day-to-day expenses. This is because most often receiving their incomes and incurring expenditures do not coincide. While incomes (either from work or business) are received at discrete intervals of time, such as once a week, month or year, expenditures are carried out at more frequent time intervals. Households do incur some kind of expenses almost daily. Similarly, business enterprises have to purchase various raw materials, pay wages to the labourers on a weekly, if not daily basis but they receive payment for their products at a later date. This lack of synchronisation of income and expenditure requires, for individuals and businesses, to keep a certain amount of cash holdings with them – or demand for money for these transactions (in modern times, due to developments in the functioning of the banking system, deposits kept in the current account may also be treated as money for transaction demand).

Transaction demand for money is largely dependent on the level of income, either individual income or business income. As the level of income rises, so does the demand for money for transaction purposes rise.

Now, at the more aggregate level, (the national economy level), we may say that the national income is the main determinant of the transaction demand for money. In other words, as the national income of a country rises, the transaction demand for money also rises. However, at what proportion the demand for money rises depends on several factors including the speed of money circulation in the economy and the people's habit of using money in the transaction process.

Using symbols, we can, therefore, state as follows:

$L_1 = L_1(Y)$, with $L'_1(Y) > 0$, where, L_1 is the transaction demand for money, Y is the national income and L'_1 signifies the functional relationship, (here positive relationship).

(b) Precautionary demand for money: Precautionary demand for money is aimed at meeting the emergency needs of the households or businesses and generally described as "rainy days". There are various types of uncertainties such as medical needs, unforeseen circumstances like accidents and the uncertainties of receiving expected payments for businesses, etc. People generally set apart a certain amount of cash balances for meeting these circumstances. Such demand for money generally depends on the level of income. Higher level of income will require a higher sum of money to be kept for such purposes. However, for business firms, precautionary demand for money also depends on another factor, the possibility of availability of bank credit such that higher availability of bank credit will reduce the precautionary demand for money.

Now, just as precautionary demand for money is true for individuals and businesses, this is equally true for the national economy as well. Hence, we can say that both transaction and precautionary demand for money, by and large, depends on the level of national income.

(c) Speculative demand for money: Speculative demand for money refers to the money kept for speculative purposes, the purposes for earning interest income from investments in financial assets (bonds or equities) by "reading ahead of the market" for such assets, often referred to as 'knowing better than the market'. Hence, such demand is also known as the asset demand for money. The asset demand for money may be symbolised as L_2. The asset demand for money is mainly related to the rate of interest. Hence,we can express it as $L_2 = L_2(r)$ with $L'_2 < 0$. We explain below in what specific way L_2 function is related to the rate of interest.

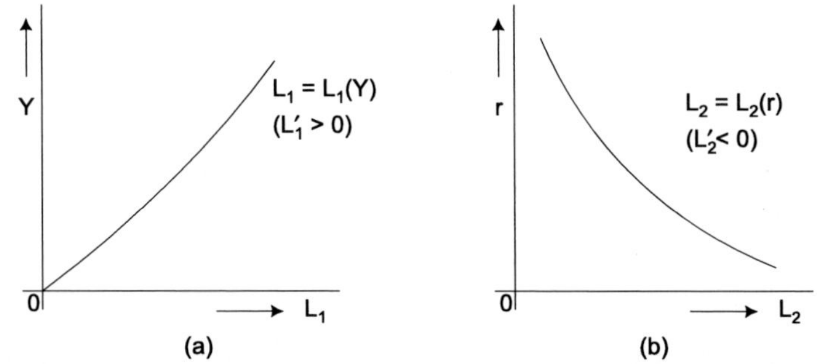

Figure 7.2 *Transaction demand for money, Fig. (a) and speculative demand for money, Fig. (b).*

Keynes' theory of interest is known as the 'liquidity preference' theory. Liquidity preference refers to the demand for money since the reasons why individuals and the community prefer liquidity (or money in its most liquid form (cash)) are the same as to why people demand money. Now, since total demand for money can be lumped together as $L = L_1 + L_2$, we can express in functional form as $L = L(Y, r)$, that is, total demand for money depends on both the level of income and the rate of interest.

Keynes defined interest as the 'reward for parting with liquidity'. This means that people generally have preference for cash or liquidity because this is the most secure form of money holding. When they part with or sacrifice this most liquid form of money holding they must be rewarded with an incentive for doing this in the form of interest. Now, when this incentive (i.e., interest rate) is lower as compared to some normal rate people generally have in their mind, they have greater preference for liquid money. Similarly, when the interest rate is higher, people have smaller preference for liquid money. Now the question is what is the alternative to liquidity preference? As we have noted earlier, L_2 is also known as the 'asset demand' for money since money serves as an asset in addition to being a medium of exchange. To understand the logic of this asset demand and its relationship with the rate of interest, we assume that there are several alternative financial assets such as bonds, equities and a variety of other alternative assets. However, Keynes assumed that there is a single alternative to cash holding viz., 'bonds'. So, people who wish to hold money as an asset have two options: either they can keep money in which case they get no reward at all, or they can buy 'bonds'. In the latter case, there is a 'return' attached with bond holding. This return is of two kinds: (a) interest rate applicable to each bond and (b) capital gain/loss in case of rise/fall in the price of bonds. The price of bond is, however, inversely related to the rate of interest, that is, if the rate of interest rises the price of bond falls and if the rate of interest falls, the price of bond rises. The inverse relationship can be illustrated with an example:

Supposing a bond worth ₹ 1000 with 5 per cent rate of interest on its face value is issued by the government or any private company with a view to raising capital from the market. Now somebody buys this bond which carries an annual yield of ₹ 50 (5% of 1000 = 50). This means that the purchaser of this particular bond will continue to receive an annual return of ₹ 50 so long as he holds the bond. In case he sells it to some other person, the new purchaser will continue to enjoy the advantage. Now, if the rate of interest falls to 4%, for instance, which is applicable to all newly issued bonds, the price of existing bond rises since, at the old price of ₹ 1000 it is not able to produce an annual yield of ₹ 50. In fact, now, its price rises to ₹ 1250 (₹ 1250 × 4% = ₹ 50). Hence, the relationship between price of bond, rate of interest and its annual payment (known as coupon payment) can be expressed as:

$$b_r = \frac{c}{B_p},$$

where, c = annual coupon payment, B_p = price of bond and b_r = bond rate of interest. Clearly, if b_r falls, c being fixed, B_p rises and conversely, if b_r rises, B_p falls.

The other kind of return attached with bond holding is the 'expected capital gain'. This depends upon the future price of the bond. If the price of bond rises in future, bond holders stand to gain if they sell it in the market. On the other hand, if the price falls they stand to lose. Thus, capital gain or loss is uncertain and depends upon the behaviour of the market rate of interest. Most bond holders would expect the yield on bonds (interest rate) to remain at low level so that they can be capital gainers. The coupon payment is, however, a constant annual sum regularly received by the bond holder.

Now, when the price of bond becomes higher (interest rate lower) people will be buying less bonds and hold more money. The opposite happens when the interest rate is higher (or, bond price lower) – people's preference will swing towards buying more bonds and keeping less money in cash. This inverse relationship, therefore, explains also the inverse relationship between the rate of interest and the demand for money (downward sloping speculative demand for money).

However, what is more important and relevant in the context of Keynesian theory of interest is not only the current rate of interest but the *expected future rate of interest.* With movement of interest rate upward or downward, the bond holders form a certain expectation about future interest rates (or, expected future price of bonds). For instance, when interest rate is increasing, holders of bonds might consider a particular rate to be highest and expect the future rate to be decreasing thereafter. Similar perception might prevail when interest rate is moving downward and reaches a certain level which the bond holders/asset holders would consider *minimum*. Their expectation, in such a situation, would be a movement upward of the interest rate in future. Based upon such a *state of expectation* about future movement of interest rate, the bond holders would either prefer to hold money or bond. For instance, when the current interest rate is regarded as the highest, wealth holders would tend to hold maximum amount of bonds, since they would expect future rate of interest to be on the lower side. By doing so, they can reap maximum capital gains by selling their bonds at higher prices. Conversely, when current interest rate is regarded as the lowest (highest bond price) they would like to hold most of their wealth in money because they expect the rate of interest to rise in the next move (bond price to fall) so that they can, then, buy bonds and subsequently gain from bond holding. This latter situation of falling interest rate to the minimum is known as "*liquidity trap*" when the demand for money is infinitely large. It must be noted, however, that all bond holders do not have the same 'state of expectation' about future movement of bond prices. Has it been so, at lowest price of bond, there would be very high demand for bonds which would raise their prices in the bond market. Opposite would be the case when bond price reaches the highest (expected) level.

As far as the supply of money is concerned, Keynes assumed that supply of money is "institutionally" determined – by the central banking authority at a point in time. So, supply of money is said to be exogenously or autonomously determined. Graphically, the interest rate determination (i.e., the equilibrium rate with demand for and supply of money) can be illustrated as follows (Fig. 7.3).

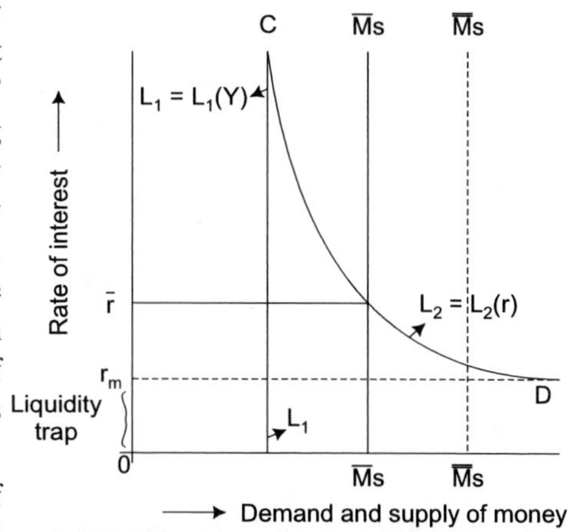

Figure 7.3 *Equilibrium rate of interest with demand and supply of money and 'liquidity trap'.*

Figure 7.3 shows the rate of interest on the vertical axis and demand and supply of money on the horizontal axis. The vertical line L_1 represents the transaction demand for money, which is insensitive to interest rate. The speculative demand for money, L_2 is, however, inversely related to the rate of interest, hence it is downward sloping. However, when interest rate reaches Or_m – considered as minimum, the demand for money, L_2 is infinitely elastic. Hence, L_2 curve is horizontal at this minimum rate of interest. This is the situation of 'liquidity trap'.[1]

[1] The total demand for money is represented by CD curve, which is the horizontal summation of L_1 and L_2.

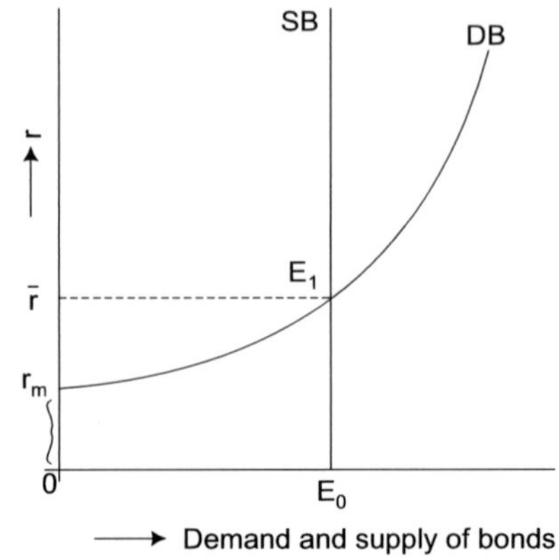

Figure 7.4 *Relation between interest rate, demand and supply of bonds.*

The corresponding demand for bond curve can also be shown side by side as shown in Fig. 7.4. The equilibrium rate of interest is $o\bar{r}$, where total demand for money is exactly equal to the total supply of money (Fig. 7.3).

Similarly, in Fig. 7.4 the equilibrium rate of interest ($o\bar{r}$), or equilibrium price of bonds is determined where total demand for bonds is exactly equal to the total supply of bonds. The demand curve for bonds is just opposite of the demand curve for money.

Now, if the supply of money, $\overline{Ms}$ (Fig. 7.3) is changed consequent upon Central Bank's policy change, the equilibrium rate of interest also changes. For instance, if $\overline{Ms}$ is increased to $\overline{\overline{Ms}}$, money supply will increase and more money will be made available to the public which will lead to lower rate of interest such as $o\bar{\bar{r}}$. Opposite will be the case if supply of money is reduced.

Referring to Fig. 7.4, money supply increasing would mean supply of bonds is reduced so that *SB* curve will be shifted leftward leading to the lower equilibrium rate of interest. In the opposite case, *SB* will shift to the right and thus the equilibrium rate of interest will be higher.

While concluding the Keynesian theory of money and interest, we may mention, at this stage that the Keynesian theory of demand for money has undergone, at a later stage, significant modifications, at least on two aspects. On the one hand, the transaction demand for money has been modified and shown to be the function of the rate of interest as well (Boumol and Tobin). On the other hand, since bond holding involves risk, the theory has been significantly modified in line with microeconomic decision-making under risk and uncertainty (J. Tobin). We have taken up these aspects in Section 7.3 of the present chapter.

7.2.1 A Note on Bond Market

A bond is a negotiable or saleable financial instrument which promises to pay the holder a certain fixed return for a time period (generally a year) which is known as 'coupon payment'. The bonds are of two kinds: bonds to perpetuity, (also known as consol bonds), and bonds with a fixed maturity period. The holder of the perpetuity bonds is entitled to receive the annual coupon payments for infinite time period but not necessarily the principal amount/the bond value. The holder of bonds to fixed maturity period (e.g., 10 years or 15 years), receives back the principal amount at the expiry of the maturity period besides the fixed annual coupon payments. Let us suppose, an individual purchases a perpetuity bond for ₹ 1000 with a yearly coupon payment of ₹ 50. The present value of this perpetual sum of ₹ 50 per year can be calculated on the basis of the standard discount formula:

$$PV_B = \frac{50}{1+r} + \frac{50}{(1+r)^2} + \frac{50}{(1+r)^3} + \ldots + \frac{50}{(1+r)\infty} \qquad \text{(i)}$$

Now, multiplying eqn. (i) by $(1 + r)$ we obtain,

$$PV_B\,(1+r) = 50 + \frac{50}{1+r} + \frac{50}{(1+r)^2} + \ldots + \frac{50}{(1+r)\infty^{-1}} \qquad \text{(ii)}$$

Subtracting (i) from (ii), we get,

(since all other terms cancel and the last term can be ignored due to its very small value)

$$PV_B\,(1+r) - PV_B = 50 \qquad \text{(iii)}$$

$$\Rightarrow \qquad PV_B\,(1 + r - 1) = 50$$

$$\Rightarrow \qquad PV_B\,(r) = 50$$

Hence,

$$PV_B = \frac{50}{r}$$

For instance, if the rate of interest, r as in this case is 5 per cent, the present value of the bond will be 50/0.05 = ₹ 500.

This is the price of the bond that the purchaser will be willing to pay for it.

It is now obvious from eqn. (iii) that there is a unique relationship between the present value (or, the demand price) of bond and interest rate (r). If the interest rate rises, demand price of bond falls and if the interest rate falls, demand price of bond rises. In other words, falling interest rate means bond price rising and vice versa. Due to this unique inverse relationship, the price of bond can also be expressed as $1/r$.

A community's asset holding in terms of money or bonds can be viewed in terms of demand and supply of bonds. Given the assumption that regular and adequately developed bond market exists in the economy let us examine how the equilibrium position in the community's asset holding is achieved. This is possible only when each wealth holder is satisfied with his portfolio of assets viz., the combination of the amount of money and bonds that he actually holds. When each one of the asset holder is holding his optimum combination, the community's asset market will be in equilibrium. Now, at a certain point in time, a certain asset holder may or may not be satisfied with his asset holding. In such a case, he may dispense with either money or bond — someone buying while some one selling bond and thus changing his individual preferences. Through such regular trading in bond market corresponding to the money market it can be argued that the rate of interest is determined by the demand for and supply of bonds as well. Since the information of the bond market — the price of bond and interest rate (or, sometimes referred to as yield rate) are immediately and constantly known to all participants in the market, it can be assumed that the market is almost nearly in equilibrium – individuals or institutions actually hold which they desire to hold at the prevailing price of bonds. This naturally refers to the quantity of money (L_2) that the individuals desire to hold at the same time.

There is, however, the other side of the bond market – the supply of bonds. Just as at a given point in time, the total supply of money is fixed, so is the total supply of bonds. Given the supply of bonds therefore, their demand would determine the rate of interest (or, yield rate) on bonds. Higher the interest rate, higher is the demand for bonds and lower the interest rate lower is the demand for bonds.

Bonds are supplied or, issued by governments as well as corporates. The basic purpose of issuing bonds is to raise the finance capital. The government however, may issue bonds in order to raise revenue to meet its budget deficit as part of government borrowing program from the market. At the time of issue, the bonds are generally auctioned and sold to the highest bidder. Once issued, these bonds become negotiable instruments in the money market and are fit to be regularly traded in the secondary market at the prevailing price of bond.

The price of bond now increases or decreases according to the pressures of demand and supply of bonds and so yield rates on them fluctuate accordingly (in the reverse direction of course). Just as government can issue bonds to make up for its budget deficit, it can also buyback or purchase its already issued bonds and redeem its debt at the time of budget surplus. Then the bonds are destroyed. In the market for bonds, therefore, there are generally three types of bonds.

(a) The outstanding government bonds – the supply of which at a point in time is fixed.

(b) Newly issued government bonds.

(c) Private or corporate bonds.

It would be clear now that the new government bonds and private corporate bonds compete with each other insofar as their response to rate of interest is concerned. In a situation of total investible fund being limited in the market, if the rate of interest is higher (price of bond lower) government bonds gain an edge over private bonds. Since the government as well as private corporate together increase the supply of bonds in the market, each with a view to collect their resources from the market, this naturally pushes up the rate of interest in the market of bonds. Then the result is generally "crowding out" of private corporate bonds.

7.2.2 An Example with Indian Bond Market

The government of India has been issuing, from time to time, various dated bonds. For instance, in February 2009, the Government of India issued a 10-year bond at 6.815% interest rate at its value. Again, in July 2009, Government issued another 10-year bond at 6.9% interest. This is in keeping with Government's plan of borrowing a sum of rupees 4.51 trillion in 2009-10 from the market in order to bridge the gap of its budgetary deficit. In May 2010, the Government issued another 7.8% 10-year bond to be maturing in May 2020. By auction sale conducted by RBI on behalf of the Government of India, these bonds were sold. This is a part of the government's public borrowing programme. These bonds, once issued, become financial instrument in the secondary market where regular trading takes place. Buyers and sellers of these bonds transact at day-to-day price of bonds depending upon their relative demand and supply. If, in a particular day, demand for bonds is relatively high, their price goes up pushing down their yield rate. Similarly, if the demand is relatively low (oversupply of bonds), their price goes down and yield rate goes up. Those transactors (bondholders) who want to make capital gains sell their bonds at higher price while at lower price they may buy some bonds. Thus, the trading goes on until the maturing period of bonds when final holders of bonds get redemption of the principal amount from the government. We may remember during the entire 10-year period, the holders, whoever they may be, continue to get the fixed coupon payment per year.

7.2.3 The Factors Influencing the Bond Market

It is now clear that like any commodity market, price of bond is influenced by their demand and supply. More generally, we may say that the price of bond depends upon the demand and supply of loanable funds which include, besides bonds, other instruments of money and capital market, and therefore, the forces of demand and supply depend upon several factors operating in the money market. Overall liquidity position in the banking and financial system and the expectation of market about the availability of liquidity mainly cause fluctuations in the price of bonds. The Government of India, for instance, issued several bonds in the financial year 2010-11 alongside other treasury bills, thus sucking out a substantial part of liquidity from the banking and financial sector. One immediate reaction was observed at the end of 2009-10 with the banking sector parting with a fair amount of money in the shape of payment of income tax from corporates and individuals and for payment of 2G and 3G spectrum purchases by the corporate houses to the government. This created a situation of liquidity crunch and so pushed the yield rate higher.

Apart from these domestic factors, international factors do influence the availability of investible funds; for instance, inflows and outflows of FDI and FII occasionally influence the investible fund's availability.

7.3 POST-KEYNESIAN DEVELOPMENTS—BAUMOL, TOBIN AND FRIEDMAN

In this chapter, we present certain extensions of post-Keynesian theories of demand for money, particularly those attempted by W.J. Baumol[1], James Tobin[2] and Milton Friedman[3]. These theories particularly the first two, are extensions of basic Keynesian interest-elasticity of the demand for money. As we have seen in Chapter 3, Keynes' speculative demand for money (L_2) is interest-elastic in the sense that money demanded as an asset is responsive to interest rate. While Baumol's theory leads to the conclusion that transaction demand for money (L_1) is equally responsive to the rate of interest besides it being a function of the level of income (Y), Tobin's analysis is much more general in the sense that 'bonds' representing the only alternative to money, bears certain 'risks' to the wealth holder. Therefore, in situation of risk and uncertainty, Tobin analyses the behaviour of asset-holder when returns are associated with risks.

7.3.1 Baumol's Inventory – Theoretic Approach to Demand for Money

Boumol views the problem of demand for money for transaction purposes similar to maintaining an inventory by producing firms. Just as keeping inventory of goods is advantageous so it involves costs as well. So, the question of maintaining an optimal inventory level (of raw materials, semi-finished and finished products) by firms becomes important. This applies equally to cash balances that firms need to keep for meeting their transaction demand (both for transaction motives and precautionary motives). The basic question is, then, 'whether there is some way in which an optimal cash balance can be computed and, if so, how this optimal cash balance figure will be affected by changes in incomes and interest rates. These are obviously important questions for business management as well as for economic theory.[4]

'A firm's cash balance can usually be interpreted as an inventory – an inventory of money which its holder stands ready to exchange against purchases of labour, raw materials, etc. It is really no different in principle from a shoe manufacturer's inventory of footwear which he stands ready to trade for distributor's cash'.[5] Therefore, the technique of determining optimal inventory levels can be used to balance off the advantages of sizeable cash balance against its costs.

---

[1] "The Transaction Demand Cash: An Inventory Theoretic Approach", Originally, *Quarterly Journal of Economics*, Nov. 1952, reviewed in WJ Baumol, *Economic Theory and Operations Analysis*:, Prentice-Hall of India Ltd., 1966. Also see RL Crouch, *Macroeconomics*, Harcourt Jovanovich, 1972. J. Tobin, "Interest Elasticity of Transaction Demand for Cash", *Review of Economics and Statistics*, Aug. 1956.

[2] J. Tobin, "Liquidity Preference as Behaviour Towards Risk", *Review of Economic Studies*, Feb. 1958.

[3] M. Friedman, "The Quantity Theory of Money: A Restatement" in M. Friedman ed. *Studies in Quantity Theory of Money*, Chicago, 1956.

[4] Boumol, Economic Theory (1966) p. 350

[5] Baumol, Economic Theory (1966) p. 350

No doubt, it is convenient for firms to keep cash balances in hand for their expenditures, particularly when it is not possible to foresee the future requirements exactly. But, it is not prudent to involve large sums in cash when it can otherwise be utilised with suitable return. The situation can be illustrated with a numerical example. Let us suppose, a producing firm receives a sum of ₹ 1 lakh at the beginning of the year to spend it for the whole year at equal, monthly instalments. So, at the end of the year it ends up with zero cash. Next year also it gets similar amount (₹ 1 lakh) to be similarly expended over the year, and so on. Since it does not need the entire cash balance to be kept for the entire period (year), it can think of investing some of it in interest-earning securities at least for some period of the year. But, it has also to meet certain costs in terms of brokerage fees when sums are invested and withdrawn as also the real cost (opportunity cost) in terms of interest amount forgone for the period that money is held in cash.

The time profile of its expenditure and money balance will appear as shown in Fig. 7.5. Let the periods of time (years) be denoted by T_1, T_2, ..., T_n and let the inflow of money (₹ 1 lakh) be denoted by M. The firm spends all this money during T_1 at a constant rate so that at the end of T_1 its total expenditure will be equal to M and his money balance will be zero. Similarly, for T_2 period and so on. The firm's average balance is, however, $M/2$ $[(M + O)/2 = M/2]$. That is, if M = ₹ 1 lakh, the average balance will be ₹ 50,000 approximately – the balance for the sixth month. Clearly, for the first six months, of the year, ₹ 50,000 remains idle. Even for the entire period of the first six months, only $1/6^{th}$ of ₹ 50,000 is used during the first month, another 1/6th is used for the next month, and so on. Obviously, the firm can invest in securities the sterile money for the period it remains unused and thereby earns interest for that period. Let us suppose, out of M amount of inflow of money at the beginning of the period, it invests I rupees in securities and keeps the rest R rupees in cash; so that, $M = I + R$.

However, out of the invested I rupees in securities, the firm has eventually to withdraw them for use for transaction purposes – preferably, in batches. Each withdrawal involves costs. The number of batches, however, varies inversely with

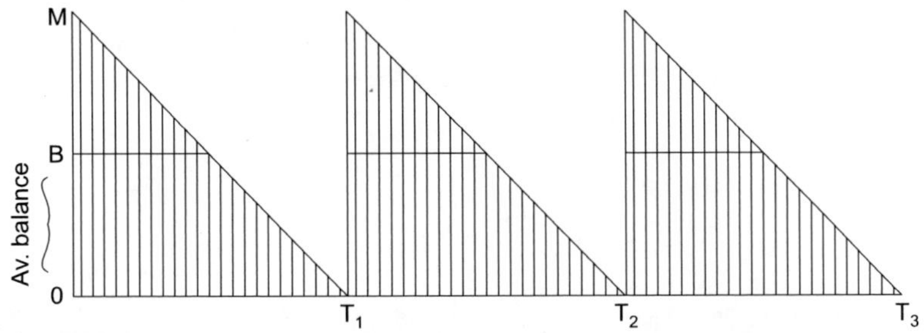

Figure 7.5 *Firm's time profile of expenditure and average balance.*

their size, that is, if the size of each withdrawal is large in amount, the firm will need small number of withdrawals and vice versa. For instance, supposing the firm decides to keep ₹ 20,000 and invests the rest ₹ 80,000 in securities. If it withdraws ₹ 10,000 each time, the number of withdrawals will be 8. However, if he withdraws ₹ 20,000 each time, the number of withdrawals will be only 4. So, if C stands for size of withdrawal smaller the value of C larger is the number of times of securities selling and larger the value of C, smaller is the number of times of selling securities. Now, let us examine the costs associated with securities transactions, i.e., buying and selling.

1. One part of the cost is, of course, the opportunity cost or, real cost – the interest forgone on the amount retained initially, i.e., R.

   But since this amount of R serves only for the fraction of the year equal to $\frac{R}{M} = \frac{M-I}{M}$, this is the period of time for which the interest forgone is associated. Thus, the opportunity cost is equal to:

   $$\frac{R}{2}\left(r\,\frac{M-I}{M}\right) = \frac{M-I}{2}\left(r\,\frac{M-I}{M}\right)^{*} \tag{7.6}$$

2. Every time, investment is made in securities some costs appear as fixed costs which do not vary with the volume of investment, for instance, the telephone charges. On the other hand, there are costs which vary directly with transactions, e.g., the brokerage fees. Thus, costs of security investments can be expressed as a linear function of the volume transactions with a positive constant:

   $$b_d + k_d\, I \tag{7.7}$$

   where b_d stands for fixed costs and k_d is the variable costs and I is the volume of investment. Transactors dealing with D-mat A/c through computers have to bear similar costs: some fixed and some variable.

3. Just as there are costs of investment, there are certain costs of withdrawals also. If C rupee batches are periodically withdrawn, the number of withdrawals will be I/C, if I is the original amount of investment. The cost of each withdrawal can also be expressed as a linear function of C such as $b_w + k_w\, C$ where, again, b_w stands for fixed cost part and k_w stands for variable cost part. Now, by multiplying this cost function by the number of withdrawals $\left(\frac{I}{C}\right)$ we can get the total cost of security withdrawals such as:

   $$(b_w + k_w\, C)\,\frac{I}{C} \tag{7.8}$$

---

* For instance, in the above example, if ₹ 20,000 is initially retained and ₹ 80,000 is invested for 12 months, ₹ 20,000 serves for $\frac{20,000}{1,00,000} = \frac{1}{5}$th of the year, i.e., $\frac{12}{5} = 2.4$ months. The interest forgone for this period at 10% per annum (for instance) will be: $20,000 \times \frac{1}{10} \times \frac{1}{5} =$ ₹ 400.

4. Yet another cost in terms of opportunity cost is involved in (7.8). The interest forgone on the amount withdrawn for the part of the year has also to be estimated. This will be equal to the average balance held during this part of the year, i.e., $\frac{C}{2}$, multiplied by the rate of interest, r and the fraction of the year this average balance is held, $(I/M)^*$, i.e.,

$$\frac{C}{2}\left(r\,\frac{I}{M}\right) \tag{7.9}$$

Thus, the total cost of the firm's decision to invest in securities, besides retaining a portion of the cash will be the sum total of (7.6)-(7.9). That is:

$$K = \frac{M-I}{2}\left(r\,\frac{M-I}{M}\right) + b_d + k_d I + (bw + kw\ C)\,\frac{I}{C}$$
$$+\,\frac{C}{2}\left(r\,\frac{I}{M}\right) \tag{7.10}$$

Our aim is now to obtain the optimum size of withdrawal, C, i.e., the value of C which minimizes the total cost, K. We get this value by differentiating K with respect to C and set it equal to zero (according to the first order condition of minimization). Thus,

$$\frac{\partial K}{\partial C} = -\frac{b_w\, I}{C^2} + \frac{r\, I}{2M}^* \tag{7.11}$$

(since the derivative will be applicable to last two terms: $(b_w + k_w\ C)/\frac{I}{C}$ and $\frac{C}{2}\left(r\,\frac{I}{M}\right)$)

Now, setting eqn. (7.11) equal to zero gives,

$$\frac{b_w\, I}{C^2} = \frac{rI}{2M}$$

$$\Rightarrow \qquad C^2\, r\, I = 2M.b_w\, I$$

---

* If $\frac{M-I}{M}$ is the period (fraction of the year) for which $\frac{R}{2}$ is held, the rest of the period (fraction of the year) for which $\frac{C}{2}$ is held will be:

$$\left(1-\frac{M-I}{M}\right) = 1-\left(1-\frac{I}{M}\right) = 1-1+\frac{I}{M} = \frac{I}{M}.$$

* $$\frac{\partial K}{\partial C} = \frac{\partial}{\partial C}\left\{b_w\cdot\frac{I}{C} + (k_w\ C)\cdot\frac{I}{C}\right\} = \frac{C\,.\,\frac{\partial}{\partial C}\cdot b_w\, I - b_w\, I\cdot\frac{\partial}{\partial C}(C)}{C^2} = -\frac{b_w\, I}{C^2}$$

and, $$\frac{\partial K}{\partial C}\frac{C}{2}\left(r\cdot\frac{I}{M}\right) = \frac{1}{2}\cdot r\,\frac{I}{M} = \frac{rI}{2M}.$$

$$\Rightarrow \qquad C^2 = \frac{2M\, b_w\, I}{rI}$$

$$\Rightarrow \qquad C = \sqrt{\frac{2M\, b_w}{r}} \qquad (7.12)$$

Equation (7.12) shows clearly that optimum withdrawal size C is inversely related to r, the rate of interest: as the interest rate rises, the optimum withdrawal will fall – withdrawing less when interest rate is high and vice versa. At the same time, it is also to be noticed that C varies in proportion with the square root of M – i.e., by less than in proportion of M.

Two conditions emerge from the above derivation:

(a) transaction demand for money varies inversely with the rate of interest; and

(b) economies of scale operate in the transaction demand for money – C (or $C/2$) varies by less than proportion to M. Thus, as M is carried in larger scale, C per withdrawal falls.

Alternatively, we can also determine the optimum size of R – the initial cash balance kept – by rewriting eqn. (7.10) in terms of R,

$$K = \frac{R}{2}\left(r\,\frac{R}{M}\right) + b_d + k_d\,(M - R) + (b_w + k_w\,C)\,\frac{M-R}{C} + \frac{C}{2}\left(r\,\frac{M-R}{M}\right) \qquad (7.13)$$

and differentiating (7.13) with respect to R:

$$\frac{\partial K}{\partial R} = \left[\frac{R}{2}\cdot\frac{r}{M} + \frac{1}{2}\cdot r\,\frac{R}{M}\right] - k_d - \frac{b_w}{C} - k_w - \frac{Cr}{2M}$$

$$= \frac{Rr}{M} - k_d - \frac{b_w}{C} - k_w - \frac{Cr}{2M} \qquad (7.14)$$

Setting this equal to zero gives,

$$\frac{Rr}{M} - k_d - \frac{b_w}{C} - k_w - \frac{Cr}{2M} = 0$$

$$\Rightarrow \qquad R = \frac{C}{2} + \frac{b_w\,M}{Cr} + \frac{M(k_d + k_w)}{r}^{*} \qquad (7.15)$$

---

* $$\frac{Rr}{M} = k_d + \frac{b_w}{C} + k_w + \frac{Cr}{2M}$$

$$\Rightarrow \qquad R = \frac{M\left\{k_d + \frac{b_w}{C} + \frac{Cr}{2M}\right\}}{r}$$

$$\Rightarrow \qquad \frac{Mk_d}{r} + \frac{Mb_w}{Cr} + \frac{Mk_w}{r} + \frac{MCr}{2Mr}$$

$$\Rightarrow \qquad \frac{M(k_d + k_w)}{r} + \frac{b_wM}{Cr} + \frac{C}{2}$$

Equation (7.15) suggests that the size of R (and hence its average $R/2$ is inversely related to the rate of interest. It follows, therefore, that if the initial average cash balance (not invested) ($R/2$) as also the average balance maintained throughout the rest of the year, i.e., $C/2$ are inversely related to the rate of interest, the average balance maintained throughout the year is also inversely related to the rate of interest. Therefore, the transaction demand for money is equally responsive to the rate of interest. If this is true for individual firm (as also for an individual investor), this will be true for market demand curve for the money (and bonds) as well – bonds being positively related to rate of interest.

An Evaluation

Most often we club the two demands for money, viz., transaction and precautionary demand and label L_1 – the transaction demand. Baumol's extension of the demand for money as explained above may be applicable to big asset-holders and corporate houses but normally, smaller asset-holders and individuals seldom act in a manner to take advantage of the high rate of interest and part with transaction balances so frequently. The precautionary aspect in the transaction balance plays an important part in taking decision in this respect. In spite of such limited applicability, Boumol's extension of transaction demand for money is certainly an useful addition to the theory of the demand for money.

7.4 TOBIN'S PORTFOLIO BALANCE APPROACH

James Tobin provides a more general theory of the demand for money in terms of the decision rule under risk and uncertainty. This theory is known as the 'portfolio balance' theory. Specifically, it tries to explain how an asset-holder allocates his portfolio of assets between money and bonds given that bond holding is risky.

Money and bonds differ in two fundamental senses:

1. Money is fixed in price at all times – a hundred-rupee note is hundred rupee worth. So, one can get hundred rupees in exchange at any time. On the other hand, the price of bond is not fixed. Its price fluctuates – it may either rise or fall (having an inverse relationship with rate of interest).
2. Money is most liquid. As an asset, it can be immediately used. The bond, however, cannot be used immediately. It has to be converted into cash before it can be used and this process may take some time.

But why is bond 'risky' in relation to money? Risk arises from the fact that its future price is uncertain – the future price may rise or fall. If the price rises there is a capital gain and if the price falls, there is capital loss to the bond holder. Thus, the more an asset-holder allocates his fund to bonds – he undertakes more risk and the less he allocates to bonds he undertakes less risk.

But it is also a fact that more risk taking provides him chance of getting higher return in terms of interest income as well as capital gain. This return, of course, is viewed in terms of expected gain or expected monetary value. Let us see how this expected value is obtained.

The existing theory of decision making under risk and uncertainly states that people take decision on the basis of expected utility or expected monetary value (EMV) which is consistent with risk-averse behaviour of such decision maker; and it is assumed that most decision makers are risk-averters. Therefore, they aim at maximising expected monetary value (or, expected return in the present case). To state the same thing, they aim at minimizing risk for a given value of expected return. Since, total returns in the case of the asset-holding in terms of bonds consist of two parts: interest income (or, yield on bonds – the fixed annual payment to bond holder) and capital gain. The second component is uncertain although the first is certain. This is, because, the possibility of capital gain is equally true as for capital loss so that there is always 50 : 50 chance of each to happen. Thus, the bond holders generally have in mind (though implicitly) a 'probability distribution' of capital gain/loss which can be approximated to a normal distribution with its mean value centred at zero and variance being constant as shown in Fig. 7.6. Now, the mean value is the expected return and variance is an index of its variability. Using symbols, $E(g)$ is the expected return and $\sigma^2 g$ is the variance of g—the expected gain/loss (or, its positive square root, σg, the standard deviation of g).

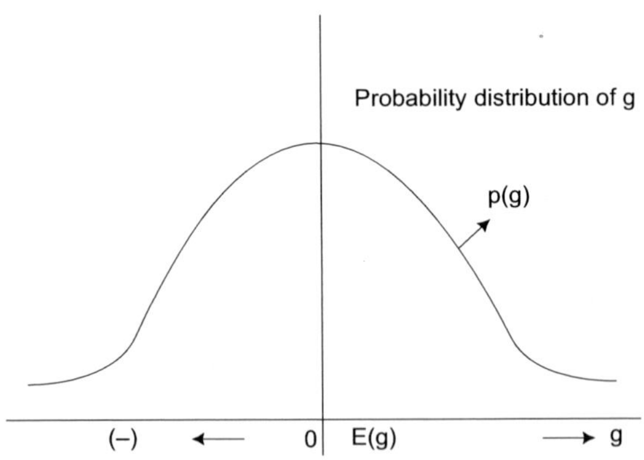

Figure 7.6 *Probability distribution of g.*

Now, if TA stands for total assets; M and B for money and bonds, respectively, then returns on total assets, $R(TA)$ can be written as:

$$R(TA) = R(M) + R(B)$$

$$\Rightarrow \quad R(TA) = R(B) \tag{7.16}$$

(since money holding gives no return).

The total portfolio of assets being

$$TA = M + B,$$

in proportion of the total, this can be expressed as:

$$\frac{TA}{TA} = \frac{M}{TA} + \frac{B}{TA}$$

$$\Rightarrow \quad \frac{M}{TA} + \frac{B}{TA} = 1 \tag{7.17}$$

To simplify the symbols, we write A_1 for $\frac{M}{TA}$ and A_2 for $\frac{B}{TA}$, so that we can write now as,

$$A_1 + A_2 = 1 \tag{7.18}$$

We may express eqn. 7.18 as $A_1 = 1 - A_2$ and $A_2 = 1 - A_1$. For example, if $A_2 = 60\%$. $A_1 = 40\%$.

Now, total return on the above portfolio can be written as:

$$TR = A_2 (r + g) \tag{7.19}$$

where, r is the interest rate on bonds and g is the capital gain/loss and A_2 is the proportion of assets in bonds. Hence, the expected value of TR can be expressed as:

$$E(TR) = E\,[A_2 (r + g)] \tag{7.20}$$

But, as we have seen above (Fig. 7.6) that expected value of g, i.e., $E(g) = 0$. Hence, equation (7.20) can be written as:

$$E(TR) = A_2 r \tag{7.21}$$

(since amount of bonds is certain and r is fixed).

Equation (7.21) indicates that as the proportion of A_2 (proportion of bonds) increases for a given interest rate, r, the expected return of the asset holder will increase and vice versa.

Now, let us see what is the total risk involved in such an exercise of holding the above combination of assets. As we noted above, the riskiness of A_2 is indicated by its variability, σg, the standard deviation of g for each unit of bond. This means the total risk involved in A_2 is the multiple of A_2 and σg, i.e., total risk (Tot. Rsk.) = $A \cdot \sigma g$. This can be represented by the expectations – variance frontier (E – V frontier) technique. Thus,

$$A_2 = \frac{\text{Tot. Rsk}}{\sigma g} \quad \left\{ \text{since } \frac{A_2 \sigma g}{\sigma g} = A_2 \right\}$$

$$\Rightarrow \quad A_2 r = \frac{(\text{Tot. Rsk})\,.\,r}{\sigma g} = E(TR) \tag{7.22}$$

(substituting from eqn. (7.21)

Equation (7.22) states that expected returns $E(TR)$ and total risk (Tot. Rsk.) are positively related for given levels of r and σg. For given values of these parameters, r and σg, therefore, more the expected returns from bond holding, more is the amount of risk involved. This relationship can, thus, be treated as 'constraint' for the asset-holder, giving a straight-line relationship $r/\sigma g$) as shown in Fig. 7.7. The slope of the straight line (or, constraint line increases or decreases according as r—the rate of interest rises or falls. Thus, if r_1 is the rate of interest ($r_1 > r$) the constraint line shifts upward to $r_1/\sigma g$.

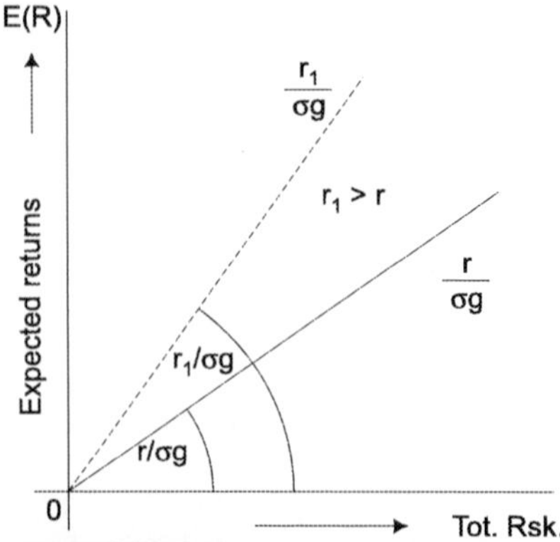

Figure 7.7 *Expected returns and total risk for an asset holder.*

Now, we should look for the asset-holder's indifference map – the various possibilities of combinations between expected returns and variance (or, s.d.) in terms of expectations. Such an indifference map would suggest the asset-holder's preferences between expected return and risk like those shown in Fig. 7.8. The set of indifference curves in Fig. 7.8 are having positive slope and concave from above. Let us consider I.C., I_1. The concavity property suggests that expected return per unit of risk rises as the asset holder moves along I_1 from left to right. This means $ef/ed > bc/ab$ (or, $ef > bc$, since $ab = ed$). In other words, if the asset holder undertakes a lower level of risk, TR_1, his expected return is only $E(R_1)$. But if he takes a higher level of risk, TR_2, his expected return increases to $E(R_2)$. In fact, this is necessary to keep him on the indifference curve I_1. This suggests risk-aversion behaviour of the asset holder. Higher levels of indifference curves (I_2, I_3...) are associated with higher levels of returns; hence I_2, I_3... lie above I_1. An asset holder will find him indifferent between any two points on any single indifference curve. Why should an asset holder prefer a higher I.C.? Because, for a given level of risk, a higher I.C. gives higher level of return or, to put it another way, for a given level of expected return, a higher indifference curve means lower level of risk.

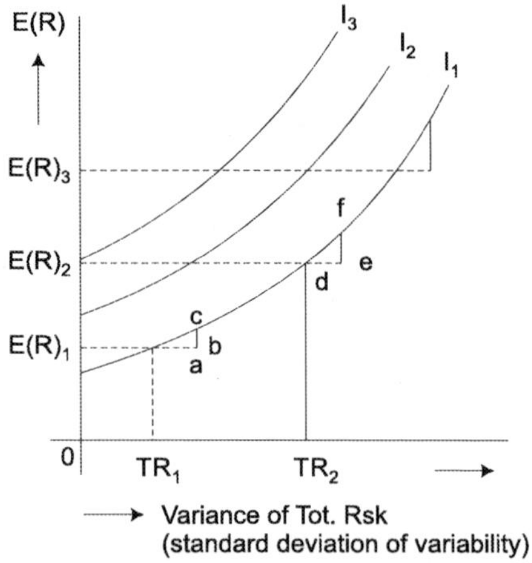

Figure 7.8 *Asset holder's preference map (expected returns and risk).*

Let us now combine the preference-map and the constraints faced by an asset holder as shown in Fig. 7.9. The equilibrium of the asset holder is located at E_1 where his constraint $\frac{r}{\sigma g}$ is just tangential to his indifference curve, I_1. Thus the asset holder's optimum combination of bond and money is, OA_2^* and 1 – OA_2^* respectively, with his total risk equal to TR^*.

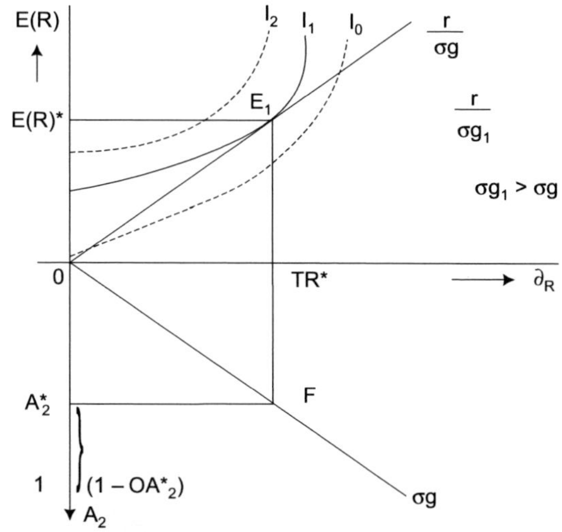

Figure 7.9 *Asset holder's equilibrium position.*

Now, how would his optimum combination change if rate of interest changes. For instance, if rate of interest rises, his constraint shift to the left (since $r_1 > r$, so $\frac{r_1}{\sigma g} > \frac{r}{\sigma g}$). The asset holder would find himself to an upper indifference curve I_2 and a new optimum combination will be located at E_2 as shown in Fig. 7.10. As compared to E_1, E_2 suggests that with rise in rate of interest, the asset holder would be preferring a greater proportion of bonds (A_2) and thereby incur greater risk as well. However, there can be two effects and hence two possibilities. Analogous to consumer's indifference map and his reaction to the change in the relative price (and consumer's budget line) here also, our asset holder can experience two types of effects: income effect (or, wealth effect) and substitution effect, of a change in the rate of interest. First, the substitution effect can be analysed by a parallel shift below of the new opportunity locus (constraint) $\frac{r_1}{\sigma g}$ just touching another point of the I_1. This results in increasing the proportion of A_2 in his portfolio. Thus, his demand for money would consequently fall. However, rise in interest rate raises his level of wealth (income).

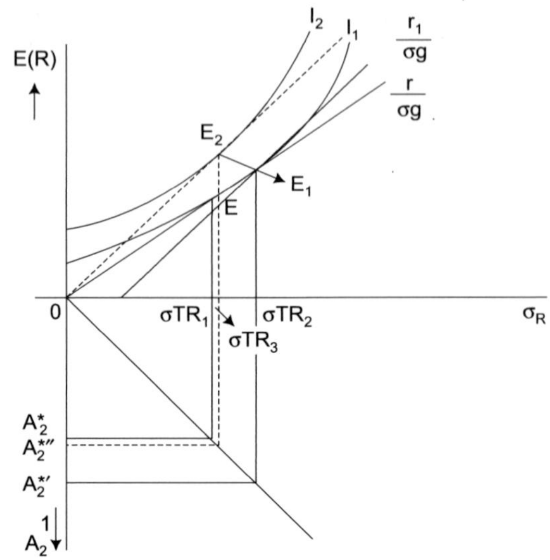

Figure 7.10 *'Income' and 'substitution' effects of the asset holder.*

There are now two different possibilities:

1. Income effect may either be positive or negative depending on whether he considers bond as a normal or inferior good. This can now be understood by locating the movement from E_1 to E_2. If E_1E_2 is backward (as shown in the diagram), resulting in lesser proportion of A_2 (such as $A^{*''}_2$), this means 'bond' is considered inferior. But if, this income effect is still less than the substitution effect, the overall position of the asset holder would be to increase the proportion of bond and decreasing that of money. However, if the backward movement of E_1E_2 would have been large enough to more than compensate the substitution effect, this could mean preferring lesser proportion of bonds to money as compared to his original position of equilibrium as a result of rise in rate of interest.
2. The income effect may be positive resulting in positive or forward movement of the E_1E_2 (not shown in the diagram). In this case, the substitution effect is reinforced so that the total effect would be to bear a larger level of risk and hold larger proportion of bonds (greater than A^*_2). Correspondingly, the asset holder's preference for money would go down. Thus, the conclusion is that the opportunity cost of holding money in the asset portfolio depends equally on the rate of interest and the riskiness of the alternative asset, viz., the bonds.

7.5. MILTON FRIEDMAN AND THEORY OF DEMAND FOR MONEY

Milton Friedman attempted a reformulation of the old Quantity Theory (Q.T.) of money of the classicals. According to Friedman, the Q.T. is a theory of demand for money, not of output, money income or prices. Secondly, money is an asset or capital good so that demand for it is a problem in capital theory. However, while old Q.T. and its Cambridge version limited itself to transaction demand for money, Friedman was concerned with Keynesian speculative (asset) demand for money relating it to the rate of interest. At the same time, this approach to the concept of wealth is not only different but broader from that used by Keynes. Wealth compries all sources of income including 'human beings'. This broader concept of wealth is then related to the demand for money as wealth which can be held in alternative forms and so a source of expected future streams of money income. In this sense, it can be said, that "the Keynesian view of the speculative demand for money as a store of wealth is carried to its logical extreme in the Friedman's reformulation of the quantity theory by suggesting that the demand function for money has to be considered only as an asset simultaneously with other major types of assets in the economy. In other words, while the traditional quantity theory was almost exclusively preoccupied with the transaction demand for money as the medium of exchange, its 'modern' preoccupation is exclusively with the demand for money as asset... the pendulum then swung from one extreme to the other – from money only as a medium of exchange to money as a 'store of wealth'.[1]

Friedman presumed that any wealth holder may be imagined to select between money as an asset and at least four other major types of assets in an economy. There are bonds, equities, physical goods and even 'human capital'. Money is only one of these five major forms in which wealth can be held. Consequently, in this framework, the demand for money as an asset is governed by all the factors that determine the net rates of return on the five major types of assets plus a budget constraint for total wealth.[2]

Thus, the reformulated demand function for money takes into account the rates of return of alternative assets and other factors which are broadly as follows:

1. A list of interest rates on bank deposits (as a form of money) (r_m), on bonds (r_b) and on equities (r_e).
2. Percentage change in the interest rates mentioned in (1) viz., on bonds and equities expressed as:

   $$\frac{1}{r_b} \cdot \frac{dr_b}{dt} \quad \text{and} \quad \frac{1}{r_e} \cdot \frac{dr_e}{dt}$$

   (these are same as $dr_b/dt/r_b$ and $dr_e/dt/r_e$ which may be expressed in percentage terms).
3. The general price level, P and its percentage change expressed as:

   $$\frac{1}{P} \cdot \frac{dP}{dt}$$

   which governs real yield on money and on physical goods.

---

[1] Amit Bhaduri, Macroeconomics: The Dynamics of Commodity Production, pp. 132-133, Macmillan India, 1990.

[2] Same as above, p. 133.

4. The overall budget constraint for wealth in terms of Friedman's notion of permanent income*, Y_p.
5. A ratio of non-human to human wealth which also acts as a kind of subsidiary constraint and symbolised as w.
6. The objective factors which affect tastes of ultimate wealth-owning units and business enterprises.

The demand function, thus reformulated, is expressed as:

$$\frac{M_d}{P} = f\left(r_b, r_e, \frac{1}{P} \cdot \frac{dP}{dt}, w, \frac{Y_p}{p}, u\right)$$

$$\Rightarrow \quad M_d = f\left(r_b, r_e, P, \frac{1}{P} \cdot \frac{dP}{dt}, w, Y_p, u\right) \tag{7.23}$$

Explanation of Variables

- M_d/P is the real demand for money, i.e., monetary demand deflated by price-level.
- r_b is the nominal rate of interest on bonds. Since bonds stand for assets which promise the holder (of bonds) a perpetual income stream of constant amount, this rate is affected by the rate of change of its price, which is $\frac{1}{r_b}$. Therefore, if the rate of interest on bonds is r_b, nominal rate of return can be approximated by $r_b - \frac{1}{r_b} \cdot \frac{dr_b}{dt}$, where $\frac{1}{r_b} \cdot \frac{dr_b}{dt}$ measures the rate of capital appreciation due to changes in the rate of interest (fall in this case).**
- r_e is the rate of return on equities, which promise to pay the holder a perpetual income stream of constant *real* amount. This means the change in the general price-level is also taken into account in this case. If r_e represents the nominal rate of return on equities, its capital appreciation rate can be approximated by $r_e - \frac{1}{r_e} \cdot \frac{dr_e}{dt} + \frac{1}{P} \cdot \frac{dP}{dt}$. (Needless to say

* This constraint of permanent income is central to his hypothesis of permanent income as an alternative theory of aggregate consumption behaviour.

** $\frac{dr_b}{dt}$ is the rate of change, per period, of bond rate of interest, r_b. The expression $\frac{1}{r_b} \cdot \frac{dr_b}{d_t}$ is the same as $\frac{dr_b}{dt} \Big/ r_b$ measuring the proportionate or percentage change in r_b suggesting capital gain/loss per period.

The permanent income can be viewed as a sort of weighted average of the current and past values of income most recent values commanding relatively great weight.

that in case of capital depreciation (capital loss), this expression would be: $r_e + \frac{1}{r_e} \cdot \frac{dr_e}{dt} - \frac{1}{P} \cdot \frac{dP}{dt}\bigg)$.

- *Return from physical goods* is generally in kind in terms of their services and their exchange or purchasing power. Hence, the return from physical goods is affected by the change in the price level. For instance, if general price level falls, the physical goods appreciate in terms of money; and in case of rise in price level, they depreciate in monetary terms. Thus, the rate of price-level change $\left(\frac{1}{P} \cdot \frac{dP}{dt}\right)$ may be treated as return from physical goods worth their value.
- *The return from human capital* (investment in education, training, etc.) is, in fact, difficult to measure from theoretical as well as practical point of view. This is because, there is no market substitutability of human capital for other forms of capital. Friedman has used a ratio of non-human capital (physical capital) to human capital or, income from non-human wealth to that from human wealth as an explanatory factor. For a given total stock of wealth, the higher its human component, the greater may be the demand for money to compensate for the lack of marketability of human wealth.
- The concept of permanent income, is perhaps, the central element of Friedman's demand function for money. It refers to a steady flow of income over the working life of a wealth holder which, in turn, is able to maintain a steady flow of consumption expenditure. Conceptually, it includes all past levels of income and expected future stream of income, If Y_p denotes permanent income, Y_p/P is the value in real terms. This notion of permanent income is different from Keynesian concept of current income insofar as the latter does not include past or even future (expected) levels of income. However, we shall soon examine below that on empirical level the difference between permanent income and current income is much narrowed down for all practical purposes.

Lastly, the form of the function is determined by the preference pattern. Friedman suggests, in this regard that 'explicit allowance can be made for some changes in tastes so far as such changes are linked with objective circumstances'. Therefore, a separate variable, u, is included in the explanatory variables group to capture the effects of changes in tastes and preferences.

7.5.1 The Empirical Estimate of Friedman's Demand Function for Money

Looking at Friedman's money demand function, it is clear that the specification of the equation involves several variables that are not empirically observable.

For instance, the percentage changes in interest rates which govern capital gains/ losses on bonds and equities $\left(\frac{1}{r_b} \cdot \frac{dr_b}{dt} \text{ and } \frac{1}{r_e} \cdot \frac{dr_e}{dt}\right)$ are, in fact, expected changes and not actual changes. Hence, they are statistically not observable. Similarly, expected price change $\left(\frac{1}{P} \cdot \frac{dP}{dt}\right)$ is also not actually observed. The parameter w – the ratio of non-human to human capital is almost impossible to measure. For these reasons, all the above-mentioned variables are dropped when the question of empirical determination of the demand function arises. For the three rates, which appear in the function (r_b, r_e and r) only one rate is used for all practical purpose. Hence, the empirical version is simplified and narrowly specified as follows:

$$\frac{M_d}{P} = f(Y/P, r, u)$$

or, $$M_d = f(Y_p, r, u) \tag{7.24}$$

where, Y/P is the permanent income deflated by price-level, r and u are variables as explained above.

7.5.2 Comparison with Keynesian Theory

The empirical testable form of the Friedman's demand function for money (eqn. 7.24), does not appear to be radically different from Keynesian version which is simply a function of two major variables, viz., income and interest rate – the former determining the transaction demand (including precautionary demand) and the latter determining the speculative demand. The only difference lies in the concept of income used by Friedman – the permanent income. In practice, permanent income refers to the weighted average of the past periods of income. But the weights used are such that the most recent periods are given the greater weights as compared to other periods. The more remote the periods of observation are, the lesser the weights. Thus, relatively current incomes have the greater chance of inclusion in the income variable for estimation purposes. Thus, the difference between Keynesian current income and Friedman's permanent income is very much unclear. Indeed, the ultimate empirical determinants – income (current or permanent) and the interest rate – are so similar in both the theories that it is only in the special equational form, rather than in introducing new conceptual determinants of the demand for money that the 'modern' quantity theory can be said to differ from the Keynesian view.[1]

7.6 EMPIRICAL RESULTS AND NEW QUANTITY THEORY

The monetarists (followers of Friedman's Chicago School) have attempted empirical estimation of demand function for money. The main results which they

[1] Amit Bhaduri (1990) p. 136.

claim to be supporting the basic conclusions of classical quantity theory are as follows:

1. Demand for money is a stable function of the level of income in the long run. Further, such a stable function by and large, suggests a linear relationship between the demand for money stock and the money income – thus implying a stable 'velocity of circulation' of money which is the central idea behind the old Q.T.
2. The rate of interest as determinant of the demand for money is not important. In fact, this relationship between speculative demand for money and interest rate is relatively weak in most empirical findings. Thus, the modern quantity theorists more or less reject the rate of interest as 'influencing' the demand for money.

   Several other empirical research findings, however, have expressed doubts on the empirical findings mentioned above supporting stable velocity function.
3. The supply of money is exogenously determined. This is one of the basic assumptions of the new Q.T. This is mainly because of the specific way money supply is defined. Money supply is defined as consisting of money in circulation plus bank deposits (or, credit money). It does not include the debt obligations of the other non-banking financial institutions which are governed by the demand for money. In other words, supply of money and demand for money are not independent to each other. Part of the money supply is endogenous in character. Besides monetary history of early period, even recent history, particularly in U.S. and other western capitalist countries (including some of the developing countries) has lent support to the fact that a substantial part of money supply in the form of debt obligations, has been in response to its demand.
4. The equational form of the new version of the quantity theory requires explanation in terms of the exact cause of the stability of the demand function of money or the velocity of circulation. In other words, there is lack of substantial theoretical basis behind the demand function specified by the new Q.T. – without a clear theoretical scheme advanced in support of its central hypothesis of constant velocity of circulation of money, the modern Q.T. often assumes the character of a 'black-box' magic; empirical tests are performed to support a hypothesis which has no theoretical basis.[1]
5. *Lack of a proper transmission mechanism*: From the new formulation of Q.T. the link between the supply of money and demand for it in terms of a transmission mechanism is largely lacking. For instance, if there is a

[1] Bhaduri, op. cit. p. 137.

change in the supply of money, the process through which this change is reflected in the corresponding change in demand for it is not explained in the new version, neither was it given in the old version. On the other hand, the theory asserts that the corresponding change in the money income has to adjust itself to wipe out any gap between demand and supply of money.

Comparing the Keynesian transmission in this regard makes things clear. In Keynes' theory, an increase in the potential money supply (through higher cash reserves) means higher debt obligations of commercial banks. If the central bank purchases securities in the open market to increase the cash reserves of commercial banks, then the price of securities increases and the corresponding interest rate decreases. Given the state of expectation about the 'normal' rate of interest, at the lower current interest rate, the demand for money by the public (M_d) also increases. Thus, the higher potential for the money supply by the banks can be realised at higher demand for money by the public. Consequently, an equilibrium between higher (actual) supply of money and its higher demand by the public can be reached at a lower interest rate. A lower interest rate, in turn, reduces the cost of borrowing finance from commercial banks by investors in physical goods.

As far as the significance of the variables, viz., income and rate of interest appearing in Keynes and Friedman, the difference between the two theories is glaring. While Keynes attaches greater importance to the rate of interest as principal determinant of the demand for money (speculative demand in particular) while reserving the due importance to income for transaction demand, Friedman gives greater importance to income and neglects rather the importance of rate of interest based mainly on the long-run behaviour of the demand for money.

APPENDIX 7A

We examine below the behaviour of income velocity of money as a ratio of nominal GNP and money supply, (V) as also its inverse (k) in the context of Indian economy for a period of 60 years (1954-55 to 2013-14).

Table 7.1 and the associated graph give these ratios alongside the nominal GNP at current prices and the money stock (M_3). If we carefully examine the table, we find that except during the first 18-19 years of observations, there is no overall stability in the behaviour of either (V) or (k) over the entire period. By and large, V exhibits a tendency of gradual decline, while k, the demand for money, shows clear signs of gradual increase over the period. The non-stability of the value of V contradicts the classical assertion that velocity of money is stable in the long run or the demand for money is stable. It is worth mentioning here that in the advanced economy like U.S., the relationship between GDP and money supply might exhibit stability as Prof. Gregory Mankiw has tried to show[1], but in a less developed economy like India, this could not be established.

1 N. Gregory Mankiw, Principles of Macroeconomics, 6th Edition, Cengage Learning, p. 355.

There might be several explanations for this. During the early years of India's development era,money supply growth, by and large, kept pace with GNP growth, but during the later years, there has been uneven growth of money supply. Also, the monetary growth in India was not guided by any policy rule. In an advanced economy like the US, on the contrary, a definite policy rule (such as Tayler's rule[1]) might have presumably been followed so that a stable relationship between GDP and money supply was observed.

Appendix Table 7. A

Table 7.1 *Behaviour of V and k in the Indian economy (1954-55 2013-14)k*

Year Ending	GNP@current prices amount in ₹ Billion (A)	Money supply (M3) amount in ₹ Crores (B)	V (A*100/B)	K (B/A*100)
1955	111.41	2379	4.683060109	0.2135355893
1956	113.61	2683	4.234439061	0.2361587888
1957	135.3	2869	4.715928895	0.2120473023
1958	139.31	3164	4.402970923	0.2271193741
1959	155.16	3476	4.463751438	0.224026811
1960	163.27	3883	4.204738604	0.2378269125
1961	178.7	3964	4.508072654	0.2218242865
1962	189.12	4247	4.453025665	0.2245664129
1963	203.21	4560	4.456359649	0.2243984056
1964	233.5	5037	4.635695851	0.2157173448
1965	272.22	5498	4.951255002	0.2019689957
1966	286.93	6134	4.677698076	0.2137803645
1967	324.39	6817	4.758544814	0.2101482783
1968	380.03	7450	5.101073826	0.196037155
1969	402.57	8306	4.846737298	0.2063243659
1970	443.34	9639	4.599439776	0.2174177832
1971	473.54	11020	4.297096189	0.2327152933
1972	507.08	12693	3.994957851	0.2503155321
1973	559.12	15013	3.724238993	0.2685112319
1974	680.95	17624	3.86376532	0.258814891
1975	804.79	19549	4.116783467	0.2429080878
1976	864.52	22480	3.845729537	0.2600286864
1977	931.89	27781	3.354414888	0.2981145843
1978	1056.15	32906	3.209597034	0.311565592

[1] Discussed in detail in chapter 9, p. 536.

1979	1144.91	40112	2.854283008	0.3503506826
1980	1258.82	47226	2.665523229	0.3751608649
1981	1499.87	55774	2.689192097	0.3718588944
1982	1758.45	62752	2.802221443	0.3568597344
1983	1960.1	73184	2.678317665	0.3733687057
1984	2280.77	86595	2.633835672	0.3796744082
1985	2551.87	102933	2.479156344	0.403363024
1986	2880.95	119394	2.412977202	0.414425797
1987	3221.44	141632	2.274514234	0.4396543161
1988	3655.92	164275	2.225487749	0.4493397011
1989	4323.97	193493	2.234690661	0.4474892286
1990	4961.97	230950	2.148504005	0.4654401377
1991	5786.67	265828	2.176847435	0.4593799197
1992	6637.98	317049	2.093676372	0.4776287365
1993	7629	364016	2.095786998	0.4771477258
1994	8792.75	431084	2.039683681	0.4902720992
1995	10325.07	527596	1.957003086	0.5109853977
1996	12132.41	599191	2.024798437	0.4938763197
1997	14061.95	696012	2.020360281	0.4949612252
1998	15591.89	821332	1.898366312	0.526768724
1999	17884.1	980960	1.823122248	0.54850957
2000	20076.99	1124174	1.785932605	0.5599315435
2001	21546.8	1313220	1.640760878	0.6094733325
2002	23357.77	1498355	1.558894254	0.6414803297
2003	25196.37	1717960	1.466644741	0.6818283745
2004	28207.95	2005676	1.406406119	0.7110321736
2005	32198.34	2245677	1.433792126	0.6974511729
2006	36672.53	2719519	1.348493245	0.7415684165
2007	42614.72	3310068	1.287427328	0.7767428719
2008	49665.78	4017882	1.236118433	0.8089839725
2009	55971.4	4794812	1.167332525	0.856653934
2010	64398.27	5602731	1.149408565	0.8700126572
2011	77023.08	6564116	1.173396083	0.8522271506
2012	89328.92	7384831	1.20962714	0.8267010281
2013	99965.15	8389190	1.191594779	0.8392114652
2014	111919.63	9497326	1.178433066	0.8485844708

Source: rbi.org.in, and calculation by author.

Behaviour of V & k in the Indian Economy (1955-2014)

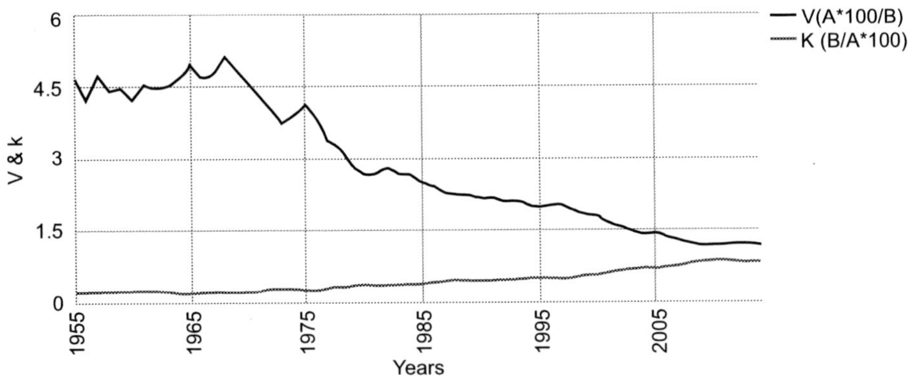

SUMMARY

1. The theory of demand for money has been extended in, at least, three ways during post-Keynesian era:
   (a) in terms of interest elasticity of the transaction demand
   (b) in terms of portfolio balance analysis of money vis-a-vis bonds or assets, and
   (c) in terms of reformulation of the old classical quantity theory of money.
2. Baumol and Tobin together have dealt with the first category of extension. Specifically, Baumol looked upon the transaction demand very similar to the business firms' inventory analysis of maintaining an optimum inventory (of raw materials and finished goods) to tackle the short run fluctuations of demand. The precise argument of Baumol was that there is no point in holding idle money for transaction purposes particularly when opportunities for earning interest income are available. It is advantageous to invest the idle money in secutiries and thereby earn income though the firm can subsequently resort to periodic withdrawal of such securities.
3. Calculating the total cost of such operations – oppotunity cost of interest forgone and costs involved in the process of investment and withdrawals and then minimizing the total cost gives the final result of minimum inventory cost of money holding. This result proves that the transaction demand for money is inversely related to the rate of interest. At the same time economies of scale is quite visible in this operation suggesting that as the volume of transactions in money is large, the cost per unit decreases.
4. Tobin, in his portfolio balance analysis, invokes the decision theory under risk for a rational asset holder who is generally a risk-averter.

The analysis is carried out in the EMV-variance framework. An EMV (or, expected monetary value) and variance (an index of risk) frontier relates the expected return from bonds and their respective risk-levels which behaves like an indifference curve of the consumer's behaviour theory. By establishing the asset-holder's equilibrium position in terms of tangency between EMV frontier and his constraint level, the author derives an optimum combination of assets (money and bonds).

5. Tobin's analysis also reveals that the optimum combination might change due to change in the rate of interest. A higher rate of interest, for instance, induces the asset holder to keep a larger proportion of bonds, although at a higher level of risk.
6. In the present-day scenario, there are a number of alternative assets, besides bonds, which have different levels of risks and returns. A risk-adverse asset holder would, therefore, weigh the different combinations of risks and associated returns from these alternative assets to arrive at final decision.

   A risk-taker, however, might behave differently and prefer to gamble and go for greater risks along with larger returns.
7. Milton Friedman, breaking away from Keynesian tradition, tries to reformulate classical Quantity Theory of Money but restates that quantity theory is a theory of demand for money and not of output, money income or prices. Money is just one of several types of assets which depends upon several rates of return on these assets as also other factors. Income, according to Friedman, is viewed in terms of permanent income which is the weighted average of past and future stream of income taken at their present discounted value.
8. There are different rates of return attached to different alternative assets such as bonds, equities, physical goods, ratio of human and non-human wealth, etc., which the asset holder keeps in mind while expressing demand for money in real terms.
9. Friedman's demand for money function has been criticized by several economists on grounds of practical applicability and on measurement of variables. In the final analysis, therefore, Friedman's demand for money has been found to be no different from Keynes'.
10. Several researchers have attempted to empirically verify the Friedman's theory by relating the demand for money with the money income for a relatively longer period of time. The findings generally have close correspondence between demand for money and money income and suggesting constant velocity of money.
11. The classical monetary theory views the demand for money as arising from the transaction purposes only which involve purchase-sale of all kinds of goods and services in the economy. This means that money

has the main role to play, that of medium of exchange in society as well as the unit of account. As such it depends on the level of income, be it individual income or business income. This implies that, at the national level, demand for money depends on the national income.

12. The Keynesian theory of the demand for money, on the other hand, is a more broad based one and includes in the list three principal motives out of which money is demanded by the community. These motives are transaction, precautionary and speculative motives, the last two are new additions.
13. The first motive is the same as that of classical theory. The precautionary demand is that which arises due to various emergency needs of the individuals or the businesses. The speculative motive is, in fact, special to Keynesian theory in as much as it arises out of the desire to speculate, to earn an income by investing in bonds or equities, an attempt to read ahead of the market about financial investment.
14. The speculative demand for money is responsive to the rate of interest, the return to the bond holders who desire to obtain speculative gain. However, this demand is inversely related to the rate of interest, while the transaction demand is directly related to the level of income.

EXERCISE

1. A business firm has an inflow of income at the rate of ₹ 60 lakh per annum. It's estimated expenditure pattern is ₹ 5 lakh per month. If it wishes to keep two months' expenditure at the beginning of the year and invests the rest amount in securities to withdraw ₹ 5 lakh every month thereafter, calculate the total costs of the firm of keeping the initial cash balance if the rate of interest is 10% and if the transaction costs on securities dealings are as follows:
   (a) ₹ 100 is fixed cost
   (b) 2% of the volume of transaction (either investment or withdrawal) is the variable cost
2. In problem (1), if the rate of interest is 6%, recalculate the total cost. Separately calculate the opportunity cost of holding the initial cash balance of ₹ 10 lakh and ₹ 20 lakh at 5% and 6% rates of interest.
3. How is riskiness measures? Examine the relationship between risk and expected return of an asset holder.
4. Explain the behaviour of risk-averse asset holder and examine the impact of a fall in the rate of interest.
5. How did Milton Friedman differ from J.M. Keynes in reformulating his demand function of money?
6. Explain Friedman's notion of permanent income.

7. Distinguish between 'transaction velocity' and 'income velocity' of money. What are the main determinants of velocity of money circulation in the society?
8. In the classical quantity theory of money, why are T and V independent of M?
9. Derive the demand function for money from the quantity theory (income version) of money. Distinguish between 'nominal' and 'real' demand for money and show the factors determining the 'real' demand for money.
10. Distinguish between 'income elasticity' and 'interest elasticity' of the demand for money.
11. Rate of interest and price of 'bond' are inversely related, prove this inverse relationship with illustration.

REFERENCES

1. Mankiw, Gregory, N. (2006), Macroeconomics, 6th Edition, Worth Publishers.
2. Mankiw, Gregory, N. (2012), Principles of Macroeconomics, 6th Edition, South Western Cengage Learning.
3. Crouch, R.L. (1972): Macroeconomics: Harcourt Brace Jovanovich, 1972.
4. Ackley, G. (1978): Macroeconomics: Theory and Policy, Macmillan.
5. Baumol, W.J. (1971): Economic Theory and Operations Analysis, Prentice Hall.
6. Bhaduri, A., (1990): Macroeconomics, Macmillan India.
7. Friedman, M. (1956): The Quantity Theory of Money: A Restatement in 'Studies in Quantity Theory of Money', Chicago University.

PART-4

Integration of Product and Money Markets

8

The IS-LM Model

The present chapter aims to provide a post-Keynesian macro model, known as *IS-LM* model. Here, *IS* stands for investment-savings while *LM* stands for liquidity-money supply (liquidity signifies demand for money, to be symbolised as L). A little pondering will suggest that the model deals with goods market and money market equilibrium simultaneously. As we know from previous chapters, the goods market attains equilibrium when the total demand for goods is exactly equal to the total supply of goods. Viewed from another angle, when total savings are equal to total investment ($I = S$), the goods market is said to be in equilibrium. Similarly, the money market attains its equilibrium when total demand for money is equal to the total supply of money ($L = M$). Thus, *IS-LM* model is a model of simultaneous equilibrium of both the goods market and the money market. In a sense, the model is an integration between classical and Keynesian theories of income and interest rate determination. This integration (or, synthesis) was first attempted by famous British economist (and Nobel laureate) Sir J.R. Hicks[1] and later popularised by American economist, A.H. Hansen[2].

One of the basic differences between classical and Keynesian theories is that while the classical economists thought that savings and investment are determined by the rate of interest in the economy, the Keynesian view is that income is the main determinant of savings and investment in the economy. Integration attempt of these two approaches began with the idea that there can be different combinations of interest rates and income levels at which the savings will be equal to investment (or, the goods market will be in equilibrium). Similarly, in the money (or, asset) market, while classical monetary theory asserts that income determines the demand for money, the Keynesian theory stresses that income and the rate of interest together determine the demand for money while

1 J.R. Hicks "Mr. Keynes and the classics: A suggested Interpretation," (1937), In: E. Shapiro (ed.), Selected Readings in Macroeconomics, Harcourt Brace Jovanovitch, 1970.

2 A.H. Hansen, Monetary Theory and Fiscal Policy, McGraw Hill, 1949.

the supply of money is exogenously fixed. An integration attempt of the classical and Keynesian monetary theories would, thus, suggest that there can be different combinations of interest rates and income levels at which the money market (or, asset market) will be in equilibrium. Thus, interest rate and income appear as common elements in both the goods market as well as money market.

In fact, when the classical economists say that savings and investment are determined by the rate of interest, they assume that the level of income is fixed at some level, presumably at full employment level. Similarly, when Keynes says that savings and investment are determined by the level of income, he presumably holds that the interest rate is fixed at some level. Thus, whereas in the classical scheme, the level of income can be taken as a 'parameter', in the Keynesian scheme, interest rate can be taken as a 'parameter'.

Before we proceed towards understanding the basics of the *IS-LM* model, we assume that the price level is constant. This refers to the first sub-model of our model-building part of the introductory chapter of the book where we have assumed the "short run" model of Keynesian variety with the aggregate supply curve being horizontal where the suppliers are willing to supply any amount of output at the given price level in accordance with the quantities of aggregate demand.

8.1 THE DERIVATION OF *IS-LM* CURVES AND EQUATIONS

While deriving the *IS* curve or equation, one can proceed either from classical position or from Keynesian position and include respective elements of the other in each of them.

An *IS* curve is defined as all such combinations of interest rates and real income levels at which the goods market is in equilibrium. Taking interest rate on the Y-axis and real income on the X-axis, the *IS* curve appears as a downward sloping curve from left to right.

Combining the classical and Keynesian views, thus gives us:

$I = f(r, Y)$, with $I'(r) < 0$ and $I'(Y) > 0$ and $S'(r) > 0$ and $S'(Y) > 0$.

In simple words, these expressions mean that investment is a decreasing function of the rate of interest but an increasing function of the level of real income. Similarly, the savings are an increasing function of both the rate of interest and the level of income. In order to draw relevant graphs, we can assume the level of income (Y) as a parameter and draw the I and S curves as shown in Fig. 8.1 (a).

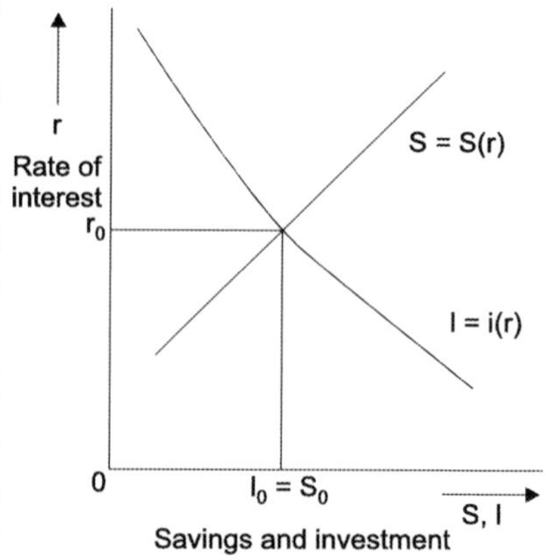

(a)

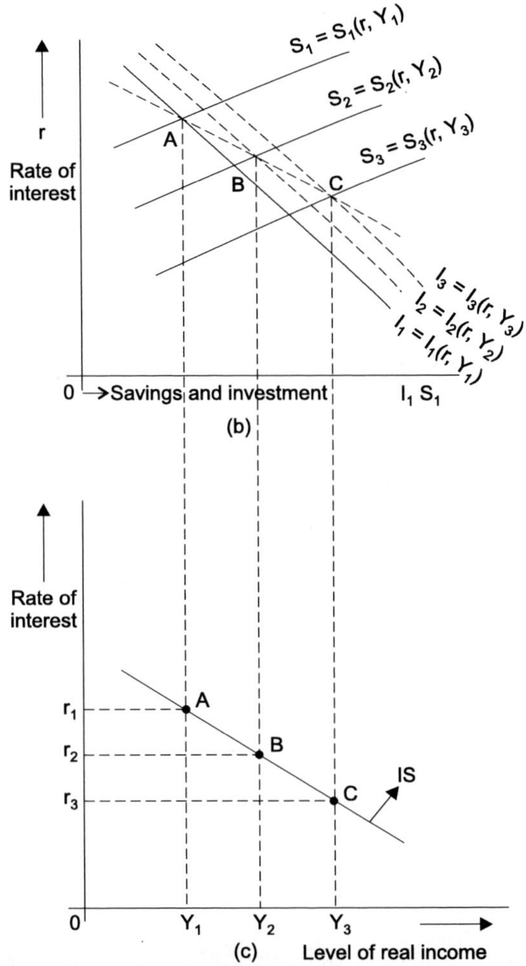

Figure 8.1 *The IS curve.*

Another graphical method of deriving the *IS* curve is to use the classical *I*-curve which is a decreasing function of the rate of interest – as rate of interest falls, the volume of investment rises – and includes this relation in the Keynesian aggregate demand function taking interest rate as a parameter. Thus, at one rate of interest, there will be a certain amount of investment. At another rate of interest (if it is lower) there will be a higher level of investment and so on. The higher level of investment, when added to the aggregate demand curve will raise the planned expenditures which will lead to higher real income. Hence, a relationship seems to exist between the rate of interest and the level of aggregate income (a negative relationship indeed) which is shown in Fig. 8.2 with *I*-curve and Keynesian aggregate demand curve.

The advantage with this method of deriving the *IS* curve is that we can now include the role of government and thus handle fiscal policy variables like government expenditures and taxation along with other 'autonomous' factors which play important parts in the equilibrium process of the goods market.

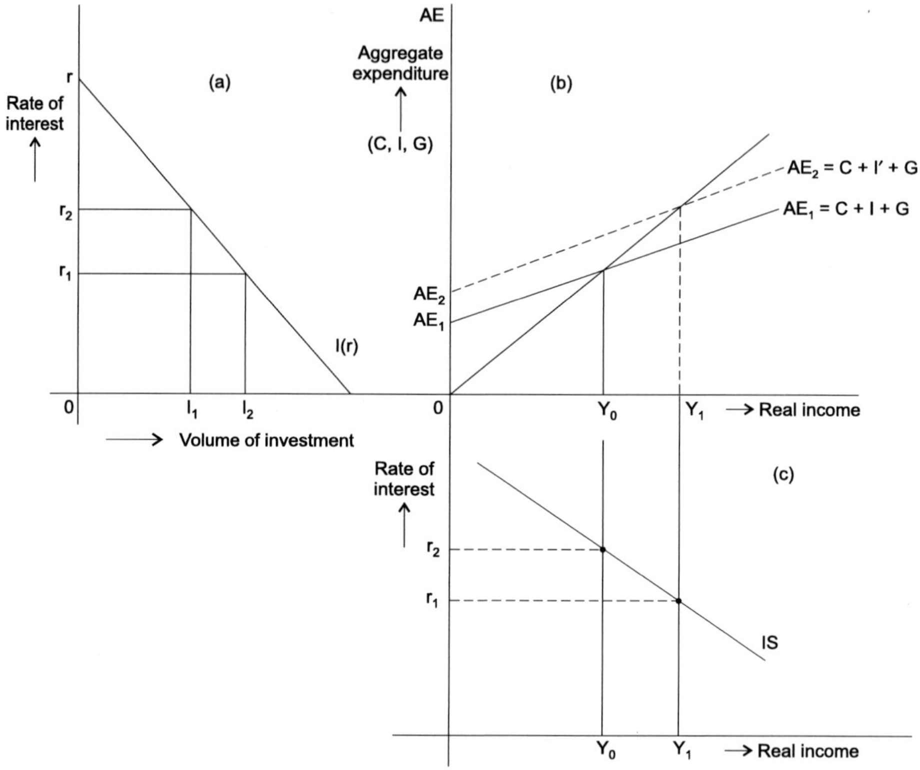

Figure 8.2 *Rise in aggregate demand due to fall in interest rate which raises the volume of investment.*

8.2 DERIVATION OF *LM* CURVE

An *LM* curve is defined as the locus of all such points where the money market is in equilibrium, that is, the demand for money is equal to the supply of money. The real demand for money, (Md/P) as in the classical model, is a function of the level of real aggregate income, Y, (transaction demand for money), while in the Keynesian theory, it is a function of both the level of real income and the rate of interest. Demand for money rises with the rise in the level of real income (transaction demand) but falls with the rise in the rate of interest (speculative demand). On the other hand, the supply of money is determined independently (or, exogenously) by the monetary authority, that is, the central bank of the country. At a certain point in time, the supply of money is, therefore, fixed at a certain level.

We draw the two curves–demand for money, L, and the supply of money, Ms, in [Fig. 8.3(a)] based on a certain level of income, Y_1. The two curves intersect at point F-1 showing money market equilibrium at an income level OY_1 and interest rate of Or_1. Hence, the demand function of money, L_1, is labelled L_1, Y_1. Now, if we take another level of income, say Y_2 ($Y_2 > Y_1$), this will shift the L function upward to the right (since, at a higher level of income, demand for money is also higher). With the vertical (fixed) supply curve of money, a new equilibrium point is established at F_2 where we have a higher rate of interest at Or_2. The pairs of interest rates and levels of income can now be isolated and taken to another figure shown below in Fig. 8.3(b) which shows an upward rising curve of different combinations of rate of interest and the levels of real income, to be known as LM curve.

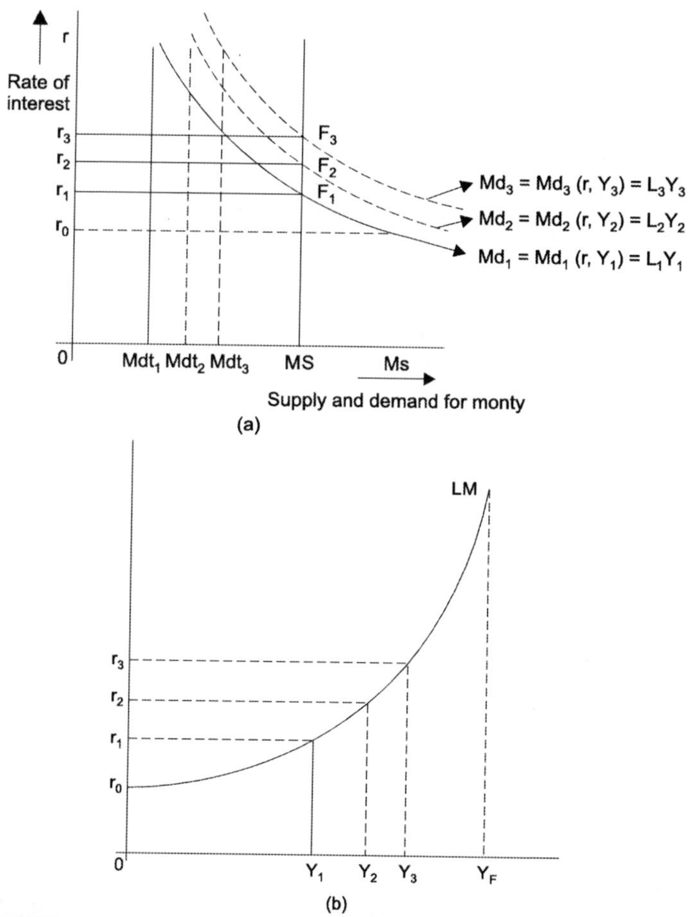

Figure 8.3 *Derivation of LM curve.*

Slope and position of the *IS* curve: The slope of the *IS* curve depends on the sensitivity of the investment curve or function to the interest rate. If the *I* curve is very sensitive to interest rate, that is, even a small change in the interest rate causes large change in the volume of investment, the *IS* curve will be relatively flat which will mean a small change in the rate of interest will bring about relatively large change in the level of income. On the other hand, if the investment function is less sensitive to the interest rate, so that even a large change in the rate of interest brings about very small change in the volume of investment, the *IS* curve will be relatively steep or, the slope of the curve will increase. Figures (8.4 and 8.5) illustrate these two cases. In extreme case, the *IS* curve takes horizontal shape if the *I* curve is highly sensitive to the interest rate. Similarly, if the *I* curve is completely insensitive to interest rate, *IS* curve becomes vertical in shape. In general, we can say, that the slope of the *IS* curve gradually decreases from left to right or, the curve rotates anticlockwise.

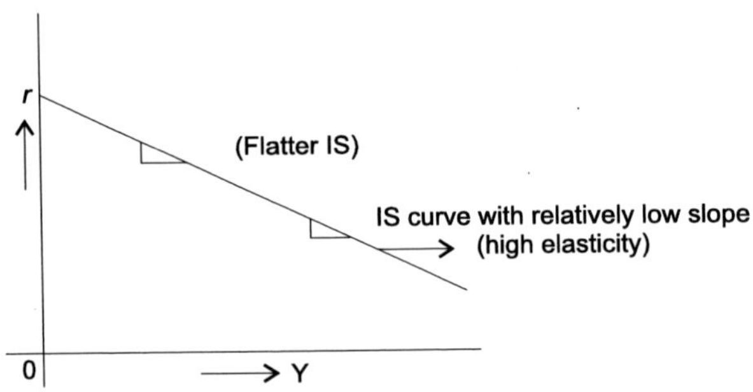

Figure 8.4 *IS curve relatively flat.*

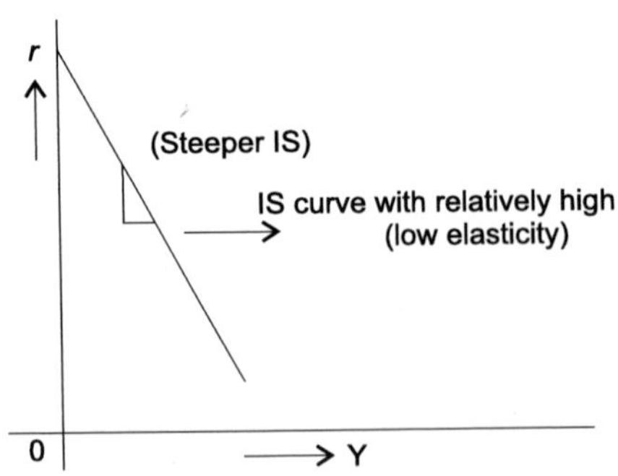

Figure 8.5 *IS curve relatively steep.*

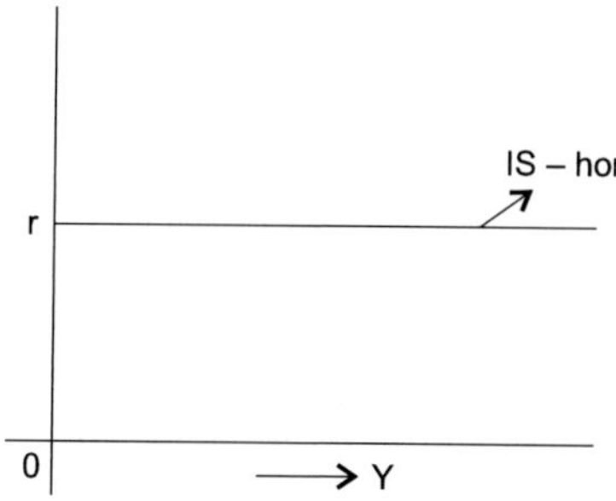

Figure 8.6(a) *IS curve — horizontal.*

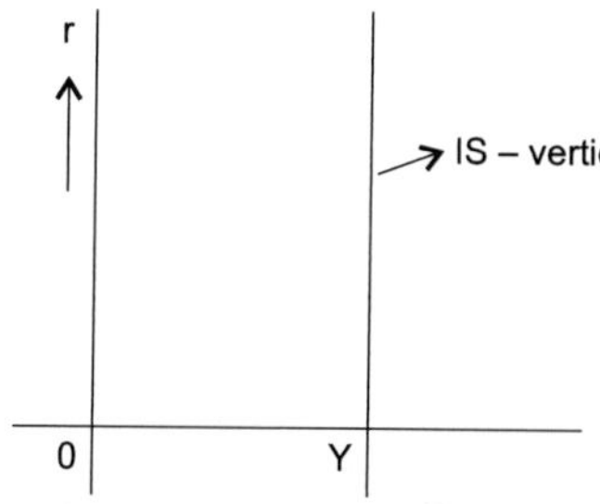

Figure 8.6(b) *IS curves - vertical.*

As far as the position of the *IS* curve is concerned, it depends on the size of the intercept of the *IS* curve. All the autonomous components such as autonomous consumption, autonomous investment and autonomous tax functions and the size of government expenditures together compose the intercept term. In the mathematical derivation section below, these autonomous components have been denoted by b_0, i_0, t_0 and G. Any change in the value or values of these components will be reflected in the shifting of the *IS* curve either to the right or to the left as the case may be. For instance, if there is increase in the autonomous consumption (that is, consumption expenditures unrelated to the level of income, for instance, consumers become less thrifty in habit, or, they have certain special items of expenditures which they have to incur even by borrowing from friends or relatives), the value of the intercept term b_0 will be higher so that there will be a rise in aggregate expenditures as also the level of equilibrium income and so the *IS* curve will shift to the right. Similarly, if autonomous investment, i_0, increases, the aggregate demand will increase and so will aggregate income which will be reflected in the shifting of *IS* curve to the right. It may be recalled here that we have assumed a certain level of entrepreneurial expectations about the investment curve which is normally downward sloping. Now, if there is a rise in the entrepreneurial expectations, the investment curve will shift to the right, given the rate of interest, thus shifting the *IS* curve to the right. In the opposite case, that is, if entrepreneurial expectations are subdued, investors are not sufficiently enthusiastic (lack of "animal spirit"), the *I* curve, and hence the *IS* curve shifts to the left. Rise in government expenditures will have the impact of shifting to the right of the *IS* curve. Only in case of t_0, the autonomous part of tax function, the reaction will be the opposite, that is, a rise in this component will mean shifting leftward of the *IS* curve and a fall in this component (or, a fall in the average tax rate) will be reflected in the shifting rightward of the *IS* curve. Figure 8.7 shows how the position of the *IS* curve gets shifted as a result of changes in the intercept term.

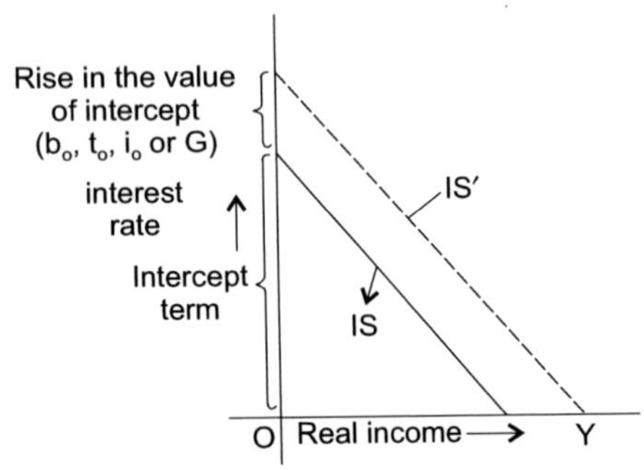

Figure 8.7 *Shifting of IS curve due to change in intercept term.*

Slope and position of the *LM* curve: As we know, *LM* curve generally slopes upward from left to right. Its slope depends on the interest rate sensitivity of the demand for money function. If the function is highly sensitive to the rate of interest, the function, or the relevant *L* curve is flatter. It becomes perfectly elastic or horizontal in shape if the demand for money is extremely sensitive to the rate of interest. In such a case, the *LM* curve also becomes perfectly elastic or horizontal in shape. On the other hand, if the demand for money is relatively insensitive to interest rate, the *LM* curve is relatively steep. In the extreme case, if demand for money is totally insensitive to interest rate, so that even a large change in the interest rate fails to bring about any change in the demand for money, the *L* curve, and hence, the *LM* curve will be completely inelastic or vertical in shape. We can say that in this case, demand for money is influenced only by the level of income.

The position of the *LM* curve depends on the intercept coefficient. In the next section on mathematical derivation of *LM* curve, we have derived the intercept term as $(m_0 - Ms)/m_1$. Since, the *LM* curve is normally upward sloping, an increase in the intercept coefficient will mean *LM* curve shifts to the left. Similarly, a decrease in the intercept term will mean that the *LM* curve shifts to the right. Now, in the intercept term, *Ms* stands for the supply of money. Thus, if the supply of money increases, m_0 and m_1 being constant, the value of the intercept term decreases. This means that the *LM* curve shifts to the right downwards. On the other hand, if m_1 increases, the intercept value decreases which implies that the *LM* curve shifts to the right. However, if m_0 increases, the intercept increases which means that the *LM* curve shifts to the left upward.

The implication of m_0 being higher is that the liquidity preference in general rises, people prefer to hold more money than other assets, thus demand for money goes up. This means the *LM* curve would shift to the left. The opposite will be the case if m_0 is lower. Since m_1 symbolises demand for money in response to the level of income, a rise in the value of m_1 also means a rise in the demand for money but it may suggest a shift away from speculative demand to transaction demand for money. (Figs. 8.8 &. 8.9 illustrate these cases.)

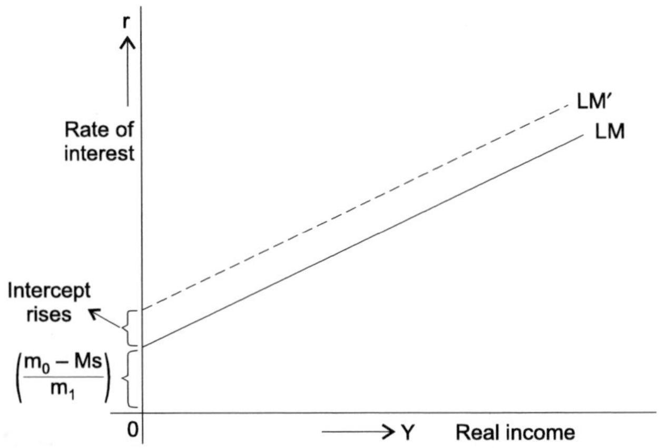

Figure 8.8 *Liquidity preference of the people rises: Intercept term rises (LM shifts upward to the left).*

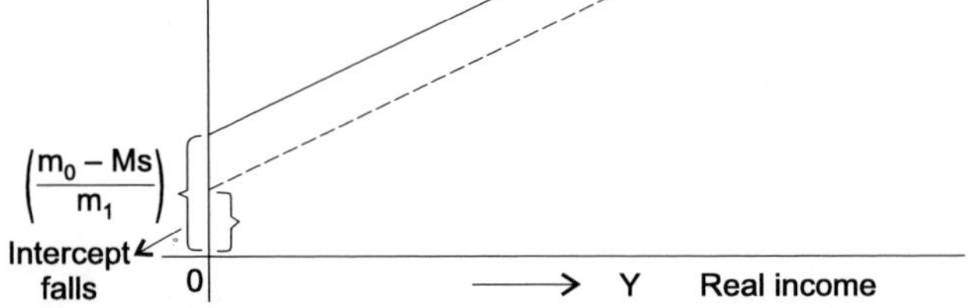

Figure 8.9 *Liquidity preference of the people falls: Intercept term falls.*

The liquidity trap and the *LM* curve: In chapter 7, we have dealt with Keynesian theory of demand for money in which context we have come across the concept of liquidity trap. Liquidity trap is an exceptional situation when the demand for money becomes infinitely large at a very low rate of interest as perceived by the investors so that the demand for money curve becomes horizontal or perfectly elastic. In fact, under such circumstances, people would prefer to keep money in cash (the most liquid form) rather than investing it. Corresponding to this situation, the *LM* curve too has a completely flat stretch at a very low rate of interest (horizontal). Thus, economists often use such a case along with its normal behaviour showing upward rising part leading up to the vertical portion as well and divide the whole curve into three segments as shown in Fig. (8.10).

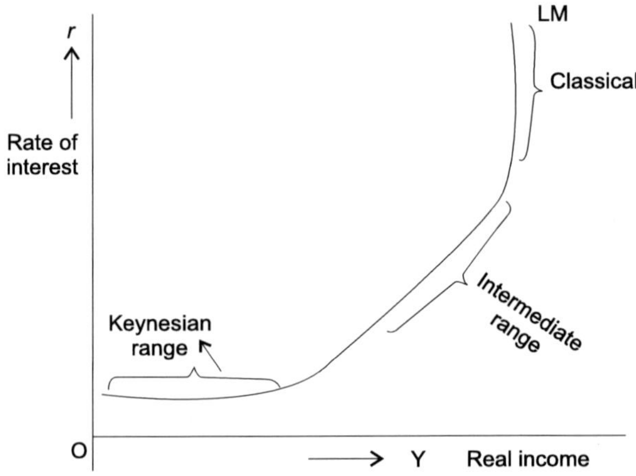

Figure 8.10 *Keynesian, intermediate and classical ranges of LM curve.*

Thus, the beginning part is described as the "Keynesian" range of the *LM* curve, while the next range is called the " intermediate " range followed by the "classical" range. It may be mentioned that Keynes specifically emphasised upon the liquidity trap as a case characteristic of the depression economy of 1929-30. However, it needs to be remembered that liquidity trap type of situations have been revisiting from time to time in advanced economies since then, the recent one occurring in 2008-09 in the US in the shape of what is described as 'great recession'. In European Union and Japan also,'liquidity trap' kind of situation prevails even to this date (see chapter 15 on Growth).

However, we may conclude that liquidity trap is not a normal phenomenon but a special case in the money and asset market.

8.3 SIMULTANEOUS EQUILIBRIUM OF THE GOODS AND THE MONEY MARKET (IS AND LM CURVES)

We are now in a position to bring together the conditions of equilibrium of the goods market as well as money market and find out how simultaneous equilibrium position is attained in both these markets. Figure (8.11) illustrates this position with *IS* and *LM* curves intersecting each other at point E_1 which, in turn, defines the corresponding equilibrium levels of income and the interest rates of OY_1 and Or_1 respectively. Thus, at point E_1, both the money and goods markets are simultaneously in equilibrium. All other points which are lying away from the equilibrium point, therefore, indicate disequilibrium situations of the economy where either goods market or the money market or both do not reach equilibrium. For instance, all points lying either to the left or to the right of *IS* curve show disequilibrium situations in the goods market while those lying to either left or right of the *LM* curve indicates disequilibrium in the money market. Let us now examine what kind of disequilibrium do these points suggest.

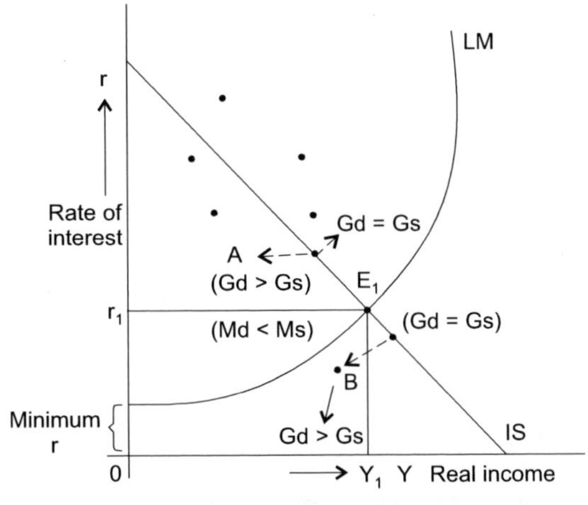

Figure 8.11 *Simultaneous equilibrium in the goods and money market (E_1) and points away from equilibrium (A,B).*

We have located at least two points to the left of the *IS* curve, *A* and *B*, each of which is characterised by excess demand for goods ($Gd > Gs$). This can be verified by simply referring these points to any corresponding point/points on the *IS* curve where $Gd = Gs$, that is, goods market is in equilibrium. One can argue then that if a point on the curve shows $Gd = Gs$, at a certain rate of interest, then, at the same rate of interest, a point lying to the left of the equilibrium point would naturally show less amount of supply of goods or real income. Hence, at point *B*, aggregate supply of goods will be less than aggregate demand for goods. Similarly, comparing point *A* with the one that touches the *IS* curve as shown by the vertical line, one can find that while the goods market clears at a higher interest rate (on the *IS* curve), at a lower point, with lower interest rate, demand for goods must be higher than the supply of goods.

On the other hand, points located to the right side of the *IS* curve, suggest supply of goods being higher than the demand. By similarly referring these points to those lying on the *IS* curve, we can verify these conclusions as shown in Fig. 8.11.

Now we can take the *LM* curve and do the same type of exercise as in the case of *IS* curve. Thus, as shown in Fig. (8.12), points lying to the left of the *LM* curve (D) indicate excess supply of money (total supply of money is greater than total demand for money) while points located on the right of *LM* curve suggest excess demand for money (C). We can verify these conclusions as follows.

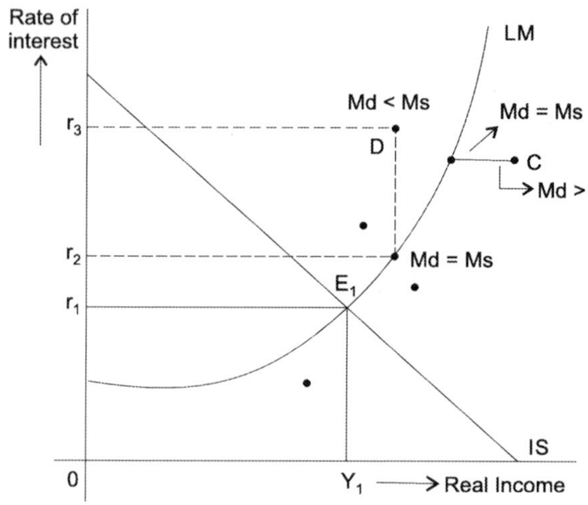

Figure 8.12 *Points away from LM cure (C, D).*

Let us consider point (*D*) which lies to the left of the *LM* curve. Comparing this point with one downwards on the *LM* curve which shows clearing the money market (demand for money = supply of money), it becomes clear that if the money market clears at a lower interest rate, it certainly cannot clear at a higher interest rate at point (*D*) since, demand for money will be less at a higher interest rate. Therefore, supply of money will be greater than the demand for it. Let us now take a point lying to the right of the *LM* curve such as *C*. This point is characterised by excess demand for money (*Md* > *Ms*). To verify this, we compare this point with one that lying just on the *LM* curve by drawing a horizontal line from point *C*. Since, money market is in equilibrium on the curve with a lower level of income, a point giving a higher level of income as on *C* will result in higher demand for money. Therefore, at *C* demand for money is higher than the supply. To generalise, therefore, we can say that all points away from the equilibrium points either on the *IS* or the *LM* curve are disequilibrium situations such that, points to the left of *IS* curve are characterised by excess demand for goods but excess supply of money. Similarly, all points to the right of *IS* curve indicate excess supply of goods but excess demand for money. In Fig. (8.13), we have tried to distinguish four segments along with their characteristics as far as the money and goods market are concerned.

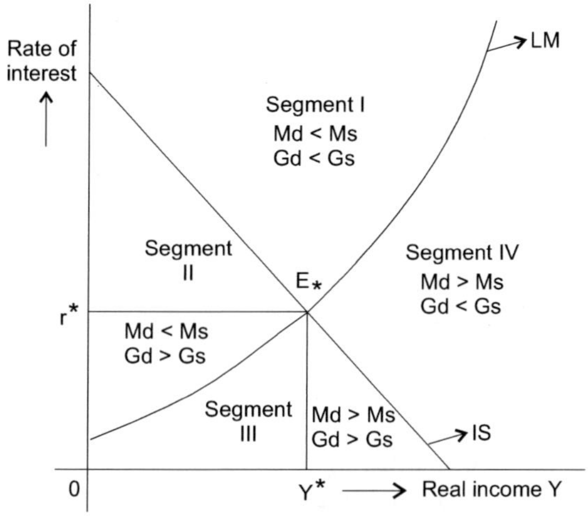

Figure 8.13 *Four segments of IS–LM system with characteristics of money and goods markets.*

Dynamics of IS-LM model: We can now attempt a simple dynamics of *IS LM* model in terms of the possible course or path that the economy might follow from an initial position of disequilibrium.

Figure 8.14 illustrates this simple dynamic. Earlier, we have explained that the actual situation in the economy at a particular point in time will, most likely, be that of disequilibrium, occurring either in the goods market or money market or both. The adjustment process in either of the two markets involves time lags although it is argued that the process of adjustment takes relatively less time in the money market. We shall maintain, however, that the actual time lag in the money market depends on several factors particularly, the extent of development of the money market and the soundness of the transmission mechanism of the monetary policy. Dealing with the dynamic aspect of the *IS-LM* system is certainly a complex issue that involves dynamic models. But we shall simply illustrate here the underlying factors that drive the disequilibrium position towards the equilibrium one. In Fig. 8.14, we reproduce the same *IS-LM* curves with four different disequilibrium positions, *A*, *B*, *C* and *D*. Starting from point *A*, where the rate of interest is higher as compared to one that clears the money market, there will be a force operating in the economy driving down the rate of interest so that point *A* could reach some point on the *LM* curve (shown in arrow). This will be due to the existence of excess supply of money in the money market. At the same time, another force will be in operation due to the existence of excess demand in the goods market. Thus, simultaneously, two forces will be in operation, one vertical and the other horizontal as have been shown by arrows. It will, eventually, take a path in between the two arrows and reach some point on the *LM* curve. However, so long as the goods market is not in equilibrium, the aggregate supply of goods will continue to expand so that it reaches the overall equilibrium point, *E*. Other disequilibrium points and their suggested movements are shown on different points of the Fig. 8.14.

We have explained above that the actual situation in the economy at a particular point in time will, most likely, be that of disequilibrium, occurring either in the commodity market or money market or both. It is important, therefore, to understand the 'dynamics' or the time-path through which the economy attains its equilibrium again. The adjustment process in either of the two markets involves time-lags although it is argued that the adjustment takes a relatively less time-lag in money market. We shall maintain, however, that the actual time-lags in the money market depends upon several factors – particularly how developed the money market is and what is the 'transmission mechanism'.

Dealing with the dynamic aspect of *IS-LM* system certainly is complex and involves dynamic models. But, we shall simply illustrate here the underlying factors that drive the disequilibrium position towards equilibrium one. In Fig. 8.14, we reproduce the same *IS-LM* curves with four disequilibrium points – *A*, *B*, *C* and *D*. Starting from *A*, where rate of interest is higher as compared to one which clears the money market, there will be a force operating in the economy driving down the rate of interest so that point *A* could reach a point on LM curve.

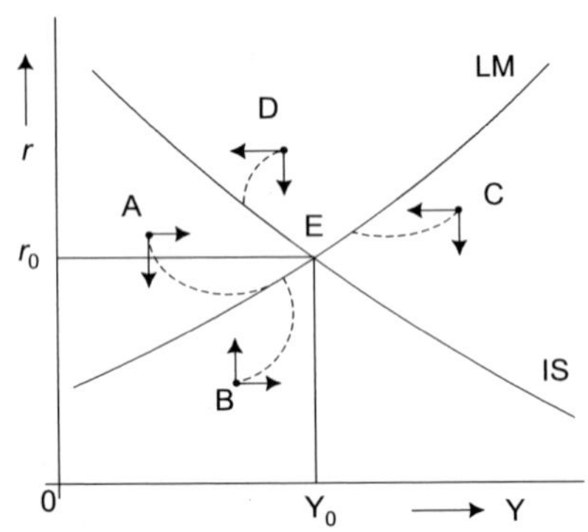

Figure 8.14 *Dynamics of IS-LM model.*

This will be due to the existence of excess aggregate demand in the commodity market as also excess supply of money. Therefore, simultaneously, two forces will be in operation – one vertical and the other horizontal as shown by the arrows. It may, eventually, take a path in between the arrows and reach some point on LM curve. However, so long as commodity market is not in equilibrium, the aggregate supply of commodities will continue to expand so that it reaches the overall equilibrium point *E*. Other disequilibrium points and their suggested movements are shown in the similar patterns.

8.4 THE IS-LM MODEL AND THE EFFICACY OF MONETARY – FISCAL POLICIES

The *IS-LM* model has proved to be an important and effective tool to apply monetary and fiscal policies for macroeconomic management. The model ruled for over four decades and represented broadly the Keynesian tool of management. Let us examine how the twin policies can be applied in different macroeconomic situations of the economy to bring about desired results.

Monetary policy refers to the central bank's policy of manipulating interest rate and money supply through the entire banking and financial sector. On the other hand, fiscal policy refers broadly to the expenditure and taxation policies of the government implemented mainly through government budgets and other related documents.

While analyzing the impact of monetary – fiscal policies, we shall first use the *IS-LM* framework in the context of certain limiting cases such as a situation of 'depression' or 'extreme recession' or of high inflation and full employment and real GNP. Figure 8.15(a) gives a picture of the economy undergoing depressionary condition. This is reflected in the LM curve which has a horizontal stretch in the beginning, showing 'liquidity trap' at Or_0 rate of interest. Lack of sufficient aggregate demand has led to a situation where investors' confidence has sunk so low that monetary demand has also come down to a level that even very low rate of interest has not been able to spur investment activities. The economy is in equilibrium (IS = LM) at Or_0 rate of interest and OY_1 level of income. Now let us see if further monetary policy stimulation would be of any use in raising the level of aggregate demand. Any attempt in this direction – by releasing more money supply in the economy will result simply in shifting the LM curve to the right as shown by the new dashed part of the LM curve – LM′. But the economy still operates at the old level of income. In fact, the extra money supply leads to the rise in 'idle balance' – people not willing to spend it. If, however, the IS curve is made to shift to the right – by increasing government expenditure ($\overline{G}$) or providing other 'fiscal stimulus' – as shown by IS′ curve, the level of income can be raised. This means, in this type of situation, only fiscal policy works and monetary policy is totally ineffective.

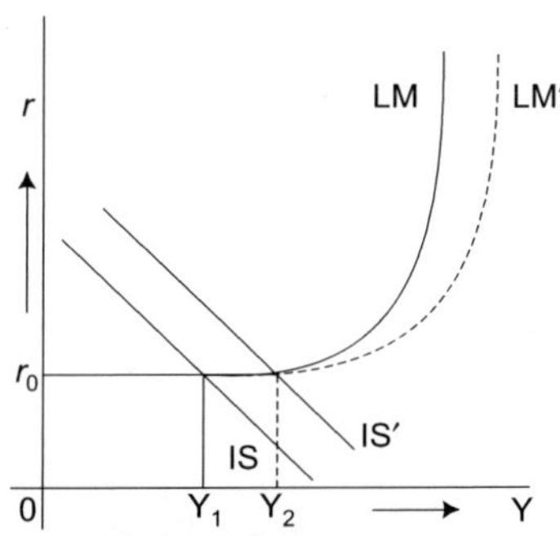

Figure 8.15(a) *LM with liquidity trap.*

One can find evidence in the US economy during the early years of 'great recession' of 2008-2010. The Federal Reserve responded by lowering the rate of interest to near zero which continued for pretty long period of time. Even after three years since recession set in, the Fed. Reserve continued to pursue the low rate regime. Later, several rounds of fiscal stimulus in the shape of stepping up government expenditures on health education and other social sectors followed with only marginal positive results visible in the last quarter of 2011-12 as is evident from reports. The current global recession said to have originated in US, created a situation of 'liquidity trap' in the monetary sector. Evidently, although monetary policy was also vigorously pursued (through two rounds of 'quantitative easing'), fiscal policy was concurrently followed. However, given that US policy makers are more inclined towards using monetary policy as better policy tool to tackle a situation of depression or great recession it must be conceded that Keynesian type of fiscal policy tool has also been revived in this case.

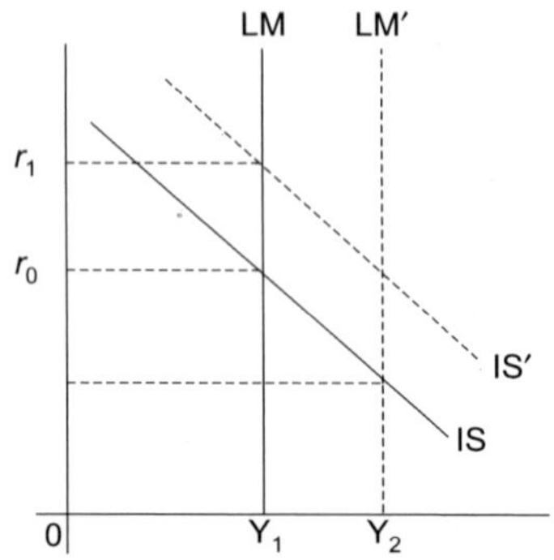

Figure 8.15(b) *The case where LM curve is vertical.*

We now examine other limiting case where LM curve is vertical in shape. Figure 8.15(b) shows this position. We have earlier explained that LM curve being vertical means LM is totally insensitive to interest rate so that whatever be the interest rate, money demand/ supply remains at the same level. In this situation, however, fiscal policy is totally ineffective while monetary policy is all powerful. Figure 8.15(b) illustrates that LM curve is vertical while IS curve has normal shape. Given IS and LM curves, they give equilibrium combination of interest and income levels of Or_0 and OY_1. Any attempt at boosting the economy through fiscal policy – shifting it to IS′ by any fiscal policy instrument raises only the interest rate, from Or_0 to Or_1 without raising the level of income.

On the contrary, if monetary policy is used – by increasing the money supply (and thus making LM curve shift to LM′) the level of income is raised from OY_1 to OY_2 while reducing the rate of interest. There is another extreme case where IS curve takes a vertical shape while LM curve behaves normally as illustrated in Fig. 8.15(c). Since, we have seen that IS curve becomes vertical when it is not sensitive to interest rate, use of fiscal policy by allowing it to shift to IS′ raises the level of income from OY_1 to OY_2 but also rate of interest is raised from Or_0 to Or'. However, at the shifted IS′ curve (as also in IS), the level of Y is independent of interest rate because, whatever be the

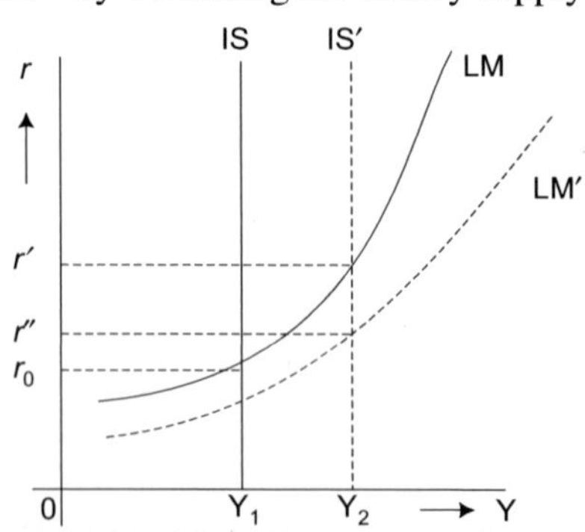

Figure 8.15(c) *The case where IS curve is vertical.*

interest rate Y would not change. Now, here, if monetary policy (expansionary in nature) is also used in conjunction, the result is the reduction in the rate of interest but level of income remains unchanged. The monetary policy works in the money market in the following manner. Without monetary policy, an increase in Y could have resulted in shifting the monetary demand from speculative balance to transaction balance (necessary to maintain the level of increased Y). Hence, there was higher rate of interest. However, since this increase in interest rate does not affect any part of consumption or investment expenditures (IS is insensitive to interest rate) the level of income achieved is not affected. However, with monetary policy and LM curve shifting to the right, the transaction balance could be shifted back (at least to some extent or to full extent) to the speculative balance resulting in lower interest rate.

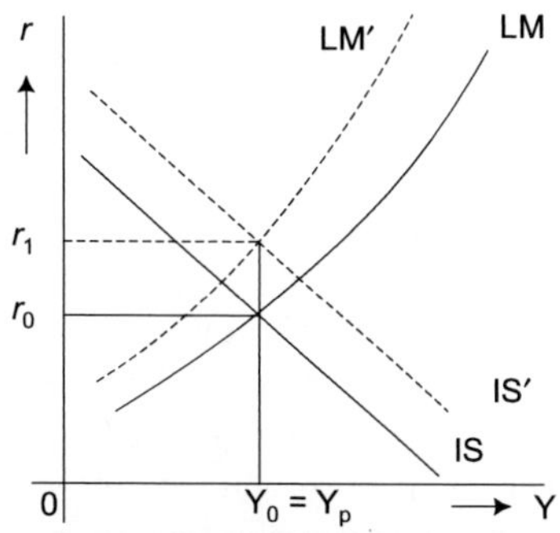

Figure 8.15(d) *The case where IS curve is insensitive to interest rate.*

Thus, in this situation, fiscal policy works in raising the level of income but monetary policy does not.

Just as the use of monetary – fiscal policy was applicable in situations of less than full employment (and less than real potential GNP), it is equally relevant in full or near full employment situation. Figure 8.15(d) illustrates one such situation. The full employment equilibrium is shown at OY_0 (= Y_p) level of income where all productive resources (including labour and capital) are assumed to be employed at their respective factor prices. Now, if an expansionary fiscal policy is applied as shown by shifted IS curve (IS′) total output and hence income is not going to increase. But extra expenditures (on C or I or any part of IS) will push the wage rate, interest rate and other factor prices due to their higher demand. This will ultimately result in leftward shift of the LM curve (LM′) due to rise in interest rate (along with other rates). Thus, the situation of excess demand will be wiped out and the equilibrium level of income will resettle at full employment level (with higher interest rate). Economists often associate such situation with classical full employment situation where any increase in money supply increases the transaction demand for money in the money market but since output is fixed at full employment level, it leads to proportionate increase in price-level. In Fig. 8.15(d) increase in price-level is not shown, but the effect is shown through increase in interest rate.

8.5 THE CROWDING OUT AND THE IS-LM SYSTEM

The concept of 'crowding out' often refers to the situation of a type of competition between the government investment through borrowing of funds from the market and that of the private investment. In a capital market marked by limited investible funds, when both groups of participants (government and private borrowers) compete, the result is the rise in interest rate. This rise in interest rate is described as partly crowding out the private investment. Thus, rise in interest rate over and above the expected level particularly in case of government borrowing, is the symptom which may ultimately adversely affect the output and employment growth. This, rather limited meaning of crowding out is now being increasingly used in broader sense, to cover areas other than the investment activity.

The broader concept of crowding out would generally cover the general shortage of productive resources. Thus, when productive resources are limited, their use by particular user-group in an increasing manner is said to crowd-out other user groups by bidding up their prices. This phenomenon applies to several uses of one particular productive factor such that when one or two uses intensify, other uses are crowded-out.

Using *IS-LM* framework, the phenomenon of crowding-out can be illustrated in the following figure (Fig. 8.16). The original *IS-LM* curves, are shown by heavy lines, with equilibrium rate of interest, r_0 and income level of Y_0. Now, when, due to government's fiscal policy operations, public expenditures, $\overline{G}$ is increased, the IS curve shifts to IS′. Supposing this rise in government investment expenditure is financed by public borrowing from the market where other private investors also draw funds from. This raises the level of income to OY_1 no doubt, but also raises the rate of interest to Or_1. This rise in interest rate discourages some of the private investment, thus preventing a part of income from rising. Hence, it is said that private investment is partially crowded out. Of course, if the central banking authority adopts an accommodative monetary policy simultaneously (which would shift the LM curve to the right) as shown by LM′ curve, and releases equivalent amount of monetary resources, the rate of interest is prevented from rising and it may settle at the old or near old rate (depending upon the size of the monetary release). Not only this, adoption of such simultaneous monetary policy will increase the level of income to still higher level to OY_2, as shown in the Fig. 8.16.

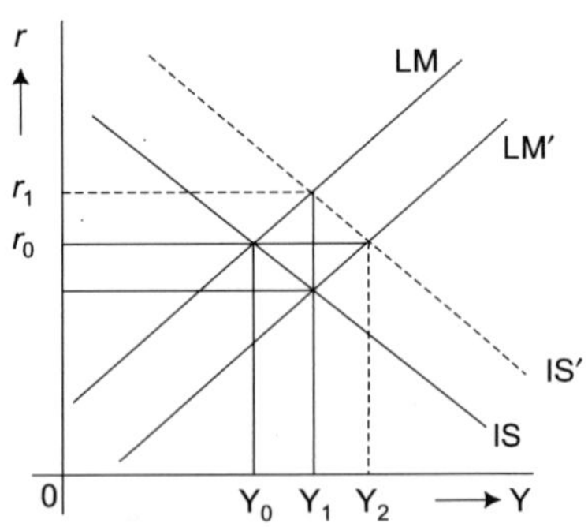

Figure 8.16 *The case of crowding out.*

The crowding-out problem has several instances witnessed in recent years in Indian economy. Being persistently pressed by the burden of increasing fiscal deficit, the government has been stepping up its borrowing programme through sale of government bonds. This naturally shifts away a sizeable portion of lendable funds to the government account and limits its size for private investors, thus pushing up the market rate of interest (or, 'yield rate' on bonds). Such a phenomenon might lead to 'liquidity crunch' in the banking and financial sector and ultimately compel the RBI to meet with such situation. Rising bond yields mean falling prices of bonds. The banking or other financial sectors holding bonds as assets find their asset value depreciate and hence loss in their balance sheets. A recent example of government's, (Govt. of India) programme to meet the fiscal deficit of the 2011-12 budget (which is projected to have increased to 5.5% of GDP from budgeted 4.6% by selling government bonds worth ₹ 40,000 crore in addition to earlier (October) programme by ₹ 52,872 crore. The Indian corporate bond yields rose on "crowding out" fears following the announcement of a $ 2.8 billion unscheduled federal debt sale. The 5-year corporate bond yield rose to 9.49% and 10 year bond to 9.46% – by 8 bsp and 6 bsp respectively. (Mint, Dec. 28th, 2011 and Dec. 31st 2011). Similar situations arise from time to time.

8.6 APPLICATION OF IS-LM MODEL

IS-LM model and the monetary-fiscal policy: We can now handle two of the main macroeconomic policies of the government or the central bank. The first is the fiscal policy and the second is the monetary policy. Further, these policies are of two varieties, expansionary and contractionary. The expansionary fiscal policy refers to increasing the government expenditures on various goods and services with a view to raising the aggregate demand. Another type of expansionary fiscal policy may be to reduce the tax rates of various goods and services. Similarly, expansionary monetary policy means expanding the money supply by the central bank/reduce the short term lending rates. Alternatively, contractionary fiscal or monetary policy means reductions in government expenditures or money supply respectively.

From the above discussion, we conclude that the government's expansionary fiscal policy action has the effect of shifting the *IS* curve to the right while the expansionary monetary policy action of the central bank has the effect of shifting the *LM* curve to the right. The contractionary fiscal or monetary policy has the opposite effect, i.e., the curves shift to the left. We are now concerned with the extent of the shifts of *IS* or *LM* curve due to these policy actions resulting in the net increase in equilibrium income or what may be called fiscal policy multiplier (or, simply fiscal multiplier and monetary policy multiplier or, simply monetary multiplier. (The present author, however, prefers the term monetary policy multiplier simply to avoid the confusion between 'money multiplier' and 'monetary multiplier.' Accordingly, we can define the fiscal policy multiplier as the increase in equilibrium income due to a given increase in any of the fiscal policy variables mentioned above while keeping unchanged the monetary policy variable. In mathematical symbols, we express fiscal policy multiplier as: $\Delta Y/\Delta G$, where, Y and G represent, respectively, the increase in equilibrium income and increase in government expenditures (which is one of the fiscal variables). The other fiscal variable is the reduction in taxes (either on average or marginal tax rates). Similarly, monetary policy multiplier may be defined as the increase in equilibrium income due to a given increase in real money stock while keeping unchanged the fiscal policy variables. In symbol, we express it as $\Delta Y/\Delta(M/P)$, where, (M/P) is the real money stock.

8.6.1 IS-LM Model with Government Sector

Fiscal policy multiplier and the *IS* curve: We would, first, analyse the impact of a given increase in government expenditures on equilibrium income through graphical exposition in terms of *IS-LM* model as shown in Fig. 8.17.

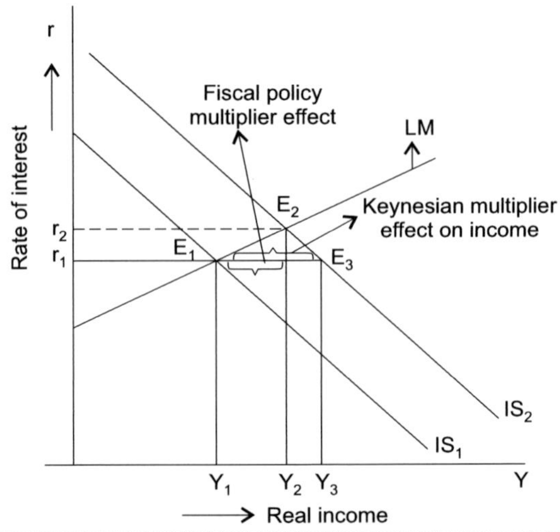

Figure 8.17 *Fiscal policy multiplier.*

The original equilibrium position in the goods as well as money market is attained at point E_1 where both the *IS* and *LM* curves intersect. The corresponding interest rate and income levels are, respectively, Or_1 and OY_1. Supposing now that government expenditures have increased by ₹ 100 crores, i.e., ΔG = ₹100 crores. This leads to the shifting of the *IS* curve to the right parallelly by ΔG. The resulting equilibrium position now is at E_2 giving a new combination of income and interest rates where both the income level and the rate of interest have increased. The effect of this increase in G on income is captured by the coefficient ΔG times the multiplier.

However, this multiplier is relatively less as compared to that of the Keynesian income determination model for, had there been no rise in interest rate, the equilibrium income would have increased to OY_3 (at the old rate of interest of Or_1). But the existence of the upward rising *LM* curve results in a lower level of income at OY_2 instead of OY_3. Had the *LM* curve been horizontal in shape suggesting that money demand is perfectly interest elastic or, to say the same thing, money does not matter, the rise in income would have been to the full extent of OY_3. In fact, the monetary phenomenon in the asset market exerts its influence in raising the rate of interest. The exact process of adjustment of the rise in government expenditures takes the route of first raising the level of aggregate demand which, in turn, raises the level of income. This leads to rise in the demand for money (transaction demand for money) thus pushing up the rate of interest, given the supply of money exogenously determined. Thus, the result is a rise in interest rate from Or_1 to Or_2 and rise in income from OY_1 to OY_2 at equilibrium point.

The difference between Keynesian income determination model and the present *IS-LM* model is now clear. The asset market in the guise of *LM* curve ensures that the multiplier effect is relatively less due to the negative impact of higher interest rate because the higher interest rate dampens the investment demand which is one of the components of aggregate demand. This is known as the "crowding out" effect. The actual calculation of the multiplier is given in the mathematical derivation section.

Monetary policy multiplier and the LM curve: We know that the *LM* curve represents money market equilibrium such that each point on the curve shows the equality between demand for money and the supply of money. A typical *LM* curve (along with the *IS* curve) is given in Fig. 8.18. Now, let us suppose that the monetary authority, the central bank, decides to increase the real money stock by ₹ 500 crores, symbolised by $\Delta(M/P)$. As a result, the *LM* curve shifts to the right downward, labelled LM_2. A new equilibrium point also occurs at point E_2 giving increased level of equilibrium income of OY_2 with decreased level of interest rate of Or_2. However, it is to be noted that the extent of the increase in income is relatively less as compared to a situation when interest rate would have fallen so low to a point on LM_2 (E_3) so that the multiplier effect will be less. Let us understand the process of adjustment that takes place in the money and asset market. An increase in *Ms* leads to an increase in real money balances (M/P), since *P*, the price level is fixed in the short run. Now, when the central bank increases the supply of money, the people have more excess money than what they desire to hold at the prevailing interest rate. They would, therefore, dispose of the excess money by either depositing it in banks or buying bonds with it. Buying bonds would lead to the higher price of bonds which means low rate of interest (since, bond price and interest rates are inversely related). The process continues until the extra supply of money is willingly held by the people.

Thus, a new equilibrium point is reached at a low interest rate. Initially, though, the interest rate falls so quickly as to reach as low as Or_3 at point E_2 on the ML_2 curve since, the money market responds to changes relatively quickly. From point E_3, however, the movement is along LM_2 upwards to finally settle at E_2. Now, the lower interest rate gets transmitted to the real sector of the economy through higher investment expenditures so that aggregate demand rises and so does the level of income from OY_1 to OY_2. Thus, the monetary policy, operating through the money and asset market, exerts its influence on the aggregate demand by stimulating private investment expenditures. Clearly, in this process, the entire banking and financial sector is involved. This is because, the effectiveness of such monetary policy action depends much on how the lower interest rate is translated into the entrepreneurs' planned investment or, better known as monetary policy transmission mechanism. However, if the lower interest rate is not fully transmitted to the real economy due to some reason or other, investment activities are not sufficiently stimulated so that aggregate income does not rise to the desired extent. Hence, the multiplier effect is less.

An example can be cited with reference to the Indian economy during the early quarters of 2019-20. Amidst claims of financial sector suffering from credit shortage and the RBI obliging the market with three consecutive policy repo rate cuts, it was alleged that interest rate cuts were not transmitted fully to the real sector of the economy. This was a case of poor transmission mechanism of the central bank's monetary policy. In fact, emanating from repeated banking scams and the bank's bad loan problem, they have become more risk–averse in recent years and are not willing to advance credit to less creditworthy customers.

Mathematical derivation of fiscal policy multiplier and monetary policy multiplier:

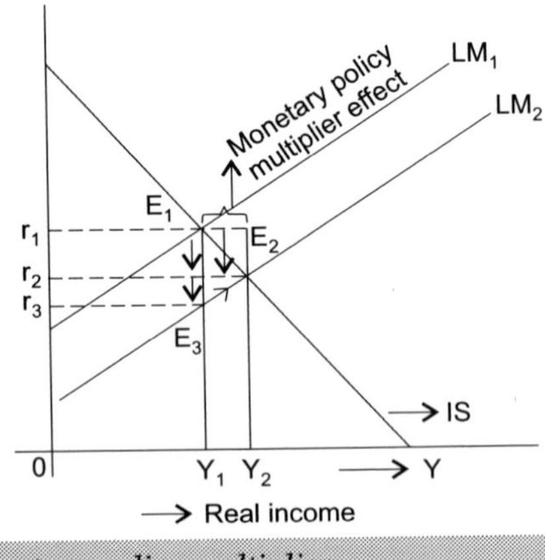

Figure 8.18 *Monetary policy multiplier.*

The equation of the *IS* curve: We begin with the Keynesian Aggregate Demand function: (in a closed economy model)

$$AD = C + I + G, \qquad (8.1)$$

where, C is the consumption function being dependent upon disposable income, that is,

$$C = b_0 + b_1\ Yd \qquad (8.2)$$

where, Yd is the disposable income, ($Yd = Y - T$; $T = t_0 + t_1Y$.). ($T = Ta - Tr$).

b_0 is the autonomous consumption and $b1$ is the slope of the consumption function, C, (mpc)

$$I = i_0 - i_1r \qquad (8.3)$$

where, i_0 is the autonomous investment, r is the rate of interest and i_1 is the interest sensitivity of the investment function.

T is the tax function, where t_0 is its autonomous part, may be called average tax rate (total tax divided by total income multiplied by 100) and t_1 is the marginal tax rate.

$$G = \overline{G} \qquad (8.4)$$

where, $\overline{G}$ is the size of government expenditures.

Now, substituting eqns. (8.2), (8.3) and (8.4) in equ. (8.1), we get

$$AD = b_0 + \mathrm{b}_1\ (Y - t_0 - t_1\ Y) + i_0 - i_1r + \overline{G}, \qquad (8.5)$$

In equilibrium,

$AD = Y$, (aggregate demand = aggregate real income/output)

Substituting, we obtain

$$Y = b_0 + b_1\ Y - b_1t_0 - b_1t_1\ Y + i_0 - i_1\ r + \overline{G} \qquad (8.6)$$

Collecting terms, we get

$$Y - b_1Y + b_1\ t_1\ Y = b_0 + i_0 - i_1\ r - b_1t_0 + \overline{G} \qquad (8.7)$$

$$\Rightarrow Y(1 - b_1 + b_1t_1) = (b_0 + i_0 - b_1t_0 + \overline{G}) - i_1\ r \qquad (8.8)$$

$$\Rightarrow Y = (b_0 + i_0 - b_1t_0 + \overline{G}) - i_1\ r/(1 - b_1 + b_1t_1) \qquad (8.9)$$

Equation (8.9) clearly shows that there is an inverse relationship between equilibrium income, Y, and the rate of interest, r. This relationship has been demonstrated in Fig. (8.15). Hence, eqn. (8.9) is the equation of the *IS* curve which expresses Y in terms of r. Alternatively, r can be expressed in terms of Y as shown in equation ....(8.10).

$$r = \{(b_0 + i_0 - b_1t_0 + \overline{G})/i_1\} - \{(1 - b_1 + b_1t_1)/i_1\}Y \qquad (8.10)$$

Thus, eqn. (8.10) is also an alternative expression of *IS* curve of which the first term within { } bracket is the intercept and the second term within { } is the slope of the *IS* curve.

Equation of the *LM* curve: We know that the demand for money function can be written as:

$$Md/P = m_o + m_1\ Y - m_2\ r \qquad (8.11)$$

where, Md/P is the demand for real balance or, real demand for money, that is, nominal demand for money (Md) separated from the influence of price level, m_0 is the intercept of the demand function of money, m_1 is the responsiveness, or the elasticity of demand for money with respect to Y, the level of income, and, m_2 is the responsiveness of the real demand for money with respect to the rate of interest, r, or, the interest elasticity of the demand for money.

The supply of money, Ms/P, assumed to be exogenously determined by the monetary authority (the central bank), hence, is fixed independently of the rate of interest. Further, equilibrium in the money market takes place when the demand for money is equal to the supply of money, that is,

$$Md/P = \overline{Ms}/P. \tag{8.12}$$

Now, substituting for Md/P in eqn. (8.11), we obtain,

$$\overline{Ms}/P = m_0 + m_1 Y - m_2 r \tag{8.13}$$

$$\Rightarrow \quad m_2 r = m_0 + m_1 Y - \overline{Ms}/P,$$

or

$$r = (m_0 + m_1 Y - \overline{Ms}/P)/m_2 \tag{8.14}$$

Alternatively,

$$m_1 Y = \overline{Ms}/P - m_0 + m_2 r \text{ thus, giving}$$

$$Y = (\overline{Ms}/P - m_0 + m_2 r)/m_1 \tag{8.15}$$

Equations (8.14) and (8.15) are both equations of LM curve.

Simultaneous determination of *IS* and *LM* equations and the fiscal-monetary multipliers: We now proceed towards simultaneous equilibrium of the goods market and the money or asset market. In other words, we are interested in equating the *IS* and *LM* equations and solve for r in terms of Y or Y in terms of r.

Thus, equating both we have

$$(b_1 + i_1 - b_1 t_0 + \overline{G})/i_1 - \{(1 - b_1 + b_1 t_1)/i_1\}Y = (m_0. + m_1 Y - \overline{Ms}/P)/m_2 \tag{8.16}$$

$$\Rightarrow \{(b_0 + i_0 - b_1 t_0 + \overline{G})/i_0\} - 1/m_2\,(m_0 - \overline{Ms}/P)$$
$$= \{(1 - b_1 + b_1 t_1)/i_1\}Y + ((m_1/m_2)Y \tag{8.17}$$

Now, solving for Y, we get

$$Y = [\{(b_0 + i_0 - b_1 t_0 + \overline{G})/i_0\} - 1/m_2(m_0 - \overline{Ms}/P)]/\{(1 - b_1 + b_1 t_1)/i_1 + m_1/m_2\},$$

which, upon simplifying, yields

$$Y = [\{m_2(b_0 + i_0 - b_1 t_0 + \overline{G}) - i_1(m_0 - \overline{Ms}/P)\}/m_2\, i_1]/\{m_2(1 - b_1 + b_1 t_1 - i_0) + (i_1 m_1)\}/m_2\, i_1 \tag{8.18}$$

$$\Rightarrow Y = [\{m_2(b_0 + i_0 - b_1 t_0 + \overline{G})\} - i_1(m_0 - \overline{Ms}/P)]/m_2(1 - b_1 + b_1 t_1 - i_0) + i_1 m_1 \tag{8.19}$$

Now, further simplifying and separating the three terms on the right-hand side, we finally get

$$Y = [\{m_2(b_0 + i_0 - b_1 t_0 + \overline{G})\}/m_2(1 - b_1 + b_1 t_1 - i_0) + i_1 m_1)\}] - [i_1 m_0/m_2(1 - b_1 + b_1 t_1 - i_0) + i_1 m_1] + [i_1\, \overline{Ms}/P/m_2(1 - b_1 + b_1 t_1 - i_0) + i_1 m_1] \tag{8.20}$$

Equation (8.20) allows us to investigate the effects of changes in fiscal variables as well as monetary variables on the level of income which lead us to obtain the fiscal policy multipliers and the monetary policy multipliers. The fiscal policy variables are: G, t_0 and t_1 while Ms/P, m_0 are monetary variables. By getting the partial derivatives of each of these variables, we have:

$$\partial Y/\partial G = \partial Y/\partial i_0 = \partial Y/\partial b_0 = m_2/\{m_1 i_1 + m_2(1 - b_1 + b_1 t_1 - i_1)\} > = 0 \quad (8.21)$$

$$\partial Y/\partial t_0 = -m_2 b_1/\{m_1\ i_1. + m_2\ (1 - b_1 + b_1 t_1 - i_1)\} < = 0 \quad (8.22)$$

$$\partial Y/\partial t_1 = -m_2\ b_1\ Y/\{m_1 i_1 + m_2\ (1 - b_1 + b_1 t_1 - i_1)\}. < = 0 \quad (8.23)$$

(Equation (8.23) can be obtained by applying the quotient rule of partial derivation and replacing the value of Y into the result.)

Equations (8.22) and (8.23) are tax multipliers which show the negative impact of a tax increase on the equilibrium income. Contrarily, tax cuts in any form, will have a positive impact on the equilibrium income, that is, tax cuts, tax rebates or tax concessions will increase equilibrium income in which cases (8.22) and (8.23) will be greater than/equal to zero.

However, there are a few special cases to be considered. What would happen if in eqns. (8.21), (8.22) or, (8.23), m_2 is equal to zero? In that case, since the demand for money becomes interest-inelastic, the values of multipliers are zero and the impact on income will be nil.

Turning to monetary multipliers now, we get the partial derivatives of eqn. (8.20) with respect to Ms/P and m_0, respectively, thus:

$$\partial Y/\partial(Ms/P) = i_1/\{m_2(1 - b_1 + b_1 t_1 - i_1) + m_1 i_1\} > = 0 \quad (8.24)$$

$$\partial Y/\partial m_0 = -i_1/\{m_2(1 - b_1 + b_1 t_1 - i_1) + m_1 i_1\}. < = 0 \quad (8.25)$$

The multiplier in eqn. (8.24) is generally positive suggesting that increasing money supply leads to an increase in income. However, the multiplier in (8.25) is negative, generally, because change in m_0 means a shift in the demand for money function (or, shift in the liquidity preference). A shift in the demand for money function upwards decreases the level of income; hence the multiplier is negative.

Another case may be if m_2 is infinitely large, that is, demand for money becomes highly elastic. In these cases, the multipliers (8.24) and (8.25) tend towards zero. Such cases are described as "money does not matter", meaning that change in money supply does not lead to any change in income.

Illustrative examples of fiscal and monetary policy multipliers

Given the following information about the economy:

$Y = C + I + G$ where,

$C = 5 + 0.8\ DI$,

$I = 10 - 2r$,

$G = 20$

$T = 4 + 0.1Y$,

$Md/P = 2 + 0.7Y - 0.3r$,

$Ms/P = 10$

$P = 1$

where, the values in absolute terms stand for '000 crore of rupees, the symbols are as shown in the text.

Calculate:

(a) the equilibrium values of Y and r. Also, draw the relevant IS and LM curves.

(b) The values of the fiscal and monetary multipliers.

(c) If the government expenditures are increased by ₹ 1000 crores, estimate its effects on equilibrium income and the rate of interest.

(d) If there is a cut in the marginal tax rate by 10%, what will be its impact on equilibrium income?

(e) If the exemption limit of income tax is raised by 20%, what will be its impact on the equilibrium income?

(f) If the supply of money is increased by the central bank by ₹ 2000 crores, estimate its impact on the equilibrium income and the rate of interest.

(g) Due to the widespread use of ATMs, people have reduced their cash holdings and so the liquidity preference has declined by 20%. Examine its impact on the aggregate income and the interest rate.

(h) If the central bank of the country lowers its policy interest rate by 100 basis points (1 percentage point) from its equilibrium level, assess its impact on the country's equilibrium income.

Answers:

(a) IS equation: $r = 15.9 - 0.14\ Y$; LM equation: $r = -26.67 + 2.33\ Y$; $IS = LM = Y = 17.23$, $r = 13.5$

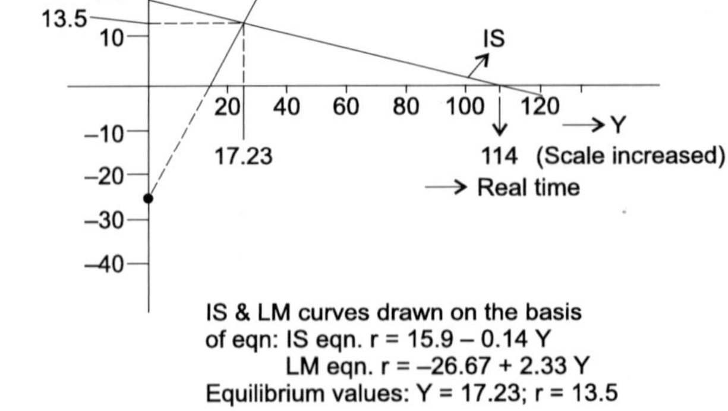

IS & LM curves drawn on the basis of eqn: IS eqn. r = 15.9 – 0.14 Y
LM eqn. r = –26.67 + 2.33 Y
Equilibrium values: Y = 17.23; r = 13.5

(b) Fiscal policy multiplier (government expenditure multiplier) = 0.157, monetary policy multiplier ($Y/Ms/P$) = 1.286

(c) In this case, government expenditures (G) will increase to 21 '000 crore of rupees. Since we have already obtained the fiscal policy multiplier (0.157), we can get the increase in equilibrium income by multiplying the increase in G with the multiplier, that is, $\Delta G * 0.157 = 157$ crores. The new equilibrium income will be 17.23 + 0.157 = 17.387 thousand crore of rupees. The rate of interest will be 13.84. Hence, the increase in interest rate = 0.34%.

(d) If there is a 10% cut in the marginal tax rate, the tax equation will be $T = 4 + 0.09\ Y$. Recalculating the new IS equation will be $r = 15.9 - 0.136Y$. With the LM equation being $r = 2.33Y - 26.67$. Solving these equations gives equilibrium $Y = 17.26$. Thus, increase in equilibrium income is 17.23 – 17.23 = 0.03 thousand crore of rupees.

(e) If the exemption limit (threshold level of income upon which no income tax is levied) is raised by 20%, the intercept coefficient of the tax equation (4) is increased by 20% so that 4 becomes 4.8. Now substituting this value in the C equation and recalculating the IS equation,we get, $r = 16.6 - 0.14\ Y$. There is no change in the LM equation. Thus, solving these two equations, we get $Y = 20.2$ and $r = 13.72$. Hence, increase in equilibrium income is 20.2 – 17.2 = 3.0 thousand crore of rupees and the increase in interest rate is 13.72 – 13.10 = 0.62%.

(f) If the central bank increases the supply of money by ₹ 2000 crores, the increase in equilibrium income can be obtained by multiplying it with the monetary policy multiplier, that is, 1.286. Thus, 2000 × 1.286 = 2286. The new equilibrium income will be 17.23 + 2.286 = 19.516 thousand crore of rupees. Alternatively, by substituting the value of money supply to $Ms/P = 12$, we can recalculate the whole process to get the new equilibrium income. The result will be the same. Fall in interest rate = 9.16%

(g) Decreasing liquidity preference is reflected in the lower value of the intercept coefficient which means rightward shift of the LM curve. The LM equation has intercept term 26.67. Reduction of 20% of (–26.67) means 5.3 will be added to 26.67 (because it is negative already). Thus, the intercept value will be (26.67 + 5.3 = –31.97). The new equilibrium income and interest rate will be 19.38 and 13.2 respectively. Hence, income will be increased by 2.18 thousand crores and interest rate will be decreased by 0.3% (13.5 – 13.2 = 0.3%). Alternatively, the intercept coefficient of the money demand function can be increased by 20% because, decreased liquidity preference means shifting upwards to the right of the money demand function, so that the intercept value increases. With new demand for money equation, the equilibrium values of Y and r can be obtained. The results will be the same.

(h) If the rate of interest is lowered by the central bank by 1%, the new equilibrium rate will be 12.5%. Putting this value in the *IS* equation and solving for *Y*, the new equilibrium income is 24.28 thousand crores, increasing by 7.08 thousand crores.

Empirical estimates of fiscal multipliers in India: The Reserve Bank of India, in its Monetary Policy Report (quoted Tulsi Jayakumar, *Mint*, January 28, 2020, has estimated different fiscal multipliers for government expenditures (revenue as well as capital expenditures) and also certain tax multipliers. For instance, the revenue expenditure multipliers for the central and state governments are 0.45 and 0.82 respectively. On the other hand, the capital expenditure multipliers for central and state governments are 3.25 and 2, respectively, which means a larger impact on GDP as compared to the revenue expenditures.

On the other hand, tax multipliers estimated for GST, corporate tax and income tax in India were around –1.08, –1 and 1.01 (reverse), respectively.

8.7 IS-LM MODEL AND THE OPEN ECONOMY

Thus far we have discussed the *IS-LM* model in the context of closed economy with no trade with any other country. When the economy becomes open, two important changes take place: (1) a part of domestic income is spent on the imports of foreign goods and (2) part of the foreign income is spent on domestic goods (exports). Thus, the consumption expenditures (*C*) in the *IS LM* model is split up into two parts: consumption expenditures on domestically produced goods and consumption expenditures on imports. Now, imports are dependent on the size of national income, *Y*. Bigger the size of national income, the bigger will be the size of imports. Assuming that imports form a constant proportional relationship with national income, we can state as follows:

$$J = j_0 + j_1 Y \tag{8.26}$$

where, J stands for total volume of imports, Y for national income, and j_0 and j_1 are, respectively, the intercept and the slope of the import function. j_1, here, denotes the marginal propensity to import, the rate at which the imports rise as a result of a unit of rise in national income; j_0, the intercept, shows that there is a certain threshold level of national income beyond which a country's imports start rising. Hence, the value of the intercept, j_0, is negative. As far as exports are concerned, these are dependent on the incomes of the foreign countries' nationals upon which the domestic residents have no control. Thus, exports can be taken as exogenously determined. Hence, exports are assumed to be fixed at a certain level at some point of time and are denoted by X.

The composition of aggregate demand is thus changed to take account of the above phenomena and written as:

$$AD = C + I + G + NX \qquad (8.27),$$

where, NX = net exports = $(X - J)$, that is, exports minus imports.

Now, $C = CD + CJ$, that is, consumption expenditure is divided into (a) consumption expenditure on domestic goods and (b) consumption expenditure on imports and both of these are functions of residents' disposable income, that is, $(Y - T)$. Thus, we can write:

$CD + CJ = b_0 + b_1(Y - T) + j_0 + j_1 (Y - T)$, where $T = t_0 + t_1Y$ hence,

$CD + CJ = b_0 + b_1Y - b_1t_0 - b_1t_1Y + j_0 + j_1Y - j_1t_0 - j_1t_1Y$, and by substitution,

$$AD = b_0 + b_1Y - b_1t_0 - b_1t_1Y + j_0 + j_1Y - j_1t_0 - j_1t_1Y + i_0 - i_1r + G + X \quad (8.28)$$

Since, in equilibrium, $AD = Y = AS$, we can further write

$$Y = b_0 + b_1Y - b_1t_0 - b_1t_1Y + j_0 + j_1\ Y - j_1t_0 - j_1t_1Y + i_0 - i_1r + G + X \quad (8.29)$$

Collecting terms and solving for Y, we get

$$Y = (1/1 - b_1 + b_1t_1 - j_1 + j_1t_1)\ [b_0 - b_1t_0 + j_0 - j_1t_0 + i_0 - i_1r + G + X] \quad (8.30)$$

Equation (8.30) is the equation of the *IS* curve – expressing Y in terms of r which appears in the negative. Alternatively, eqn. (8.30) can be written as:

$$r = \{b_0 - b_1t_0 + j_0 - j_1t_0 + i_0 + G + X\}/i_1\} - Y[1 - b_1 - b_1t_1 + j_1 - j_1t_1]/i_1 \quad (8.31)$$

which expresses r in terms of Y.

Let us now examine the basic difference between the closed economy *IS* and open economy *IS* curves. The introduction of import function, J, makes all the difference in the value of the multiplier. In the denominator of the multiplier, j_1 and j_1t_1 appear, the former with a negative sign while the latter with a positive sign. Since both are fractions, we expect that in sum, the denominator will be higher in value so that the multiplier will be less as compared to the closed economy multiplier. One can intuitively argue that with the economy opening up to trade, a part of the domestic income which is spent on imports, flows out from the country and hence domestic income is reduced to that extent.

The *IS* curve is no doubt downward sloping as is evident from the negative relationship between r and Y in eqn. (8.31). However, the slope of the curve is steeper. This is evident from the inclusion of additional coefficients of j_1, the marginal propensity to import in the second part of the eqn. (8.31).

We must now examine the effect of the change in the exogenous variables like G and X. For instance, an increase in X – the exports, will shift the *IS* curve to the right and hence result in a higher level of income (with a lower multiplier though). Similarly, an increase in government expenditures, now, will surely result in increased income but since a part of it is likely to have some import content and so that will be spent on imports, the increase in income will be relatively less.

The *LM* curve and the open economy: As far as *LM* curve is concerned, there is no change in its structure, so we present it in the same form as in the closed economy model:

The demand for money: $Md/P = m_o + m_1 Y - m_2 r$;

where, the notations are as explained above.

The supply of money is exogenously fixed, so $Ms = \bar{M}s$.

Equilibrium in the money market is ensured by $Md/P = \bar{M}s/P$. After substituting the values, we get:

$$\bar{M}s/P = m_0 + m_1 Y - m_2 r,$$

$$\Rightarrow \quad r = (m_0 + m_1 Y - \bar{M}s/P)/m_2 \tag{8.32}$$

Now, equating eqns. (8.31) and (8.32) and solving for Y, we get,

$$Y = [\{b_0 - b_1 t_0 + j_0 - j_1 t_0 + i_0 + G + X\}/i_1 + \{\bar{M}s/P - m_0\}/m_2]$$
$$[\{1 - b_1 - b_1 t_1 + j_1 - j_1 t_1\}/i_1] + (m_1/m_2) \tag{8.33}$$

From eqn. (8.33), we can get the partial derivative of Y with respect to G as well as X and examine their signs to know the impact of fiscal policy (government expenditures) changes and the exports on the aggregate income/GDP.

Thus:

$$\partial Y/\partial G = \partial Y/\partial X = 1/\{(1 - b_1 - b_1 t_1 + j_1 - j_1 t_1)\}/i_1 + (m_1/m_2) \tag{8.34}$$

Equation (8.34) indicates a smaller multiplier as compared to that of a closed economy since, $(j_1 - j_1 t_1)$ being positive, is added to the denominator thus making it larger and the multiplier smaller.

Figure (8.19) depicts the *IS-LM* model in an open economy.

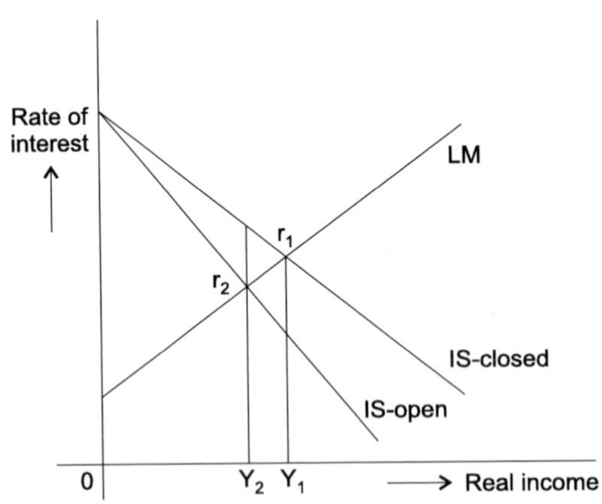

Figure 8.19 *IS curves - closed and open economy.*

8.8 A CRITICAL EVALUATION OF IS-LM SYSTEM

The *IS-LM* model and its applicability as described in the previous pages provides a very useful framework of macroeconomic behaviour. Although it could not be possible to work out some of the practical implications of the model, these could be developed by use of insight by interested readers. The *IS-LM* framework of analysis remained an unquestioned tool of macroeconomic policy during much of the post-Keynesian era and is still equally relevant today. In fact, economists have, since then, refined this tool of analysis in several ways. They have given it a more general shape by incorporating more classical/neo-classical elements (like wage price flexibility) on the one hand and more Keynesian elements (rigid money wages) on the other hand. Most of the underdeveloped and emerging economies (including India) still have great reliance on *IS-LM* model and, in fact, use it to their own convenience.

Only in the wake of 'rational expectation theory' developed by Robert Lucas and his associates in Chicago University and shunning most of the Keynesian tools like Phillips curve and *IS-LM* model that a new set of theory and policy was made increasingly polular and implemented to their economies during the period of last 30 years or so. We have discussed these new developments elsewhere in this book (Chapter 11).

One major limitation of the model is that it has been developed on the assumption of constant price level. Hence, there is no effect of the change in general price-level on either the commodity market or money market. However, one can conceive, by logic, the effect of any change in the price-level on the components comprising either the money demand/supply or the aggregate demand for commodities. We shall try to develop a model in terms of aggregate demand and aggregate supply with explicit reference to general price level in Chapter 9 p. 207.

During early sixties, Clower and Leijonhufvud provided a new interpretation of Keynesian economics and the concept of equilibrium as being essentially a 'disequilibrium' concept which arose from the market's inability to clear (total demand = total supply). This is as much true for labour market as for other markets. In the authors' view, therefore, the so-called classical-Keynesian synthesis attempted by the neo-Keynesians failed to capture the fundamental difference between classical and Keynes' economics.

Thirdly, the entire Keynesian and post-Keynesian apparatus is based on 'adaptive expectation' theory. This theory asserts that expectations are largely formed on the basis of 'lagged values' of the variables – such as one year or two year past values (or, other remote past values) with greater weight being attached to recent past. This theory of expectation is criticized by many modern economists who claim that expectations are 'rational' – based more upon current information than past trends.

In spite of these shortcomings, the *IS-LM* model as a classical-Keynesian synthesis model remains as one of the powerful tools of macroeconomic analysis and policy.

SUMMARY

1. The *IS-LM* model provides an important framework of macroeconomic analysis. It is a classical-Keynesian synthesis model. The earliest attempts to do so were made by JR Hicks and AH Hansen, so that it is also known as Hicks-Hansen analysis.
2. *IS* stands for equilibrium in the commodity or goods sector while *LM* stands for equilibrium in the monetary sector. Hence, *IS-LM* system represents the equilibrium in both sectors simultaneously.
3. The starting point in the *IS-LM* discussion is the derivation of IS and *LM* curves. There are basically two methods of derivation: graphical method and mathematical method. Again, the derivation process may take either of the two routes. One may start from classical equilibrium system in terms of equality of savings and investment determining the rate of interest and then include the Keynesian basic feature in terms of income as determining both savings and investment.

   Alternatively, one may start from Keynesian income determination process and insert in it the rate of interest as an additional variable determining consumption and investment expenditure (and hence the level of income).
4. Both the methods (routes) can be illustrated graphically as well as mathematically as has been done in the basic text. Comparatively, however, the Keynesian route allows us to identify all the parameters involved in the whole *IS-LM* system amenable for further analysis.
5. The diagrammatic method, in turn, can be represented either in a single positive quadrant – or in four phases utilizing all four quadrants showing positive values from opposite sides. From analytical point of view, the four-phase diagram is preferable.
6. In a similar manner the *LM* curve can be derived with features of demand for money both in the classical and Keynesian formulations, viz., transaction demand for money being a function of level of income while speculative demand being a function of rate of interest. Taking Y as a parameter, *LM* curve can also be drawn by assuming different levels of income in a single phase diagram; or, using four-phase diagram by taking both types of demand for money on the same scale.

   As far as shapes of *IS* and *LM* curves are concerned, *IS* is normally downward sloping while *LM* is, generally, upward sloping except the 'liquidity trap' situation when *LM* is partially horizontal in the beginning.

7. Mathematical method of derivation, though seemingly cumbersome, is simply substitution of one function into another when each of the underlying relations are specified in mathematical equations. The Keynesian route, in this case is considered better due to reasons explained above. The solution of the *IS-LM* system then follows either expressing rate of interest (r) in terms of Y along with other parameters or expressing income (Y) in terms of the rate of interest and the parameters.
8. The mathematical method allows us to work out a 'multiplier' which, in turn, permits us to calculate precisely, the increase in income for a given increase in any one of the parameter values. Alternatively, it permits to calculate the change in interest rate for a given change in any of the parameter values.
9. Shifts in IS curve occur due to change in any of the parameter values—the autonomous terms shift the curve parallelly while other terms shift along with its slope. There are certain special cases of both IS and *LM* curve systems when *IS* becomes vertical (being uninfluenced by rate of interest) or when *LM* is vertical (situation of full employment). Similarly, *LM* becomes horizontal when L becomes infinitely elastic, as happens when longer recession or depression type situation develops.
10. Simultaneous equilibrium in both commodity and money/asset markets occurs when we combine both *IS* and *LM* curves with reference to the rate of interest and level of income. This is the overall equilibrium in the economy with equilibrium values of interest rate and level of income.
11. The actual situation in an economy in a particular point in time is, however, a situation of disequilibrium except by accident, which, in the present model, is to be located away from the equilibrium point. Thus all points lying either to the left or to the right of both *IS* and *LM* curves represent disequilibrium points – characterised by either excess or deficient aggregate demand in the commodity market or excess or deficient demand in the money/asset market.
12. Disequilibrium characteristics suggest some dynamic behaviour — showing the time-path of the movement of the economy either independently or under the pressure of the monetary – fiscal policies. Such time paths generally suggest a gradual movement of the economy towards stability, i.e., towards the original equilibrium. However, much depends on the relative slopes of *IS* and *LM* curves and the strength of the policy actions, if they are applied.
13. Macroeconomic policies like monetary and fiscal policies have an impact on *IS-LM* system and hence on the management of the economy. Any expansionary fiscal policy (raising government expenditure and/ or lowering tax rates) has the effect of shifting the *IS* curve to the right

and raising the level of income (as also the interest rate) *LM* remaining the same. On the other hand, contractionary fiscal policy (lowering government expenditure and/or raising tax rates) shifts the IS curve to the left and lowers the level of income. Similarly, increasing the supply of money (and credit) by any method shifts the *LM* curve to the right, lowers the rate of interest and, under normal situation, raises the level of income as well. Under 'liquidity trap' situation, however, the expansionary monetary policy does not work. Here, only fiscal policy is able to raise the level of income. On the other hand, when *LM* becomes vertical (full or near full employment situation) fiscal policy becomes ineffective.

Under normal conditions judicious combination of monetary and fiscal policies yields desirable results.

14. A phenomenon known as 'crowding out' is often associated with a situation when public (or government) investment and private investment compete with each other resulting in raising the rate of interest if public investment programme is largely financed by borrowing investible fund from the market which is limited in nature. The 'crowding out' (of private investment) however, can, to a large extent, be tackled by expansionary monetary policy.
15. In spite of significant merits of the *IS-LM* system, there are certain drawbacks in it. It is based upon constant level of prices.

EXERCISE

1. Derive the equation of the *IS* curve if you proceed from classical equilibrium position to the Keynesian equilibrium position.
2. Given the following values for *IS-LM* model, solve for the equilibrium values of variables asked for:

$$Y = C + I + \overline{G}$$

$$C = 15 + 0.6\ DI - 0.05\ r$$

$$I = 10 + 0.7\ Y - 0.25\ r$$

$$\overline{G} = 25;\ T = 0.02 + 0.03\ Y$$

$$Md = 0.4\ Y - 0.5\ r;\ r = 0.06$$

$$Ms = 30$$

where, values in absolute terms stand for '000 crore of rupees, the symbols are as given in the text:

(a) find the equilibrium values of Y and r.

(b) find the value of the income multiplier.

(c) if the supply of money (*Ms*) is decreased by ₹ 10,000 crore, what will be its effect on equilibrium rate of interest and income?

(d) if government expenditure increases to ₹ 30,000 crore estimate its effect on equilibrium income and rate of interest.

(e) if the crowding-out of private investment is sought to be avoided, what will be the net increase in money supply required?

3. If GNP (Y) increases by 10 per cent what is its possible impact on the other variables of the system?
4. If marginal tax rate is reduced to 20% from the existing 30%, what will be its effect on equilibrium income and interest rate?
5. If community's preference for liquid money increases by 10%, with GNP value of Example, calculate the equilibrium condition in the money market and then examine its impact on equilibrium GNP and interest rate.
6. In the *IS-LM* model, explain the role played by autonomous consumption and autonomous investment components.
7. Derive graphically the *IS* and *LM* curves and explain their basic characteristics.
8. Under what conditions does the *IS* curve become horizontal and vertical?
9. If the government intends to promote growth of the economy (raise output by public expenditures) from the equilibrium level by 10%, but the central bank wants to keep interest rate constant, what is the policy option available to the government/ central bank?
10. How would you evaluate the *IS LM* model as a short-run macroeconomic model?
11. Derive mathematically the equations for *IS* and *LM* curves and obtain the overall equilibrium conditions for the economy.
12. How can the *IS-LM* model be extended to the open economy case? Illustrate graphically as well as mathematically.
13. Given the following information about an economy, calculate the government expenditures multiplier and monetary policy multiplier.
14. $Y = C + I + G + NX,$ $\qquad (NX = X - J)$

    where,

    $C = 600 + 0.6\ Yd;\ I = 400 - 800\ r;\ G = 200;\ T = 500;\ Yd = Y - T;$
    $X = 100,\ J = 0 + 0.1\ Y.\ Md/P = 2\ Y - 10000\ r$

    $Ms = 2000$

    $P = 1$

15. Given the following information about a certain economy:

    $Y = C + I + G$

    where $C = 50 + 0.8\ Yd$

    $I = 100 - 0.7\ r$

    $T = 4 + 0.2\ Y$

    $G = ₹\ 2000$

    $Md/P = 5\ Y - 2\ r$

    $Ms/P = 1000.$ $P = 1.$

    (figures in the absolute value are in crores of rupees)

(a) Obtain the equations for *IS* and *LM* curves.

(b) Obtain the appropriate values of interest rate and income levels at which the goods and money markets clear simultaneously.

(c) If there is a 10% increase in the level of equilibrium income desired by the policy makers, what are the policy alternatives available?

(d) If the government expenditures on public health increases by ₹ 1000 crores, what will be its effects on the equilibrium income and interest rate?

(e) If the central bank wants to prevent the interest rate from rising in the above case,what policy requirements will be necessary?

REFERENCES

1. Edward Shapiro (ed.) Macroeconomic Readings Harcourt Brace Jovanovitch, 1970.
2. A.H. Hansen, Monetary Theory and Fiscal Policy, McGraw Hill, New York, 1949.
3. Gardner Ackley, Macroeconomics: Theory and Policy, Macmillan, 1978.
4. R.L. Crouch, Macroeconomics, Harcourt Brace, 1972.
5. Mint, New Delhi, daily, various issues.
6. N. Gregory Mankiw, Macroeconomics, Sixth Edition, Worth Publishers, 2006.
7. R. Dornbusch, Stanley Fischer and Richard Startz, Macroeconomics, 9th Edition, McGraw Hill, USA, 2009.

9

Aggregate Demand and Aggregate Supply

9.1 AGGREGATE DEMAND AND AGGREGATE SUPPLY

In the previous chapter, we prepared the background for the final analysis of the economy in terms of aggregate demand and aggregate supply. In fact, the *IS-LM* framework is the building block of the aggregate demand-aggregate supply (*AD-AS*) model. In the present chapter, we will attempt to derive the *AD-AS* model primarily from the *IS-LM* model with the relaxation of the basic assumption of constant price level of the model. In other words, we will now assume that price level is changeable and there can be different equilibrium situations of the *IS-LM* system under different price levels.

Secondly, in deriving the *AD-AS* model, we will invoke the 'real balance effect' the effect of the price level change on the real value of assets, as propounded by economist Don Patinkin. In particular, a fall in the price level raises the real value of money/assets and a rise in the price level lowers the real value of money/assets. It may be mentioned here that the famous British economist, AC Pigou had termed this the 'wealth effect' while advancing his argument in favour of full employment.

Before we actually dwell on the derivation of *AD-AS* model, we would like to refer to the classical quantity theory of money which, by implication, reveals an inverse relationship between general price level and aggregate demand. We reproduce here the quantity theory equation: $MV = PY$, where, PY represents the nominal national income (P being the price level and Y being the real national income). The left side of the equation shows the total quantity of money in circulation that is released by the central bank multiplied by the average number of times each unit of money circulates in the economy. Now, supposing M remains constant because of the monetary authority's policy decision and V also does not change for a considerable period of time, (since it is determined by institutional factors), there appears to be a mutual relationship between P and Y such that if P rises, Y has to fall or, if P falls, Y has to rise in order for the equation to hold (PY to remain constant). Not only this, P and Y behave in a manner which, translated into a curve, produces a 'rectangular hyperbola'–proportionate rise or fall in P will be followed by proportionate fall or rise in Y, as shown in Fig. 9.1. This curve represents the aggregate demand curve in the classical system. Also implied in the quantity equation is that every increase/decrease in the quantity of money will lead to the rightward shift/leftward shift of the aggregate demand curve. Aggregate supply is, of course, constant in the classical system because of the full employment assumption in the long run. Hence, the aggregate supply curve is vertical in shape.

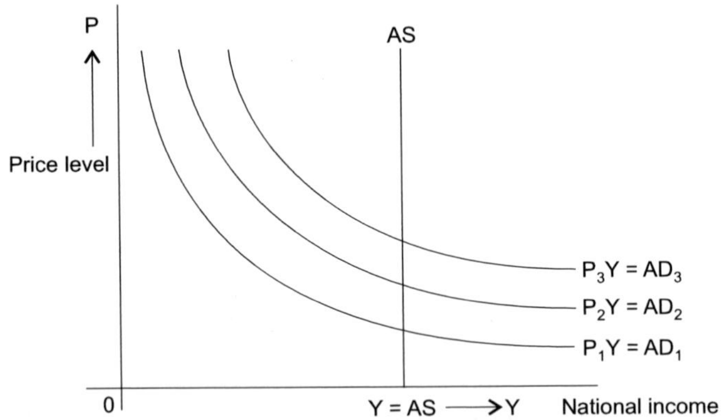

Figure 9.1 *Aggregate demand & aggregate supply (derived from classical quantity theory of money).*

We now attempt to derive the aggregate demand curve/function using *IS-LM* model.

Let us start with an initial equilibrium position in the *IS-LM* model based on one fixed level of price, denoted by P_1. Accordingly, the *LM* curve is labelled LM/P_1. Now, if, for instance, the price level decreases, the *LM* curve will be shifting down to the right. Why? Because lower price level means higher value of money as an asset (real balance effect). This means real supply of money is increased. The opposite happens in case of rise in the level of prices. These changes can be separately plotted in another curve as shown in Figs. 9.2 and 9.3. Evidently, the new curve is a downward sloping curve from left to right.

Thus, by relaxing the assumption of constant price level in the *IS-LM* model we obtain a general *AD* curve for the economy as a whole. It represents simultaneous equilibrium in all major markets (goods and money) at different levels of prices.

The second method is derived from the general *IS-LM* model by relaxing the assumption of fixed price level of the model, which is illustrated in Fig. 9.2. The reasoning behind this method is that a change in the price level brings about change (shift) in the *LM* curve. If the price level falls, for instance, the real value of money (and other assets) increases. Thus, as it happens in the case of *LM* curve, the real value of money balance rises. This causes shift in the *LM* curve to the right.

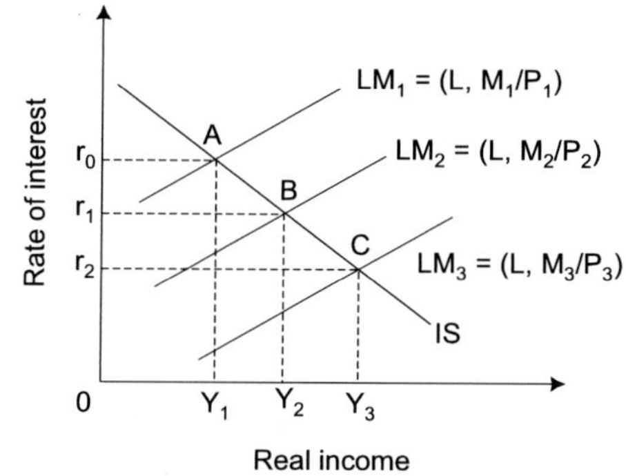

Figure 9.2 *Impact of real balance effect on LM curve.*

We can label the real value of money balance as *M*/*P*. If we assume three prices such as P_1, P_2 and P_3 and assume that $P_1 > P_2 > P_3$, then as price level falls L, M_1/P_1 shifts to L, M_2/P_2 and similarly L, M_2/P_2 shifts to L, M_3/P_3. The new equilibrium points as shown in Fig. 9.2 are *A*, *B* and *C* respectively. If we plot these points and join them by a straight line (Fig. 9.3) while showing different price levels P_1, P_2 and P_3 in the vertical axes, the downward sloping curve will represent aggregate demand (*AD*) curve.

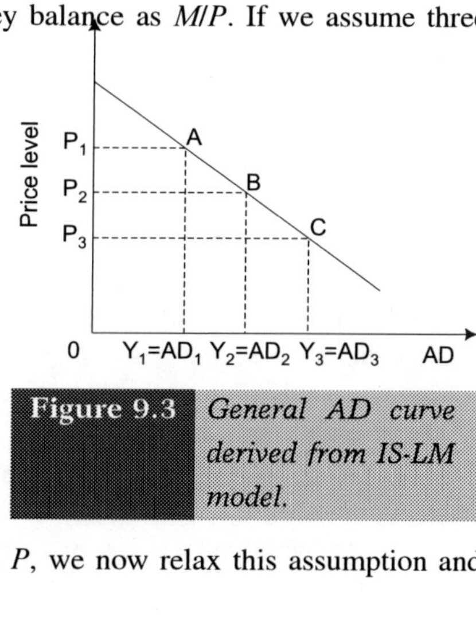

Figure 9.3 *General AD curve derived from IS-LM model.*

Mathematical derivation of the *AD* curve from the *IS-LM* system: From the *LM* equation with a fixed price level, *P*, we now relax this assumption and allow *P* to vary.

$$LM \text{ equation: } \frac{Ms}{P} = m_0 + m_1 Y - m_2 r \ldots\ldots \tag{9.1}$$

$$\Rightarrow \quad r = \left(m_0 + m_1 Y - \frac{Ms}{P}\right) / m_2 \tag{9.2}$$

$$\Rightarrow \quad m_2 r = m_0 + m_1 Y - \frac{Ms}{P}$$

$$\Rightarrow \quad \frac{Ms}{P} = \frac{m_0 + m_1 Y}{m_2 r}$$

$$\Rightarrow \qquad \frac{P}{Ms} = \frac{m_2 r}{m_0 + m_1 Y}$$

$$\Rightarrow \qquad P = Ms\left[\frac{m_2 r}{m_0 + m_1 Y}\right] \qquad (9.3)$$

Now, for getting the equilibrium income in the IS-LM frame, we can substitute the value of r from equation (8.14) into the IS equation (8.9) and obtain,

$$Y = \frac{(b_0 + i_0 - b_1 t_0 + \bar{G}) - i_1\{m_0 + m_1 Y - \bar{M}s / P\}}{m_2(1 - b_1 + b_1 t_1)} \qquad (9.4)$$

After collecting terms for Y to the left side of equation, and further simplifying we obtain,

$$Y = \frac{(b_0 + i_0 - b_1 t_0 + \bar{G}) - i_1\{m_0 - \bar{M}s / P\}}{(1 + i_1 m_1) \times m_2(1 - b_1 + b_1 t_1)} \qquad (9.5)$$

This is the equilibrium IS-LM at a certain value of P, for instance, $P = P_1$. From equation (9.5), it is obvious that Y and P are inversely related – thus giving a downward sloping AD curve (Y representing aggregate demand). Similarly, changing the value of P to P_2 (where, assumedly, $P_2 < P_1$), we can get another LM curve and so another set of equilibrium Y and P. This way, we can map the whole AD curve.

From equation (9.5), we can analyse the impact of monetary variables as well as fiscal variables on the aggregate demand. Monetary variables are: (1) Change in the real money stock ($\bar{M}s/P$) and interest rate while the fiscal variables are change in government expenditures and tax rates. Equation (9.5) shows that if real money stock increases, aggregate demand will rise, i.e., AD curve will shift to the right. However, if interest rate (m_2) rises, Y will fall, i.e., AD curve will shift to the left.

As far as the fiscal variables are concerned, the equation (9.5) reveals that rise in government expenditures, $\bar{G}$, will raise the level of Y–AD curve will shift to the right; while, tax rate (t_0 or t_1) has negative impact on AD-AD curve shifts to the left.

Hence, P is inversely reláted to Y, giving a downward sloping aggregate demand (AD) curve, given other parameters.

Aggregate Supply Curve: Aggregate supply refers to the total supply of goods and services in the economy during a certain time period. This is equivalent to the concept of real GDP. The aggregate supply curve is derived from the short-run supply curves of individual firms' production and supply behaviour and aggregating them over the whole economy. However, since individual supplies are normally responsive to individual price level, aggregate supply curve is also responsive to general price level. But, there is some basic difference between short-run and long-run supply behaviour at the individual (micro level) and (macro-level) aggregate level. Microeconomic theory suggests that short-run supply curve is either vertical or upward rising with relatively greater slope due to the existence of fixed factors of production with the producers. The long run supply curve is, however, upward-rising with relatively lesser slope (or greater elasticity) due to flexibility in factor supplies. In fact, all factors of production, in the long run become variable in nature.

The macro level or aggregate supply curve, however, differs from their micro level counterparts in terms of 'expectations' as well as basic assumptions of the different schools of thoughts. The macro level aggregate supply curve in the short run is upward rising with price level particularly so long as unemployed resources exist in the economy. For instance, existence of unemployment of labour may induce the firms to exploit this opportunity and expand output at lower wage rate. This is possible, however, with money wage rates and other resource prices remaining unchanged in the short run. The rising price level, therefore, allows the producers to reap short-run profits which induce them to increase output and supply of goods and services. But in the long run, when the economy reaches its 'potential' or full employment stage, the supply curve becomes vertical in nature. Figure 9.4 illustrates the nature of short run as well as long run aggregate supply curves.

In Fig. 9.4, SAS is the short run supply curve which is upward sloping from left to right—showing positive relationship between aggregate price level and the total quantities of goods and services in the economy (real GDP). This is because, in the short run, as we know, at least some of the factor services, such as certain types of capital and technology are fixed so that necessary adjustments in the aggregate supply, even if required, against any change in aggregate demand (except changes in inventories) are difficult to be made. However, other factor services such as labour and raw materials, already in stock, and unused land resources can be utilized for making adjustments with *AD*. Thus, if *AD* is increasing in the short run, *AS* can respond by increasing output until all unused or partially used resources are fully utilized. Once the potential output (or potential GDP) is achieved with full utilization of unused productive resources, further increase in output is not possible, but this can happen only in the long run. In other words, full employment is a possibility in the long run—a classical/ new classical proposition. The long run supply curve is, therefore, vertical in nature as shown by the LAS curve. This does not however mean that short run supply stops at potential output level if price level continues to rise and labourers fail to realize that their real wage rate has fallen and the price level has not affected other resource prices and hence employers' cost of production (price rise is, mainly, demand-driven). The producers may continue to increase output and exceed the level of potential output as shown in Fig. 9.4 at point OS_2. However, as soon as money wage rate increases to compensate for falling real wage rate, the employers' profit margin stops increasing. Therefore, they would cut back output and return to the potential output level. The long-run supply curve (LAS), therefore, is not sensitive to price level changes and hence becomes vertical in nature. (We should remember here that potential output level is not necessarily a fixed quantity but it refers to growth rate of output.) It may be a matter of empirical investigation if in the long run price changes are followed by full percentage change in money wage rates. If not, LAS will not be necessarily vertical.

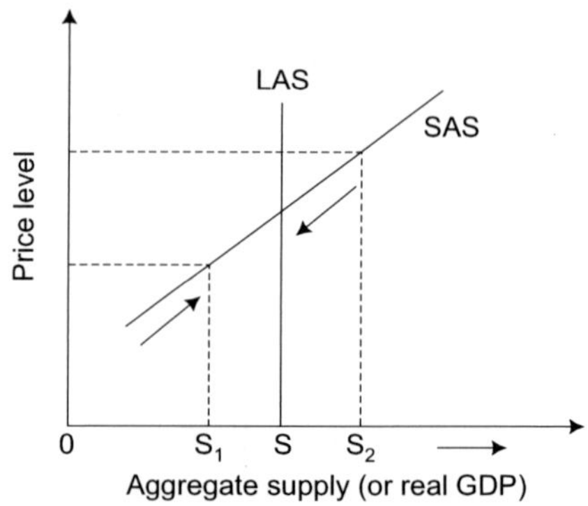

Figure 9.4 *Short run and long run aggregate supply curve.*

9.2 SHIFTS IN AD AND AS CURVES

As far as the components of *AD* and *AS* are concerned these can be expressed in terms of the following symbols:

$$AD = C + I + G + NX \qquad (9.6)$$

where C = consumption demand,
I = private investment demand
G = government demand (purchases of goods and services)
NX = net export demand (exports-imports).

The *AD* components are the same as used in the Keynesian *AD* model.

$$AS = f(L, K, T) \qquad (9.7)$$

Here, *AS* has been expressed in functional form since supply of goods and services depends upon supplies of factors of production such as labour (L), capital (K) and the state of technology (T).

$f(L, K, T)$ is the expression for aggregate production function.

If we distinguish between short run and long run production functions, we can rewrite 9.7 as follows:

$$AS = f(L, K, \overline{T}), \qquad (9.8)$$

where $\overline{T}$ is the given state of technology in the short run. The production technology is, in fact, a relatively long run phenomenon because changes in technology take longer time.

Shifts in AD Curve

The aggregate demand for the economy can be affected by (1) Government's macroeconomic policy, namely, fiscal and monetary policies and (2) exchange rate policy. We discuss below how changes in these macro policies cause shifts in *AD* curve.

Fiscal Policy and AD

Fiscal policy of the government refers to the expenditure and taxation policies which influence real income levels of the citizens of the country and, through them, the aggregate demand. Government's expenditure policy can be either expansionary or contractionary in nature. Increase in government expenditure (expansionary fiscal policy) leads to the rightwards shift of the IS curve as we have already examined in Chapter 8 in *IS-LM* model. This leads to the rightward shift of the *AD* curve even at the same price level. On the contrary, decrease in government expenditure (contractionary fiscal policy) leads to leftward shift of the IS curve initially, and finally to the leftward shift of *AD* curve. Similarly, changes in tax rates lead to shifts of *IS* curve and hence to *AD* curve. For instance, decrease in tax rate has the impact of increase in disposable income and has the similar impact like increase in expenditure so that IS curve shifts to the right and also *AD* curve shifts to the right. Tax break, increase in the exemption limit has the similar impact on *AD* as the cut in tax rate. Increase in tax rates on the other hand, has the opposite effect—leftward shift of *AD* curve. Figure 9.5(a to h) shows the effects of fiscal policy changes on the *AD* curve.

Monetary Policy and AD

Monetary policy changes work through the money market, i.e., through the *LM* curve. We have already examined that *LM* curve is influenced mainly by change in the rate of interest and change in the supply of money. An increase in the rate of interest, for instance, decreases the demand for money so that *LM* curve shifts to the left. This has the effect of decrease in the real GDP demand (or aggregate demand). On the other hand, a decrease in the rate of interest increases the demand for money-shifting *LM* curve to the right and ultimately increasing the real GDP demanded (or, aggregate demand).

An increase in the supply of money, other things being equal, shifts the *LM* curve to the right, thus, increasing the purchasing power of the community. This leads ultimately to increase in aggregate demand. In fact, aggregate demand shifts to the same extent as the shift in *LM* curve. The opposite effect takes place when there is a decrease in the supply of money. These shifts in *AD* curve are shown in Fig. 9.6 (a to h).

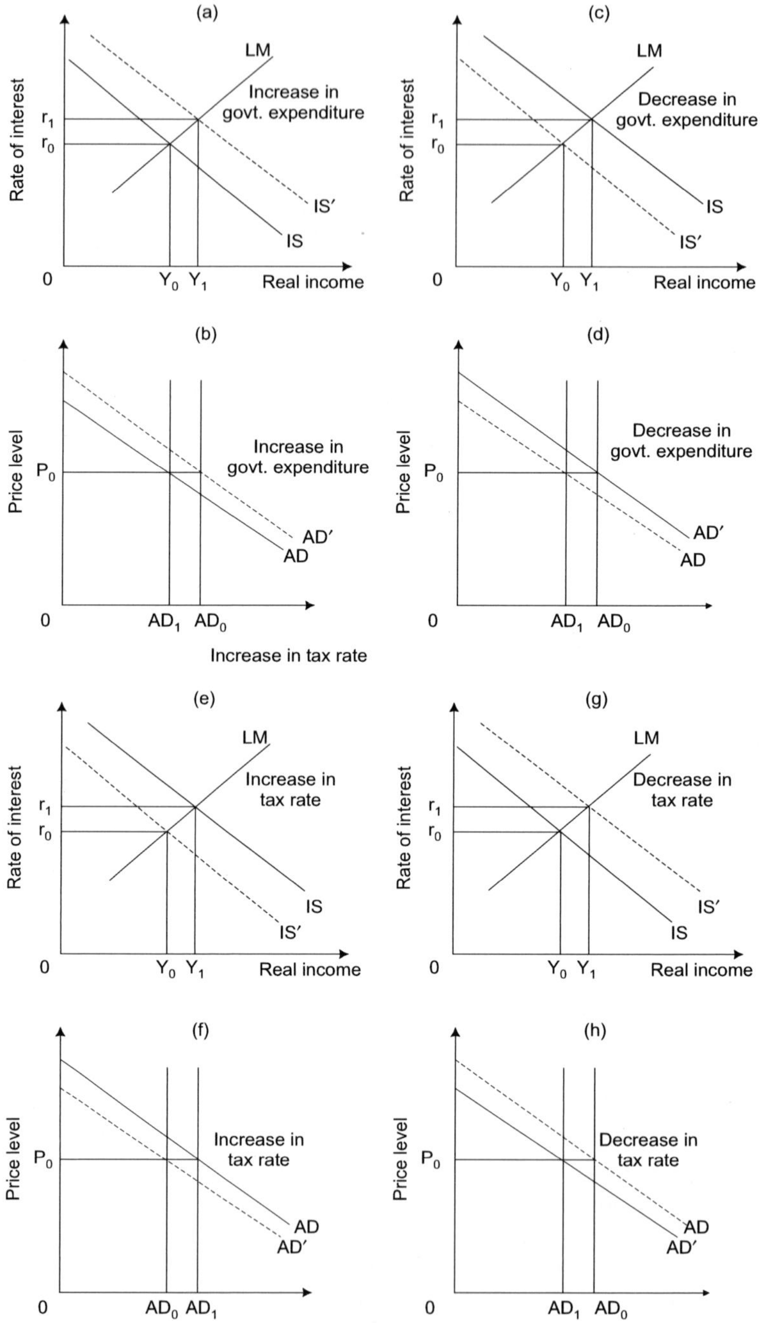

Figure 9.5 *Effects of fiscal policy changes on AD.*

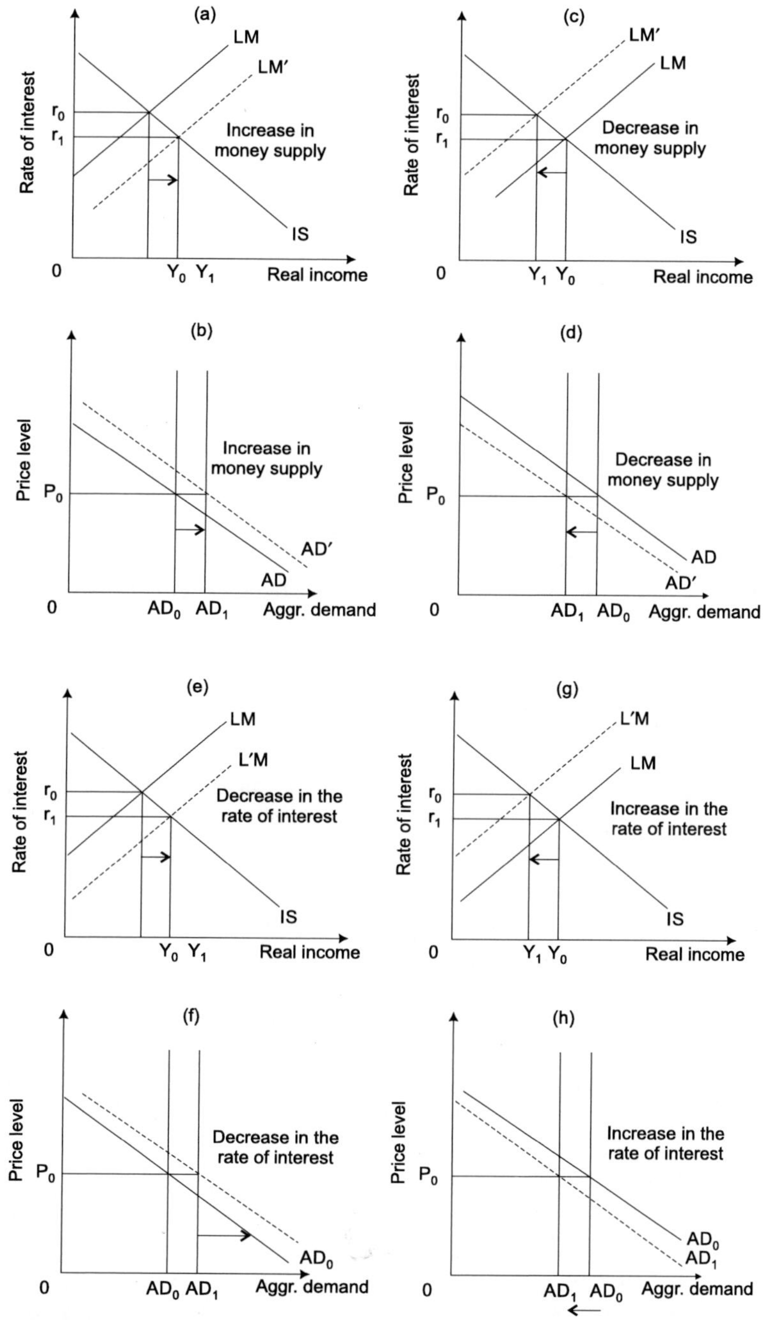

Figure 9.6 *Effects of monetary policy changes on AD.*

It is to be noted that monetary policy changes such as increase in the supply of money (decrease in supply of money) has the similar effect on aggregate demand as the decrease in rate of interest (increase in rate of interest). The point of difference, however, lies in the chain of causation. Rate of interest change either lowers or raises the cost of borrowing by the banking and financial sectors and hence either enhances or lowers the expenditure levels of the firms and individuals. The change in the supply of money—either increase or decrease-mainly effected by the central banking authority works through open market operations (purchase or sale of securities) to the banking and financial sectors, increase in net credit to the government or monetization of government debt. However, to the extent that the supply of money is created through the banking sector (credit money) the effects are similar.

Expectations and AD

Generally, expectations about four important factors and their changes in future cause shift in *AD* curve. These are (a) expectation about future income, (b) expectation about future inflation (c) expectation about future profits and (d) changes in world economy.

(a) Expectation about Future Income If there is widespread optimism that real income levels of individuals are likely to increase in future, the present *AD* curve is most likely to be shifted to the right. This may be due to several factors. For instance, if the existing stocks of assets provide a promise of increase in future earnings, if there is prospect for good monsoon and expectation of good crop production, aggregate demand curve would shift to the right. On the other hand, pessimistic outlook about future incomes would shift the *AD* curve to the left.

(b) Expectation about Future Inflation If inflation expectation is high implying that there will be a price rise in future, the buying plans for the present appear to be worthwhile. Hence, current aggregate demand, even at unchanged prices is likely to shift to the right. Opposite will be the case if future inflation rate is likely to fall. These are causes of preponement or postponement of current demand by the community.

(c) If the business community and investors have reasons enough for their future profits to rise, they would increase their demand for raw materials and other capital goods so that aggregate demand shifts to the right. Expansion of market for product in future has the potential for increased future profits which would, most likely, shift *AD* curve to the right.

(d) Changes in World Economy and AD Globalised economies with exposures of exports and imports of goods and services are affected by changes in (i) exchange rate and (ii) incomes of foreign countries. These, in turn, have impact on domestic countries' *AD*. For instance, if the exchange rate of domestic currency rises (more dollars per unit of rupee or less rupees per unit of dollar) imports become cheaper and exports become costlier. This leads to fall in exports and rise in imports so that net exports (*X-M*) falls leading ultimately to leftward shift of *AD* curve. On the other hand, if the rate of exchange falls (less dollars per unit of rupee or more rupees per unit of dollar), exports become cheaper and imports costlier, net export earnings rise and domestic *AD* curve shifts rightward. These outcomes are possible despite the fact that there is no change in the price level of the domestic economy.

International income effect also takes place when there is a rise in the level of real incomes of the foreign countries which have significant show up in demands for the domestic goods and services. This leads to unilateral increase in exports of domestic goods and services ultimately leading to rightward shift of *AD* curve. On the other hand, opposite impact is felt in case of fall in real incomes of foreign countries in which case *AD* curve shifts to the left.

(e) **Demand shocks: positive and negative:** Besides the above-mentioned factors, there are possibilities of sudden change/changes in the domestic or global scenario which may raise real incomes of the citizens. For instance, if there is a sudden rise in population of a certain country owing to influx of refugees due to political disturbances, the aggregate demand schedule will be shifting to the right thus raising the demand for goods and services. This will, likely, raise the price level ultimately. On the other hand, if a sizable population of a certain country dies due to a certain epidemic or war (spread of Coronavirus in China and other countries for recent example), aggregate demand may be suddenly falling although demand for selective categories of goods and services may rise.

During a recession or slowdown or certain disruptive policy decision of the government (India's demonetisation in 2016, for example), there are sudden job losses and income losses of the people. These obviously have negative shock on aggregate demand so that demand for many goods and services suddenly fall.

Expectations: Expectations play a very important role in determining human behaviour, particularly in the economic decision making of individuals and society. In the context of aggregate demand, there are certain kinds of expectations such as people's expectations about general outlook of the economy, future inflation, expectations about recession or cyclical downturn of the economy or overall perception of the economy in the minds of consumers, investors and the general public. If there is widespread optimism about the prospect of the economy in the people's mind, the current aggregate demand curve is likely to shift upward to the right. In the opposite case, there will be a leftward shift of the *AD* curve. As an example, the Indian economy has shown signs of slowdown in the early 2019-20 as evident from data thrown up by the official as well as non-official sources. Producers and manufacturers have resorted to cut back in production due to shortages in demand in major manufacturing sectors. The so-called "animal spirit" is said to be suffering a setback for investors. In terms of our analysis, the aggregate demand curve has virtually shifted backward to the left. Not only in the case of India alone, the current scenario in the global economy is beset with uncertainties of various kinds (economic as well as political) resulting in the recessionary conditions in major advanced economies of the world thus giving signals of shifting backward of the aggregate demand curves.

The aggregate supply: As far as the aggregate supply (*AS*) curve is concerned, its behaviour depends on the time horizon to be taken into consideration. If a short-run time horizon is taken into consideration, the supply curve will be upward sloping from left to right suggesting that suppliers are willing to supply greater and greater amounts of supply at higher prices of output. However, if a long-run time horizon is taken, the aggregate supply curve will be vertical in shape. This is because, in the long run, the real output or, (real GDP) becomes equal to the potential output (or real GDP). Hence, there is no scope for output level to change. It is the full employment level of output where all the economic resources are fully employed. Figure (9.7) illustrates this. It is pertinent, at this stage, to understand the difference between potential output and actual output (see chapter 2).

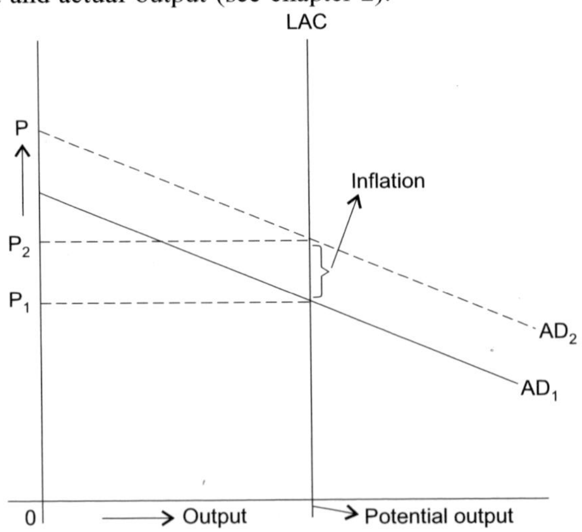

Figure 9.7 *Long-term supply curve: AS curve at potential output.*

In the introductory part (xxv) of the book, Fig. 0.1, on formal model building, we have distinguished three models, the first being the constant, price level based horizontal supply curve of Keynesian variety where, most prices are assumed to be constant because they are sticky in nature. Some prices are, of course, flexible. Therefore, we revise our position now to allow the aggregate supply curve to be upward sloping– responding to the rising price level. This supply curve is, of course, short run or, at best, medium run. Figure 9.7 depicts short-run along with long-run supply curves.

9.3 SHIFT IN LAS CURVE

Shift in LAS curve takes place when potential GDP changes. For instance, when potential GDP increases in the long run LAS curve shifts to the right. However, along with it SAS also shifts to the right. Potential GDP changes due to the following factors:

1. Change in the full employment quantity of labour.
2. Change in the quantity of capital (physical or human).
3. Advancement in technology.

1. Change in the availability of labour either due to population growth particularly the proportion of labour force (population in the working age group) or their qualitative improvement through education and training leads to the expansion of the base of the economy—the full employment or potential quantity of labour force.
2. Similar change in the availability of capital such as raw materials (new sources through invention) and other forms of capital help expand the productive base of the economy. Easy availability of raw materials, for instance, reduces the production cost so that firms can produce and supply more. Qualitative improvement in such capital goods also leads to increased supply even at the existing price level.
3. Technology advancement brought about by investment leads to productivity improvement. Thus, more output can be raised by the same or lower input costs. Long run supply curve therefore, shifts to the right due to all these factors. The shifts in LAS curve are shown in Fig. 9.8 (a) & 9.8 (b).

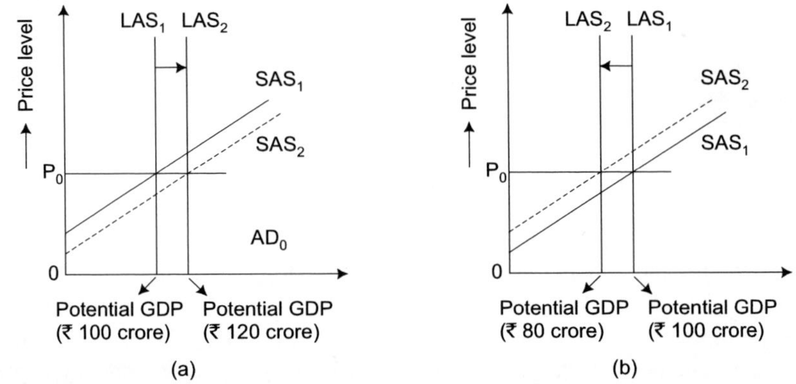

Figure 9.8 *Shifts in LAS curve due to change in potential output.*

9.4 EQUILIBRIUM OF THE ECONOMY IN THE AD-AS FRAMEWORK

The equilibrium of the aggregate economy can be understood in terms of *AD-AS* framework when both the curves are put together and jointly they determine the aggregate price level as well as output (or real GDP). Clearly, the equilibrium set of price-output is determined at the point of intersection of both *AD* and *AS* curves when the quantity of real GDP demanded is equal to the quantity of real GDP supplied. Figure 9.9 illustrates this position. As the figure shows, there is short run equilibrium of the economy with ₹ 1000 crore of real GDP demanded as well as supplied at P_0 price level. However, in the short run, real GDP may be below or above this equilibrium GDP. If real GDP is below equilibrium GDP (for instance ₹ 800 crore), this means the supply falls below demand, the firms raise prices and increase production by moving along SAS. On the other hand, if the real GDP is above equilibrium GDP, e.g., ₹ 1020 crore firms decrease production and lower prices again moving along the SAS. This means supply rises above demand. This way short-run equilibrium in the economy is re-established. It may, however, be noted that in the short run, actual real GDP may be either lower or higher than the potential GDP. If it is less than potential GDP, it results in Keynesian-type involuntary unemployment.

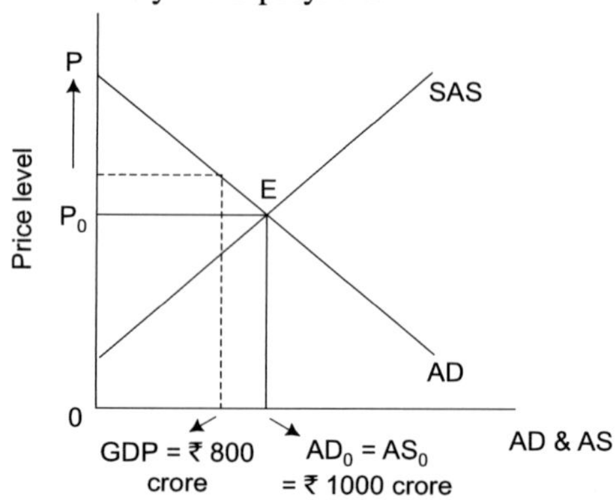

Figure 9.9 *Short-run equilibrium of the economy: AD and SAS with Keynesian involuntary unemployment.*

9.5 LONG RUN EQUILIBRIUM OF THE ECONOMY

Long run macro equilibrium of the economy occurs when real GDP equals potential GDP and when the economy moves along the long run aggregate supply curve (LAS) as shown in Fig. 9.10. The figure shows long run equilibrium reaching point *E* with *AD* and LAS intersecting each other. The economy in the short run might have been moving along SAS but, given sufficient time, price level, money wages and other input costs might have been fully adjusted to come back to LAS. Also, in response to change in aggregate demand, the economy would likely move along LAS.

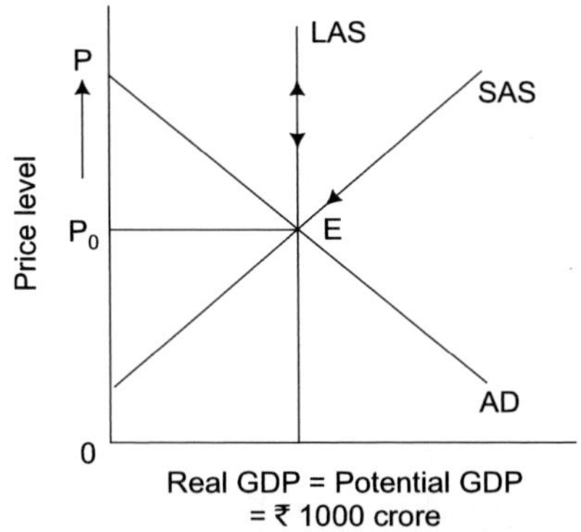

Figure 9.10 *Long-run equilibrium of the economy: AD and LAS intersecting each other.*

9.5.1 Analysis of Inflation and Recession in AD-AS Framework

Inflationary situation occurs in the economy when *AD* increases by more than the increase in LAS. According to current thinking, when money supply increases faster than the potential GDP, *AD* increases also faster than long run *AS* curve. The situation is depicted in Fig. 9.11(a). In the figure, two *AD* curves are shown AD_1 and AD_2. The *AD* curve has shifted to a greater extent from AD_1 to AD_2 rightward than the LAS curve. This has resulted in increase in price level from P_0 to P_1. However shift in LAS curve to the right implies economic growth taking place. During this course, it is possible that money supply increases faster than the requirement of economic growth. This causes increase in *AD*—very often faster than the desired extent and causes inflation in the economy. (For detailed theoretical discussion on inflation, refer to Chapter 17).

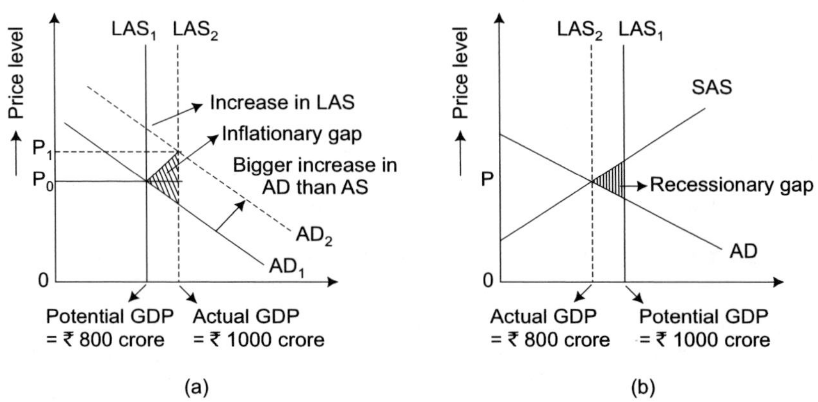

Figure 9.11 *Inflationary gap and recessionary gap.*

A recessionary gap in the output takes place when actual GDP is less than the potential GDP as shown in Fig. 9.11(b). As is evident from the figure, the equilibrium in the economy is at below full employment level at ₹ 800 crore of GDP, while the potential GDP is ₹ 1000 crore, hence ₹ 200 crore of GDP is the recessionary gap. Thus recession (or downward phase of business cycle) takes place because aggregate demand and short run aggregate supply fluctuate but the money wage rate doesn't change rapid enough to keep real GDP at potential GDP.

9.6 FLUCTUATIONS IN AGGREGATE DEMAND

The short run and long run effects of fluctuations in aggregate demand can also be analysed in the present framework. Figure 9.12 shows the effects of an increase in *AD* as it shifts from AD_1 to AD_2. The initial position is the long run equilibrium when AD_1 intersects the LAS curve at point E_1 with ₹ 1000 crore. Now, as the *AD* curve shifts rightward, firms in the short run would increase output and raise prices. Thus, real GDP increases to ₹ 1100 crore from the initial ₹ 1000 crore. As a result, the price level (here shown in terms of index number) has gone up from 110 to 115. The firms have moved along SAS-from E_1 to E_2. In this situation, there is an inflationary gap of ₹ 100 crore. Now the money wage rate begins to rise and short run aggregate supply begins to fall. SAS curve moves leftward along AD_2. The price level rises and real GDP falls until it has returned to potential GDP. This is the long run effect of the fluctuation in aggregate demand.

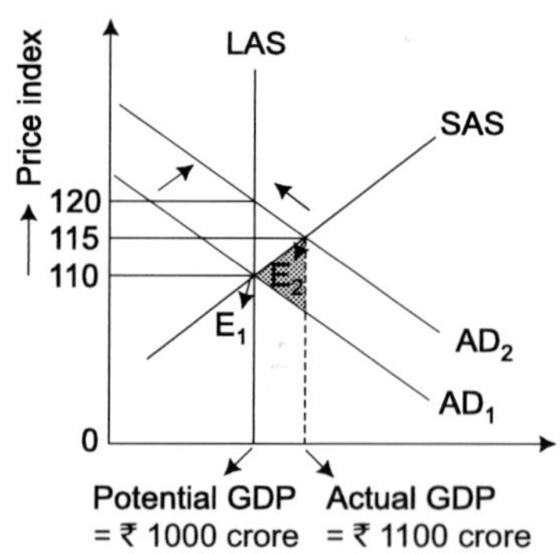

Figure 9.12 *Fluctuation in aggregate demand and inflationary gap.*

9.7 FLUCTUATIONS IN AGGREGATE SUPPLY

Now the short run and long run effects of fluctuations in aggregate supply can be analysed in terms of shifts in *AS* curve as shown in Fig. 9.13. The figure shows how a situation of stagflation develops when there are fluctuations in aggregate supply. With initial *AD* and LAS and SAS_1, the long run equilibrium position is at E_1 with ₹ 1000 crore of GDP. Supposing there is an oil-shock so that the price of crude oil goes up suddenly. This results in reduction in aggregate supply. The SAS curve shifts to the left to SAS_2. The new short run equilibrium is now at point E_2 with actual GDP equal to ₹ 800 crore. The price level has also increased and aggregate supply has decreased. This illustrates the situation of stagflation—a combination of inflation and stagnation (lower GDP growth)-coincide.

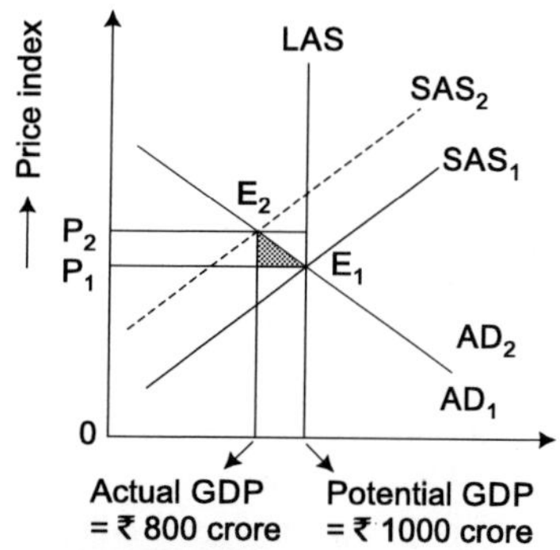

Figure 9.13 *Fluctuation of aggregate supply and stagflation.*

9.8 THE REAL BALANCE EFFECT: A DIGRESSION

Real balance refers to the real value of money and other forms of wealth that the community holds. When these values are expressed in monetary terms or nominal terms, they are known as nominal balance. Now given the nominal balance of wealth of the community at a certain point in time, if there is a change in the price level (which includes the prices of all such wealth held by the community), there will be a change in the real value of the wealth. If the price level rises, the real value of wealth falls and if the price level falls, the real value of the wealth rises. Accordingly, the real purchasing power of the wealth holders falls or rises. This is precisely "the wealth effect" advanced for the first time by classical economist, A.C. Pigou in 1941. Pigou's wealth effect on consumption came as a defence of the classical theory of employment when Keynes' General Theory largely challenged the classical postulates to ensure full employment. When Keynes argued that full employment was not achievable due to inadequate aggregate demand in the short run, Pigou's wealth effect tried to establish that given the sufficient wage-price felxibility, this will still be possible through the wealth effect. For instance, if price falls (or, price deflation takes place) then the real value of all wealth will rise. This will have a favourable effect on consumption expenditure—people will spend more due to their increased level of real wealth. Thus, it assumes that wealth has positive effect on consumption and hence will expand aggregate demand; employment and output will also increase in the face of unemployment and this will ultimately restore full employment. This wealth effect on consumption is also known as "Pigou effect" since then.

Later on, the idea was more fully expanded by Don Patinkin in his book, *Money, Interest and Prices: An Integration of Monetary and Value Theory*, 1956. Patinkin, using rigorous mathematical analysis proved that monetary sector and real sector of the economy are interdependent and not separable as argued by the classical writers. The so-called 'dichotomy' postulate of the classicals is, therefore, demolished. The reasoning Patinkin gave is that the effect of changes in the price level on the real value of the people's wealth holdings disturbs the households' consumption behaviour and, in fact, affects the relative prices of commodities in the real sector. The two sectors – monetary and real – are, therefore, integrated and do not any longer stand separated. Henceforth, the effect is known as 'real balance effect'.

Critics of Pigou effect have, however, expressed doubts about price deflation method as an effective channel to restore full employment. Firstly, even if it has some favourable effect on consumption, it may not be sufficient to promote the required level of aggregate demand and hence employment. Secondly, community's asset holdings mainly consist of money and bonds (although other forms of wealth are also available). Now, if price level falls, generally, it is followed by fall in the rate of interest as well. Falling interest rate means rise in the price of bonds. In such a situation, as we have seen in Chapter 3, bond holders would not purchase more bonds; rather they would prefer more money. Lesser demand for bonds means less investment expenditure and so, lower aggregate demand, lower employment and output.

The other forms of wealth, for instance, house property, generally follow market rule of demand-supply. If price level increases, the nominal value as well as real value of houses also increase and similarly, if price level decreases, their nominal and real values decrease too. Even if general price level does not change, but demand for houses goes up, their prices go up. Thus, not all forms of wealth experience the real balance effect in both directions of price level changes.

In spite of these shortcomings, modern-day economists tend to believe that real balance effect works at least in case of some assets—particularly liquid money and nominal interest payment (of debt). If price level rises (or, inflation rate rises), real value of money balance falls and so also the real interest rate.

SUMMARY

1. The model of aggregate demand and aggregate supply has been extensively used by western economists in order to explain short-run and long-run equilibrium conditions of the economy in the *AD-AS*-price level framework. The derivation of the *AD* curve follows either by direct implication of Keynesian *AD-AS* (with constant price level) and introducing change in the price level as a parameter or introducing real balance effect in the *LM* function in the *IS-LM* framework of analysis.

2. Aggregate supply behaviour differs from individual micro-level supply behaviour in certain respects. While microeconomic theory suggests a short-run as well as long-run upward sloping supply curves with price level (varying in their slopes only), macro-level aggregate supply behaviour suggests a short-run upward sloping supply curve but a long-run vertical supply curve.
3. Aggregate demand components are: (a) consumption demand, (b) private investment demand, (c) government demand (or, government purchases of goods and services) and (d) net external demand (exports-imports). Aggregate supply is a derived concept—derived from supplies of basic factors of production such as (a) raw materials, (b) different components of other capital goods, (c) labour supplies, (d) land, water and other natural resources harnessed by human efforts and (e) entrepreneurial abilities. These are sometimes conveniently subsumed as land, labour, capital and entrepreneurship.
4. Shifts in *AD* and *AS* curves take place under the impact of different forces in the economy including economic and non-economic policies of the government. For instance, shifts in *AD* curves occur due to changes in monetary and fiscal policies of the government, change in expectations about future income changes, future inflation and future profits. In an open economy, with greater globalised environment, income changes in the importing countries cause change in *AD* in the exporting countries through rise/fall in the incomes of their population.

EXERCISE

1. Explain methods of derivation of aggregate demand curve.
2. What is real balance effect? Illustrate its inherent meaning and implication for the value of money and other assets.
3. Enumerate the main factors that influence the changes in aggregate demand.
4. Explain the behaviour of short-run and long-run aggregate supply curve. What will be the behaviour of aggregate supply curve under very long run?
5. Explain under what conditions 'stagflation' occurs. Compare the situation of stagflation with inflation and recession.

REFERENCES

1. Mankiw, G.N. (2006), Macroeconomics, 6th Edition, Worth Publishers.
2. Don Patinkin (1965), Money, Interest and Prices. 2nd Edition, Harper and Row.
3. Dornbusch, R., Fischer S. and Startz R. (2012), Macroeconomics, 10th Edition, McGraw Hill Education (India), New Delhi.

PART-5

Post-Keynesian Macroeconomics

10

Monetarism

10.1 THE ORIGIN OF MONETARISM

Monetarism emerged as a school of thought originated and nurtured in the hands of late Professor Milton Friedman and his associates at the University of Chicago. Prof. Friedman received the Nobel Memorial Prize in Economic Science in 1976 for his contribution to the field of monetary history, theory of consumption and theory and complexity of stabilisation policy.

Professor Friedman's contribution to economics is immense as is evident from his creation of a 'new school of thought', called 'monetarism'. In almost all his writings, the dominant role of money in the economy is clearly visible. At a time when Keynes dominated in all theoretical and policy domains in economics, Milton Friedman's economic thought came as a great turning point and, in fact, a formidable challenge to Keynesian thought.

Milton Friedman drew great inspiration from the Classical School of Economics, so that he can be called a classical economist. His reformulation of Classical Quantity Theory of Money as well as his assertion of full employment in the long run along with the natural rate of unemployment hypothesis bear testimony of his belonging to the classical tradition and faith.

Although it is difficult to evaluate or even broadly summarise Milton Friedman's contribution in the limited space of a short chapter, we will attempt to discuss at least two of his famous works, namely, *A Monetary History of the United States, 1867-1960,* and *The Quantity Theory of Money: A Restatement.*

10.2 MONETARY HISTORY OF THE U.S. 1867-1960

In their *A Monetary History….*, Milton Friedman and Anna Schwartz (one of his prominent associates in the Chicago School) studied the relationship between the money supply and the price level in the US covering a period of almost a hundred years and found a remarkable direct association between the two. Largely, this was the main basis of the emergence of the new theory of monetarism in as much as attempting to provide an empirical basis of the said relationship.

When the book was published in 1963, it was hailed as a 'classic' in the academic circle. For instance, economist Alan Meltzer wrote in 1965: "The book is clearly destined to be a classic, perhaps one of the few emerging in that role rather than growing into it." Similarly, economist R. Clower praised the book thus: "The book offers an almost inexhaustible supply of worthwhile conjectures. I have no doubt that it ...will be the focus of a major share of scholarly research on money and income during the coming decade". James Tobin, the future Nobel laureate, praised the book even more eloquently in the following words: "This is one of those rare books that leave their mark on all future research on the subject. "Similarly, Hugh Rockoff, in a retrospective review article in 2000, called it "the most significant book in the field of economic history in the twentieth century".

Friedman and Schwartz, while conducting their research on monetary history, drew substantially from Wisley Clair Mitchell's *Business Cycles* (1913). From the historical data of the earlier period of business cycle (1897-1914), Friedman and Schwartz concluded that the discovery of new gold fields in South Africa and other countries as well as new methods of extracting gold from ore were examples of independent change in money stock which was responsible for increased money supply leading to the rise in price level during that period. So the authors argued that some changes in the stock of money could occur for reasons independent of current and future changes in economic activity (Hugh Rockoff, 'On the origins of '*A Monetary History* ….., 2006'). They further argued that the combination of independent changes in money, which could be observed by looking closely at the historical circumstance in which changes in money occurred, and the resulting changes in the economy provided persuasive evidence that "money mattered" (Rockoff, op. cit.).

10.3 DIRECT LINKAGE BETWEEN RISE IN MONEY STOCK AND PRICE LEVEL

Thus far there was near agreement between the analyses of Mitchell and Friedman-Schwartz. But Mitchell recognised the role of bank lending (credit) as the most important part of the transmission mechanism linking change in money supply to the change in economic activities. For example, an unexpected increase in bank reserves would produce an increase in bank lending, a fall in interest rate and an increase in investment that would generate increased economic activity (Rockoff, op. cit.). Friedman-Schwartz, however, did not agree with this transmission channel. The latter insisted that there existed a direct linkage between increase in money stock and the price level. Thus "money matters" entered as a powerful argument in monetarism.

10.4 MONEY SUPPLY AND BUSINESS CYCLES

Hence, expansion and contraction of money supply were viewed as the main factors behind business cycles. While Friedman-Schwartz did recognise other non-monetary factors behind business cycles, they did not discuss them in detail in their analysis. For instance, they discussed good harvest in the US with poor harvests in Europe on a number of occasions in the 19th century, the stock market crash of 1929, wartime mobilisation and demobilisation and the rise of labour unions in the 1930s. Similarly, they assumed that there was an inherent tendency for the economy to recover from recessions. Regarding the role of monetary policy during recession or depression, Friedman and Schwartz viewed them being the effect of the decrease in the stock of money either during the Great Depression of 1929-30 or 1937-38 recession and as " a factor that significantly intensified the severity of the decline", (Friedman and Schwartz, 1963b, p. 544, quoted, Rockoff, 2006). Similarly, they held the view that excess expansion of money stock is the reason behind the cyclical boom.

10.5 MONETARISM AND QUANTITY THEORY OF MONEY

Monetarism signalled the revival of the old quantity theory of money of the classical economists, as explained below, which established the direct (and, of course of proportional) relationship between the quantity of money and the price level. In fact, monetarism provided the empirical basis for the conclusions of the quantity theory.

The other main ideas of monetarism are: (1) by controlling the money supply in the economy, inflation can be controlled and (2) monetary policy plays a more important role than fiscal policy, in fact, fiscal policy has a dismal role in the management of the economy.

As has been mentioned above, before monetarism as a school of thought gained currency, Keynesian economic thought or Keynesianism influenced and dominated the economic policy domain and that the role of fiscal policy rather than monetary policy was considered to be more important for controlling the economic fluctuations. Keynesianism continued to dominate almost four decades post Great Depression. However, the later events of stagflation, a situation of inflation and stagnation, of the mid-1970s and 1980s baffled the Keynesian policy which failed to explain stagflation. Monetarism flourished during this critical period of history.

In Friedman's view, supply of money in the economy should be increased by a certain fixed rate per period depending on the growth of output and productivity in the economy. This is known as the 'monetary targeting' policy, targeting a certain rate of growth of money supply.

It may be recalled here that Friedman differed with the Fed Reserve's policy of not maintaining the smooth and continued money supply during the Depression years and maintained that the Great Depression could not have happened had the Fed continued its money supply unabated. Subsequently, on the 90th birthday of Friedman in 2002, the then Fed chairman, Ben Bernanke admitted having committed a mistake by the Fed. During the Depression years but he assured Friedman to be amending the next time if it would happen. During the 2008-09 Great Recession, it may be recalled, Bernanke kept his promise of continued money supply and also applied several unconventional monetary policy tools. It is a different matter to assess whether Bernanke's monetarist policy tools resulted in desired effects post-2008 years which many commentators differed even to this date.

On the question of unemployment, Milton disagreed with the Keynesian view that there exists 'involuntary unemployment' in the economy. On the contrary, he believed that there is full employment just in line with the arguments of the Classical economists. However, he supplemented his argument with the 'natural rate of unemployment hypothesis' clause which he denied being 'involuntary unemployment' but which is quite common in an economy given its dynamic nature with labour market flexibility. At the same time, Friedman also believed, as in the classical tradition, that without the government intervention, a free society would attain full employment with flexibility in the wages and prices.

However, monetarism fell in terms of its diminished influence in the wake of the rise of New Classical as well as New Keynesian economic thoughts in the eighties and nineties with their continued debates on major economic issues till date even though certain areas of agreements and disagreements remained between Keynesianism and monetarism on the one hand and between monetarism and New Classical Economics on the other.

In recent years, though, to revive the low growth and low inflation economies of the west, economists of the Chicago School tradition mooted the idea of "helicopter drop of money" which was in line with the doctrine of monetarism. The helicopter drop of money may be looked upon as a policy tool for direct transfer of money to the public in general which would expectedly raise aggregate income in the recession hit economies. Although these monetarist ideas have not been tried in policy circles, a number of modern economists have recommended their use in modified forms.

10.6 MILTON FRIEDMAN AND THE DEMAND FUNCTION FOR MONEY

Any discussion on monetarism is incomplete without reference to Friedman's reformulation of the Quantity Theory of Money and his programme for monetary stability for the US. In his lead paper, titled The Quantity Theory of Money: A Restatement, in *Studies in the Quantity Theory of Money* (1956), Friedman started with the cash balance version of the demand for money and expanded it as a broader theory of the demand for money, money viewed as a form of the wealth which depends on income and on rates of return on several alternative assets such as bonds, equities, physical assets, the ratio of non-human to human wealth (which represents a form of human capital) as also a variable, u, reflecting the factors affecting the tastes and preferences of individuals and the institutional factors like the payment practices of businesses (see section 7.3

on Friedman's Demand function for money for details). On the left-hand side of the quantity equation, Friedman specified the supply of money, *Ms*, and its determinants in terms of (a) reserve money (or high powered money), which depends on two crucial (proximate) determinants, namely, currency-deposit ratio of the public and the reserve-deposit ratio of the banks which, in turn, depend on the respective behaviours of the two entities (public and the banks), (b) aggregate money supply and (c) the money multiplier as applied to the money creation process of the banking system (see sections 6.3 & 6.4 for details of money supply sources).

What is relevant here to remember is that the rates of returns on various assets, mentioned above, represent the 'expected' nominal rates of returns. Secondly, in Friedman's view, any change in any of the underlying factors that change the supply of money is likely to change, initially, the level of nominal income or other nominal rates, but ultimately and predominantly change in the level of prices. Thus, money supply remains the principal determinant of price level.

On the theory of inflation, Friedman-Schwartz were clear in their view that "inflation is always and everywhere a monetary phenomenon". Friedman's views on inflation were hugely supported by Philip Cagan's econometric work on inflation (Cagan, 1956). They have, in fact, cited examples of various countries suffering from high inflation as being the result of high rates of money supply.

Thus, the policy implications of Friedman's quantity theory that he enunciates are as follows:

The acceptance of quantity theory means that the quantity of money is a key variable in policies directed at controlling the level of prices or of nominal income. Inflation can be prevented if and only if the quantity of money per unit of output can be kept from increasing appreciably. Deflation can be prevented if and only if the quantity of money per unit of output can be kept from decreasing appreciably (Milton Friedman, *Collected Works*, op. cit.).

In *A Program for Monetary Stability*, Friedman submitted three proposals with respect to US monetary policy in 1960. (1) to switch from the pegged exchange rates of the Bretton Woods system, then in place, to freely floating exchange rates, (2) to impose 100% required reserves on deposit- issuing banks and (3) to direct the Federal Reserve to maintain a constant growth rate of the stock of money. It may be mentioned here that out of the three proposals, listed above, at least two have been wholly or partially implemented: (1) has been implemented to a substantial extent although interventions by the central banks have been witnessed from time to time. Regarding (3), the Federal Reserve is understood to have followed this suggestion but perhaps not seriously enough.

It ought to be mentioned here that the New Keynesian scholars have criticised the Quantity Theory of Money, as had Keynes himself done, principally on two grounds: (a) the velocity of money (V) is not stable on empirical grounds and (b) P, the price level of the component, PY on the right-hand side of the quantity equation, is "rigid", thus any change in M is most likely to influence Y, the real national income in the first place.

10.7 CRITICISM OF MONETARISM

Critics of monetarism (hailing mainly from the neo- Keynesian group of economists) argue that the historical method of correlating the growth of money stock and the price level changes do not, in fact, prove any 'causation'. For example, it is difficult to say whether money stock changes caused money income changes or money income changes caused money stock changes. In the critics' view, therefore, *Monetary History* of Friedman and Schwartz placed too much weight on historical evidence without taking recourse to mathematical models or statistical tests of causation. The critics were sure that Friedman and Schwartz had confused between "correlation" and "causation". For example, money might be correlated with national income because changes in money caused changes in national income or because money and changes in national income were produced by some third factor, say changes in fiscal policy. So the critics think that Friedman and Schwartz might have fallen into this trap.

Another scathing criticism has been levelled by James Tobin (Nobel laureate) and a well known neo-Keynesian economist. Based on his 1970 paper, "Money and Income: Post Hoc Ergo Propter Hoc.?", Tobin presented an ultra Keynesian model in which money did not matter that fit Friedman-Schwartz's findings regarding the relationship between money and income better than a Friedman model. Friedman-Schwartz, however, countered while stressing the important role that historical evidence played in their conclusion that money mattered.

Another important criticism came from economist Peter Temin, who in his book, *Did Monetary Forces Cause the Great Depression*? (1976), commented that the chapter 7 of Friedman-Schwartz's *Monetary History* which specifically dealt with the 'Great Contraction, 1929-33', was "merely a detailed description of how the supply of money and other variables had changed during the contraction. Temin thinks that the main conclusions of the *Monetary History* … are that the level of income fell as sharply as it did in the early thirties because of a massive fall in the stock of money. This stock of money, in turn, fell because of sustained effects of multiple banking crises, that is because of a restriction in the supply of money. But an account of the supply of money cannot be taken for an account of the stock of money, unless it is known that demand plays no role. The *Monetary History* appears to have been designed to show just this ….but it turns out to be a narrative based on such an assumption, not an argument for it." Friedman and Schwartz, writing elsewhere, tried to show that the stock of money was historically determined independently of income and that the correlation between money and income, therefore, must be interpreted to mean that movements in the stock of money determine movements of income. The *Monetary History*, however, does not provide independent evidence for this proposition. It follows that the hypothesis about the cause of the Great Depression must be regarded as unproven as well (Temin, op. cit.).

Temin would like to look for, instead, a contrasting hypothesis for determining the causative relationship between money and income or any other variables. For example, the money hypothesis, as he uses the term for Friedman-Schwartz hypothesis, would predict a rise in short-term interest rates during 1929-33. On the other hand, the spending hypothesis, as Temin prefers to call for the Keynesian hypothesis, would predict a fall in short-term interest rates. Since, during the Depression years (1929-33), the short-term interest rates had fallen, Temin concluded that the monetary forces did not cause the Depression. Peter Temin, therefore, did not approve of the methodology adopted by Friedman and Schwartz for determining causation. In his view, chapter 7 of *Monetary History* is, essentially, a narrative constructed on the assumption that money matters. It contributes to the case for believing that money matters only to the extent that it provides another data point. For Friedman and Schwartz, the conclusion that the decline in the stock of money aggravated the contraction, and that it could have been prevented by appropriate policy measures, follows from the whole body of evidence. According to critics, therefore, the Great Depression was just a separate case history. The monetary factors that Friedman and Schwartz emphasised so forcefully, could be established only by a large number of similar case studies.

SUMMARY

1. Monetarism is a school of economic thought that grew and nurtured by Nobel laureate economist Milton Friedman and his team at the Chicago School of Economics, USA.
2. The main thesis of monetarism is to establish and substantiate the classical view that money stock/supply plays the key role in determining the price level in the economy.
3. Milton Friedman co-authored with Anna Schwartz, studied the monetary history of the U.S. for a period of about one hundred years (1867–1960) and found remarkable direct relationship between the growth of money stock and the price level. This major finding was the basis of monetarism. The study emphasized and reaffirmed the conclusion of the classical quantity theory that money supply and price level are directly related and that growth of money supply is directly responsible for rise in the price level.
4. Monetarism also stresses the point that business cycles and inflation are caused primarily by excessive growth of money supply. Hence, Friedman held the view that inflation is always and everywhere a monetary phenomenon'. On Great Depression, 1929-30, Friedman's view was

that US Federal Reserve's faulty monetary policy was responsible for failing to halt the simple recession from drifting into depression. This could not have happened, as Friedman argued, had the Fed Reserve continued unabated the supply of money in the economy during the entire Depression years.

5. Having his allegiance to the classical school of thinking, Friedman presented the Quantity Theory of Money in a reformulated form—particularly the demand function of money and generalised it to include several alternative assets to money with their respective rates of return. The particular emphasis that he put on the ratio of non-human to human assets is an attempt to broaden the whole idea of the demand for money.
6. Monetarism was criticised by several authors, particularly by the New Keynesian economists. While monetarism argued for the view that 'money matters' (emphasizing the role of money) the New Keynesianism held that' money does not matter' and instead, 'aggregate demand' plays the dominant part.
7. New Keynesians further challenged the monetarist view of direct relationship between money stock and the price level and argued that the growth of money stock did not ensure the growth of money supply unless aggregate demand is influenced. In fact, rise in aggregate demand only raises the demand for money. So, aggregate demand and not the money stock growth is responsible for the rise in the price level.
8. The critics further argued that Milton Friedman confused between 'association' and 'causation'. 'Association' between two variables did not mean that one caused the other so that one could not conclude that growth in money stock caused the rise in price level.

EXERCISE

1. Which names are associated with 'monetarism'? When did monetarism flourish?
2. What are the main tenets of monetarism? Explain.
3. Who wrote 'A Monetary History of the United States—1867-1960 and when?
4. State if Milton Friedman belonged to (a) classical economists (b) Neoclassical economists, (c) Keynesian economists (d) New Keynesian economists
5. What do the terms 'money matters' signify? How do they differ from the terms, 'money does not matter'?
6. What causes business cycles according to monetarist view?
7. What is classical demand for money? How did Friedman reformulate the classical Quantity Theory of money?

REFERENCES

1. Hugh Rockoff (2006): "On the Origins of a Monetary History of the United States, 1867-1960", NBER, Working Paper 12666, November.
2. James R. Lothian (2009): Milton Friedman's Monetary Economics and the Quantity Theory Tradition, Fordham University, New York, USA.
3. www.hoover.org "*From the Collected Works of Milton Friedman*", compiled by Robert Leeson and Charles G. Palm.
4. P. Cagan (1956): "The Monetary Dynamics of Hyperinflation," In: M. Friedman (ed.) *Studies in Quantity Theory of Money*, University of Chicago Press, USA.
5. Peter Temin (1976) *Did Monetary Forces Cause the Great Depression*?

11

New Classical Macroeconomics/ Supply Side Economics

In the present chapter, we will discuss the essentials of new classical economics often clubbed with supply side economics also which came into prominence in the later half of 1970s and 1980s. After the Keynesian revolution, during the previous decades, the major macroeconomic problem gripped the western capitalist economies in the form of stagflation – a combination of stagnation and inflation. In other words, it was at the same time a combination of high rate of unemployment and low growth rate of the economy. The new classical economics at this juncture was, in a sense, a paradigm reverse shift in economic thought. It is a revival of old classical economics along with certain specific prescriptions for economic policies. It may be mentioned here that Phillips curve as also *IS-LM* model played, until then, a significant role as twin policies of macroeconomics.

11.1 SUPPLY SIDE ECONOMICS

The new thinking on Supply Side Economies was popularized by the works of Robert Mundell, Arthus Laffer, Victor Kanto and J. Wanniski during the same period of '70s and '80s. The supply side model was put into practice by the then US President Ronald Reagan and British Prime Minister M. Thatcher in their respective countries and economies. Hence, supply side economics is also known as Reaganomics and Thatcherism. The supply side theory has its intellectual root in early economic thoughts of Austrian and old Classical school of thought as propounded by economists like Adam Smith, David Hume and Alexander Hamilton. The theory is largely based upon central classical law known as Say's law of market (discussed in Chapter 2) which is expressed as "supply creates its own demand". To repeat the idea, Say's law states that whenever a good is produced and supplied it automatically creates demand equivalent to its own value. It argues that, in a barter type economy, a good is supplied in a market not for itself but for some other good that the supplier needs. Even in a complex economy involving money, the purchasing power for the good is created in the process of its production through the payments made to the factors of production. In fact, at the aggregate level, i.e., when all new goods are added together, the aggregate supply will be exactly equal to aggregate demand and there will be no overproduction or under-consumption of any good in the economy. Additionally, the economy will be operating at full or near full employment level.

The supply side economists have rekindled their faith in the Say's law by advocating that ensuring adequate supply will take care of everything including economic growth and distribution of income. As for specific economic policies, supply siders would argue for cuts in tax rates—both of income and capital gains tax rates, which would, in their view, enhance tax revenues for the State. In fact, supply siders have great faith in the "**Laffer Curve**" which relates tax revenue collections with tax rates such that at a relatively low rate of taxation the tax revenue increases and attains maximum at a certain optimum rate. At higher rates thereafter, however, tax revenue begins to fall. Figure 11.1 illustrates Laffer curve. As is evident from the figure, if the actual tax rate is above the optimum point *E*, tax cut would generate tax revenue. If however, tax rate is at a very low level, then raising the tax rate would increase the tax revenue also. The crucial question is to determine the actual tax rate in the economic system, whether it is above the optimum point or below it.

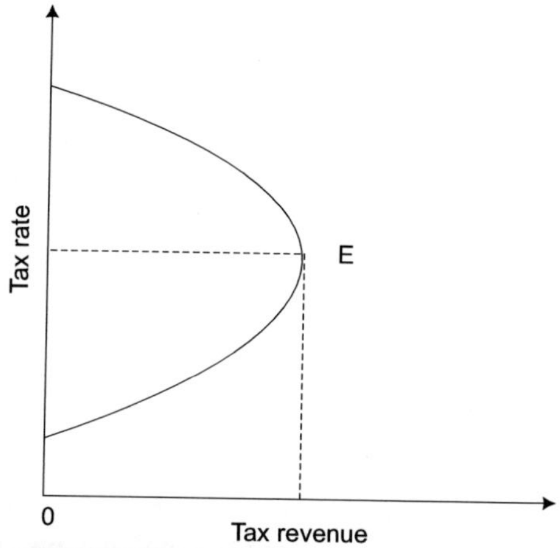

Figure 11.1 *Laffer curve.*

In the case of US economy, as supply side economists view, the then existing tax rates were much higher and above the optimum point of the Laffer curve, hence they advocated for tax cut with a view to generating the tax revenues for the State on the one hand and releasing resources for the manufacturing firms thus lowering their cost of production. Additional investment would thus, expectedly, be forthcoming both for the firms as well as for the government. The supply of goods and services would consequently be enhanced which would lead to economic growth. One more argument in favour of tax cut is that such a measure increases the tax payer's "incentives to work and save". They would thus work more and enhance their incomes; this would ultimately raise GDP as well as tax revenue through greater collections rather than decreasing them. The other tenets of supply side economics are as follows:

11.1.1 Free Trades

Since taxes act as trade barriers, their reduction would lead to increase in total income. This applies as much in case of domestic trade as to trade among nations. This essentially is the free trade argument of old classical thinkers. The principles of comparative advantage advocated by classical economists like Adam Smith, David Ricardo, Bastable, etc., states that when the free trade principle is applied in the field of international trade, it enhances the incomes of all trading countries.

Supply side economists also advocate free movement of goods as well as capital among nations and removal of all kinds of trade barriers. We may mention here that during the last 30 years or so one of the integral policies of the supply side/new classical economics has consistently been to implement the free trade principle with modifications made through the newly established organization of World Trade Organisation (WTO).

11.1.2 Indexed Marginal Income Tax Rates

Supply side economists argue that monetary inflation pushes wage earners into higher marginal income tax brackets which remain static. This means that as wages increase to maintain purchasing power with prices, income tax brackets are not adjusted accordingly, so that wage earners are pushed into higher income tax brackets than the income tax policy intends. Therefore, they advocate for indexed marginal income tax rates – i.e., rates must be properly indexed to adjust for monetary inflation (price rise).

Supply siders, however, do not have much to say on the budget deficit arising out of cut in marginal tax rates. As Mundell has pointed out "Fiscal discipline is a learned behaviour". To put it another way, eventually the unfavourable effects of running persistent budget deficits will force governments to reduce spending in line with their levels of revenue. They also sometimes cite Robert Barrow's work which states that rational economic actors will buy bonds in sufficient quantities to reduce long term interest rate so that government will be able to sufficiently enhance resources to reduce budget deficits. Critics however, argue that the standard exchange rate theory could predict instead a devaluation of the currency of the nation running high budget deficit and eventual crowding out of private investment. In fact these are the outcomes of the recent post-global recession era not only in US but also in the European countries which are facing the great debt crisis.

Certain empirical findings on US economy's tax cut policy are summarized below:

President Ronald Reagan, after his election victory in 1980 promised and, in fact, executed an across-the-board reduction in income tax rates and even larger reduction in capital gains tax rates. When the US economy, after suffering nearly 16 months of recession during 1981-82, experienced economic revival, these tax cuts were seen as the most important contributing factor. The critics however, were of the view that the rebound was not due to any supply side policy but rather due to federal budget deficit acting as "pump priming" which was quite in line with IS-LM model of late 1970s. The critics also point out that during the immediate post-1981 years after the tax rate cuts, tax revenues as a share of GDP dropped even though nominal revenues increased. The question of whether the tax cuts proved Mundell's prediction as correct (tax cut would increase national output so much that tax revenues would also increase and economic expansion would also mop up excess liquidity and bring inflation back under control) has sparked much debate between supply siders and mainstream economists. According to the latter group of economists, while nominal revenues rebounded after the tax cuts comparing nominal tax collections overtime, fails to take account of inflation. Thus, by converting tax revenue from nominal to real terms, these economists have shown that tax revenues didn't surpass their 1981 levels until 1987.

The defenders of supply side economists complain that the focus of the debate on government revenue tends to ignore the societal benefits of economic growth – primarily lower levels of unemployment, higher wages for workers and lower prices for consumers. However, this argument, better known as "trickle down economics", according to critics, should be viewed as distinct from the economic theory of supply side economics.

Critics of supply side economics claim that it failed to produce much of the exaggerated gains promised by some supply siders. Paul Krugmann, Princeton University Professor and 2008 Nobel Laureate in Economics, summarized the situations thus "when Ronald Reagan was elected, the supply siders got a chance to try out their ideas. Unfortunately, they failed". Describing the supply side theory as "free lunches" along with other critics Krugman emphasized on the increased budget deficit during Reagan administration as proof that Laffer curve was wrong.

The supply side advocates however asserted that revenues increased but spending increased even faster. They typically point to total revenue in this regard even though it was only income tax rates that were cut. For instance, of the total increase in tax revenues from $600.6 billion in 1983 to $ 666.5 bn in 1984, 26 bn was due to inflation alone., $18.3 bn to corporate taxes and $21.4 bn. to social insurance revenues (mostly FICA taxes). Thus, the critics argue that the income tax revenue in constant dollar decreased by $ 2.77 bn in that year. Supply siders cannot legitimately take credit for increased FICA tax revenue because in 1983, FICA tax rates were increased from 6.7% to 7% and the ceiling was raised by $2100. For the self-employed, FICA tax rates went up from 9.35% to 14%.

Some critics of supply side economics has branded it as "tape-worm theory" implying that the way to get rid of a tape worm is to stab your patient in the stomach (P. Samuelson). Similarly, Gregory Mankiw called the new theory as

"Fad economics" – to describe the notion of tax rate cuts leading to increase in revenue. To quote him "Lower tax rates might encourage people to work harder and this extra effort would offset the direct effects of lower tax rates to some extent but there was no credible evidence that work effort would rise by enough to cause tax revenue to rise in the face of lower tax rates ... People of fad diet put their health at risk but rarely achieve the permanent weight loss they desire".

Economist J.K. Galbreth commenting upon supply side economics wrote "Mr. David Stockman has said that supply side economics was merely a cover for trickle down approach to economic policy – what an older and less elegant generation called the horse-and-sparrow theory – if you feed the horse enough oats some will pass through to the road for sparrows".

Other critics of supply side economics dismiss the entire project as a "Trojan horse" for reducing marginal tax rates for upper income brackets and ultimately a failure (since real productivity fell under supply side taxation regime on a unit worker basis). Paul Krugmann called the supply side economics "peddling prosperity" and dismissed it as being unworthy of serious economists (Paul Krugmann 1994 quoted in Hoover, www.econ.lib.org.)

The debate on supply side economic policy continued even after 2000. For instance in 2003, the Wall Street Journal declared it to have ended after extensive modeling done by Congressional budget office failed to support the most extreme claims of supply side policy – that tax cuts can completely compensate for the initial loss of revenue due to the cut, but does acknowledge that resulting growth from the tax cut does replace some of the lost revenue. On the other hand, just before president Bush's 2003 tax cut proposal, the partisan Economic Policy Institution (EPI) released a statement signed by the Nobel laureates entitled "Economists' statement opposing the Bush tax cuts" which states that "passing these tax cuts will worsen the long term budget outlook adding to the nation's projected chronic deficits. This fiscal deterioration will reduce the capacity of the government to finance social security and medicare benefits as well as investments in schools, health, infrastructure and basic research. Moreover, the proposed tax cut will generate further inequalities in after tax income". However, Bush's tax cut plan did materialize on arguing that further evidence suggested that during 2001 and 2005 fiscal years although cut in income tax rates resulted in lower income tax revenues compared to 2000 level but by 2006 revenues exceeded the 2000 level.

A recent working paper sponsored by IMF shows that the Laffer curve can arise even with very small change in labour supply effects but that labour supply changes do not cause the Laffer effect. This is contrary to the supply side explanation in which the increases in tax revenue are held to be the result of an increase in labour supply. Instead, their proposed mechanism for Laffer effect states that tax rates cut can increase revenues by improving tax compliance. The study referred in particular, in case of Russia with a high rate of tax evasion where their tax compliance model did yield significant revenue increases. For instance, Russia introduced a flat 13% personal income tax rate replacing the earlier 12%, 20% and 30% rates. The tax exempt income was also increased further decreasing the tax burden. Besides, social securities reforms were carried out at the same time so the tax rates were cut substantially for most tax payers in response to these measures, personal income tax revenues have increased significantly by 4.6% in nominal term and 26% in real terms in the following years. Even more interesting is the revelation that personal income tax revenues have increased from 2.4% to 2.9% of GDP – a more than 20% increase relative to GDP.[1]

The nomenclature of New Classical Macroeconomics is similarly given to the school of economic thought that originated in early 1970s in the works of economists centred at the universities of Chicago and Minnesota – particularly of Robert Lucas (receipent of Nobel prize of 1995) and Thomas Sargent (recipient of Nobel prize in 2011), Neil Wallace and Edward Prescott (corecipient of Nobel prize in 2004). Old classical economists (Adam Smith, J.B. Say, David Recardo, A.C. Pigou, J.S. Mill and others including Alfred Marshall held the view that the price system in a free competitive economy was efficiently guiding the mutual adjustment of supply and demand in all markets including the labour market. Unemployment, therefore, could arise only because of market imperfection – either due to intervention of the government such as (enactment of minimum wage legislation) or the actions of labour unions. By removing such market imperfections, therefore, unemployment could be eliminated. It may be remembered that J.M. Keynes had shifted the focus of wage analysis from individual markets to the whole economy and argued that even without market imperfections aggregate demand might fall short of the aggregate productive capacity of its labour and capital or what Keynes called 'potential output'. In such a situation, unemployment is largely 'involuntary', i.e., workers may be unemployed even though they are willing to work at a wage lower than the wage the firms pay their current workers.

11.1.3 Microfoundations for Macroeconomics: The Origin of New Classical Macroeconomics

As stated above, the New Classical macroeconomics suggests a revival and refinement of old classical economics. In a large measure, it is so. The New Classical writers attempted to provide microfoundations for Keynesian labour market. They applied the rule that in case of labour market, involuntary unemployment is exactly a situation when the amount of labour supplied exceeds

[1] www.wikipedia.com (anonymous).

the amount demanded which is not a case of equilibrium. Hence, their analysis leaves no room for involuntary unemployment.

Keynes viewed that recessions occur when aggregate demand falls largely as a result of fall in private investment causing firms to produce below their capacity. Firms, therefore, need less workers and so employment falls. Firms fail to cut wages to as low a level that job seekers will accept (wages are inflexible or sticky downwards) leading to a situation of involuntary unemployment. The New Classicals reject this step as irrational. To them, involuntary unemployment would present the firms with an opportunity to raise profits by paying workers lower wages (Pigou's wage-cut policy in revival?). The firms would not be optimizing if they fail to take their opportunity. Employed workers should not be able to resist such wage cuts effectively since the unemployed stand ready to take their place at lower wages. According to New Classical economics, thus, Keynesian economics rests on either market imperfections or irrationality, but Keynes denied both these conditions.

Fundamental conditions of new classical economics are as follows:

1. **Individuals are optimizers:** All individuals are optimizers in the sense that they all attempt to maximize their respective gains. Given the prices they face and the assets they hold, (including human capital in the shape of education and training) all individuals, whether they are acting as consumers or producers or traders or entrepreneurs, choose the best options available to them. Therefore, consumers maximize utilities, while firms maximize profits.

   This fundamental condition is mere restatement of the basic economic instinct of individuals but all of us know that in the real world situation maximizing behaviour is an idealized situation. Most individuals have to work under several kinds of constraints.

2. **Prices adjust, to a first approximation** What this condition implies is that the price in the market gives the individuals or firms to react quickly to changing incentives and therefore, to revise their choices, to make suitable adjustments in the quantities supplied and demanded.

3. **Business cycles** Business cycles pose a challenge to the New Classicals because large fluctuations in output are not compatible with the above mentioned conditions or tenets of new classical economics. What the new classicals have to say on business cycles can be put as under.

   In the economy, there can be demand shocks or supply shocks which are often unexpected. For instance, shocks in the aggregate demand are unanticipated changes in monetary or fiscal policy while shocks in aggregate supply are typically changes in productivity that may result from transient changes in technology, prices of raw materials or the organisation of production. When the economy is hit by favourable shocks, firms would choose to produce more and pay the workers higher wages. The workers would also be willing to work more when productivity and wage rates are higher. On the other hand, when the economy suffers from unfavourable shocks, firms would be producing less, pay their workers less while workers would like to enjoy more leisure. For both, the rule is "make hay while the sun shines." But the fact that economy experiences good and bad shocks is not enough to explain business cycles. The financial crisis and the resulting global recession of 2008-10 is a case in point. Therefore, an adequate theory must account for the persistence of the fact that business cycles typically display long runs of good times followed by shorter but still significant runs of bad times. Those new classicals who regard demand shocks as dominant, argue that the shocks are propagated slowly. It is always costly to adjust production levels quickly. Similarly, when higher production requires new capital, it takes time to build it up and when lower production renders existing capital redundant, it takes time to wear it out or use it up. New classicals belonging to their "real business cycle school" (led by Edward Presscott and Finn Kydland) regard changes in productivity as a driving force in business cycles. Because changes in technology may also come in waves, runs of favourable or unfavourable productivity or technology shocks may account for some of the persistent characteristics of business cycle.

4. **Non-acceptance of involuntary unemployment** The new classicals do not accept the involuntary unemployment to exist. But why would employment rise in periods of boom and fall in periods of slump? The new classical explanation is that when a worker is laid off, he must seek a new job. He weighs the value of taking a lower paid job that might be easily available (a machinist might become a day labourer) against the value of a better paid, more suitable job that is harder to find. The worker chooses what he regards as the best available options even when the options are poor. To remain unemployed and to show up in unemployed statistics – something that he chooses based on his judgement that the benefits of search outweigh the cost. The new classicals aptly argue that such a situation is consistent with the equilibrium condition, i.e., the amount supplied = amount demanded and not an exception to the rule. If at all, this may be called the *search unemployment* situation.
5. **Rational expectations and new classical economics** The new classical adopted John Muth's rational expectation hypothesis. Muth argued that an economic model in which people's expectations differ from the outcomes predicted by the model itself is poorly formulated.

> If the predictions of the model were correct – and therefore, people's expectations were wrong – then they could use the model to correct their own expectation. To fail to do so would result in economic losses and would be irrational. At one level, Muth's hypothesis is just a technical consistency criterion for a model. At another level, it appeals to economic insight that people will not persist in easily correctible systematic and costly errors. The new classicals appeal implicitly, and sometimes explicitly, to Abraham Linchon's adage: 'You can fool some of the people all the time and all the people some of the time, but you cannot fool all the people all of the time'. They warn policy makers that a policy that depends on the assumption that public systematically misunderstands its own interest is likely to fail.

With particular reference to Phillips curve, which Keynesian economists used to appeal as a 'trade-off' between unemployment and inflation and to the question of the appropriateness of monetary and fiscal policy, the new classicals argue that since there exists a trade-off between unemployment rate and inflation rate, a policy that lowered unemployment rate also caused higher inflation rate. The new classicals were concerned with the question: how much extra inflation was a 1% point fall in unemployment rate worth. They rejected the idea that there was any useful trade-off at all. They argued that an expansion of aggregate demand lowered unemployment only because the acceleration in prices was not anticipated. Firms that mistook higher market prices for higher real returns would be willing to produce more. Workers who mistook higher market wages for higher purchasing power would be willing, if unemployed, to take a job sooner. Increased output and lower unemployment would, however, be temporary because neither the return to firms nor the purchasing power of workers was, corrected for inflation, really higher. As soon as they realized the mistake, firms and workers would return to old levels of production and labour supply.

Besides, what is more, having made the mistake once, they would not be easily fooled again by the same policy. The combination of rational expectations and the central tenet of new classical analysis that quantity supplied equals quantity demanded ensures that systematic pure aggregate demand policies (Keynesian policies) do not have real effects on the economy. The Phillips curve trade-off can be observed in the data because some part of policy is always unanticipated but policy makers cannot exploit it because the public will see through any systematic policy. Because it rejected the prevailing Keynesian view that fiscal policy could offset a recession, this came to be known as *policy ineffective proposition* of the early new classical macroeconomics.

11.1.4 Ricardian Equivalence

One of the propositions of new classical economics is what is known as Ricardian equivalence. This refers to the argument that whether a given path of government expenditure is financed through taxes or debt is unimportant. Substituting debt for taxes appeared to increased disposable income today but since the debt has to be repaid with interest, a rational tax prayer would save the entire windfall gain in order to afford the future tax bill, thus leaving his expenditure unchanged. However, the Ricardian equivalence remains controversial because it depends on assumptions about public foresight as well as the grasp of the fiscal system closely related to the rational expectations hypothesis. Also, there are debatable assumptions about the incidence of taxes and expenditures.

11.1.5 Lucas Critique

Robert Lucas, a great champion of the new classical economics was of the view that any policy which is unanticipated is not systematic and therefore cannot be used to direct the economy. On the other hand, a systematic element of a policy can be viewed at least implicitly as a policy rule. Illustrating from Phillips curve, he argued that to the question of how much does unemployment fall from one percentage point increase in inflation, the answer depends on the policy rule. If the rule had been one that held the inflation rate to zero (prices are constant) then the increase (in inflation rate) would be unanticipated and unemployment would fall. If the rule had been one that maintained as steady one percent rate of inflation (each year prices grow by one per cent) then the increase would be just what systematic policy implied and the inflation would be perfectly anticipated, but unemployment would not change. But if the rule had been one that maintained a steady two per cent rate of inflation then a one percentage point increase (in inflation) would fall short of what had been anticipated and then unemployment would rise.

These different trade-offs suggest that there is a different Phillips curve for each policy rule. A Philips curve estimated under one policy regime would not predict accurately what would happen under a different regime. On this basis, Lucas suggested that what is true of Phillips curve is also true of the most important relationships in the econometric models in macroeconomics used to evaluate economic policy. In other words, he is critical of macroeconomic models estimated by econometric methods for policy purposes.

Conclusion

Economists now have widely accepted Lucas critique discussed above. They sought ways to predict exactly how estimated relationship would change with the change in policy regime by integrating rational expectations and the public response to policy rules into their model. Because rational expectation depends on the structure of the whole economy, the program of micro foundations is no longer satisfied to look at different markets separately but concentrates on general equilibrium among them. Thus, dynamic models have replaced static models. Policy actions, therefore, cannot be evaluated merely for what they do today, but for how they change people's judgment about the future.

In spite of this, many economists are skeptical of the rational expectations hypothesis as a description of people's actual expectations. Some, including founding new classicals such as Sargent have, in fact explored models of learning that emphasize that overcoming expectation errors is a process that may take some time. Secondly, most economists no longer accept the policy ineffectiveness proposition. It is widely agreed that wages and prices do not move quickly and smoothly to the values needed for long run equilibrium between quantities supplied and demanded. Consequently, even if monetary policy is ineffective in the long run, it may be of considerable use in the short run. Similarly, many economists question whether optimal search and voluntary changes in labour supply hypothesis can explain the high unemployment rates during recessions evident from recent global recession, particularly in US and Europe) nor could it explain the 25% unemployment rate of the Great Depression of 1929 as the result of a mass decision to take a vacation.

SUMMARY

1. The precurser of new classical macroeconomics was the supply side economics which became popular in the late 1970s and 1980s in the hands of Margaret Thatcher in UK and Ronald Reagan in the US.
2. The classical dictum, 'Supply creates its own demand' or Say's law of market found its place in the revamped supply side economics which laid stress on strengthening the supply side of economics , thus ignoring or neglecting the demand side which had, hitherto, been the main plank of Keynesian economic policy making.
3. Among noted authors who propagated supply side economics were Robert Mundell, Arthur Laffer, Victor Kanto and others, although the intellectual root of the theory was found in the writings of David Hume, Alexander Hamilton and of course, Adam Smith.
4. The supply side economists rekindled their faith in the Say's law by advocating that ensuring adequate supply will take care of everything including economic growth and distribution of income. Specifically, the cut in tax rates would, in their view, enhance tax revenues for the state. Arthur Laffer, in this connection, provided 'Laffer curve'—relating tax rate and tax revenues which argued that both very high tax rate and very low tax rate resulted in lower tax revenues for the State. This clearly suggested an optimum tax rate—neither very high nor very low.
5. Laffer curve further argued that lower tax rate would release economic resources for the individuals and society which would ultimately help economic growth. Another argument advanced in favour of tax cut was that tax cut raises the taxpayer's 'incentives to work and save'.

6. Some other tenets of supply side economics were: free trade and indexed marginal income tax rate.
7. Critics have, however, argued that tax cut results in budged deficit on which the supply siders have no answer. Critics have further criticised the supply side as either fad economics' or that it failed to produce much of the exaggerated gains promised by supply siders.
8. A full-fledged new classical economics was advocated by economists like Robert Lucas and Thomas Sargent, Neil Wallace and Edward Prescott who revived the view that the price system in a free competitive economy was efficiently guiding the mutual adjustment of supply and demand in all markets including the labour market. Therefore, unemployment would arise only because of market imperfection either due to government intervention (in the shape of minimum wage legislation) or actions of labour unions.
9. New classical economists tried to provide micro foundation for Keynesian macroeconomics, particularly the labour market and asserted that involuntary unemployment is just a situation of supply of labour exceeding the demand for it which is not a case of equilibrium Hence, there is no scope for involuntary employment.
10. Other important tenets of New classical economics are:
    (a) individuals are optimisers in the sense that all of them attempt to maximise their respective, gains.
    (b) Prices adjust quickly with respect to their demand and supply conditions as well as incentives given to firms and individuals.
    (c) They advocate what is known as 'real business theory' which they say that business cycles are caused by 'demand stocks' or supply shocks which are often unexpected. For example, on the supply side, changes in productivity due to transient changes in technology is often responsible for occurrence of business cycles.
11. Ricardian Equivalence is another interesting thesis of new classical scholars. This relates to the question of government's financing of deficit in the budget either by taxes or by incurring public debt. Ricardian equivalence argues that taxes or 'public debt' are equivalent in terms of their final impact on the economy or society.
12. Rational Expectation hypothesis is, perhaps, the most important contribution that new classical economists provided in their analyses. In line with John Muth's argument that expectations are 'rational' which arrived at based upon all the current informations. At the same time, any economic model will be poorly formulated one in which people's

expectations differ from the outcome of the model. If expectations are rational, there will be no 'systematic error'. In fact, people will rarely persist easily correctible systematic and costly errors. The new classical economists would appeal to Abraham Lincoln's adage: you can fool some of the people all the time and all the people some of the time but you cannot fool all the people all the time, so that poorly framed models will not meet people's expectations. A warming for policy makers thus comes that a policy that depends on the assumption that the public systematically misunderstands its own interest is likely to fail.

Besides this, having made the mistake once, people would not be easily fooled again by the same policy.

13. Lucas critique was much more emphatic by stating that any policy which is unanticipated is not systematic and therefore, cannot be used to direct the economy. Illustrating from Phillips curve, the author argued that the inflation-unemployment trade-off depends on the systematic element in it which is the policy rule. So, much depends on the 'policy rule'. For example, if the policy rule had been one of zero inflation rate but actually the inflation rate rises, then this would be unanticipated and unemployment would fall.

EXERCISE

1. What is supply side economics? Who were the main propounders of supply side economics?
2. Discuss the behaviour of Laffer curve. When and where was the Laffer curve put to empirical test? What are the main criticisms levelled against Laffer curve?
3. What do you understand by 'indexed marginal income tax rate'? Explain the supply siders' argument in favour of indexed marginal income tax rate.
4. When and where was the new classical economics propagated?
5. Examine the main areas of disagreements between New Keynesian and new classical economists.
6. What is rational expectation hypothesis? Examine its role in the formulation of new classical economists.
7. Discuss, in brief, the 'policy ineffective proposition'.
8. Write short notes on the following:
   (a) Ricardian equivalence
   (b) Natural unemployment
   (c) Real business cycle theory
   (d) Micro foundations of macroeconomics

REFERENCES

1. Ackley, G. Macroeconomics: Theory and Policy, Macmillan US 1978.
2. Kevin D. Hoover, "New Classical Macroeconomics" http://www.econlib.org/library/Each/NewClassicalMacroeconomics.html.
3. An anonymous article: www.wikipedia.com

12

New Keynesian Macroeconomics

The publication of Keynes' *General Theory of Employment, Interest and Money* in 1936 marked the beginning of a new era in macroeconomic thinking while largely discarding the hitherto accepted perceptions about the functioning of the economy.

Since then Keynesian theory and policy ruled the economic policy domain for the next four decades or so. Early followers of the Keynesian Economics in UK and USA included the great economists like J.R. Hicks, Mrs. Joan Robinson, A.H. Hansen, Paul Samuelson, James Tobin, to mention only a few who refined, extended and modified the original Keynesian theories to a significant extent: hence they are branded as 'neo-Keynesian' economists.

Since the mid-60s, however, a new wave of macroeconomics initiated by economist Milton Friedman in Chicago University, regarded as the father of 'monetarism', swept most of the 1970s with the gradual diminution in influence of Keynesian Economics and policies. In particular, the 'stagflation' of the late 1970s and early 1980s culminated in the virtual rejection of the Keynesian influence on economic policy and emergence of another turning point in terms of the ' Supply Side Economics'. Suggestively, this particular thought attempted to implement a set of specific economic policies known as 'Thatcherism' in the UK and 'Reaganomics' in the US, after the names of the then British Prime Minister Margaret Thatcher and the American President, Ronald Reagan. During this era, although Keynesian Economics and writings in the Keynesian tradition were continued, the actual influence on policy domain was largely dominated by a revival of the old Classical theory, the "supply creates its own demand". While the supply side economic thinking was creating ripples in the policy implementation circles, a full-fledged classical revival in its new garb, nurtured by economists like Robert Lucas,Thomas Surgent, Robert Barro and Thomas Prescott in the US rechristened the title 'New Classical Macroeconomics'. "By about 1980, it was hard to find an American academic macroeconomist under the age of 40 who professed to be a Keynesian. That was an astonishing intellectual turnabout in less than a decade, an intellectual revolution for sure" (Alan Blinder, 1988).

In the later part of the 1970s (1977-78), however, several writings came up that marked the revival of Keynesianism. Similarly, in the late 1980s, a number of post-Keynesian economists sprang up with their new research on Keynesian Economics and policies which appropriately bagged the title of New Keynesian Economics. These economists include Joseph Stiglitz, Paul Krugmann, James Tobin, (all Nobel Laureates), N. Gregory Mankiw, Alan Blinder, R.J. Gordon, David Romer, John B. Tailor, Stanley Fischer, Janet Yellen, Olivier Blanchard, Larry Summers, George Akerlof, John Cooper and several other noted economists.

It ought to be mentioned here that the terms 'neo' and 'new' attached to Keynesian Economics differ as much as the former referring to the immediate followers of Keynes' writings in the Keynesian tradition while the latter referring to the recent works on reemergence of Keynesian Economics as a response to the attacks by the New Classical Economists and focusing more on providing microeconomic foundations of Keynes' macroeconomics thus making its basic tenets stronger. (Similar prefixes with Classical Economics also carry the similar meanings.)

In the present chapter, we will try to present the essential elements of the New Keynesian Economics as propounded by the various authors mentioned above. Before we actually proceed to examine the main developments of the New Keynesian Economics, we would mention the central points of New Keynesian propositions at the beginning. These can be broadly put as under.

Keynesian Theory is basically a theory of aggregate demand and of the effects of aggregate demand on real output and inflation. The following tenets directly follow from this basic proposition.

12.1 CENTRAL IDEAS OF NEW KEYNESIAN ECONOMICS

1. Keynesian economists believe that aggregate demand is influenced by a host of economic decisions, both private and public and sometimes behaves erratically (private investment, for example). Decades back, there were active debates over the relative roles of monetary versus fiscal policies in controlling aggregate demand. But in subsequent periods, these issues are no longer debatable because modern Keynesians and most monetarists (followers of Milton Friedman) now believe that both monetary and fiscal policies affect aggregate demand even though the possibility cannot be ruled out that monetary policy might cancel the macro effects of fiscal policy by controlling nominal GNP (Blinder, 1988). This view is in contrast to the New Classical economists who believe that fiscal policy does not affect aggregate demand. Ricardian Equivalence in which the New Classical economists repose their faith,

stresses the point that a public debt or tax (for bridging the fiscal gap) is neutral in its effects, hence fiscal policy has no impact on aggregate demand (see New Classical Macroeconomics in the previous chapter).

2. According to Keynesian theory, changes in aggregate demand, whether anticipated or unanticipated, have their greatest short-run impact on real output and employment, not on prices and the short run lasts long enough to worry about (Blinder, 1988).

   In the textbook exposition, this idea is conveyed through the short-run aggregate supply curve which is highly elastic (see model one in the model building chapter, 0.1) so that changes in aggregate demand are not normally dissipated at higher prices. Thus, output and employment are treated as demand determined while inflation is left to be determined by the Phillips curve (inflation, unemployment trade-off). However, in order to understand the real effects (effects in real terms as against monetary or nominal terms), of anticipated monetary policy, it ought to have some sort of 'nominal rigidity' in any model that intends to investigate the real effects of monetary policy. Hence, nominal rigidity is an important ingredient of the New Keynesian models.
3. Keynesians believe that goods markets and, especially the labour markets respond only sluggishly to shocks. In other words, wages and prices do not move quickly enough to clear markets. New Keynesians have attempted to verify, in several ways, these propositions with microeconomic data to substantiate their findings. Various price and wage rigidity models have sprung up in this connection.
4. Regarding the business cycles, which the Keynesians consider as one of the most important economic problems, an activist stabilisation policy is recommended in order to reduce the amplitude of the cycles while this is virtually no problem for the rival New Classical group.
5. For New Keynesian economists, unemployment is a bigger problem than inflation, hence most New Keynesians are more unemployment fighters than inflation fighters.

12.2 MICROFOUNDATIONS OF KEYNESIAN MACROECONOMICS

The major areas of new research mainly centre around providing the microeconomic foundations of the main tenets of Keynesian macroeconomics which were largely lacking in the older or original presentations. For instance, the existence of "stickiness" in the wage and price systems lacked solid empirical support in their favour for explaining 'involuntary unemployment', one of the key tenets of Keynesian Economics. Stanley Fischer (1977) and J.B. Tailor (1979, 1980), in their studies, brought into focus the "staggered" or overlapping wage setting by firms which signal the stickiness in wages which ultimately lead to involuntary unemployment. Joseph Stiglitz-C. Shapiro (1984) Janet Yellen (1984) and George Akerlof (1986) and Larry Summers (1988) developed the

Efficiency Wage models to illustrate the case of firms paying their employees a wage rate greater than the market clearing wages even amidst the prevalence of involuntary unemployment. The real-world situation of imperfect competition, particularly, the monopolistic competition, which the Keynesians accepted as the norm presented another example of price stickiness in the new Keynesian framework. A model of "menu cost" and imperfect competition was developed by Gregory N. Mankiw and others. We try to present each of these models as far as possible.

(a) **The efficiency wage theory:** Firms seek to maximise the productivity for their firms. They are guided by the notion that by offering better wages to the labour, somewhat higher than the equilibrium wage rates, they would be hiring relatively more efficient workers capable of producing more productive output and thus enhancing their profits. This means that a sizable number of unemployed workers wait outside the firms willing to work even at lower wage rates but the employers are not willing to hire them. This creates a pool of involuntary unemployment. The first group of economists to propose efficiency wage theory include Janet Yellen (1984) and George Akerlof (1984, 1986), C. Shapiro and Joseph Stieglitz (1984) followed by L. Summers (1988) and Weiss (1990).

12.3 YELLEN MODEL

Yellen explains the efficiency wage model as follows:

Let us think of a production function of output being a function of labour being the only variable factor, but labour expressed in terms of the 'efficiency units'(effort per labour unit) as expressed in the following equation:

$Y = f(eL)$, and total labour cost being $w.L$, where, w is the real wage rate and L is the labour input, e indicates effort per unit of labour. Starting with the hypothesis that e rises with real wage rate, and further assuming that $e'(w) > 0$ and $e''(w) < 0$, the total profit for a firm is expressed as:

$$V = f(e(w\ L)) - wL \tag{12.1}$$

where V is profit and wL is the total wage cost.

Now, (12.1) will be maximised when two conditions hold: (1) the marginal product of labour must be equal to the wage per efficiency unit that is, $f'(eL) = w/e(w)$ where, $f'(eL)$ is the marginal product of labour and $w/e(w)$ is the wage per efficiency unit, (2) wage must be set at a point at which the function $e(w)$ has unit elasticity (the formal proof is given in footnote 1). The second condition fixes the equilibrium wage, w^*, on purely technological grounds. Given w^*, the first condition then determines optimal employment, L^* as long as labour supply at w^* is at least as great as L^*(Blinder, 1988, p. 290). An equilibrium with unemployment arises if L^* happens to fall below labour supply at w^*. It is a true equilibrium, not just a long lasting disequilibrium, because profit maximising firms have no interest in reducing wages. It has involuntary unemployment that persists for an indefinite period of time because at wage w^*, labour supply exceeds labour demand. Translated into graph, the equilibrium unemployment may be shown as shown in Fig. 12.1.

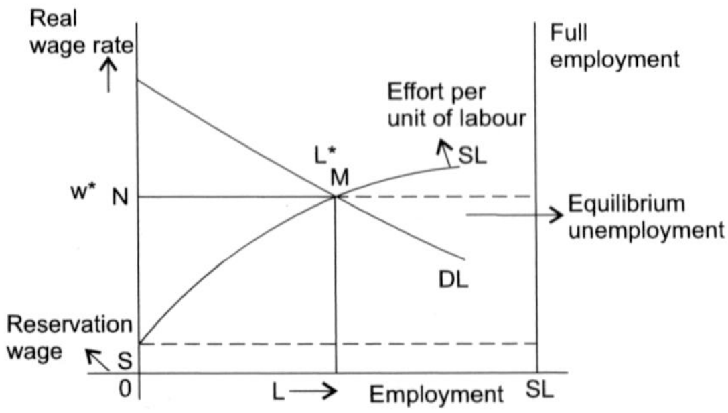

Figure 12.1 *The equilibrium unemployment in Yellen's model.*

Footnote 1:

1. Proof: $V = f(e\ (wL) - wL)$,
   $d\,V/d\,w = L.\,f'\ (eL).e'\ w - L.$ ....(fn 1),
   Setting (fn 1) equal to 0, for the first order condition of maximisation of profit to hold, we have
   $L.\,f'(eL).\ e'\ w = L.$
   $= f'\ (e\ L)\ .\ e'\ w = 1$......................($fn$ 2)
   $dV/d\ L = f'(eL)\ .e\ (w) - w = 0$
   $= f'\ (e\ L)\ e\ (w) = w$
   $= f'\ (eL) = w/e\ (w)$..............(fn 3)

12.4 SHAPIRO-STIGLITZ MODEL

Shapiro-Stiglitz model of equilibrium unemployment points towards the existence of efficiency wage as a measure for preventing the shirking habits of the workers since firms fail to fully monitor the worker efforts. They illustrate the phenomenon in terms of a diagram (Fig. 12.2).

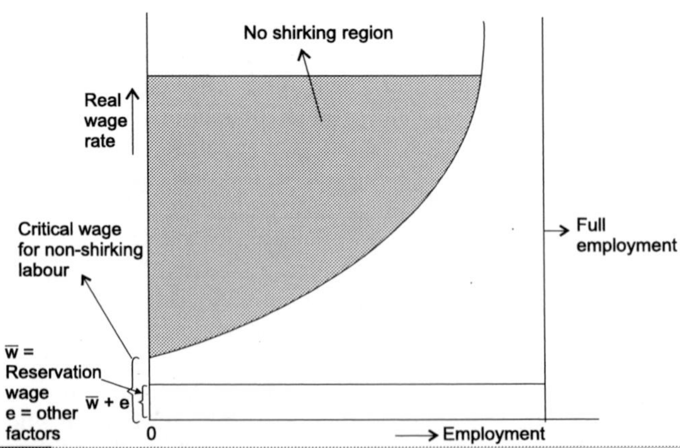

Figure 12.2 *Efficiency wage and no shirking condition of labour.*

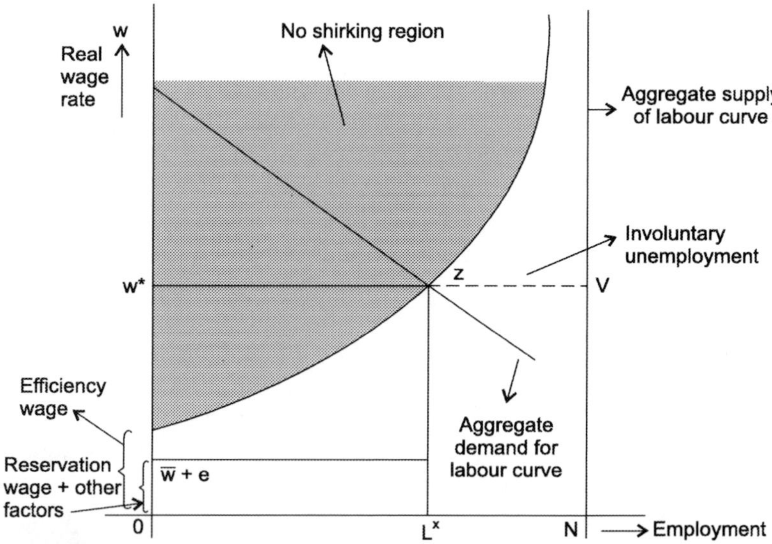

Figure 12.3 *Equilibrium unemployment and no shirking condition.*

Like Yellen, Shapiro-Stiglitz also adopts a production function for a perfectly competitive firm in the form $Q = (e(w)\ N)$, where, N is the number of employees, e is the effort per worker, and w is the real wage. A profit maximizing firm which can hire all the labour it wants at the wage it chooses to offer, will offer a real wage, w^*, which satisfies the condition that the elasticity of effort with respect to wage is unity $(de/d\,w)\ (w/e) = 1$, or to state the same thing as the proportionate change in the effort put in by labour is equal to the proportionate change in the wage paid by the employer. Since, the proportionate increase in effort in the case of efficiency wage is higher, so will the wage rate be higher. The wage, w^* is known as the efficiency wage and this wage choice minimises the labour cost per efficiency unit. The NSC curve shows the non-shirking condition for labour. The whole region to the left of the curve represents the non-shirking region. The labourers would not shirk as long as the wage rate continues to rise and the (NSC) increases with an increasing rate. It does not touch the labour supply at full employment (the vertical line) simply because full employment is inconsistent with NSC. It is to be noted that the NSC curve starts from a level of wage which is above the 'reservation wage' of the labourers. This is the critical wage for the non-shirking labour which depends on several factors like (a) the reservation wage, (b) probability of detection of shirking, (c) efforts of labourer, (d) the quit rate, (e) the interest rate, (f) the unemployment benefit and (g) flows out of unemployment. All the factors mentioned above except (b) are positively related to the level of critical wage so that an increase in any or all of these factors will raise the intercept and so will shift the NSC curve backward to the left while an increase in (b) shifts the curve to the right. It is not difficult to imagine the effects of these different factors. In case of the NSC curve shifting to the left, the size of the equilibrium unemployment becomes bigger. Now, to understand the labour market equilibrium we need to introduce the labour demand function. The aggregate demand curve for labour which is downward sloping cuts the NSC labour supply curve at point Z showing the equilibrium unemployment of the labour market, equilibrium coexisting with unemployment, since the supply of labour exceeds the demand for it by the distance ZV (Fig. 12.3). Why is the situation called 'involuntary unemployment'? This is because the unemployed workers would strictly prefer to work at the real wage, w^* than to be unemployed, but firms would not hire them at that wage or at a lower wage for the simple reason that any reduction in the wage paid would lower the productivity of all employees already in the job.

Existence of efficiency wages have other explanations apart from preventing the shirking habits of the workers. Workers generally have a tendency to shirk or avoid work if they are not monitored adequately and properly. Also, the workers need to be aware of the risk of being fired in case they shirk labour so that they need to be incentivised and encouraged to stay at their current jobs. Since each firm pays its worker more than the market wages, the aggregate labour market fails to clear. At the same time, the workers are given to understand that there is the risk involved, risk of losing their current job and searching for another one, so this is a big disincentive to shirking.

It is to be noted here that efficiency wage theory can adequately explain the inter-industry wage differentials in different countries of the world, advanced and low income countries alike. Also, the theory helps to explain a few other labour market phenomena like real wage rigidity, dual labour market (highly paid and lowly paid labour), existence of wage distribution for workers of identical characteristics and labour segmentation.

Critics have pointed out that efficiency wage theory is just a case of relative wages and not so much of stimulating the nutrition level of the workers as often argued because workers' nutrition is not a problem for the developed countries. In fact, workers compare the efficiency wages offered by their employers with those of other workers in the industry to be encouraged to put their best efforts to the production process.

Some economists (Akerlof, 1984, for example), try to explain the efficiency argument in terms of 'gift exchange' by both the employers to workers on the one hand and by the workers to the employers on the other. While the employers offer gifts in terms of efficiency wages to the workers while the workers, with the implicit understanding, offer their productive efforts without shirking in any way.

For the employers, there are certain other benefits of higher (efficiency) wages.

For instance, in case of frequent quitting of workers, there will be higher turnover cost involved in terms of cost of fresh recruitment, training, etc., which they can avoid by paying higher wages. Similarly, there is the risk of adverse job selection since the employers might not be fully aware of the actual abilities of the individual workers and so the actual selection of workers may be faulty. By paying efficiency wages, the average quality of job applicants may be improved.

Higher wages also are most likely to boost the morale of the workers and their attachment to the firm.

(b) Imperfect competition and price setting: Imperfect competition, particularly the monopolistic competition as a market structure provides the new Classical economists good ground where price rigidities persist. How this plays out can be understood in terms of 'menu cost' hypothesis of Gregory N. Mankiw and others. Mankiw, however, advanced another hypothesis in terms of "aggregate demand externality" to explain price stickiness. In a monopolistic competition, the firms are not inclined to cut prices frequently because there is a cost involved in this exercise, each time forwarding a new price list of products to the customers, known as 'menu cost'. It may be a small cost for each firm, but taken together for the whole market, it is significantly large. Secondly, given the nature of the individual market demand curve being downward sloping with relatively high elasticity, the firms want to increase their sales as much as possible at the current price level. They would, thus, avoid frequent changes in the prices since these would lead to more uncertainties about their sales. A slight decrease in the price leads to relatively higher sales if other firms do not follow suit, but a slight increase in price leads to greater fall in sales, hence the uncertainty.

In terms of 'aggregate demand externality', Mankiw argues that if firms cut their prices, it has real income effects on the part of the consumers of not only the present firm but also of other firms, and so the aggregate demand rises thus producing a welfare effect of the society. A small menu cost is likely to be more beneficial to society and economy. This is, precisely, the aggregate demand externality because its effects go beyond the firm and its customers.

The argument can be stated in alternative ways as well. "If starting from the monopolistically competitive equilibrium, a firm decreases its price, this would lead to a small decrease in price level and to a small increase in aggregate demand. While the other firms and households would benefit from this increase in aggregate demand, the original firm cannot capture all of these benefits and thus has no incentive to decrease its price" (Kiyotaki and Blanchard, 1987 p. 653). The menu cost and price stickiness are certainly harmful to society in terms of large welfare costs to society but the existence of price stickiness is a reality.

(c) Staggered wage setting model: Stanley Fischer (1977) and J.B. Tailor (1979, 1980), in their early studies on new Keynesian Economics, adopted a "staggered" or "overlapping" contract model which illustrates the case of wage stickiness or inflexible wages. They take the example of two worker unions in the economy who take turns to make decisions on wage fixation. The first union, when its turn comes, sets wages that remain in force for the next two periods (two years, for example). Then comes the turn of the second union which sets wages for the next one or two periods. But this union may be using the latest information in the wage setting exercise and thus may differ from the former or "overlap" with each other. This outcome makes the wages sticky due also to sticky information. Tailor's model, however, keeps the 'nominal' wages constant over the contract period. In any case, both Fischer and Tailor have the common feature that only the unions setting the wage in the current period are using the latest information: wages in half of the economy still reflect the old information. Tailor model, thus, have both the sticky nominal wages as well as sticky information in that nominal wages had to be constant over the length of the contract period.

During the 1990s and 2000s, advancements in New Keynesian Economics along different lines have taken place to further enrich the basic Keynesian tenets with a certain degree of inclusion of new classical ideas into the New Keynesian framework. For instance, Keynesians have now accepted the rational expectations hypothesis into the Keynesian theory while calling for a new neoclassical synthesis (the old neoclassical synthesis was coined by Paul Samuelson in 1950s after the integration of basic Classical and Keynesian theories were carried out by early post-Keynesian economists like Hicks, Hansen and Samuelson himself).

Co-ordination failure: The coordination failure problem arises in the economy due to the existence of many kinds of agents pursuing their respective profit maximisation goals but having inability to coordinate their actions successfully in a many-person decentralised economy. For example, there are many sellers selling their goods in a monopolistically competitive market where one agent's action depends on other agents' actions. There exists what may be called "strategic complementary" of each other's actions in such a market condition. Any failure to identify such complementary and to optimise the opportunities out of this, leads to coordination failure. Thus " the optimal level of 'effort' of a particular agent depends positively on the levels of effort of other agents in the economy. In such circumstances, an all round expansion of economic activity might be desirable, but an individual increase in effort may not be to the advantage of any given single agent." (Russell Cooper and Andrew John, 1988). The authors analysed a number of papers presented in a seminar which used game theory to arrive at optimum equilibrium levels of the agents. They used models with multiple equilibria where agents could coordinate to improve (or, at least not harm each one of their respective positions. The general equilibrium analysis of L. Walras and the auctioneer is absent in the real world.

The general coordination failure problem can be depicted in a simple diagram as shown in Fig. 12.4.

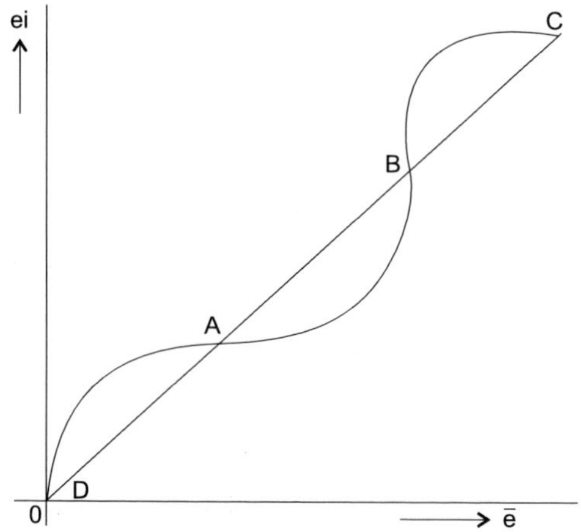

Figure 12.4 *Coordination failure.*

Figure 12.4 shows that there is a representative firm, *ei*, which takes its output decision based on the average output of all firms, *e* (bar). When the representative firm produces as much as the average firm, (*ei* = *e*(bar)), the economy is at equilibrium represented by the 45 degree line. The firm's actual decision curve intersects with the equilibrium line at more than one point which shows that the firm fails to produce at the optimal point due to the lack of coordination. Had they coordinated they could have produced at the optimal point, *A*. But, failure to coordinate results in less optimum or less efficient equilibrium point, either *B*, *C* or *D*.

SUMMARY

1. During the post II World War period, Keynesian Economics and Policy dominated the world economy for about four decades. During the 1970s, however, the Keynesian influence began to wane with the rise of Milton Friedman's monetarism and the occurrence of 'stagflation' which Keynesian Economics failed to explain in terms of the standard Phillips curve.
2. Certain theoretical works during the late 1970s and 1980s, however, laid the foundation at the microeconomic level of some of the basic tenets of Keynesian Economics. This marked the reemergence of what is now being called New Keynesian Economics. Economists like Stanley Fischer and John Tailor and a few others brought to the fore the Keynesian characteristics of stickiness in the price and wage systems in several cases. This was followed up by a number of studies during the 1880s in the new Keynesian tradition. Notable among these studies were Janet Yellen and Joseph Stieglitz on the efficiency wage

model revealing the case of involuntary unemployment. These studies were also supplemented, in several ways, by a number of other studies confirming the efficiency wage model.

3. One important aspect of "stickiness" in the wage and price setting exercises were due to what the authors like Gregory Mankiw, Akerlof, Yellen and Kiyatoki and Blanchard called 'menu cost', the cost of frequent changes in the firms' catalog or menu. These menu costs are not liked by the firms but their small reduction leads to bigger benefits to the economy in terms of 'demand externality'.
4. Another case of market failure arises from the 'coordination failure' among the economic agents. Such lack of coordination often results in the less than optimum equilibrium situation in the economy and, in fact, results in multiple equilibria. In an imperfectly competitive situation, which is nearer to real-world situation, Walras' auctioneer is absent.

EXERCISE

1. What do the terms New Keynesian macroeconomics signify?
2. Discuss the main tenets of New Keynesian macroeconomics.
3. What is 'efficiency wage'? Is it consistent with involuntary unemployment?
4. What do you understand by 'no shirking condition' of labour? Explain the relationship between 'no shirking condition' and efficiency wages.
5. Define 'reservation wage'. Explain the different factors which determine the critical real wage rate below which the labourers are most likely to shirk labour.
6. Explain Prof. Gregory N. Mankiw's 'menu cost' and price stickiness model.
7. What do you understand by 'staggered wage' setting? Explain its relevance to New Keynesian hypothesis of sticky wages.
8. What is 'gift exchange' model of Prof. Akerlof. Explain its importance in the New Keynesian economics.

REFERENCES

1. Alan S. Blinder (1988): The Fall and Rise of Keynesian Economics, Economic Record, December (academia.edu).
2. R. J. Gordon (1990): "What is New Keynesian Economics," *Journal of Economic Literature*, 28(3), September, published by American Economic Association (www.jestor.org).
3. Gregory, N. Mankiw (1985): "Small Menu Costs and Large Businesses Cycles : A Macroeconomic Model of Monopoly", *Quarterly Journal of Economics, May*.

4. Abid A. Burki (1995): "A Review of Efficiency Wage Models of the Labour Market: Theory and Evidence," *Asia-Pacific Development Journal*, 2(2): 73-90.
5. Stanley Fischer (1977), "Long Term Contracts, Rational Expectations and Optimal Money Supply Rule", *Journal of Political Economy*, Vol. 85, No. 1 Feb., University of Chicago Press.

6 & 7. "Staggered Price and Wage Setting In Macroeconomics," In Handbook of Macroeconomics, Vol-1, Chapter 15, (ed), J.B. Tailor and M.Woodford, 1999, pp. 1013-1030, Elsevier Science, B.V.

8. George Akerlof (1984), "Gift Exchange and Efficiency Wage Theory: Four Views", *American Economic Review*, 74(2): 79-83.
9. Janet Yellen (1984), "Efficiency Wage Model of Unemployment", *American Economic Review*, 74(2): 200-205.
10. C. Shapiro and Joseph Stiglitz (1984), "Equilibrium Unemployment as a Worker Discipline Device", *American Economic Review*, 74(3): 438-439.
11. Nobuhiro Kiyotaki, and Olivier Blanchard (1987), "Monopolistic Competition and the Effects of Aggregate Demand", *American Economic Review*, 77(4): 647-666.
12. Russell Cooper and Andrew John (1988)," Coordinating Coordination Failures in Keynesian Models", *Quarterly Journal of Economics*, 103(3): 441-463 (PDF).
13. Lawrence F. Katz (1986), Efficiency Wage Theories: A Partial Evaluation, Working Paper No 1906, NBER, 1050, April.

PART-6

Macro-theories of Consumption/Savings

13

Macro-theories of Consumption/Savings

In Chapter 4 we discussed consumption and savings behaviour in the context of basic Keynesian macroeconomics. Also, saving was viewed as the reverse (or, complement) of consumption. However, there exist, in the literature, several other theories which aim at explaining the "aggregate" behaviour of consumption/saving. Such aggregate behaviour generally refers to the "sum total" or "average" consumption or savings behaviour of either the group, community or national averages.

In microeconomics, we confront theories of consumer's behaviour which attempt to explain individual or household level decision making process as consumer. Generally, such decision behaviour is based on standard utility maximization assumption subject to certain constraints. We also identify in this context, the main determinants of consumer's behaviour, viz., real income level, relative commodity prices and expectation of future prices of goods, given, of course, the taste pattern of consumers.

In the present chapter, our emphasis is on aggregate consumption/savings behaviour. In particular, we shall attempt to review the main theories or 'hypotheses' that are currently prevalent and which purport to explain the aggregate consumption/saving behaviour. It is worth mentioning here that the reason why these theories are also expressed in terms of hypotheses is that these can be and actually have been formulated in testable forms. In other words, they can be and are still capable of empirically verified by facts. Secondly, even though the theories/hypotheses seek to explain macro behaviour, most of them originate or are verifiable at the micro level (either individual or family level). In fact, what is suggestive is that the theory or hypothesis which is applicable at the macro level, should equally be applicable to micro level as well-albeit with some exceptions.

Currently, there are mainly four such hypotheses:

1. Absolute Income Hypothesis,
2. Relative Income Hypothesis,

3. Permanent Income Hypothesis
4. Life cycle Hypothesis.

These hypotheses have been developed from time to time by several authors as major explanatory factors of aggregate consumption behaviour. However, of these, the last two hypotheses are essentially not different from one another.

13.1 ABSOLUTE INCOME HYPOTHESIS

Lord Keynes' statement appearing in his General Theory..., "men are disposed, as a rule and on the average, to increase their consumption as their income increases but not by as much as the increase in their income" is perhaps the first statement of absolute income hypothesis; at least, this is what most economists think. Thus, aggregate consumption expenditure depends largely on the level of absolute income — absolute income here means consumer's real absolute current level of income — unrelated with incomes of any other person or groups of persons in any way. This is true as much for individual consumers' as for consumers at the aggregate level. Keynes' consumption function, we have discussed in Chapter 3 is based on this hypothesis. We virtually restate here Keynesian version of the consumption function showing a relationship between consumption expenditures and consumers' real (disposable) current income. It should be remembered that Keynesian consumption function is a short-run consumption function; but can be extended to long-run behaviour as well.

The relationship does not necessarily show a linear or straight-line behaviour but one that suggests a declining trend with rise in income levels. Figure 13.1 presents the relationship in the short run and hence a linear one. In symbolic terms, we can write:

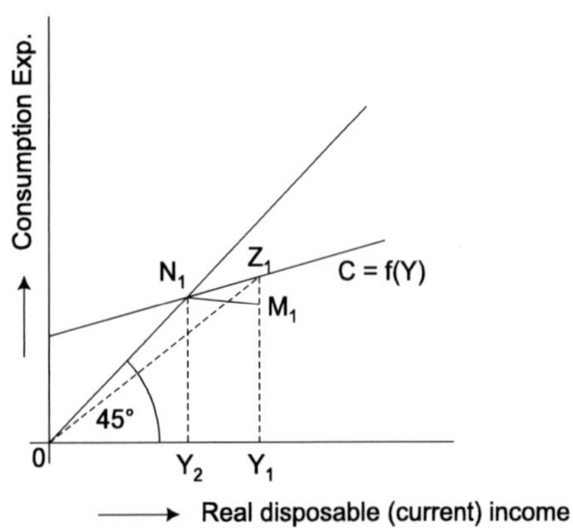

Figure 13.1 *Keynes' consumption function.*

$$C = f(Y)$$

with $1 > C'(Y) > 0$

The above symbolic expressions suggest that aggregate consumption expenditures generally rise with the level of real disposable income so that the slope of the $C = f(Y)$ curve in Fig. 13.1 is positive but its value is less than one implying that for every increase in the disposable income, the increase in consumption expenditure is always less.

Secondly, for income level below OY_2, consumption expenditure is higher than income which means "dissaving" or "borrowing" since extra expenditure has to be met by either drawing down past savings or borrowing from other sources.

There are two essential features of this function:

1. Real consumption expenditures are a stable function of the real income which means that the function generally does not fluctuate.
2. Marginal propensity to consume (MPC) is positive but less than one.

   Two additional features are also implied by the Keynesian consumption function, although they were not explicitly stated:

3. Marginal propensity to consume is less than the average propensity to consume (MPC < APC), and
4. As income level rises, APC itself declines.

Marginal propensity to consume $C'(Y)$ or $\left(\frac{\Delta C}{\Delta Y}\right)$ is measured by the slope of the function at any point. For instance, at point Z_1, it is measured by Z_1M_1/M_1N_1. That it is less than one is clear from visual inspection since the distance $Z_1M_1 < M_1N_1$.

Similarly, we measure average propensity to consume C/Y at point Z_1 by the slope of the line connecting Z_1 with the origin, i.e., Z_1Y_1/OY_1. That APC > MPC is also clear visually. APC is, therefore, the consumption income ratio. However, as income level rises, APC falls.

The obverse of consumption function — the savings function, is equally true. As income increases, savings, generally increase too. Since marginal propensity to save (MPS) is 1 – MPC — the residual from unity — it is also less than unity. Secondly, while consumption-income ratio declines with income the saving-income ratio rises with income.

13.1.1 Empirical Testing of Absolute Income Hypothesis

Extensive empirical tests have followed to verify if actual empirical data on consumption expenditures and absolute (real) incomes really support the basic as well as the related implications of the hypothesis. Most of these tests have, by and large, confirmed the basic conclusions of the hypothesis. However, certain inconsistencies were noticed between the micro-level or family budget studies and the macro-level data and between short-run and long-run behaviour of the consumption function. For instance, Simon Kuznet's family budget study revealed that while short-run saving-income ratio had been rising with income levels, the long-run national aggregates on saving-income ratio showed almost constancy. Many economists, since then, have tried to reconcile this inconsistency. The reasoning advanced is that in the cross-section family budget samples, individuals of different categories varying with age, family size, and social obligations, etc. (although within the same income-groups) reveal a certain kind of consumption or saving behaviour in the short run. But over the long run, these parameters undergo changes thus causing shift of the consumption function upward in most cases. This means, in the long run, consumption-income ratio as also saving-income ratio will have a tendency to be constant.

Secondly, while Keynesian consumption function based on absolute income hypothesis, when estimated using regression technique gives essentially an average relationship with all the implications (such as 1 > MPC > 0 and MPC < APC); when aggregated at the macro level and estimated with national level data on time-series basis, most likely, it would provide either a constant or a rising consumption-income coefficient. In other words, as compared to short-run behaviour, long-run behaviour will show higher MPC and, of course, higher APC.

Many other empirical testing on cross-section budget studies have, by and large, confirmed the validity of the absolute income hypothesis. Some studies, slightly different in nature, have been conducted to verify what is known as Engel's law[1]. In the process, however, a relationship between total family expenditures on all consumption items and the levels of family income is automatically established which confirm, rather than reject, the conclusions of the Keynesian absolute income hypothesis.

Although it is beyond the scope of this chapter to list all empirical studies which have grown enormously, we shall mention here at least two — one done by G. Ackley relating to US economy on cross-sectional budget data for the year 1960-61, collected both from urban as well as rural families and the other estimated by the present author for the Indian economy using macro-level data. Ackley's results are given in Fig. 13.2.

The curve connecting the dots represents the consumption function — relating average annual consumption expenditures and money incomes after taxes (i.e., disposable incomes). The curve has all the characteristic features of Keynesian consumption function, viz., marginal propensity to consume is positive but less than one. Average propensity to consume is greater than MPC and with rise in levels of incomes MPC (and so also APC) declines.

However, as pointed out by the author himself, each dot represents the average income and average consumption expenditure of families whose incomes were within the income brackets shown by the vertical lines. The curved line, therefore, shows the average relationship of consumption to income.

However, within each income brackets, among individual families, actual consumption expenditures varied widely. For instance, within income bracket

1 Following E. Engel, (1895), a German Statistician, whose study concluded, long before Keynes' consumption function, that as income levels of individuals rise, the percentage of expenditure on different consumption items change such that the percentage on food and housing fall, those on clothing and household operations remain constant while those on education, health and entertainment increase. Engel function was most extensively tested by H.S. Hauthakkar (An International Comparison of Household Expenditure Patterns, Econometrica, 25 October, 1957) who, of course, confirmed the conclusions related to expenditures on food and housing only.

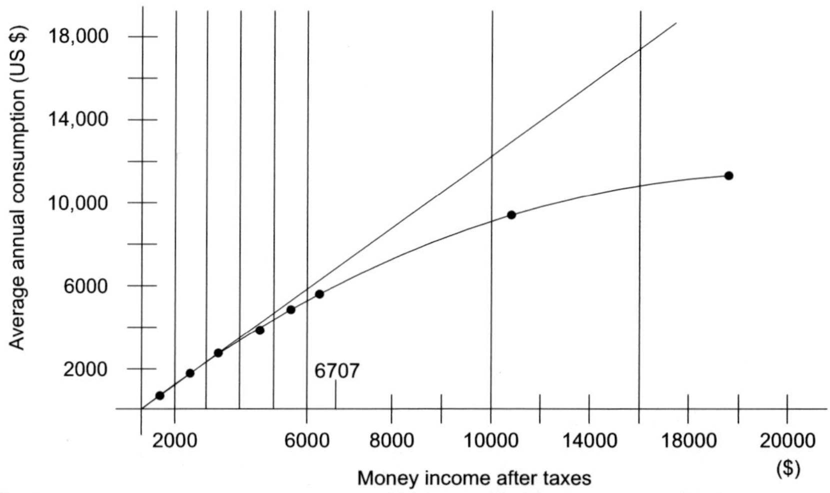

Figure 13.2 *Average consumer expenditures of US families according to money income after taxes, 1960-61.*
Source: G. Ackley, Macroeconomics: Theory and Policy, 1978, p. 552.

of $6000-7500, the average income after taxes was 6707 and the average consumption expenditures, $6125. But individual consumption spending ranged widely around this average. For example, some families in this income bracket may have spent as little as $ 3000 others $ 12000 or more. Obviously, many other factors were responsible for actual individual expenditures other than absolute income. Other theories/hypotheses (which we deal with later in this chapter) have tried to capture these factors and presented in systematic ways. It may be pointed out here that the usual linear regression technique (based on least squares analysis) that is adopted for estimating the Keynesian consumption function, interpret these factors as 'disturbance' terms or 'error' terms whose average value is assumed to be zero.

The present author attempted to examine the consumption-income/saving-income ratios for the Indian economy for the period 1952-53 – 2009-10. These ratios are presented in Table 13.1.

The consumption-income ratios calculated for the period 1952-53 to 2009-10 suggest a clear declining trend over the period. While the ratios ranged between 1.065 in 1952-53 and 0.943 in 1969-70, it has almost been consistently declining since then. During 1970s the average consumption-income ratio was 0.944 (or, 94%) while during 1980s, it gradually declined to 0.881 (or, 88%). On the average, the post-1990s period was similarly marked by lower consumption-income ratios as compared to earlier period (0.784 and 0.744 during 1990s and 2000s, respectively).

That the obverse is also true can be inferred from the data. The saving-income ratio has been, by and large, rising over the whole period of 59 years. Indian macro data, thus, provide evidence of at least the fourth important proposition of Keynesian consumption function – consumption-income ratio (or, average propensity to consume, C/Y) declines with increase in the levels of income. Needless to say, over the years the levels of income (personal disposable income of the economy as a whole) has been rising (Table 13.1). The evidence also suggests that consumption function has, possibly, been shifting over time, although no conclusive result is obtained short of estimation of the consumption functions for different time periods.

Table 13.1

Year	*Personal Disposable Income (at current prices), ₹ crore, base 1999-00 (Y)*	*Private final consumption expenditure (at current prices), ₹ crore (C)*	*Ratios of C/Y*
1952-53	9237	9841	1.065
1953-54	10125	10708	1.057
1954-55	9392	9966	1.061
1955-56	9794	9968	1.017
1956-57	11692	11757	1.005
1957-58	11933	11926	0.999
1958-59	13362	13539	1.013
1959-60	13971	14074	1.007
1960-61	14983	15207	1.015
1961-62	15719	15902	1.011
1962-63	16698	16747	1.003
1963-64	19077	18593	0.974
1964-65	22515	21889	0.972
1965-66	23569	23105	0.980
1966-67	26957	26908	0.998
1967-68	31931	32067	1.004
1968-69	33692	32082	0.952
1969-70	36797	34704	0.943
1970-71	38898	36819	0.946
1971-72	41151	39411	0.965
1972-73	45523	43768	0.961
1973-74	55923	52762	0.943
1974-75	61968	63925	0.983
1975-76	69233	65374	0.944
1976-77	73824	67968	0.920
1977-78	85267	78268	0.918
1978-79	91507	85122	0.930
1979-80	99632	92433	0.928

Contd..

Contd..

1980-81	123067	111961	0.909
1981-82	142181	128598	0.904
1982-83	157291	141608	0.900
1983-84	185749	166542	0.896
1984-85	207491	184216	0.887
1985-86	229527	201783	0.879
1986-87	256413	226596	0.883
1987-88	291585	253924	0.871
1988-89	345011	293708	0.851
1989-90	395239	328875	0.832
1990-91	465097	376943	0.810
1991-92	531515	435723	0.819
1992-93	618587	490823	0.793
1993-94	716964	562932	0.785
1994-95	842261	651951	0.774
1995-96	959733	751734	0.783
1996-97	1145206	886559	0.774
1997-98	1236982	965336	0.769
1998-99	1474404	1121595	0.761
1999-00	1617965	1253643	0.770
2000-01	1773250	1339274	0.755
2001-02	1954839	1667196	0.750
2002-03	2064836	1551365	0.751
2003-04	2282148	1633485	0.745
Base 2004-05			
2004-05	2582283	1917508	0.742
2005-06	2910078	2152599	0.739
2006-07	3327745	2476389	0.744
2007-08	3734543	2840421	0.760
2008-09	4488770	3257800	0.726
2009-10	5122132	3782013	0.738

Source: Reserve Bank of India, estimates own.

Estimating Procedure of Consumption/Saving Function

At the empirical level, the absolute income hypothesis can be tested using econometric technique in two forms:

$$C = a + bY + u \quad \text{Consumption Function} \qquad (13.1)$$

or, $$S = a' + b'Y + u' \quad \text{Savings Function}$$

$$\frac{C}{Y} = c + dY + u \quad \text{Consumption Income Ratio} \qquad (13.2)$$

or, $$\frac{S}{Y} = c' + d'Y + u' \quad \text{Saving Income Ratio}$$

where, C is consumption expenditure

Y is disposable income

S is savings

And parameters a, a', b, b', c, c', d and d' are the parameters and u and u' are the disturbance/error terms.

The first version in eqn. (13.1) expresses consumption expenditures or savings as related to absolute disposable incomes, while the second version in eqn. (13.2) shows the relationship between consumption-income/saving income ratios as functions of absolute incomes. The two versions are basically the same from theoretical point of view (since consumption and saving are complement to each other) but empirically there may be certain differences arising from individual differences in behaviour, measurement errors or some other factors.

While a, a' or c, c', are known as intercept coefficients (or, parameters), b, b', d and d' are the crucial parameters (or, coefficients) which capture the influence of income on consumption/saving, measured either as absolute variables or ratios.

Two essential points need to be remembered in the process of estimation. First, the equations to be estimated are linear in form. This means that the slope coefficients, viz., b, b' represent constant MPC or MPS in equation form (13.1) while d, d' represent constant APC or APS. Thus, even if actual observational data might suggest some curved relationship, as they ought to, the data are taken at their logarithmic values in order to render the relationships linear. Secondly, the interpretation of the results, in this case, will change such that b or b' estimates will mean the percentage change in consumption/savings due to one per cent change in disposable income instead of unit change in consumption/saving due to one unit change in disposable income. Similarly, in equation form (13.2), the interpretations will be as follows: percentage change in consumption income or saving-income ratios due to one per cent change in disposable income.

As far as data are concerned, the researcher can either use the cross-section (family-level) data for scientifically selected sample of appropriate size or he may make use of the macro level data. It is easier, however, to handle the cross-section data. The macro-level data for the economy as a whole (which are normally available at the time-series levels), although can be handled, need careful measurement and interpretation.

13.2 RELATIVE INCOME HYPOTHESIS

Relative income hypothesis was originally suggested by James Duesenberry as early as in 1949[1]. Duesenberry argued that consumption functions are

1 Income, Saving and the Theory of Consumer Behaviour, Cambridge, Mass, 1949.

inter-related or, to say the same, consumption functions of individual consumers are not independent, rather they are related with one another in such a manner that when they come in contact with one another, they have a 'demonstration effect' on each other. Thus, those with relatively higher levels of consumption exert an influence on the consumption pattern of others with lower level of income and consumption. The latter, therefore, have a tendency to imitate the consumption pattern of those of higher income groups. From this basic thesis, it can be concluded that consumption patterns of individuals living within a society are interrelated in a manner that income levels are also interrelated. Since, consumption depends on income, it is not the absolute level of income alone rather 'relative income' of individuals which goes a long way to explain consumption behaviour and consumption expenditures. Further empirical support was also provided by Modigliani[1]. Relative income, in a broader sense, can be understood if we have a picture of distribution of incomes of different income-earning groups — such as decile or percentile groups. Thus, a particular person's relative position in such an income scale speaks of his relative income. To be precise, we can express relative income of an individual X, relative to that of Z as Y_X/Y_Z for a particular point in time. Similarly, relative income of a certain community or group of population can be expressed as its position in the relative income scale (community-wise or population group-wise). In the same vein, relative income of a particular country will mean that country's GNP(real) relative to that of some other country which is either contiguously situated or otherwise related economically and culturally. For instance, $\text{Y}_\text{R}\text{IND}/\text{Y}_\text{R}\text{CHINA}$ will refer to India's relative real GNP to that of China. The concept can also be extended to include a country's or community's or individual's income levels at two different periods of time — such as, Y_t/Y_{t-1} where, Y_t and Y_{t-1} signify incomes at two periods of time, t and $t-1$, respectively.

A formal model to test the relative income hypothesis can be formulated as follows:

$$C_i = a + bY_i + c\frac{Y_i}{Y_j} + u \tag{13.3}$$

or, alternatively,

$$C_i = a + bY_i + c\frac{Y_i}{\overline{Y}} + u \tag{13.4}$$

The corresponding relative saving hypothesis can be formulated as:

$$\frac{S}{Y} = a' + b'\frac{Y}{\overline{Y}} \tag{13.5}$$

[1] "Fluctuations in Saving-Income Ratio: A Problem in Economic Forecasting", National Bureau of Economic Research, Studies in Income and Wealth, Vol. 11, New York, 1949 quoted in Ferber op cit.

where, C_i is the consumption expenditure of the ith individual, Y_i is the absolute income of the ith individual and Y_j is absolute income of the jth individual; hence the ratio Y_i/Y_j is the relative income of the ith individual, $\overline{Y}$ is the average income of the group, and a, b and c are coefficients related to absolute income and relative income, respectively.

For empirical estimation of the coefficients, one can use cross-section data relating to individuals across income groups in a society who often come in contact with each other. After suitably standardising the data, a multiple regression analysis can be done to obtain the estimated values of a, b and c. What is important to be examined in this case, is the sign as well as size of the estimates which would test the adequacy of the verification of both absolute and relative income hypotheses of consumption behaviour.

The idea as well as the procedure can also be taken to the macro level. However, in this case, we need to compare inter-country or inter-regional consumption-income data and convert them into relative income ratios. Also, we need to use time-series data in this case such as for different years provided such time periods do not exhibit any abnormal conditions. The results of regression analysis (with their appropriate statistical tests) would suggest the strength of the hypotheses.

One important aspect of relative income hypothesis is the change in consumption behaviour between two or more business cycles. Normally, during the upswing or prosperity phase of the business cycle, people's as well as businesses' incomes rise rapidly. Consequently, their consumption patterns also change and they typically spend more on consumption items of all varieties. Their standard of living improves significantly. This tendency continues throughout the boom phase. Now, when the business cycle enters the downward phase and remains in longer recession (or, enters depression), the income levels suddenly fall. In such a changed situation people try to maintain their consumption behaviour earlier attained during the "peak" of the business cycle. But since their current incomes (both from work and assets) have fallen sufficiently, their consumption expenditures are also reluctantly curtailed. However, the consumption expenditures fall by relatively lesser extent as compared to the rate at which they had risen during the boom phase. This is known as "consumption ratchet" (or 'ratchet effect') which is shown in Fig. 13.3.

A linear consumption function is shown in Fig. 13.3 along with 45 line. Upswings and downswings of trade cycle are shown above and below the point of intersection between $C = C(Y)$ curve and the 45 line. Levels of income and consumption expenditures are represented in the horizontal and vertical axes, respectively. Beyond C_1, consumption expenditures are rising consistently with rising incomes. Consumers develop the 'habit' of improved consumption

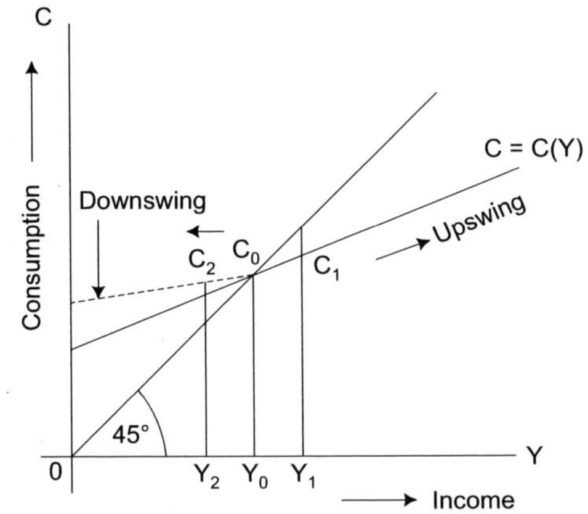

Figure 13.3 *Relative income hypothesis with consumption ratchet.*

behaviour and it continues till the 'peak' level of the cycle when consumers reach highest possible level of consumption. Now, during downswing of the trade cycle (shown to the left of C_0), when income levels are falling continuously, it becomes difficult for consumers to shun such habits to which they have already become accustomed — somewhat addicted to. But consistent fall in income levels makes them reluctant to reduce consumption expenditures; else they would fall in debt trap. However, it is certainly not the same level of consumption they return to when they were on upward movement during upswing but to a lesser extent. This is shown by the falling dashed curve below point, C_0.

The relative income hypothesis with 'habit persistence' as explained above can also be verified with relevant data regarding consumption behaviour of a sample of households during two phases of a business cycle, provided the selected households remain the same. But such disaggregated sample is difficult to be selected unless the researcher is careful enough to identify the peak level of households' income and consumption levels and observe their changed pattern during the downward phase or recession. However, when such recession is well under way, a researcher can form a sample of households and through well-thought out questionnaire or schedule of information, collect relevant data on consumption behaviour just before the onset of recession and the present consumption behaviour along with their income levels.

At the macro level, the hypothesis can be tested by making use of historical data on aggregate consumption expenditures (and also at disaggregated community-group levels) and aggregate incomes (GNP/GDP/DI) during two different phases of the cycles. It is possible, however, that habit persistence, if at all present, may be different among major income-earning groups. In that case, the above approach of investigation will show up only the average behaviour of habit persistence of the aggregate level consumers.

The relative income hypothesis can also be verified in the context of cyclical consumption behaviour using the model spelt out in eqns. 13.3 or 13.4. The only change that needs to be done is to substitute the second explanatory variable–

$$\frac{Y_i}{Y_j} \text{ or } \frac{Y_i}{\overline{Y}} \text{ by } \frac{Y_{\text{current}}}{Y_{\text{peak}}}$$

where, Y_{current} and Y_{peak} indicate "current level" and "peak level" of incomes. The corresponding coefficient will, hopefully, reflect the strength and weight of the relative income, that is, current income relative to the highest achieved level of income in explaining aggregative consumption behaviour.

The role of demonstration effect as evidence of relative income hypothesis can also be understood from regional or geographical differences in savings rates. Duesenberry himself found that Negro families saved more than the white families in US in 1935-36 and 1941 and that dissaving at a given level of income was less frequent in 1941 than in 1935-36. James Tobin provided an explanation in terms of wealth differences among different regions or population groups rather than income differences. Similarly, higher savings rates of farm families were observed than nonfarm families.[1]

In India, we can observe enough evidence in support of relative income hypothesis. Here also, rural families save more (in terms of rates) than their urban counterparts. Certain specific population groups or communities have a tradition to save more. For instance, Marwaries, Gujaratis, Parsies are havitual savers.

In the context of present globalized world, relative income hypothesis has great relevance in explaining strong demonstration effect on consumption behaviour. The economies of the world today have come closer due to revolution in information technology. International mobility of capital and labour has increased manifold and allowed easy access of information to underdeveloped countries from developed ones. The economic prosperity witnessed during last two three decades or so of the major developed countries along with liberalization and globalization process has been responsible for high rate of imitation of the life-style, consumption and spending behaviour prevalent in developed countries – notably US by the underdeveloped and emerging economies. With liberalised trade and easy flow of financial resources and import of goods and services international demonstration effect is taking deeper root. The implication of this trend is clear: developing and emerging countries with their higher relative incomes achieved compared to their recent past, are now increasingly coming in closer contact with their developed counterparts resulting in higher spending on newer consumption items and lesser savings percentages. Although in a country

[1] Robert Ferber, "Household Behaviour" in Surveys of Economic Theory, Macmillan, 1967 Vol. III, p. 119.

like India, savings rate has been showing consistently rising trend (despite the one or two recession years of 2008-09), but one can argue that the rate could have been even higher short of demonstration effect.

Current international economic environment, therefore, provides sufficient empirical ground for testing the relative income hypothesis and its fall-out insofar as the consumption behaviour is concerned. In fact, the effect is so pervading that the enquiry could extend beyond economics sphere and include cultural and social spheres.

13.3 THE PERMANENT INCOME HYPOTHESIS

This hypothesis was propounded by Milton Friedman and his associates at Chicago School, U.S. Friedman introduced the notion of 'permanent income' that a consuming unit (individual or household) earns or expects to earn over his entire period of earning (may be called planning horizon). According to Friedman, 'measured' or 'current' income of a consuming unit at a certain period of time has two components, viz., 'transitory' component and 'permanent' component. Similarly, 'measured' or 'current' consumption during a given period of time of a consuming unit consists of 'transitory' part and 'permanent' part. Symbolically, therefore, we can write, by segregating these components as:

$$y = y_p + y_t$$

and $$c = c_p + c_t$$

where, y is total income, c is total consumption, y_p and y_t are permanent and transitory incomes and c_p and c_t are permanent and transitory consumption respectively.

According to this hypothesis, there are two kinds of relations between consumption and income: apparent and true relations. The true relation between consumption and income is that which exists between permanent income and permanent consumption. This is the long-run behaviour of consumption function. Any short-run relation between consumption and income — the apparent relation — reflects its transitory nature which obscures the true relation. This is further elaborated as follows.

A certain consuming unit has a long-term horizon within which he expects to receive a stream of income from his work and wealth. How much income he would expect to get at the end of the time horizon depends on his present decision to save more or less. For instance, if he saves more now, he can expect to receive more and if he saves less, he would receive less at the end of the period (such as at his retirement from work). So, the choice of his decision is inter-temporal in nature (involving two distinct periods of time—present and future). Clearly, different consuming units will have different perceptions about their choices regarding present versus future consumption and saving behaviour since they depend largely upon size and age composition of their family members, their present and future needs and obligations which are likely to fall within their time horizons and of course, the total constraint of wealth at the turn of this planning horizon. However, as argued by Friedman, these individual differences influence more the transitory part of their income and consumption but not the permanent part.

Now, transitory components may be higher or lower than the permanent ones and hence may fluctuate. For instance, an individual might face sudden jump in his current income during a certain period for some reason or other. Accordingly, his consumption expenditures may also go up for short time – interval. However, they would soon return to their long-run or trend levels as suggested by permanent income hypothesis.

However, permanent income or permanent consumption are not observable. What is observable is a hybrid mixture of permanent and transitory components and is reflected in current measured incomes and consumption data. There is, therefore, a difference between short-run and long-run consumption-income relationship such that in the short-run, consumption-income relationship does not show any proportionality while in the long-run the relationship is proportional. Milton Friedman is much more concerned about long-run trend rather than short-run one. His argument is that the mean value of the transitory elements of consumption, over a long period, will be zero; thus leaving the permanent parts unaffected. On this basis, it has been further argued that permanent consumption is a certain fixed fraction of permanent income which can be written as:

$$C_p = kY_p \tag{13.6}$$

where k is some fixed fraction. It needs to be clarified here that k is independent of the *level* of permanent income.

Further, even though k is assumed to be a fixed fraction, it depends upon certain variables like rate of interest, the ratio of non-human wealth to total wealth and a stochastic variable which includes age and taste of the consuming unit. We take these other variables as parameters which vary with individual cases. For instance, one individual consuming unit may have one ratio of non-human to human wealth (and hence to total wealth), another may have another ratio. For each case, therefore, the value of k will be different. Similarly, for stochastic variables. Symbolically, we can state:

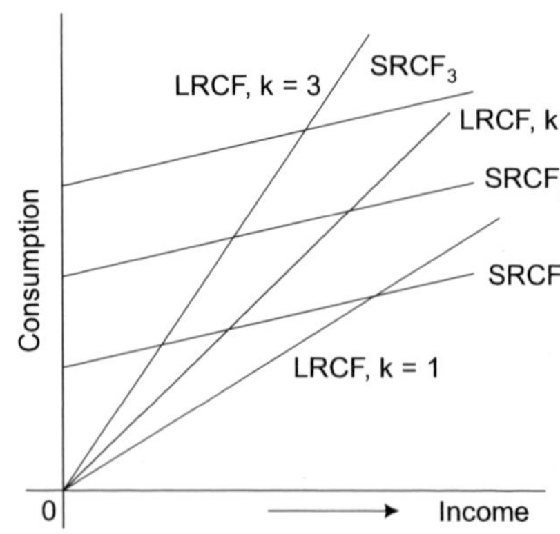

Figure 13.4 *Short run and long run consumption functions.*

$$k = f(r, w, u), \tag{13.7}$$

where r stands for rate of interest, w for ratio of non-human to total wealth and u for the stochastic variable. Figure 13.4 captures the effects of k on short-run and long-run consumption functions.

Equation 13.6 suggests a constant proportional relationship between permanent consumption and permanent income and hence, C_p/Y_p, remains, by and large, constant in the long run.

Another important implication of the relationship is that transitory and permanent incomes, transitory and permanent consumption as also transitory income and transitory consumption all are uncorrelated. To use statistical terms (of correlation coefficients), these can be written as:

$$r_{y_p y_t} = 0, \quad r_{c_p c_t} = 0, \quad \text{and} \quad r_{y_t c_t} = 0$$

Lack of correlation between the variables ensures that transitory and permanent components of income and consumption do not move in any systematic manner. So is the case with transitory income and transitory consumption.

There are three basic questions concerning the permanent income hypothesis:

1. How to estimate permanent income?
2. What is the appropriate test of the hypothesis?
3. How to establish the underlying assumptions/implications?

Regarding the estimate of the permanent income, it mainly depends upon two factors, viz., (a) the expected stream of income coming due during the whole working period of the consuming unit and (b) the standard rate of interest which can be used as discount rate. In all probability, this rate may be some weighted average of the rates of interest. Obviously, the first factor is practically difficult for all categories of consuming units to arrive at except certain non-wage earning units with certainty of earnings both from work and wealth. In any case, if the expected future income stream is known, its present value can be worked out by using the 'present value' criteria. Thus, if the income series are:

$$y_1, y_2, \ldots, y_n,$$

and the discount rate is r, the present value of the income series can be written as:

$$W = \sum_{i=1}^{n} y_i/r \tag{13.8}$$

(assuming that y_i (i = 1, 2, …, n) are the same and the series is infinite)

or, $$W = \frac{Y_0}{r},$$

where Y_0[1] is the permanent income — a steady flow to perpetuity.

[1] The flow of income has to be steady and to perpetuity because the life, generally, lasts even beyond the earning period but consumption is essentially a continuing process.

This present value of income stream is the accumulated wealth, W (see Chapter 9: Theory of Demand for Money – Post Keynesian Developments).

As far as the empirical test of the hypothesis is concerned, it is certainly very difficult due mainly to the problem of measuring permanent income as well as permanent consumption. Nevertheless, certain indirect tests have followed relying mainly on long-term trends of consumption-income relationships.

1. As Friedman himself has emphasized, the time-series aggregates (on income and consumption) provide some results which are consistent with permanent income hypothesis. For example, marginal propensity to consume is invariably less than the average propensity to consume; if due allowance is given to the variability in the observed consumption-income ratio due to transitory factors, the ratio of permanent consumption to permanent income, k, appears to remain constant for a fairly, long period; in the case of a fitted consumption function to observed data of time-series, the income elasticity of consumption (estimated $b \quad \overline{Y}/\overline{C}$ where $\overline{Y}/\overline{C}$ are measured at their mean values) has a tendency to rise as the period of observation increases. This might be an indication of the fact that transitory factors in the long run are less important.
2. Similarly, with regard to cross section budget data, the author has noted, that the average propensity to consume (C/Y) showing relatively constant values over different times and different groups indicates that transitory incomes and transitory consumptions are not as important as permanent ones. Secondly, the results based upon cross section data – consumption-income ratio declines with rise in income — is not consistent with time-series aggregates.
3. A regression (log-linear) run on observed consumption-income data in the form:

   $$C = a + bY,$$

   gives b the slope of the function as representing income elasticity of consumption, (mentioned above). From permanent income point of view, b is equivalent to kP_y, where P_y is the ratio of the variance of permanent component of income to total variance of income, i.e.,

   $$P_y = \frac{\Sigma\,(P_y - \overline{P}_y)^2}{\Sigma(y - \overline{y})^2} \tag{13.9}$$

Since k is constant, by assumption, this means that fluctuations in the slope of measured income reflect fluctuation in the relative importance of the permanent component of income. In other words, if there are no significant fluctuations in the slope of consumption function based on measured income and consumption, the relative importance of permanent income is higher.

In econometrics, errors – in variables model can be applied. In terms of this model, the transitory consumption and income variables can be expressed as:

$$C_t = C_t^p + u_t \quad (13.10)$$

and

$$y_t = y_t^p + v_t \quad (13.11)$$

where, u_t and v_t are error terms that capture the factors giving rise to transitory elements. These error terms are assumed to have zero mean with no correlation between them, i.e.,

$$E(u_t) = 0, \quad E(v_t) = 0 \quad \text{and} \quad {}^{r}u_t v_t = 0,$$

Now, if the distributions of u_t and v_t are specified (e.g., whether they follow standard normal distribution with constant variance (σu^2, σv^2 being constant) and the related co-variance are zero then k appearing in eqn. (13.6) can be estimated which would suggest the long-run marginal propensity to consume (LRMPC) or slope of the long run consumption function. In that case, long-run MPC will be the same as long-run consumption-income ratio (C/Y). However, if the two significantly differ in value, relative importance of permanent income hypothesis is far from being proved.

13.3.1 Limitations/Criticisms of Permanent Income Hypothesis

Criticism of permanent income hypothesis has been levelled both on theoretical as well as empirical grounds.

1. On theoretical point of view, two basic assumptions and their validity have been questioned: (a) k (eqn. (13.6)) is independent of the level of income; and (b) there is no correlation between transitory consumption and transitory income. One implication from (a) is that whatever be the level of income, level of consumption will form a constant proportion — like either 80% or 90% or 70%. Thus, possibly, low-income families will have no greater preference for purchase of future goods (savings) than high-income families. But families at different levels of income may have different pressures and motivations as a result of which consumption-income (or, saving income ratio will differ. Regarding (b), i.e., transitory consumption is uncorrelated with transitory income, (implying in turn, the zero MPC out of transitory income) is also questioned on grounds of logic. If low income families get unexpected rise in income, there is, generally, strong pressures to spend it on current consumption items. Similarly, when there is unequal distribution of wealth in the society, low income families (with low wealth and experiencing generally dissaving) with rise in their transitory income will be stimulated to resort to maintaining consumption when there was temporary decline in income.

2. On empirical ground as well, research findings have suggested that most of the implications of the permanent income hypothesis are also found in evidence from absolute income hypothesis. For example, empirical results that MPC is positive but less than zero, APC being more than the MPC are equally true in the case of absolute income hypothesis. In addition, results obtained from consumption-income regression analysis have suggested that for different groups of families classified by income levels the slope of the function is steeper than the overall regression. Similarly, Tobin, has tried to reconcile between constancy of long-run propensity to consume (C/Y) with the variability of short-run C/Y implied in absolute income hypothesis.

   Certain empirical evidence have also been provided to contradict the lack of correlation between transitory income and transition consumption (or to say the same thing as having zero marginal propensity to consume out of transition income). For instance, it has been found that unexpected dividends received as transitory income have a higher propensity to consume than from regular income.

   Referring to our findings on Indian data, it is sufficiently suggestive that at segregated levels of NI by different periods (particularly with their rising levels), savings ratio is rising. This would further suggest that slopes of the consumption function would be gradually rising.

   Thus, in many instances, permanent income hypothesis has remaind from being proved even though it has provided a major contribution in this field of study.

3. Perhaps, the most important limitation of permanent income hypothesis arises from the problem of measurement or estimation of permanent income. Most individuals or consuming units do not have any fair idea of the expected income stream over the entire earning period due to imperfect knowledge of the various forces affecting the future flow of income. There are, for instance, various kinds of uncertainties which the individuals are unable to discount. However, at least, some individual units with more stable income growth and stable resource flows can make 'educated guess' about the expected future income from work or wealth.

13.4 FISHER'S INTER-TEMPORAL CONSUMPTION THEORY

Professor Irving Fisher, an American economist, provided a consumption theory which is essentially inter-temporal in nature, that is, consumption decisions by the consumers between two distinct periods of time such as the present and the future. In other words, Fisher's theory tries to throw light on how a particular consumer, when faced by the choice of allocating his available resources to his present and future needs and requirements.

Prof. Fisher applied the Hicksian type of indifference curve technique to analyse the problem of consumer's/saver's choice as mentioned above. (inter-temporal) As we have seen in our microeconomic theory, a consumer faces certain 'constraints' with regard to his income which he likes to allocate between two competing goods with a view to maximise his gain or welfare. This gain or welfare is represented by a family of indifference curves which he confronts. He has, then, to adjust his constraints with this set of indifference curves.

Here, the problem before the consumer is his choice between the two time periods, viz., present and future consumption or saving. In fact, the consumer has two options: how much of his income to spend on his present consumption and how much to save for future requirements for, if he spends more today, he will have less to be spent tomorrow. But, if he spends less today, he will have more for tomorrow's spending. So, how does he take his decision with regard to consumption and saving? The problem can be settled with the indifference curve analysis which we explain below.

Let us first examine the consumer's constraint. The constraint consists of the consumer's present income as well as expected future income. Since, the expected future income is to be available in some future date, it can be estimated using a certain rate of discount for its present value. In Fig. 13.5, the relevant constraint has been drawn as a straight line sloping downward from left to right suggesting that the present income and expected future incomes are competitive in nature, more of present income means less of future income and less of present income means more of future income. Let his present income be denoted by OY_1 and the future income be denoted by OY_2. Now, if our consumer decides to consume his entire income in period 1, and does not save anything for the future, his position will be located at point C_1. On the other hand, if he decides to save his entire income to be spent in period 2 and does not spend anything in period 1, then he is to be located at point C_2. But, in practice, he is most likely to divide his income to be spent in the two periods. Thus, our consumer has another option, he can spend part of his income in period 1 and save the rest to be spent in future. In that case, his position will be located at any point between C_1 and C_2. Our consumer has yet another option to explore, he can "borrow" from others, individuals or institutions such as banks.

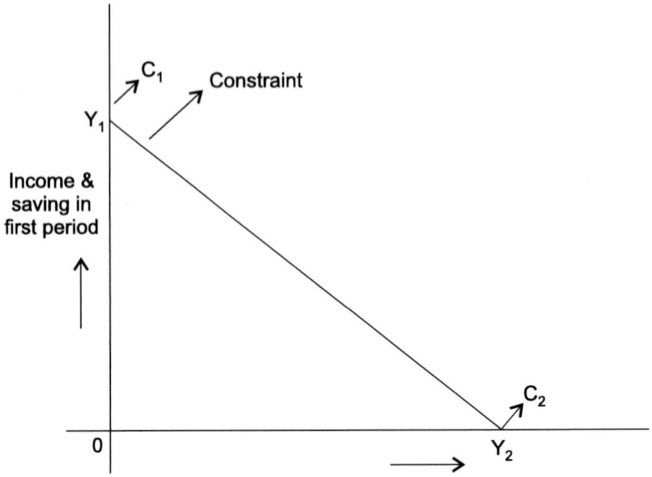

Figure 13.5 *Consumer's constraint.*

Now, the consumer's constraint can be shown as a straight line joining C_1 and C_2. With the constraint thus defined, we now look at our consumer's preferences, between his present utilities obtainable from the present incomes and future utilities from expected future incomes. More specifically, how much can he sacrifice his present wants and preferences for his future wants and preferences? In other words, can there be any combination of the present and future wants between which he may be indifferent? These are the questions whose answers can possibly be provided by an indifference curve projecting the inter-temporal utilities.

Figure 13.6 shows the consumer's preference map, a family of indifference curves representing different levels of utilities, each one drawn parallel to the other. An indifference curve here shows a locus of all such combinations of two goods (here present and future goods) where our consumer finds himself at the same level of utility. Thus, point '*a*' gives him the same level of utility obtained from the present and the future goods as that obtained from point *b* on IC_1. What is the rationale behind this? This is because point '*a*' represents a relatively greater amount of the present good but a smaller amount of future good when compared with point '*b*'. But if our consumer is induced to move from point *a* to point *b*, that is, a movement downward from left to right on IC_1, it is necessary that any sacrifice he makes by foregoing the present good, must be compensated by the future good. In other words, IC_1 (as also all other indifference curves) are downward sloping from left to right, i.e., it has a negative slope.

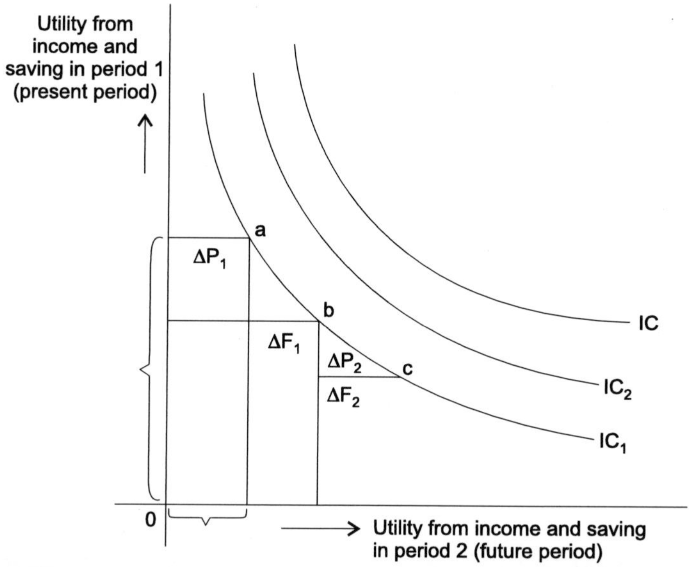

Figure 13.6 *Consumer's preference map: a family of indifference curves.*

Secondly, the indifference curve is convex to the origin, i.e., its slope gradually decreases (in absolute terms) as one moves from one point to the other downwards on the same indifference curve. The reason behind this is that as our consumer is induced to sacrifice more and more of the present consumption, he has to be compensated by gradually greater and greater amounts of the future consumption. To state the same thing somewhat differently, for a given amount of sacrifice of the present consumption, our consumer needs to be compensated by a greater amount of future goods as he moves along the same indifference curve from left to right. For instance, let us take another point, '*c*' on the IC_1 curve and compare the amounts of changes of the present and future goods between points '*a*' and '*b*' and then between '*b*' and '*c*'. It will be evident that the ratio of the amount of sacrifice of the present good and future good, $\Delta P_1 / \Delta F_1$, between '*a*' and '*b*' is greater than that between '*b*' and '*c*'. This is clearly visible since we have set $\Delta P_1 = \Delta P_2$ in both the ratios but, ΔF_2 in the second ratio is visibly greater than that of the first ratio, i.e., ΔF_1.

Now, our rational consumer will always prefer greater amounts of both present and future goods to lesser amounts of them. In other words, he will prefer to be on a higher indifference curve to a lower indifference curve, hence, the *IC* curves are parallel to each other upwards.

We now bring together both the constraint and the preference map for the consumer to reach his optimum decision. Such an optimum solution is feasible only at the point of tangency between the constraint line and the highest attainable indifference curve which is shown in Fig. 13.7.

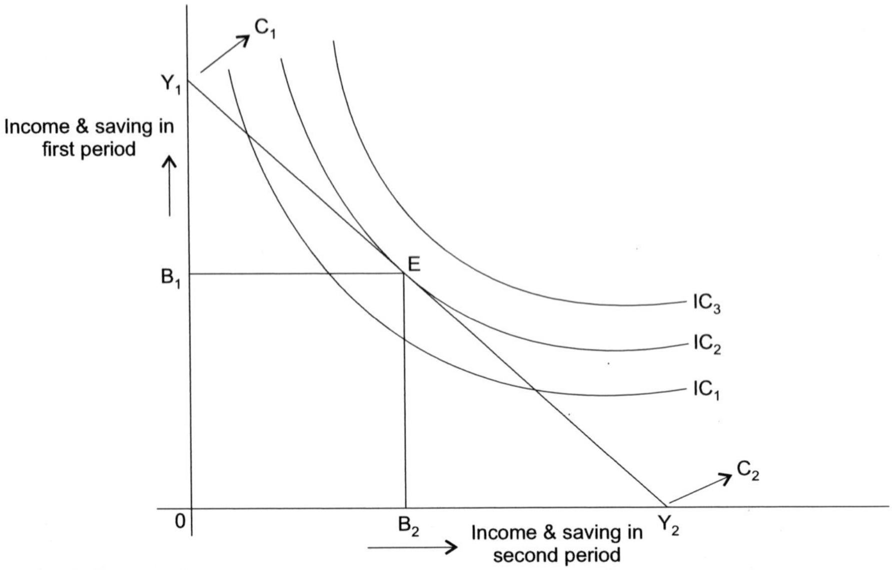

Figure 13.7 *Consumer's equilibrium: the tangency between budget line and the IC curve.*

What is relevant, now, is to understand how our consumer relates his income to the consumption in the two periods. In order to understand this, we proceed as follows:

In the first period, our consumer's saving (S) will be equal to his income (Y_1) minus consumption (C_1) from which we can write

$$C_1 = Y_1 - S \tag{13.12}$$

But, in the second period, consumption will be equal to his accumulated savings in the first period (with its interest thereon) plus his expected income in the second period. This can be expressed as:

$$C_2 = S(1 + r) + Y_2 \tag{13.13}$$

where, r is the rate of interest.

By combining the two equations (showing the consumption of both periods), we can write

$$C_2 = (Y_1 - C_1)(1 + r) + Y_2 \qquad \text{(since, } S = Y_1 - C_1\text{)} \tag{13.14}$$

$$= Y_1(1 + r) - C_1(1 + r) + Y_2 \tag{13.15}$$

Now, by slight rearrangement of terms of eqn. (13.15), we can further write:

$$C_2 + C_1(1 + r) = Y_2 + Y_1(1 + r) \tag{13.16}$$

Further, dividing both sides of eqn. (13.16) by $(1 + r)$, we obtain

$$C_1 + C_2/(1 + r) = Y_1 + Y_2/(1 + r) \quad (13.17)$$

Equation (13.6) shows consumption in both periods are related to incomes of both periods. The equation is also an expression of the budget line. The total consumption in the periods is limited to the consumer's total income. Further, by differentiating eqn. (13.4) with respect to C_1, we can get the slope of the budget line. Thus,

$dC_2/dC_1 = -(1 + r)$ which is negative.

Let us now find out the consumer's equilibrium position (optimum condition) given his preferences and his constraint. As demonstrated in Fig. 13.7, clearly this happens on the point where his constraint line just touches the IC_2 curve, i.e., at point E. This is the point where the slope of the budget line will be equal to the slope of the indifference curve, the so-called marginal rate of commodity substitution (MRS). At the point of equilibrium, therefore, he will spend/consume OB_1 of his first period income while saving the rest, C_1B_1 for the second period. Thus, the second period consumption will be equal to $OB_2 = C_1B_1(1 + r)$. Hence, $OB_2 > C_1B_1$.

Further implication of the equilibrium condition is that the slope of the indifference curve coincides with the slope of the budget line. Since, the slope of the budget line is equal to $(1 + r)$ = MRS, we conclude that in equilibrium, MRS equals 1 plus the rate of interest.

From the above analysis of the consumer's inter-temporal consumption decision, it appears that the two important factors that influence the optimum decision are: income and the rate of interest. We shall, therefore, examine the effects of these factors on the optimum choice of the consumer.

1. **Change in income:** Any change in income implies a shift in the consumer's budget line either upward to the right or downward to the left. Let us suppose, there has been an increase in the consumer's income so that the budget line shifts upward to the right as shown in Fig. 13.8. The old budget line is represented by AB while the new shifted budget line is shown by AB'. The AB' line indicates an increase in income in both periods. Our consumer moves on to a higher indifference curve, IC_2. The optimum choice, the point of tangency between IC_2 and the new budget line, indicates that the consumption in the periods have increased. However, this ought to happen provided both goods are treated 'normal', i.e., the present good as also the future good are thought of as normal or are treated equally important to the consumer.

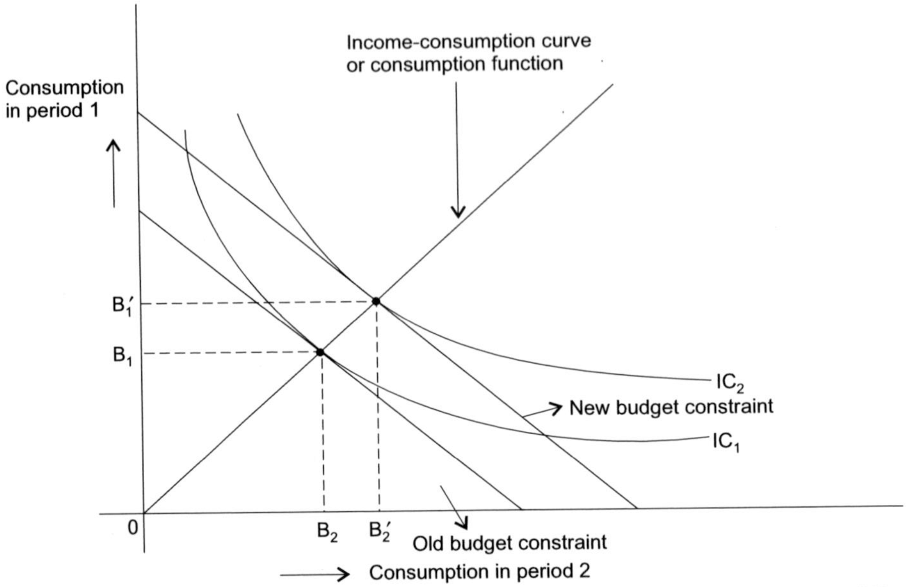

Figure 13.8 *Effect of a change in income on the equilibrium present and future consumption/saving.*

2. **Change in the rate of interest:** If there is a rise in the rate of interest, our consumer is most likely to be tempted to save in the present period in favour of higher consumption in the future. Thus, his present consumption might be falling. (In fact, this is the principle behind the classical economists' theory of saving, saving is an increasing function of the rate of interest). However, a rise in the interest rate also implies a rise in the interest income for our consumer particularly if he is a lender. This may produce a positive income effect which means that the consumption might be higher in both periods. Here is a conflicting situation. In the former case, our consumer prefers future consumption (saving) to present consumption in response to a rise in the rate of interest. We may call this the substitution effect of the interest rate change. In such a situation, it is difficult to conclude whether a rise in the rate of interest will induce saving in the present period or not. However, if our consumer is a borrower, his burden on interest payments on his borrowed capital will increase. This may lead to a reduction in his present consumption. Figure (13.9) shows the effects of a change in the rate of interest on current and future consumption/ saving. Our consumer's original equilibrium position is shown at point E_1 with the budget constraint being R_1R_1. A rise in the rate of interest creates a substitution effect such that the budget constraint line shifts down to

R_2R_2 while still touching the indifference curve IC_1 at point E_2. Thus, E_2 is the new equilibrium point. Clearly, there has been a reduction in the current consumption to the extent of ΔC_1, while the future consumption/saving has increased by ΔC_2. Thus, the consumer has substituted saving for consumption. It is also clear that the increase in future consumption (saving) has been to a greater extent than the reduction in current consumption. This is the incentive for saving that has been created by the increase in the rate of interest.

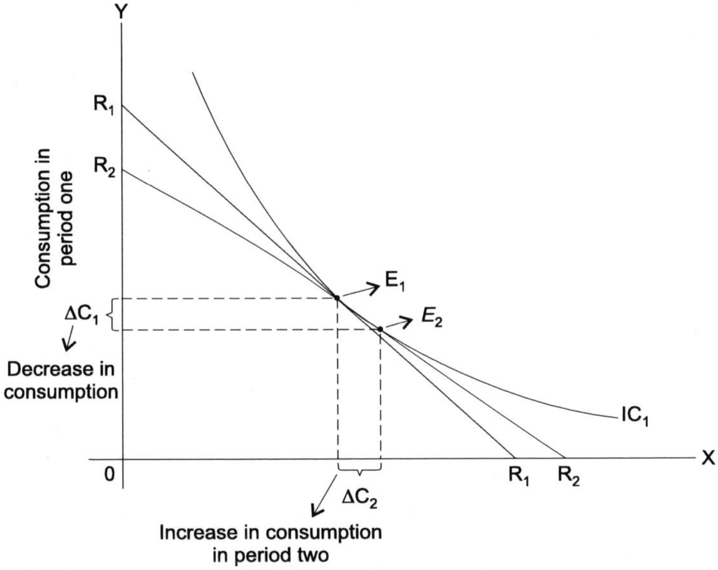

Figure 13.9 *Effect of a rise in the rate of interest on present and future consumption/ saving.*

Professor Fisher's inter-temporal consumption/saving theory provides the background for the lifecycle theory as also the permanent income theory, the former by three authors (Ando, Modigliani and Brumberg) while the latter by Milton Friedman which we are now going to discuss.

13.5 LIFECYCLE HYPOTHESIS

Life cycle hypothesis was advocated by three economists, viz., Franco Modigliani, R.E. Brumberg and Albert Ando, popularly known as Modiliani-Brumberg-Ando (MBA) version of the theory of consumption/saving. Basically, there is not much of difference between Friedman's approach and that of MBA except the concepts used. Firstly, the life cycle hypothesis extends the time horizon of the consuming unit to the entire life period, i.e., until the end (death) of the consuming unit. Secondly, while Friedman uses the concept of "permanent income" determining the long-term consumption behaviour, MBA uses the concept of "permanent wealth" which influences the whole life-time consumption as well as saving behaviour. That the wealth happens to be an important determinant of consumption behaviour is reminiscent of "Pigou effect" (also known as wealth effect) on consumption in the classical macroeconomic discussion.

Life cycle hypothesis is also essentially inter-temporal in nature (involving present consumption/saving vs. future consumption/saving). We attempt to explain the hypothesis assuming only two periods (or, two-halves) of the life cycle of a certain consuming unit. Figure 13.10 illustrates the case of two period income-consumption/saving options to the consuming unit and its optimal decision. The vertical axis measures the first period life cycle (and the consumption and resources) – assuming from the start of the earning period until the finishing of the children's education and their entry into earning period. The second period is assumed to start from the end of the first period till the death of the members of the consuming unit (generally husband and wife) and is represented in horizontal axis. There is also an additional assumption of some 'estate' leaving for the next generation (i.e., positive bequests). To quote the authors, at this stage, "The household or consumer unit is assumed to determine the amount available for consumption over life, which is the sum of the household's net worth at the beginning of the period... plus the present value of its non-property income... minus present value of planned bequests"[1]. This is the total available resources which he is expected to allocate for consumption between two periods. The resources, thus, act as "constraints". Although Modigliani and others assume that consumption will form a fixed relationship with the total resources, actual consumption will differ due to individual preferences and needs.

Let us now define the following terms:

1. Y_1 = the unit's income from work and wealth in period one.
2. Y_2^e = the expected earnings from work in period two.
3. W_1 = the current existing wealth of the consuming unit in period one which he might have inherited.
4. i = the rate of interest at which the unit can borrow as well as lend its resources.

The total resources available to the unit in period one is the sum total of Y_1 and W_1 and the total resources expected to be available in period two will be only Y_2^e. Now we refer to Fig. 13.10 which represents the consuming unit's different opportunities of allocating its resources between the two periods, subject to the resources constraint. The line $R_1R_2^e$ is such an "opportunity locus" or "resources constraint".

[1] F. Modigliani and Albert Ando, "The Permanent Income and Life Cycle Hypothesis of Saving Behaviour: Comparison and Tests", quoted in Ferber, 'Household Behaviour in Essays in Economic Theory: III, MacMillan, 1967.

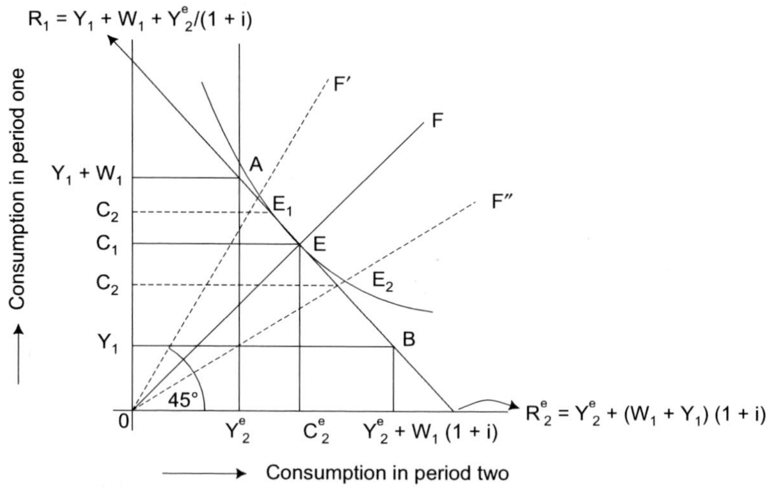

Figure 13.10 *Inter-temporal consumption income relationship in life-cycle hyothesis.*

The opportunity locus, $R_1R_2^e$ shows all possible combinations of its consumption and saving in each of the two periods for the consuming unit. For instance, if it plans to consume all its resources of period one $(Y_1 + W_1 + Y^e{}_2/1 + i)$ in period one itself and leaves nothing for period two, its position will be located at point R_1. On the other hand, if it consumes nothing in period one and saves its entire income and wealth — the maximum possible second period resources that it is able to consume — is $Y_1 + (W_1 + Y_1)(1 + r)$ and will be located at point $R^e{}_2$[1]. However, R_1 and $R^e{}_2$ are the two extreme positions. In between two points, the consuming unit chooses any of the several points depending upon its plan of consumption and saving, his decision about how much he would borrow in the first period to be paid back in the second period and also on how much he "dissaves" (draws down his wealth or saving) without resorting to borrowing or partly dissaves and partly borrows. For instance, if he decides to consume all his income plus all his wealth in period one; that is, he 'dissaves' all wealth but does not borrow, its consumption in period two will be limited to its entire second period expected income — Y_2^e — and his position will be located at point A. If he consumes his entire first period income, Y_1, but neither saves for second period nor dissaves his wealth, W_1, his consumption in the second period would be equal to $Y_2^e + W_1(1 + i)$ — the combination represented by point B. Similarly, the consuming unit has the option of choosing any other point of alternative combinations on the opportunity locus. For instance, if he

---

1 The first period resources include Y_2^e, the 2nd period expected income at its present value, hence, it is divided by $(1 + i)$ to get its discounted present value – the discount rate being i. Similarly, the 2nd period resources include compounded value of $(W_1 + Y_1)$ – the remaining 1st period income and wealth – with accumulated interest on it hence multiplied by $(1 + i)$.

is on some point between R^e_2 and B, this means he saves certain part out of his current income. Similarly, choosing any point between B and A would mean some current 'dissaving' since the entire W_1 is not exhausted although Y_1 is. But selecting a point between A and R_1 means the consuming unit exhausts all first period income and wealth and plunges himself into debt possibly with the hope of repaying it with his second period expected income. In case he has no wealth, the points A and B will coincide[1].

The line (ray), OF from the origin represents the ratio at which the total life-time consumption of the consuming unit is divided between the two periods according to his own preference for current vs. future needs and requirements. If, for instance, it attaches the same importance to its current needs and requirements as its future ones, the line OF will form a 45 angle with the origin. In that case, the unit's consumption will be located at the point of intersection between OF and $R_1R^e_2$ lines, i.e., at point E. At this point, the consumer unit consumes OC_1 amount of first period resources which includes total income of the period and some part of its current wealth (i.e., 'dissaving') but he does not need to borrow. The rest of his wealth he plans to use during the rest of his life cycle.[2]

If, however, our consuming unit considers that his present needs are more important than future needs, the OF line would shift to the left of 45 line (such as OF') implying that the present resources will be used to a greater extent. He will find himself at point E_1 with OC_1 amount of consumption, involving more dissaving, though not all. In the similar vein, if he considers future needs to be more important than the present ones, OF will rotate to the right forming less than 45 angle such as OF'. For instance, if an Indian family unit has three daughters to marry off as also a house to build in the second period of his life cycle, future needs will be considered more important than the present needs. Now, his equilibrium position will be at E_2. Here, he would exhaust all current income and will also resort to some amount of dissaving. But, a portion of current wealth would remain intact. He will now be consuming OC_2 of his current resources and leave the rest for future consumption.

We may now attempt to analyse the effects of three influencing variables on the consumption decision of the consuming unit between the two periods of its life cycle: (a) change in income, (b) change in wealth and (c) change in the rate of interest. In this respect, there is close similarity between consumer's behaviour in terms of income effect and substitution effect of a price change as it appears in microeconomics and which we analyse in terms of indifference curve analysis and the present inter-temporal consumption decision.

[1] The slope of the opportunity locus, $R_1R^e_2$ indicates the rate at which the present resources can be converted into future resources.

2 We assume that the releveant indifference curve, IC_1, showing possibilities of present vrs. future consumption, is just tangential at this point (E).

(a) Change in income: We first assume that there is an increase in the first period income while other two variables are assumed to remain constant. The second period expected income is also assumed to be unchanged. Figure 13.11 illustrates the effects.

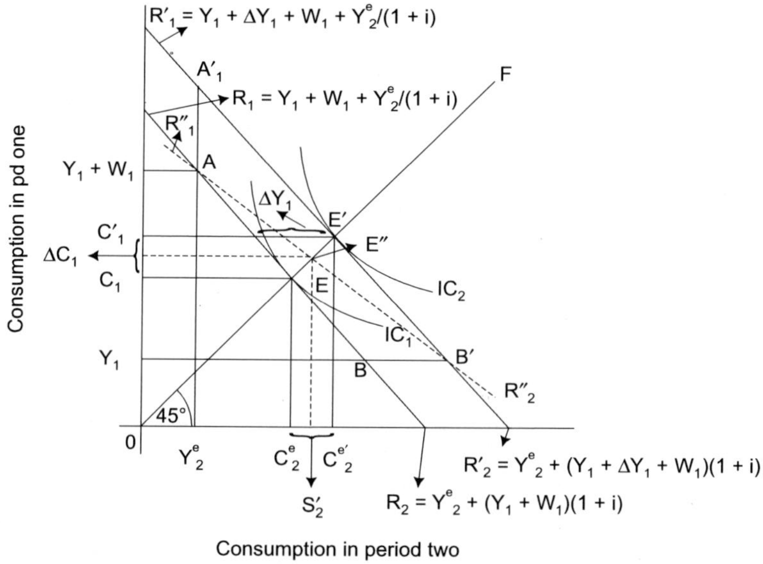

Figure 13.11 *Impact of change in income and interest rate.*

The opportunity locus or, constraint has shifted to $R'_1R'_2$. Now, given the same perception of our consuming unit regarding the present needs vs. future needs (the ray *OF* remaining unchanged) the unit's optimal behaviour will now be located at point E' with relevant IC_2 curve being tangential at this point. The new line will pass through point A'_1 since we have assumed the Y^e_2 level to be unchanged. The first period increase in income is shown by the amount ΔY_1, shown in the figure. Now, the new combination of first period and second period consumption will be C'_1 and $C^{e'}_2$, respectively which show increased amounts of consumption in both periods. Similar effect can be felt if the second period expected income rises. In such case, R_1, R_2 line will shift still further to the right, thus causing combined positive effects on consumption.

(b) Almost similar effect can be observed in case W_1, that is *wealth level* in the first period is increased while other variables remain unchanged. In fact, rise in income and wealth have same positive effects on consumption of both periods.

(c) Change in the rate of interest: Now, if there is a change in interest rate, (other variables remaining unchanged), it will have differential impact on different categories of consumers. If our consuming unit is a lender, a rise in interest rate will raise its interest income (and a fall in interest rate will lower his interest income), but if he is a borrower, a rise in interest rate will push up his interest burden and so he may, quite likely, have to revise downward his consumption plan because his disposable income falls. However, the value of his wealth, if evaluated at higher interest rate will certainly rise, of course, depending upon the composition of wealth. For instance, if wealth is held mainly in the form of bonds, a rise in interest rate will lower its market price (since there is inverse relationship between the rate of interest and price of bond). In that case, the capital value of the existing bonds falls. If wealth is held in the form of other securities, generally, rise in interest rate raises the price of securities and there is the possibility of rise in income; at least in the first period. Values of other forms of wealth generally have positive impact upon consuming unit's level of consumption and saving. Thus, the final impact on the consumption plan depends upon the total net effects of all forms of wealth and income. Just as rise in interest rate has these effects, a fall in interest will have opposite effects and hence on consumption/saving plan.

Referring to Fig. 13.11, impact of interest rate changes has been shown by rotating the opportunity locus, $R_1R^e{}_2$ through point A, assuming expected second period income (Y_2^e) remains unchanged. In case of rise in interest rate $R_1R^e{}_2$ line will rotate to the right via A, as shown by the dashed line, R'_1 R'_2 while its effects are shown by corresponding dashed lines on OR_1 and OR_2 axes. Clearly, the consumption in both periods go up. Similarly, it can be visualized that in case of fall in interest rate the opportunity locus will rotate to the left via A and the corresponding impact on consumption will be to decrease in both periods.[1]

However, income and wealth effects of interest rate change may become opposite in case of lender and borrower. For instance, if our consumer unit is a lender, a rise in interest rate may produce both positive income and positive wealth effects. But if the consumer unit is a borrower, income effect will be negative but substitution effect (from wealth value) will be positive. However, whether the total effect on consumption will be positive or not depends on how much is the positive wealth effect and how much is the negative income effect if the consumer unit is a borrower.

Now, since a substantial section of society consists of both groups of lenders and borrowers, at the macro level these opposite effects on lenders and borrowers, presumably will cancel out.

[1] We have not shown relevant indifference curves, but can easily be visualized as being tangential at these points.

13.5.1 Limitations of the Hypothesis

In spite of a considerable amount of truth and novelty in the life cycle hypothesis explaining saving or consumption behaviour over the consumer's entire life period, there are certain limitations of this hypothesis which are broadly listed below:

1. **Inaccurate expectations of the future income/wealth:** As has been mentioned in connection with permanent income hypothesis, people as consuming units are most likely to falter in estimating correct expected future earnings from work or wealth due to the complicated nature of calculations as also the presence of a number of uncertainties. Values of many forms of wealth, for example, stocks and shares or bonds or even such durable assets like houses are subject to 'shocks' leading either to abrupt fall or rise in their values. Similarly, the government's macroeconomic policy changes in future (which are mostly unpredictable); for instance change in tax rates might change the future value of wealth or income which is likely to influence the long-term consumption/saving behaviour of the consuming unit.
2. **Individual/cross-section vs. Aggregate consumption behaviour:** Like permanent income hypothesis, life cycle hypothesis also implies proportional long-run relationship between income saving/consumption, which may or may not be reflected in cross sectional individual short-run sample studies. Among other factors such as family size and composition, number of earners per family unit etc., what is more relevant is the actual stage in the life cycle of the consuming unit. For instance, whether the unit is in its youth or at middle stage of its career or at its retirement stage; whether it is suffering from some acute and prolonged illness, are also equally important. In the Indian social system, we can add, if our consuming unit is having girl child to marry off or other adults to be properly educated and settled in life and for which consistent saving or dissaving of wealth at some stage becomes necessary, the behaviour towards consumption and saving becomes different in such cases.

   The theorists rationalize by arguing that the average behaviour, when aggregated over large number of families would cancel out leaving the presumed long-run relationship — a constant proportionality — between consumption and income or saving and income intact. But such relationship, to a large measure, also depends on the social structure, norms and traditions of the society as also the composition of different social groups (for example, the proportion of habitual savers or habitual spenders, etc.) To quote Ackley in this regard, "The most basic deficiency of life cycle of behaviour is not its oversimplified concept of individual behaviour but rather its lack of recognition that consumption and saving are forms of social as well individual behaviour"[1].

However, according to life cycle hypothesis, the main conclusion that emerges is that life-time income as well as wealth are equally influencing factors of consumption and saving. Now, at the macro-level, the testing of the hypothesis would require both long-run income and wealth data to put along side consumption/saving data and to study the relationship in a multiple regression model. However, it may be mentioned here, that the author's own findings suggest relatively large influence of income rather than wealth on consumption. Secondly, income and wealth have grown more closely over the long period in history to suggest a multi-collinearity between them. In sum, therefore, income remains a single most important variable to explain consumption as well as saving, thus lending support to Keynesian consumption function[2].

3. **Population growth and other demographic changes:** The life cycle theory does not apparently consider the population growth factor and certain related changes in demographic pattern which presumably have influence over the long-run saving/consumption behaviour. For example, population is growing and people's life-time incomes, measured by any standard, are also rising either steadily or rapidly in different economies over time. With this, the demographic structure is also changing such that greater and greater number of younger families are adding to the population while retired families are dying. This implies that while those who presently save for retirement are saving at a rate higher than the rate of dissaving of the currently retired/retiring units/families — thus providing a picture of gradually higher rate of saving on the average. Similarly, the rising average life-span of the consuming units would tempt them to save more on the average than the dissaving taking place.
4. **Treatment of planned bequests:** According to the life cycle theory, consumers save only because they 'dissave' or spend their entire saving in their later life. Further, they spend the entire life-time resources (including the wealth they receive in the form of 'bequests/estates from older generations) within their life-time. Their 'planned bequests' therefore necessarily form part of their saving. But bequests may be planned or unplanned for future generations because consumers save for many other reasons. Also, they may or may not receive wealth as

---

[1] G. Ackley, Macroeconomics: Theory and Policy, MacMillan, 1978, p. 570.

[2] Ando and Modiliani fitted a regression model using US data with wealth and income as explanatory variables on consumption. They used the following model: $C_t = \alpha_1 W_t + (\alpha_2 + \alpha_3 T_\beta) Y_t$. The result they obtained for α_1 was ranging between 0.05 and 0.07 while for the combined coefficient $(\alpha_2 + \alpha_3 T_\beta)$ the values ranged between 0.65 and 0.75. One can approximate these values at average values to suggest a regression result: $C_t = 0.06W_t + 0.7Y_t$ (See Ackley, op. cit, p. 558)

bequests. If we include several generations and if there are traditions of leaving 'estate' for next generations this may be one reason for saving for the purpose of bequeathing. In developed countries, many reputed and wealthy families may have such tradition in vogue. But, many families also dissave all or substantial part of their bequests for some purpose or other.

In an underdeveloped country like India, poor family units do not receive any bequest or receive very little; they may not be able to save for any bequests to be left. On the other hand, there are laws of inheritance in existence which entitle the heirs to receive whatever amount is left as 'estate' or wealth in the form of savings. So, 'planned' or 'unplanned', certain bequests may or may not continue to accrue over the next generation.

Besides, there are many other reasons why people save during the first period of their life cycle, as also leave certain 'bequests'. Parents generally have a desire to remain attached to their children because:

(a) They have love and affection for them as also their grand-children.

(b) They wish that their children take proper care for them at their advanced old age.

(c) Their children regularly visit them or keep contact on phones if they are away from home.

The wealthier families may use their wealth (likely to be bequeathed) as a kind of 'tacit threat' – that if their children do not fulfil their wishes they may be deprived of such 'bequests'. Looking exclusively from the point of consuming families, when they grow old and lack adequate social security (as in most underdeveloped economies), their saving during their early life (the first period) are generally intended to satisfy "precautionary" needs arising out of uncertainties of various kinds. Necessary medical expenses at the old age is one of the vital reasons for such needs. Secondly, no one can predict or precisely estimate the occurrence of death. Saving, for these purposes, are considered essential and not necessarily for "dissaving" at the later life or leaving bequests. In fact, some savings would naturally continue to accrue even after the life ends.

5. **Liquidity of assets:** One implicit assumption of the life cycle hypothesis is that any future assets acquired by way of present savings or ones that are received as gifts or bequests, by inheritance or so, can be easily converted into present ones whenever required. In other words, assets are fully liquid. But in actual practice, there are good number of assets which cannot be easily converted. For example, house properties are not easily disposable without incurring heavy losses at times of

recession. In a country like India with social divide and institutional obstacles to sale, landed properties of all categories cannot be sold at will nor can borrowing be made against them. This kind of 'liquidity constraint' can limit the amount of 'dissaving' that consumers might require during their temporary fall in current income or when family needs are most urgent. In India, particularly during some decades past, numerous instances of 'distress sale' of property or other forms of assets were reported.

6. **Buffer stock savings:** People also resort to buffer stock savings, the savings which they keep as 'precautionary' or emergency fund to tide over the contingent situations. The changing behaviour of savings during people's difficult times such as sudden shutdowns of working places leading to job losses, national emergencies (epidemics or pandemics that has currently gripped the world economy in the form of COVID-19) or long recession, floods and famines is an example of buffer stock savings. The people generally create a sort of "buffer" against these emergency situations. As has been observed during the outbreak of the COVID-19, many individuals as well as businesses have utilised their buffer stock savings (those who maintain) when they suddenly found that they are in the midst of national lockdown and are prevented from going to their workplaces for earning of incomes. However, these buffer stock savings are subject to change and are likely to decrease or increase depending on the severity of uncertainty as well as government policy responses.

We can conclude, therefore, that life cycle theory/hypothesis is not an adequate explanation of why consumers save or consume over their whole life cycle. In fact, there are numerous reasons and motives and pressures – individual, social, cultural and religious – that prompt the consumer units to spend as well as save their resources. A satisfactory theory should possibly include all these factors but to provide such a unified theory is far from being easy.

SUMMARY

1. Macro theories of consumption/saving relate the aggregate consumption/saving behaviour with different variables like absolute disposable income, relative income, permanent income and life-time resources etc. Different economists have proposed these theories in terms of major hypotheses from time to time. While absolute income hypothesis was proposed by Keynes himself on which basis his consumption function was based, relative income hypothesis was given by Duesenberry. The permanent income hypothesis was advanced by M. Friedman. The life cycle hypothesis was proposed by three economists — Modigliani, Bramberg and Ando known, in short, as MBA hypothesis.

2. Although these hypotheses are known as macro theories, these have their foundations also at the micro levels (individual household levels, for instance). All the hypotheses are capable of being tested with relevant empirical data. In fact, many studies have been conducted by different economists for different countries including India. Most of these studies have confirmed the validity of Keynesian consumption function. There have been huge differences, however, with regard to other hypotheses; either on measurement ground or empirical testing levels.
3. Absolute income hypothesis tries to emphasize that absolute disposable incomes of the individual households as also at aggregate levels, are major determinants of the consumption expenditures. The consumption function when estimated gives the values of marginal propensity to consume (MPC) whose value generally lies between zero and one. Also, the value of average propensity to consume (APC) lies between zero and one; but the value of MPC is less than APC. APC is the same as consumption-income ratio and has a tendency to fall with rise in levels of income.
4. The relative-income hypothesis is more relevant when viewed in combination with absolute income. Relative-income hypothesis can be explained in two ways: (a) taking incomes relative to other families' incomes within the society who live in close contacts. If other families' incomes rise relative income of original family falls and so it feels a sort of dissatisfaction within. This is reflected in rising consumption expenditure because of 'demonstration effect' of higher consumption pattern of other families. Thus, consumption functions are interrelated and not independent. In a broader sense, the relative income hypothesis can be viewed as income-levels falling within the income distribution scale or ranges (like different decile or percentile groups). Incomes of those lying in the relatively lower ends, feel the effect of demonstration effect and hence go for higher level of consumption expenditure.

   The hypothesis is also applicable to different phases of business fluctuations with rising and falling income levels.
5. Milton Friedman's permanent income hypothesis introduces the concept of 'permanent income' and relates it to the permanent consumption of any individual consumer or family over the earning period. He distinguishes between transitory income and permanent income. The permanent income is the expected stream of income over the earning period discounted for the present. This component of the income alone affects the consumption pattern of the individual consumer units. Other components like transitory income fluctuates over this permanent component and does not explain the long-run consumption behaviour.

Friedman tries to correlate the permanent income and permanent consumption at the macro level and finds certain empirical support. However, many economists have criticized this hypothesis as practically unmeasurable and not very different from Keynesian hypothesis.

6. The life cycle hypothesis also tries to correlate long-term consumption behaviour with the long-term life-time resources of the consuming units. The resources include income earned and expected income as well as wealth received in the beginning of the life cycle. The consuming units, while taking decisions on consumption expenditures keep in mind present needs and requirements as also the future requirements till the end of the life-period including certain 'bequest' desired to be left for the posterity.

   Essentially, both the permanent income hypothesis and life cycle hypothesis are not different except the approach towards income concept adopted and the perception of life and earning period and certain other considerations affecting the consumption decisions. However, there are several practical merits of the life cycle hypothesis.

EXERCISE

1. Explain 'absolute income' hypothesis as an explanation of macro level income-consumption relationship.
2. Distinguish between short-run and long-run consumption behaviour. How would you resolve the conflict between the two?
3. Examine James Duesenberry's 'relative income' hypothesis as an explanation of consumption/saving behaviour.
4. What is 'consumption ratchet'? What relationship does it have with relative income hypothesis?
5. What do you understand by 'inter-temporal' consumption saving behaviour? Explain what factors influence the equilibrium of an inter-temporal consumer/saver.
6. Distinguish between 'transitory' income and 'permanent income. How can 'permanent income be estimated at its present value?
7. What is 'life-cycle hypothesis? To what extent this is an adequate explanation of 'inter-temporal' consumption saving behaviour?
8. Enlist all other factors for life-time behaviour of aggregate savings.

REFERENCES

1. Robert Ferber, "Household Behaviour", in Surveys of Economic Theory, Macmillan, 1967.
2. N. Gregory Mankiw, Macroeconomics, Cengage, 2008.
3. G. Ackley, Macroeconomics, Theory and Policy, Macmillan, USA, 1978.

14

Theories of Investment and Capital Accumulation

It has long been recognised that investment is the most volatile determinant of aggregate demand. Hence, it is also the cause of fluctuations of economic activities in the economy. Therefore, it is important to analyse the behaviour of investment in much more detail. In chapter 4, section 4.4, we have explained the meaning of investment and the basic Keynesian approach to the problem of determination of investment. Also we have discussed the more general supply-demand (or stock adjustment) approach of investment behaviour. In the present chapter, we intend to go deeper to examine some other widely discussed theories such as flexible accelerator theory, Tobin's Q-theory and neoclassical theory of investment (Jorgenson's model).

We begin with the flexible accelerator theory of which an early version was presented by R.M. Goodwin (1955).

14.1 THE FLEXIBLE ACCELERATOR MODEL

Goodwin's investment function: Goodwin suggested an S-shaped investment function as shown in Figure (14.1). Although Goodwin developed his theory in the context of the business cycle model, this is equally relevant to the investment behaviour of the firms, since fluctuations in investment are believed to be the prime determinant of the business cycles.

The figure shows two crucial non-linearities. A lower limit to net investment is set by capital wastage (leftward portion of the curve in the negative zone where gross investment is zero or the disinvestment is maximum). The upper limit is set by the 'capacity' or the maximum output of the new capital goods obtainable with given capital and labour supply. The vertical axis of the figure shows the rate of change of capital stock (investment) while the horizontal axis shows the difference between the desired and actual capital stock. As a certain firm experiences that the gap between its desired and actual capital stock is increasing, it is taking up more and more investment and the rate of investment is determined by the slope of the investment curve which appears to be, by and large, of *S* shape.[1]

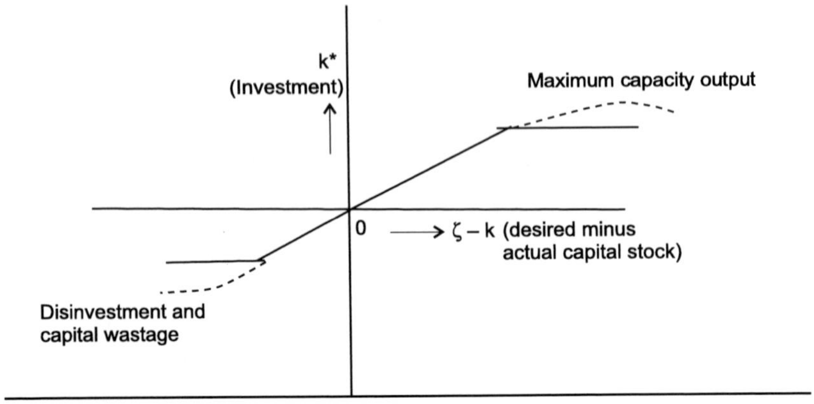

Figure 14.1 *Goodwin's investment function.*

In Goodwin's model, the desired level of capital is proportional to output, except for modifications brought about by technical change as symbolised by the following equation:

$\zeta = v\,y + \beta\,(t)$, where, ζ = desired capital, y = output, v is the accelerator coefficient, and $\beta(t)$ is the technical change function. In Godwin's model, the actual investment is a function of the discrepancy between desired and actual capital, thus:

$g(k^*) = \zeta - k$, where, k is the actual capital and k^* is the rate of change in capital stock (= net investment). Figure 14.1 illustrates this investment function.

Goodwin's system contains a variable representing *desired* capital (which is a subjective variable). This, in itself, has not been measured on any broad scale. By substitution, this subjective variable can be eliminated from his system to derive a relation making investment a function of output and capital stock as shown in eqn. (14.1),

$$g\,(k^*) = v\,y - k + \beta\,(t) \tag{14.1}$$

Equation 14.1 shows that investment is a rising function of the growth of output, y and a falling function of the actual capital stock, k, with v being the accelerator. This further means that if the actual capital stock is lower compared to the desired capital stock (so that the discrepancy between the two is large), the rate of investment will be higher. In this formulation, the variables are observable, hence can be estimated empirically to obtain the value of the accelerator, v. However, in this model, there is no explicit mention of the rate of interest as a determinant of the investment.

1 R.M. Goodwin, quoted in Lawrence R. Klein, *An Introduction to Econometrics*, Prentice Hall, India, 1969, pp. 216-221.

In chapter 4, in the context of the Keynesian theory of investment, we mentioned the role of a simple or rigid accelerator which assumes that the gap between the desired (or optimum) capital stock and the actual capital stock is immediately filled or, it is filled in the same period without any 'lag'. Thus, if K_t and $K_t - 1$ stand for the actual capital stocks of the current and past periods, and if the difference between the two, i.e., net investment (ignoring the depreciation, for the time being), is a function of the change in income $(Y_t - Y_{t-1})$, (in fact, it is actually the expected change in income), which is rising, then, under the simple accelerator model, the stock of actual capital will quickly be adjusted to the optimum stock in the current period itself. That is to say that $K_t = K_t^*$, where, K_t* stands for desired or optimum stock of capital. However, it has been argued by various authors that there are definite time lags involved in the adjustment process between the two levels of capital stock. In fact, there are various kinds of lags that appear in the process such as: (1) decision lag, (2) installation lags, (3) delivery lags, (4) financial lags and (5) other administrative lags. Obviously, the length of time that these processes require may vary greatly among firms as also among different types of capital expenditures. For example, if national income is rising thus stimulating expectations among the investors, they are likely to take a decision to increase their existing capital stock to the level of their desired or optimum capital stock (or net investment). However, this decision itself takes time to take a final shape. Then, placing an order for capital goods and getting delivery of the same is time taking. This is precisely the delivery lag. Similarly, installing a big factory for output, (for instance, an automobile factory or telecommunication tower network) will involve another time lag. Thirdly, if the investor is hopeful of getting financial funds from the banks or other financial institutions, it will create some more delay which is the financial lag. Lastly, the entire process will surely entail a certain amount of administrative delay in terms of clearance of the project at various levels which may be called the administrative lags.

The presence of the above-mentioned lags is most likely to cause a slow and time taking adjustment process so that we can say that the simple accelerator model will be unable to fully explain the business investment behaviour. Hence, we have to search for an alternative model which can take account of the lag coefficients and their behaviour. In econometrics, there exists one of the most popular and widely used lagged-variables models known as Koyck's distributed lag model.

We shall, first, derive the flexible accelerator and then try to fit it with the Koyck's distributed lag function.

Let us define K_t^* as the desired capital stock and K_t as the actual capital stock in period t. If the actual capital stock at any period is less than the desired one, then every firm will be trying to achieve the desired level of capital for meeting with the rise in income that the firm expects to be happening in the market or in the larger economy. Let us define Y_t - Y_{t-1} as the increase in income in period t over its previous period, $t - 1$, and β as capital output ratio (units of capital required to produce one unit of output, see chapter 4 p. 79-80) which is assumed to be constant, particularly in the short run, suggesting a fixed proportion production function, then we can say that:

$$K^* - K_{t-1} = \beta\,(Y_t - Y_{t-1}) \qquad (14.2)$$
$$= \beta\,\Delta\,Y_t$$

where, ΔY = change (increase) in income.

Since, change in capital stock is defined as net investment (without depreciation), we can write

$$I_t = \beta\,\Delta\,Y \qquad (14.3)$$

where, I_t is the net investment.

Thus, net investment is proportional to change in income or output. Now, in the case of simple accelerator, the lag in capital stock between the two periods of time, *t and t* – 1 is zero, so that,

$$I_t = (K_t^* - K^*_{t-1}) = \beta\,\Delta\,Y \qquad (14.4)$$

But if we allow for lagged response to investment in equation (14.3), it becomes

$$I_t = (1 - \lambda)\,(K^*_t - K_{t-1}) \qquad (14.5)$$

where, $1 > \lambda > 0$.

What the lagged response behaviour means is that investment takes place with a certain time lag and in fact, changes not by the full extent of the difference between the desired and the actual capital stock but by a certain fraction of this difference. This fraction may be ranging between 0 and 1 depending on how investment responded in previous periods to change in income.

At this stage, a distributed lag model may be utilised to obtain the value of the lag coefficient, to understand the nature of adjustment (or the speed of adjustment) and substitute the same in eqn. (14.1). In econometrics, as we have mentioned above, an extremely popular distributed lag model, known as Koyck's distributed lag model is available to be accessed for further study.

It will be obvious, now, that the present accelerator model incorporates lagged variables in the capital accumulation process, thus making the investment respond slowly over time to changes in output. This is a special feature of the "flexible" accelerator model.

It needs to be mentioned at this point that in this accelerator model, it is assumed that price level is constant and quantity is taken as variable. Thus, it is in the tradition of Keynesian short-run models. This assumption implies that only quantity changes in the investment (or, stocks of capital) have been considered having assumed no change in the price level.

The flexible accelerator model has been empirically put to test in several studies and has been found to be largely consistent with the prediction of the model. For instance, Koyck himself implemented his model to the railroad industry (along with some other industries) using data for the years 1894 to 1940 and found consistent results suggesting slow adjustment in bridging the gap between the desired and actual capital stocks. In recent years, similar empirical studies have come up using flexible accelerator models. Since our focus is mainly limited to the theoretical aspect of the model, we would not explore further this aspect.

Limitations of the flexible accelerator model

1. The first limitation of the flexible accelerator model is its assumption of constant capital output ratio which suggests a fixed proportion production technology, which, in turn, suggests that all output can be raised with only a single process using a fixed proportion of factors of production. There is, thus, no alternative process or processes available with the producing firms, particularly in the short run. This assumption does not allow any flexibility in the factor used as in the case of more general neoclassical production functions which generate smooth and continuous isoquants.
2. Keeping the price level constant and focusing only on quantity, as is typical with all Keynesian models, restrict the model's applicability to micro level studies because a number of price variables (such as interest rate and exchange rate changes) or government's fiscal policy changes bring about changes in the general price level as well as firm's investment decisions even in the short run.

14.2 NEOCLASSICAL THEORY OF INVESTMENT

The neoclassical theory of investment is the most popular as well as widely debated theory of the business investment behaviour. There are two versions of the theory—the early neoclassical version and the modern neoclassical version, particularly the Jorgensonian version and its development thereafter. The early version of the theory dates back to the classical (Adam Smith, Ricardo, J. M. Mill and other classical-neoclassical theories) which present an investment theory based on the classical capital theory. The behaviour of investment, according to this theory, is explained in terms of a decreasing investment function with rate of interest with a fairly high degree of elasticity. Basically, this version of the theory tries to derive the investment function from the demand for capital—capital which has been argued to be intrinsically "productive" due to the round- about process of production. Adding more capital to the process of production, therefore, adds to the output several times larger. But the addition of capital would come from savings of the community which it brings by foregoing the present incomes in lieu of a certain amount of interest. Now, more and more capital can be added to the production process only if the cost of obtaining it (the rate of interest) is lower in relation to the additional output that it brings about. Hence, a negative relationship between investment and the rate of interest is easily established.

This investment-interest relationship was developed in the context of the macro economy as a whole. Secondly, this theory accepted the notion of capital as a single homogeneous factor of production. Thirdly, this is a long period investment theory with reference to a free competitive capitalist economy. However, a theory of investment based on this concept of capital which, in fact, consists of a large number of heterogeneous elements besides the fixed elements in it, was criticized by a group of economists of the Cambridge school known as "Cambridge capital controversy". The fixed element in capital is a lumpy factor obtained at some rate (price) at one point in time that provides a flow of services from the 'stock' element over the whole of its lifetime while the whole group of heterogeneous capital — the different raw materials, energy and other intermediate capital goods are generally obtained at different rates. Secondly, some of these fixed or circulating capital may be owned by the producers themselves. In a free competitive economy, a suitable theory was required to be developed to compensate the producing firms for the different types of capital costs that they incur on account of being their owners.

Let us illustrate the early neoclassical theory of investment in terms of a graph showing a production function with two factors–labour and capital–and a couple of isoquants. Figure (14.2) gives one such isoquant, Q_1, based on two different capital labour ratios. One of these factors, labour, is held at a certain fixed level assuming full employment in the labour market. Based on a certain capital labour ratio, α, ($K/L = \alpha$), a ray arising from the origin is intersecting the isoquant, Q_1, and with labour curve L = [drawn vertically downward at point Z_1. Since this capital labour ratio is based upon the marginal productivity conditions of factors, this is also consistent with their equilibrium factor price ratios, that is, $K/L = MPk/MPl = r/w$. (neoclassical theory of the firm with regard to factor use). At a different factor price ratio, (for example, due to capital becoming more costly), the firms will change their K/L ratio in the direction of substituting more labour for capital so that the K/L will now be less. The demand for capital in the industry as well as the economy as a whole will be falling. The firm will be operating at a lower point intersecting the vertical L *curve* on a lower isoquant, Q_2. A different ray generates from the origin through this new K/L ratio, β. For more output, the firm will be expanding along this path and therefore adding more capital in the same ratio so long as the relative factor price ratio does not change. However, in the process of reorganising the capital labour ratio, some capital in the form of old plants and machinery will have to be scrapped or withdrawn which means the labour employed in them will be rendered unemployed. If full employment assumption of labour is retained, additional investment will be needed for re-employing them or re-skilling them suitable for the new plants with less capital labour ratio. So the investment (new capital addition) will be limited to that extent only. However, the net result will be a fall in the capital intensity of production as well as a fall in output along with the disinvestment equal to $OK_1 - OK_2$.

Thus, a competitive firm with the long run goal of profit maximisation will be required to equate the value of the marginal product of each factor of production to its price, that is, value marginal product of capital to the real interest rate (interest rate/price level) and the value marginal product of labour to the real wage rate (nominal wage rate/price level). This is the static equilibrium condition of the firm. The equilibrium condition will however change in response to change in the factor price ratio, so the movement will be from one equilibrium position to another.

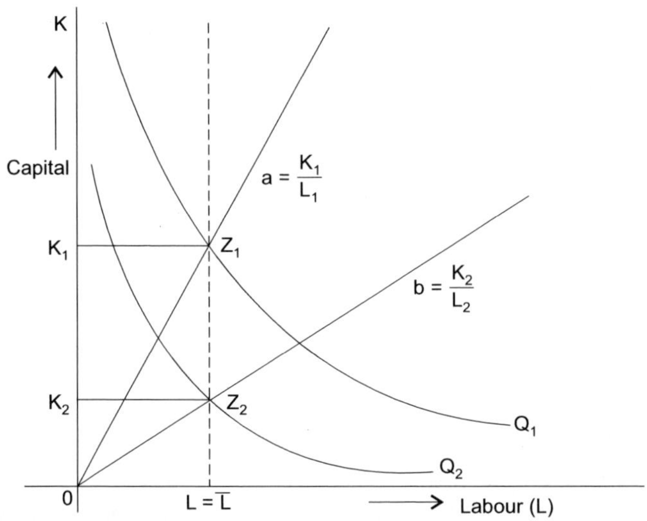

Figure 14.2 *Changing capital labour ratio and investment: Early neo-classical theory of investment.*

In the context of the specific neoclassical production function like the Cobb-Douglas production function such as:

$$Q = A\, K^{\alpha}\, L^{\beta} \tag{14.6}$$

$$\partial Q/\partial K = \alpha\, A\, K^{\alpha-1}\, L^{\beta} \text{ and } \partial Q/\partial L = \beta\, A\, K^{\alpha}\, L^{\beta-1},$$

$$= \alpha\,(Q/K) \qquad \text{and} \qquad = \beta\,(Q/L)$$

In equilibrium, the value of marginal products of capital and labour will be equated to their respective factor prices— rate of interest (r) and real wage rate (w), thus:

$$p(\alpha\, Q/K) = r, \text{ and } p(\beta\, Q/L) = w \tag{14.7}$$

Now, taking the ratio of the above two equations, we have:

$p\ (\alpha\ Q/K.)/p\ (\beta\ Q/L) = r/w$ (14.8)

$\Rightarrow (\alpha/\beta)\ L/K = r/w.$

$\Rightarrow L/K = (r/w)/(\alpha/\beta)$ ....

$\Rightarrow K/L = (\alpha/\beta)/(r/w)$ ....

$\Rightarrow K/L = \alpha\ w/\beta\ r.$ ....

If L is constrained to $\overline{L}$, we can express K in terms of r

$K^* = \{r\ \overline{L}^{-\beta}/\alpha\ A\}^{1/\alpha-1.}$ (14.9),

and the rate of change of K^* with respect to r, $\partial K/\partial r = \gamma\ r^{(1/(\alpha-1)-1)}$

(14.10)

where, γ is constant.

$$\gamma = \{(\alpha\ A)^{1/\alpha-1}.\ \overline{L}^{(-\beta/\alpha-1)}\}/(\alpha-1)$$

A careful examination of equation (14.10) reveals that the exponent to r comes with a negative sign which suggests that K^* has a negative relationship with the rate of interest, so long as (γ) is positive and (γ) will certainly be positive given the signs of α and β.

The above results clearly show that the equilibrium or optimum capital stock held by all firms in the aggregate economy, K^*, increases with the decrease in the rate of interest and vice versa as exhibited in the equation 14.10. The rate of increase in the capital stock, $\partial K/\partial r$, that is, investment, is also a decreasing function of the rate of interest provided the production technology is putty clay–meaning that the factors are substitutable only ex-ante, that is, at their planned level (before the plant and machinery have been installed).

Thus, the traditional neoclassical investment theory suggests a static equilibrium model that states that the macro (aggregate) investment function can be derived from the capital theory (capital labour ratios of the economy) based on the concept of capital as a single homogeneous factor of production.

Jorgenson's neoclassical model of investment and capital accumulation.

Dale Jorgenson (1963) provided an investment model which has evoked enormous interest and lively debate among economists. At the same time, the model has been criticised from several points of view. Jorgenson's approach is essentially microeconomic in nature—taking a single producing firm for investment analysis. For a firm operating in a competitive environment and wishing to remain in existence for an indefinite time period with profit maximising goal, will be trying to maximise the firm's net revenue or net cash flow over the whole time period which can be evaluated by taking the summation of the periodwise net revenues. This will be the compounding process, given a certain rate of compounding. The reverse process, that is, the discounting, when applied, will mean that the firm tries to maximise the present value of the discounted sum of all future net revenues for an indefinite period. This process can be expressed in the following integration formula assuming that the summation takes place continuously. Hence, this is a dynamic model of investment.

$$V = \int_0^{\infty} e^{-rt} R(t)\, dt \tag{14.11}$$

where, $R(t) = p(t)\, Q(t) - w(t)\, L(t) - q(t)\, I(t)$,

$Q(t) = F(K_t, L_t) = A\, K_t^{\alpha}\, L_t^{\beta}$

Subject to the constraint:

$K^*(t) = I(t) - \delta\, K(t)$.

where, R are net revenues, r is interest rate, p is output price, w is wage rate, q is the price of capital good (price of machine, for example), Q is the quantity of output, L is the quantity of labour, δ is the rate of depreciation and I is the investment (expressed in physical units), K^*_t= time rate of capital services at time t.

The constraint here means that the net investment, $\{I(t) - \partial K(t)\}$ will be equal to the time rate of change of the flow of capital services at time t. In other words, this constraint ensures that the flow of capital services per unit of time will be proportional to the net investment. (All variables have been expressed in real terms, that is, after being deflated by the price levels).

A few points need to be clarified at this stage. There can be two types of factor services available to the firm for use besides labour services. The firm may own some of the factors themselves such as a machine. The other alternative is to hire the machine from the market — from those who hire them out on a per day, per hour or per year basis. The second type of factor services offer their own market prices at which they can be easily purchased. But the first type of factor services like machines (or any such fixed factor) owned by the firm need to be compensated fully. At least three key elements, in this connection, enter into the firm owner's cost calculation. These are: (1) the depreciation cost on the machine's wear and tear per period of time. Generally, such depreciation is evaluated on a straight line basis—at a certain fixed rate of say 10% per year on the purchase price of the machine. Depreciation cost or depreciation allowance is, in fact, set apart on a regular basis in order to replace the machine at the end of its lifetime, in other words, to have the machine forever. Thus, the firm's owner, to remain the machine owner forever, needs to be compensated for this cost, (2) the opportunity cost in terms of the interest cost foregone on the capital cost incurred for purchasing the machine. For instance, if the owner would have sold the machine and purchased bonds of the same amount, he would have earned interest on bonds (annuities), and (3) any decrease in the market price of the machine that would have taken place during the time period. This is because in the case of such decline in the machine's market price, its potential resale value falls so this needs to be compensated too. However, in the case of rise in the market price, the amount needs to be suitably deducted.

Jorgenson has called the sum total of these costs the "user cost" of capital.

We now come back to the basic equation expressing discounted present value function given above and take up for further analysis.

On applying the maximisation conditions with respect to the variable factors and the constraint of the production function as presented in eqn. 14.11 above, we have to following marginal productivity conditions:

$$\partial Q/\partial L = w/p \text{ and } \partial Q/\partial K = \{q(r + \delta)\}/p = c/p,$$

where, $c = q(r + \delta)$. Further, $q(r + \delta)$ has been defined as the 'user cost of capital'.

Let us try to understand these marginal productivity conditions.

The marginal productivity condition, $\partial Q/\partial L = w/p$, simply states that the marginal product of labour is equal to the real wage rate (nominal wage rate divided by the general price level, p).

The second condition means that the marginal product of capital is equal to the 'user cost of capital' in real terms, that is, the sum total of qr and $q\delta$, *deflated by the general price level.* While qr is the component of total interest cost (quantity q multiplied by the rate of interest) forgone and $q\delta$ is the component of total amount of depreciation cost (the machine cost times its rate of depreciation). The sum of these two costs, termed as 'user cost' as mentioned above in (1) and (2) are relevant here because the third component is uncertain depending on the future market price of the owned capital good and, in fact, the owner's 'compensation' is applicable only in case of falling price of the capital good. Jorgenson has also shown that the marginal productivity condition for capital, $\partial Q/\partial K = q(r + \delta)/p$ is the implicit rental value of capital services supplied by the firm to itself.

The firm's main objective in this connection is to choose the optimal paths for capital (K_t) *and* labour (L_t) while fulfilling the maximisation criterion. In this context, Jorgenson has proved that the firm's equilibrium condition in terms of the maximisation of the present value of net revenues (or cash flow) at continuous times to indefinite future will be the same as in the case of point to point (or at discrete intervals of time) maximisation.

Secondly, he has also proved that instead of owning a capital good, if the firm hires the capital services from the market, assuming a competitive rental market for capital exists, (such as machine per hour, machine per day or the like) and pays rent accordingly, the conclusion will be the same.

Now, let K^* represent the desired amount of capital stock. Assuming that the production function is Cobb-Douglas with constant returns to scale (CRS), such that the coefficients/output elasticities (or exponents) of the factors of production, labour and capital, add to unity ($\alpha + \beta = 1$), then the marginal productivity condition for capital leads to the following conclusion:

$$K^* = \alpha\,(pQ/c). \tag{14.12}$$

However, to understand our competitive firm's investment behaviour, it is suggestive from equation 14.12, that the firm will be accumulating more and more capital so long as it's marginal productivity remains higher than the user cost or the rental price of capital services which, of course, includes the rate of interest, r. This means that if the user cost, c is lower, the firm will be tempted to acquire more and more capital (i.e., the firm will be undertaking more and more investment), given its expansion path and the paths of w and p (wage rate and price level). Secondly, investment is a rising function of the output (Q), given p, the price level. In order to achieve the desired capital stock, the firm in question, initially starts with a certain capital stock and then proceeds on a trial and error basis until it reaches the desired or optimum capital stock level. There is no formal proof nor any example to illustrate the conclusion.

Critical evaluation of Jorgenson's investment model

Jorgenson's investment model has been criticised from several angles. Most criticisms have come from the neo-Keynesian group of economists.

1. Jorgenson's model of investment is essentially a microeconomic approach to investment behaviour which analyses the equilibrium condition of an atomistic firm that faces a production function and basically two goods—one variable factor input (capital) and one output (labour is assumed to remain at full employment). The firm is assumed to operate in a perfectly competitive market. The model's basic objective, as the author himself states, is to arrive at an optimum capital stock for the firm and then to derive an investment function through the capital accumulation process. However, critics have said that Jorgenson's results lead to an indeterminate solution which is broadly termed 'indeterminacy' problem (Giradi, 2017). At best, the model is able to determine the optimum K/L ratio but not the optimum K^*.

   Jorgenson argues that the indeterminacy problem can be solved by simply taking an initial capital stock and then going in for an 'iterative process' that is, adopting a trial and error method to arrive at the optimal capital stock. The author believes that this process will eventually converge to the optimum or desired capital stock. He also believes that in this process, particularly in the second stage of the iteration, both output and employment should be held at a certain level. At this point, Giradi has argued that this way of arriving at the optimal capital stock is not convincing since, if both employment and output are held constant at a certain level, no change in capital (K) is possible. Thus, either employment or output should be assumed to be given in the second iteration stage.

2. In a fully competitive market economy, an atomistically small firm is free to hire any amount of capital or labour. Hence, labour need not be constrained to a full employment level. Secondly, for the production

process to be continued uninterrupted, capital and labour are both needed to be available unhindered at their prevailing prices, i.e., capital costs and wage rates. But with full employment in the labour market, any rise in the labour demand on the part of the atomistic firm will mean the rise in the wage rate thus disturbing the basic equilibrium condition.

3. The use of neoclassical production function in its Cobb-Douglas form with its Constant Returns to Scale (proportionate increase in the labour and capital leads to an equal proportionate increase in total output) as a special property has been criticised by many critics. In fact, a well known problem in neoclassical production theory is that under constant returns to scale, the profit function of a price taking firm is linear in the capital stock so the optimal value of the latter is not determined. In fact, under such conditions, the optimal size of a profit taking firm is either zero, infinite or undefined depending on whether the unit production cost is higher, lower or equal to the unit price of output (Giradi, 2017, p. 13).
4. Critics have pointed out that the adjustment problem is invariably associated with the acquisition of the capital stock. Jorgenson assumes that adjusting the capital stock is cost less (besides the cost of acquiring the new capital good). He recognises the 'delivery lags' but assumes that firms take every change in the capital stock as permanent, so they do not influence the process of optimisation. As a result, the firm makes its choices as if adjustment was instantaneous and cost less. The critics have, however, argued that to explain short-run investment dynamics, one needs to model not only the optimal capital stock but also the choice of the speed at which the gaps between the actual and optimal capital stock are filled and hence the adjustment process must be modelled explicitly. The adjustment problem has been forcefully advocated by economist Haavelmo.

   In spite of the above-mentioned drawbacks, Jorgenson's model is a standard representative of the neoclassical investment theory that has attracted the attention of economists. The model has been put to wide empirical tests also.

14.3 TOBIN'S Q-THEORY OF INVESTMENT BEHAVIOUR

James Tobin, a Nobel laureate (1981) and a neo-Keynesian economist, advanced a theory of investment, which is essentially a financial theory of investment. His view is that the investment behaviour of a modern firm is influenced by its market value in the stock market (or, the market capitalisation) relative to its asset value. Tobin's investment theory is known as Tobin's Q-theory.

Tobin argued that a firm's investment level should depend on the ratio of the present value of its installed capacity to its replacement cost of capital. If this ratio is greater than one ($Q > 1$), that would mean that the firm would like to increase its capital stock while in the opposite case, i.e., if the ratio is less than one ($Q < 1$), the firm would decrease its capital stock. Investment, therefore, responds positively with Q-ratio being greater than one and negatively Q-ratio being less than one. The Q-ratio is expressed as follows:

Q-ratio = The total market value of the firm/Total asset value of the firm.

Here, total asset value is the same as the total replacement cost of the firm, since at this cost, the firm can be replaced, i.e., a new firm can be purchased with the same asset value. The rationale behind the decision to invest more in case of the market value being higher than the asset value is that the firm is able to buy a ₹ 100 worth of capital at replacement cost and earn profit that has present value in excess of ₹ 100.

On the contrary, if the Q-ratio is less than one, the present value of the profits earned by installing new capital is less than the cost of capital so that more investment means lower profits. Further, in this case, if some firms want to enter the industry, they can acquire the necessary capital assets more cheaply by buying an existing firm than by building a new one with new capital. In fact, most transactions in the stock markets are carried out, by and large, on this basis. Rational investors often take recourse to the Q-ratio before making investments in a particular firm. In financial jargon, Tobin's Q is expressed in the following way:

Tobin's Q = Equity market value + Liabilities market value/Equity book value + Liabilities book value.

In this formula, a comparison is made between a firm's market value as evident in the stock market and its equity book value. The equity book value is calculated according to the initial financial position of the firm. Similarly, liabilities are calculated on the basis of total loans and other liabilities both at their current market value and at the initial financial position of the firm.

If the assumption is made that the market value and the book value of a firm's liabilities are equivalent, then the above formula becomes:

Tobin's Q = Equity market value/Equity book value

This formula implies that if the Q-ratio is less than one, the cost of replacing a firm's assets is greater than the value of its stocks which means that this stock is undervalued. In the opposite case ($Q > 1$), the firm's stock is more expensive than the replacement cost of its assets which means that the stock is overvalued. In fact, this measure of stock valuation is the driving factor behind the investment decision.

From the individual firm in the market, one can move to the market as a whole to understand whether the market is overvalued or undervalued. Thus, from this aggregative point of view, the Q-ratio is expressed as:

Tobin's Q (market) = Market capitalisation of all firms / Replacement value of all firms.

Thus, $Q > 1$ indicates that the market is overvalued. Similarly, $Q < 1$ would indicate that the market as a whole is undervalued. The undervalued firms in the market naturally become the object of attraction for prospective purchasers who would go in for purchasing rather than creating a new firm. On the other hand, the overvalued firms are most likely to witness higher competition in the market due to their earning higher profits (rate being higher than their replacement cost) and thus inducing other firms to create similar businesses. As a result of the entry of new firms into the businesses, the old firms' market share will be reduced thus resulting in the fall of their market price. This means the numerator of Tobin's Q falls in value thus reducing their Q-ratio.

Tobin's Q-ratio helps a great deal to determine the ideal or fair market value of the firms in the aggregate which suggests its value to be equal to one. This can be termed as the market equilibrium value for the aggregate stocks. Market watchers are interested to see how far the Q-ratio fluctuates around the value of one.

It may be mentioned here, that in periods of swings of the business cycles, the Q-ratio also fluctuates such that during periods of upswing (particularly when these are not backed by real factors), the value of the ratio rises too much above one. Similarly, during downswing, the value of the ratio falls below one. This is why, during peaks of every business cycle leading to their bubble formation stage, maximum values of Q-ratios have been witnessed.

Limitations of *Q*-ratio: Tobin foresaw that the movements in the stock prices will be reflected in the changes in the community's investment as well consumption behaviour. However, on an actual empirical level, critics have not found strong evidence on the correlation between these variables.

Tobin's Q has been consulted by a good number of companies to make investment decisions no doubt. But, the other models have made better predictions regarding the fixed business investment. During certain periods of time, particularly during the early 1970s, the Q-ratio was able to predict business behaviour well in the US economy, but during other periods of time it failed. In fact, the firms take into consideration not only the Q-ratio but also other determinants like the current and expected future interest rates as well as the present value of the expected rate of profits before a final decision on investment is taken.

14.4 TYPES OF INVESTMENT: RESIDENTIAL INVESTMENT, BUSINESS FIXED INVESTMENT, AND INVENTORY INVESTMENT

In the earlier chapter, we have seen that private consumption and investment expenditures are the two vital components of aggregate demand which are responsible for creating employment and income in the economy. We have also discussed the general principles of investment function from both the demand and supply sides.

There are certain specific types of investments which deserve mention since these involve the decision-making process from both the investors as well as consumers. Investment in residential houses (or, real estate) is one such category of investment.

While for the investors, it provides huge opportunities for earning profit incomes, to the larger economy also, it creates opportunities for greater employment and incomes through the multiplier effects as well. The consumers or the purchasers of the residential houses are benefited in several ways. For instance, they enjoy the benefits of living in good and comfortable houses on relatively easy terms from their financiers (the banks or other financial institutions). Also, in most cases, they get tax benefits from the government in terms of tax-free interest on housing loans.

However, there is a downside story attached with investment in this segment. It is susceptible to risk — the risk of over investment and glut if the market crashes due to shortage of purchasers and there is inventory build-up of unsold houses.

We may recall here the great housing market collapse (the sub-prime crisis) causing the financial crisis leading ultimately to the Great Recession in the US during 2008-09. Thus, if there are fluctuations in investment activities in this area, they might be responsible for causing crises in the economy.

We examine, in this section, the main determinants of residential investment from both the demand and supply sides.

Demand for residential investment: Residential investment can be basically viewed from two angles: (a) from using the residencies for living/self-consumption and (b) for using them as investment/assets categories.

(a) Individuals need houses to live in: This is an essential part of the lives of the people. For building a house they require extra funds which they can provide from their own savings or they can obtain as a housing loan from the banks and other financial institutions. In the latter case, the land as well as the house remains mortgaged with the concerned bank or financial institution until the loan amount is fully repaid. However, they have another option — of renting in a house provided there is a flexible and nearly perfect lease market for houses.

The house-less people have a special urge for houses since ownership feeling attached with their own house gives them a feeling of security for individual house owners. Also, house ownership gives the house owner a permanent address and other advantages like children's schooling facilities, etc.

With population growth, gradual subdivisions of the existing family size and urbanisation, the demand for houses is rising (albeit with rise in incomes). Secondly, with economic growth and change in the living standards, demand for better and comfortable houses is also on the rise.

(b) For using residential houses as an "asset" is basically the result of the speculative motive of the rich property owners who either sell them at exorbitant prices when the demand for houses is high in the market or put them on rent and thereby earn rental income. Often the rents are fairly high compared to the computable cost of production (keeping the average life period of a housing unit — around 50 years).

The demand for residential investment, thus, arises from consumer demand for houses, particularly in the urban segments of the economy as also the rising prices of urban land and houses.

Of course, the demand for housing depends on its relative price—price relative to the general price level—which negatively influences its demand as is normally the behaviour of the demand curve.

As far as the sources of funds for investment are concerned, the availability of such funds at lower costs is an important factor influencing the extent of investment demand. And, obviously, the rate of interest at which such funds are available from financial institutions, is an important component of the cost such that at lower rate of interest, the demand for investment is higher and at higher rate of interest, the demand is lower thus suggesting an inverse relationship between the rate of interest and the volume of such investment (see Figure 14.3). However, as with the behaviour of investment in general, investment in housing too is influenced by the prospect of expanding market availability as well as risk and return of undertaking such investments.

Supply of residential investment: As far as the supply of residential investment is concerned, it can be taken as a fixed stock at a particular point in time. However, over time, this stock can be increased. Any addition to the existing stock adds up to the gross investment (or, net investment), which may also be called 'capital formation' in the residential segment. However, we have to keep in mind that the existing stock of houses has a certain depreciation cost — the life of houses gets shortened by wear and tear and requires replacement. Thus, the supply curve of residential investment is vertical in nature.

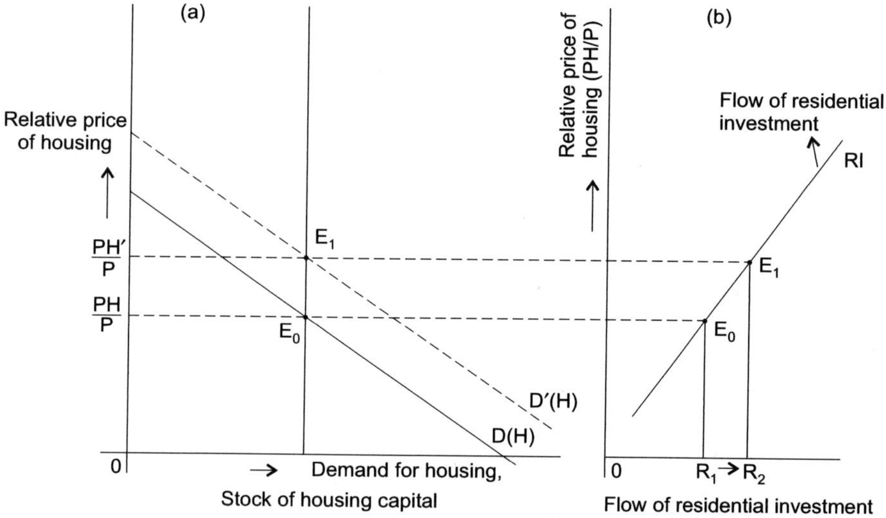

Figure 14.3 *Demand and supply of residential investment.*

Thus, the intersection of the demand and supply curves of investment determines the equilibrium price of houses. Clearly, with a rise in demand (shift in demand curve upwards), the housing prices will be rising, while with a rise in the supply (stock) of housing units, the prices will be falling. The main shift variables, in this case, are population growth, migration of people from rural to urban areas and change in the pattern of living consequent upon rise in incomes of the people. From the supply side, gradual shrinking of the urban and semi-urban land areas (particularly, in a country like India), pushes up the price of such land leading to the higher cost of houses.

Effect of interest rate changes and tax benefits to housing investment: When does a crisis arise in the housing sector? Clearly, an oversupply of housing units or crash in demand in the housing market or both can cause turbulence in the economy. In such situations, the link of the investment channel is disrupted somewhere, most often by the credit channel by the financial institutions. In fact, an oversupply is often caused by over investment spree in the real estate sector particularly, during the upward phase of demand which is carried far enough without proper estimate of the demand ahead. Similarly, a crash in demand may be caused by the drying up of the credit flow from the banking sector.

The above model of the demand, supply and equilibrium prices, by and large, explains the fluctuations in the residential markets with variations across cities and towns or other locations.

Business fixed investment: This is a type of investment every business enterprise, big or small, has to undertake before it starts the business operations. Expenditures on acquisitions of factory buildings, machines, implements, warehouses, etc., are included in this category. The main property of these categories of investment is that they provide a flow of services over a long period — the lifespan of the machines. Secondly, such fixed investments represent lumpy factors of production which cannot be obtained in very small parts so that a relatively greater investment has to be made for acquiring them at the beginning of the production cycle. Thirdly, they incur a certain depreciation cost which is normally estimated by dividing the total cost of such machines by their lifespan. In order to possess such a machine forever, the entrepreneur needs to estimate the accumulated sum of depreciation costs (along with its interest amounts) as well as the maintenance costs of such machines including the interest cost on borrowed capital for acquiring the machine. Let us now examine the main determining factors of these fixed investments.

From the above discussion, it will be clear that estimation of the expected profit (or prospective yield) of the machine over its life period and the marginal efficiency of capital (or, its internal rate of return) is the most important part of the entrepreneur's decision on business fixed investment. Using the standard formula for discounting, the entrepreneur can arrive at the net present value (NPV) and then compare it with the total cost of the machine (or any such fixed capital). A typical example has been given in chapter 5, section 5.7. (Readers are advised to consult this section for further discussion on this topic as also chapter 14 on theories of investment.)

Inventory investment: Inventory investment refers to the expenditures by the firms on maintaining the stock of raw materials, semi-finished (or, goods in process) as well as finished products. The main purpose for such investment expenditures is to ensure smooth production and sale of the firms' products. This is because the businesses very often face short-run fluctuations in demand for their products. There are periods when the market demand for the products is fairly high during which the firms need to maintain adequate inventory of finished goods. Also, sufficient quantities of raw materials and intermediate goods have to be procured for ensuring timely delivery of orders. On the other hand, during periods of slack demand, as often happens during recession or slowdown, the firms require to maintain lower inventory. Thus, it can be said that the inventory investment bears a certain fixed relationship with the total output of the firm. It may be 20%, 25% or 30% of the total output depending on the firm's perception about the market size and its capacity to maintain the inventory since the inventory has a cost which needs to be balanced with its returns. In fact, there exists a theory of optimum inventory accumulation—the level that minimises the cost of maintaining a certain amount of inventory.

For smoothening their output, firms need to concentrate on a steady rate of production of their goods. For example, car makers might aim at producing ten cars per month. Now, when the market demand is fifteen cars per month on average, they will be able to meet the demand by drawing down their stock or inventory of cars (since, they will be producing fewer cars than they are able to sell). Thus, there will be negative investment on inventory. On the other hand, when the market demand for cars is slack (say, five cars per month) there will be an accumulation of inventory investment—more cars in the waiting. Thus, without inventory investment of proper size, the production process cannot be smooth.

Another reason for investment on inventory is the relatively cheap purchases of raw materials when they are purchased in bulk. This way, the firms are relieved of frequent small quantities purchases from the markets. Of course, this means that the firms are required to maintain sufficient warehouses also.

Inventory investment is also important from the point of view of reaping the best opportunity of the market in terms of prices and profits of the products.

Just as there is a general theory of investment as we have explained in the beginning of this chapter, there is also a specific theory of inventory investment which, in essence, is no different from the general one. Readers are, therefore, advised to follow the same theory (the acceleration theory) to explain the formation and size of inventory investment.

SUMMARY

1. Among the principal determinants of aggregate demand, namely, private consumption, private investment and export demands, the investment demand plays a crucial part since it is the most volatile element of all. Fluctuations in investment demand are primarily responsible for most business cycles.
2. Business investment behaviour depends on several factors. Hence, there are several theories explaining its behaviour. Keynes' theory which we discussed in chapter 4 that came out in 1936 in his *General Theory of Employment, Interest and Money*, focused on one of the key elements, viz., the marginal efficiency of capital relative to the interest cost being the determinant of private investment.
3. The accelerator theory of investment that followed examined mainly the relationship between net investment and aggregate income/output through the capital output ratio, also known as accelerator. This theory particularly emphasises upon the lags of various kinds that stand in the way of immediate response of the capital stocks to output. Rather, the actual stock depends on several time lags. Specifically, the actual capital stock is a certain fraction of the difference between the capital stocks of two or more time periods. In case the response is in the same period, the accelerator model is known as a simple or rigid accelerator model. But in case the response is spread over several past periods with weights being highest in the immediate past and lowest in the remote past, it is known as the flexible accelerator model.

4. The neoclassical investment theory stresses upon the negative functional relationship between the real rate of interest and the investment demand which is derivable on the strict neoclassical principle of maximisation of profits or net incomes of individual firms. In fact, there are two versions of the theory—the early neoclassical theory and later neoclassical theory. The early neoclassical theory suffered from two defects. It recognised the concept of capital as a homogeneous factor of production. Secondly, the theory was static in nature applicable to a certain point in time. But the early version was concerned with the aggregate investment behaviour for the economy as a whole.
5. The later version, pioneered by D.W. Jorgenson emphasised upon the present value maximisation of the net revenues over the indefinite future periods of a competitive firm. Applying the standard neoclassical principles of maximisation on the assumption of a Cobb-Douglas production function, Jorgenson derives the factor demand functions of labour and capital and specially focuses upon the cost of capital. Jorgenson's main concern, in this regard, is the owned fixed capital units to which 'user cost of capital' applies. Based upon this formulation, Jorgenson derives the capital demand function and finds that the net investment is a falling function of the rate of interest while it is a rising function of the output.
6. Tobin's Q theory of investment is essentially a financial theory of investment. Tobin believed that business investment decisions are reflected in the functions of stock markets. Tobin defines Q as a ratio of the market value of the firm divided by the replacement cost of the firm. The higher value of this ratio, particularly in the case of higher than one suggests higher investment in the market while lower value (the ratio being less than one) suggests that the market is undervalued so less investment in the market. This applies as much to the whole market as to the individual firms or companies.

EXERCISE

1. Identify the main factors responsible for the investment expenditures of a given firm.
2. What do you understand by the flexible accelerator model? How does it differ from a static accelerator model? Give a suitable example.
3. Explain the various 'lags' involved in the process of investment of a certain firm.
4. Examine Goodwin's investment model as a suitable flexible accelerator model of investment.

5. Do you think D.W. Jorgenson's neoclassical model of investment behaviour is an improvement over other models? Give reasons.
6. What is 'user cost' of capital? Discuss the different components of 'user cost of capital'.
7. Define Tobin's *Q*. How is it important in influencing the investment behaviour of the firm?

REFERENCES

1. L.R. Klein (1969): *An Introduction to Econometrics*, Prentice Hall, India.
2. D.W. Jorgenson (1967): *Capital Theory and Investment Behaviour*, nber.org (pdf).
3. Jeffrey Parker (2010): *Theories of Investment Expenditures*, www.reed.edu
4. Daniel Giradi (2017): "Old and New Formulations of the Neoclassical Theory of Aggregate Investment, A Critical Review", Working Paper, Department of Economics, University of Massachusetts, Amherst, USA., scholarworks.umass.edu
5. www.investopedia.com: *Q*-Ratio - Tobin's *Q*, by Adam Hayes.
6. www.wikipedia.com: Tobin's *Q*.

PART-7

Economic Growth and Business Cycles

15

Theories of Growth and Development: Macroeconomic Equilibrium in the Long Run

15.1 ECONOMIC GROWTH AND ECONOMIC DEVELOPMENT

When we talk about economic growth, we usually refer to the growth of certain economy over a long period of time, as suggested by yardsticks like Gross Domestic Product (GDP) or Gross National Product (GNP)/Gross National Income (GNI). However, since GDP or GNP does not necessarily reflect the living standard of the population of a country, economists often prefer another yardstick, Per Capita GNP/GDP/GNI, since this is obtained by dividing the total GNP/GNI by the size of the population of the country concerned. This, in a sense, gives an idea of average living condition or the level of living or well-being of the average population.

Sometimes, rate of industrialization is associated with economic growth. In fact, there are instances in history of certain countries' pace of industrialization being responsible for their economic growth.

The concept of economic development is, however, a broader concept which considers, besides GDP/GNP/GNI/PCI, the overall development of the economy in terms of changes in institutional set-up, changes in people's attitude towards development, better distributional effects on population, improvement in quality of labour force, etc. In other words, economic development implies growth and expansion in the overall productive capacity of the economy. Changes in the structure of the economy take place when its structure of production, compositional share of different components of GDP, etc., undergo significant changes. For instance, if a predominantly subsistence economy (agriculture and other primary sector) gradually transforms into predominantly manufacturing and services dominated economy so that the share of manufactured and services products rises while that of primary products declines. Similarly, the quality of labour force also changes with economic development taking place. Unskilled labour becomes semi-skilled and fully skilled ones. Education and training for labourers become important for them since demand for such labourer rises rapidly. With this, female labourers/workers participate in a greater percentage in the outside jobs.

Institutional set-up, too, must change with economic development. Banking and financial institutions, for instance, play a greater role in credit advancement, old institutions and practices like tenancy system or other feudal and semi-feudal institutions in agriculture give way to new and better system. Many other institutions and practices must eventually undergo change. People's attitude, in general towards development also gradually changes with economic development. Most people become inclined towards development; in fact, the process of economic development induces this positive attitude of the masses rather than attitudinal changes taking place by themselves.

Economic development is a process which results in better distribution of the fruits of development. Only then, economic development turns into overall social development. Not necessarily, however, that economic growth will be able to distribute its benefits to all sections of population. It is possible that growth may result in greater concentration of wealth and income in relatively few hands in which case development will be far from being desirable and equitable.

We can summarise the above discussion by stating that economic growth and economic development are strictly not the same – the latter being much broader a concept, although very often we get confused and use the terms interchangeably. But one thing is perhaps, obvious: economic development is possible only with economic growth by whatever method it takes place.

In more recent periods, particularly during the last two decades or so, the concept of economic development has been expanded and broadened to take yet another dimension, viz., human development. To capture the impact of economic development on overall quality of life primarily in terms of health improvements and educational attainments, the United Nations Development Programme (UNDP) is engaged in preparing human development index and ranking different countries of the world on achievements on human developments. The UNDP has since been refining and including other indicators which are considered appropriate for human development. The studies of UNDP have revealed that there are many countries whose performance on human development are far from being satisfactory although on economic development as such they have ranked better.

15.2 ECONOMIC GROWTH AND ITS MEASUREMENT

Economic growth is generally measured by calculating annual or decadel growth rates of GDP/GNP/PCI etc. In order to free these measures from mere price-level changes, growth rates are measured in terms of real GDP/real GNP/real PCI etc. which are based on some base year constant price-level (see Chapter One on National Income Analysis).

During a decade or so, measuring annual growth rates are likely to change from year to year due to changes in base-year values. An average annual growth rate is sometimes, obtained to represent the average growth rate of the decade as a whole. But since this measure is also not free from defects, the most preferred measure is the compound annual growth rate (CAGR). Using a relatively longer period of time, this method uses a "trend regression" method and estimates "trend" growth rate. It ignores minor year-to-year variations but reveals the trend rate at which GDP/GNP etc. are changing.

In recent years, economists and policy makers are interested in figuring out 'quarterly' growth rates of GDP and other related variables with a view to monitoring the economy more closely. Also, GDP growth is decomposed into sectoral GDP growth rates such as agricultural GDP, manufacturing GDP (factory output and non-factory output) services GDP) etc. to isolate the principal sources of growth from overall GDP. However, annual growth rate still occupies the central place in thses exercises from short period point of view.

15.3 KEY FACTORS OF ECONOMIC GROWTH

Economic Growth is primarily influenced by the following contributory factors which may also be called the key sources of economic growth.

1. Endowment of natural resources
2. Accumulation of capital
3. Availability of human resources
4. Advancement in productive technology

We explain below the relative importance of each one of these with suitable illustrations from historical records.

15.3.1 Endowment of Natural Resources

Economies sufficiently endowed with natural resources and able to exploit them profitably have become primary beneficiaries of these resources. A number of industries based on these resources could have been set up in these economies which, in turn, proved to be important sources of economic growth. Those producing surplus have been able to export them to other countries and earn substantial income from external sources and thereby help their growth process. Abundance of crude oil and other petroleum products in Middle East countries has been instrumental in bringing about economic growth in this region of the world. Rich mineral deposits in Australia, earstwhile USSR, China and India have helped their respective economies to set up industries based on such minerals. France and USA have big deposits of uranium and nuclear fuels besides possessing other natural resources. In India, availability of coal and iron ore and gypsum quite in abundance has helped set up large and medium sized iron and steel plants and other core-sector industries which are producing a variety of products for domestic use as also for exports. In USA, Canada and Australia, large tracts of agricultural land have made them surplus producers of agricultural products. For many years now, these countries, besides meeting their domestic needs, partially feed the rest of the world through exports and concessional grants to poor countries.

However, endowment of natural resources is a necessary factor but not a sufficient cause of economic growth. Mere availability of natural resources will not be enough unless other co-operating factors like capital and technology are also combined to properly tap them if they remain unutilized or underutilized. The role of these co-operant factors is separately explained below. But it can be said and, in fact, established by evidence that even such richly endowed countries may remain only primary producing countries without experiencing much of economic growth.

15.3.2 Accumulation of Capital

Capital accumulation is, perhaps, the most important source of economic growth. In most of the developed countries of the world (U.K., U.S.A., Canada, Germany, France, Australia and other European countries) capital has been the dominant co-operant factor for bringing about a rapid rate of economic growth. More and more capital accumulation means larger availability of investible funds for industrialization, harnessing of existing natural resources and encouraging entrepreneurs to undertake innovations for development. Capital is chiefly responsible for industrialization process. Thus, rising share of industrial products in the GDP with their higher market value has raised the value of GDP and GNP of developed countries. Capital- rich countries can benefit also by exporting capital to other countries via different routes and thereley earn factor incomes from overseas investments.

This way, capital receiving countries can also accelerate their growth process as the recent history has thrown enough evidence in cases of some of the emerging countries like China, India, Brazil, South Africa, Indonesia, South Korea etc.

Capital consists of physical as well as financial capital. Finance capital and its availability is as important as the physical capital. Developed countries, by creating a systematic structure of finance capital has been able to help the process of industrialization in their own countries as also sending them to other countries for the latter's growth process provided adequate institutional mechanism is in place. Recent developments in the world economy, thanks to the globalization process, have amply revealed that investment flows through finance capital have played a big role in the development process of developing countries. Specifically, investments in the form of foreign direct investment (FDI) are contributing in a big way to the process of economic growth of these countries. Besides, the foreign institutional investment directly investing in the stock markets of the recipient countries are also bolstering the capital market of these countries in spite of some of the shortcomings and vulnerabilities of such finance capital. This way, both the capital rich as also the capital poor countries are benefiting themselves and economic growth is transmitted across the national boundaries. During the industrial revolution of Britain in the later half of eighteenth century and early nineteenth century, mobilization of private savings, credit through private-commercial banks and London money market helped a great deal towards the success of industrial revolution. Similarly, recent historical evidence of technological revolution in western capitalist countries including Asia's Japan points toward liberal availability of financial capital.

15.3.3 Economic Growth and Human Resources

Resources in the shape of skilled, trained and educated manpower are equally powerful agents of growth. Countries like Japan, Hongkong, Singapore, even with paucity of natural and capital resources, succeeded tremendously in terms of raising their GNPs through their highly skilled manpower resources. Through innovations, this section of manpower has been able to produce newer and newer goods and services which are able to compete in international markets. Different countries are, however, not equally efficient in producing different goods and services. While some are much better in certain products, others excel in other products. Thus, US has been able to produce a variety of high-tech products like computers, medical instruments, chemicals etc. partly with the help of high-skilled manpower resources and partly due to heavy investments in the production of these goods. Early scientific inventions of high standard mostly in western capitalist countries like U.K., USA and Canada and their successful commercial uses have indeed helped their respective economies to become high-tech high income economies.

More recently, emerging countries like India and China have practically thrown up challenges to the rest of the world in terms of the significant contributions of their skilled and educated manpower to the path of their economic transition. India is now judged as one of the fast growing countries where relatively high-skilled and educated manpower particularly in the services sector (like information technology and related services) is providing high contribution to the GNP growth. China, too, has been able to achieve its high growth rate (around 9-10 percent till recently) not only through manufacturing output of high standard (textiles, toys, watches etc.) but also mobile phones and other fine quality products at relatively low prices which are widely exported to developed as well as developing countries thus providing opportunities for earning foreign exchanges.

15.3.4 Advancement in Technology

Educated manpower and technological advancement are somehow inter-related in the sense that technological advancement is not generally possible without education. If production techniques are available, their acquision by the people can be possible through education and training. In fact, technological change is basically a function of technical knowledge and its application. This, is turn, is the function of scientific invention and engineering. A greater share of national output to research and development activities only can bring about such scientific results which can subsequently be put into practice for furthering economic growth. Greater and greater availability of goods and services would then be possible through such advancement of production technology. Thus, advancement in technology in all fields of production as well as distribution has been a prime mover of economic growth. Right from the period of industrial revolution in Great Britain till date, ample evidence can be easily gathered from the historical records of most of developed nations as also some of the recently developing nations.

Advancement in technology, in sum, brings about expansion of the country's production possibility curve (or, production possibility frontier – PPF) which shows the maximum possibilities of combinations of two or more goods/services that a given country can produce with its available technology or productive capacity. Figure 15.1 illustrates PPF for a country.

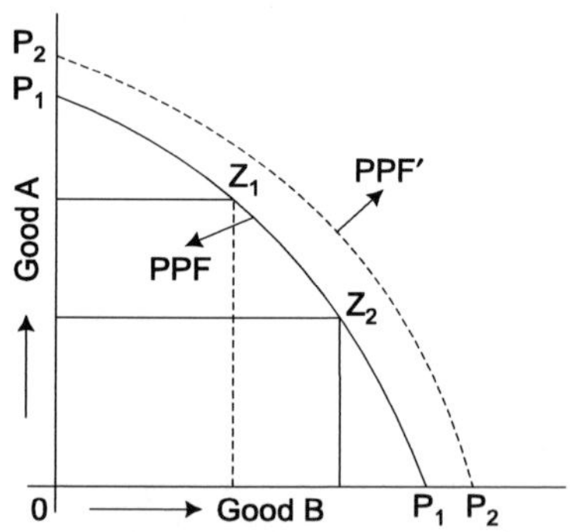

Figure 15.1 *The production possibility curve/production possibility frontier (PPF) of a country.*

Let us suppose a country is initially operating within the PPF bounded by points P_1P_1. The PPF thus shows the maximum possibilities of two goods, A and B with its given production technology. Z_1, Z_2, or any such combinations of the two goods are possible to be produced but not beyond this boundary. Now, when economic growth takes place, it brings about expansion of productive capacity as shown by the outward shift of the PPF- to PPF′. As a result, larger volumes of output of both the goods can be possible with technological advancement. Here, we have illustrated the role of technological progress and its application with the help of PPF in the limited two dimensional space. One may, however, imagine many dimensional space where expansion of output capacity of many goods is possible resulting in larger supplies of goods and services.

The above discussion on key sources of economic growth suggests that the sources mentioned above are, in a way, interdependent. Even though some countries are richly endowed with natural resources, their exploitation and use for industrial and commercial purposes requires the co-operation of other factors such as capital, technology, knowledge and entrepreneurship. Unless these are made available in proper proportion either from domestic sources or, from outside the domestic sources, growth of real GDP will not be possible. This is the reason why most primary producing countries (producers of basic raw materials, agricultural and related products, plantation crops like tea, cocoa, forest produce etc.) are still in the category of either underdeveloped or developing countries.

15.4 THEORIES AND MODELS OF GROWTH

Theories of growth can, broadly, be classified as (a) pessimistic theories and (b) optimistic theories. While Classical, Marxian, and 'Limits to Growth' models are essentially pessimistic, the Neo- classical and Harrod Domar models are essentially optimistic.

Economic growth has always been the subject of interest for economists right from the classical days. In fact, without understanding the process of growth, the significance of macroeconomics can not be properly understood. Classical economists, particularly Adam Smith and David Ricardo provided a long-run theory of growth of the capitalist economy. While Smith stressed upon some of the fundamental elements which induce the process of growth, such as capital accumulation, division of labour and specialization, he did not present the theory in an explicit manner. But eventually, according to Smith, due to certain limitations imposed by the extent of the market, law of diminishing returns to agriculture, falling wage-rate for labour to the level of subsistence and population growth drive the economy to a "stationary state" where growth would stop. As against Smith's non-systematic theory, David Ricardo advanced a more explicit and systematic theory. According to Ricardo, the capitalist economy advances on the path of growth through changing relative shares of major factors of production such as rent, wages and profit; the initial motive force of growth is, however, the same as in Smith, ie., capital accumulation. But Ricardo explained that as this process goes on, eventually the law of diminishing returns would operate and total output would increase by less than proportion to factor inputs, because factors like land would be available in limited supply. But, the share of rent in total output would gradually rise and landlords would gain in the process. On the other hand, wage rate of labourers would be driven down even though initially it may increase above subsistence level. The most important impact would be felt on the share of profit which would be falling due to larger and larger accumulation of capital (and hence leading to fall on the rate of profit) on the one hand, and decreasing rate of total volume of output on the other. Along with this, the theory of population growth as profounded by T.R. Malthus, poses another limitation which predicts that population growth by geometric progression but food grains production by arithmetic progression ultimately imposes a population pressure thus making the process of growth more and more difficult to feed the growing population. The entire process- the declining profit, dampening entrepreneurial propensity to plough back larger shares of profit in further output, rising rent and falling wages would lead the economy to stationary state with zero profit, subsistence wages and highest rent. The classical economists thus presented a pessimistic theory of growth.

It is clear from the classical theory that the fundamental feature of economic growth is capital accumulation although it is an oversimplified theory and presents a pessimistic outlook of long-run growth of the economy. In fact, both Ricardo's historical diminishing returns and Malthus' population growth principle seriously underestimated the possibility of technological progress countering the tendency towards diminishing returns.[1]

Karl Marx, a great visionary of the nineteenth century, analysed deeply the development of the capitalist economy and predicted that the capitalism is inherently unstable and suffers from a number of contradictions. These contradictions would ultimately lead to the downfall of the system. Like the classical economists, Marx too relied on the labour theory of value arguing that labour is the only source of value in all commodities. It is able to produce surplus over its own subsistence. This surplus is appropriated by the capitalists which they transform into capital for reinvestment. Capital accumulation goes on and so does the profit of the capitalists. But as the process of capital accumulation continues, the rate of profit begins to fall due to the competition among capitalists. With a view to retain their position they resort to mechanization thus replacing capital for labour. This leads to still more exploitation of labour- extracting more and more surplus value from them. The rate of profit, however, ultimately, falls and capitalism meets with crisis. Marx developed his theory with the help of a

[1] G.M. Meire and R.E. Baldwin, Economic Development: Theory, History, Policy, Asia Publishing House, Bombay, 1964, p. 46.

number of accompanying theories such as (a) theory of surplus value, (b) theory of exploitation, (c) theory of under-consumption and (d) theory of crisis.

In the classical scheme, particularly in Ricardo's, improvements in technology are not sufficiently powerful to prevent the ultimate arrival of the stationary state. They only delay, temporarily, its arrival. As against this, in the Marxian scheme, technological improvements in the capitalist system takes place at a rapid rate which ultimately leads the capitalist class to its eventually doom.[1]

Thus, once technological progress is introduced, instead of accumulating by duplicating old productive methods, capitalists now are able to expand their surplus value even more by labour-saving inventions which raise the productivity of a give amount of labour time. Theory of exploitation along with technological improvements leads ultimately to the fall in the price of the product which, in turn, leads to the rate of profit to decline.[2]

Marx clearly foresees the capitalists' attempt to venture into the financial capital by speculative means to have an access to such capital in the event of continuously falling rate of profit. This rush for speculative ventures precipitates the crisis in capitalist system that arises earlier with falling rate of profit. It paralyses the function of money as a medium of exchange. The chain of payments due at a certain time is broken in a hundred places and the disaster is intensified by the collapse of the credit system".[3]

Interestingly, one can find resemblance of this type of crisis in the capitalist economies of the west, as it developed in 2008 financial crisis leading to the Great Recession which continued for more than four years now. In fact, during that time, economists and other academics including those in charge of policy making, were invoking the teachings of great masters like Marx and Keynes.

When the rate of profit continues to fall as described above, the capitalists commit further errors such as wrongly estimating their market so that there is general over production and under consumption of goods. This aggravates the crisis.

Marx contents that the consuming power of the capitalist class is restricted by the tendency to accumulate, the greed for an expansion of capital and a production of surplus value on an enlarged scale. This is a law of capitalist production imposed by incessant revolutions in the methods of production themselves, the resulting depreciation of existing capital, the general competitive struggle and the necessity of improving the product and expanding scale of production, for the sake of self preservation and on penalty of failures.[4] Thus the consumption power of the workers is limited by their poverty, whereas that of

[1] G.M. Meier and R.E. Baldwin, op. cit. p. 54.

[2] G.M. Meier and R.E. Baldwin, op. cit. p. 57.

[3] K. Marx, Capital Volume III, p. 298, quoted in Meier and Baldwin, op. cit, p. 59

[4] Marx, op. cit. p. 286-287, quoted, Meier and Baldwin, op. cit. p. 60

the capitalists is limited by their greed for accumulation. The resultant inability of consumption goods industries to absorb the output of capital goods causes a persistent tendency for general overproduction which manifests itself in periodic crises and economic stagnation.

15.5 HARROD-DOMAR MODEL OF GROWTH

One of the celebrated growth models that came up in the post Keynesian period is by the two economists-Evesy Domar from U.S.A. and Roy Harrod from U.K. Both of them employed Keynesian tools and analyzed the problem of maintaining a steady growth in the long run after the economy having achieved the full employed equilibrium. Essentially, the problem of steady growth is the problem for the developed economies since it is believed that only advanced developed economies would have achieved a stage of full employment equilibrium while most of the underdeveloped economies are believed to be in the phase of transition and moving towards the goal of full employment.

Both Harrod and Domar would pose the problem of steady growth as follows:

In the process of economic growth, investment plays a crucial role. But, investment has twin role to play. On the one hand, it increases income in the economy several times via its multiplier effect as Keynesian theory adequately explains. However, at the same time, investment expands the productive capacity of the economy thereby capacity to produce more and more goods and services requiring additional purchasing power (income) to be created. This suggests that if both sides of this process of investment expenditure are to be matched, both sides must actually be equal.

Even though Harrod and Domar approach the problem somewhat differently, essentially, they reach the same conclusion and, in fact, Domar's result can be arrived via Harrod's result or vice versa.

Let us first begin with Domar's approach. Let us suppose a newly created capital, e.g., a machine, of ₹40,000, raises the capacity to produce output worth ₹10000 annually; so that we can say, annual output to capital ratio is 10,000/40,000 or, . Using symbols, the same can be stated as: $\sigma = \Delta Y/\Delta K$, where, ΔK is the amount of newly created capital and ΔY is the resultant increase in real income (or, output). In other words, σ stands for the ratio of increase in income to increase in capital or, output-capital ratio (inverse of capital-output ratio). Since ΔK is the net increase in capital stock (gross investment minus depreciation), and is equivalent to net investment, In, we can rewrite:

$$\sigma = \Delta Y/\Delta K = \Delta Y/In;$$

$$\Rightarrow \quad \Delta Y = In\,\sigma \quad (15.1)$$

From Keynesian multiplier analysis, we know that multiplier is the ratio of increase in income to increase in investment, i.e., $\Delta Y/\Delta I$ (due to certain increase in investment, income increases by a certain multiple, say, k times), so that the relationship can be expressed as:

$$\Delta Y = k\Delta I \tag{15.2}$$

where, k is multiplier and is equivalent to 1/mps, where, mps is marginal propensity to save ($\propto$). Relations (15.1) and (15.2) can now be combined and expressed as:

$$k\Delta I = In\ \sigma$$

$$\Rightarrow \quad 1/\text{mps}\ \Delta I = In\ \sigma$$

$$\Rightarrow \quad \Delta I/In = \sigma\propto \tag{15.3}$$

Equation (15.3) reveals that $\Delta I/In$ is the rate of increase in investment per period (annually, for example) $\propto$ is the mps and σ is the inverse of capital output ratio (in the incremental sense) or, accelerator coefficient. Equation (15.3) states that in order to maintain full employment output in the long run, annual percentage rate of increase in investment should be equal to the multiple of the mps times the inverse of capital output ratio.

Domar himself provides a numerical example. Let σ be 25% per year; let $\propto$ be 12% per year and let Y initially be \$150 billion. If full employment is then to be maintained, investment must equal 150 12% = \$18 billion; that is, investment must offset the amount of full employment savings. But this investment will raise productive capacity by the amount invested (\$18 billion) times σ that is, by 150 12% 25% or, \$4.5 billion. If unused productive capacity is not to result, national income will have to rise by \$4.5 billion. However, relative rise in income will be equal to the absolute increase divided by the income itself that is,

$$(150 \times 12/100 \times 25/100)/150 = 12/100 \times 25/100$$

$$= \propto\sigma = 3\%$$

Thus, income must grow at a rate of 3% per annum if full employment is to be maintained and there is not to be excess of capital goods.

Harrod's analysis follows almost the similar reasoning. Harrod starts with the basic equilibrium condition of the economy in terms of savings and investment as expressed in the equation:

$$GC = s \tag{15.4}$$

where, G stand for the rate of growth of income (or, output), C stands for capital requirement, i.e., additions to capital per unit of output (or, ratio of investment to increase in income) and s is the saving income ratio. Here, G, C, and s are all "actual" or, "realized" magnitudes, i.e., actual rate of growth of income, actual investment to income ratio and actual savings income ratio, respectively, that an economy experiences at a certain period of time. Equation (15.4) represents the basic equilibrium condition of the economy in terms of savings investment equality. This can be easily verified by rewriting eqn. (15.4) as follows:

$$\Delta Y/Y \quad I/\Delta Y = S/Y$$

$$\Rightarrow \qquad I/Y = S/Y$$

$$\Rightarrow \qquad I = S \tag{15.5}$$

Since G is $\Delta Y/Y$ = rate of growth of income, $C = I/\Delta Y$ = ratio of investment to increase in income and $s = S/Y$ = saving income ratio, Harrod's second fundamental equation is presented as:

$$Gw\ Cr = s \tag{15.6}$$

where, Gw is defined as the warranted rate of growth; Cr is defined as capital requirement or, capital output ratio – C/O, and s is the required saving income ratio. Equation (15.6) states that if the economy wishes to maintain its full employment equilibrium in the long run and ensure full utilization of its growing stock of capital, without any fluctuation like inflation or unemployment, its income must be growing at a certain required rate or warranted rate, Gw, while Cr is capital required to sustain this growth rate. It will be pertinent here to state the basic assumptions of both models of Harrod and Domar:

1. The saving income ratio (S/Y) remains constant and is equal to marginal propensity to save ($\Delta S/\Delta Y$) which also remains constant in the long run.
2. The capital output ratio (C/O) remains constant.
3. There will be no government intervention in any form and the economy, by and large, will operate on laissez-faire principle.

Returning to eqn. (15.6), it can be said that, given Cr, the capital output ratio, s, the savings rate becomes the crucial variable in the model, since savings rate provides the required capital for investment purposes.

Now what happens if the actual growth rate, G, deviates from the warranted growth rate, Gw? If, during any particular period of time, an economy is growing at a rate higher than the warranted rate, so that $G > Gw$, the higher and higher growth of aggregate demand creates more and more productive capacity. This means that capital requirement for this increased productive capacity is more than C – the actual growth, i.e., $Cr > C$. This implies that the existing capital stock is not sufficient to either produce or maintain the existing level of output, G. In the short run, this situation leads to inflationary condition which will be felt more in the capital goods sector. According to Harrod's model, such discrepancy ($G > Gw$) gradually widens and the economy advances more and more away from the steady growth path.

In the opposite case, when $G < Gw$, the actual growth rate of the economy is lower than the warranted rate. In this case, $C > Cr$, that is the actual capital is greater than the required capital. In other words, there is excess supply of capital goods. The entrepreneurs, therefore, are not interested in undertaking further net investment. Excess capacity develops and output growth slackens. Economy will experience a downward trend and possibly a situation of unemployment and recession will be in sight. In the Keynesian sense, aggregate demand will be less than the aggregate supply. This trend will further aggregate and will push G further downward thus reducing aggregate demand. Just as in the case of $G > Gw$, leading the economy farther and farther away from Gw in the upward direction, in the case of $G < Gw$ also, the movement becomes cumulative by pushing the economy away from the steady path downward.

15.5.1 Upper and Lower Limits of Growth-Gn-the Natural Growth Rate

Even though the growth path, once deviated, departs farther and farther away suggested by Gw, there is an upper limit beyond which it cannot go. This upper limit is set by what Harrod calls 'the natural rate of growth'. This is defined as maximum growth rate permissible by the economy's natural resources, population and other factors. The available natural resources and their productive capacity are the real limitations on the growth of the economy. Similarly, population growth puts a ceiling on the growth of the economy. These are, therefore, the sources of potential growth of the economy. Harrod symbolizes the natural growth rate as Gn. Thus, actural rate of growth may be either greater or less than the warranted rate of growth, but it cannot exceed natural rate of growth. Hence,

$$Gn > Gw > G \tag{15.7}$$

The natural rate of growth, Gn, is also called the 'full employment ceiling' on growth where, all labour and capital are fully employed (potential growth rate).

Just as there is an upper limit to the growth, there is also a lower limit of the growth process which is given by the "autonomous" investment of the economy. Since autonomous investments are independent of the growth rate of the economy, they provide the "floor" of the economic growth. Similarly, there is always a level of actual consumption being greater than zero and correspondingly a certain level of income which it supports. This point may be called the 'break even point' of the consumption function below which consumption expenditure is always greater than income. Another factor that explains the floor level of growth path is that the gross investment (net investment + replacement investment) is seldom negative. This means there will always be some replacement investment due to depreciation of fixed capital which will be greater than the net investment in the event of the latter becoming negative (or, disinvestment). These three factors together provide the minimum or floor of the downward direction of the growth process.

An Evaluation In spite of the elegance of the Harrod-Domar model in presenting conditions for steady growth in the long run, it suffers from certain shortcomings which are discussed below.

1. The underlying assumption of the model is the "fixed proportions" production function. The implication is that production process follows the fixed proportions in which capital and labour are combined. The possibility of substitution of labour for capital or capital for labour is ruled out. This follows directly from the assumption of constant capital-output ratio. This is a rigid assumption. The entire production process is restricted in such a manner that only a single process of capital labour ratio is allowed. However, if the more flexible neo-classical type of production function is allowed so that substitution between factors of production is relaxed as is possible through technological changes, the steady growth path of the economy (warranted growth) can be more easily followed. Perhaps it is for this reason alleged that Harrod's growth model suggests a "knife edged" path on which walking is very difficult and unstable. But the above mentioned relaxation of the fixed proportions of the production function will, possibly, free the model from this defect.
2. Secondly, Harrod-Domar model fails to consider the favourable effects that flexibility in the price system may bring about in restricting the run away movement of the actual rate of growth deviating from the warranted rate. Supposing thet $G > Gw$ (in Harrod's case) economy is departing farther and farther away from the steady growth path, the actual requirements of new investment will be greater but if price rises are, at the same time, allowed to a certain extent, a given level of actual expenditure will be inflated to give higher monetary (nominal) expenditures which will produce lower level of real outputs. This means less real net investment will be required. Thus the requirement of steady growth will be less. For example, given the rise in price level, a 10% increase in expenditure may result in less than 10% (say 8%) rise in output. In other words, real output growth will be less; hence capital requirement for this output growth will also be less.
3. Economists have, in fact, analysed these effects and modified the Harrod-Domar model accordingly.

15.6 NEO-CLASSICAL MODEL OF GROWTH

Neo-classical economists departed from classical economists in terms of their outlook from being pessimistic to being optimistic. As far as growth theory is concerned, their views were sufficiently aided and supported by technological progress that took place around their time in the field of scientific inventions in different aspects of social life. A new and modified approach to economic growth and development was, therefore, presented by a number of neo-classical economists, notable among them being Marshall, Meade, Solow, Swan, Mrs Joan Robinson, Clark and others.

The neo-classical approach was based upon the following premises:

1. Growth is a smooth, continuous and harmonious process.
2. Capital accumulation occupies the central place as in the classical case but here, capital is allowed to be substituted by labour and hence even without the corresponding growth in labour force, capital stock can be increased which, in turn, increases output and income.
3. Technological progress brings about shifts in production function upward- thus making it possible for larger and larger productivity of factors of production.
4. Population growth may act as a constraint to the process of capital accumulation; but it can be taken care of by higher productivity brought about by technological progress.

15.7 TECHNOLOGY OF PRODUCTION

Most neo-classical models would stress that technology of production as suggested by aggregate production function would provide the link between output supply and factor supplies- supplies of land, labour, capital and technology. Of these, technology during a certain period of time is given by the state of knowledge of the society. In fact, changes in this body of knowledge do come but they often come in waves and not continuously. For this, we can take technology as given, at least for the time being. Then the output supply behaviour can be captured by the production function as shown in eqn. (15.8)

$$Q = f(K, L, T) \tag{15.8}$$

where, Q is total output, K is capital input, L is labour input and T is technology which, for reasons explained above, is constant at $T = \overline{T}$ and taken out of the function. Equation (15.8) can, therefore, be rewritten as:

$$Q = f(K, L) \tag{15.9}$$

This function is further assumed to obey the law of constant returns to scale. This means that if the factor inputs K and L are increased by some constant proportion, output, Q, will also increase by the same constant proportion.

In mathematical terms, the function is linear and homogeneous or homogeneous of degree one. We illustrate this case as follows:

Let K and L increase by λ times (or, 100%) then the function will also increase by λ times (or, 100%), so that we can write

$$\lambda Q = f(\lambda K, \lambda L) \tag{15.10}$$

In other words, if this happens then only the function (15.9) can be called linear homogeneous one, or, obeying the law of constant returns to scale.

One such empirical production function has become highly popular in the literature, known as Cobb- Douglas production function which has been specified and empiricially estimated in the context of American economy with a purpose of assessing the labour's share in total output. The Cobb- Douglas production function possesses all the characteristic features of neo-classical production function, viz, obeying the law of constant returns to scale (a long run characteristic) with the law of variable proportions with individual factor inputs- labour and capital (a short-run characteristics) as also the coefficients of factors representing their relative shares in total output.

A typical Cobb- Douglas production function is specified as:

$$Q = AK^{\beta} L^{\alpha} \tag{15.11}$$

where, Q is physical output (or, output in physical terms), K and L are, respectively, capital and labour inputs, A is intercept term capturing the contribution of non-included variables and β and α, are, respectively, the coefficients (or, elasticities) of capital and labour inputs. The values of these coefficients are constrained to less than unity but each is positive ($1 > \beta, \alpha > 0$). However, their values taken together can not exceed unity; in fact, in this case, their sum is exactly equal to unity ($\beta + \alpha = 1$). This is a special constraint aimed at allowing the constant returns to scale to hold. The neo-classical economists have, by and large, adopted this form of production function as sufficiently explaining the real world production behaviour.

Now, with these basic characteristics of Cobb-Douglas production function, a modified version of production function can be specified in terms of output per labour unit (or, average productivity of labour) thus:

$$Q/L = f' \, (K/L)^{\beta} \, (L/L)^{\alpha} \tag{15.12}$$

$$= f' \, [(K/L)^{\beta} \times 1] \tag{15.13}$$

(This is the same as multiplying the function given by (15.11) by $1/L$ times, because the function obeys the law of constant returns to scale and so, doing this exercise does not affect the total output).

Now, in eqn. (15.13) we can ignore the constant number 1 and rewrite it as:

$$Q/L = f' \, (K/L)^{\beta}$$

or, using small letter, for Q/L and K/L we can write:

$$q = f' \, (k)^{\beta} \tag{15.14}$$

Equation (15.14) expresses output per unit of labour (or, average productivity of labour), as a function of capital per unit of labour (or, capital-labour ratio). Since the value of β lies between zero and unity ($1 > \beta > 0$), this further means that as capital labour ratio increases, output per labour unit increases by less than proportionately – thus obeying the law of variable proportions in the short run. A typical production function in terms of total output curve is drawn in Fig. 15.2.

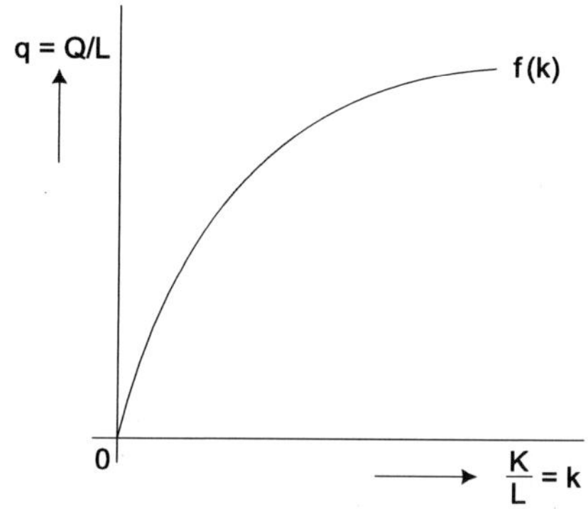

Figure 15.2 *Cobb-Douglas production function with per capita capital labour ratio.*

15.8 CONSUMPTION, SAVING AND INVESTMENT

In the next part, we examine how the total output, q, is allocated between consumption and saving. If we assume that the propensity to consume is 75%, i.e., 75% of total output is devoted to consumption then the remaining 25% of total output (which is equivalent to total real income), is saved by the community. Since output or income per labour is now a function of capital-labour ratio, k (= K/L), we can derive the savings function also being a function of the capital-labour ratio, k, so that we can write.

$$s = s(k) \tag{15.15}$$

Assuming now that all savings are converted into investment, we can further write:

$$s = i = i(k) \tag{15.16}$$

where, i is investment.

(We have seen earlier that investment means net addition to capital stock, i.e., $i = \Delta k$, so that eqn. (15.16) can be rewritten as:

$$s = f(\Delta k) \tag{15.17}$$

In other words, savings is a function of increase in capital-labour ratio. The savings function, along with production function is shown in Fig. 15.3.

Figure 15.3 illustrates that at a certain level of capital stock per unit of labour at a certain point of time, the economy produces a certain level of output which is then divided between consumption and saving or consumption and investment.

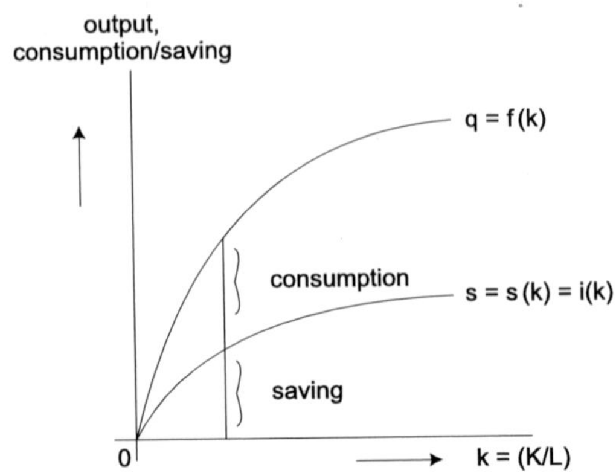

Figure 15.3 *Behaviour of output, consumption and saving.*

The figure also shows that as the capital stock per labour is growing, investment per labour is also growing but, following the behaviour of production function it is growing gradually slower and slower.

15.9 THE CONCEPT OF STEADY STATE

The steady state is defined as a state of the economy when the capital stock per labour unit is just equal to its rate of depreciation. The rate of depreciation is the rate at which the capital stock wears out per period of time. For example, if the annual rate of depreciation of the capital stock is 2% (straight-line fashion) and if the capital stock per labour at a given point of time is 5 units, then we will say that capital stock at that point of time grows, net of depreciation, at 3 units (5-2). However, overtime, capital stock is growing at a slower rate as Fig. 15.3 reveals. Now, for an economy, it is possible that it starts with higher capital stock per labour than the depreciation rate, or, to say the same thing, net capital stock is positive. In this case, the economy would grow with higher output and capital stock growing overtime. Thus, so long as the actual capital stock is growing and is greater than its annual depreciation rate, we may say that the economy is approaching towards the steady state. Eventually, since the capital per labour unit grows slowly overtime, a stage will be reached when the actual capital stock would grow at the same rate as the rate of depreciation. In other words, the new capital stock will just replace the old worn-out ones.

At this stage, there will be no further incentive for capital stock to grow and the economy would have a tendency to remain "steady" at this situation. This is the steady state condition. On the other hand, if the economy starts operating at a stage where annual depreciation rate is higher than the capital stock growth, the economy has a tendency to slip back to steady state condition. Such a steady state is illustrated in Fig. 15.4. In the figure, *S* represents the steady state growth of capital stock. At point *T*, the economy is approaching towards the point *S* and the capital stock is continuously growing. But, at point *V*, since new capital stock is not even able to replace the depreciated ones, the economy will eventually fall back and come to stay at the steady state.

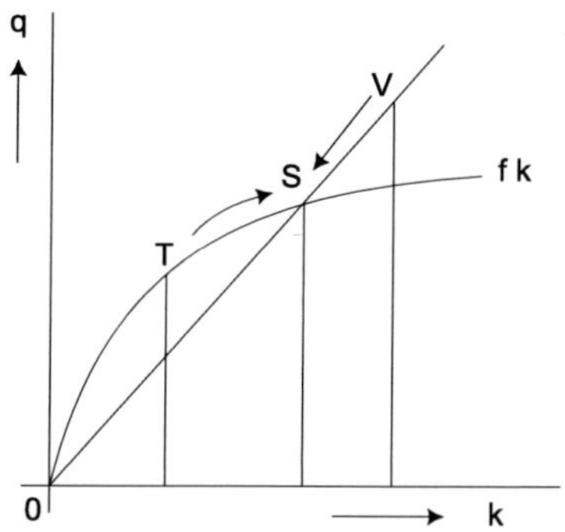

Figure 15.4 *The steady state.*

15.10 POPULATION GROWTH AND THE STEADY STATE

Thus far we have assumed that there is zero growth of population (or, population is constant). Now, we introduce population growth and examine the position of steady state. For all practical purposes, population can be assumed to be growing "continuously" at a certain compound rate. Let this rate be denoted by *n*. Thus, *n* is the annual compound rate of growth of population. This obviously provides increased labour force (workers) to work with the old ones, so that now the capital per unit of labour becomes lower. In other words, capital accumulation process is now dampened. It is not only reduced by the rate of 'depreciation' of the capital assets but also by the population growth rate of *n* percent. For instance, if the existing rate of investment (addition to capital per labour) is 5% per annum, depreciation rate is 1.5% and population growth rate is 2%, the effective rate of investment is only 1.5% (5% – 3.5% = 1.5%). This is because, part of the investment is meant for 'wear and tear' of old capital stock and part of it is meant for providing the new workers with required capital.

As far as the attainment of steady state growth of capital is concerned it can be stated now that so long as rate of effective investment continues to remain positive and does not become equal to zero (so that the rate of investment is just equal to the sum of the depreciation and population growth rates) capital accumulation will continue. It will reach the steady state at the new but lower than earlier steady state. This is illustrated in Fig. 15.5.

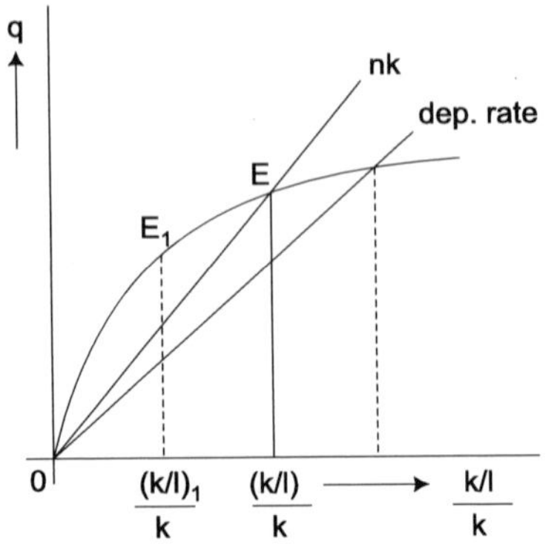

Figure 15.5 *Population growth and the steady state.*

The straight line *nk* shows that there is minimum rate of investment necessary for taking care of both the depreciation of existing capital as also making provision for new workers with extra capital. Now, so long as the actual investment rate is above this 'minimum', capital stock will continue to grow as shown at point E_1 (or, on any point between *O* and *E*. However, beyond *E*, when the actual investment rate is less than the required minimum, it will eventually slip back to point *E*. Thus, *E* is the steady state growth of capital per labour because the economy will have the tendency to remain steady at this state. This new steady state represents a position where actual savings rate *s* is equal to investment rate both of which are equal of *nk*, the rate of growth of capital stock times the population growth rate ($s = s(k) = i(k) = nk$). Every country will have its own steady state which defines its long run growth. It depends on its current savings and investment rates, the existing stock of capital, the rate at which it wears out and the rate of growth of its population.

15.11 FACTORS EXPLAINING ECONOMIC GROWTH

In explaining 'steady state' we identified some of the constraints-depreciation of capital stock and population growth – beyond which there is little possibility of sustained economic growth. But, rise in savings rate and technological progress are the two main sources of sustained growth while any increase in the population growth rate is a source of further constraint to economic growth. We shall, therefore, try to examine the effects of these factors now:

1. **Rise in savings rate** A rise in the rate of savings for an economy is reflected in the upward shift of the savings curve as shown in Fig. 15.6. In Fig. 15.6, we have drawn into savings curves, *s* and $s' - s'$ being the new shifted one-showing larger amounts of savings per unit of capital labour ratios. *nk*, as earlier, is the required rate of investment to account for population growth and labour supply. Since the higher savings curve

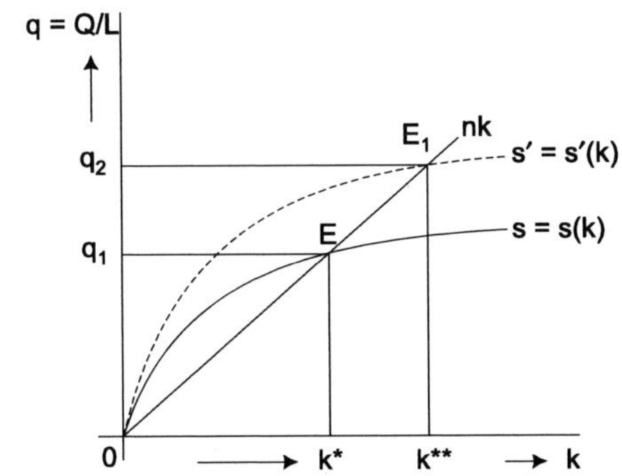

Figure 15.6 *Rise in savings rate and economic growth.*

cuts the *nk* line at a higher point, E_1, this means E_1 is the new steady state where capital-labour is higher induced by higher rate of investment. This has made possible the higher level of income per labour unit as shown by point Oq_2 as compared to Oq_1.

2. **Rise in population growth rate** If we now assume that population growth rate has increased – say from n to n_1 ($n_1 > n$) – then the *nk* line will be shifting to the left forming a new ray from the origin as shown in Fig. 15.7. In this case, the required investment rate is higher as compared to the earlier *nk* line. If we take the savings rate as unchanging, then the new n_1k line lowers the steady state and so lowers the actual capital labout ratio. The result is lower income per unit of labour from Oq_2 to Oq_1 as shown in F\ig. 15.7. If both these factors mentioned above are at work simultaneously, one can imagine that the positive effect of rise in saving rate may be to some extent neutralized by the negative effect of higher population growth rate, depending upon their relative shift.
3. **Technological progress** Technology of production refers to the technical relationship existing between product output and various inputs as thrown up by a certain body of knowledge provided by engineers, technocrats and scientists to the society at a certain period of time. When we talk of technological progress it naturally refers to the 'change' to this available body of knowledge. Most often technological progress results in improved knowledge about the existing technical relationships among output and inputs as also the methods of combining them. Thus, technological progress, in the context of production function, would suggest an upward shift of the production function (or, the total output curve). This leads to higher output per unit of input or, to say the same thing, input requirement per unit of output is less. Technological progress thus suggests that the qualities of both output as well as inputs

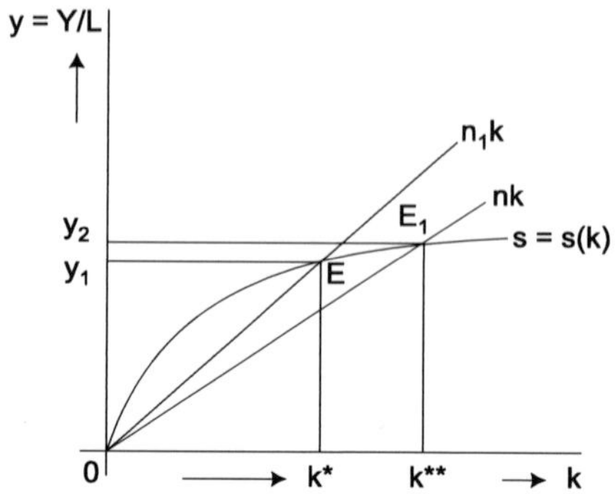

Figure 15.7 *Rise in population growth rate and economic growth.*

are significantly improved. In terms of cost of production that means that cost per unit of output is lowered. Since technological progress improves the efficiency of labour it enhances the effective supply of labour and hence it is known as labour augmenting technological progress. Inventions of different kinds of machines which replace the use of labour are examples of such technological progress.

It is clear, therefore, that by continuous technological progress, economic growth process can be sustained at a rising rate. Figure 15.8 illustrates the technological progress in terms of shifts of production function. As a result of upward shift of total output curve from q_1 to q_2 resulting in higher level of output when the same level of capital per labour unit is used. Thus at *ok*, capital-labour ratio, the output rises from OZ_1 to OZ_2. As the technological progress proceeds further through newer and newer discoveries and inventions and the subsequent enhancement of knowledge, the production function continues to shift upward in different periods of time.

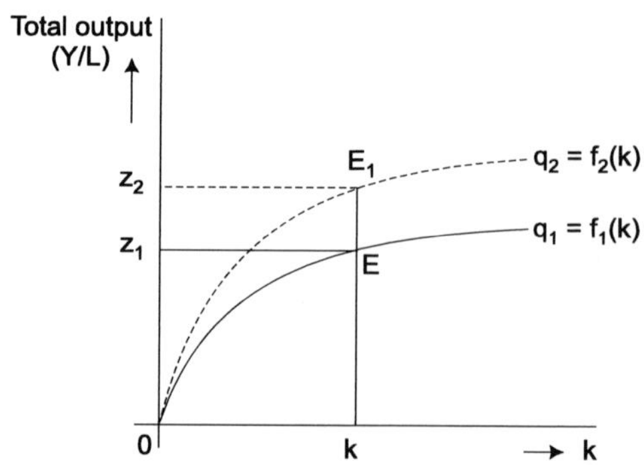

Figure 15.8 *Technological progress and economic growth.*

From the above discussions, it would be clear that three key factors – savings and investment rates, population growth and technological progress – determine largely the long run growth pattern of most countries of the world. In the case of developed countries of the world, capital accumulation and technological progress have been chiefly responsible for higher economic growth. In most under-developed economies with higher rate of population growth, a larger proportion of growth in output is devoted to maintaining the larger population size and hence, even if there is evidence of rising saving rate helping capital accumulation process the rate of growth of the economy is relatively low.

15.12 THE CONVERGENCE HYPOTHESIS

The neo-classical models make certain predictions about convergence of growth rates of different economies starting at different levels of development at different points of time in history. For instance, poor and rich countries have wide differences in terms of per capita income levels, standard of living and other criteria of development. But, overtime if the poor countries starting late on growth path catch up with their richer counterparts, then this property is known as the convergence property. If they fail to catch up then the poor countries starting late would remain poor in the long run. The hypothesis of convergence suggests however that countries with same savings rates, same population growth rates and labour efficiency would most likely to converage even though they start off at different periods in history or they have different capital stock. The convergence hypothesis can be verified with reference to growth stories of developed and developing emerging economies of the world in recent decades.

The neo-classical models of growth no doubt try to explain long run growth process in terms of supply and demand aspects of growth – supply being determined by the technical conditions of production and factor supplies (labour, capital and technology) and demand being determined by consumption, savings and investments. However, the models have failed to take account of certain non-economic factors of growth such as the role of education and political leadership. Investment in education and health (human capital) can raise the efficiency of workers which contributes to growth process of an economy at a relatively early stage as evidenced in the case of some of the emerging economies of Asia notably Singapore, Hongkong, South Korea. Therefore, the role of human capital as distinguished from pure material capital might be helpful in explaining the growth process of some other recently developing economies including India where knowledge-based contributions to growth have become significantly high.

In the similar vein, role of political leadership in shaping and implementing appropriate economic policies for growth is equally important. Historical evidence of the later 20th century and early 21st century of the role of political leadership at crucial junctures of nations prove that without strong political will, economic theories and models would have remained mere dogmas. However, within the strict economic growth model it is not possible to quantify the role of political leadership.

The golden rule: The implication of the above discussion of Prof. Solow's growth model is that capital accumulation, savings rate and the technological progress of an economy are the chief determinants of the growth rate of an economy. This might suggest that maximum rate of saving is the best thing for the economy's well-being. However, if the entire income of the people is saved and none is consumed, the result will be disastrous. In fact, the ultimate aim of the welfare of the people is to attain a maximum level of consumption of goods and services. Therefore, it will be useful to understand the concept of maximum level of consumption at which the rates of savings (and investment) attain "steady states". Such steady-state saving, investment rates are referred to as the "golden rule" levels of saving and capital investment.

As we know from our earlier discussion on neoclassical production function, consumption is simply income minus saving or, to state the same thing, total output minus total investment ($C = Y - I$ or, $c = y - i$ in per capita terms). The behaviour of output (y), investment (i) and consumption (c) with capital stocks would suggest that there must be a certain steady-state capital stock which would give maximum per capita consumption. This is the "golden rule" capital stock. Corresponding to this capital stock, there will be a certain saving rate, called "golden rule" saving rate. Such a saving rate would, suggestively, be a permanently sustainable saving rate for the economy. We illustrate these concepts in Fig. 15.9.

Three curves are shown in Fig. 15.9 – steady-state output, being a function of capital stock, k^*, steady-state depreciation of capital, $(n + d)k^*$ and steady-state saving, s^*. Clearly, there can be several steady-state saving rates, but, among these, there is only one saving rate which allows maximum consumption per capita. Below this saving rate, consumption is less than optimum, while above this saving rate too, consumption is less than optimum. In other words, below the optimum rate of saving, the required capital stock per worker is lower while above the optimum rate, capital stock is higher than required for optimum. Thus, steady-state capital stock will be too low at less than optimum consumption while it will be too high at more than optimum level of consumption.

Conditions for golden rule

1. The rate of growth of steady-state output – a function of capital stock – which is the marginal product of capital (MPK) is equal to depreciation rate of steady state capital : MPK = $(n + d)$.
2. Steady state saving rate (s^* gold) is equal to steady-state investment rate (i^* gold) which, in turn, is equal to steady state output growth: s^* gold = i^* gold = MPK.

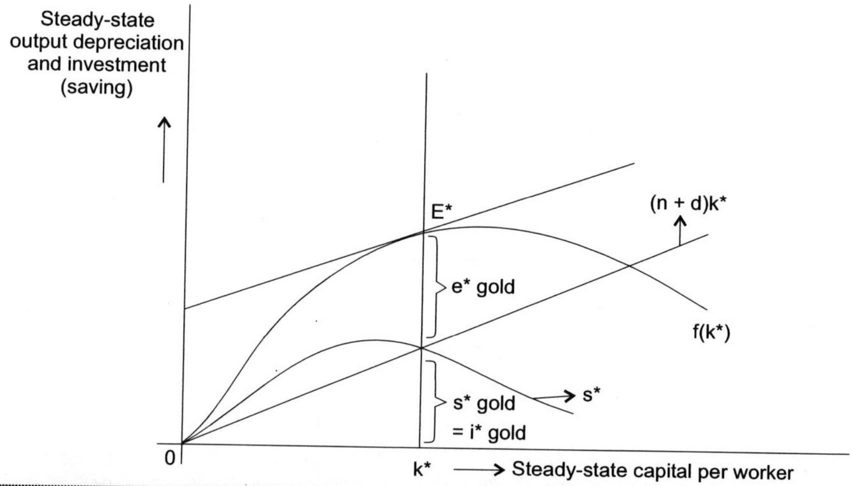

Figure 15.9 *Golden rule capital stock and golden rule saving rate.*

The first condition is evident from the equality of the slopes of steady state output and depreciation rate at point E^* in Fig. 15.9. The second condition follows logically, since consumption is the difference between output and investment.

We now use mathematical symbols to illustrate the above results:

$$c = y - i. \tag{15.18}$$

that is, per capita consumption is the difference between per capita income and per capita investment. At steady state,

$$c^* = y^* - i^* \tag{15.19}$$

Since, y^* and i^* are both functions of k^* and investment is always equal to depreciation, we can write

$$c^* = f(k^*) - f(n + d)k^* \tag{15.20}$$

where, $(n + d)k^*$ is the amount of depreciation.

Now, since we are interested in maximisation of consumption, we obtain $\partial c^*/k^*$ and set it equal to zero to fulfil first order condition of maximisation.

Thus,

$$\partial c^*/\partial k^* = f'(k^*) - (n + d) = 0,$$

$$\Rightarrow \quad f'(k^*) = (n + d) \tag{15.21}$$

Equation (15.21) states that at the golden rule, rate of output growth per unit of capital stock is equal to the rate of depreciation, i.e., addition to depreciation amount, since slopes of both the output curve and depreciation curve are the same (parallel to each other)[1]. A numerical example may support this result. For instance, let the stock of capital, k^*, for a certain point in time for an economy stands at ₹ 5 billion when it produces an output worth ₹ 1 billion. If this economy increases its capital stock by ₹ 1 billion more, and the output rises to ₹ 1.5 billion so that ₹ 0.5 billion worth of extra output is the marginal product of capital (MPK). Similarly, at ₹ 5 billion stock of capital, the total amount of depreciation is ₹ 1 billion and at ₹ 6 billion stock of capital, the amount of depreciation is ₹ 1.1 billion, then the rate of depreciation is $(1.1 - 1.0)/1.0 = 0.1/1.0 = 1/10 = 10\%$. Thus, MPK = ₹ 0.5 billion and depreciation rate is ₹ 0.1 billion. Here, MPK is greater than the depreciation rate so that consumption per capita is on the rise due to increase in capital stock. In other words, MPK is greater than $(n + \delta)$.

If this process continues, then eventually MPK will be declining while $(n + \delta)$ will remain the same and a stage may be reached when MPK = $(n + \delta)$ which will ensure the attainment of "golden rule". If MPK < $(n + \delta)$, this means further increase in capital stock leads to decrease in consumption per capita.

Thus, only at the golden rule level of capital stock will consumption be maximum.

Now, if economies are positioned at different steady states other than the 'golden rule', the following are the inter-temporal growth implications for the present versus future generation of consumers:

1. For economies starting with less capital stock than one required for golden rule, policy makers would go for capital accumulation which means higher rate of saving and investment but lower rate of consumption. Thus, the present generation is likely to suffer in terms of current consumption, since current consumption will fall below the maximum. But, future generation of consumers is likely to gain, since both saving and investment curves would be higher which would promise to provide higher goods and services in future. Thus, there is a trade-off before the policy makers whether to give more weightage to the present generation or to future generation of consumers. Those who will be more concerned about the present generation will favour a policy to discourage savings to provide more resources for consumption. However, those policy makers who are interested more for future generations of consumers will encourage more savings at present to provide room for more investment and so higher consumption in the future.
2. For economies starting with more capital stock than necessary for golden rule, the policy maker would favour lower saving and investment rates

1 $(n + d)k^*$ shows the amounts of depreciation at each level of capital stock, while it's slope $(n + d)$ is the rate of depreciation (which takes into account the population growth also).

to ensure higher consumption; so the present generation is sure to gain. But if the economy aims at moving towards the 'golden rule' steady state, future generations of consumers too are likely to gain since, this will ensure long-run equilibrium at the Golden Rule steady state of the economy.

Actual data of an economy and achieving a 'golden rule': If a certain economy regularly throws up data, on time series basis, on national output (GDP), capital stock (k), savings rate (s), investment rate (i), estimated rate of depreciation (δ), population growth rate (p), estimated marginal product of capital (MPK), then one can identify the following steady states for the economy:

1. the initial steady-state condition by equating the rate of investment with the rate of depreciation, and
2. the golden rule steady state by equating MPK with the rate of depreciation (δ) or by locating the maximum level of consumption among various levels of saving rates.

For carrying out such an exercise however, one needs first to specify the underlying production function in the Cobb-Douglas framework by assuming certain numerical values of the coefficients of inputs-labour and capital.

Decomposition of the sources of growth: the neoclassical approach:

According to the neoclassical model of growth, there are mainly three sources of growth : (1) growth of labour, (2) growth of capital and (3) technological progress. Of these, (1) and (2) are factor inputs while (3) is such change that occurs overtime to influence productivity of both labour and capital (also known as total factor productivity). We try to account for these sources of growth by decomposing their factor contributions.

In terms of production function, the total output is expressed as a function of labour, capital and technology:

$$Y = f(L, K, T) \tag{15.22}$$

where, Y is total output (or GDP), L is total labour input, K is total capital input and T is technology. Since, technology can be separately treated for reasons we explain below, we succinctly write eqn. (15.22) as follows:

$$Y = f(L, K) \tag{15.23}$$

Now, if we are interested in knowing how a given increase in Y, say ΔY, is obtained through factor inputs, L and K, we obtain total differentiation of the function (15.23) as follows:

$$\Delta Y = \partial f/\partial L * \Delta L. + \partial f/\partial K * \Delta K \tag{15.24}$$

which can be alternatively expressed as:

$$\Delta Y = (\partial f/\partial L * L) * \Delta L/L. + (\partial f/\partial K * K)\, \Delta K/K \tag{15.25}$$

Now, dividing through by Y, we obtain

$$\Delta Y/Y = (\partial f/\partial L * L/Y)\, \Delta L/L + (\partial f/\partial K * K/Y)\, \Delta K/K \tag{15.26}$$

Equation (15.26) expresses growth rate of output ($\Delta Y/Y$) being equal to the sum total of two components: growth rate of labour input ($\Delta L/L$) multiplied by the elasticity of output with respect to labour ($\partial f/\partial L * L/Y$) and growth rate of capital ($\Delta K/K$) multiplied by the elasticity of output with respect to capital ($\partial f/\partial K * K/Y$). This is how the growth rate in total output is decomposed into growth rates of factor inputs. Thus, the main sources of growth in output or GDP can be traced to the growth rates of factors–labour and capital along with their respective shares in total GDP. The respective input elasticities – ($\partial f/\partial L * \Delta L/Y$) and ($\partial f/\partial K * \Delta K/Y$)–represent their respective shares in total GDP. It is to be noted that these relative factor shares have two components: (1) marginal products of factors: $\partial f/\partial L$ and $\partial f/\partial K$ and average products of factors: Y/L and Y/K respectively. Each elasticity coefficient is obtained by dividing the marginal component by the average component as is the normal case for all elasticity formula.

Now, if we can develop a method of evaluating the marginal products of factors, then their factor share components can be easily estimated. Then the growth rates of GDP, labour and capital over a fairly long period of time can be obtained from observable data with the help of which growth rate of GDP can be traced to relative contributions of factors of production – labour and capital. Such a method of evaluating marginal products is available in terms of real wage rates for labour and rental values for capital under the assumption of competitive market economy. Thus, if labour's share in total output (L/Y) at any given period of time is assigned the value of real wage rate (money wage rate deflated by price level) and capital's share in total output (K/Y) is assigned the value of rate of interest (which is the rental value of capital in terms of its opportunity cost) and then these values are multiplied by the growth rates of factors ($\Delta L/L$) and ($\Delta K/K$), then we approximately account for growth rate of output (GDP).

Effects of technological progress: The second source of GDP growth is technological progress. Earlier, we have defined technological progress as improvement in the whole body of knowledge relating to the new techniques and methods of production and their application to actual production process. Technological progress over time can be captured either by introducing a new factor, T in the production function framework or accounting for change in the total factor productivity through rise in the value of the intercept term, A, which is normally associated with a specific production function. In fact, the intercept term is capable of capturing a number of factor contributions other than the measured variables such as labour and capital. Important among such factors are: (a) effects of managerial ability and efficiency, (b) education, training and overall skill development and (c) effects of government regulations on measured factors. Since technological progress as such is difficult to be precisely quantified and measured separately, it is captured by "change" in the intercept term which represents 'total factor productivity'. This is because these nonquantifiable variables are, to a large extent, influenced by technological progress. Professor Solow suggested measuring total factor productivity as "a residual" factor contribution. By residual he meant the remainder of total output growth after deducting the contributions of measured factors (labour and capital). This is what is known as "Solow residual". Accordingly, we can rewrite our production function as:

$$Y = A\ F\ (L, K) \tag{15.27}$$

where, A, the intercept, is a measure of total factor productivity.

By decomposing now eqn. (15.27), we get

$$\Delta Y = \Delta A + \partial F/\partial L * \Delta L + \partial F/\partial K * \Delta K$$

And dividing through by Y, we get

$$\Delta Y/Y = \Delta A/Y + (\partial F/\partial L * L/Y) * \Delta L/L + (\partial F/\partial K * \Delta K/Y) * \Delta K/K) \tag{15.28}$$

Thus, one additional term. $\Delta A/Y$ appears in eqn. (15.28).

This additional term shows the growth rate of total factor productivity. However, the growth rate in total factor productivity is not directly observable. Hence, it is measured by Solow residual, after deducting the factor contributions of labour and capital from total output growth. If we observe total output growth over a period of time which is in excess of measurable factor contributions, then the 'excess' output growth can be attributed to total factor productivity. In terms of eqn. (15.28), it can be stated as:

$$\Delta A/Y = \Delta Y/Y - (\partial F/\partial L * L/Y) * \Delta L/L - (\partial F/\partial K * K/Y) * \Delta K/K \tag{15.29}$$

Total factor productivity growth in India in recent years: an illustration

According to a recent study by Karan Bhasin, (Mint, January 8, 2020), on GDP growth and total factor productivity growth of India as well as emerging markets and developing economies, over the period 2007 and 2018, India's adjusted GDP growth in 2005 was 9%,while total factor productivity growth was 3.5%, in 2006, growth was 9.3% while TFP growth was 3.3%, in 2007, the figures were 10.1% and 3.1% respectively. In 2016, India's TFP growth was 3.5% while in 2017 and 2018, these figures were, respectively, 1.6% and 2.4%. This empirical study is based upon the Total Economy Database.

The message this study gives is that total factor productivity growth has a great role to play in economic growth. Total factor productivity can be improved by structural reforms of the economy which can enhance productive capacity (for example, investment in physical infrastructure of the economy, including the human capital). Recent slowdown of Indian economy during 2018-19 and 2019-20 can be traced to this factor.

Appendix-15 A: A Digression on Cobb-Douglas Production Function

In the beginning of our discussion on neoclassical growth model, we have mentioned that Solow model of growth has assumed a specific form of production function known as Cobb-Douglas production function mainly due to its simplicity of obeying the law of constant returns to scale in the long run while fulfilling other characteristics of neoclassical production function. Here we are going to examine in detail these characteristics of Cobb-Douglas production function.

The *C-D* production function is generally expressed as:

$$Y = A\ L^{\alpha}\ K^{\beta}. \qquad (15.\ A1),$$

where, Y is total output, L and K are physical inputs of labour and capital, A is the intercept term and α and β are coefficients of labour and capital, respectively, also known as elasticities of output with respect to labour and capital, respectively. These elasticities indicate the responsiveness of output due to certain changes in amounts of inputs. The general formula for elasticity, as we know, is the ratio of marginal value to average value. Therefore, we need to compute the marginal product and average product of labour and capital in eqn. (15. A1).

Marginal products are obtained by taking the first partial derivatives of Y with respect to L and K which are given below:

Marginal product of L : $\partial Y/\partial L = \alpha.A\ L^{\alpha-1}\ K^{\beta} = \alpha.\ (A\ L^{\alpha}\ K^{\beta})/L = \alpha.\ Y/L$

Marginal product of. K : $\partial Y/\partial K = \beta.\ A\ L^{\alpha}\ K^{\beta-1} = \beta.(A\ L^{\alpha}\ K^{\beta})/K = \beta.\ Y/K$

On examining the behaviour of the marginal products (MP s), we find that,

(1) as amounts of L are gradually increased, (α . Y/L) decreases, and

(2) similarly, as amounts of K are gradually increased, (β. Y/K) decreases.

Therefore, both the marginal products: MP_L and MP_K, obey the normal behaviour, the law of diminishing returns – they are positive but diminishing within their relevant ranges.

Constant returns to scale: Let us now examine what happens to total output when both labour and capital are simultaneously changed by certain constant proportion, say μ times.

$$Y = A\ (\mu\ L)^{\alpha}\ (\mu K)^{\beta}$$

$$\Rightarrow \qquad A\ \mu^{\alpha}\ L^{\alpha}\ \mu^{\beta}\ K^{\beta} = \mu^{(\alpha+\beta)}\ A\ L^{\alpha}\ K^{\beta} = \mu^{(\alpha+\beta)}.\ Y$$

Thus, total output changes by $\mu^{(\alpha+\beta)}$ times. Now, if (α + β) sums to unity, then we can say that total output also changes by μ times. In the case of Cobb-Douglas production function, it is assumed that the contributions of labour and capital taken together always add up to total output. (In fact, this result is suggested by Euler's theorem.) This means that if labour's contribution to total output is 70 per cent, that of capital is 30 per cent or, for that matter, any such proportions conceivable. Therefore, it is asserted that $(\alpha + \beta) = 1$; or, $\alpha = 1 - \beta$ or, $\beta = 1 - \alpha$. And so, the production function is also expressed as $Y = L^{\alpha}\ K^{1-\alpha}$. From this constraint, it is concluded that if the contribution of one factor (either labour or capital) is known, that of the other is easily obtained.[1]

1 The assumption of constant returns to scale is often justified on empirical ground. Supposing there are two identical firms with the same number of labour with equal efficiency and same amount of capital and also the same managerial efficiency. Now, if firm no. 1 produces an output of 100 tonnes of steel, there is apparently no cause to prevent the firm no. 2 to produce the same output of 100 tonnes of steel. In other words, if factor inputs are multiplied by any constant times (doubled or tripled), output is also likely to increase by the same constant times

The elasticity coefficients, α and β are obtained simply by dividing the marginal products of factors by their average products. Thus,

$$\alpha = \alpha \cdot (Y/L)/(Y/L) = \alpha; \qquad \beta = \beta \cdot (Y/K)/(Y/K) = \beta$$

It may be noted that α and β also indicate the respective factor shares in total output. From eqns. (15. A2) and (15. A3), we get an idea of total returns to labour and capital (marginal products times their quantities). Thus, total returns to labour = $(\alpha \cdot A\ L^{\alpha-1} \cdot K^{\beta}) \cdot L$ and to capital = $(\beta\ A\ L^{\alpha}\ K^{\beta-1}) \cdot K$ and so their shares in total output = $(\ (\alpha \cdot A\ L^{\alpha-1} \cdot K^{\beta}) \cdot L)/Y$ and $((\ \beta\ A\ L^{\alpha}\ K^{\beta-1}) \cdot K)/Y$

which yield to $\alpha\ A^{\alpha}\ K^{\beta}\ /Y$ and $\beta\ A^{\alpha}\ K^{\beta}\ /Y$ which further lead to

$\alpha \cdot Y/Y = \alpha$; and $\beta \cdot Y/Y = \beta$

Thus, α and β represent the factor shares in total output.

The convergence hypothesis and neoclassical growth: One of the implications of the neoclassical growth models is that advanced and poor economies, since they differ with respect to factor resources like capital and labour (capital is scarce while labour is abundant in poor economies while opposite is true for the advanced economies) the marginal productivity of capital in the poor economies being higher than that in advanced economies, in the long run, as the former acquire more and more capital, they would, subsequently, catch up with the advanced economies even though they start from different levels of growth paths with initially suffering from low level of savings. Obviously, this would require the poor economies to move faster; for those who would either be laggard or move with the same speed as their advanced counterparts, would remain at the same relative positions as before.

Convergence hypothesis emerged as an excellent idea of the neoclassical growth theory which, on implementation, promised an egalitarian world where income inequalities would be reduced to the minimum among the countries in the long run particularly if it is played out with freer trade and investment regimes.

If we look at the real world situation, the early post-War ll had ravaged the countries like Germany, Italy, Japan and some of their European allies. But, thanks to their perseverance and capital transfers from international institutions, they managed to move on the fast track to emerge in the following decades as economically strong nations. Thus the theory and its policy outcomes appeared to be true.

In more recent periods, particularly in the post-1990s, with substantial liberalisation and openness of trade and capital investment among nations (globalisation), the convergence hypothesis was expected to come true on real grounds. In fact, in the case of emerging economies, the prediction of the hypothesis appeared to be true since these countries experienced the fastest ever growth rates of their economies to close the existing gaps in growth and development levels. Instances of emerging economies like India, China, South

Korea, Brazil, Russia, South Africa and their growth histories in recent years speak for themselves.

However, a recent report by the World Bank (quoted by economist Vivek Dehejia, Mint, 27 January, 2020) reveals that there is a trend of slowing productivity growth in the emerging economies in recent periods which is preventing the process of further convergence.

15.13 ENDOGENOUS GROWTH MODELS

During 1980s, growth models developed by economist Paul Romer and others at New York University, US gained currency and became popular in the following decades. It is worth mentioning that Romer was the co-recipient of the Nobel prize in Economics (along with William Nordhaus) in the year 2018 for his significant contribution to economic growth theory and its application.

The endogenous growth model has tried to explore the sources of growth not in the exogenous factors like capital accumulation and technological progress as suggested by the neoclassical growth models of economist Robert Solow, T. Swan and others, but in the endogenous factors like human capital, knowledge and innovation which are internal to the particular firm and are generally affected by economic forces and not merely technological forces. In fact, technological progress is essentially a scientific process which creates "inventions" in the social domain and from which the neoclassical economists can assume a certain growth vision in their growth models.

The most striking fact about the endogenous growth theory is that while the neoclassical growth theories predict the inevitable law of diminishing returns to the factor inputs like capital and labour, the endogenous theory rules out the application of this historical law to factors like knowledge, human capital and new ideas or innovations which accompany the capital accumulation process. Thus, the theory predicts that there is ample possibility of the law of increasing returns or, at least, the law of constant returns to the variable factors instead of the law of diminishing returns to capital. We can illustrate this new phenomenon with the help of the following Fig. 15.10.

Professor Romer has demonstrated how investment in new ideas and knowledge capital has tremendous scope for growth in emerging and less developed economies. In fact, some of the Asian economies like South Korea, Vietnam, Singapore and some other Latin American countries have already experienced this new growth potential. A country like India, the theory has predicted, has enough experimental fields for realising the growth potential through greater investment in new knowledge capital.

The other striking feature of the endogenous growth theory is the spillover effects of the investment in knowledge capital and new ideas. For instance, if a certain firm produces a drug based upon the formulation of a scientist or a group of scientists, it creates spillover effect in that the benefits of the drug are not confined to the producing firm alone, but is spread over to all other firms who would be interested in replicating and enhancing its production (after obtaining licences) and thereby benefiting the society at large. This is called the positive externality of such spillover effects. This is because these effects result in benefits whose costs are borne by other firms (external benefits without costs). It is needless to say that in the event of such positive externality, an increasing volume of the good will be produced with their better qualities and thereby raises the value of the new product manifold.

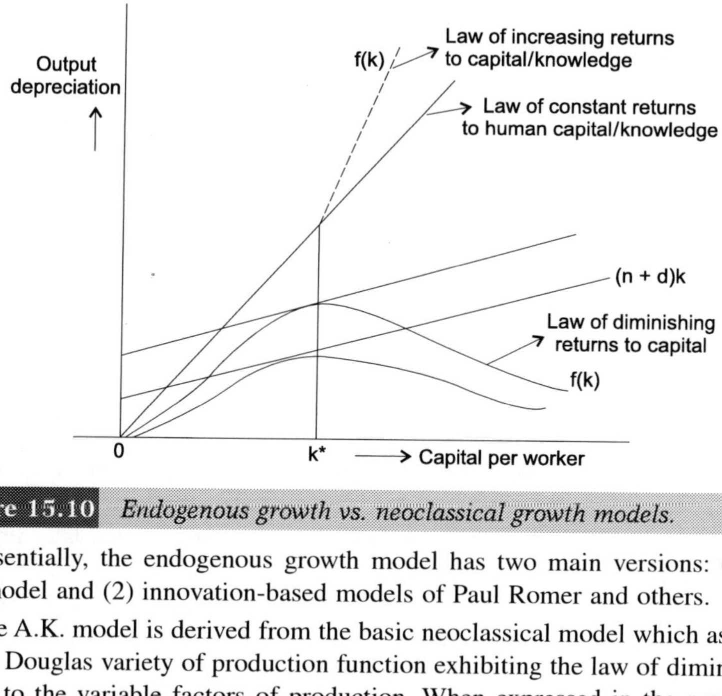

Figure 15.10 *Endogenous growth vs. neoclassical growth models.*

Essentially, the endogenous growth model has two main versions: (1) the A.K. model and (2) innovation-based models of Paul Romer and others.

The A.K. model is derived from the basic neoclassical model which assumes a Cobb Douglas variety of production function exhibiting the law of diminishing returns to the variable factors of production. When expressed in the per capita terms (K/L), as we have seen in the case of Solow model, in a special case, when the value of k (= K/L) is one, that is when the output elasticity of capital per labour unit becomes unity, $(dy/dk).(k/y) = 1$, the production function becomes one that exhibits the law of constant returns to the variable factor, k, thus preventing the operation of the law of diminishing returns. The Fig. 15.10 also represents this. Hence the Cobb Douglas function collapses to:

$$Y = AK \tag{15.30}$$

where, Y is total output, A is the intercept term (here a positive 'constant') and K is output elasticity of capital. In graphical terms, it shows a straight line upwards from the origin. Obviously, it shows that a proportionate increase in K leads to the proportionate increase in Y. We can easily obtain the growth rate of output using the basic equation of the A.K. model as shown below:

The growth rate is measured by the derivative of Y with respect to time, expressed as

$$(dY/dt)/Y, \text{ or, } (dY/dt).\ 1/Y. \tag{15.31}$$

Now, from eqn. (15.30),

$$(dY/dt).1/Y = (dK/dt).1/K \tag{15.32}$$

Since A is a positive constant. Now, assuming an economy saves a certain fixed fraction of total output, s, and there is a fixed rate of depreciation, d of the capital, then the rate of aggregate net investment (dK/dt), that is, gross investment minus depreciation, (investment = net addition to capital) is,

$$(dK/dt). = s\ Y - d\ K \tag{15.33}$$

Since net investment = net savings. Now, putting the result of (3) in (2), we obtain the growth rate of output,

$$(dY/dt).\ 1/Y = (sY - d\ K).1/K = s\ Y/K - d$$

$$= s\ A - d, \text{ since, } Y/K = A \tag{15.34}$$

Thus, an increase in the rate of savings, s, will lead to a permanently higher rate of growth of output (s is obviously an endogenous variable).

The main explanation lies in the productivity increases (total factor productivity) inherent in the intercept term, A, which captures several variables influenced by non-observable factors like innovations, new ideas, etc., which depend largely on the extent of expenditures on research and development (R & D) by the concerned firm. The actual process through which the capital accumulation converts the physical and human capital into intellectual capital is that some part of the physical or human capital is absorbed and later reflected in the innovations, the new way of doing the old thing or doing a new thing altogether. 'Learning by doing' gives the necessary experience to the workers of the firms. The neoclassical growth models failed to recognise this aspect of growth coming from new sources of intellectual capital.

It is also evident that incentives like intellectual property rights in the form of patent rights play a very important role in allowing firms to reap the benefits of innovations. Also important are the government policies of subsidies and other benefits towards innovations.

Since innovation results in a new product or a new process of an old product, the patent rights and other intellectual property rights obviously provide the patent holders certain monopoly power over their products. This means that government policy towards competition also has a role to play to regulate the resulting market structure. These are some of the various incentives as well as opportunities on which the pace of innovations depends leading ultimately to growth of output.

It may be remembered here that Austrian economist Joseph A. Schumpeter's innovation theory predicts that every innovation (product or process) leads ultimately to the destruction of the old product and emergence of the new ones which he calls the "creative destruction". This creative destruction, according to the author, is actually good for the market although many producers lose their existence. But this is a natural process and, as the author thinks, there is no need for government intervention in any respect since this is in line with the Darwinian principle of the "survival of the fittest".

As regards the role of population growth, the endogenous growth theory implies that population growth is a big opportunity for undertaking innovations for growth by way of a big market as well as a larger supply of labour. This has been quite consistent with evidence in several Asian and African countries. A large and expanding market provided by population growth gives enough room for innovations of various kinds. This is in contrast to the neoclassical growth model where population growth is seen as a dampening factor for long-run growth.

In recent years, instances are aplenty how new innovations followed by technological changes are taking place in the domain of digital technology replacing the older modes and the more recent ones being "virtual" or remote modes of working or teaching particularly in the emergency situations like COVID-19 and its follow-up era. Similarly, encouraging the new innovations in the form of "start-ups" and their success stories in the field of economic growth bear enough testimony of the endogenous growth model being unfolded in practice.

To conclude our discussion on endogenous growth theory, the theory emphasises on the factors that are within the economic system such as investment in knowledge, education and innovations that lead to technological progress and hence long-run economic growth. The returns to these factors do not necessarily exhibit the operation of the law of diminishing returns as suggested in the neoclassical growth models.

15.14 THEORY OF SECULAR STAGNATION

The term secular stagnation means persistently falling long-term economic growth, that is, when economic growth continues to fall and remains at low level for a considerable period of time. The theory of secular stagnation was first brought into discussion in economics literature in the aftermath of the Great Depression of 1929-30 by economist Alvin H. Hansen in 1938. In his presidential address to the American Economic Association that year, Hansen expressed apprehension that the Great Depression caused massive fall in aggregate demand during the years that followed. There was sluggish recovery after the Great Depression, as Hansen observed. Among the major causes, he found, were the slower growth of population and lower speed of technological progress which, together, contributed to the unemployment remaining persistent along with lack of wage growth for workers. Thus, "without new people entering the workforce and without new inventions coming into the market, there would be less investment in new goods, employees and services. Without investment, fewer businesses would open or expand, growth would slow and more workers would be unable to find jobs….." This is the essence of secular stagnation, observed Hansen. Subsequent events, particularly the outbreak of World War II belied Hansen's fears because the war encouraged defence production of weapons and investment in many types of infrastructure projects. Since then, it has been observed that after every big recession that occurred in the advanced capitalist economies, saw the reemergence of the secular stagnation like situation. In particular, since the Great Recession of 2008-09 following the housing market crash in the US, economists have been debating over the secular stagnation hypothesis, a persistent fall in GDP growth rate along with low levels of inflation and almost zero interest rate of the major central banks of the world. The most surprising fact is that despite continued attempts at reviving the aggregate demand and growth, nothing tangible has yet happened. As evidence, we may cite the US GDP growth hovering around 2% during the most of the post-2008 period. Similarly, the EU's growth rate remained below 1.5% and Japan had already experienced near zero growth for more than two decades. The story on the inflation front is the same as the US has been missing its inflation target of 2% despite persistent monetary policy easing efforts (near zero interest rates by the Federal Reserve). For nearly more than a decade, the EU's inflation rate too has been, by and large, not above 2%. In fact, some of these economies are showing signs of deflation.

Larry Summers (2013), former treasury secretary of the US under president Bill Clinton, revived the debate on secular stagnation in the US in a speech in the IMF and, in fact, warned that the secular stagnation fear was real. Summers called for new approaches to deal with the sluggish growth, low interest rates and an absence of inflation. Summers observed that during the post-2008 financial crisis and Great Recession, there have emerged clear trends of consistently falling investment alongside the rising savings thus creating a growing gap between the two. Normally, such a scenario, as the economic theory suggests, would lead to a fall in interest rate to so low that investment demand would rise while savings would fall to ultimately equate the two and restore equilibrium. But, in an environment of secular stagnation, falling interest rates are unable to stimulate investment no matter how low the rate falls. In fact, in the entire positive interest rate zone, it has been found, investment sentiments are largely absent. It is perhaps in the negative zone only that investment might be activated. Even in the negative zone, how much negative rate will be required is not yet known and central banks over the entire advanced world are grappling with this problem with resulting changes in the behaviour of the saving community so much so that the savers are shying away from bank deposits and frantically finding alternative avenues of saving. At the same time, savers are also experiencing a negative real rate of interest too. In the familiar *IS-LM* framework, it can be suggested that the *IS* curve is not able to meet the *LM* curve in the positive quadrant. They would require extending downward below zero interest rate possibly to meet somewhere in the negative range as shown in Fig. 15.11. The theory of secular stagnation has since received recognition in the writings of economist and Nobel laureate Paul Krugman, Berry Eichengreen, the economic historian of California University, Berkeley, Kenneth Rogoff, Harvard University Professor and Robert J. Gordon. Professor Summers have further enumerated the main reasons for dearth in investment in the post-2008 recession era. These are, changing demographics and technological changes which are further elaborated below:

(1) Decline in working age population: Slow growth of population in the advanced economies and the resulting decline in the working age population has greatly reduced the demand for new capital goods and equipment for the workers to work with as well as for housing the growing workforce. Within the workforce, the participation rate for male workers has declined while that of the females has increased thus giving the employers the options for saving on costs. The phenomenon of a falling working age population is not only seen in the advanced capitalist economies but also in a country like China. According to a recent report, between 1961 and 1990, the global working age population (comprising people in the 15-64 age group) grew by 2.05% every year on an average. In fact, in 25 of 30 years, the working age population grew by 2% or more while economic growth during this era averaged 4.11% per year. In 1991, the growth of the working age population fell below 2% and has stayed like that ever since. This has primarily caused the slowing down of economic growth over the last three decades. In 2017, the growth of the working age population has further fallen to just 1% and has since stayed there.

More significantly, the growth in the working age population between 1991 and 2019 has averaged 1.53% per year. During this period, global

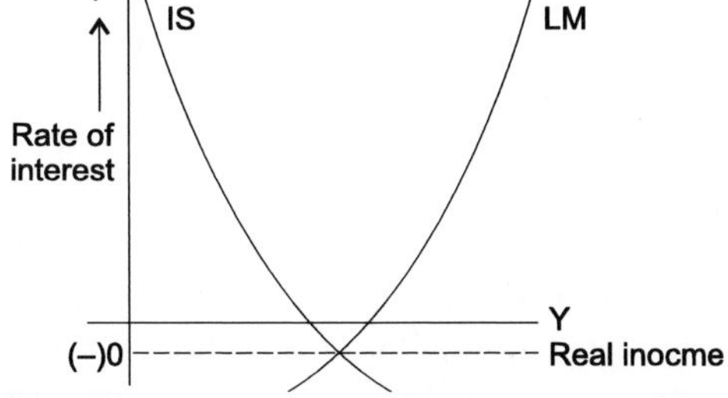

Figure 15.11 *Secular stagnation hypothesis: equilibrium at the negative range of interest rate.*

economic growth slowed down to 2.83% per year. Since the global recession of 2008, the working age population growth has dropped to 1.21% per year with the economic growth slowing down to 2.5% per year (Ruchir Sharma, *Times of India* 2016 and Vivek Kaul, 2020).

According to author Sharma, this is not limited to the western capitalist countries alone. Even in India, the growth rate of the working age population was 1.4% in 2019 while it was 2% in 2009. Thus, growth in the working age population in any country is a significant factor in ushering in long term growth and any country not able to register growth 2% or above will find it hard to consistently grow at a rapid rate.

(2) **Rise in the old age population:** Another significant development has been the rise in the aging population in the developed countries of the world including those of Japan in Asia. On the one hand, the older population has lesser propensity to spend, resulting in lesser consumption demand while they have higher propensity to save, thus stimulating more savings. Of course, certain investments in old age care activities, such as old age homes, are encouraged.

(3) **Technological changes:** Technological changes, particularly in the field of 'Internet' and computer applications and emerging areas of mobile technology and cloud computing and the like, are making possible substantial reduction in investment demand as well as consumption demand of several goods and services. For instance, digital technologies are much less capital absorbing, creating only little new investment demand relative to other revolutionary technologies. At the same time, during the entire decades of the 21st century, there has been a reduction in the prices of capital goods, especially those of the information technology. In fact, new innovations have replaced the old versions of a certain product thus making older investments obsolete but adding unemployment numbers. All this leads to slowing growth.

(4) **Rising inequality of income and wealth:** There is now ample evidence of growing inequality in the distribution of income and wealth in the advanced economies more so in the Internet era. Thus, a small percentage of people in the income distribution scale owns a considerable percentage of income and wealth while a large percentage of people owns only a small percentage of income and, what is more, over time, this distribution has worsened even more. The French economist, Thomas Picketty (2014) has thrown considerable evidence of growing inequality of income and wealth. In particular, his argument is that when the rate of return on capital is greater than the rate of GDP growth, the wealth and income gets concentrated in the top 1% of the wealth holders. The implication of growth stagnation is that more incomes tend

to be concentrated in fewer hands who have lower propensity to spend but higher propensity to save thus further distorting the environment of both consumption and investment demand. Economists and policy makers are now suggesting that it is better to accept the low growth–low inflation–low interest regime as the 'new normal'.

15.15 THE LIMITS TO GROWTH MODEL

The neo-classical economists are highly optimistic as evident from their models of growth. According to them, continuous technological progress in different dimensions can sustain the growth process without any fear of 'doomsday' overtaking the capitalist economy. However, skeptics have posed questions such as: growth rates and developments to what extent? Technological progress to what extent? Are there no limits to growth and no limits to resources exhaustions? It is in this context that 'Limits to Growth' model was advanced by the Club of Rome in 1972 based on their project 'Predicament of Mankind and designed in the department of Economics, MIT, USA, by professor Jay Forrester, known as world 2 model. Later, Meadows and others presented a modified world 3 model and is contained in their book, Limits to Growth. This book evoked a controversy on economic growth and was followed by a symposium on different dimensions of growth controversy by eminent economists and social scientists at the Centre for Social Research, Lehigh University, Bethlehem, Pennsylvania, USA, in October, 1972. The proceedings of the symposium are contained in the book, The Economic Growth Controversy.

The limits to growth model, in its analysis of the growing world population and level of pollution, the depletion of natural resources and the need for an ever increasing food supply, has specifically predicted that unless the economic growth and population growth are halted immediately, the situation will be alarming for human race in next 100 years or so (the prediction came in early seventies). In other words, the model argued for zero economic growth rate with population stabilized at a certain size.

The main concern of limits to growth model is that known reserves of all natural resources are finite and exhaustible and most of them are non-renewable – most important of them being the sources of energy – oil, coal and other minerals – which are increasingly being used for industrial and other purposes. At current rate of depletion they are estimated to last not more than seventy years from now (date of prediction). On the other hand, population world over is growing with density increasing in urban areas causing congestion and pollution along with industrialization. The world food production is lagging behind population growth making it increasingly difficult to feed the millions of mouths.

Critics have taken these views as extremely pessimistic. The neo-Malthusian fears of world food supply declining while world population growth rising with its attendant problems have, in a sense, resurfaced in the 'Limits to Growth model. The optimists, on the other hand, would argue that just as spectacular technological development in the field of agriculture in the shape of 'Green Revolution' was successful in raising agricultural output several times – thus belying the earlier Malthusian 'spectre', this time around also, technological changes will, most likely, come to the aid of meeting the impending challenge.

Neo-classical thinkers who are, among the chief critics of Limits to Growth model, once again pin their faith on the possibility of appropriate technological progress to deal with world food crisis, reduction of pollution levels or rapid depletion of natural resources and substitution of alternative sources of energy.

In spite of these optimistic views, certain pessimistic postures are not entirely out of place particularly in view of problems of poor and underdeveloped countries of the world.

In fact, the current decade of 21st century is full of warnings from various quarters (World Bank, FAO etc.) regarding the impending dangers of food crisis and food security over the world. (We have discussed certain aspects of this problem in Chapter 17 on Inflation). As historian Kranzberg rightly remarked, "... we can not dismiss lightly the warnings of the Club of Rome. Just because the Malthusians and neo-Malthusians proved wrong in the past does not mean that they might not be correct now in their forebodings. If we compare them to the boy in the fable who cries "Wolf!" we must remember that, at the end of the story, the wolf finally did come and made a clean sweep of the lambs. In other words, this might not be another false alarm; this might be the real thing."[1]

SUMMARY

1. Economic growth is often identified with growth in national income, gross domestic product or gross national product. A better index to reflect average living condition of a nation is per capita income or per capita GDP.
2. Economic development is a broader concept which considers, besides economic growth, overall development of the economy in terms of changes in institutional set up, people's attitude towards development, improvement in quality of labour force, etc. leading to expansion of productive capacity of the economy.
3. Economic growth is measured often by annual or decadal growth rates of GDP, GNP or PCI or, better, by the growth rates of real GDP etc. A better measure is however, annual compound rate of growth using a relatively longer period of time.

[1] In Economic Growth Controversy, (eds.) Weintraub et al., Macmillan, USA, 1973.

4. Among the key factors of economic growth are: (a) endowment of natural resources, (b) accumulation of capital, (c) availability of human resources and (d) advancement in production technology.

   These factors have, either singly or jointly, played major roles in the process of economic growth of different developed countries of the west or east as is evident from historical records. However, advancement in technology and accumulation of capital appear as crucial factors explaining economic growth process.
5. There are different theories and models of economic growth propounded by different schools of economists from time to time. Broadly, these theories can be grouped as either 'optimistic' or 'pessimistic'. While classical, Marxian and Limits to Growth models are essentially pessimistic, the neo-classical as also Harrod-Domar growth models are optimistic in character.
6. Classical economists notably Adam Smith, Ricardo and Malthus together advanced a theory that capital accumulation, division of labour and specialization are the factors that induce growth process. Eventually the operation of the law of diminishing returns, falling wage-rate of labourers to the subsistence level and limitation imposed by the extent of the market drive the economy to a 'stationary state' where growth would stop. Ricardo specifically analysed now this stationary state is arrived through the changing relative factor shares such as rent, wages and profits in a capitalist economy. Thus, as the economy advances in the path of growth, share of rent rises while those of wages and profits would eventually fall.
7. Marx's theory of growth of the capitalist economy relies on his theory of surplus value and theory of exploitation along with the theory of accumulation of capital. Marx's analysis suggests inner contradiction of the functioning of the economy – falling rate of profit – increasing accumulation (of capital) by the capitalists – falling wage rate-increasing mechanization adopted by capitalist – all ultimately lead to the crisis and downfall of the capitalist system.
8. Harrod and Domar take up the case of the problem of steady growth beyond full employment of the advanced capitalist economies. They argue that investment has twin functions to play – increasing income via multiplier process as also creating productive capacity of the economy. If, therefore, having achieved full employment state, the economy has to grow without interruption such as inflation or, excess capacity, both sides of the growth in aggregate income and the growth of capacity creation must be equal. This is the essence of the equational expression of Harrod-Domar model of growth. Thus, while Domar argues that in order to maintain full employment income growth over a long run, the

rate of investment must be growing at the multiple of the savings rate and output-capital ratio (or, accelerator coefficient), Harrod talks about 'warranted' rate of growth (Gw) which must be equal to the savings rate multiplied with capital output ratio (or, capital requirement). Harrod further visualizes the possibility of actual rate of growth deviating from warranted rate in which case, the economy either experiences continuous inflationary condition or, unemployment and recession of continuous nature.

9. The upper limit of the growth path is, however, set by the natural rate of growth (Gn), determined by the natural resources, population and other factors which are the sources of potential growth of the economy. Similarly, the 'lower limit' of growth is conditioned by the 'autonomous investment' of the economy which is independent of the growth of income.
10. Harrod-Domar growth model is based on certain restrictive assumptions such as 'fixed proportions' production function and inflexibility of the price system. Relaxation of the 'fixed proportions' production function and allowing for substitution between capital and labour frees the model from this defect. Similarly, flexibility of the price system would restrict the possibility of run away movement of the economy from the 'warranted' path.
11. Neo-classical economists look upon growth as a smooth, continuous process and present an optimistic theory of how an economy advances towards a steady state. By and large, neo-classical thinkers would begin with the technology of production defined by the production function allowing for capital-labour substitutability and one that follows constant returns to scale. Expressing the production function in terms of output being a function of capital-labour ratio and then deriving the consumption – saving functions, the neo-classical model then specifies a particular state of the economy called steady state – when the economy would advance at a particular rate in the long run. In a situation when population growth is assumed to be zero, such a steady state is reached when the rate of investment is just equal to the depreciation rate of the existing capital stock. However, with population growth at a certain constant rate, the steady state is attained when the rate of investment is not only equal to the depreciation rate but is also equal to the population growth rate.
12. The growth process of an economy is most likely to be influenced by the savings rate, the population growth rate and technological progress. While rise in savings rate and technological progress help achieving steady state at a relatively higher levels of capital-labour ratios the rise in population growth rate shortens the level.

13. In the early seventies, the Club of Rome advanced the 'Limits to Growth' model which, to many authors, is a 'doomsday' model. The model is principally concerned with the rate of natural resources depletion, the rising population and level of pollution, falling food production causing food crisis in the world over. The model predicts that the present rate of resource depletion and energy use for industrialization and domestic use, the growth will reach a limit in abort 70-75 years from the date of prediction, unless the population growth and economic growth rates are stopped immediately.
14. The 'Limits to Growth' has been branded as extremely pessimistic, neo-Malthusian in spirit which fails to visualize the tremendous possibility of technological progress in all spheres of human life which could easily bypass the dangers of the pessimists.
15. As the current decade is full of warnings from various international agencies regarding the main issues raised by the Limits of Growth model, there is surely some room to be pessimistic and urgent need to reverse the course of world economic development on several fronts.

EXERCISE

1. Distinguish between economic growth and economic development and discuss the main indicators of economic growth.
2. What are the main properties of Harrod-Domar model of growth. Also, discuss the limitations of the model.
3. Why is Neoclassical model of growth so popular? Examine Solow's model of growth.
4. Explain the concept of 'steady growth'. Discuss the main factors that determine the steady growth.
5. Define 'golden rule'. How is golden rule steady state is attained in an economy?
6. Obtain the golden rule condition of an economy with suitable example.
7. How is decomposition of growth derived? Explain, in this context, the concept of 'total factor productivity' and the actual method of measuring total factor productivity.
8. What is 'convergence hypothesis'. How far has it been realized in real-world situation?
9. Explain the concept of 'endogenous growth' model. How does the endogenous growth model differ from the neoclassical growth models? Give some recent examples of endogenous growth model.

REFERENCES

1. G.M. Meier and R.E. Baldwin, Economic Development: Theory, History, Policy, Asia Publishing House, Bombay, 1964.
2. N. Gregory Mankiw, Macroeconomics, 6th Edition Worth Publishers, New York, 2006.
3. Weintraub, A., Eli Schwartz, J.R. Aronson (eds.) The Economic Growth Controversy, MacMillan, USA, 1973.
4. Laurence H. Summers (2020), *Accepting the Reality of Secular Stagnation*, Finance and Development March, volume 57, No. 1 (PDF version).
5. Jacob Davidson (2016), This Theory Explains Why the US Economy Might Never Get Better, *Time*, March 25.time.com
6. Julius Probst (2019), "Secular Stagnation: it is time to admit that Larry Summers was right about this global economic growth trap", conversation, Doctoral Researcher in Economic History, LUND University, March 12.
7. Thomas Picketty (2014), *Capital in the 21st Century*.

16

The Business Cycles: Theory and Policy

16.1 THE FORMATION OF A TYPICAL BUSINESS CYCLE

One of the baffling problems that capitalist economies suffer from, is the business cycles (or, trade cycles/economic fluctuations) which have appeared from time to time in the history of capitalist economies. These business cycles are characterised by booms and busts in businesses and the whole economic activities causing mild to enormous disturbances in the economy. Thus, there are prosperity phases when businesses grow, raising incomes and employment of the people as also of the national economy which may be short-lived or may be relatively lengthy before falling through causing incomes to fall, making people out of jobs and bringing hardships to the millions of citizens of the country. The latter phase, the downturn of the economy, is known as *recession* which, if left unchecked, ultimately leads to depression. In some cases, recovery of the economy might take place before the depression stage is reached.

Business cycles are caused by a variety of factors. Based on these factors, economists have built various theories explaining the upswing and downswing of business cycles. Economists have also investigated the formation of bubbles and sometimes warned the people and the policy makers of their timing of bursts.

However, as the experience has revealed, most of the time, these warnings go unnoticed and finally the bubbles burst causing different sectors of the economy out of track which turn the economy or economies from prosperity phase to depression phase.

Figure 16.1 shows a typical business cycle, around a trend growth rate of a certain economy, starting with upswing, the rising phase of economic activities such as business profits, prices, incomes, employment and demand, gradually or rapidly reaching the peak of the cycle, continuing for some time before the formation of the bubble and then bursting of the bubble (or crash as it is sometimes called) when the downswing begins with slowing of the economy.

The next phase of the cycle, the recession begins when the painful period starts and all economic parameters, output, employment, income, demand, price level and business expectations are on the falling phase. All these have a chain reaction reflected first in the falling sales and output of businesses firms followed by employment and income fall and so on. The extreme part of the recession is called depression when the economy is nearly shattered. Then starts the recovery phase, may be well before the depression phase is reached, and gradually gathers momentum to lift the economy from recession with output and employment being in the positive territory. After some time, with support from the financial sector, the pace of the economy becomes faster and all indicators of economic and social progress are within sight once again. It goes on well on the rising path unless another bubble of some variety is formed and unless the policy makers are able to detect and suitable policy actions are applied to check it in time.

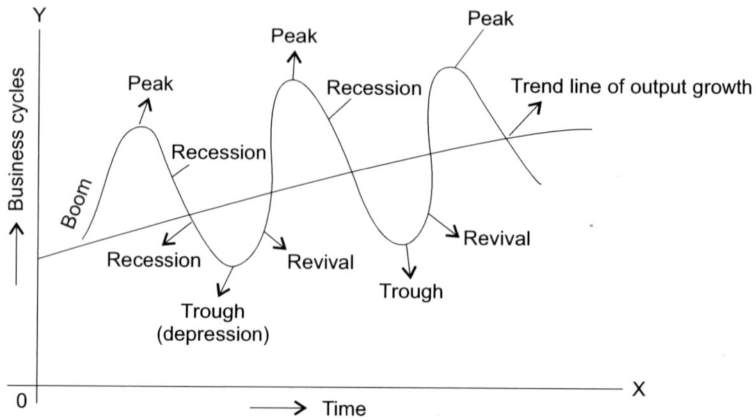

Figure 16.1 *A typical business cycle*

When the economy enters the depression phase, the entire banking and financial sector becomes panicky and loses confidence in the market so that they are reluctant to lend to the businesses and the individuals. It is this phase which requires strong policy intervention so that the economy can be revived and the cycle is reversed to get an upturn from the 'trough', the lowest level of the recessionary phase. If the policy becomes successful in bringing back the confidence and expectations of the investors and, most importantly, the financial sector is revived and begins lending to the market, the upturn of the cycle is said to have begun. However, one cannot predict how long the revival phase will take. Moreover, the revival may take various forms like V-shaped, U-shaped or W-shaped ones depending on whether the upturn takes the shortest, smooth but relatively longer or a jerk or double-dip type of recovery.

As mentioned above, the business cycles are caused by a variety of factors. Secondly, there are different sets of factors for the upswing and downswing phases of the cycle. We shall mention here a few best known factors as explained by eminent economists, right from the classical era to the recent period. Classical economist, J.S. Mill, in his famous book, *Principles of Political Economy* (1848), dealt at length the causes of economic booms and busts. According to him, booms or business prosperity are caused by some 'external shocks' or some "accidents", for instance, a new market that sets speculation at work. As prices rise, the sight of others growing rich "calls forth numerous imitators and speculation not only goes much beyond what is justified by the original grounds for expecting rise in price but extends itself to articles in which there never was any such ground: these, however, rise like the rest as soon as the speculation sets in. Price gains beget more price gains and a self-sustaining bubble forms.[1]

16.2 THE MAIN FACTORS BEHIND THE OCCURRENCE OF BUSINESS CYCLES

Joseph A. Schumpeter, one of the foremost economists of the Austrian school, examined the crisis in capitalism and viewed it in terms of what he described as *creative destruction*. Crisis occurs, according to Schumpeter, within a long process beginning with economic growth that results from 'innovation' by either a single or a group of entrepreneurs. In fact, Schumpeter developed a theory of growth known as *innovation theory of growth*. According to him, innovation is not merely invention but economic and commercial application of that invention. Even a new idea and its application, a new method of doing a particular thing may act as an innovation. Innovation, therefore, sets in motion a chain reaction to various activities gradually followed by others and allows markets to expand and raise expectations all around. Thus, innovations are responsible for the creative phase of the cycle. In this phase, incomes rise manifold, profits of entrepreneurs rise consistently and so do employment and price levels.

In Schumpeter's view, capitalism consists of waves of innovation in prosperous times, followed by a crucial winnowing in times of depression.[2] This is a natural process. The boom and bust cycle will end with the Darwinian principle of 'survival of the fittest'. Thus, only the ablest innovators / entrepreneurs will survive in the end. Schumpeter thinks that there is absolutely no need for government intervention; it is a painful but necessary adjustment process, the 'destruction'.

16.3 THE GREAT DEPRESSION: DIFFERENT VIEWS OF ITS CAUSES

We now turn our attention to the Great Depression of 1929-30 which was the turning point in economic history at least from two points of view: it ruined the economies of the large western capitalist countries and made them feel strongly for setting up regulatory bodies and secondly, it changed the entire thinking as well as the doctrine of economic theory. It inspired the greatest economist of

1 N. Roubini, Crisis Economics, Allen Lane, USA. p. 48.

2 Roubini, N., op.cit. p. 54.

the 20th century, John Meynard Keynes, to come out with his 'magnum opus', *General Theory of Employment, Interest and Money* which was published in 1936. The *General Theory* provided the world a new vista in terms of a set of theories which largely challenged the then prevailing Classical and Neoclassical theories.

Scholars have debated over the exact cause of the Great Depression. However, the general assessment of the crisis is that it followed the ever rising prosperity phase in the early 1920s mainly unleashed by the rise in stock prices in the USA. Inspired by the phenomenal success in the stock market, people, including those with smaller means, began purchasing stocks even by mortgaging their homes or with borrowed money with the hope of paying back the debt with their speculative gains. However, the prices of stocks increased to the extent of creating ' bubbles' which did not justify the growth in the real economy. Ultimately, there was a crash in the stock market, known as the Wall Street Crash which led to enormous loss of incomes of the people. This was followed by panic in the banking sector. Banks became reluctant to lend because they were not sure to get their loans back. The depositors too, with a view to withdrawing their deposits, flocked to their banks resulting in the bank-run. As panic was widespread, amidst falling prices of assets and goods, the situation worsened with people trying to liquidate their assets to pay off their debts. Thus, there were bank failures.

The result was that there was a great fall in consumption since the people held back their money being reluctant to spend. The investment demand too fell significantly because the investment sentiment (the so-called animal spirit of the entrepreneurial class) suffered a setback. Thus, the aggregate demand fell dramatically in the US, Britain and other western capitalist countries. Subsequently, the other countries of Asia were also affected like a contagion.

America's agricultural sector saw a great deal of overproduction and price crash while facing competition from other European countries. There was fall in agricultural incomes as well which also contributed to fall in aggregate demand.

Besides, in those days, countries were on gold standard; on the international trade front, countries were obliged to pay or receive in gold at a fixed rate, which created additional difficulties because of cheaper American goods abroad. While other countries continued purchasing American goods, the Americans reduced their purchases of foreign goods. This resulted in a huge trade surplus for the US. For the importing countries, however, this meant rapid depletion of the gold reserves. This led to the abandonment of the gold standard gradually, one country after another.

Since Keynes' view was that the main cause of the Great Depression was the dramatic fall in aggregate demand, he obviously recommended massive public expenditures to stimulate aggregate demand. It may be mentioned here that after the Depression years were over, public expenditures became the essential features of the public policy/fiscal policy of most governments.

However, scholars like Irving Fisher developed a theory known as debt-deflation theory. It suggested that during the depression phase, prices were falling a great deal (deflation) and in such an environment, people's debts were ever on the rise because the value of the debt was rising in real terms. To quote the author, "the very effort of individuals to lessen their burden of debt increases it because of the mass effect of the stampede to liquidate each dollar owed... the more the debtors pay the more they owe... the more the economic boat tips the more it tends to tip"[1]. How this happens is when debtors owe a certain amount of debt in nominal terms (e.g., $ 1000) and when deflation sets in, as during depression, prices of goods fall but the real value of the debt ($1000) rises. If the debtors as a group try to repay their debts, the prices of assets (as also of all goods) go down and so they incur still more debt. Thus, Fisher concludes, "debt and deflation which has wrought havoc up to March 4, 1933, were then stronger than ever and if left alone would have wrecked even greater wreckage than even after March 4"[2]. Thus, Fisher's analysis of the cause of the Great Depression lay in over-indebtedness due to easy money during the boom phase but debt and deflation during the bust phase of the cycle.

Milton Friedman, the father of monetarism (or, the Chicago School of Economics), had a different view about the Great Depression since he thought that the fault lay in the inadequate money supply by the central banks, especially the Federal Reserve Bank of the US. Friedman further stated that had the Fed Reserve continued the money supply unabated, the confidence of the market and the entire credit channel would have been restored and the economy would not have drifted into the Great Depression from what seemed to be an ordinary recession. It is worth remembering here that on one birthday ceremony of the great economist (Friedman) in 2002, Ben Bernanke, who later became the Fed chairman, assured him that he would not repeat the old mistake of the Fed, in case any such situation would arise. Bernanke kept his promise when the Great Recession following the financial crisis of 2008 took place. Not only did he adopt ultra-loose monetary policy by lowering the Fed rate to almost 0%, but he kept continuing money supply by trying unconventional monetary tools for a long period of time. The result was that the recession did not turn into depression although low growth and low inflation prevailed over a long period in the U.S.

Hyman Mynsky, a neo-Keynesian economist, who studied Keynes in great depth and analysed some of the neglected chapters of Keynes' ' *General Theory....* and *A Treatise on Money,* which deal with banks, credit and financial sector functioning has, in fact, proposed financial instability hypothesis to explain business cycle booms and busts. Mynsky believed that profligacy in the financial sector (advancing credit to the borrowers too liberally, often exceeding the justifiable limits), ultimately leads to the crash in the financial sector.

---

1 I. Fisher, The Debt-deflation Theory of Great Depression, 1933, quoted in V. Moorthy. The Neglected Part of Fisher, Mint, Delhi, March 3, 2009.

2 Fisher, quoted in Moorthy, op.cit.

"Instability", he wrote "is an inherent and inescapable flaw of capitalism which originates in the very financial institutions that make capitalism possible....this flaw exists because the financial system necessary for the capitalist vitality and vigour which translates entrepreneurial 'animal spirits' into effective demand for investment contains the potential for runaway expansion, powered by an expansion boom". This runaway expansion, Minsky explained, can readily grind to a halt because " accumulated financial changes render the financial system fragile"[1].

In his book, *Stabilising an Unstable Economy (1986/2008),* Minsky categorised three types of borrowers, namely, (a) hedge borrowers, (b) speculative borrowers and (c) ponzi borrowers, each having a particular behaviour during the 'boom' phase of the cycle. While the hedge borrowers use their borrowed money that they can make payments on both the interest and principal amounts of their debt from their current cash flow, the speculative borrowers' current income covers only the interest payments but not the principal amount. Ponzi borrowers, on the other hand, can neither cover the interest nor the principal payments. The only option left to them is to mortgage their future finances by borrowing still further in the hope for a rise in the value of their assets that they purchase with borrowed money. During the boom period of the cycle, the number of speculative and ponzi borrowers grow relative to the hedge borrowers. The asset prices during the boom go on rising and encourage all borrowers to borrow still more. But time comes when the debts cross the limit of their serviceability (interest payments fall due) and take the shape of a balloon. This is the stage for causing a financial crisis. Any failure anywhere by any institution could trigger the onset of bust as it had happened in the case of 'Lehman Brothers' and 'American International group (AIG)' in 2008 in the US economy (Roubini, 2010).

The financial crisis of 2008: In the US, the housing bubble and its subsequent bust in 2008 caused a massive financial crisis. It not only substantially reduced asset values of the thousands of investors but also ushered in a long recession which gradually spread to other countries of the world. We will briefly review the origin of the financial crisis of 2008 and how it impacted the US economy in subsequent years resulting in the Great Recession.

During the early 2000s, there was a significant shift in the US' housing policy in terms of providing liberal credit to the citizens and thereby favouring house ownership to all. This was, no doubt, a noble public policy since community living is relatively peaceful and ensures greater social welfare. Inspired by this motive, the important financial institutions were instructed to advance house loans at liberal terms. But, later on, with the gradual rise in the house prices in America, people, particularly the Wall Street people, dealing with financial market transactions, began to look for innovative ways of raising profits from

1 Hyman Minsky, quoted in Roubini, op.cit., p. 50.

the housing stock market. In the initial stage, the big loan associations thought of the mortgage papers to be converted into 'securities' (or bonds) called Mortgage Backed Securities (MBSs) to be sold in the market like any other bond. This way, the so-called 'financial engineers' hoped to raise speculative profit incomes of the investors as well as other stakeholders although at the cost of incurring a certain amount of risk. This was the first stage of innovation, called "securitisation". With further liberalisation of the loan market, banks, non-bank institutions and loan associations all gradually plunged into this game of earning ever rising profits. This spree of getting rich led the financial engineers to go one step further by dividing the house stocks/securities into smaller parts or tranches and selling them to the investors. For instance, if initially, one stock of $1000 million was issued, then lower valued stocks of $1000 each numbering 1000 stocks were issued by pooling together the earlier stocks. But since these stocks were risky of different levels, they needed some kinds of ratings by the rating agencies. So, in the next step, these financial experts approached the rating agencies and got these new bands of securities rated as AAA, BBB, CCC, etc., in accordance with their relative risk levels. Obviously, the first category of securities would be rated as least risky but fetching lowest returns as well. The next batch of securities, BBB rated, would be more risky than the AAAs with higher rate return and so on. In yet another stage of innovation, in order to make the more risky securities more attractive, they again pooled them together and sliced them into several new securities, each of lower denominations and getting them rated as AAAs, BBBs, etc. But, as in the earlier case, the AAA-rated ones faced no difficulty in selling while others had. This time they invented the 'credit default swaps' to guarantee any default in the loan repayment schedule. These new financial products were termed the Collateralized Debt Obligations (CDOs) in the next stage known as 'leveraging'. This way, the financial experts tried to make sure that the housing stock market runs smoothly while the system is insulated from any risk while the investors were kept in the dark about the exact character of the securities.

So long as the house prices in America were rising, the investors too were highly attracted to reap as much advantage as possible by investing in the housing stocks. But, once there was a default in repayment of interest and / or principal amounts, the entire network of the financial institutions received a jolt and the cracks in the system began to surface. So long as the default cases were few, there was not much worry. But as the number gradually increased, the financial flows to different stakeholders began to dry up which adversely impacted their own balance sheets. Ultimately, the financial market crashed. In fact, what actually happened is that many risky or toxic assets were made to appear as not so risky before the purchasers. Thus came the bust of the cycle with the biggest ever financial institutions, development banks, insurance companies and loan associations becoming bankrupt and the wealth valued billions of dollars was lost.

Now, the efforts began to rush to rescue the failed institutions with massive financial grants from the government treasury at the first instance followed by monetary policy initiatives. The US Fed. reduced the lending rate of interest to near zero to create an atmosphere of revival of the investment sentiment. Unfortunately, however, no improvement was in sight for a long time. Macroeconomists over the whole of the US came forward to criticise the wrong macroeconomic policies of the three decades long neo-liberal and largely unregulated financial markets. The 'efficient market hypothesis' propagated by Prof. Eugene Fama, – any snag in the functioning of the asset market will be immediately reflected and that if there is, for example, a rise in the prices of assets, that would signal its efficient functioning, hence, there was no cause of worry over the housing stock prices, proved to be utterly wrong.

The Great Recession of 2008-09: With the crumbling of the financial market and its attendant adverse impact on the real economy, output of goods and services began falling continuously for more than two quarters to qualify (technically) for the economy to have entered the recessionary phase. Unemployment rose to more than 9% in the US by 2010. The Industrial production fell by over 15%, worse than all previous recessions. Similarly, manufacturing trade sales, adjusted for inflation, fell by about 11% since the peak of November, 2007. The recession began extending beyond the national boundary and gradually spread to the European and Asian countries because of the financial and trade links following globalisation of the early years. In particular, the subprime related financial products like MBS and CDOs were purchased by the financial institutions of other European and Asian countries which saw their values fall dramatically. In subsequent periods, the inability of these institutions to advance credit to the manufacturing sector led to the recession in their economies. The worldwide recession slashed both production and international trade and the impact was felt most in the export driven economies of Asia.[1]

The Great Recession divided the macroeconomists of the US and elsewhere into two groups: the Keynesian group and the new classical group. The former (Keynesian) included Joseph Stiglitz, Columbia University Professor and Nobel Laureate (2001), Paul Krugman of Princeton University and Nobel Laureate (2008), Brad DeLong of the University of California, Berkeley, William Buiter of London School of Economics and others. These economists were vehement critics of neo-liberal and new classical policies of market fundamentalism, the so called 'efficient market hypothesis' mentioned above which favoured complete absence of market regulations. These policies continued to be pursued for the last thirty years prior to the Great Recession. According to the critics, markets are subject to failure due to imperfect information and lack of adequate regulations in place.

---

1 Reported in Mint daily. April 27, 2009.

In the second group of economists were included those belonging to the new classical school, the proponents of the existing policies. Prominent among them were Robert Lucas of Harvard University and Nobel laureate (1995), Robert Barrow of the University of Chicago and their followers. In fact, Prof. Lucas was so hopeful about the tremendous success of the market economy that he once said that his group of economists had been able to control the forces responsible for the business cycles at least for the next two three decades to come. But the economist's prediction failed miserably with the occurrence of financial crisis and the Great Recession of 2008. When asked about why the macroeconomists turned a blind eye to the formation of bubbles in the financial market and failed to give signals to the impending dangers of big recession coming, these economists simply avoided by saying that the macroeconomists had much less business meddling with finance and the financial market functioning.

On the Great Recession, the critics further argued that the economists missed the origin of the crisis, failed to appreciate its worst symptoms and then could not agree about the cure. In other words, the economists misread the economy on the way up, misread the way down and now mistook the right way out. Many of them thought that the housing bubble would pop or the dollar would fall but they did not expect the financial system would break. .... Most were quite sanguine about the prospect of Lehman Brothers, too big to fall.[1] The critics further accused the proponents of the new policy of failing to have learnt from the great masters of the past like Keynes, Fisher and Minsky. As the Chinese economist, Prof. Fan Gang remarked rightly that the problem for the world economy is that everybody remembers Keynes' lesson about the need for counter cyclical policies only when the crisis erupts after demanding to be left alone, with no symmetric policy intervention, during the preceding boom. But managing the boom is more important because it addresses what causes the crisis in the first place.

The early revival efforts of the great recession: The government of the US initially began with the fiscal policy response by releasing big bailout funds which included the bailout of certain failed or bankraft financial institutions.

At the same time, the Federal Reserve, US central bank, reacted initially with monetary policy by lowering the Fed rate almost near zero, thus sending a signal that banking and financial institutions would lower their rates of lending. However, for a considerable period of time, monetary policy didn't seem to work since banks were reluctant to lend and wanted to protect their reserves as far as possible. In effect, Keynesian "liquidity trap" seemed very much at work. The then Federal Reserve Chairman Ben Bernanke, however, tried several other non-conventional monetary policy tools such as buying some toxic assets with Fed fund and certain other monetary interventions in the financial sector. Reduction of Fed policy rate in US to zero was followed by other central banks of European

1 The Economist, July 18, 2009.

countries since, by that time, recession had already hit their economies as well like the contagion of a disease.

What was required now was a big push fiscal stimulus in the form of public expenditures programme as also certain tax relief to the citizens. President Barack Obama had earlier announced a $250 billion bail out plan for the banking sector, half of which was to go to big banks reporting bankruptcy while the rest half was to be given to smaller banks needing rescue capital. However, the first fiscal stimulus bill was passed by the US Congress, amid controversies among members, in January 2008 thereby approving $152 billion package of tax breaks granted to individuals and businesses. Later, American Recovery and Reinvestment Act 2009, was passed approving a massive $787 billion towards a wide range of fiscal stimulus. Of this, government expenditure on goods and services took the lion's share while expenditures on infrastructure and energy projects and miscellaneous items of public expenditure including health care and education got the rest. Besides the above, a substantial amount was earmarked to tax-credits and tax cuts to citizens ($237 billion), and on other social welfare programmes such as unemployment allowances, old age welfare schemes, etc. Keeping in view the global nature of great recession, the heads of G-20 countries met in London on 2nd April 2009 and resolved to release $1.1 trillion as further stimulus package to be executed through IMF besides agreeing to create $250 billion of SDRs (Special Drawing Rights) with IMF. The critics, however, blamed the G-20 meet for failing to take concrete steps to solve some of the burning issues afflicting the functioning of the world economy such as dominance of dollar as reserve currency, global liquidity and a system to tackle financial crisis in future.

At a later stage, when conventional monetary policy measures failed to respond and the economy did not show signs of revival, the then US Fed Chairman, Ben Bernanke, started adopting non-conventional monetary policy measures like (a) large-scale asset purchases of US government bonds from the market and releasing dollars with the hope of creating demand through the purchasing power in the economy. These asset purchase programmes were designated as Quantitative Easing (QE) programmes. From 2008 onwards, the Fed. started releasing dollars through QEs till 2016 in different instalments amounting to trillions of dollars. Alongside, a very low rate of interest was also announced earlier, representing ultra loose monetary policy. Unfortunately, however, these monetary policy measures failed to revive the financial sector and the economy. On the contrary, the new dollars, instead of being invested in reviving the domestic economy, were invested in the overseas markets of the emerging economies including India where relatively the rates of interest were higher and thereby earning better returns of their investments.

However, many economists were critical of using this ultra loose monetary policy for too long thereby creating an unbalanced and divisive world economy where continuous dollar inflows to the emerging economies created inflationary conditions thus wiping out much of the competitive advantage of such economies.

By the end of 2015 and beginning of 2016, the US economy began showing signs of revival from low growth as well a low and subdued inflation while the E.U. countries and Japan still continued to remain low growth economies which had also followed the US like quantitative easing (QE) programmes to stimulate their own economies. It may not be unfair to conclude that the advanced economies could not fully recover from the recession–effects till date with growth being tepid and inflation not being consistent with growth.

The Coronavirus (COVID-19)-triggered Recession of 2019-20: A new brand of recession arising out of a global coronavirus outbreak, a deadly viral infection originated in China in late December, 2019, but which subsequently engulfed as many as 180 countries of the world by the third week of March, 2020 is now assuming a threatening proportion in terms of its infection rate as well as fatalities. In China, 3231 people reportedly died while the number of infected people stood at more than 20000. In countries like Italy, Iran, US, France, Germany, Britain and Spain, the casualties as well as the number infected were relatively large while in other countries the number of deaths or infected were rapidly rising. The international organisation like the World Health Organization declared the outbreak of the pandemic as a 'health emergency' for the whole world. By the end of June, 2020, the number of infected cases reached nearly 10 million worldwide with fatalities reaching 5 lakhs while by the third week of September 2020, these figures rose to above 30 million and 9.5 lakh, respectively.

In India, the virus reached late, sometime in late February, 2020 but seemed to be threatening with first appearing in small parts of the country but gradually covering almost the entire country. Also, the most cases of infected persons seemed to be 'imported' in the sense that it was carried through the foreign tourists or through the Indian nationals who had returned recently from their foreign tours. However, this new virus gradually began infecting many more people through social contacts with one another.

The significant fact about the COVID-19 virus is that no preventive medicine had been found by this time, to arrest the spread of this disease hence it was called the new Coronavirus. There is also no curative medicine either available till date. Till the third week of March, 2020, the total number of infected cases reached nearly 5,00,000 while more than 20,000 people died of this viral disease over the world with the number daily increasing. There is, no doubt, Corona virus has become the most challenging menace before the governments of the world as well as the international institutions like World Health Organizations, World Bank and the IMF and has resulted in almost standstill position of the economies of the world because of the lockdown policy adopted by most of them which has been recommended as the only precautionary/preventive measure to check the spread of the pandemic. What is more significant about this virus is its pattern of spread such that in the beginning, it spreads slowly particularly till it reaches the second stage. But thereafter, that is, as soon as it enters the third stage, it multiplies rapidly and results in the community transmission of the disease. The evidence from different medical reports suggest that while in the first 67 days of its infection, it has been able to infect about 1,00,000 people, it took only 11 days to infect another 1,00,000 people and only four days to cause another 1,00,000 infections. In other words, at the later stage, the virus continues to grow 'exponentially'.

No doubt, a certain number of patients are recovering by sheer strength of their immunity when properly kept in isolation in hospitals and taken care of by the medical personnel. But the rate of recovery of such patients is not above 10% of the number infected. In the early period, China recorded a higher number of patients with a rapid rate of rise. However, subsequently, it has been able to contain the spread and the rate gradually slowed with lower numbers reported although it has not yet been completely freed from the scourge of the disease till date (end of March, 2020).

It is worth mentioning here that certain countries of the east Asia such as South Korea, Singapore, Vietnam, Taiwan, etc., were able to contain the spread of the virus by their strict public hygienic policy of early testing of the infection, in fact, South Korea followed the policy of completely testing each member of its population, and then isolating them for further treatment, thereby achieving great deal of success. However, for larger countries like India, the task is extremely difficult, short of adequate testing facilities, supply of testing kits, personal protective equipment (PPEs) and the number of hospitals and medical and paramedical staff.

Among advanced countries, the position of the US is worst in terms of the number of infected patients and the number of deaths occurred followed by Italy, Spain, France, Germany and other EU countries as reported till 31st March, 2020.

According to the World Health Organization (WHO), the COVID-19 pandemic "is one of humanity's darkest hours". According to the IMF, the current COVID-19 induced recession is worse than the 2008 recession and even comparable to the 1929-30 Great Depression.

The economic impact of COVID-19: After the outbreak of COVID-19 pandemic over the whole world, countries have been adopting different strategies to fight the virus. Since, this virus has been found to be spreading through human contacts in a complex way and also there is no proven vaccine available till date, one consensus view that has emerged and which also got the approval of the WHO is the complete or partial lockdown of the area or areas where the disease occurred and then systematically isolating the individual cases for further treatment. The other agreed upon effective measure is the social distancing, that is, leaving sufficient space (about 1 to 1.5 metres) between two individuals when they come out of their houses for essential work with their face masks on as a mandatory measure and an advisory to frequently wash their hands with soaps or sanitisers. For those suspected to be infected need to be completely isolated for a certain period not less than two weeks.

The above mentioned measures, particularly the lockdown of the country, partially or wholly, however important they may prove to be, from the point of view of public health, obviously have a great adverse effect on the economic and social life of the masses and the economy at large. In fact, the public authorities including the policy makers are faced with a dilemma between saving the life and saving the livelihood of the people. In the western countries like the US, UK, Italy and others, the policy response from the government side is centred around a trade-off between saving the lives of the people and the livelihoods at large given the limited resources of medical facilities relative to the sharply rising virus infected cases demanding proper testing, ICUs and ventilators. The so-called trade off mentioned above became a topic of hot discussion in a country like India also. However, it must be said that there is absolutely no place for such debate. Human lives are uppermost and must be saved on a priority basis. If the virus is brought under control by a sizable proportion, then appropriate policy should be devised to gradually reopen the various segments of the economy on priority basis. Perhaps this paramount goal that the government of India set before it prompted it to go in for a policy of complete lockdown of the country as announced on 25th March, 2020 for a period of 21 days followed by an extension by another 19 days thus totalling 40 days at a stretch. There was further extension of lockdown till 31st May, 2020 in four phases in all. This was the strictest lockdown world over almost crippling the economic and social life of the people. Perhaps the most pathetic fall out of this lockdown was witnessed when the migrant labourers who had migrated to big cities like Mumbai, Delhi, Surat, Ahmedabad, Amritsar and Bengaluru were given to understand that their factories have been shut for an indefinite period and they were virtually forced to take a drastic decision to walking down hundreds of miles to their homeward journey resulting in several deaths on the way. This pitiful incident might have been due to the co-ordination failure among the three players, the workers, the factory owners/ employers and the government.

At a later stage, the government realised that both life and livelihood have to be taken care of with proper protective measures since the respite from the virus seemed far away until a vaccine was discovered and made available to the general public. The government thus adopted the policy of unlocking the economy in a staggered manner on priority basis. But by this time enough damage had been done to the valuable lives and livelihoods and to the economic, social and other aspects of life.

As far as the economic impact of the COVID-19 is concerned, almost the entire world economy has been pushed to another Great Recession which is evident from the fact that the whole production and distribution machinery has been disrupted. The transportation system has been suspended, the rail, air and road, except certain essential services. The factories have been shut and trade and commerce have virtually stopped functioning. The workers have been rendered jobless on a massive scale leading to unemployment. In fact, this recession has thrown up twin shocks at a time, the demand shock as well as the supply shock_and both of these are negative in nature. The negative demand shock has arisen from the substantial fall in aggregate demand, the pandemic has prevented the people to come out of their houses to come to the marketplace for making purchases or for the businesses to carry out sales while job losses have reduced their incomes. The negative supply shock has been the result of great disruption in the supply chain, the important raw materials, components and parts of the factories and firms have been blocked in the international value chain system which has become very complex in modern times. For instance, a number of factories located in China which happen to be the producers of relatively cheap raw materials or component parts for the producers of various final products located in other countries have now faced disruptions in their value supply chains due to the coronavirus outbreak in China's Wuhan province and the consequent closure of those factories.

The COVID-19 has impacted the different sectors of the economy differently. For instance, the transportation, hospitality and trade and tourism sectors have been the worst victims rendering many workers jobless, wholly or partially, thus slashing their incomes and purchasing power. In a country like India, a huge number of migrant labourers who usually migrate to the cities from their villages to seek jobs of different varieties and live in slums or slum-like conditions have faced pitiable conditions in the wake of lockdowns enforced by the COVID-19 pandemic as has been mentioned in the above paragraph. The education sector has got a setback inasmuch as the schools, colleges and universities have all been shut for indefinite periods. The hotels, restaurants and other food delivery businesses are virtually closed. Even the on-line businesses are in a dilapidated condition. The agricultural and rural economy initially faced a different problem. Here, the farmers raised their crops but there were no customers in sufficient numbers, hence facing oversupply conditions leading to price crash. In cities and big towns, on the other hand, prices ruled higher because goods were unable to reach the mandies or from mandies to retailers in adequate amounts.Similarly, a number of agricultural products like wheat in Punjab and various categories of vegetables were either facing the shortage of labourers who had left for home due to virus scare or lack of purchasers in the retail markets.

Meanwhile, growth forecasts for the world economy by international institutions like IMF and the World Bank for 2020-21 and 2021-22 have been made which are highly disappointing. While the IMF has projected that the world economy will contract by 3% due to COVID-19 impact and remarked that the present crisis is the worst fallout since the Great Depression of 1929 (reported *Economic Times*, 10.4.20), the World Bank along with IMF have recast their growth forecasts for the Indian economy at 1.5% to 4% and 1.9% respectively. Similarly, global funding and rating agencies like Moody's, Fitch, Barclays and Nomura have cut down their forecasts for India respectively at 2.5%, 0.8% and 0%. (*Mint*, April 24, 2020). The SBI's Research Wing has cautioned that the Indian economy may contract by 6.8% in the fiscal year 2020-21 while Crisil Rating predicted 5% contraction of the economy in the current fiscal. Referring to the loans to the MSME sector, the SBI Research wing further remarked that these loans will be of little use to them for why will they take on debt when there are no customers? It further suggested that businesses needed direct support like the government purchasing corporate bonds. Only then would investment, jobs, incomes pick up.

As reported on 15th April, 2020, more than 14 million Americans filed claims for unemployment benefits last month while the International Labour Organisation (ILO) warned that almost 25 million jobs would be lost if the virus is not quickly contained. According to a report in the *Economic Times* dated 9th April, 2020, the world merchandise trade was set to decline by 13-32% in 2020 and may rebound 21% in 2021 depending largely upon the duration of the COVID-19 outbreak and the effectiveness of policy responses." As we confront what may well be the deepest economic recession or downturn of our lifetime, we should aim to make the most of all potential drivers of sustainable growth to reverse this situation", the Director General of WTO, Roberto Azevedo said in a virtual news conference in Geneva.

"The decline in trade will likely exceed the trade slump brought on by the global financial crisis of 2008-09; as "today the spread of disease means that labour supply, transport and travel are directly affected in ways they were not during the financial crisis", commented the IMF. The IMF further remarked that this is the worst fall out since the Great Depression of 1929-30, "with over 170 countries likely to experience negative per capita income growth due to the raging Coronavirus pandemic", IMF Managing Director Kristalina Georgieva said while addressing on ' Confronting the Crisis: Priorities for Global Economy' (*Economic Times*, 10.4.2020). She further observed, "Today the world is confronted with a crisis like no other. COVID-19 has disrupted our social and economic order at lightning speed and on a scale that we have not seen in living memory". Observing that the world is faced with extraordinary uncertainty about the depth and duration of this crisis, she said that it is already clear, however, that the global growth will turn sharply negative in 2020. The US Commerce Department announced in late April, 2020, that the US GDP fell by 4.8%, the worst economic decline since 2008 during the quarterly drop (January-March).

While the economies over the world were on a contraction track with differences at the country levels, responses at the policy levels were pouring in by various international institutions like IMF, World Bank, Asian Development Bank and the individual sovereign governments. These policy responses covered largely the monetary, fiscal and health and pandemic related measures while at the same time, researches on COVID-19 vaccines were initiated at nearly a hundred centres over the world. But the rate of infection of this deadly virus continued to rise in spite of other precautionary measures taken at the individual or community levels.

On 25th May, 2020, the European Union unveiled a big fiscal recovery package of € 750 billion ($ 826 billion) for its 27 economies while Japan approved a new $ 1.1 trillion stimulus package that included significant direct spending to shore up the economy. With this, Japan's spending stimulus totalled $ 2.18 trillion or about 40% of GDP (*Mint*, 28.5.20).

India has thus far recorded the most alarming picture with regard to the progress of the virus and the government's lukewarm response to the containment efforts and in providing adequate medical facilities to the suffering masses. This is evident from the simple fact that India has marched from the 7th-8th position in the corona graph to 2nd position (after the US) as on September 18, 2020 and culminating in the infection rate rising to as high as ninety six thousand per day.

Meanwhile, the Centre for Monitoring Indian Economy (CMIE), in its 3rd May, 2020 survey report, recorded an unemployment rate of 27.1% rising from 23.5% in April 2020. India's services sector, accounting for more than 50% of the nation's GDP, collapsed to the lowest level in the world. The Services Purchasing Managers' Index (PMI) for India sank to an unprecedented level of 5.4 in April from 49.3 in March, 2020, the sharpest deterioration in services activity since IHS Markit started collecting data from December, 2005 (a reading below 50 indicates activity is shrinking). Added to this, the *Mint* reported that 27 million youth in the age-group of 20-30 years lost their jobs in April 2020 following a nationwide lockdown to prevent the spread of novel Coronavirus. (*Mint*, 7th May, 2020). In September 2020, came the first quarter (April-June) reading of the growth downfall for Indian economy which presented a shocking 23.9% contraction in GDP.

The policy response of COVID-19 in India: Unlike other recessions, this recession is markedly different in the sense that the recovery from the current recession hinges upon the progress of the corona fight, the availability of the vaccine for the infection for the general public and the efficiency of the government machinery in containing the spread of the virus any further. That remaining the primary focus, the government has, no doubt, responded with measures ranging from providing maximum medical facilities to other monetary and fiscal policy measures to protect the vulnerable sections of the population and also to save the affected sectors of the economy. The Prime Minister Narendra Modi announced the first fiscal package of about ₹ 21 lakh crore on 13th May, 2020 followed by Finance Minister, Nirmala Sitharaman's detailed distribution of the amount among different sectors. Earlier, the RBI had announced a slew of monetary policy measures amounting to ₹ 5.2 lakh crore followed by policy interest rate cut by 40 bsp (from 4.4% to 4%).

On closer examination, however, the economists have criticised the fiscal package of the finance minister as being largely, guaranteed cheap credit through banks to the country's MSME and other sectors while ignoring the direct transfer of funds and supporting the income loss of a large section of population. The current measures are largely the supply side measures which fail to address much needed demand revival problems since the recession has been caused by more a demand crash than a supply shock. In this context, a few comments by some members of the Monetary Policy Committee of the RBI, at the conclusion of its 22nd May meeting, are worth examining. Michael Patra, the Deputy Governor of RBI commented thus: the damage is so deep and extensive that India's potential output has been pushed down and will take years to repair. Governor Shaktikanta Das said "looking ahead, the growth outlook has deteriorated sharply. There is still uncertainty as to when the COVID curve will flatten. Even as the supply side is expected to ease gradually, as the lockdown related restrictions are phased out, it is the demand side which will continue to weigh heavily on economic activity for some time to come". Patra further observed that the spending patterns have altered drastically away from the "discretionary" to the "essential". The destruction of economic activities by COVID-19 and ensuing lockdowns is much more deleterious in terms of loss of basic livelihood, economic security, health and confidence than the range of estimates/projections of GDP and other macroeconomic aggregates suggest. The deputy governor added further that the large monetary stimulus and fiscal effort are striving to put a floor under the aggregate demand and, at the current juncture, the all out effort is to maintain and sustain with the hope that when the life is secure, resources, energy and time can be marshalled to rebuild and revive.

At this stage, a few remarks by Ruchir Sharma, the global investor and author, are worth mentioning in an interview (published in the *Economic Times*, dated 22nd September, 2020), Sharma said that the Indian economy is unlikely to achieve the same level of output that it had before the COVID-19 pandemic until possibly March-April, 2022 as he argued that two years of output growth have been wiped out. He estimated that given India's trend growth rate is about 5%, we will have basically 10% below our trend growth rate in the middle of 2022. This is the huge loss due to massive damage inflicted in one quarter (April-June, 2020) by the most draconian lockdown imposed by any country in the world.

The second wave of COVID-19 (SARS-COV 2), vaccine roll out and impact on the economy:

The first phase of COVID-19 attained its peak sometime in October, 2020 followed by diminishing case load as also rising recovery rate of the corona-infected patients. By this time, loud talk about the emergence of a number of vaccine candidates by a handful of developed countries and a couple of emerging countries brought a sigh of relief as well as hope to the world community. First, AstraZeneca, a British-Swedish multinational company in collaboration with Oxford University, announced their readiness to roll out its vaccine candidate, called AstraZeneca. The Indian version of this vaccine, called 'Covishield' was manufactured by the Serum Institute of India, located at Pune, Maharashtra. The second candidate, Covaxin, manufactured by Hyderabad-based firm, Bharat Biotech, in collaboration with Indian Council of Medical Research, also showed its readiness to roll out its own vaccine. Both these vaccines are, obviously, indigenous, being manufactured in India. Serum Institute of India, it may be noted, is adjudged as the world's biggest vaccine manufacturing company. Thus, when the first phase of COVID-19 seemed to peter out around the close of the year (2020), two India-made vaccines were set to be rolled out and available primarily to the Indian population.

On the other side of the globe, two big giants in vaccine manufacturing, Pfizer-BioNTech and Moderna in the US came out with their respective vaccines followed by Johnson and Johnson. Thus, while India started her vaccination drive on 16th January, 2021, as promised by the Indian Prime Minister, Mr. Narendra Modi, the US rolled out the vaccine around the same time. Subsequently, Russia and China also came out with their own vaccine candidates called Sputnik-V and Sinofarm, respectively.

In most European countries however, the Oxford-AstraZeneca vaccine was mostly in demand. Different governments in the European Union allowed the vaccine to be used by their medical professionals after meeting due regulatory processes. It may be mentioned here that in the initial stage, AstraZeneca faced an unpleasant situation of certain adverse effects following vaccination such as cases of recipients' death due to blood dotting. In some countries of E.U., the governments even stopped vaccination and demanded thorough investigation of such adverse cases. The public were found to be hesitant to take the AstraZeneca jabs. Countries like Norway, Germany and France even rejected the vaccine for some time. However, after several research studies found such events to be 'rare' and unrelated to the jabs, people resumed accepting the vaccines. Even in India, as many as 80 plus recipients met with similar adverse events after receiving the 'Covishield' (which is the Indian version of AstraZeneca).

Later, these cases too were dismissed as arising out of causes unrelated to jab-taking.

The plan of the vaccine administration in India

The vaccine administration in India (as also in most other countries) has been finalised by prioritising the various vulnerable groups of population as listed below:

1. To vaccinate, first, the health workers like doctors, nurses and other medical and paramedics who are directly involved in the treatment of the Covid-19 patients.
2. In the second category are included all the frontline workers such as the members of the police force, military and paramilitary forces including the sanitation workers.
3. The third priority group consists of the senior citizens (above 60 years of age) who are supposed to be highly vulnerable to Covid-19.
4. Then comes those above 45 years of age-group.
5. Lastly, 18-44 age groups of adults are included in the vaccination schedule.

The children group – below 18 years of age – have not yet been included since the vaccination trial has not yet been completed in India although in the US they have been recently included. Thus, vaccine administration in India got started in order of the preferred group but it lacked the required pace due to several impediments including the vaccine hesitancy among a sizeable section of the population. The major glitch, however, appeared in the supply-demand gap (supply falling short of demand) of the available stock of vaccines that led to a change in the existing vaccine policy of the government in favour of sufficient flexibility in the purchase policy of the state governments and the private sector hospitals besides the central government. Now, the state governments could procure vaccines from any manufacturer including the foreign based companies at any negotiated prices. But the new policy not only created confusion but also led to failure in arriving at a negotiating process. In particular, the dual pricing of vaccines to be charged in government hospitals and private hospitals/ vaccination centres; in the new policy was widely criticised by the public and several state governments. Meanwhile, valuable time was lost in the vaccination drive which proved to be immensely costly, which soon was evident with sudden upsurge of the second wave of Covid-19 (identified by WHO as Delta variant of the virus) towards the end of February, 2021 which fully played out in March and April, 2021. The second wave, being highly infectious and quickly transmissible, devastatingly baffled the entire health care system in India by simply overwhelming the health infrastructure—the hospitals beds, medical ambulances supply of medical equipment, including essential medicines, medical oxygen as also the medical personnel (doctors, nurses, paramedics). Over the whole country, the patients outnumbered the hospital beds on most occasions, the death rate of patients being higher than that of the first wave. At one point of time, the number of infected persons rose to over 4,00,000 per day with the total infections reaching 26,50,00,000. While before the second wave, the death rate was around 1% of the infected cases, during the second wave, the death rate went up to 3.5%. The second wave worsened the situation so much that it became the "cause of concern". even for the world community (WHO).

As on 17 May 2021. India became second, after the US, to cross 25 million cases – the last 5 million cases took just 14 days. A cursory glance at the progress of the virus is given below:

1 to 5 million	219 days
5 to 10 million	104 days
10 to 15 million	121 days
15 to 20 million	15 days
20 to 25 million	14 days

Source: *The Times of India*, dated 18.5.2021.

The second wave of the COVID-19 has impacted India the most in terms of severity as well as fatality caused by the virus such that the death rate in India during the second wave reached 3.5%, as mentioned above, with daily death counts being more than 4,000 the total deaths reaching nearly 3 1akh as on 20 May, 2021 while the confirmed cases reported were 26,03,199. At the same time, in the world as a whole, the Covid-19 caseload reported was 16,52,53,588 lakh. In terms of a simple graph, the progress of the corona cases is presented here which shows the peaks of the two waves of the virus (first and second) as also the flattening thereafter.

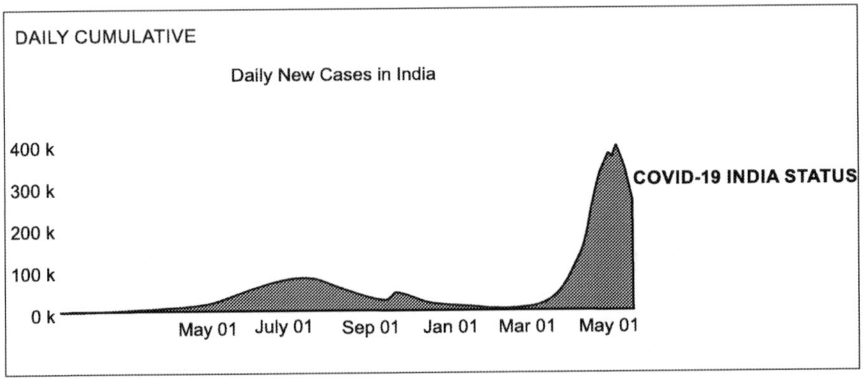

Source: Times of India, May 22, 2021

In States like Maharashtra, Delhi, Chhattisgarh, Punjab, UP and some other states, there was acute shortage of hospital beds, oxygen cylinders, oxygen concentrators which were highly on demand at the time when the virus was at its peak bringing a large number of patients in its fold and the cases proved to be fatal. The death rate too was high overwhelming even the crematoria so much so that there was almost a scramble for such places. There seemed to be a complete "pandemonium amidst pandemic". People were found to be rushing from pillar to post taking their patients along in search of oxygen and hospital beds but a sizable number met with failure with their patients succumbing to death. Even though the number of actual deaths is still not available, the official figures are much on the lower side. A recent study by Washington based Centre for Global Development, outlined in a report released on July 20, 2021 'three death estimates in India' all of which pointed to multiples of the official 4 lakh count. Even a moderate estimate outlined in the study based on extrapolation of state level civic registration from seven states, suggested 3.4 million excess deaths. In a second calculation, applying international estimates of age-specific infection fatality rates (IFR) to Indian seroprevalence data implied a higher toll of around 4 million. A third calculation in the report based on the analysis of Consumer Pyramid Household Survey, a longitudinal panel of 8,00,000 individuals across all states, yielded an estimate of 4.9 million excess deaths.

While the progress of vaccination in India was going on, by and large, according to prioritised targets of population, there was a sudden shortage of vaccines available in the country causing a big confusion among the potential recipients, vaccine suppliers, government agencies and the public in general. While the potential recipients of the vaccines were anxiously waiting for their turns, vaccine suppliers expressed their inability to produce sufficient volume of vaccine vials due to several supply constraints. Some of them, notably the Serum Institute of India — the manufacturer of the prime vaccine, the Covishield — at one occasion complained of the lack of order, public outcry was centred around faulty vaccine policy, the obligation of meeting export orders while ignoring domestic requirements. For example, people were made to wait for vaccine doses only to be told that there were no vaccines at the centre. Even the Supreme Court of India had to intervene, at this stage, and comment that the central government's vaccine policy was "arbitrary and irrational" causing concern to the country's highest court of law. We quote below the relevant section of the Supreme Court's judgement.

"Due to the importance of vaccinating individuals in the 18-44 age group, the policy of the central government for conducting tree vaccination for groups under the first two phases (healthcare and frontline workers and those above 45 years) and replacing it with paid vaccination by state and Union Territory governments and private hospitals for those between 18-44, is, prima fade, arbitrary and irrational". The Supreme Court further asked the central government to explain the rationale behind the vaccination policy. Specifically, the top court asked why the budgetary allocation of 3500 crore for vaccine procurement could not be used to inoculate this group (18-44) free of cost. Lastly, the Supreme Court reminded that the Union of India should consider utilising its position as the monopolist buyer in the market and pass down the benefits to all persons. The Centre and States/Union Territories operate in the service of the Indian population, and raise and disburse funds in their name. While concluding the judgement, the Court opined, "We find that the liberalised vaccine policy may not be able to yield the desired results of spurring competitive prices and higher quantities of vaccines."

The new vaccine policy of the Government of India

India's Prime Minister, Mr. Narendra Modi on 7th June, 2021 announced on TV, the new vaccine policy, largely replacing the old policy as also largely meeting the concerns of the Supreme Court, the salient features of which are as follow : According to the new policy, the central government would procure 75% of the vaccines and distribute them to the State governments, free of cost for vaccinating all the adult population aged between 18 and 44 years. The rest 25% of the vaccines are to be allocated to the private hospitals and nursing homes who would be allowed to charge not more than 150 as their service charge over and above their pre-determined prices for the different vaccines currently available in the country.

While the much needed policy change in the vaccination process was expected to solve some problems in this regard, the fact remains that even till date (mid-July), there exists a glaring shortage of vaccines in different parts of the country while the government at the centre is reportedly exploring different sources from countries including the US' Pfizer-BioNTech and Moderna. The Government of India, meanwhile, has announced plans to vaccinate the entire adult population (18-44 years) by the end of the year 2021. Several estimates have, however, suggested that this will be an enormous task given the current slow pace of vaccination and a large segment of the population to be vaccinated.

Economic impact of the second wave of Covid-19

It ought to be mentioned at the beginning that during the falling phase of the caseload of the first wave of Covid-19, the government relaxed the major restrictions imposed on the economy like lockdown and movement restrictions and gradual opening of the markets as also the transportation sectors. But, with the second wave of Covid-19, the government decided to leave the decision on further lockdown to the respective state governments depending on severity of their caseloads. As subsequent assessment of the impact on economic fronts has shown, the second wave impact was not so severe as that of the first wave due to the avoidance of complete lockdowns even amidst alarming situations of Covid patients dying and infection rate rising sharply.

We shall present below the GDP growth forecasts by certain reputed institutions—both the original and the revised ones.

Table 16.1 *Revised growth projections*

Revision in 2021-22 GDP growth projections by different agencies					
RBI		*Moody's*	*CMIE*	*W.B.*	*SBI*
Old	10.5%	13.7%	9.2%	10.1%	11.0%
New	9.5%	9.3%	8.7%	8.3%	7.9%

Source: *The Times of India*, June 10, 2021.

The above estimates have been made on the basis of the lower base of GDP of the last fiscal, i.e., 2020-21. Obviously, the estimates appear to be on the higher side. The RBI, in its June 16, 2021 State of the Economy Report, has clearly mentioned the loss of economic output likely to be about ₹ 2 lakh crore during the current fiscal (2021-22). The RBI's output loss has been factored into its revised GDP forecast as revealed in the Table above (Table 16.1). In fact, GDP growth had crashed by 7.6% in the last fiscal, the first such collapse in over 40 years (*The Times of India*, 10 June, 2021). The RBI has lowered its growth projection for 2021-22 to 9.5% from 10.5% white the World Bank has slashed its growth forecast to 8.3% from 10.1%. The State Bank of India (SBI) has a sharper slashing from 11% to 7.9%. Two other private research firms, namely, Centre for Monitoring Indian Economy (CMIE) and Moody's have also revised their forecasts on the lower side the latter to a much greater degree than the former.

On 27 July 2021, International Monetary Fund (IMF) also slashed India's growth projection for 2021-22 to 9.5% from its earlier April's projection of 12.5% citing a slow recovery in consumer confidence because of the ferocious second wave of the pandemic and a tardy vaccination programme. In its updated biannual World Economic Outlook, the IMF noted, "Recovery has been set back severely in countries that experienced renewed waves—notably India. Growth prospects in India have been downgraded following the severe second wave during March-May and expected slow recovery in confidence from that setback". The chief economist of the IMF, Gila Gopinath further noted that the Delta variant of the virus (Covid-19) is dominant around the world right now, and it has already affected IMF's growth forecasts.

The employment effects of the second wave

As reported in the weekly surveys of the CMIE, the unemployment rate crept up into double digits for the consecutive weeks for the first time since last year's lockdown, reaching 13.6 per cent on 6 June 2021 as against May's 11.9%. (reported 10 June 2021). The inability of the economy to absorb labour force has led to the loss of approximately 7.35 million jobs in the country.

As for the labour force participation rate, between May, 2020 and April, 2021, it fell to 39.98% from 40.7%.

Another CMIE survey report (ET 24 September 2021) says that India's swift recovery after the COVID-19 lockdowns seems exhausting and discriminatory as incremental improvement in job generation has diminished drastically and salaried jobs have witnessed greater job losses than any other sector.

On the other hand, the Government of India's quarterly employment survey of the Labour Bureau says that 2.3 million organised sector jobs were lost in the country between 25 March 2020 and 30 June 2021 when the government had imposed nationwide lockdown to contain the pandemic. As per the survey, 28.4 million people were employed across 9 sectors as on 1 June 2020, down from 30.7 million in March just before the lockdown. The survey further says that employment decreased due to the pandemic in 27% establishments and while 81% of the workers received full wages during the lockdown period, 16% received reduced wages and only 3% were denied any wages.

The latest CMIE weekly report dated 8.10.21, (E.T.), however, notes that India's unemployment rate fell sharply in September to 6.86% from 8.32% in August, 2021, on the back of the creation of 8.5 million additional jobs, most of them in the rural India, as construction activity picked up pace.

Income distribution effect

While the Covid-19 has depressed incomes of a large section of population particularly in the lower and lower middle bracket, there is evidence that those in the higher brackets have added to their incomes substantially. Several factors have contributed to this development. Even though people's savings have fallen in general many savers have shifted to the stock market and have taken advantage of the buoyant stock market conditions thus earning their incomes manifold from the capital market. This clearly indicates that the income distribution effect has worsened. The process has been facilitated further by the falling rate of interest offered in the fixed deposit accounts of banks and other non-banking institutions.

This situation is not limited to a developing country like India but is applicable to developed countries also where stock markets have been showing buoyancy in recent years even amid Covid prevalence.

Inflation impact

Following the pandemic, particularly the second wave, prices of certain items in the wholesale as well as consumer price segments have shown rising tendency in recent months. For example, there has been a spike in the wholesale price segment than those of the consumer price segment. While the CPI inflation rate (in terms of consumer price index) was recorded as 3.5% in January 2020, WPI increased to 10.5% in April 2021, thus showing a 6 percentage point divergence in the CPI inflation causing a concern for the consumers. However, normally, we observe changes in both segments of inflation data in the same direction but with different rates— WPI changing at a slower rate than the CPI— the current observation as reflected in the RBI study, is perplexing. The analysts have interpreted these data as reflecting, on the one hand, fall in consumer demand during the pandemic accompanied by the lack of 'pricing power' on the part of the producers. Also, there has been a rise in the food and fuel prices in recent months— fuel prices rising constantly over the period (reported in the *Times of India* 10 June, 2021). According to some economists, the recent spike in inflation in India is mainly due to supply side constraints— supply of essential inputs to manufacturing products such as fuel, coal and steel, etc., being hampered thus pushing the prices of manufactured products. The rising global commodity prices are squeezing producer margins and costs are being passed to consumers (Sonal Verma, *Times of India*, October 4, 2021).

The future outlook of the pandemic and the speculation for revival of the economy

The delta variant of COVID-19 is still active not only in India but also in major parts of the world including China, Indonesia, Malaysia and South Korea in Asia; Russia, Australia, U.K., USA, France, Germany and Brazil. In fact, altogether, 127 countries are, presently, remain affected by the Delta variant of the virus. Different vaccines are now being manufactured at selected locations but the question of unequal distribution of the vaccines, particularly among the developing and poor countries remains a big worry. It ought to be mentioned here that "COVAX.", an international initiative by WHO, has already been started which aims at solving this problem by requesting the developed and emerging countries (producers of vaccines) to channelise certain quantities of vaccines to the poor countries. However, much depends upon the progress of vaccination at ground level.

Outlook for revival

As for the recovery of the economy from the current slowdown, it is now being observed in different parts of the world economy that there are signs of revival of demand— both consumption and investment demand— in different sectors like manufacturing and services. However, it is still in the nascent stage and requires policy intervention in a big way. Economists expect that the recovery of the economy will depend on the revival of the 'pent-up' demand which has been slashed greatly during the first wave of the pandemic. Recent evidence, however, suggests the recovery of the economy is very much in sight in terms of revival of growth— particularly in manufacturing and services. As a result, employment growth has also picked up and the unemployment rate has also fallen. But, what exactly will be the policy requirements most suitable for the revival of the economy is now drawing the attention of the economists. Most of them agree that it is time that massive fiscal policy actions — public expenditures on direct income transfers to the vulnerable sections of the population, on infrastructure development including health infrastructure and compensation expenditure— ought to be taken up by the government. Certainly, such fiscal expenditures will be a drag on the fiscal burden of the government resulting in the fiscal deficit size being significantly higher than the budgeted number. The basic question is then how will the government meet these additional expenditures? The first measure, obviously, would be to resort to borrowing, both from the central bank as well as other banks. This can happen by way of selling the sovereign (government) bonds to the central bank (including other banks) as well as the public, which, in turn, would release money to the government to compensate for the fiscal expenditures gap. Although this is not a novel method (in fact, this is called 'quantitative easing') which has been tried on many earlier occasions by the governments of developed countries as also recently by the RBI (Government Securities Acquisition Programs, or, G-sec SAP), there is a limit to this exercise in so far as this may lead to building of inflationary pressures within the economy. At the same time, this measure may lead to a very low rate of interest regime which will not be in the interest of the economy since such situations will, most likely, cause capital flight from the country.

Some western economists (Chicago School, in particular) also argue for unlimited fiscal deficit under such a situation by directly printing money by the central bank (Modem Monetary Theory). This latter approach, however, has not found favour with Indian economists.

Notes:

1. Quoted, in N. Roubini and Stephen Mihm, *Crisis Economics*, (2010), Allen Lane, USA, pp.43-44.
2. Joseph A Schumpeter, quoted Roubini and Mihm, op.cit. p. 54.
3. Irving Fisher (1933), The Debt-Deflation Theory of Great Depression, quoted, Vivek Murthy, The Neglected Part of Fisher, Mint, Delhi, March 3, 2009.
4. Irving Fisher, quoted in Murthy, op.cit.
5. Hyman Minsky, quoted in Roubini, op.cit. p. 50.

SUMMARY

1. Business cycles happen to be one of the common features of capitalist economies. There are cycles in the economic and business activities— cycles of upswing and downswing characterised by rising incomes, employment and overall economic growth along with high expectation of future growth of the economy followed by falling incomes, employment and low expectation and other parameters. The rising phase of these activities, often result in 'boom' with most parameters at their highest levels. The boom, however, does not last long and often results in 'bust'. It is followed by recession—the falling trend of output, employment and incomes of businesses and individuals.

2. The recession/downtrend of business cycle continues until business sentiments are reversed. Government's monetary/fiscal policies, if applied properly, do help 'recovery' to some extent. However, if these policies fail, recessions may lead to 'depression'. In recent history, the Great Depression of 1929 occurred in USA, U.K. and other capitalist economies with disastrous consequences.
3. Besides the above short recessions have been occurring from time to time in most advanced capitalist economies with their adverse consequences on low income underdeveloped economies.
4. What causes business cycles? To this question, economists have differed widely. Some hold the view that very often, sudden discovery of certain goods, changes in technology of production and distribution (like industrial revolution' in Europe) cause great rise in economic output resulting in rise in levels of living of the masses and welfare of the society. Manifold rise in incomes and employment, ultimately lead to prosperity and boom. However, the downtrend of the business cycle may start with sudden "shock"—either due to geopolitical or other disturbances.
5. On Great Depression 1929 the scholars have differed too. While J.M. Keynes held the view that great and sudden fall in 'aggregate demand' was the main cause of the Depression, I. Fisher was of the opinion that 'debt' and 'deflation' were the chief causes that compounded the problem to lead to the Depression. Milton Friedman, on the other hand, held a different view about Great Depression. According to him, Central bank's reluctance to lend money unabated in the country like the U.S. converted a simple recession like situation to the Great Depression. Had the US Fed. continued money supply without interruption, the Depression could have been avoided.
6. The 'great recession' occurred in the U.S. in 2008-09, causing financial crisis of big magnitude with its effects on other countries and economies. This time, however, the policy of the US Fed. did not allow the recession to drift into Depression by continued 'asset purchase' policy and releasing money supply.
7. Scholar like Hyman Minsky advanced the view that disorder in the financial market and advancing reckless credit of unworthy borrowers were responsible for financial crisis leading to recession or even Depression.
8. Sometimes, big 'shocks' do occur in the health economy in the shape of Covid-19 pandemic and the like Covid-19 has caused both 'demand shock' as well as 'supply shock'—demand shock from sudden fall in people's employment and income due to countrywide lockdown in the

initial stage, while the supply shock arising out of sudden supply chain disruptions around the world as well as government's failure to deliver the right medicines and other health care products.

EXERCISE

1. Given a typical picture of business cycles in diagrams.
2. Explain which factors are responsible for 'prosperity' phase of the business cycles.
3. When did the 'Great Depression' occur? Examine the main causes of the Great Depression.
4. Explain the monetary explanation of the business cycles.
5. The great recession in the U.S. was due to 'over exuberance' and greed', discuss with reference to the great recession of 2008.
6. What do you understand by the 'black swan' event? Who coined the phrase 'black swan' and why?
7. Explain how the Covid-19 pandemic caused recession of different type. To what extent did it impact Indian economy?

REFERENCES

1. Nassim Nicholas Taleb (2007): *The Black Swan: The Impact of the Highly Improbable*, Random House, USA.
2. Nouriel Roubini and S. Mihm (2010). *Crisis Economics*, Allen Lane, USA.
3. Nouriel Roubini (2020a), "The White Swans that could set off the next major global crisis, *Mint* 24 February.
4. _____________ (2020b): "The Great Depression that we might be staring at this decade", *Mint*, April 30.
5. Kaushik Basu (2020), "Economic Policy must account for varied effects of epidemics", *Mint*, March 12.
6. Pankaj Mishra (2020), "The COVID pandemic will revive the idea of an all-powerful State", *Mint*, March 23.
7. Dani Rodrick and Stefani Stantcheva (2020), A Redesigned Social Contract for Altered Post-Pandemic Realities ", *Mint*, June 16.
8. Klaus Schwab (2020), "Let us prepare for the Great Reset of Modern Capitalism", *Mint*, June 5.
9. LN. Dutta (2014), *Modem Macroeconomics*, I.K. International Publishing House, New Delhi.
10. *The Economist, Weekly Report* (2021), Infections in India: The Other Side, May 24th.

PART-8

Inflation and Phillips Curve

17

Inflation

In this chapter, the readers will be acquainted with the following:

1. Meaning and types of inflation
2. Measurement of inflation
3. Effects of inflation
4. Theories of inflation
5. Inflation and unemployment–the Phillips curve
6. Phillips curve and rational expectations
7. Inflation problem in India

For convenience of discussion, these have been arranged under the following sections: Section I discusses the meaning, types, measurements and effects of inflation while Section II deals with major theories of inflation. Phillips curve is the subject of discussion of Section III. In the last section (Section IV), inflation problem in India has been taken up for a brief analysis and discussion.

SECTION I

17.1 MEANING AND TYPES OF INFLATION

Inflation is a situation of sustained rise in the level of prices in an economy. By sustained rise in prices is meant almost a continuous rise in price level. Price level here refers to the "general" price level which takes into account prices of all major commodities and services. Fluctuations in prices of some or all items for a very short period, do not necessarily suggest an inflationary situation. Figure 17.1 illustrates the condition of inflation. Thus, it is the overall continuous (sustained) increase in the level of prices that indicates an inflationary situation.

In any economic system, there are hundreds and thousands of goods and services being produced and consumed. When these goods and services are sold to the consumers, there are various points at which they are sold. For instance,

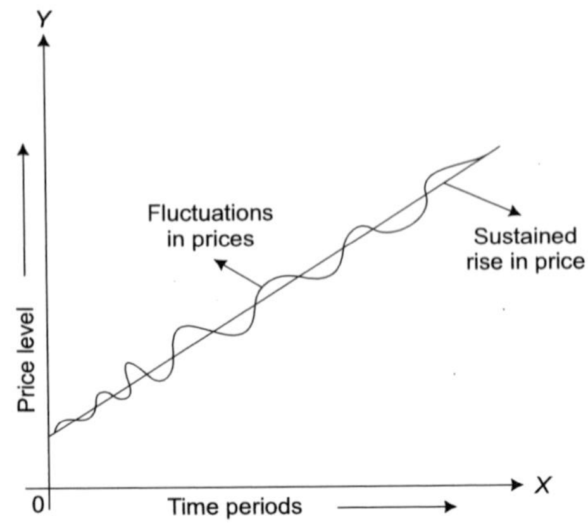

Figure 17.1

first of all of these are sold at the wholesale point — sold at bulk to some immediate customers — known as wholesalers. These wholesalers, then sell them to different retail sellers. These retail sellers ultimately take the goods to the final consumers. Accordingly, selling prices are not the same at all stages. Retail prices are, obviously, higher than wholesale prices to cover transportation, retailers' profit and other related costs.

17.1.1 Types of Inflation

Depending upon the rate or pace at which prices rise, inflation is often classified as: (a) creeping inflation; (b) moderate inflation; (c) runaway inflation and (d) galloping or hyper-inflation.

When the rate of inflation is very low such as creeping like a baby, it is known as creeping inflation. The rate may be as low as 0.5 to 1.0% annual in such a case. Normally, creeping inflation does not pose any problem for the economy and society. Nevertheless, prices keep rising and have certain social and economic consequences.

Moderate inflation refers to inflation rising at a moderate rate not exceeding 3 to 4 per cent per annum. This moderate rate, however, depends upon the nature and stage of development of an economy and the perception of the policy makers. In developed countries, inflation rate below 3 per cent is considered moderate. In countries where the economies are experiencing growth and development at relatively rapid rate, the inflation naturally picks up a higher pace due to several structural factors. In such cases, inflation rate even upto 5 per cent may be considered 'moderate'.

Runaway type of inflation exceeds 4-5 per cent annually and goes on increasing year after year reaching beyond 10 per cent. Such runaway inflation poses serious problem not only for the economy but also for polity and society at large. Political stability is threatened since this may result in social unrest.

If the rate of inflation is 'galloping' like galloping of horses, the result is very rapid rate of price level increase. The rate may range between 50 per cent or beyond per annum. Examples of galloping inflation are found in the post-war Germany and Russia during 1920s, China and Hungary during 1940s.

In more recent times, following Korean war in 1970s or whenever war-like situations occurred in different parts of the world, inflation of runaway type came to the surface. During 1970s, when stagflation gripped the western capitalist countries (US, UK, and other countries) high inflation was combined with unemployment.

Sometimes inflation is distinguished between '*open*' and '*suppressed*' inflation. Open inflation is the actual condition of persistent price-rise reflected in market demand and supply conditions. But, if by imposition of price controls, the government suppresses the rise in prices, it is called 'suppressed' or 'repressed' inflation. Such inflation generally resurfaces once the price controls/rationing are lifted.

Structural inflation exists when structural imbalances — either due to continuous supply shortage or demand pressures in some sectors of the economy — lead to the rise in prices. This type of inflation generally lingers for a longer period unless structural imbalances are addressed.

Depending upon the groups of commodities included in the inflation calculation and emphasizing upon responsible areas/ segments, inflation is categorized as *headline* inflation, *food/fuel* inflation, and *core* inflation.

Headline inflation (or, WPI-based overall inflation) is based upon wholesale price indices. In India, this is widely referred to as inflation rate. Food inflation exclusively takes account of major food articles while fuel items, particularly imported crude oil and petroleum products, are sometimes separated out or clubbed with food items. *Core* inflation is referred to the prices of the manufactured goods. In other words, core inflation includes non-food, non-fuel items. This is said to be the result of spreading of inflation to manufacturing sector.

17.2 MEASUREMENT OF INFLATION

The average level of prices is expressed by some indicator known as price-index or price-index number. At different points in time, e.g., once in a year, once in a month or once in a week, etc., data relating to prices of major commodities or groups of commodities are gathered by designated agencies appointed by the government or certain independent research agencies. These data are then processed and converted into index numbers with reference to certain base period. These index numbers expressed for different points in time suggest whether there is any sustained increase in prices or not.

As mentioned above, since the price levels can be collected either at wholesale stage or retail stages, index numbers, accordingly, may be either on wholesale prices basis or on retail prices basis. The index number constructed on the basis of wholesale prices is called wholesale price index (WPI) and that on retail price level is called consumer price index (CPI).

In India, overall inflation is measured by wholesale price index (WPI) although at the same time, other commodity groups' inflation measurement is also available. For instance, food inflation — inflation of major food items — manufactured goods' inflation, etc., are also available. At the same time, certain categories of consumer price based inflation (CPIs) are measured for policy purposes aimed at such categories of consumers. For example, CPIs for industrial workers, for agricultural labourers urban non-mannual workers are separately constructed and inflation based on them are measured in India.

17.2.1 The Inflation Rate

The inflation rate or the rate at which prices are rising, is measured typically by comparing WPIs (or CPIs) at different points in time and expressing the changes in percentage terms. An illustrative example of inflation rate based on WPIs in India is given in Table 17.1.

Table 17.1 *WPI inflation rate in India (April 2009–May 2010)*

Months	*Inflation rate (%)(Y-O-Y)*	*Month*	*Inflation rate (%) (Y-O-Y)*
April 2009	1.31	November '09	5.6
May 2009	1.38	December '09	8.1
June 2009	- 1.01	January '10	9.44
July 2009	- 0.6	February '10	10.06
August 2009	- 0.2	March '10	11.04
September 2009	0.5	April '10	11.23
October 2009	1.46	May '10	1.16

Source: Dept. of Industrial Policy and Promotion, Govt. of India quoted in *Mint* 23, 2010.

Here, year-on-year inflation rate means that the rates have actually been calculated on the basis of comparing WPI's of the concerning month (April, May etc.) with those of the corresponding month/months of the previous year. The rate of change is, then, measured and expressed in percentage terms. For instance, if WPI for April 2008 is 150 and that of April 2009 is 180, the rate of change will be (180-150)/150 = 5 per cent.

The negative figures shown in Table 17.1, for June, July and August, 2009 suggest that the average level of prices was actually declining instead of increasing. Similarly, zero rate of inflation (not shown in the table) would mean that, on the average, prices are constant. Inflation rate is also measured on weekly basis and is widely referred in media and policy circles. In fact, monthly inflation rates, mentioned earlier, reflect the average of all weeks of each month. Again, when we talk of weekly inflation rate, it refers to the rate relating to the price index number of the same week of the same month of previous year. It is also known as week-on-week inflation rate.

17.2.2 Base Effect and Inflation Rate

Since inflation rate is measured with reference to a certain period in the past, it may happen that previous year's rate may affect current year's rate even if prices remain unchanged during the current year. This is known as 'base effect'. For instance, if price indices (WPI) for January and February, 2009 are, respectively 150 and 160. Now, if price indices for January and February, 2010 are, respectively, 170 and 170 (same for both months), the inflation rate for Januray, 2010 would be calculated as [(170 – 150)/150] 100 = 13.3 per cent. For February, 2010, however, the rate will be calculated as [(170 – 160)/160] 100 = 6.25 per cent. Thus, inflation rate for February, 2010 is substantially lower when compared to the same period a year back. Thus, even if price levels between January and February are unchanged, the rate of inflation may show up differently due to 'base effect'.

According to the Annual Report of RBI, 2009-10, the base effect of high prices in the first half of 2008-09 contributed to low inflation during the first half of 2009-10. However, the waning base effect along with sharp increase in food and oil prices on account of lower agricultural production and increase in international commodity prices, specially oil, contributed to the faster rise in inflation during the second half.

The base effect, needless to add, may be at work in the opposite direction as well (i.e., in case of falling rate of inflation in the previous periods).

In advanced and some emerging countries like US, UK, Germany and some other countries of EU and Asian countries (Japan, China) consumer price indices are regularly published and such price-index based inflation rate is used for policy purposes. In India, although consumer-price indices for different categories of consumers, as mentioned earlier, are prepared, they are seldom used for measuring overall inflation rate. According to a recent information, the Government of India's Department of Statistics has prepared such consumer price indices which are likely to be used for policy purposes.

17.2.3 The New CPI Launched on February 18, 2011: A Report

There will be separate CPI data for rural and urban areas to measure inflation along with a combined all India index. A CPI for states and UTs would be compiled, which will help monitor the price movement in different parts of the country and provide as better picture of the price situation. The first series of the new indices, to be released on 2010 price level, would be available for five major groups: food, beverages and tobacco, fuel and light, housing, clothing, bedding and footwear and miscellaneous items.

"The present CPI numbers do not encompass all segments of the population and as such they do not reflect the true picture of price behaviour", the Statistics ministry said... It said, it was necessary to compile a CPI which takes into account the consumption patterns of all segments of population.

17.2.4 Inflation, Deflation, Disinflation and Reflation

While inflation is a state of rising prices (with rate either rising or constant), deflation is the condition characterised by falling price level. So, in this sense, deflation is opposite of inflation. Generally, deflation follows recession or depression in the context of business cycles. In such a situation, most prices start falling. In terms of rate of inflation, deflation can be expressed as characterizing negative zone. An example of deflation is the recent recession of 2008-09 and the resulting deflationary situation in US and parts of Europe (Greece, Ireland, Poland) where price level reached significantly low level. In India also, during the months of June to August, 2009, the average level of prices was falling suggesting a deflationary tendency but, thereafter, prices started rising and moved in the positive zone.

Disinflation: When the rate of inflation is brought down from higher to lower level (for example, from 10% to 6% or so) and the trend continues for some time, the situation is known as 'disinflation'.

Reflation: A relatively lower level of inflation which generally follows the recession/depression stage is known as reflation.

Figure 17.2 illustrates all four phenomena.

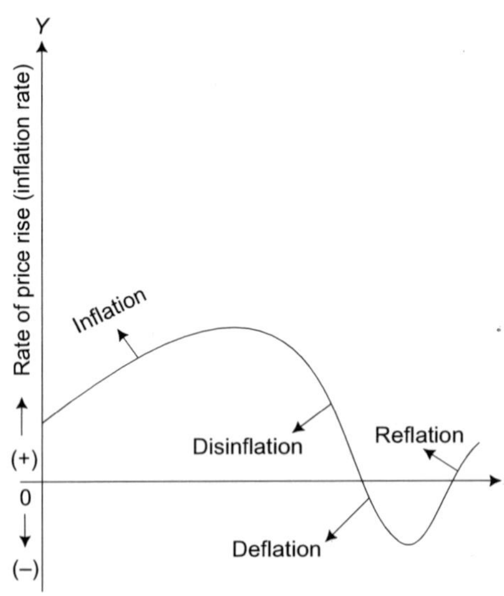

Figure 17.2

The commodity groups included in calculating inflation rate and their weights

In India, as also in other countries, the major groups of commodities are also segregated, although their weights differ from those in India. For instance, Table 17.2 shows some latest inflation data for the following groups of commodities.

Table 17.2 *Inflation (%) for the week-ended June 19, 2010 (excluding manufacturing items)*

Commodities	*Latest WoW*		*YoY*		*Average*
	08-09	*09-10*	*08-09*	*09-10*	*09-10*
Primary Articles	2.65	0.17	7.57	14.75	13.24
A. *Food Articles*	3.88	0.34	12.57	12.92	16.19
Rice	0.21	0.20	17.22	6.44	12.43
Wheat	0.04	0.31	6.40	4.49	10.33
Pulses	1.47	- 0.47	18.53	31.57	31.84
Vegetables	6.57	3.35	25.19	1.17	12.81
Fruits	4.96	0.51	5.09	8.74	9.81
Milk	4.5	0.0	9.51	15.91	14.32
B. *Fuel, Power, Light*	0.24	0.0	- 12.42	12.90	2.24

Source: ET, July 2, 2010.

17.2.5 Weights Assigned to Different Commodity Groups in India

Weights signify the relative importance of the different commodity groups in the overall final consumption basket. In calculating the index numbers of prices, when weights are assigned, they become weighted index numbers. In India, following weights have been assigned to different commodity groups.

Commodity groups	Weights (%)
1. Primary Articles	22.02
2. Fuel, Power, Light and Lubricants	14.23
3. Manufactured Products	63.75
4. All commodities	100.00

The weight used for food articles, separately and for different price indices (WPI, CPI-IW, CPI-AL/CPI-RL) are as follows:

Food Articles	Weight
Food (WPI)	25.43
Food (CPI-IW)	46.20
Food (CPI-AL)	69.15
Food (CPI-RL)	66.77

New series of CPI'11

Weights	R	U	C
Food Beverages & Tobacco	59.31	37.15	49.71
Fuel and Light	10.42	8.40	9.49
Clothing, Bedding & Footwear	5.36	3.91	4.7
Housing	—	22.53	9.7
Misc.	24.91	28.00	26.3

How are these weights determined? The weights are largely determined by the percentage of consumer expenditures made on different commodity groups and by different consumer groups. These weights, obviously, do not remain stable but actually change overtime with changing real income levels of the consumers. However, due to the limitations of obtaining consistent data on consumer expenditures, the weights are assumed to remain stable for relatively longer period of time, although they are updated from time to time.

Table 17.3 *Annual average inflation rate based on WPI (%)*

Year	*Primary articles*	*Fuel, power, light & lubricants*	*Manufactured products*	*All commodities*
Weights (%)	*22.02*	*14.23*	*63.75*	*100.00*
2000-01	2.8	28.5	3.3	7.2
01-02	3.6	8.9	1.8	3.6
02-03	3.3	5.5	2.6	3.4
03-04	4.3	6.4	5.7	5.5
04-05	3.7	10.1	6.3	6.5
05-06	2.9	9.5	3.1	4.4
06-07	7.9	5.6	4.4	5.4
07-08	7.6	0.9	5.0	4.7
08-09	10.1	7.5	8.1	8.4
09-10	22.2	13.8	5.2	10.2

Source: Dept. of Industrial Policy and Promotion/Economic Survey 2009-10.

Annual inflation as per different price indices (%)

Month	*WPI*		*CPI-IW*		*CPI-UNME*		*CPAL*		*CPI-RL*	
	08-09	*09-10*	*08-09*	*09-10*	*08-09*	*09-10*	*08-09*	*09-10*	*08-09*	*09-10*
April	8.0	1.3	7.8	8.7	7.0	8.8	8.9	9.1	8.6	9.1
May	8.9	1.4	7.8	8.6	6.8	9.7	9.1	10.2	8.8	10.2
June	11.8	- 1.0	7.7	9.3	7.3	9.6	8.8	11.5	8.7	11.3
July	12.4	- 0.5	8.3	11.9	7.4	13.0	9.4	12.9	9.4	12.7
Aug.	12.8	- 0.2	9.0	11.7	8.5	12.9	10.3	12.9	10.3	12.7
Sept.	12.3	0.5	9.8	11.6	9.5	12.4	11.0	13.2	11.0	13.0
Oct.	11.1	1.5	10.4	11.5	10.4	12.0	11.1	13.7	11.1	13.5

Contd..

Contd..

Nov.	8.5	4.8^P	10.4	13.5	10.8	13.9	11.1	15.7	11.1	15.7
Dec.	6.1	7.3^P	9.7	15.0	9.8		11.1	17.2	11.1	17.0
Jan.	5.0		10.4		10.4		11.6		11.4	
Feb.	3.5		9.6		9.9		10.8		10.8	
March	1.2		8.0		9.3		9.5		9.7	
Average	8.4		9.1		8.9		10.2		10.2	

Source: Dept. of Industrial Policy & Promotion, Labour Bureau and CSO.

IW = Industrial Workers, UNME = Urban Non-Manual Employees, AL = Agricultural Labour, RL = Rural Labour. P = Provisional

Table 17.4 *Food inflation based on WPI, CPI-IW, CPI-AL/RL*

		2009								
	Wts(%)	*Apr.*	*May*	*June*	*July*	*Aug.*	*Sept.*	*Oct.*	*Nov.*	*Dec.*
Food (CPI-IW)	46.20	10.42	11.72	12.24	14.67	13.73	13.55	13.84	17.61	21.29
Food (CPI-AL)	69.15	9.09	11.16	12.44	13.96	14.13	14.63	15.33	18.14	20.22
Food (CPI-RL)	66.77	9.09	11.16	12.44	14.22	14.13	14.63	15.33	18.14	20.43
Food (WPI)	25.43	9.04	9.56	10.80	12.67	13.32	14.67	14.24	17.78^P	19.77^P

Source: Dept. of Industrial Policy & Promotion, Labour Bureau; P = Provisional.

For purposes of computing the food index, the components of food articles in the primary articles group and manufactured products group are clubbed. The overall weight of the composite food index in the WPI is 25.43%, which comprises food articles with a weight of 15.40% and manufactured food products with a weight of 10.03% (after adjusting for oil cakes, weight = 1.42% and cattle feed, weight = 0.01%.

17.2.6 Inflationary Expectations

Inflationary expectations refer to the perception of the public with regard to the expected inflation rate in near future, i.e., in the short and medium term. Such inflationary expectations are, generally, based upon the following factors:

(a) past trend of price-changes

(b) government policy of dealing with present inflation

(c) current outlook about climatic conditions affecting agricultural output

(d) sudden changes in external and internal factors (such as rise in prices of crude oil, wars with any country or floods and famines of dangerous scale.

(e) some authors add current real interest rate, i.e., nominal interest rate minus the rate of inflation, to this list which together contribute to formation of inflationary expectations.

These factors are explained below:

(a) Past trend of inflation or 'lagged inflation' by one or two year period, according to some authors, contribute almost 50 per cent in explaining the formation of inflationary expectations.[1]

Thus, if past trend of inflation suggests a higher rate, the people will, most likely, form their expectations about the current as well as future inflation rate to be on the higher side. This kind of inflationary expectation is rather of adaptive variety. People are used to think more in terms of the past rates of inflation and accordingly adapt their expectations about future inflation rate. However, modern economists, particularly those having faith in New Classical Economics, think that expectations are formed on "rational" grounds. In other words, people form their expectations largely on current information of the economy and predict rationally on such information.

(b) The policy actions of the government, to a large extent, influence the people's expectations. If the government policy (such as monetary policy, fiscal policy or administrative policy) is seriously and sufficiently directed towards inflation management, people will begin to think that expected rate of inflation in future will be lower than at present. On the other hand, if there is confusing and vague monetary policy pursued by the country's central bank or other agencies of the government or the policies are unable to deliver goods, expectations will be on the higher side.

(c) In a predominantly agricultural economy like India where agricultural production is primarily dependent on rainfall and favourable weather conditions, the current outlook about climatic conditions, such as timely, adequate and regionally well distributed rainfall contributes significantly to forming expectations about agricultural output and hence future price trend of agricultural products. Secondly, agricultural products have a higher weightage particularly in constructing certain CPI-based price indices.

(d) Certain unpredictable changes which are either external to the domestic economy or internal, besides raising the current price level, affect people's perception about future course of inflation. Fuel price hikes, for example, very often act as 'shock' factor in determining inflation expectation. In recent years, for instance, oil importing countries have been rather forced to follow the dictates of OPEC countries which have virtually formed 'cartel' regarding price and output decision of crude oil.

[1] Machael D. Patra and Partha Ray, "Measuring Inflation Expectation and Monetary Policy in India: An Empirical Exploration", IMF Working Paper, 2010, quoted, *Mint* July 10, 2010.

Similarly, war with any country (e.g., Iraq-US war, Afghanistan-Russia US) involves excess expenditures of various kinds which not only push up the current level of prices but also raise expectation of future price-rises particularly if the wars are long-drawn in nature (in fact, in most cases they have been in the past).

Floods can damage crops on a large scale (as has been frequently in India and other countries) and create obstacles to transportation. Even though ravages of floods are temporary in nature, in the short-run, they can influence expectations about future prices of food and other primary articles.

(e) Lastly, as mentioned above, real interest rate (nominal interest rate deflated by inflation rate) affect inflationary expectations. For instance, if real interest rate is high, people will begin thinking that future course of inflation will also be high. If, on the other hand, real interest rate is low, opposite will be the thinking. In fact, actual inflation rate and real interest rate usually move in the same direction.

Most authors feel that it is inflationary expectations rather than actual inflation which is the cause of greater worry. If expectations about future inflation are strong, people's present behaviour will be such as to affect the present inflation to go up. On the other hand if expectations are weak this will impact the present inflation also to remain at lower level.

17.2.7 Surveys of Inflationary Expectations in India

India's RBI has been conducting surveys on inflationary expectations from time to time. Table 17.5 gives the results of some of these surveys:

Table 17.5

Survey round	*Percentage of respondents (who think price-rise will accelerate one year ahead)*
March, 2009	59.7
June, 2009	64.7
September, 2009	62.8
December, 2009	69.5
March, 2010	68.2
June, 2010	62.8
September, 2010	70.8
December, 2010	77.4

Source: RBI.

Another round of the survey was conducted between January and March, 2011 on 4000 urban households across 12 cities in India. This survey has captured the inflation over the next three months and for the next one year. The survey results show that 34% respondents feel that RBI is taking necessary action to control inflation while 39.6% feel otherwise. Out of these 34% respondents, 61% are aware that RBI's action has got an impact on inflation. As against the current expectation of 11.5%, according to the survey, households expect inflation to rise to 11.9% during the next quarter and 12.7% next year.

Further, the present survey shows that inflationary expectations of households have come down compared to previous round survey. In the earlier round, the inflation expectations for next three months and next one year were 12.4% and 13.1% respectively, while in the present survey, these are 11.9% and 12.7% respectively. The percentage of respondents expecting price rise has gone down for all product groups such as general level of prices, food products, non-food items, household durables, housing and services. (Reported *ET*, June 11, 2011). Similar surveys are conducted by RBI on regular basis.

17.3 EFFECTS OF INFLATION

Inflation, particularly if it is rising at a relatively high rate (generally more than 5-6 per cent annually) is said to be beyond tolerable limit for the economy. It has a wide-range of consequences for the economy, society and the polity. However, tolerable level of inflation generally helps growth process of the economy. We discuss below these consequences.

17.3.1 Inflation and Cost of Living

If prices of most commodities rise, people's purchasing power is proportionately reduced. Their cost of living, therefore, increases and finally disturbs the household budget. People are forced to revise their regular purchase plans and often have either to postpone or drop some current purchases. Often they have to resort to past savings or seek loans from others. Thus, household savings are also adversely affected.

Even if assuming that inflation is adequately taken care of by protecting the incomes of the people so that their real incomes remain more or less constant, people would not simply remain satisfied because they would expect a rising level of real incomes for improving their standard of living. If food inflation occupies a significant position in the overall inflation, as it happens in most low-income and underdeveloped countries, this may lead to public protests (street protests) and may often be the cause of political instability. For instance, recent global inflation — particularly food inflation has been a cause of worry and subject of serious discussion in international forum such as (World Economic Conference, Davos, Switzerland, 2011). According to a report from Davos, "higher food costs would have a significant impact in China and India since food accounts for 47 per cent of the basket of products that make up India's consumer price index and

34 per cent of China. In Tunisia, Algeria and Egypt, rising food costs — such as Tunisia's 30 per cent increase in cooking oil prices — have been a spark for street protests". In India, high price of onion, has, in the past, led to the downfall of the government. Even present Indian government has not yet been able to grapple with food inflation and is facing constant protests in parliament and elsewhere.

If, however, people's incomes are protected from ravages of inflation to leave their real incomes unaffected, the impact on cost of living is largely compensated. However, in most cases, particularly for unorganized sections of society, such compensation is not practically possible. Only if the nominal incomes like wages and salaries are linked to inflation (or, inflation-indexed) by payment of appropriate dearness allowances, the concerned consumes are relatively protected from inflation. The wages of labourers in the unorganized sector are immediately affected by inflation although their wages rise with a time-lag. But in any case, nominal wages are not able to fully compensate the rising cost of living.

Rising prices for food, energy and other commodities are reducing the disposable incomes of poor people across the planet, providing a trigger for street protests in North America and posing a deep conundrum for policy makers world wide. This is one of the issues on the agenda of the World Economic Forum in Davos.

Though the phenomenon hits the hardest in poor countries where people spend most of their incomes on food and to a lesser extent on energy it is also a worry in countries such as UK. New British data this week showed the economy did not grow in the fourth quarter even as inflation has accelerated that raises the spectra of stagflation — high inflation and low growth — that last hit Britain in the 1970s.

In India, CEOs of some of the country's largest companies cited quickly rising food prices as a problem because it hurts the poorest sections of India's population and could translate into political uncertainty. Zhu Min, a Chinese economist who advises IMF told one of panel that higher food costs would have a significant impact in China and India. He said the world was experiencing a three-speed economic recovery, with advanced countries likely to grow at just over 2.5% in 2011 and the emerging economies at just under 7% with US growing at 3%. Nouriel Roubini, a Professor at New York University's Stern School of Business said, political instability deriving from higher food and energy and commodity prices as seen in North America was one factor that could hurt world growth. However, he saw new risks between economic growth and contraction evenly balanced.

17.3.2 Inflation and Distribution of Income

Inflation has significant impact on redistribution of incomes in the society. In particular, incomes are transferred from the consumers to producers, business community and profiteers. When prices of goods and services rise the producers and businesses are the immediate gainers who experience higher profits, particularly in the short run. So, profit incomes increase while wage/salary incomes are reduced. For instance in India, according to a study of 450 companies by *Economic Times*, corporate profits in Q_3 of 2010-11 grew by 25% over the period year ago and this was largely attributed to current inflation rate which was 8.4% in December 2010. Rentier class, owning house property and other assets are also generally losers since they find their rentals falling in real terms due to rising price level. Similarly, interest income-earners are not benefited in real terms in the face of rising inflation. In fact, real interest rate decreases since the investors discount real interest rate as nominal interest rate minus the rate of inflation. For instance, if nominal market rate of interest is 8 per cent per annum and annual inflation rate is 6 per cent, the real interest rate is 2 per cent (8-6). In case the inflation rate is still higher, e.g., 10 per cent, then real interest rate becomes negative (– 2 per cent).

However, moderate level of inflation acts as an incentive to producers and entrepreneurs since in the allurement of rising levels of profits they would be tempted to increase output and employment. Thus, it helps the process of economic growth.

However, much depends on the major source inflation, i.e., whether it is the result of excess aggregate demand (demand pull inflation) or due to rise in input costs to producing firms (cost-push inflation) or due to supply shortage (separately discussed in the next section).

17.3.3 Debtors vs. Creditors

Inflation makes debtors gainers but creditors losers. Debtors generally obtain credit whose amount remains fixed (apart from regular interest payment at fixed rate). They are expected to refund the principal amount after the agreed period of time. Now, meanwhile, if the price level rises, the real value of the debt amount is reduced. The debtors thus gain in the sense that they have to refund virtually a lesser amount in real terms. Conversely, the creditors are losers in the same sense that they get back lesser amount in real terms because of inflation.

If, however, the creditors discount the expected rate of inflation in future and adds to the interest payment, they may be, at least partially, compensated for the loss on credit amount. But expected rate of inflation itself is not reliable since expectations are formed on imperfect informations. However, in modern times, most bank-financed credits are advanced on variable rate of interest. With change in the cost of credit (interest rate hike by banks) the rate of interest charged to debtors is also changed; hence, creditors are seldom losers. However, outside the institutional finance, debtors and creditors remain the gainers and losers, respectively.

17.3.4 Inflation and Project Cost

Most development projects are prepared on the basis of current costs of inputs and services. But very often projects have long gestation periods — longer periods of time to be completed. Some are launched belatedly. By the time the projects are completed actual project cost may be higher than estimated due to rise in several of the input costs resulting in frequent upward reversion of the project costs. To allow for inflationary expectation in future, some projects may have certain built-in flexibility. But actual inflation may be different from expected inflation due to unforeseen rise in prices of at least some input materials and services. Thus, inflation enhances the estimated project costs. This is true as much of government projects as of private corporate projects.

17.3.5 Inflation and Government Budget

Government's budgetary estimates are also affected by inflation. Expenditure budget is, very often, escalated and results in higher actual expenditures at the end of the fiscal year. Similarly, government's revenue budget (tax collections in particular) might be adversely affected since higher inflation implies lesser disposable income with consumers and lesser consumption expenditure resulting in lower tax collection. Capital expenditures are similarly affected. If expenditures are in the form of direct government purchases, the price-rise leads to higher purchase cost. Other capital expenditures are affected by inflation in the same manner as through project cost escalation. Wage-bill, in particular, will be pushed higher in total capital project cost.

17.3.6 Relative Inflation in a Global Environment

In an open economy where trade and investment relations are established among nations, international capital movement becomes a part of the process of macro-economic development. However, among other factors, global capital movement is influenced by the real interest rates prevailing in different countries. This, in turn, is affected by the relative inflation rates in the destination countries. For instance, if nominal interest rate is higher in India than in US, it is likely that there will be greater capital inflow from US to India for investment purposes.

However, if at the same time, inflation rate is relatively high in India than in US or any other comparable nation, US investors may become shaky to invest in India. After all, foreign investment flows are attracted by the prospects of growth in the country concerned and rising inflation rate acts as obstacles to growth. This is reflected in the fluctuations in share price indices. For instances, in India, recent high level of inflation and continuous hikes in RBI's interest rates have affected the growth prospect in the economy. The impact was felt in the sell-off of FII funds. Between January 24, and January 27, 2011 alone, the total equity sell-off was of the order of US $ 105.02 million resulting in BSE sensex falling to four and a half month low from 21,000 to 19,000, (*ET*, January, 31, 2011).

17.3.7 Inflation and Currency Exchange Rate

Persistently high inflation rate can lead to depreciation of domestic currency. If high interest rate can attract foreign investment in a liberalised global environment, inflows beyond the absorption limit may initially lead to appreciation of domestic currency. But accompanied by high inflation and low real interest rate, there is likely to be capital flight from the country . This will ultimately depreciate the domestic currency and have the adverse impact on current account deficit in the balance of payments.

17.3.8 Inflation and Economic Growth

The relationship between inflation and economic growth has evoked controversy among economists and policy-makers. Whether inflation helps economic growth or adversely affects it depends, to a large extent, on the level and nature of inflation; particularly the rate of price-rise and its sustainability. If inflation continues to rise in accelerated pace and takes the form of "spiralling" one — product price inflation entering into factor price inflation and latter affecting, in turn, the product price and so on — or if the inflation tends to become 'stubborn' in nature, the economic growth process is most likely to be affected adversely. Current inflation situation in India (during 2010-11) bears a clear testimony of this. In such situations, policy measures taken in one particular direction (for example, monetary policy alone as largely adopted in India) fail to tackle the situation. Most economists today agree that inflation, if it is creeping or moderate — rising not beyond 3-4 per cent and capable for the economy to tolerate or absorb it is consistent with economic growth. However, this again depends on the nature of the economy itself — whether it is a mature and developed economy or underdeveloped and emerging economies on the road towards achieving a higher state of economic development — the latter putting growth at top of their economic and political agenda.

SECTION II

17.4 THEORIES OF INFLATION

Inflation is a process of persistent rise in price level. Any theory trying to explain inflation ought to investigate this process. Among major theories, there are: (a) classical theory, (b) Keynesian theory and (c) modern version of a combination of demand inflation, cost inflation and economic growth theory of inflation.

The classical theory of inflation based on the quantity theory of money, states that if the quantity or supply of money is in excess of the total quantity or supply of goods and services, the price level increases. The total supply of goods and services is constrained by the total available productive resources. In other words, when productive resources are fully employed so that output is at potential level, there is no further scope of expanding output. In such a situation, if supply of money is increased leading to excess purchasing power of the people, the general level of prices must rise. Often this phenomenon is described as 'too much money chasing too few goods'.

In addition, the classical quantity theory stresses that price level will be increasing exactly in proportion to the increase in quantity of money. For instance, if quantity of money increases by 10 per cent, price level will also rise by 10 per cent. It is immediately obvious from this classical explanation that inflationary process can be controlled by controlling the quantity of money, since there is direct linkage between the two.

This simple version of quantity theory, however, failed to identify the channel through which excess money supply results in excess purchasing power and expenditure made by the public on available constant level of output. It was **K. Wicksell** (belonging to the Swedish school of economics) who identified this channel by pointing out that excess supply of money would come through the banking system in the form of bank loans to business community who would use them in financing new investment. The investment will be in excess of the current rate of saving. This divergence between investment and savings will mean net increase in aggregate demand for goods and services. This will ultimately result in higher price level. But, since consumers' real incomes will be lower now at higher level of prices, their money incomes, after some time lag, will also rise in proportion to price level rise and they will come back to the same earlier position. However, if the banking system continues to advance further loans to investors, this process of rising prices will continue. If, however, the banks stop advancing loans, the excess of investment over savings will raise market interest rate to equate with 'natural' (or, equilibrium) rate of interest. This will choke off investment demand and possibly also the consumption demand (via the encouragement of saving). Thus, the aggregate demand which was now 'excess' in nature will be wiped out. The inflationary process will be halted.

In the later half 1950s, a full-fledged monetary theory of inflation under the influence of Milton Friedman of Chicago School was developed. Friedman's famous quote "inflation is always and everywhere a monetary phenomenon" is worth remembering. A dynamic model under the adaptive expectation assumption was presented by Cagan[1] which proved that the rate of increase in price level was exactly equal to the rate of growth of money supply. The policy implication of this theory is that inflation rate can be controlled by controlling the supply of monetary growth rate and hence monetary policy plays a vital role in controlling as well as monitoring the inflation in the economy.

17.4.1 Keynes' Inflationary Gap Analysis

Lord Keynes, in his 'How to Pay for War' (1940), provided an analysis in terms of "inflationary gap" which is essentially excess demand version of inflation. Figure 17.3 captures the condition under which inflationary gap develops.

Figure 17.3 shows that *C* curve is the consumption function suggesting *C* as a function of real income *Y* as in the Keynesian income determination model. Let us assume there is relatively high level of *I* + *G* (investment + government spending) which has been made independent of the price level (for example, war expenditure). The total desired real expenditures at each possible level of real income are shown by *C* + *I* + *G* curve. If there were no limit on real output, income would rise to Y_0 where real expenditures would equal real output (at the intersection of 45 line). But if there exists a full-employment limit on real output, Y_p, real income cannot reach Y_0. At Y_p, total demand (*C* + *I* + *G*) exceeds total output leaving an inflationary gap equal to *AB* (in the figure). This is the amount by which aggregate demand at full employment exceeds output at full employment. This inflationary gap causes prices to rise. Now, the question is whether this inflationary gap will be automatically closed or will continue to widen leaving room for ever increasing inflationary process.

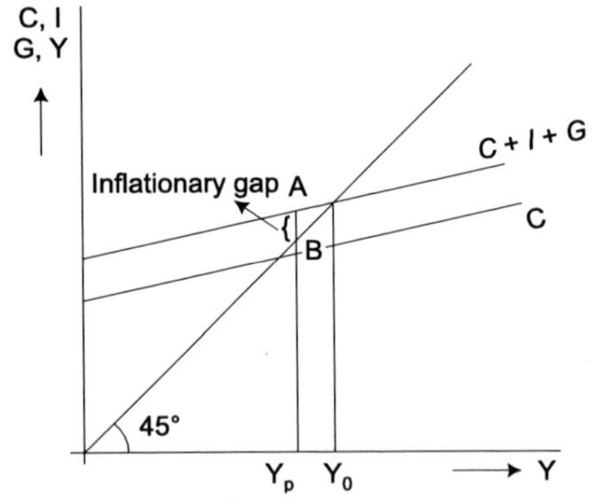

Figure 17.3

There are several possibilities on which this depends:

1. If money supply (*M*) is constant or rises in smaller proportion than price level, the rate of interest (*r*) will rise; so investment (*I*) will be reduced, thus keep reducing the inflationary gap. This may also, to a certain

[1] P. Cagan, "Monetary Dynamics of Hyper Inflation", in M. Friedman (ed.), Studies in Quantity Theory of Money, University of Chicago Press, 1956.

extent, reduce consumption expenditure (since higher rate of interest may promote savings tendencies).

2. Higher prices may produce "Pigou effect" by reducing the real value of wealth held in the form of government debt and other forms of wealth. In addition to this price effect, higher rate of interest means lower price of bonds. So bond incomes decline with its adverse effect on the consumption expenditure implying a shift in C curve downward. The inflationary gap is thus likely to be reduced.
3. With international trade and "net exports" (exports – imports) forming a component part of aggregate demand, inflation raises the domestic price of goods, so domestic goods become costlier relative to foreign goods. This tends to increase imports and reduce exports. The net exports part, therefore, gets reduced and the inflationary gap is likely to be reduced.
4. The redistribution of income in favour of the profit earners, as we have already seen earlier, results in lower aggregate demand provided the m.p.c. + m.p.i. (marginal propensity to consume and marginal propensity to invest) of the profit earners is less than those of the wage earners (which is the most likely case). So, inflation, through such distribution helps reduce aggregate demand and also the inflationary gap. However, given that permanent redistribution of income due to inflation is not possible and possibly, after a time lag, money wages tend to rise in proportion to price rise, inflationary gap via this route is likely to remain there.
5. The inflationary gap may be induced in case rising prices induce the consumers and investors to expect further price rise in future. This expectation may tempt them to purchase more and invest more in the present to "beat" the likely price rise. Thus, the current aggregate demand will be pushed up and the inflationary gap will be widened. On the other hand, if the expectation is that the current rise in prices is temporary and likely to be followed by price decrease even to a greater extent, both consumers and investors may postpone some of their current purchases (or, reduce inventories by investors), the aggregate demand curve may be shifted downward and help reducing the inflationary gap.

Thus, the extent the inflationary gap will be automatically bridged depends upon several factors. While some factors help reduce the gap, others may accentuate and widen it. In fact, the entire process of price rise is dynamic in nature and without understanding the underlying dynamic behaviour it cannot be predicted if the inflationary process will be halted.

17.4.2 Inflation as a Dynamic Process

Inflation is a process of persistent rise in price level. It is also a dynamic process in the sense that once the initial cause of inflation takes place, the process starts but the prices do not rise instantaneously. Prices rise over a certain period of time — may be over five years, seven years, ten years or more depending upon several other factors influencing the process. It may be self-propelling in nature or induced further by exogenous forces. It may possibly be halted or its pace and speed may be slowed by appropriate anti-inflationary measures. In any case, it is the rate of inflation which assumes significance.

The dynamic behaviour of inflation is complex in nature. Thus, ultimately, how much prices will rise depends upon the dynamic adjustment. In fact, what may possibly happen, once the process of inflation gets started, is that initial basic conditions which determine the size of 'inflationary gap' (e.g., the excess of government expenditures) as also the circumstances which might lead to the closing of this gap, could themselves change.

We now attempt to examine some of the factors which determine this dynamic process:

1. The rate of price increase (or, the speed at which prices rise) depends primarily upon the *size of the inflationary gap.*[1] Bigger this size, larger will be the rate of price-rise, provided all other factors remain unchanged.

With the help of a simple dynamic analysis (period analysis) in the following Keynesian framework, the dynamic process of inflation can be illustrated:

Let

$$Y_t = C_t + I_t = Y_p \tag{17.1}$$

where, Y_t represents current real demand for output, consisting of real consumption demand (C_t) and real investment demand I_t and where Y_p is a fixed potential output (full employment output). Setting $Y_t = Y_p$ means that we are assuming no unsatisfied demand; that is, all markets are cleared. The consumption function implies that current real consumption is proportional to current real income as shown below:

$$C_t = c_1 \left(\frac{(Y_{t-1})\, P_{t-1}}{P_t} \right) \tag{17.2}$$

where c_1 is the marginal propensity to consume and $Y_{t-1} \cdot P_{t-1}$ is the money income arising from sale of output at an earlier date. Dividing by P_t converts it to real income $\left(\frac{Y_{t-1} \cdot P_{t-1}}{P_t} \right)$.

From (11.2), inflationary gap (*IG*) can be measured as:

$$IG = I_0 + c_1 Y_p - Y_p;$$

$$\Rightarrow \quad IG = I_0 - (1 - c_1)\, Y_p \tag{17.2a}$$

where, $c_1 Y_p$ is the equilibrium consumption expenditure.

[1] We may call it any such demand-inducing shock.

$$I_t = I_0 \tag{17.3}$$

where I_0 is a (constant) real investment demand. Eqn. (17.3) states that all real investment demands are carried out regardless of current prices.

Now, by substituting equations (17.2) and (17.3) into (17.1), we obtain the following simple result:

$$Y_p = c_1 \frac{Y_{t-1} \cdot P_{t-1}}{P_t} + I_0$$

$$\Rightarrow \qquad Y_p - I_0 = c_1 \frac{Y_{t-1} \cdot P_{t-1}}{P_t},$$

By taking reciprocals of both sides we get,

$$\frac{1}{Y_p - I_0} = \frac{1}{\dfrac{c_1\, Y_{t-1} \cdot P_{t-1}}{P_t}} = \frac{(c_1\, Y_{t-1} \cdot P_{t-1})/P_t}{Y_p - I_0} = 1$$

$$\Rightarrow \qquad \frac{c_1 Y_p}{Y_p - I_0} = \frac{P_t}{P_{t-1}} \tag{17.4}$$

(since $Y_{t-1} = Y_p$; all markets are cleared)

$\dfrac{P_t}{P_{t-1}}$ indicates the rate of price level increase. Equation (17.4) suggests that the inflation rate $\left(\dfrac{P_t}{P_{t-1}}\right)$ depends positively on c_1, i.e., m.p.c. and I_0, the constant level of real investment (I_0 with negative sign appears in the denominator). However, the effect of Y_p on inflation rate is uncertain, since Y_p appears both in the numerator as well as denominator. But while in the denominator Y_p is independent in the numerator it is associated with c_1 (where its value is less than one). Hence, depending on the relative size of c_1, Y_p and I_0, the inflation rate is accordingly influenced.

A numerical example will illustrate the point:

Let $Y_p = 100$, $c_1 = 0.75$ and $I_0 = 40$, then

$$\frac{P_t}{P_{t-1}} = \frac{0.75(100)}{100 - 40} = \frac{75}{60} = 1.25$$

That is, prices rise by 25% per period. What annual rate of price increase this implies, depends on the length of period – length defined by the length of income-payments lag. For instance, if this lag is 6 months, prices rise by 50% per year. If the lag is 2 years, prices rise by 12.5% per year. Obviously, longer this lag, other things equal, the slower the rate of inflation.

The above model also suggests that the rate of inflation is a direct function of the size of inflationary gap. Let us take another example:

Let $Y_p = 150$, $c_1 = 0.75$ and $I_0 = 50$, then

$$\frac{P_t}{P_{t-1}} = \text{(Inflation rate)} = \frac{0.75(150)}{150 - 50}$$

$$= \frac{112.5}{100} = 1.125$$

That is, prices rise by 12.5% per period [(1.125 – 1.000) 100]. Again, if the length of the period is 6 months, prices rise by 25% but if it is 2 years, then prices rise by 6.25%. Here, in this case, the size of inflationary gap is smaller (since Y_p is higher) but I_0 is slightly higher — but not as high as to offset the fall in inflation rate. Obviously, as compared to the original level of $I_0 = 40$ in which case the inflation rate could be still lower), the rate is somewhat higher. Therefore, the inflation rate depends on both, the size of the inflationary gap as well as the constant level of autonomous investment (I_0).

Alternatively, we can test these conditions assuming given values of other variables (except any one) and verify if the same rate of inflation yields the value of the unknown variable. For instance, let us suppose mpc = 0.75, $Y_p = 100$ but I_0 is unknown. Then if $P_t/P_{t-1} = 1.25$, by substituting other values in the equation (11.4) we obtain:

$$1.25 = \frac{0.75(100)}{100 - x}$$

(where x is unknown)

Solving this equation gives,

$$1.25\ (100 - x) = 75$$

$$\Rightarrow \quad 100 - x = \frac{75}{1.25}$$

$$\Rightarrow \quad x = 100 - \frac{75}{1.25} = 100 - 60 = 40$$

So, $\quad I_0 = 40.$

Similarly, let us assume mpc is unknown while other values are known. We substitute other values in eqn. (11.4) and get:

$$1.25 = \frac{x\ \ 100}{100 - 40} = \frac{100\ \ x}{60}$$

$$\Rightarrow \quad 60\ \ 1.25 = 100x$$

$$\Rightarrow \quad x = \frac{60\ \ 1.25}{100} = \frac{3\ \ 1.25}{5} = 0.75$$

In the similar way we can also obtain the size of the inflationary gap.

From eqn. 2(a), the size of inflationary gap is

$$IG = I_0 - (1 - c_1)\ Y_p$$

In the given example,

$$IG = 40 - (0.25) \quad 100 = 40 - 25 = 15.$$

Now, let us suppose that the value of I_0 (autonomous investment) is higher at 50, then

$$\frac{P_t}{P_{t-1}} = \frac{0.75 \quad 100}{100 - 50} = \frac{75 \quad 2}{50 \quad 2} = 1.50.$$

That is, inflation rate increases to 50%.

Now, if IG increases to 20;

$$20 = 40 - 0.25Y_p = 40 - 0.25Y_p$$

$$\Rightarrow \qquad 0.25Y_p = 40 - 20 = 20$$

$$\Rightarrow \qquad Y_p = \frac{20}{0.25} = 80.$$

Now substituting $Y_p = 80$ in eqn. (11.4), we get,

$$\frac{P_t}{P_{t-1}} = \frac{0.75 \quad 80}{80 - 40}$$

$$= \frac{60}{40} = 1.50.$$

Again, the rate of inflation rises to 50%.

Thus, it is clear that inflation rate is directly related to the size of inflationary gap as well as the size of autonomous investment.

However, the simple mathematical (as also numerical examples) presentation may not give expected results because: (1) the rate of inflation may not remain uniform over the whole period; (2) within the period, so many reactions from different groups of society might be at work which may either speed up or slower the pace of price rise or even help closing the gap.

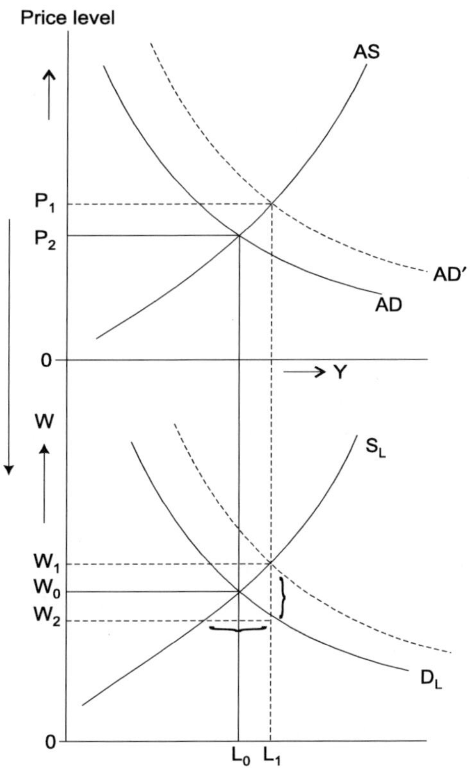

17.4.3 Wage-Price Spiral in Case of Demand Inflation

We have assumed, in the analysis of excess-demand inflation that all the markets are cleared instantaneously. Notably, the output market and the labour markets are cleared simultaneously. But very often this is not the case. Thus, while there exists excess demand in the output market — causing prices of goods to rise, however, after a time-lag, money wages tend to rise following rise in the cost of living of workers. Initially, at lower real wage rate, (since inflation reduces the real wages of workers) workers are unwilling to supply labour unless their money wages are also raised to compensate for the loss. So, labour supply curve shifts to the left and the labour market clears at a higher wage rate (demand for and supply of labour are equal). When this lag ends, there will be further extra expenditures in the output market since at new prices, the expenditures will be enhanced. Again, there will be inflationary gap in the output market leading to further rise in prices. This will be followed by wage rate rise with a lag. The labour market will be in disequilibrium leading to shift in labour supply curve. This process will continue until the entire inflationary gap is eliminated. This is the case of wage-price spiral arising out of excess demand in the output market.

17.4.4 Demand Pull and Cost-Push Theories of Inflation

The Keynesian inflationary gap analysis represents a variety of demand pull inflation. Using the general analytical framework of aggregate demand and aggregate supply (see Chapter 5), the demand pull inflation can be explained in the following manner:

Demand pull inflation can develop irrespective of the full employment level of output (potential output) provided one or more components of aggregate demand gets boosted – for instance, consumption expenditure, private investment expenditure, government investment expenditure or net export – and supply of output fails to respond to sufficient extent, prices will rise in the short run. Private consumption demand might be boosted due to rise in income levels of individuals arising out of better employment opportunities and government or private expenditures on various kinds of development and social projects.

Similarly, private investment demand may rise due to massive innovations, opening of new territory, etc. An example, in this regard, is the telecom sector development in India and elsewhere which have encouraged enormous private sector investment. Similarly, real estate sector development in India has been largely responsible for growth of private investment since these investment projects have been mostly financed by the banking and financial sectors.

However, the most typical of the demand-full inflation is the government expenditures incurred in times of wars or war-like situations. In the recent past many such situations have occurred (US-Iraq, Russia-Afghanistan) including constant preparations and arm-build up between India and Pakistan. These war and defence expenditures from the side of the government greatly boost government demand for various goods and services with immediate impact on the price level to go up.

Lastly, if the "net exports" of a country rise resulting in higher net incomes from abroad, these are translated into higher price level at home country.

Using the aggregate demand-aggregate supply framework (AD-AS framework), the phenomenon of inflationary process can be explained as shown in the figure below (Fig. 17.4).

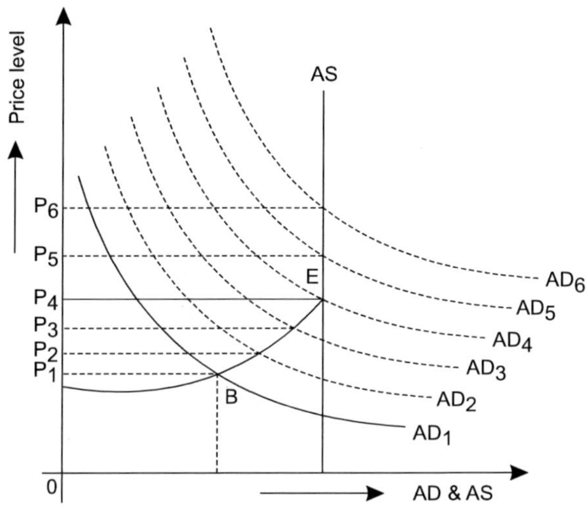

Figure 17.4

Given the original aggregate demand curve, AD_1, and short-run AS curve AS, price level settles at point P_1. For every rise in any the components of AD, AD curve shifts to the right, for instance to AD_2, AD_3 and so on and with it the price level also rises. However, it rises in response to the supply elasticity. Since aggregate supply curve also rises in the short run, price level rises but not quite sharply. Only beyond point *E*, aggregate supply curve is unable to respond to rise in AD. AS curve is completely inelastic. Hence, beyond point *E*, price level rises more rapidly — from P_4 to P_5 and P_5 to P_6. This is how the demand-pull inflation arises and continues unabated until appropriate demand management policies are applied to check the inflationary process.

17.4.5 Cost-Push Inflation

Cost-push variety of inflation is, in fact, the result of rise in various input costs of production being passed on to the price level of final products — by producers, by service providers, by businesses and also by the government. On most occasions, wage-bargaining by labour unions can act as market power in raising wage rates which are ultimately included by the employers in their product prices.

Mark-up pricing by sellers is one of the elements of cost-push type of inflation. In most situations, sellers add, over and above the total cost of production, a certain percentage to their product prices – known as 'mark-up' by sellers. In fact mark-ups are done to ensure a certain target rate of return for the producers. There are many items of costs which are "fixed" in nature — not directly varying with output changes, for example, in plant and equipment, big machinery, costs incurred on research and development, advertisement and administration, etc. These costs are ultimately so designed that certain amounts are additionally "marked up" in prices of final product. This part is not separately dealt but rather generally treated as one of cost-items. Besides these, the firms which acquire sufficient market power or market share in a more or less oligopolistic market situations, can and are able to raise their product prices even in the conditions of moderate rise in demand. The early phase of mobile revolution with only few market players saw the service charges as well as hand-set prices at a relatively high levels.

The most glaring example of cost-push inflation is the continuous rise in fuel prices. Fuel being an important input in a number of production activities, naturally finds its reflection in the price level of final products.

In agricultural production process, if prices of fertilizers, water charges for irrigation, cost of transportation or agricultural wage rates rise, these are normally reflected in higher prices of agricultural produce.

If government imposes levies or taxes on any item of industrial product, agricultural product/ inputs or services of any kind, prices of related products are bound to go up.

Cost-push inflation can be illustrated with the help of cost curves that characterize individual producing firms. As we know from microeconomics, short-run cost curves can be shown in terms of marginal cost and average cost curves. We also know that the industry supply curve can be derived from the firm-level marginal cost curves. Now, when raw material costs rise (or, any item of variable costs rises) for firms, their marginal cost curve (and, of course, associated average cost curve) shift upward for each level of output as shown in Fig. 17.5(a). Figure 17.5(b) has been obtained by showing MC curve as supply curve for the firm since, in the short run, the rising part of MC curve represents the supply curve. For the industry as a whole, individual supplies are aggregated to get industry supply curve.

Figure 17.5(a) depicts two MC and two associated AC curves which have their usual shapes in the short run.

MC_1 (and AC_1) have been drawn on the assumption of no increase in any of the variable cost items. Shift of MC_1 and AC_1 to MC_2 and AC_2 indicates that

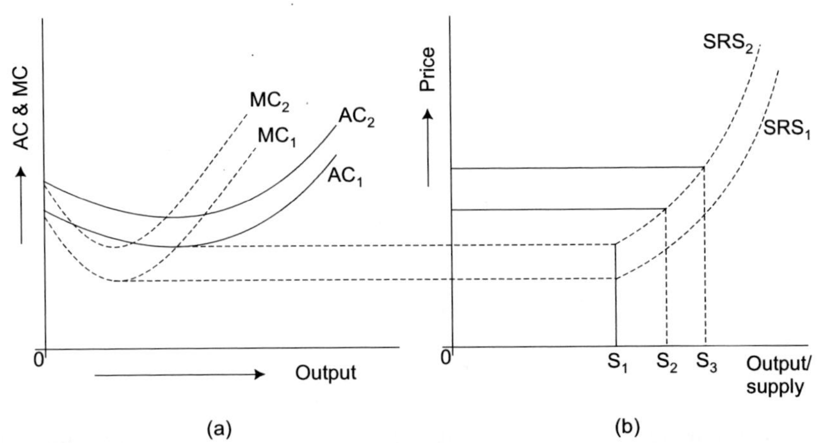

Figure 17.5 *Cost push inflation: from firm's cost to supply.*

any or some of the items of marginal cost (short-run variable costs are marginal costs) increase for the firm which it adds to the original marginal cost.

By horizontally summing the MC curves across firms and relating them with output prices, we obtain the short-run supply curves of the firm. We may mention here that we are particularly interested in the rising parts of the MC curves, which, translated into supply curves, look like SRS_1 and SRS_2. While SRS_1 shows different levels of output (and supply) at each price of output, SRS_2 shows that for the same level of output (and supply) now the firms charge higher price. Hence, the parallel shift in the SRS curves.

17.4.6 The Wage-price Spiral (The Case of Cost-push Inflation)

If cost inflation is the result of wage-rate rise which is incorporated in marginal cost by the firms, the situation may ultimately lead to wage-price spiral as it happens in the case of demand inflation. For instance, the rise in product-price of not only the present firm but also of other firms may raise the cost of living of the workers who find their real wage rate diminished. They now begin demanding higher money wages. This leads to wage-price spiral: higher wages leading to higher prices, higher prices leading to higher wages and so on.

17.4.7 The Supply Shock and Inflation

Inflation may be caused by supply shock or supply shortage thus acting directly towards shift in supply curve. The most relevant examples are: (a) fuel supply shock (of imported crude) from OPEC countries; and (b) shortage of foodgrains leading to rise in food grains prices.

(a) OPEC countries have formed cartels to have a control over the supplies of their crude. Supply shocks have occurred from time to time in the international fuel market mostly due to political disturbances in the Middle East and North African countries. But sometimes the supply cut and raising crude price follows the deliberate policy decision of OPEC countries.

(b) As witnessed recently in India and elsewhere in the world, agricultural production was hit by persistent failure of rainfall as also floods in certain parts of the country thus leading to rising food inflation. In some countries including India, agricultural lands have been converted into non-agricultural uses and food crops (sugar, maize) are being used for fuel production (ethanol, for example). Such substitution combined with some other factors have made the food inflation a global phenomenon (see Section IV on Inflation in India).

However, such supply driven inflation may be temporary in nature and once seasonal supply constraint improves, inflation rate might soften, provided that rise in cost of living due to inflationary pressure does not enter into workers' wages.

17.4.8 Cost-Push vs. Demand-Pull Theories

Richard Lipsey[1] has nicely drawn a distinction between demand-pull and cost-push theories of inflation. Thus, looking simply at the causal sequences involved, the cost-push theory says that it is increases in factor prices that cause increases in final goods prices, and that these changes in factor prices can occur independently of the state of excess demand. The demand-pull hypothesis reverses this order of causation and says that it is increases in the demand for final goods (consumers' goods or investment goods) that causes increases in the prices; these price increases cause a rise in the demand for factors of production which in turn cause an increase in factor prices; thus it is the increases in the level of goods prices which cause increases in the level of factor prices.

Thus, demand-pull sees changes in the demand for goods as the main cause of price level changes, while cost-push sees prices changing when exogenous changes in factor prices are passed in the goods markets – through shifts in the supply curves for goods. Thus, the manifestation of a successful cost-push will be a supply curve shift in the markets for goods.

Within the factor market, however, the cost-push theories can be distinguished between market force and extra-market force theories, the former explaining factor-price changes by the state of excess demand in the factor market and the latter explaining factor-price changes in terms of forces which are independent of the state of excess demand.

[1] R. Lipsey, An Introduction to Positive Economics, ELBS, 1969, pp. 722-23.

SUMMARY

Concepts and Measurement

1. Inflation is a situation of sustained rise in price level in the economy. Price level means the average level of prices of all major goods and services.
2. Price levels are measured with the help of index numbers that are constructed at different points in time. There are mainly wholesale price index numbers and consumer price index numbers which are used in most of the economic systems of the world. Wholesale price index is also known as headline inflation indicator and is still the principal device used in India.
3. The rate of inflation refers to the percentage change in the price index numbers over two points in time or two periods of time. The first type of inflation rate is known as year-on-year (or, point to point) while the second type is known as annual average inflation rate.
4. Price index numbers are constructed on the basis of a base period when prices are expressed as 100. The other period which is used for measurement is known as 'current period'. When rates of inflation are measured, it is possible that base period rate may affect current period rate even though price indices may remain the same in the current period. This is known as 'base effect'.
5. Related to price movements there are related concepts like 'inflation', 'deflation', 'disinflation' and 'reflation'. While inflation is a condition of sustained rise in prices, deflation is a condition of falling prices. Disinflation refers to the falling rate of price rise, i.e., from high rate to low rate of inflation. Reflation generally accompanies the *revival* of the economy from the condition of recession/depression and is characterized by relatively low level of inflation.
6. Inflationary expectations refer to the people's perception about the expected inflation rate in near future, i.e., short and medium term. Such perception is formed on the basis of certain factors such as past trend of price changes, government policy actions about the present inflation, sudden changes in external and internal conditions like 'oil shocks', wars with any neighbouring country, floods and famines, etc.

Effects of Inflation

1. Inflation has wide ranging effects on different sections of society. It raises the cost of living of most people. The salaried class people whose salaries are protected by inflation-indexed allowances are relatively less affected by inflation while poorer sections are most affected.

2. Inflation redistributes incomes in favour of the producers and business community from the consumers. So profit incomes rise while wage/ salary incomes decline. Rentier class owning house property and other assets are also losers since their incomes in real terms fall. However, company shareholders may stand to gain by inflation. Interest income earners also lose since real interest rate falls by general price-rise.
3. Debtors gain while creditors lose by inflation except when credit money is so adjusted with regular interest payments that inflation is, at least partially, taken care of.
4. Inflation raises the costs of projects particularly those having larger gestation period. Most projects (either in the private or public sector) are, for some reason or other, delayed. Meanwhile, price rise of several inputs of the projects makes the projects more costly. Some present-day projects may have in-built flexibility in prices on expected inflation rate, but actual inflation might differ from expected inflation.
5. Government budgets are often affected by inflation and the actual budgetary expenditures increase due to unforeseen inflation rate. This not only makes the government's fiscal operations difficult but also fuels future inflation rate through rise in fiscal deficit.
6. International capital movements are influenced by real interest rate (nominal interest rate – rate of inflation). If relative rate of inflation rises in countries where capital is flowing in its real return is reduced so that capital inflow becomes shaky.
7. Persistently high inflation rate may ultimately depreciate the value of the domestic currency. If high inflation is followed by high interest rate then through capital flight domestic currency may depreciate.
8. Persistent and accelerated rate of inflation is likely to adversely affect the growth process of the economy. In spite of controversies on this point (as is the case presently with India) it is agreed that inflation affects the economic growth process through several channels.

Theories of Inflation

1. Inflation is a process of sustained rise in price level. It is also a dynamic process.
2. The different theories that attempt to explain inflation process mainly fall under two main categories: demand-induced (or, demand pull) and cost-induced (cost-push) inflation. Demand-pull theories stress upon the fact that excessive monetary expansion create excess demand in the economy beyond the economy's potential output given by total available goods and services.

3. The oldest version of the theory of demand-pull inflation is set out by classical quantity theory of money which seeks to establish direct relationship between money supply and price level. When quantity (or, supply of money) is much in excess of the supply of goods and services within the economy, the price level tends to rise and continues until the excess supply of money is mopped up.
4. The 'inflationary gap' explanation provided by Lord Keynes is also of the demand-pull inflation. But such inflationary gap arises from excess aggregate demand (either private consumption demand, or private/public investment demand or both) beyond the economy's productive capacity. Generally, such 'gap' arises from war or war type situations in the economy causing excessive government expenditures.
5. Inflationary gap in certain situations, may be gradually closed, but under other situations may go on widening. Only proper macroeconomic policies (monetary, fiscal or administrative policies) can tackle such excess demand condition.
6. The cost-inflation arises when input costs such as wage cost, other raw material costs consistently rise and enter into the producers' price-determination process leading to higher prices of output.

   In case rise in wage rates (due to supply-demand gap of labourers or wage-bargaining by trade unions) leads to rise in output price which in turn leads to the rise in wage rates (due to rise in the cost of living of the workers) and this process continues, it leads to wage-price spiral. Such wage-price spiral may either originate in the output market due to demand inflation and percolate into labour market or it may originate in the labour market and translate into output market.
7. Inflation is a dynamic process. Once an inflationary process starts, its full effect is felt only after a time gap. Therefore, it is important to understand the time path of this process. It is here we are concerned about the rate of inflation per time period.

   For instance, it is important to know the annual rate of inflation due to a given increase in investment expenditure in one period; and how the entire effect is spread over the whole period. The dynamic nature of inflation can be suitably studied by dynamic models and not by the static models.

   However, the rate of inflation depends, primarily on the size of the inflationary gap, the marginal propensity to consume, the constant level of real investment, potential level of output and the length of time period defined by the length of income-payments lag.

SECTION III

17.5 PHILLIPS CURVE: THE RELATION BETWEEN INFLATION AND UNEMPLOYMENT

In 1958, Prof. A.W. Phillips, a British economist published an empirical study of annual wage rate changes and unemployment rates for nearly one hundred years.[1] This study suggested an inverse relationships, by and large, between annual percentage changes in wage rates and the unemployment rates and known as the Phillips relationship or Phillips curve[2]. Phillips curve has since been a subject of interesting research as well as intensive debate. In initial years, following Phillips' study, wide support was provided by subsequent studies and became popular as one of the most important macroeconomic policy tools. Since the Phillips curve suggested a "trade-off" between rates of wage – inflation and unemployment, most economies of the world adopted it as a policy apparatus to decide between appropriate levels of unemployment and inflation rates.

However, Phillips curve lost much of its relevance and importance as a Keynesian demand management tool in the wake of stagflation of 1970s (a combination of inflation and unemployment recurring simultaneously in the major western capitalist economies of the world). The New Classical Economics developed during 1970s and the theory of "rational expectations" put a challenge to the Phillips curve and in fact, to the entire Keynesian framework of analysis. Nevertheless, the debate has not stopped and, in fact, two schools of thought: Keynesian and New Classical continue to debate over several of the analytical tools and policies in economics. It is worth mentioning in this regard, that the 'great recession' of 2008-09 (not to mention other earlier recessions) was attributed to the failure of the new ideas of economic policy practised over the past 30 years or so and once again, Keynesian tools seemed a comeback.

In the present section, we shall first present the basic Phillips curve model and its underlying policy implications. We shall then briefly trace the subsequent developments in studies on Phillips curve. Finally, we shall summarise our discussion.

17.5.1 The Original Phillips Curve

Figure 17.6 shows the original Phillips curve. On the vertical axis is shown the rate of wage inflation while on the horizontal axis is shown the rate of unemployment. The curve represents the empirical fact that wage rate inflation is a negative

[1] "The Relation between Unemployment and the Rate of Change of Money Wage Rates in the United Kingdom, 1861-1957", Economica, XXV, 1958, pp. 283-300; reprinted in J. Lindauer (ed.) Macroeconomic Readings, The Free Press, 1968, pp. 107-119.

[2] The term Phillips curve was later coined by Prof. P.A. Samuelson

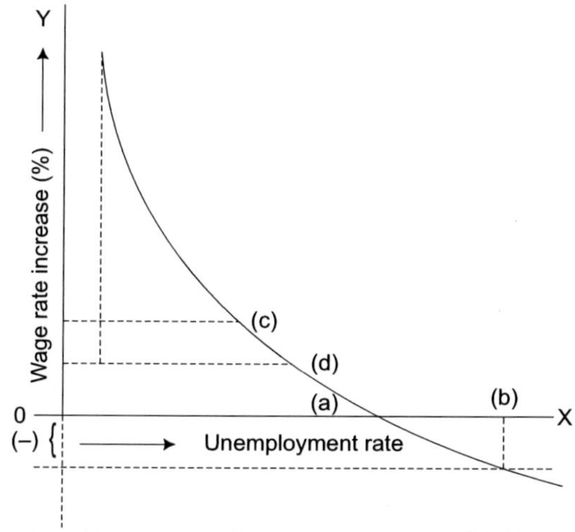

Figure 17.6 *Phillips curve: the relation between unemployment rate and wage rate.*

function of the unemployment rate, i.e., as unemployment rate decreases, rate of inflation increases. However, three distinguishing features of the curve need to be interpreted and understood: (1) the curve is downward sloping but convex to the origin. In fact, it gives a shape like rectangular hyperbola; (2) at zero rate of inflation, the unemployment rate is substantially high (point a) and (3) there is a negative zone of the curve.

1. The curve is downward sloping simply suggests a "trade-off" between inflation rate and unemployment rate — lower rate of inflation is associated with higher rate of unemployment and higher rate of inflation is associated with lower unemployment rate. In other words, if we want lower inflation rate as a macroeconomic policy we have to accept certain degree of unemployment. On the other hand, if we want unemployment rate to be at relatively low level, we have to bear relatively high rate of inflation.
2. The curve is convex, i.e., at lower levels of inflation, relatively higher rate of unemployment needs to be sacrificed for further decrease in inflation rate (e.g., from point *c* to *d*). On the other hand, at relatively low level of unemployment, the rate of inflation will be increasingly higher. So, the relationship also depends at what level of unemployment/ inflation rate a particular economy is operating.
3. Unemployment rate, however low, will never be zero. This is, because, even though unemployment rate may reach a very low level (when wage inflation is very high due presumably to rise in aggregate demand causing unemployment rate to fall) some frictional or structural unemployment will still be there.

Secondly, wages are "sticky" downwards. This suggests that in the downward direction, wages tend to be sticky — reluctant to fall due to several labour market characteristics. For example, workers are unwilling to accept lower wages even when unemployment rate is very high, neither can employers force them to accept lower wages under labour union pressures. At most, wage rates may fall but very slowly at high level of unemployment. In addition to this, there are certain institutional factors such as the existence of minimum wage legislations, the unemployment insurance, etc., which are prevalent not only in developed economies but are now gradually coming into existence in a number of underdeveloped over-populated countries (including of course, India). These factors explain the lower end of Phillips curve (P.C.) including the negative zone where unemployment rate is substantially high and there is deflationary condition when prices actually fall (as it happens in case of recession or depression). On the other hand, on the upward movement, wages tend to rise at a faster rate keeping pace with the price-rise so that they can protect their real wages intact. For this reason, at relatively low level of unemployment, wage inflation rises at higher rate. Phillips curve, therefore, appears as convex to the origin.

In terms of mathematical equation, Phillips curve can be expressed as:

$$W^* = a + b\frac{1}{U^*} \qquad (17.5)$$

(or alternatively, $W^* = a + bU^{*-1}$)

where, W^* is wage rate increase, U^* is the rate of unemployment and a and b are constants (parameters). The constant a represents the position of the curve which is influenced by factors, other than unemployment rate contributing to wage rate increases. Thus, a captures the fact that unemployment rate will never be zero due to the influence of these other factors. The term b is the rate of wage increases with a fall in unemployment rate. The shape of the curve being rectangular hyperbola is clear from equation 17.5.

In fact, Phillips himself fitted this relationship to the British economy data and obtained the following results:

$$W^* = -0.9 + 9.638\ U^{*-1.394} \qquad (17.6a)$$

or,

$$W^* = -0.9 + \frac{9.638}{U^{*1.394}} \qquad (17.6b)$$

17.5.2 From Wage-inflation to Price-Inflation

At the time when Phillips did his study, it was widely believed that wage-increases were the main contributor of price increases. At a later stage, it was empirically demonstrated that most wage increases are translated into price level increases, although with some time-lags and, of course, taking into account the average productivity of labour. In fact, price level can be expressed as

$$P^* = W^* - APL.$$

where APL is average productivity of labour.

P^* and W^* are percentage changes in price level and money wage rates, respectively. Therefore, economists like R. Lipsey and G. Ackley and others, later on, chose to substitute wage-rate increases by price level increases (or, inflation rate). Since then it has become customary to express Phillips curve in terms of inflation rate and unemployment rate. In equational form Phillips curve is expressed as:

$$P^* = a + b/U^* \tag{17.7}$$

where, P^* represents the rate of inflation while other terms are the same.

By the end of 1960s, major economies estimated their Phillips curves and obtained the values of the coefficients (*a* and *b*) and were able to determine the position and shape of the Phillips curve Accordingly, they could formulate their macroeconomic policies to tackle the twin problems of inflation and unemployment.

On further theoretical and empirical levels, continuous research on Phillips curve was conducted by several authors and debated over a few basic questions.

As it was presumed that both inflation and unemployment originated from changes in the levels of aggregate demand (a Keynesian derivation), some authors proposed that if aggregate demand was the main cause of either inflation or unemployment, by correcting the level of aggregate demand appropriately, and shifting Phillips curve downward enough applying monetary and fiscal policies, economies could even operate at zero inflation as well as zero unemployment rates. However, the main response to this argument was that besides the demand inflation there are always some sources of non-demand inflation.

Similarly, as we have seen above, unemployment rate can never reach zero since there are always some kind of frictional or structural unemployment. In fact, Phillips himself argued that Phillips curve is fairly stable (not fluctuating significantly) over time and the relevant range of Phillips curve can be usually found within much of the convex region (such as points *a* and *b*). However, theoretical explanations were still lacking for this part of the Phillips curve which provided scope for 'trade-off' between inflation and unemployment.

17.5.3 The Theoretical Basis of Phillips Curve

1. **Lipsey:** Richard Lipsey provided an explanation as to why inflation and unemployment will coexist and why there will be movement along the downward slope of the Phillips curve. His explanation was based on competitive market forces. For instance, let us suppose, there is a point *a* on Phillips curve in Fig. 17.7. Now, if the aggregate demand rises, output and employment will rise (unemployment will fall) so that there will be movement from *a* to *b* along the Phillips curve. In

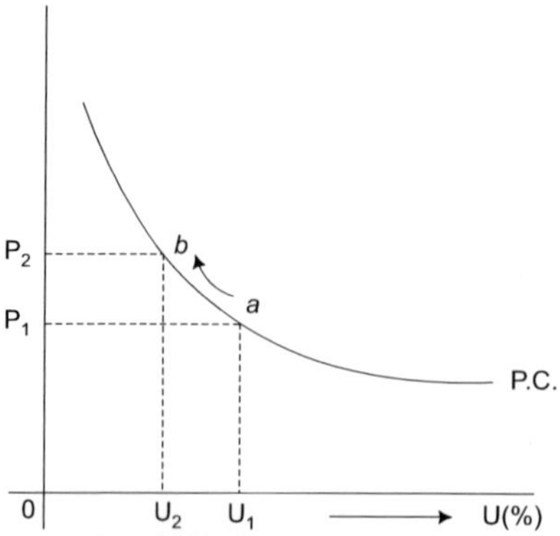

Figure 17.7 *Phillips curve: Unemployment vs. price inflation.*

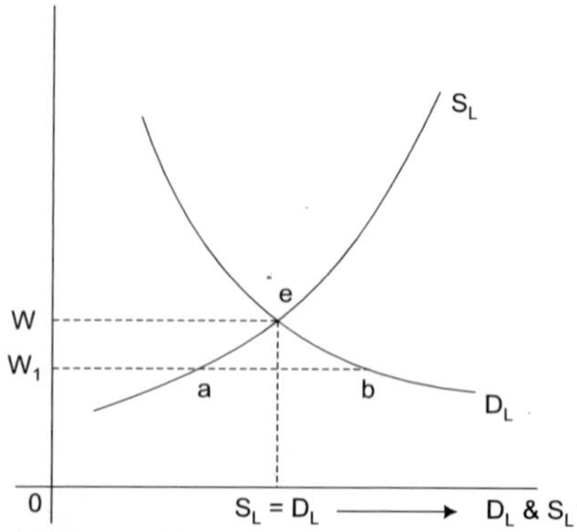

Figure 17.8 *Wage adjustment process.*

fact, rise in the demand for labour in response to the rise in aggregate demand will largely make this possible. Lipsey's theory is often referred to *wage-adjustment function* in the labour market. For instance, if the labour market situation is given by demand and supply curves of labour, as shown in Fig. 17.8, W is the wage rate at which both demand for and supply of labour are equal. Now, let us suppose, there exists disequilibrium in the labour market such that there is excess demand for labour – the demand-supply gap being equal to $a\ b$ and the wage rate is W_1. This leads to wage adjustment and will cause wage rate to rise to W. So, changes in aggregate demand in the product leads to changes in aggregate demand in the labour and automatic adjustment in wages and prices take place.

2. **Search unemployment explanation:** Provided by Phelps and others this explanation suggests that the information cost involved in searching for appropriate job vacancies on the part of unemployed workers and for appropriate workers by the employers is high. This information cost generally decreases slowly in the face of high unemployment. Even though search unemployment is, strictly speaking, voluntary unemployment since the unemployed prefer to remain unemployed rather than accept lower wage rate, the theory seeks to explain, at least partly, the behaviour of Phillips curve.

17.5.4 Policy Implications of Phillips Curve

We have mentioned earlier that Phillips curve suggests a trade-off between inflation rate and unemployment rate. In fact, welfare of the society and economy depend equally on inflation and unemployment both of which pose problems if they exceed certain tolerable limits. Therefore, for any economy, there will be certain preferable combination of inflation rate and unemployment rate. If the society prefers less unemployment rate, it has to bear higher inflation rate. On the other hand, if the preference is price stability (and low inflation rate) it will have to put up with higher unemployment rate. This means that these two goals (of low inflation and low unemployment) are in conflict. It is largely the political authorities, the policy makers and social institutions representing the society and economy which express the choice of preference between the two goals. Keeping this "trade-off" and "preference" function, economists have also estimated the so called "sacrifice ratios" for different economies. In US, for instance, according to one estimate, 5% sacrifice in annual GDP (and employment) growth will be required for 1% fall in inflation rate. This estimate is based upon certain level of existing inflation and unemployment. As we have examined (as the Phillips curve suggests) such high level of sacrifice ratio will be applicable towards the lower end of the Phillips curve. What the inflation worries most is its relatively higher level. The convexity of the Phillips curve suggests that the sacrifice ratio is likely to be lower in such a situation. An earlier study by Samelson and Solow estimated this as 5.5% unemployment being the sacrifice ratio for price stability, i.e., when inflation rate is zero (prices are held steady) provided that productivity of labour increases at 2.5% annually. This implies that wage-rate increase takes place at 3% (5.5% – 3% = 2.5%).

17.5.5 Expectation of Inflation and Shifting of Phillips Curve

Expectation plays a significant part in the behaviour of Phillips curve. The Keynesian approach to expectation is based on adaptive expectation hypothesis. Adaptive expectation is formed largely on the basis of past trend of the particular variable. For instance, in case of inflation, expected rate of inflation is based on the past rates of inflation. Of course, immediate past rates have greater weight than the remote past rates. In terms of time periods we can say that last year's inflation rate that prevailed has the greatest influence on the expectation about current year's inflation and current year's inflation rate on next year's, while inflation rates with two or more period lags have lesser and lesser influence on the formation of expectation about current or future inflation rates. This is precisely the adaptive expectation, i.e., expectation adapts to some past trends. In symbolic terms, expected inflation rate (adaptive) can be expressed as:

$$p_t^e = p_{t-1} + \alpha\,(P_t - P_{t-1}^e)$$

where p_t^e is the expected inflation rate in period t, p_t is the actual inflation rate in period t, P_{t-1} is the actual inflation rate in the previous period, p_{t-1}^e is the expected inflation rate in the previous period, and α is the coefficient whose value lies between 1 and 0 ($0 < \alpha < 1$).

More specifically, we can say that p_t^e is a weighted average of the past rates of inflation. For example, if we consider only three past periods, P_{t-1}, P_{t-2} and P_{t-3}, expected rate of inflation in period t can be expressed as:

$$P_t^e = aP_{t-1} + bP_{t-2} + cP_{t-3},$$

where, $a + b + c = 1$ and $a > b > c$.

a, b and c indicate the relative weight given to rates of inflation last year, year before last year and two years before the last year, respectively.

Now when people form their expectations (about inflation) in this manner, Phillips curve will be shifting upwards when actual inflation rates rise above the expected inflation rate. This is illustrated in the following figure (Fig. 17.9).

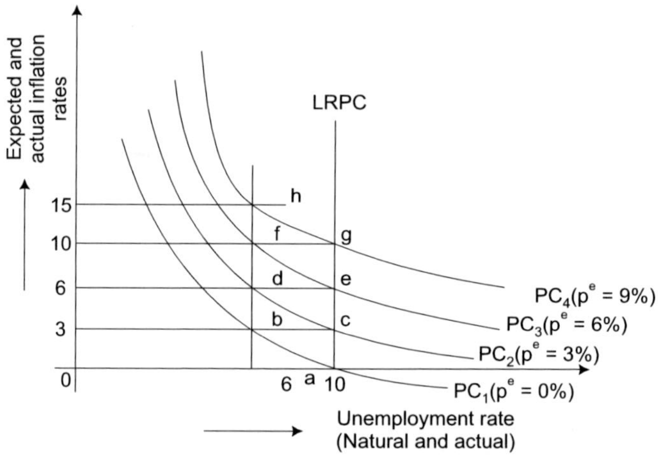

Figure 17.9 *Expectation and shifting of Phillips curve.*

Figure 17.9 shows four Phillips curve, (PC_1, PC_2, PC_3 and PC_4) for four different periods and different expectational levels of inflation. Let us suppose, in period 1, there is zero inflation with 10% rate of unemployment. The community, therefore, expects the future inflation rate also to be zero. In the next time period, however, let us suppose, the authorities intend to expand aggregate demand in order to reduce unemployment rate. They undertake monetary and fiscal policies to expand AD and thereby reduces unemployment rate to 6%. This demand management policy, results in inflation rate of 3% but reduces the actual unemployment rate to 6%. The people, however, still continue to believe that the same earlier rate of zero per cent inflation will prevail. But, as soon as they realize that increased inflation rate has resulted in reducing their real wage rate, they would demand for higher money wages, (and the economy's real AD will fall) there will be movement from point b to point c on PC_2 (PC shifts upwards). The people will now reverse their expectations in the light of the past experience and the new expected rate of inflation is 3%. But the economy will return to the unemployment rate of 10% which was prevailing at the beginning.

Again, in period three, if the government attempts to reduce unemployment rate by 4% (i.e., to 6%) and it further undertakes measures to expand aggregate demand, it succeeds in its plan and actual unemployment rate is again reduced to 6%. Expected inflation continues to be 3% (past actual rate) but AD increases supported by monetary expansion. The economy moves from point *c* to *d* on PC_2. There is further increase in inflation rate to 6% and the *PC* shifts to PC_3 due to movement from point *d* to point *e*. Unemployment will fall back to the original level of 10% due to fall in real AD and also due to higher money wage demands by workers. Similarly, every time government tries to reduce unemployment rate by applying monetary/fiscal policy in the short-run unemployment falls but at the same time inflation also rises. Subsequently, this is neutralized, Phillips curve shifts right and the economy returns to the original level of unemployment. What the analysis suggests is that the demand management, Keynesian type policies (raising aggregate demand to reduce unemployment) fail in the long run and only ends up in higher and higher rates of inflation or accelerated rates of inflation. This is known as the accelerationist of explanation of shifting Phillips curve.

This is because, in each time period the government reduces unemployment, greater is the rise in inflation in that period followed by higher expectation of inflation in the next period as also each subsequent period. Thus, rate inflation will accelerate each time. This suggests, therefore, that the long-run trade-off is between the rate of acceleration of inflation and unemployment rate and not between the typical inflation and unemployment rates of original Phillips curve.

In fact, this is precisely the view held by monetarists (followers of Milton Friedman and others) who argue that there is no evidence of the existence of long-run Phillips curve, even though there is possibility of short run Phillips curve because, in the long run unemployment that exists is, only, the natural rate of unemployment (also known as equilibrium unemployment). It is a different matter, however, that over time, due to the operation of structural factors and changes therein (for example technological innovations, government's enhanced unemployment allowance rate etc.), the natural rate of unemployment itself may change and, in fact, rise.

Also, it is clear from the above analysis that although short-run Phillips curve is downward sloping and suggests a trade-off between inflation and unemployment, the long-run Phillips curve is vertical in shape drawn along all short-run Phillips curve at natural rate of unemployment at 10% (shown in Fig. 17.9).

However, the behaviour of short-run and long-run Phillips curve are based on certain assumptions which may or may not hold true in actual practice. First, it is yet not clearly established whether expectations are actually formed on adaptive basis or more recently advocated rational expectation basis (of the new classical economists) or certain combination of the two. Secondly, the concept of natural rate of unemployment may be relevant with reference to full employment and in the long run. In most of the labour surplus underdeveloped economies the concept is irrelevant, since, even in the long run, full employment does not occur due to, among other factors, the faulty measurement of the unemployed. In such economies, fiscal policy has to be carried out with a primary purpose of promoting growth and employment although at the cost of higher level of inflation. For instance, in a country like India, the current dilemma seems to be between growth and inflation (in keeping with Phillips curve). But, it is also a fact that only monetary policy cannot solve the dilemma. Inflation, here, depends upon several factors including the government's faulty policies other than in economic spheres — inadequate implementation of development programmes (for further discussion, see next section on Indian inflation).

17.5.6 Stagflation

We have mentioned earlier that stagflation is a peculiar situation of inflation coexisting with unemployment. Thus, while inflation is rising, unemployment (and hence growth of real output) remains stagnant. During 1970s and 1980s, stagflation gripped developed economies like US and UK. Keynesian economic policies largely failed to explain such a situation. It is during this period that new economic policies were formulated and implemented which go by the name of supply-side and new classical economics.

We shall theoretically examine here how a situation of stagflation develops before we turn to the further discussion of new classical influence on the behaviour of Phillips curve. Figure 17.10 describes the phenomenon of stagflation with the possibility of Phillips 'loop' which develops in the clockwise fashion. We

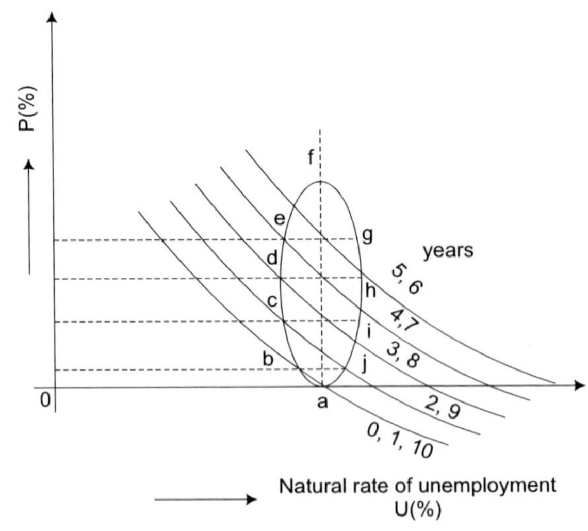

Figure 17.10 *Clockwise Phillips loop.*

consider a ten-year cycle (from 0 to 10 years). In year zero, let us suppose, the economy is at point *a* with zero rate of inflation and 0*a* amount of natural unemployment. However, as explained in the previous section, in the context of shifting of Phillips curve upwards, the government is not at peace with this rate of unemployment and therefore, undertakes expansionary fiscal-monetary policy during next two-three years. The result is that the unemployment rate falls and the economy moves to *b*, *c*, *d* positions, via shifting of Phillips curve. This results in rising inflation rates as well without reducing unemployment rate further.

When inflation gets accelerated in this way, the government becomes worried and takes steps to reduce inflation by adopting contractionary monetary/fiscal policy even at the cost of rising unemployment to a certain extent. But the unemployment rate is still below the natural rate and to left of point *a*. This means there is still some excess aggregate demand so that the pace of inflation still continues to rise. The economy now moves from point *d* to *e* which indicates that both inflation and unemployment are rising. This process continues till the economy moves to point *f* where the actual unemployment reaches point *a* (natural rate). This is because although the government adopts anti-inflationary measures, inflation expectations are still high based on previous year's actual rate.

This is exactly the situation of stagflation — a combination of rising inflation as well as unemployment. Stagflation, therefore, is mainly the product of circumstances created by false impression of shifting Phillips curve but economy operating at full or near full employment, i.e., actual rate of unemployment to rise beyond the natural rate but the expected inflation is now lower since previous year's inflation has not risen any further. The economy now moves from point *f* to *g* downward and this process continues (based on inflation expectations) till the economy is back to point *a* and unemployment is just equal to the natural rate in the tenth year. This gives a cyclical movement — may be called Phillips loop – which operates in the clockwise fashion.

According to economists of the monetarist group, stagflation is the result, primarily of adopting Keynesian demand management policy (of reducing unemployment via raising aggregate demand). The Keynesian economists, however, do not agree and they emphasize that stagflation occurs due to supply shocks and rise in input prices which ultimately shifts leftward the aggregate supply curve. Thus, while product prices rise, supply constraints develop at the

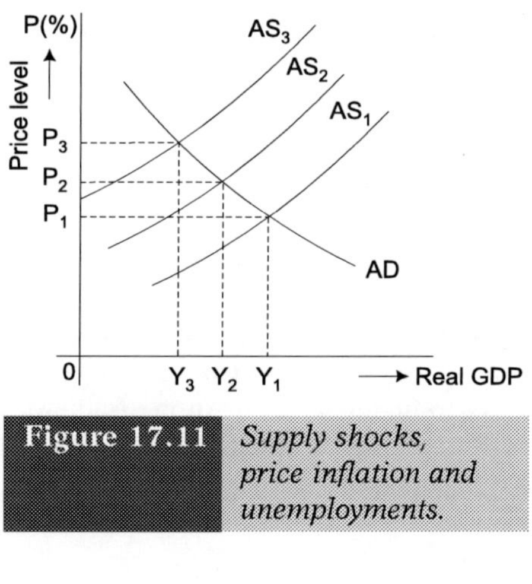

Figure 17.11 *Supply shocks, price inflation and unemployments.*

same time leading to fall in employment (and rise in unemployment) as shown in Fig. 17.11 in *AD-AS* framework.

In terms of Phillips curve underlying the shift in supply curves, the stagflation can be derived in the following manner. The occurrence of stagflation according to modern Keynesian view is that Phillips curve behaves normally but it shifts to the right as shown in Fig. 17.12. PC_1 is the original *PC* when supply shocks are not there and hence costs have not gone up. Unemployment is at U_1 and price at P_1 at point *a*. When supply shocks have taken place and costs have risen the PC_1 shifts upward to the position of PC_2. For instance, point *a* has moved to point *b*. Prices have risen to P_2 while unemployment also increases to U_2. Keynesians cite the cases of industrial unrest and growth of monopoly power, cases of mergers and take-overs of companies and the oil shocks during 1970s and 1980s in western countries which, in a combined way, pushed the costs of production upwards and caused the shift in supply curves to the left.

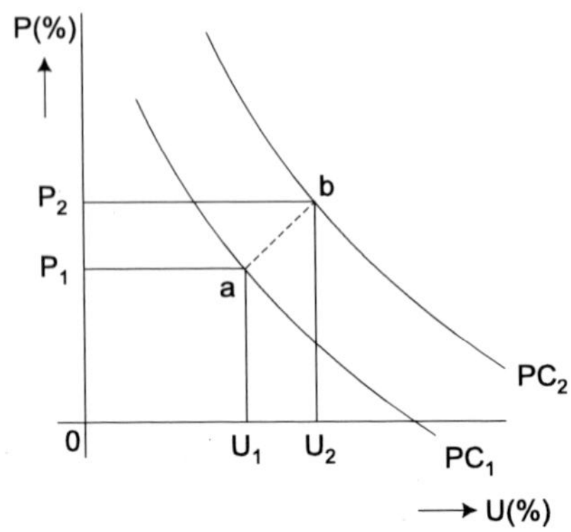

Figure 17.12 *Phillips curve and stagflation.*

17.6 PHILLIPS CURVE, RATIONAL EXPECTATIONS AND NEW CLASSICAL ECONOMICS

Rational expectation hypothesis was developed and made the basis of economic analysis by economists like Robert Lucas, Thomas Sargent and Thomas Barro of Chicago University. The new classical economics — a virtual revival and refinement of old classical economics — argued that expectations are formed largely on 'rational' basis. People, market participants and other agents generally study the current situation with all available information and thereby form their expectations about future. The hypothesis presumes, however, that information is "imperfect" but markets are "efficient" in the sense that they clear without any time lag, i.e., instantaneously. Now if expectations are rational, what will be its impact on the behaviour of Phillips curve?

In the previous section we have seen that expectations of adaptive variety produces short-run Phillips curve which is downward sloping but also a long-run Phillips curve which is vertical in shape. When expectations are rational, however, both the short-run as well as long-run Phillips curves are vertical. Let us try to understand this in the framework of AD and AS.

Figure 17.13(a) gives the initial equilibrium with AD_1 and AS_1 ($SRAS_1$) at point *a* with real output of Y_1 and natural rate of unemployment. If, now

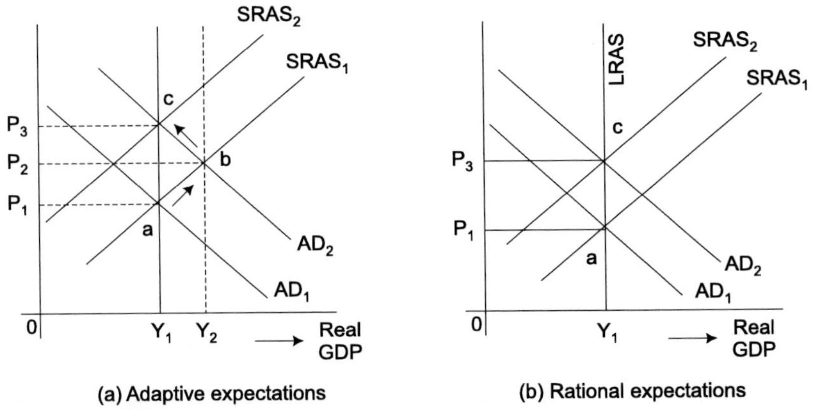

Figure 17.13 *Rational expectations and Phillips curve.*

the government attempts to raise AD by expansionary monetary/fiscal policy AD_1 shifts to AD_2 and real output is higher at Y_2. Unemployment rate falls (temporarily) below the natural rate. People continue to believe that P_1 price will prevail. Short-run AS will move along from *a* to *b* along $SRAS_1$ curve where $AD_2 = SRAS_1$. Prices have risen to P_2 from P_1 at equilibrium. Producers will now revise their expectations upward about the price level. But higher prices raise their input costs which causes leftward shift of the SRAS curve to $SRAS_2$. They will, therefore, cut their output and soon the real output will fall and come back to original level of Y_1. The new point of equilibrium at *c* will occur at higher price level of P_3. The movement of equilibrium will be first from *a* to *b* and then from *b* to *c* (shown by arrows). Unemployment will come back to the natural rate at Y_1. This implies that Phillips curve in the short run is downward sloping (between P_1 and P_2 prices), not shown in the diagram but one can easily read out (rising real output means falling unemployment rate). However, in the long run, AS curve becomes vertical (Y_1c) and so also is the Phillips curve.

Now if expectations are rational (Fig. 17.13(b)), people correctly anticipate the full long run effects of rise in AD and rise in price level directly to P_3. There will be no movement along $SRAS_1$ curve. Instead, $SRAS_1$ will totally shift to $SRAS_2$. The movement will be directly from *a* to *c* vertically. This means SRAS curve will coincide with LRAS curve and both will be vertical in shape, provided people correctly anticipate the price rise. The behaviour of Phillips curve, impliedly, will also be vertical. Thus, according to rational expectation hypothesis short run Phillips curve as well as long-run Phillips curve are vertical and there is, absolutely, no trade-off between inflation and unemployment rates. Any attempt to raise aggregate demand and thereby raising output and employment will meet with frustration. It will simply end up in raising price level (or inflation rate). As further policy implication, the rational expectation hypothesis suggests that inflation can be controlled only by monetary policy. No demand management policy (fiscal) can be used to raise aggregate output and employment.

17.6.1 Some Critical Comments

It is obvious now that rational expectation hypothesis rests upon the premise that people's expectations are based on the available current information and they draw rational conclusions and therefore they are as near as truth. Their errors in judgement are 'random'. These errors may be small or big but, on the average, they cancel out and, in fact, they are zero. But expectations often turn out to be wrong.

Secondly, information itself may be correct or incorrect. Therefore, predictions may go wrong.

Thirdly, recent events (global financial crisis) leading to 'great recession' in the economies during 2008-09 are fit examples of how the economic and financial system largely based upon new classical economic policies of past 30 years or so, miserably, failed. One may question why people and organisations could not predict rationally (and, therefore, correctly) the occurrence of 'great recession'.

Fourthly, when economic crises like recessions (or depressions) do occur it is ultimately the demand management policies of the Keynesian variety which come to the rescue and revival of the economy as has happened in major developed economies recently (post-2008).

Lastly, in forming inflationary expectations, past trends of inflation have a role to play. For example, predictions about agricultural production is still based on past or lagged output levels or adaptive expectations hypothesis.

17.6.2 Modern Keynesian Views

There is still great amount of disagreements between new classicals and Keynesians. Keynesians still believe that demand management policies play a significant role in controlling or stimulating aggregate demand. In the case of inflation management also, economists and authorities, particularly of underdeveloped world tend to believe that Keynesian demand management policy is still better than new classical principles (India, China for example).

Modern Keynesians assert that markets often do not clear neither are they efficient. Also, certain prices are always sticky in nature. However, they have now reached certain amount of compromises on different aspects of new classical theory.

First, while the earlier Keynesians did not attach much importance to expectations, modern Keynesians recognise this and advocate the incorporation of expectations in the economic models.

Secondly, they admit the possibility of 'equilibrium unemployment' and, therefore, also admit that besides 'involuntary unemployment', some unemployment will also be of voluntary nature which will always be there (for example, search unemployment).

Thirdly, while early Keynesians firmly believed that inflation was caused by excess aggregate demand alone, modern Keynesians have conceded that cost-push factors are also important in explaining inflation as also stagflation.

SUMMARY

1. Phillips curve, originally an empirical long-run relationship between percentage change in wage rates and percentage change in unemployment rates studied by British economist A.W. Phillips in 1958, suggested an inverse relationship between the two. Several other economists provided support to such relationship. It became an important macroeconomic policy tool for several economies in later years as a "trade-off" between wage inflation rate and unemployment rates.
2. Phillips curve was generalized as an inverse relationship between price inflation and unemployment since in Phillips' days inflation was believed to be caused mainly by wage rate increases. This inverse relationship or "trade-off" was expressed in several ways: simple graphical relationship or mathematical relationship to be capable of empirical estimation.
3. There are three notable features of the Phillips curve: it is downward sloping (suggesting a trade-off), it is convex to the origin and it has a negative zone suggesting the possibility of a very high rate of unemployment if price inflation is brought to zero or negative (price deflation).
4. Phillips curve remained an important Keynesian policy tool until the 1970s. However, the decades of 1970s and 1980s were marked by "stagflation" — a peculiar combination of inflation and stagnation (implying growing unemployment) that gripped western capitalist countries like US, Britain and some other European countries. Stagflation could not be suitably explained by Phillips curve and it lost much of its relevance as a policy tool.
5. A new theory of "rational expectation" was adopted by economists of University of Chicago (US) under the influence of Robert Lucas. This provided an important explanation of long run Phillips curve with virtually no "trade-off" between inflation rate and unemployment rate. Thus, when expectation about future inflation goes on higher and higher, Phillips curve continuously shifts upwards and the "trade-off" no longer holds. However, this was based upon the assumption that people would correctly anticipate the future price rise.

6. Later day economists were virtually divided between Keynesians and New Classicals (advocates of rational expectations and other related theories) and differences still continue regarding some of the major policy tools. Some sort of agreements, however, seem to have been arrived particularly with regard to Phillips curve — that while short-run Phillips curve may be downward sloping the long-run Phillips curve is vertical.
7. Recent global recession (2008-11) regarded as 'great recession', threw up a challenge to the new classical theories due to its failure to predict the recession. Once again, Keynesian demand management policies were invoked to fight the recession and "bail out" package in terms of massive public expenditures were carried out in US, EU and to a lesser extent in some of the emerging economies. This development, once again, brought to focus the limitations of the current economic policies and importance of Keynesian policy including the appropriateness of Phillips curve.

SECTION IV

17.7 INFLATION IN INDIA

In Section I of this chapter, we have discussed the concept of inflation and its measurement with examples from Indian economy. In this section, we examine the trends of inflation in India in the post-independence period. For convenience, we divide the period of observation as follows:

1. Inflation trend during 1950-1990
2. Inflation trend during 1990-2010
3. Current inflation problem: 2010 onwards
4. Food inflation: a global phenomenon
5. Summary

During the immediate post-independence period, India did not face much of inflation problem, although the spectre of 1943 Bengal famine was still haunting. Bengal was one of the chief food growing states of India, but drought and famine hit severely raising food prices manifold and to alarming levels, resulting in death of many people. However, by the time India achieved independence it largely overcame the problem.

Post-independence, India launched First Five Year Plan, beginning 1951 which put 'Agriculture and Community Development' as the main objective. During the plan period (1951-56), it is worth noting, that there was satisfactory level of food grains production. The food prices as well as other commodity prices did not rise any markedly. This favourable environment in terms of prices encouraged the government to undertake an ambitions second Five Year Plan (1956-61) by resorting to substantial amount of deficit financing in the budgets. Financing the budgetary deficit in those days involved more of printing new notes than other measures. This ultimately resulted in continuous rise in money supply without being backed by supply of goods and services. We may recall that India's second Five Year Plan emphasized upon 'industrialisation' and initiating some of the large public sector industries such as three iron and steel plants and some other giant-sized plants with longer gestation period. Consequently, during the plan period, general price level rose by as much as 20 per cent.

During 1960s, inflation problem was really of concern due to two consecutive wars — one in 1962 with China and the other with Pakistan in 1965 — and the consequent large rise in defence expenditure. This was compounded by drought and famine conditions of 1966-67. As it often happens in such situations, substantial hoarding and blackmarketing of food grains and other essential commodities took place, thus creating artificial shortage and sending the prices of these goods substantially. For instance, food grains prices rose more than 40 per cent while the general price level rose by 14 per cent and 11 per cent during the next two years, respectively. The tendency of rising prices was, however, softened with good crop production in 1967-68 and the situation improved subsequently.

However, the influx of refugees from earstwhile East Bengal (now Bangladesh) during late sixties and the extra government expenditure on the refugees and with failure of monsoon in 1972-73, once again, contributed to rising trend of price level. Then, in 1973, there was an external shock in the form of crude oil price rise. The worldwide inflation during that period resulted in depreciation of external value of rupee thus making our imports even more costly. By September, 1974, the index number of wholesale prices increased to 331 (with base year of 1961-62), i.e., prices in 1974 increased by 231 per cent, compared to 1961-62 level.

Following declaration of national emergency in June, 1975, the union government took certain monetary, fiscal and administrative measures during this period, such as Compulsory Deposit Scheme (CDS) in order to impound a part of people's incomes, credit squeeze by Reserve Bank of India and the imposition of Maintenance of Internal Security Act (MISA) against the hoarders, smugglers and blackmarketeers which together helped reduce the level of prices. Thus, the general price level which had reached 331 in September, 1974, came down to 283 in March, 1976, although for a brief period until the end of 1977.

It was during the Janata Government rule at the centre during 1977-79 that prices could be brought under control by the use of government's demand management as well as supply management policies. The result was that the WPI which was 183 in March, 1977 (with base 1971-72) rose marginally to 185 by the end of 1979. With foodgrains production reaching 131 million tonnes and industrial production showing marked improvement thus creating a favourable economic environment, the objective of price stability seemed well within sight. But, in 1979, then Finance Minister, Choudhary Charan Singh presented a deficit budget involving a massive deficit financing of ₹ 1365 crore (the largest size so far). This triggered inflationary pressures within the economy, and in consequence, by January 1980, the WPI rose to 224 from 185 in 1979 — an increase of 21 per cent.

During most of 1980s, the annual average rate of inflation (as measured by WPI) remained, by and large, satisfactory. With 1981-82 = 100, the rate of inflation varied between 4.4 per cent (the lowest) in 1985-86 and 10.3 per cent in 1990-91. Only in 1991-92, the rate increased to 13.7 per cent (Table 11.6). The average for the whole decade (1982-83 – 1991-92) turned out to be 7.6 per cent. It ought to be remembered that the years of 1990-91 and 1991-92 were the years of extreme hardships for the Indian economy. Not only in the domestic front but also in the external front, the economy was suffering from low development regime with growth rate of the economy hovering around 2-3 per cent, supply constraints of various raw materials for industrial products and serious foreign exchange crisis – even resulting in outflow of some 67 kg of gold (deposited with Bank of England) to tide over the immediate current-account payment problem.

Table 17.6 *Wholesale price index – annual average*

Year	*Index (Average of weeks)*					
	AC	*PA*	*of which*		*F&P*	*MP*
			FA	*NF*		
1	*2*	*3*	*4*	*5*	*6*	*7*
			(Base: 1981-82 = 100)			
1981-82	100.0	100.0	100.0	100.0	100.0	100.0
1982-83	104.9	106.7	111.1	100.8	106.5	103.5
1983-84	112.8	118.2	126.5	112.4	112.5	109.8
1984-85	120.1	125.5	131.8	124.6	117.3	117.5
1985-86	125.4	125.7	134.1	120.4	129.8	124.5
1986-87	132.7	137.1	147.2	134.1	138.6	129.2
1987-88	143.5	152.6	161.1	163.0	143.3	138.5
1988-89	154.2	160.1	177.1	160.2	151.2	151.5
1989-90	165.7	163.6	179.3	166.0	156.6	168.6
1990-91	182.7	184.9	200.6	194.2	175.8	182.8
1991-92	207.8	218.3	241.1	229.2	199.0	203.4
1992-93	228.7	234.6	271.0	228.7	227.1	225.6
1993-94	247.8	250.9	284.4	249.1	262.4	243.2

Contd..

Contd..

			(Base: 1993-94 = 100)			
1993-94	100.0	100.0	100.0	100.0	100.0	100.0
1994-95	112.6	115.8	112.8	124.2	108.9	112.3
1995-96	121.6	125.3	122.2	135.4	114.5	121.9
1996-97	127.2	135.8	137.3	134.2	126.4	124.4
1997-98	132.8	139.4	141.4	137.5	143.8	128.0
1998-99	140.7	156.2	159.4	151.8	148.5	133.6
1999-00	145.3	158.0	165.5	153.0	162.0	137.2
2000-01	155.7	162.5	170.5	146.5	208.1	141.7
2001-02	161.3	168.4	176.1	152.9	226.7	144.3
2002-03	166.8	174.0	179.2	165.4	239.2	148.1
2003-04	175.9	181.5	181.5	186.3	254.5	156.5
2004-05	187.3	188.1	186.3	187.6	280.2	166.3
			(Base: 2004-05 = 100)			
2004-05	100.0	100.0	100.0	100.0	100.0	100.0
2005-06	104.5	104.3	105.4	96.7	113.6	102.4
2006-07	111.4	114.3	115.5	102.3	120.9	108.2
2007-08	116.6	123.9	123.6	114.4	121.0	113.4
2008-09	126.0	137.5	134.8	129.2	135.0	120.4
2009-10	130.8	154.9	155.4	136.2	132.1	123.1
2010-11	143.3	182.4	179.6	166.6	148.3	130.1

AC: All commodities
PA: Primary articles
FA: Food articles
NF: Non-food articles
F&P: Fuel and power
MP: Manufactured products
FA and NF and part of PA.
Also see notes on Tables.

Source: Office of the Economic Adviser, Ministry of Commerce and Industry, Government of India.

Table 17.7 *Consumer price index – annual average*

Year	*Index (Average of weeks)*			
	IW	*IW-Food*	*UNME*	*AL*
1	*2*	*3*	*4*	*5*
		(Base: 1960 = 100)		
1970-71	186	202	174	194
1971-72	192	205	180	196
1972-73	207	223	192	217
1973-74	250	279	221	263
1974-75	317	358	270	354
1975-76	313	342	277	340
1976-77	301	317	277	293
1977-78	324	345	296	324
1978-79	331	347	306	317

Contd..

Contd..

1979-80	360	373	330	346
1980-81	401	419	369	395
1981-82	451	476	413	444
1982-83	486	508	446	467
1983-84	547	581	492	520
(Base: 1982 = 100 for IW and 1984-85 = 100 for UNME)				
1983-84	111	117	92	520
1984-85	118	122	100	521
1985-86	126	128	107	546
1986-87	137	141	115	572
1987-88	149	152	126	629
1988-89	163	169	136	708
1989-90	173	177	145	746
1990-91	193	199	161	803
1991-92	219	230	183	958
1992-93	240	254	202	1076
1993-94	258	272	216	1114
1994-95	284	304	237	1247
1995-96	313	337	259	1381
(Base: 1986-87 = 100 for AL)				
1996-97	342	369	283	256
1997-98	366	388	302	264
1998-99	414	445	337	293
1999-00	428	446	352	306
2000-01	444	453	371	305
2001-02	463	466	390	309
2002-03	482	477	405	319
2003-04	500	495	420	331
2004-05	520	506	436	340
2005-06	542	527	456	353
2006-07	579	575	486	380
(Base: 2001 = 100 for IW)				
2006-07	125	126	486	380
2007-08	133	136	515	409
2008-09	145	153	561	450
2009-10	163	176	634	513
2010-11	180	194		564

IW: Industrial workers UNME: Urban non-mannual employees AL: Agricultural labourers

Note: Base: 2001 = 100 for CPI(IW). Data at the new base were reported beginning January 2006; the conversion factor is 4.63 for the 'General Index' and 4.58 for the 'Food Group'. CPI-UNME has been discontinued with effect from January 2001.

Source:

1. Labour Bureau, Ministry of Labour and Employment, Government of India.
2. Central Statistics Office (CSO), Ministry of Statistics and Programme Implementation, Government of India.

However, the year 1991 was the turning point for the economy. With the new government at the centre under the Prime Ministership of Sri Narasimha Rao and Finance Minister, Dr. Manmohan Singh, the new policy regime was ushered in with 'liberalisation, privatisation and globalisation' being the new 'mantra' and with abolition of 'licence-permit raj'. In the industrial policy front gradual reduction of excise and customs duties was begun in the subsequent annual budgets of the Union Government. These measures led to reduction of input costs of various industrial products and were passed on to the consumer prices. At the same time, efforts were made towards strengthening the supply side by allowing to set up a number of new industries in the private sector. With favourable monsoon in most years during 1990s, the government was able to build a satisfactory buffer stock of foodgrains. All these factors in a combined way led to the gradual fall in the inflation rate as exhibited in Table 17.8.

Table 17.8 *Price movements and inflation rates during 1990s*

Year	*WPI*	*Annual rate of inflation (average) (%)*
1980-81	256	
1981-82	100 (1981-82 = 100)	9.7
1982-93	104.9	4.9
1983-84	112.8	7.5
1984-85	120.1	6.5
1985-86	125.4	4.4
1986-87	132.7	5.8
1987-88	143.5	8.1
1988-89	154.2	7.4
1989-90	165.7	7.4
1990-91	182.7	10.3
1991-92	207.8	13.7
1992-93	228.7	10.1
1993-94	(247.8)	8.3
	(Base, 1993-94 = 100)	
1994-95	112.6	12.6
1995-96	121.6	8.0
1996-97	127.2	4.6
1997-98	132.8	4.4
1998-99	140.7	5.9
1999-00	145.3	3.3

Source:

1. Labour Bureau, Ministry of Labour and Employment, Government of India.
2. Central Statistics Office (CSO), Ministry of Statistics and Programme Implementation, Government of India.

As the table shows annual inflation rate was lowest (3.3 per cent) in the year 1999-2000. The fall in the rate of inflation has been gradual since the beginning of 1990s.

As a result of continued policy reforms like further liberalization of industrial policy, financial sector reforms (such as low interest rate regime, banking sector restructuring with easy availability of credit) and, above all, good monsoons had a favourable impact on the supply side management. In 2003, the Fiscal Responsibility and Budget Management (FRBM) Act was passed and the Central Government was committed to limit fiscal deficit to not more than 4 per cent of GDP in a phased manner. The impact of these policy measures was felt in the relatively rapid growth of the economy as also gradual fall in inflation rate. Thus, barring the initial year of 2000-01, the annual rate of inflation ranged between 3.4 per cent (in 2002-03) and 6.6 per cent (in 2006-07). The exceptional couple of years were 2008-09 and 2010-11, recording rates of inflation at 8.1 per cent and 9.5 per cent, respectively. We may remember that in 2008, due to global recession with its partial impact on Indian economy, the government announced certain fiscal stimulus such as higher public expenditure and tax rebates as revival measures which ultimately resulted in higher percentage of fiscal deficit.

On closer analysis, however, Table 17.9 reveals that since 2003-04 itself, there is evidence of almost consistent rise in inflation rate — from 3.4 per cent in 2002-03 to 5.5 per cent the following year, 6.5 per cent in 2004-05, 6.6 per cent in 2006-07, 8.1 per cent in 2008-09 and 9.5 per cent in 2010-11.

Table 17.9 *Price movements and inflation rates, during 2001-10*

Year	*WPI*	*Annual inflation rate (average) (%)*
	(Base: 1993-94 = 100)	
2000-01	155.7	7.2
2001-02	161.3	3.6
2002-03	166.8	3.4
2003-04	175.9	5.5
2004-05	187.3	6.5
	(Base: 2004-05 = 100)	
2005-06	104.5	4.5
2006-07	111.4	6.6
2007-08	116.6	4.7
2008-09	126.0	8.1
2009-10	130.8	3.8
2010-11	143.3	9.5

Source:

1. Labour Bureau, Ministry of Labour and Employment, Government of India.
2. Central Statistics Office (CSO), Ministry of Statistics and Programme Implementation, Government of India.

Analysing the behaviour of inflation in recent years (2004-05 – 2009-10), some economists have pointed out that during this period, oil and food prices have increased consistently which have been the main drivers of inflation. But while food prices have resulted in the agricultural GDP growth (in current prices) partly due to consistent rise in the minimum support prices of major agricultural commodities, oil price being 'autonomous' (since it is determined by international crude prices and government's policy) it has essentially reflected in other commodity prices.[1]

We now look at the more disaggregated inflation numbers — by primary articles (food and non-food) fuel and power and manufactured products. (Table 17.10)

Table 17.10 *Inflation rates by commodity groups*

Year		*Primary articles of which*		*Fuel, power, light and lubricants*	*Manufactured products*	*All commodities*
		Food	*Non-food*			
	Weight(%)	*22.02*		*14.23*	*63.75*	*100.0*
2000-01	2.8	3.0	2.4	28.5	3.3	7.2
2001-02	3.6	3.3	4.4	8.9	1.8	3.6
2002-03	3.3	1.8	8.2	5.5	2.6	3.4
2003-04	4.3	1.3	12.6	6.4	5.7	5.5
2004-05	3.7	2.6	0.7	10.1	6.3	6.5
2005-06	2.9	5.4	- 3.3	9.5	3.1	4.4
2006-07	7.9	9.6	5.8	5.6	4.4	5.4
2007-08	7.6	7.0	11.8	0.9	5.0	4.7
2008-09	10.1	9.1	12.9	7.5	8.1	8.4
2009-10	22.2	15.3	5.4	13.8	5.2	10.2
2010-11	13.0	15.6	22.3	12.9	6.2	9.0

Source:

1. Labour Bureau, Ministry of Labour and Employment, Government of India.
2. Central Statistics Office (CSO), Ministry of Statistics and Programme Implementation, Government of India.
3. Economic Survey, Government of India, 2010-11

Table 17.10 shows that during the early years of the decade 2000, food inflation has not risen much, particularly, upto 2004-05 — remaining within 3 per cent. But fuel and power group exhibited relatively higher rates — for the entire period. Also, fuel inflation shows greater flexibility — 28.5 per cent in 2000-01 being the highest while 0.9 per cent in 2007-08 being the lowest. On the

[1] Mihir Rakshit, "Inflation and Relative Prices in 2006-10: Some Analytical and Policy Issues", Economic and Political Weekly, April 16-22, 2011.

average, however, fuel inflation remained at 10.96 per cent for the entire decade. Food inflation for past 2004-05 period, however, shows consistent rise — from 5.4 per cent in 2005-06 to 9.1 per cent in 2008-09. The last two years of observation exhibit abnormal rise in food inflation — 15.3 per cent and 15.6 per cent, respectively. We can conclude, therefore, food and fuel inflation have been the main drivers of higher inflation rate in recent period in India. Non-food inflation, which includes items of manufactured food (processed food items) also shows almost consistent rise in prices right from 2002-03 except a couple of years of 2004-05 and 2005-06. From 2007-08 onwards, the non-food group has been rising, by and large, at relatively greater rate compared to food group. This reflects among other factors, change in taste patterns of food consumption items in favour of processed food items arising basically from rise in income levels as also growth in urbanization or urban growth of population.

Inflation in India has become a matter of concern in more recent period since the beginning of 2010-11. The government, the RBI and the public in general have been equally concerned about current inflation. Policy makers at the government level initially were guided by the impression that current inflation, particularly food price inflation, was mainly the supply-side problem. Alongwith supply disruptions, crude oil and consequent rise in import prices of crude due to geo-political disturbances in the Middle East and North African countries (MENA) Egypt and Lybia being mainly responsible. On the other hand, RBI and the market at large felt that it is due to excess demand created by higher purchasing power of the public that was mainly responsible. Various evidence were presented in support of the demand growth both in the rural as well as urban sectors (Table 17.14).

In fact, in theoretical terms, there has been shift of the demand curve upward which means that (a) at the old price level, the quantities demanded are higher and (b) given the supply shortage in the short run (as in the case of food) the higher demand pushes up prices (Fig. 17.14). As policy measures, therefore, the demand management policy took the centrestage while certain short-run supply management measures were also simultaneously taken. The RBI has since been consistently using monetary policy — raising the policy rates (repo and reverse repo rates) — to tame inflation. It may be mentioned here that between April, 2010 and October 2011, the RBI raised its policy rates as many as thirteen times. Surprisingly, however, inflation remained stubbornly at high level — above 10 per cent most of the months. At one stage, RBI seemed to be in utter confusion regarding what ought to be its primary objective. Later on, it held a firm opinion that inflation controlling was its primary goal even at the cost of growth of the economy. At that time, some sort of policy dilemma gained currency — growth versus inflation. The government, apparently, was not in favour of excessive tightening of monetary policy lest the growth momentum of the economy

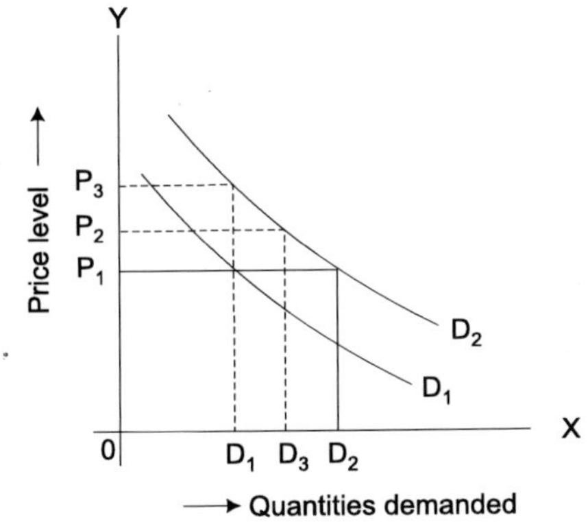

Figure 17.14 *Upward shifting of demand curve.*

would suffer. But RBI did not relent and went ahead with its rate hikes until, as announced by RBI, clear evidence would be visible of lower inflation rate. By the end of 2011 (2011-12) there were certain evidence of inflation rate softening but not before growth rate of the economy was also adversely affected. The growth rates projected during 2011-12 were revised downwards several times — from earlier 8-8.5 per cent to 7-6.9 per cent. However, it must be noted that lower growth projection had several other explanations — from domestic to international factors. The most significant international factor has been the global recession effect — slowing down of the world economy at large and adversely affecting the export sector of Indian economy. Other international factor has been the prevalence of global inflation in the earlier period sending the large number of commodity prices higher (separately dealt with later) along with global food inflation.

As RBI has observed, "… the transmission of rising international commodity prices and spillover from the past food and some wage price inflation in some sectors has been visible in recent months. Despite moderating food inflation, headline inflation remained firm in quarter-four of 2010-11 as generalized price pressures emerged with rising input costs feeding into manufactured products inflation. Risks to inflation in 2011-12 have amplified from an uncertain outlook on international commodity prices and possibility of prices of food, fuel, minerals and metals staying firm. Policy interventions are necessary to address near term and structural imbalances to bring down inflation on an enduring basis." An evidence of movement of international prices and domestic prices between March, 2010 and March, 2011 is provided in Table 17.11.

Table 17.11 *Movement of international and domestic commodity prices (%)*

Items	*Annual variation March, 2011*	
	Int. prices	*Domestic prices (WPI)*
Rice	- 1.9	2.7
Wheat	65.7	0.8
Maize	82.7	25.5
Soyabean oil	42.8	19.1
Sugar	40.6	- 7.5
Cotton	167.6	98.1
Rubber	63.8	49.1
Coal	35.6	15.9
Petroleum	37.0	6.3
Iron Ore	21.2	29.7
Fertilizers	28.4	9.4
Aluminum	15.8	1.8
Copper	27.3	0.3
Gold	27.9	33.4
Silver	109.6	68.9

Source: World Bank and Ministry of Commerce and Industry, Government of India, quoted in RBI. http//www.rbi.irg.in - Publication-VI Price Situation Review, May 11, 2011.

A further analysis of WPI-based inflation in India by details of commodity groups along with their weighted contributions to inflation is also provided by Table 17.12.

Table 17.12 *Wholesale price inflation in India (2004-05 = 100)*

Commodity	*Weight*	*Year-on-year*			
		2009-10		*2010-11*	
		Inflation	*W.C.*	*Inflation*	*W.C.*
1	*2*	*3*	*4*	*5*	*6*
All commodities	100.0	10.2	100.0	9.0	100
1. Primary articles	20.1	22.2	48.1	13.0	35.5
Food articles	14.3	20.6	31.9	9.5	18.2
Non-food articles	4.3	20.4	8.6	25.9	13.6
Minerals	1.5	37.9	7.7	12.2	3.5
2. Fuel group	14.9	13.8	20.1	12.9	22.1
(i) Coal	2.1	7.9	2.0	15.9	4.4
(ii) Mineral oils	9.4	18.6	17.1	14.7	16.6
(iii) Electricity	3.5	3.4	1.0	3.6	1.1
3. Manufactured products	65.0	5.2	32.0	6.2	41.5
(i) Food products	10.0	15.1	14.7	2.4	2.8

Contd..

Contd..

(ii) Beverages, tobacco & tobacco products	1.8	8.1	1.5	7.3	1.5
(iii) Textiles	7.3	9.1	5.4	15.6	10.5
(iv) Wood and wood products	0.6	6.6	0.4	3.2	0.2
(v) Paper & paper products	2.0	2.5	0.5	7.2	1.4
(vi) Leather & leather products	0.8	2.5	0.2	- 3.0	- 0.3
(vii) Rubber & plastic products	3.0	3.7	1.0	9.0	2.6
(viii) Chemicals & chemical products	12.0	3.7	4.1	6.6	7.8
(ix) Non-metallic mineral products	2.6	3.2	0.9	3.2	1.0
(x) Basic metals, alloys & metal products	10.7	1.4	1.5	9.3	10.6
(xi) Machinery & machine tools	8.9	1.5	1.3	2.4	2.1
(xii) Transport equipment & parts	5.2	1.2	0.6	3.3	1.7
Memo					
Food items (composite)#	24.3	18.5	46.6	6.8	21.0
Food items (protein based)$	6.4	28.7	19.5	7.5	6.7
Manufactured non-food products	55.0	3.3	17.2	7.0	38.8
WPI excluding food	75.7	7.4	53.4	9.8	79.0
WPI excluding fuel	85.1	9.6	79.9	8.3	77.9
Essential commodities	14.4	18.6	28.6	5.2	9.8

W.C. = Weighted contribution to increase in WPI

Primary food, articles + manufactured food products

$ includes milk, egg, meat and fish and pulses.

Source: RBI website: http//:www.rbi.org.in/publications = quarterly.

During 2011-12, for most of the months, inflation scenario remained on the higher side even after RBI's higher policy rate cycle continuing. Food inflation remained higher than 10 per cent while other commodity groups, viz., fuel, showed fluctuations with peak of 14.8 per cent in October, 2011. Manufactured groups inflation too rose to 7.6 per cent in October, 2011. The RBI, too responded with its continued policy of rate hike. It is worth noting that during 2010-11 and 2011-12 (till October 2011), policy rates were raised as many as thirteen times. Meanwhile, the growth forecast for the economy was revised at 8 per cent or lower, rather than 9 per cent done earlier. Later, towards the end of 2011-12 and beginning of 2012-13, the growth forecast was further reduced to 7 per cent for 2012-13. Thus, the government was caught under the "Phillips curve" type of "trade-off" between inflation and growth. Different quarterly figures for

Table 17.13(a) *Farm wages, other input costs and minimum support prices of paddy and wheat in India*

Minimum agricultural wage rate (₹)		NREGA wage rate (₹ daily)	Retail prices of key fertilizers (₹/tone)		
States	*Wage rate*			*2009-10*	*2010-11*
Assam	87	130	Imported DAP	9350	10750
Andhra Pradesh	125	121	Potash	4455	5055
Bihar	109	120	Urea	4830	5310
Gujarat	100	124			
Madhya Pradesh	110	122			
Uttar Pradesh	100	120			
West Bengal	96	130			
Haryana	167	179			
Kerala	200	150			

Source: Economic Times, April 15, 2011.

Table 17.13(b) *Minimum support prices (₹, quintal)*

Year	*Paddy*	*Wheat*
2004-05	560	640
2005-06	570	650
2006-07	580	750
2007-08	645	1000
2008-09	850	1080
2009-10	950	1100
2010-11	1000	1120

Source: Economic Times, April 15, 2011.

either index of industrial production (IIP) or purchasing managers index (PMI) prepared by HSBC indicated slowing down of the output in the real sector.

By the end of fiscal year 2011-12 (December, 2011), inflation rate somewhat softened. The WPI (or, headline) inflation rate fell to 7.47 per cent from 10.88 per cent in April, 2011. Meanwhile, in February 22, 2012, the CSO published, for the first time in independent India, all India level of consumer price-index based inflation rates (CPI). According to the newly released data, the overall inflation rate (CPI) was 7.65 per cent in January 2012 as compared to the level of January, 2011 (base year, 2010 = 100). While the rural inflation rate was recorded at 7.38 per cent, that of urban India, it was 8.25 per cent (details in Table 17.14a).

Table 17.14(a) *All India consumer price inflation: rural, urban and combined*

Base: 2010 = 100

Commodity groups	*Inflation rate (%)*		
	Rural	*Urban*	*Combined*
1. Cereals and products	3.44	0.79	2.69
2. Pulses and products	5.19	6.64	5.66
3. Oils and fats	12.65	15.11	13.47
4. Eggs, fish and meat	10.71	9.82	10.45
5. Milk and milk products	16.54	16.35	16.53
6. Condiments and spices	11.35	12.89	11.83
7. Vegetables	- 22.33	- 30.15	- 24.83
8. Fruits	9.91	11.59	10.62
9. Sugar etc.	1.94	1.43	1.84
10. Non-alcoholic beverages	11.34	11.74	11.52
11. Prepared meals etc.	10.23	10.65	10.39
12. Food and beverages	4.18	3.98	4.11
13. Fuel and light	13.70	12.43	13.13
14. Clothing, bedding and footwear	13.78	15.39	14.25
15. Overall inflation	7.38	8.25	7.65

Source: Central Statistical Organisation (CSO), Government of India. The consumer price inflation for April 2012 released on May 18, '12, shows that price pressures have again increased.

Table 17.14(b) *Inflation rate*

Commodity groups	*Rural*	*Urban*
Cereals and products	4.38	2.56
Pulses and products	6.52	5.06
Oils and fats	16.65	19.73
Egg, fish and meat	9.82	10.29
Milk and products	15.70	13.85
Condiments and species	5.37	3.19
Vegetables	21.27	32.43
Fruits	4.55	0.45

Source: CSO, quoted in *Times of India*, dated May 19, 2012.

The major inflation trackers of the economy—wholesale price index (WPI) and consumer price index (CPI) have been captured in Figs. 17.15 and 17.16 at page 460-461 for relatively recent period (2012-13–2018-19). As far as the WPI is concerned, the all commodities group has recorded a rise of 2% on the average over the six-year period while the primary articles group shows 3.4% rise during the same period. The highest rise, however, has occurred in the food articles group with as much as 5% on the average. The fuel and power groups, however, has recorded a negative rate (–0.45%), meaning that the prices of articles in this group have declined, although by a small percentage. The manufactured group of articles has recorded 2% inflation rate over the same period while the non-food group has shown 1.4% rise in prices. Thus, as far as WPI is concerned, the inflation rate over the period mentioned above, can be said to be moderate since it lies within the RBI's inflation target range of 4% ± 2%.

Let us now examine the CPI inflation figures, particularly the new CPI numbers. The combined CPI inflation rate for the said period is 6.2% while those of rural and urban categories separately, are 6.53% and 5.85%, respectively. Thus, as compared to WPI inflation, the CPI inflation rate is much higher and are on the border line of breaching the RBI's targeting limits. Similarly, the inflation rate (CPI) for industrial workers is high enough at 6.73% while those of food articles, it shows 6.43% and for agricultural labourers the inflation rate is 6.05%.

Inflation in India in recent years 2012-13–2018-19

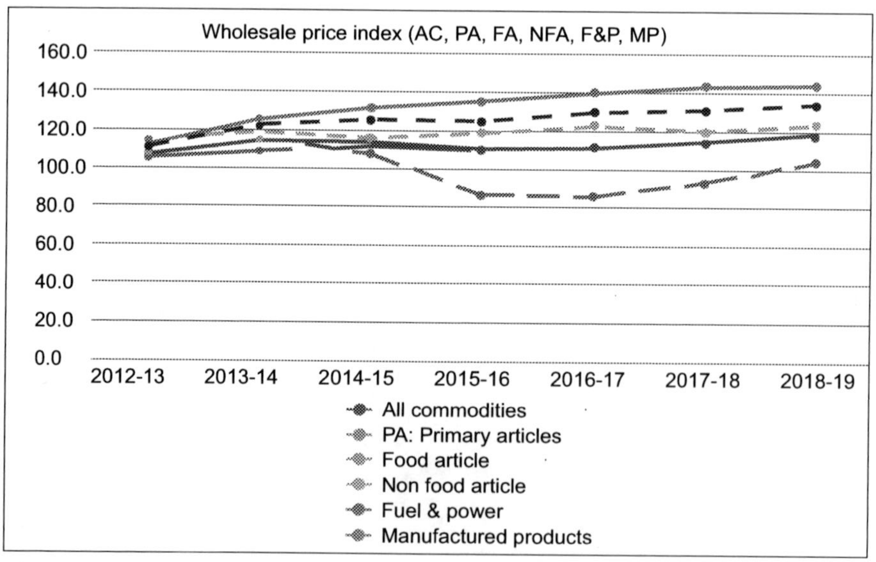

Figure 17.15 *Trends of wholesale price index.*

Source: www.rbi.org.in

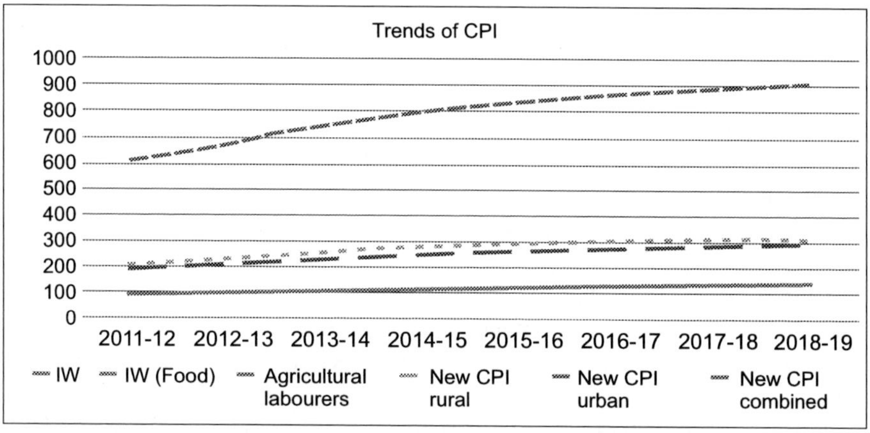

Figure 17.16 *Trends of consumer price index: 2011-12–2018-19.*

Source: www.rbi.org.in

In April 17, 2012 annual monetary policy review, the RBI, after a careful study of the economy, reduced its policy rates (repo and reverse repo rates) (by 50 basis points. Thus, repo was reduced from 8.5 per cent to 8 per cent and reverse repo, from 7.5 per cent to 7 per cent. This has been done besides the cut in CRR by 50 basis points in January, 2012 (from 6 per cent to 5.5 per cent) and another cut by 75 basis points from 5.5 per cent to 4.75 per cent in March, 2012. These rate softening measures by RBI, signals a 'reverse' cycle in the monetary policy, apparently to encourage growth prospects in near future, although RBI's so called comfort level of inflation (4 to 5 per cent) has not yet been visible anywhere. The cuts in CRR, according to RBI, have been aimed at enabling smooth flow of credit to productive sectors of the economy as also avoid temporary cash crunch in the banking sector.

17.8 FOOD INFLATION AS A GLOBAL PHENOMENON

Since food inflation has assumed special significance and has taken a global character, it is appropriate to look more analytically at the problem.

A study by Asian Development Bank (ADB) titled, Global Food Price Inflation and Developing Asia (reported in *Economic Times*, April 27, 2011) concludes: "Rising food and fuel prices could result in a major setback for Asian economies including India and China as high inflation is threatening to push millions into extreme poverty. Fast and persistent increases in the cost of many Asian food staples since the middle of last year (2010) coupled with crude oil reaching a 31 month high in March (2011), are a serious setback for the region which has rebounded rapidly and strongly from the global economic crisis".

The study warns that a sustained 10 per cent increase in domestic food prices could push an additional 64 million people — or, at least 2 per cent of Asia's 3.3 billion people — below the poverty line of US $1.25 a day. Domestic inflation in food prices in Asia has averaged about 10 per cent in the first two months of 2011 while international prices have increased more than 30 per cent in annual terms.

The study suggests that efforts to stabilize food production should take centrestage with greater investments in agricultural infrastructure to increase food production and expand storage facilities to better ensure that grain produce is not wasted.

Another report of IMF released in early April 2011 stresses that fast growing Asian economies were showing signs of overheating. The report says that structural factors such as ballooning demand due to rising population, higher incomes from economies, changing diet which were responsible for food crisis of 2007-08, continue to be relevant in the current scenario. The report further explains that in 2011, inflation has primarily been caused by large increases in the prices of cereals, edible oils and meat that were triggered by shortfalls because of bad weather. Sustained increase in oil prices due to political unrest in the Middle East has also added to the pressures. In the short run, the report predicts, the pattern of higher and more volatile food prices is likely to continue.

The Economist, in its February 26 – March 4, 2011 issue carried out a special report on 'World Food Crisis and the Problem of Feeding the World's 9 billion People'. This report mentions, at the beginning, that world food prices during the last few years have risen above the peak they reached in early 2008. Going into details, it adds that during the period 2007-08, hundreds of millions of people fell into poverty, food riots were shaking governments in dozens of developing countries, exporters were banning grain sales abroad and land grabs carried out by rich grain importing nations in poor agricultural ones were raising awkward questions about how best to help the poor.

"This time, too, there have been export bans, food riots, panic buying and emergency price controls, just as in 2007-08. Fears that drought might ruin current wheat crop in China, the world's largest producer, are sending shockwaves through world markets. Discontent over rising bread prices has played a part in popular uprising through the Middle East. There are differences between the two periods, but the fact that agriculture has experienced two big price spikes in under four years suggests that something serious is rattling the world's food chain". Among explanatory factors, according to the report, are rising demand in India and China, a dietary shift away from cereals towards meat and vegetables, the increasing use of maize as a fuel and developments outside agriculture (such as fall in dollar). Thus, the period of cheap food that started in early 1970s has come to an end. But this has coincided with growing concern about the prospects of feeding the world.

Among the principal reasons, the report lists, are the following for high food demand in recent years.

1. People, on the average, now eat more than they used to before, so that food intake in general and protein-rich intake in particular, has increased significantly. For instance, *Lancet*, a medical journal, reckons people need no more than 90 grammes of meat a day. But, on the average, they eat more than that now. Hence, there is a yawning gap between food consumption and food output. If output falls below demand, prices will tend to rise, even if "excess" calories are being produced. That happened in 2007-08 and is happening again now.

   Besides, an increasing proportion of people is living in cities and — city dwellers eat more food and especially more processed foods than their country cousins. They also tend to be richer and able to afford pricier food such as meat. So, meat demand will rise strongly. In 2000, 56% of all calories consumed in developing countries were provided by cereals and 20% by meat, dairy and vegetable oils. By 2050, according to an estimate by UN's Food and Agricultural Organisation (FAO), the contribution of cereals will drop to 46% and that of meat, dairy and fats will rise to 29%.
2. **Declining yield rate of certain cereals:** The earlier period of post-1960s was of green revolution, as exceptional time. According to UN's International Wheat and Maize Research Organisation, the farmers in developing countries could often double their harvest by switching over to HYV seeds. The constant use of these seeds absorbed more fertilizer and water. But now there is no adequate water to spare and the fertilizer use in some places has passed the 'saturation' point. A new green revolution is required to make even more efficient use of existing resources. The climate change is also a potential danger to farming which could reduce yields in future. Presently, rather surprisingly, crop yields are growing more slowly than population. "Between 1961 and 1990, wheat yields were rising at nearly 3% a year. During that period, the world's population was growing by an average of 1.8% a year. Between 1990 and 2007, population growth slowed down to 1.4% but the rise in annual wheat yields slackened to 0.5%. The growth in rice yields between the two periods halved."
3. **Government's bio-fuel policy:** Most countries of the world have been adopting a new bio-fuel policy to meet their requirements of a certain proportion of their energy needs. This has to be met from renewable fuels, most of them biofuels (i.e., ethyl alcohol made from crops, generally from maize and sugar). Countries like Brazil, Japan, Indonesia

and the European Union insist that biofuels must supply 10% of energy demand for transport by 2020. China's target for the same date is 5% while America aspires to meet 30% of such needs by 2030.

The market for energy is becoming more valuable than that of food and because even small percentage increase in fuel involves large quantities of crops, ethanol production is highly costly in terms of crops and land resources. For instance, in US, ethanol accounts for just 8% of fuel for vehicles, but it consumes almost 40% of US enormous maize crop.

World ethanol production increased fivefold between 2000 and 2010 but would have to rise a lot further to meet all the targets. In case this happens, it would divert a tenth of world's cereal output from food to fuels. Alternatively, if food crop production were to remain stable, a huge amount of extra land would be needed for the fuels or food prices would rise by anything from 15 to 40% which would have dreadful consequences.

4. **Wastage of food grains:** Both in rich and poor countries a staggering 30-50% of all food produced rots away uneaten. According to Josef Schmidhuber of FAO, in Africa, the post-harvest waste largely explains why many small holders are net purchasers of food even though they grow enough for their families to eat. In poor countries, most food is wasted on or near the farm. Rats, mice and locusts eat the crops in the field or in storage. Milk and vegetables spoil in transit. These might be considered losses rather than waste. But such losses could be reduced by half which would be equivalent to rise in output of 15-25%.

   In poor countries, much of the waste is caused by inefficient management — for example, grains are heaped on the ground and covered with just a sheet and left to waste by rains and rats. Losses, in such cases, could be reduced by investments in infrastructure such as better roads, cold storages, etc. which are, of course, expensive.

In India, too, grains collected through government procurement lack enough storage facilitlies or poor management. Enough evidence is there how every year wheat is kept in the open and left to waste. Even in the current year (2012-13), according to a recent report by Ashok Gulati, Chairman of agricultural costs and prices, the gap between procurement and storage is nearly 1/3, i.e., 1/3 of the total procurement will need proper storage.

To conclude, global food inflation has mainly four major explanations:

(a) Changing structural demand for food grains due to sustained rise in incomes and dietary shift towards more protein-rich food
(b) Falling yield rates of some main food grains
(c) Government's biofuel policy
(d) A good amount of wastage of food grains at various levels.

Food inflation in India in recent years, by and large, have similar explanations with varying degrees. However, here in India, seasonal factors like inadequate rainfall and floods in certain food growing regions often play a spoil spot in short-term supply management problem. Also, important is the speculation in food grains prices and hoarding particularly during periods of shortage.

The biofuel policy in India does not play any significant role since there has not been any policy shift towards this although it is in the offing. According to media reports, very recently the government has given directions towards blending of 5% ethanol produced from sugar (molasses) with fuel to facilitate more eco-friendly petroleum use. But certain confusion has surfaced between State Government (U.P., for instance) policy and sugar mills. However, in India, sugar cane production in some years becomes bumper thus providing a case for ethanol blending provided appropriate technology is in place and there is no supply shortage.

Other factors like sustained income growth both in rural and urban areas, shifts in diets towards more protein – rich foods and growth of urban population do equally apply to India.

According to recent reports, inflation has, again, raised its ugly head in late April, 2012. Within food inflation, vegetables and fruits have registered higher rates, although the whole of primary commodity group has shown rising trend in prices. For instance, prices of primary articles segment in April rose by 15.09%, fuel group rose by 13.04% and that of manufactured items increased by 6.8% while the headline inflation increased by 7.23% from 6.89% in March, 2012. Food inflation in April rose by 10.49% from touching negative figure of – 0.68% in January, 2012.

Rising inflation, once again, has baffled the policy makers. The RBI seems not inclined to respond by raising policy rates right at present and would prefer to maintain status quo.

SUMMARY

1. Inflation problem in India during the immediate post-independence period was not serious enough. The first decade of 1950s saw the completion of two plan periods — first and second. Partly due to the first five year plan's stress on agricultural development and favourable monsoons, prices of essential commodities did not rise; rather price index number somewhat fell. During the second five year plan, however, emphasis was shifted to industrialization. Heavy investment expenditures on setting up of a number of basic industries were followed by 'deficit-financing' policy of the plan expenditures. This resulted in the rise in money supply and rise in general price level by about 20 per cent over the plan period.

2. During 1960s, real challenge on price front took place. Two big political events — war with China in 1962 and that with Pakistan in 1965 involved heavy defence expenditures and consequent rise in price level. This was compounded by drought and famine conditions of 1966-67 resulting in food grains price-rise by 14 per cent in the following year. However, the good monsoon followed and satisfactory food grains production softened the situation to a great extent.
3. In the late sixties, there was political disturbance and civil war within the then East Pakistan (now Bangladesh) and large influx of refugees from there to India involved extra public expenditure on relief and maintenance of the refugees. In early 1970s (1971) there was another war with Pakistan over the issue of liberation of East Pakistan. India helped the liberation army of East Pakistan and on defeat of Pakistan, Bangladesh was born. But this event also involved good amount of India's defence expenditures with pressures on price-front. In 1972-73, there was another monsoon failure which further added to the pressures on prices. The first "oil-shock" of 1973 (due to Arab-Israeli war) was a major external cause of inflationary pressure not only in India but also to the world economy by and large.

   Almost the whole of 1970s saw upheavals on the inflation front. With public agitation all over the country with call for "total revolution" under the leadership of Late Jai Prakash Narayan and huge response threatened the stability of the government. This led to declaration of Emergency in 1975 by Prime Minister, Mrs. Indira Gandhi. During this period, certain stringent measures like monetary, fiscal and more importantly administrative, were taken to control prices. The situation gradually came under control and in 1976, prices fell by 16 per cent from the level in 1974.
4. During the later half of 1970s, under Janata Government rule (1977-79) price situation improved to satisfactory level. This was partly due to better combination of policy tools — monetary, fiscal as well as administrative — improved supplies of some of the basic raw materials and food grains. Price level in general virtually did not rise during this period. But, in 1979, a heavy doze of deficit financing in the budget was resorted to which again triggered inflationary pressures and by the end of 1980, price level rose substantially with WPI rising from 185 in 1979 to 224 in early 1980. During most of 1980s, the situation on the price front was, on the average, comfortable except in the late 1980s and beginning of 1990s when supply shortfalls of basic agricultural commodities and certain manufactured products caused prices to rise.
5. A significant policy shift took place during 1990s with the beginning of economic reforms era. Liberalisation and privatisation policies were

initiated with gradual reduction of tax rates, excise and customs duties and gradual rationalization of entire tax-structure. Thus 'license-permit raj' of the earlier period was largely given away. Industrial policy structure was changed substantially to give more and more place to private enterprises and reduction of public sector's role through privatization process (reducing government's stake in public enterprises). Alongside, financial and banking sector reforms were initiated with globalization of trade and financial system. As a result of combined influence of these measures, supply situation improved considerably as also the inflation trend. The annual rate of inflation, as recorded during 1990s dropped to 3.3 per cent, on the average, by the end of 1999-2000.

6. Continued economic policy reforms with higher growth rates of the economy and stepping up investment activities kept the inflation rate more or less in the satisfactory trajectory during the first half of 2000s. But external shocks in the shape of oil-crisis and income growth coupled with demand-supply mismatch in the food grains sector posed certain problems in the later half of the 2000s. By the close of the decade, global recession with financial crisis in US and European countries, with its partial impact on Indian economy, slowed the growth rate although no abatement on price front was noticed. In fact, it was in the fag end of the decade and beginning of 2011, that inflation problem proved to be a menace with little sign of softening even with continued and sometimes aggressive, monetary policy tightening. Food inflation in particular, with fresh rise in crude oil price due to political disturbance in the North and East African states causing supply disruptions contributed largely to the headline inflation. After softening to some extent in the end of November-December, 2011 and first quarter months of 2012, inflation has, once again, risen. RBI has not responded with any policy rate changes. Meanwhile, debates and discussions among economists are going on the issue of inflation and appropriate policy prescriptions.

Further information on retail price fronts have revealed that for January, February, March and April, the rate of CPI inflation, on year-on-year basis, increased by 7.65% to 8.83%, 9.38% and 10.36% respectively — thus indicating that retail prices are on the continuous increase in early 2012 — creating a fresh headache for RBI or government what further measures to take on checking this trend.

EXERCISE

1. Distinguish clearly among the terms: inflation, deflation, reflation and disinflation.
2. What do you understand by inflation rate? What are 'runaway inflation' and 'galloping inflation'?

3. Discuss the various effects of inflation.
4. Distinguish between demand-pull and cost-push theories of inflation with suitable examples.
5. Explain how Keynes' 'inflationary gap' arises in the economy.
6. What exactly does the Phillips curve try to explain? Give diagrammatic illustration.
7. How does 'expectation' impact the behaviour of Phillips curve?
8. What is 'stagflation'? How does it arise in the economy?
9. Distinguish between WPI and CPI inflation? What is core inflation? How does it differ from fuel and food inflation?
10. What do you understand by 'inflationary expectation'? How is inflation expectation estimated in India?
11. What are the main anti-inflation measures normally adopted by India's Reserve Bank?

REFERENCES

1. Economic Surveys, different years, Government of India.
2. Reserve Bank of India, various publications; (http//:www.rbi.org.in/scripts/publications – quarterly).
3. Chetan Yahya, "The Origin of India's Inflation Problem", Economic Times, 10th February, 2011.
4. Mihir Rakshit, "Inflation and Relative Prices in 2006-10: Some Analytical and Policy Issues", Economic and Political Weekly, April 16-22, 2011.
5. Jehangir Aziz, "It is Time for Aggressive Tightening", Economic Times, May 3, 2011.
6. T.T. Ram Mohan, "A New Norm for Inflation?", ET, May 12, 2011.
7. http//www.Indiabudget.nic.in, for Union Budget, 2011-12 and Economic Survey, 2010-11.
8. Mint, Delhi, Report by Investment Bank, Nomuna, dated 25 February, 2011.
9. T.T. Ram Mohan, "Higher Inflation is Here to Stay", E.T., April 27, 2012.
10. The Economist, February 26 – March 4, 2011: A Special 14 – page Report on Future of Food.
11. G. Ackley, Macroeconomics: Theory and Policy, McMillan, New York USA, 1978.

12. R. Lipsey, An Introduction to Positive Economics, ELBS Edition, 1969.
13. John Slowman, Economics, Prentice Hall, London, 1991.
14. N. Gregory Mankiw, Macroeconomics, 6th Edition, Worth Publishers.
15. R.B.I., www.rbi.org.in.
16. Handbook of Statistics of Indian Economy, Sept. 15, 2021.
17. Government of India, Economic Survey, different years. Ministry of Finance.

PART-9

International Macroeconomics

18

International Macroeconomics

18.1 THE INCOME DETERMINATION MODEL IN AN OPEN ECONOMY

Since the new variables in an open economy have emerged in the form of (a) exchange rate and (b) foreign income, they are likely to influence the domestic income determination process through the *IS-LM system* in a significant manner.

We can better look at our total expenditures or aggregate demand (*AD*) as distinguished by (a) expenditures by domestic residents on various goods and services and (b) total expenditures by domestic and foreign residents on goods and services. This is because the sources of demand for domestic goods and services are now two: the domestic sources and foreign sources. Accordingly, we can write as:

$$AD \text{ (domestic)} = C + I + G,$$

and $$AD \text{ (total)} = C + I + G + NX,$$

where, *NX* is net exports (exports - imports or (*X-M)*.

From the behavioural relationships of *C, I and NX,* we can further specify that $C = f(Y)$, that is, aggregate consumption expenditures depend on real national income while the aggregate investment expenditures depend on the real rate of interest, $I = I(r)$, (where, *r* is the real rate of interest, i.e., nominal rate of interest minus the expected rate of inflation). *The government expenditures* are exogenously determined. The exports (*X*) on the other hand, depend on foreign incomes (*Yf*) as well as the exchange rate (*RE*), while the imports (*M*) is a function of domestic income (*Y*) as well as the exchange rate (*RE*). Thus, the net exports (*NX*) depends on three variables: *Yf, Y and RE.* Considering the above modifications, we can reformulate the *IS function* as:

$$IS = AD(Y, i, Yf, RE).$$

We know that the *IS* function represents the goods market equilibrium and relates the levels of aggregate income at each level interest rate. Further, the *IS* curve is downward sloping indicating that the level of income is a decreasing function of the rate of interest. However, we have now two additional variables, viz., foreign income (*Yf*) and the exchange rate (*RE*). whose effects can be examined by assuming them as parameters, causing 'shifts' in the *IS* function.

Effects of rise and fall in foreign incomes: If there is a rise in foreign incomes, for instance, those of the US, UK, Russia, China, etc., which have trade relations with India, there will be more demand for Indian goods in those countries; India's exports will rise and, through this route, aggregate demand in India will go up. In terms of the IS curve, we can say that the *IS* curve will be shifting to the right. On the other hand, if there is a fall in the incomes of those countries,there will be fall in India's exports and hence, a fall in the aggregate demand in India, causing a shift backward to the left, of the *IS* curve. Figures (18.1) and (18.2) show the effects of rise and fall in foreign incomes on domestic aggregate demand.

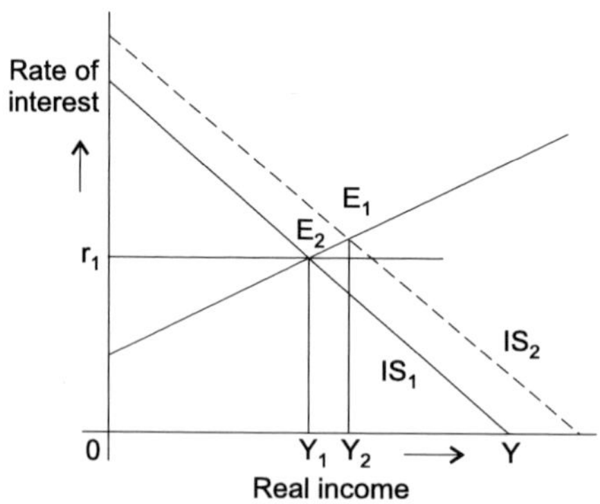

Figure 18.1 *Effect of rise in foreign income (IS curve shifts up to the right).*

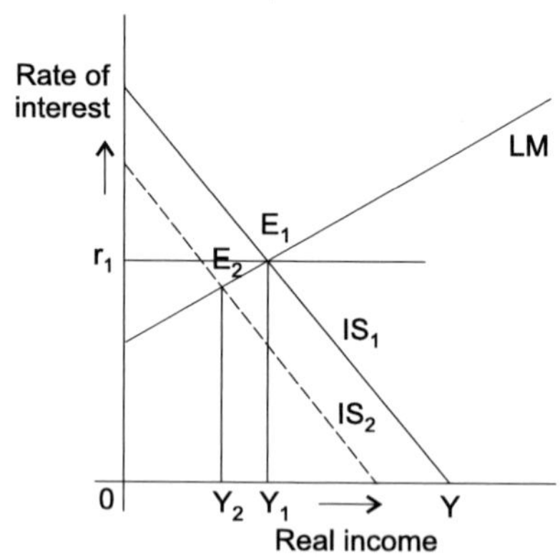

Figure 18.2 *Effect of fall in foreign income (IS curve shifts down to the left).*

Effects of rise and fall in exchange rate (RE): A rise in the exchange rate of a country means payment of more domestic currency against a unit of foreign currency which means depreciation of the domestic currency. Depreciation, as we know, makes the domestic goods cheaper in the foreign markets while it makes the foreign goods costlier. In that case, it is expected that exports will rise and so will the domestic aggregate demand. This will cause an upward shift of the *IS* curve to the right. Opposite will be the case if there is a fall in the exchange rate, i.e., domestic currency appreciates. Appreciation of currency makes the exports costly while making the imports cheap. If, therefore, exports fall and imports rise, the aggregate income (or, national income) will be reduced, thus causing the *IS* curve to shift backward to the left. Figures 18.3 and 18.4 show these effects.

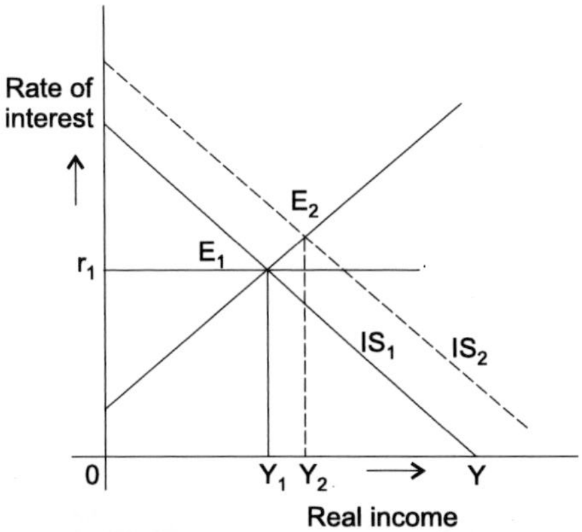

Figure 18.3 *Effect of a rise in RE (more ₹ per US $ exports cheaper, imports costly).*

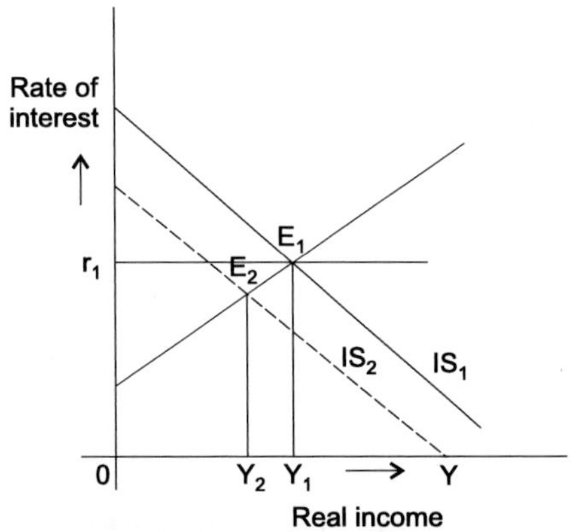

Figure 18.4 *Effect of a fall in RE (less ₹ per US $ exports costly, imports cheaper).*

However, there will also be certain interaction effects of changes in foreign incomes as well as appreciation and depreciation of domestic currency. For instance, if foreign income rises, leading to a rise in domestic demand, this, in turn, will lead to some rise in imports and hence a further rise in foreign income. In fact, this is how the countries' combined incomes rise which result in their collective growth. Opposite happens in case foreign income falls initially.

Similarly, currency appreciation and depreciation have their chain effects, causing either rise or fall in domestic as well as foreign incomes, depending on the extent to which the countries are interlinked in trade.

18.2 THE EXCHANGE RATE

Exchange rate is defined as the price of a unit of foreign currency in terms of domestic currency. If ₹100 can buy 1 US $, then ₹100/1$ is the exchange rate. However, the exchange rate can be quoted in either way, in rupee terms or in dollar terms, i.e., ₹100/ $1 or, $1/100. Change in exchange rate means change in the price of a unit of foreign money. If, instead of ₹100, it rises to ₹120 per US dollar, we say the exchange rate has risen or the Indian rupee has depreciated. Similarly, if the rate becomes ₹80 per US $, the exchange rate falls or the Indian currency appreciates. In other words, if the value of the domestic currency appreciates, it can buy more units of foreign currency and if the domestic currency depreciates, it can buy lesser units of foreign currency.

The basic question is: what determines this rate of exchange? The rate of exchange is determined in the foreign exchange market, a market consisting of a set of designated or authorised sellers and buyers of foreign money. As in the case of the ordinary domestic market, demand for and supply of foreign exchanges mutually determine the equilibrium rate of exchange. The process is explained with the help of Fig. 18.5.

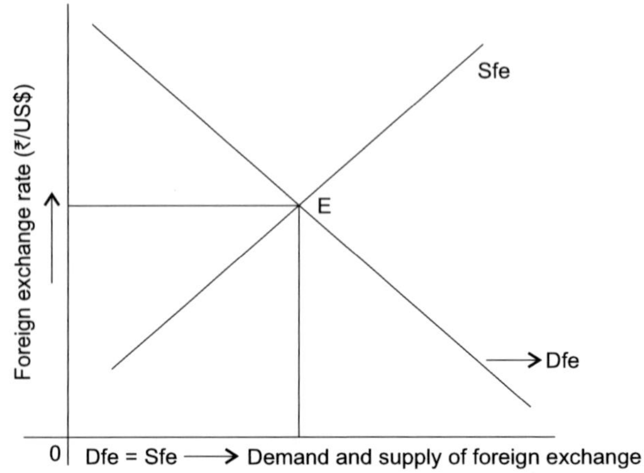

Figure 18.5 *Determination of equilibrium rate of exchange.*

In the figure, Dfe is the demand curve for foreign exchange which is downward sloping while Sfe is the supply of foreign exchange which is upward sloping. Point *E* shows the equilibrium rate of exchange at which the demand and supply of foreign exchange are equal. Now, if the rate of exchange becomes higher, the price of US goods for the Indian consumers becomes higher, so they would reduce their purchase of US goods and hence demand less of US dollars. On the other hand, if the exchange rate is lower, US goods become cheaper since the Indian buyers have to pay less for them and so they purchase more US goods. Viewed from the US consumers, Indian goods become cheaper when the exchange rate is higher, so they wish to buy more of Indian goods and thereby supply more US dollars to the foreign exchange market. Contrarily, when the exchange rate is lower, the Indian goods are costly for the US customers, so they purchase less quantities of them and release less of US dollars in the foreign exchange market, the supply of foreign exchange is less. In fact, demand and supplies of foreign exchange are "derived" demands and "derived" supplies because they are derived from demands and supplies of the goods or services being traded in the international markets. If the demand for Indian goods rises in the US market, the demand for Indian currency will also rise and so, in exchange, the supply of US dollar will increase in the Indian market. Opposite will be the case if the demand for Indian goods falls in the US market.

18.3 BALANCE OF PAYMENTS: THE BASIC ACCOUNTING TOOL

Balance of Payments (BoP) is a statement of all kinds of transactions that take place between the residents of a country and those of other country or countries including their governments, for various kinds of payments made or payments received during a specified period of time (such as a year). BoP is an accounting statement which has three broad parts: (1) Current account, (2) Capital account, and (3) Monetary movements. We explain them below as also the important items within each of them with reference to Table 18.1

1. **Current account:** It includes all transactions relating to imports and exports of goods, known as balance-of-trade (BoT) or merchandise trade, and imports and exports of different kinds of services, known as 'invisibles'. This part of the BoP is the most important item. The balance-of-trade (BoT) i.e., value of exports – value of imports (or, net exports) of goods reflects a country's capability in terms of productive resources and consumption needs. In fact, international trade is established on the basic principle of 'comparative advantage' of producing goods as also services of various kinds. Comparative advantage, however, depends ultimately on the resource endowments that a country either possesses or acquires. The more a country enjoys comparative advantage the more it can export its goods abroad and thereby earn foreign exchange. On the other hand, when a country is not able to meet its needs, it imports the deficit from other countries. In the BoP account, exports are recorded as credit items (because these are payments received) while imports are recorded as debit items (because these payments are made to other countries).

   In accordance with the present practice, as far as the valuation is concerned, exports are valued on f.o.b (free on board) basis, i.e., exclusive of all costs till shipment of exportable goods. On the other hand, imports of goods are valued on c.i.f. (cost insurance and freight) basis, i.e., inclusive of cost, insurance and freight charges.

   Invisible items include mainly the 'services' rendered by the residents or government to non-residents or foreign governments or services received from non-residents or governments outside to the residents and government, transfers and certain kinds of incomes. Services include travel, transportation and insurance services. g.n.i.e., stands for 'government not included elsewhere' and refers to the services connected with embassies and consulates of foreign countries (general administration and other kinds). The funds received by domestic government are entered as credit items while those paid to foreign governments are entered as debit items.

   Miscellaneous items include certain other kinds of services. Of these, software services, business services and communications are prominent. Transfer payments across the border are of two kinds: official transfer and private transfers. These are outright transfers. Official transfers include revenue contributions by the domestic government to the international institutions as also transfers as gifts to non-residents.

Cash remittances made by non-residents to the residents and their families form the major private transfers. Also, NRE (Non-resident External) deposits (along with their interest amount) when paid back also form part of private transfers.

Incomes under BoP current account are investment incomes as also the compensation of employees. For instance, when certain kinds of investments are made by one country to another, the incomes accruing from them are entered as debit items of the investment receiving country. Similarly, incomes from the investments made abroad by the domestic country are entered as credit items.

2. **Capital account:** Foreign capital of any nature received or transferred is recorded in the capital account. Within capital account, investment of capital in any form, loans and banking capital are the important items.

   Foreign investments are of two kinds: Foreign Direct Investment (FDI) and Foreign Institutional Investment (FII).

   Foreign direct investment, again, can be made through two routes: (a) directly investing in particular companies/projects of public or private sector units; (b) transfer of equity shares of companies to the domestic company. FDI can also come through reinvestment of earnings of the existing FDIs, apart from some other sources of capital which are not specified. The above-mentioned sources of FDI are received within the domestic country (for example, in India). But it can be received also through domestic companies operating abroad (MNC status) and they can also have all four sources (direct, equity, earnings reinvested and other types not specified).

   Portfolio investments are investments in the shares/equities of foreign companies through designated institutions known as FII. In India, for example, it is made through SEBI (Securities and Exchange Board of India). Some investments under this category are raised through Global Depository Receipts (GDRs) and American Depository Receipts (ADRs). Just as in the case of FDI, some part of portfolio investments are raised abroad through transfer of shares. Some FIIs which are not registered in India, make their investments through designated banks by participatory notes (PN) also. All inflows are credit items while all outflows are debit items.

External loans are of three kinds: external assistance, external borrowings and short term loans. Of these, first two (external assistance and commercial borrowings) are each, two-way flows. External assistance is made on soft terms — with low rate of interest. For example, external assistance to India means the assistance amount coming to India through foreign sources such as World Bank, International Development Association and several such institutions.

Assistance by India means soft loans advanced by India to other countries or institutions. All receipts are entered as credit items while all repayments (principal + interest) made are entered as debit items.

Commercial borrowings are borrowings on commercial terms, i.e., market rates of interest. These are also two-way flows like the external assistance. Short term credits are, essentially for short period of time.

Foreign assets and liabilities of the banking sector come within the category of banking capital. For example, commercial banks which are designated to deal with foreign funds deposits and disbursements deal with foreign banking capital. In the banking sector balance sheet, as the practice goes, all increases in assets are debit items while all decreases in assets are credit items. Conversely, all increases in liabilities are credit items while all decreases in liabilities are debit items. For example, non-resident deposits (NRE) are entered as liabilities of the banks since these are deposits to be repaid sometime.

Rupee debt service refers to payment of interest, periodic repayment of principal and other related charges on loans incurred by domestic country which are made in terms of Indian rupee as per contractual terms (applicable in case of India).

There are some other categories of capital which are not specified but together they make up a sizeable amount (particularly for India).

'Errors and Omissions' refer to certain discrepancies in the accounting process and timings. Necessary adjustments are, therefore, made by entering this item in the BoP.

Lastly, monetary movements consist of transactions with IMF and the Central Bank of the country regarding foreign exchange reserves. Foreign exchange reserves of the Central Bank consist of gold holdings, foreign currency reserves and SDR (Special Drawing Rights) allocations. All drawals from IMF are treated as credit items while all repayments made to IMF are debit items. On the other hand, all additions to foreign exchange reserves are entered as debit items while drawing down of all existing reserves are entered as credit items. In fact, the net deficit in the overall BoP is matched by monetary movements which are shown as credit item in the monetary movements category. Similarly, the net surplus in the overall BoP is matched by equivalent amount of debit item.

A few notable points need to be remembered in the context of BoP.

1. BoP statement is compiled on the basis of 'double-entry' accounting system. When, looked at the statement as a whole, balance of payments always balances. This is only an accounting necessity and procedure. For purposes of analysis, however, the BoP needs to be examined by parts such as Balance of Trade, Current Account Balance, Capital Account Balance and Monetary Movements.

2. The identity: Current Account Balance + Capital Account Balance + Monetary Movements (including Errors and Omissions) = 0 (This can be easily verified from any BoP data given in Table 18.1 for India). It is also obvious that if there is no monetary movement, the identity is equivalent to the following:

   Current Account Balance + Capital Account Balance = 0

   This means that any surplus/deficit in current account is fully compensated by deficit/surplus in the capital account. Such identity, however, seldom happens in actual practice.
3. Any current account deficit needs to be financed by capital account items. In other words, shortfalls in the amount of foreign exchange arising out of deficit in the current account has to be made up by adequate flow of foreign exchange in the capital account. It may be in the form of foreign investments of any kind or, loans obtained from any foreign source. In case, the flow of capital account falls short of the requirements of current account deficit, the foreign exchange reserves of the central bank are used to finance the deficit. In extreme situation gold holdings of the central bank are used for the purpose. If the current account and the capital account deficits taken together are perpetual and foreign exchange reserves too dwindle the result is 'accumulation of sovereign debt' (or, external debt). Such sovereign debt becomes a matter of serious concern when any further debt through issuance of bonds or any such pledge by the government is not acknowledged or honoured by other countries or institutions. Currently, such a situation has arisen in the case of some of the euro-zone countries like Greece, Spain, Portugal, Ireland and Italy. Such debt crisis deepens when old debts are not renewed further or restructured or the foreign investments flee from the countries for impending fears of worsening of the crisis or the domestic economy itself is running heavy fiscal deficit. Thus, sovereign debt is compounded by fiscal deficit.
4. BoP as a whole can be said to be the barometer of the country's health vis-à-vis rest of the world and is not merely an accounting statement. Its analysis, in its different segments, is very important to judge the health of the economy and apply suitable treatment, else the situation may lead to collapse of the economy particularly in an environment of fast changing globalized world.
5. Just as perpetual deficit in the BoP is a source of trouble, perpetual surplus also invites complications of different nature. Overall surplus in BoP implies accumulation of foreign exchange indicating strong economic fundamentals. The country perpetually exports more than it imports.

Table 18.1 *Key components of India's balance of payments (2001-02–2010-11)*

Item/Year	2001-02	2002-03	2003-04	2004-05	2005-06	2006-07	2007-08	2008-09	2009-10	2010-11
1	2	3	4	5	6	7	8	9	10	11
I. Merchandise										
A. Exports, f.o.b.	213345	260079	303915	381785	465748	582871	668008	857960	862333	1139517
B. Imports, c.i.f.	268300	311776	367301	533550	695412	862833	1035672	1405412	1423079	1734545
I. Trade balance (A-B)	-54955	-51697	-63386	-151765	-229664	-279962	-367664	-547452	-560746	-595028
II. Invisibles, net	71381	82357	127369	139591	185927	235579	304185	419821	380120	392494
III. Current account (I+II)	16426	30660	63983	-12174	-43737	-44383	-63479	-137631	-180626	-202532
IV. Capital account (A to F)	40167	51377	80010	128081	109633	208017	433167	30516	244863	261981
A. Foreign investment	38861	29072	71728	68366	94814	134282	249388	106619	311779	251277
B. External assistance, net	5819	-14863	-12553	8993	7876	8027	8484	13139	15357	22589
C. Commercial borrowings, net	-7543	-8263	-13274	24149	11610	73889	91212	30948	15674	52899
D. Rupee debt service	-2457	-2306	-1756	-1858	-2557	-725	-492	-471	-452	-313
E. NRI deposits, net	13127	14424	16869	-4439	12457	19574	705	20430	14254	14822
F. Other capital	-7640	33313	18996	32870	-14567	-27030	83870	-140149	-111749	-79293
V. Overall balance (III+IV)	56593	82037	143993	115907	65896	163634	369689	-97115	64237	59449
VI. Monetary movements (VII+VIII+IX)	-56593	-82037	-143993	-115907	-65896	-163634	-369689	97115	-64237	-59449
VII. Reserves (increase -/ decrease +)	-56593	-82037	-143993	-115907	-65896	-163634	-369689	97115	-64237	- 59449
VIII. IMF, net	0	0	0	0	0	0	0	0	0	0
IX. SDR allocation	0	0	0	0	0	0	0	0	-24983	0

Note:

1. Data for 2010-11 are preliminary estimates and data for 2009-10 are partially revised.
2. Capital account includes Errors and Omissions.

Also see notes on tables.

Source: R.B.I.

Contd..

Contd..

India's overall balance of payments

(US$ million)

	2014-15	2015-16	2016-17	2017-18	2018-19 P
1	2	3	4	5	6
A. Current Account					
1. Exports, f.o.b.	316545	2666365	280138	308970	337237
2. Imports, c.i.f.	461484	396444	392580	469006	517519
3. Trade Balance	-144940	-130079	-112442	-160036	-180283
4. Invisibles, Net	118081	107928	98026	111319	123026
a) 'Non-factor' services of which:	76529	69676	68345	77562	81941
Software services	70400	71454	70763	72186	77654
b) Income	-24140	-24375	-26302	-28681	-28861
c) Private transfers	66264	63139	56573	62949	70601
5. Current account balance	-26859	-22151	14417	48717	-57256
B. Capital Account					
1. Foreign investment, Net (a + b)	73456	31891	43224	52401	30094
a) Direct investment	31251	36021	35612	30286	30712
b) Portfolio investment	42205	-4130	7612	22115	-618
2. External assistance, Net	1725	1505	2013	2944	3413
3. Commercial borrowings, Net	1570	-4529	-6012	-183	10416
4. Short term credit, Net	-111	-1610	6467	13900	2021
5. Banking capital of which:	11618	10630	-16616	16190	7433
NRI deposits, Net	14057	16052	-12367	9676	10387
6. Rupee debt service	-81	-73	-99	-75	-31
7. Other capital, Net$	1109	3315	7559	6213	1057
8. Total capital account	89286	41128	36447	91390	54403
C. Errors & Omissions	-1021	-1073	-480	902	-486
D. Overall Balance [A(5) + B(8) + C]	61406	17905	21550	43574	-3339
E. Monetary Moments (F + G)	-61406	17905	-21550	-43574	3339
F. IMF, net	0	0	0	0	0
G. Reserves and Monetary Gold (Increase -, Decrease +)	-61406	-17905	-21550	-43574	3339
of which: SDR allocation	0	0	0	0	0
Memo: as a ratio to GDP					
1. Trade balance	-7.1	-3.2	-4.9	-6.0	-6.6
2. Net services	3.8	3.3	3.0	2.9	3.0
3. Net income	-1.2	-1.2	-1.1	-1.1	-1.1
4. Current account balance	-1.6	-1.1	-0.6	-1.8	-2.1
5. Capital net	4.4	2.0	1.6	3.4	2.0
6. Foreign investment, net	3.6	1.5	1.9	2.0	1.1

P: Provisional

$: Includes delayed export receipts, advance payments against imports, net funds held abroad and advances received pending issue of shares under FDI.

Note:

1. Gold and silver brought by returning Indians have been included under imports, with a contra entry in private transfer receipts.
2. Data on exports and imports differ from those given by DGCI&S on account of differences in coverage, valuation and timing.

Source: R.B.I.

18.4 BALANCE OF PAYMENTS: DISEQUILIBRIUM AND ADJUSTMENT

We have seen, later in this chapter (see 18.6), that in the open economy, the objective of macroeconomic policy is to achieve internal as well as external balance at the same time. Internal balance refers to the attaining of full employment while external balance refers to the achievement of zero balance of payments (deficit in the balance of payments is zero). However, these twin objectives of macroeconomic policy are very difficult goals to be met in practice. Often it happens that attempts to achieve one goal frustrate the achievement of the other goals.

In the context of an open economy, for a country suffering from BoP disequilibrium, particularly, BoP deficit, there are two types of policy interventions available for the government as explained below.

18.4.1 Expenditure Reducing Policy

If the country's import bill is consistently rising, one way to tackle it is to reduce the domestic aggregate demand. In terms of *IS* curve, the policy is to make it shift to the left. Reduction of aggregate demand means reducing the demand for imports and thereby improving the external balance. In order to understand how expenditure reducing policy is related to the external balance, we can make use of the open economy aggregate demand (OEAD) equation discussed in chapter 1, which is reproduced here for reference:

$$Y = C + I + G + NX. \tag{i}$$

$$NX = Y - (C + I + G) \tag{ii}$$

where, NX is the net exports (exports-imports), Y is the aggregate demand (or, aggregate expenditures), C is consumption expenditure, I is the investment expenditure and G is the government purchases of goods and services. From eqn. (ii), we can infer that if the aggregate expenditure part $(C + I + G)$ is reduced, the right-hand side component of the equation will be larger so that NX will be larger. In other words, BoP deficit will be narrowed. However, in this exercise of compressing the aggregate expenditures, caution needs to be taken that Y is not negatively impacted. For, if $C + I + G$ is somehow reduced (individually or severally) and at the same time, Y is also reduced, there will be no reduction on NX and so, BoP deficit will not be corrected. On the contrary, the size of the economy will be reduced as also the rate of growth of the economy will be slow.

Beyond the simple mathematical arrangement, it is largely left to the government to work out the detailed policy alternatives as to how and to what extent aggregate expenditures can be reduced. Private consumption expenditure on such items which have a larger import content can be discouraged by appropriate government policy. Similarly, private investment expenditure on items with higher import content should be avoided by suitable fiscal as well as monetary policy actions by the government. For example, taxes can be levied on selective basis on different items of expenditures. At the same time, the rate of interest can also be raised by the central bank to reduce investment expenditures. However, extreme care needs to be taken to see that aggregate expenditures are not adversely affected beyond a point.

18.4.2 Expenditure Switching Policy

Another set of policies that stress on switching or shifting the expenditures from "imported" goods to "domestic" goods is also suggested while largely maintaining aggregate expenditures at the original level. For such policies to be operational, domestic prices of internationally traded goods will have to be lower and competitive so that consumers may be induced to move away from imported goods to domestic goods. This is certainly not an easy task for, domestic level of prices depends on several factors including the rate of money supply and the government's fiscal policy. For instance, Indian consumers cannot be easily encouraged or induced to buy Chinese imported goods due primarily to their price differences. Prices of imported goods can be made costly by influencing the rate of exchange, i.e., depreciating the domestic currency which makes imports costly but cheapens export goods. This way, the balance of trade deficit can be narrowed. Balance of trade, as we know, happens to be the most important item in the current account balance as also the balance of payments generally.

18.4.3 Imposition of Import Tariffs

With the free trade rules under the WTO being flouted increasingly in today's international trade and business environment, countries are concerned about their own welfare and are applying protectionist measures by imposing tariffs on various items of import goods. This way, import cost is going up thus discouraging imports. However, what is needed most is to start detailed policy initiatives for export promotion of goods and services of various kinds. New and emerging areas of exports need to be explored.

The current tariff restrictions war (trade war) going on between the US and China is a matter of concern for the way world trade is going ahead. It is feared that other countries may also follow the same route in order to reduce the disequilibrium in their BoPs.

Besides the imposition of tariffs on imports, there can be restrictions on the volume of imports as well by various types of government regulations such as on gold and silver or other precious metals or various types of "sin" goods (alcohol, for instance).

18.4.4 Monetary Policy

Besides a slew of fiscal measures to compress the aggregate demand, the government and its concerned authorities can also adopt monetary policy measures, either expansionary or contractionary as the case be. For instance, if the country's BoP is suffering from extreme deficit, contraction in the supply of money by the central banks is needed to control the domestic inflation rate so that the prices are prevented from rising. The measure is likely to improve the country's competitiveness in the international markets so that exports are encouraged and the adverse BoP position is ultimately improved. On the other hand, in the case of BoP surplus, expansionary monetary policy is required to be adopted. The resulting rise in inflation rate in the domestic economy will ultimately reduce the exports and encourage imports and thereby correct the BoP situation.

The monetary policy tweaking as stated above also helps in another way, through inflow and outflow of external capital a big part of which is influenced by the rate of interest in the economy. Thus, if the relative rate of interest in the domestic economy is higher as a result of adopting contractionary monetary policy, there will be greater inflow of external capital which will help bridge the deficit in the BoP. In the opposite case, the excessive surplus in the BoP will be wiped out restoring the appropriate balance.

18.5 DIFFERENT APPROACHES TO BALANCE OF PAYMENTS DISEQUILIBRIUM

One of the basic questions macroeconomists often face is what causes disequilibrium in the balance of payments (BoP) and what determines the rate of exchange. There have been several attempts at explaining these phenomena. However, we shall review two such attempts, viz.: (1) monetary approach and (2) asset market approach.

18.5.1 Monetary Approach to BoP

The role of money supply in the long-run determination of BoP was stressed by economists Robert Mundell and Harry G. Johnson during the late 1960s which was later developed and expanded during the 1970s. Their approach can be called an extension of 'monetarism' (a Chicago school 'avatar' led by economist late Milton Friedman) to the field of international economy. In fact, one can find an obvious link between the Mundell Fleming model as applicable to perfect capital mobility under a fixed exchange rate system and the monetary approach to BoP and exchange rate determination.

According to monetary approach, balance of payments problem is, essentially, a monetary phenomenon, since monetary movements among nations ultimately cause either deficit or surplus in the BoP in the long run. In order to see how this happens and how it automatically restores monetary equilibrium, we shall examine the cases of fixed rate of exchange and flexible rate of exchange systems by turns.

(a) Fixed rate of exchange and monetary approach

In the domestic economy, as we already know, monetary equilibrium is established when the total demand for money is equal to the total supply of money. In the same vein, monetary disequilibrium occurs when either the supply of money exceeds the demand for it or, the demand for money exceeds its supply. In the context of an open economy, if there is èxcess supply of money in the domestic economy, this will find its way out in the international market. Similarly, if there is excess demand for money in the domestic economy, this will, expectedly, be compensated by an inflow of money from international markets. In the process, there occurs disequilibrium in the country's BoP via its *foreign reserve component.* If the excess supply of money goes out of the country, there will be corresponding equivalent depletion in its foreign reserves causing BoP deficit. On the other hand, if there is excess demand for money, the nation's foreign reserves increases, thus causing BoP surplus under fixed rate of exchange.

In order to better understand the whole process, we shall recall the demand function of money as also the supply function of money as discussed in our previous chapters. To recapitulate, the demand function of money can be expressed as:

$$Md = k\ Po\ Y. \tag{18.1}$$

where, Md is the nominal demand for money, $Po\ Y$ is the nominal GNP and k is the proportion of nominal GNP that is demanded by the public in the form of cash, (Po is the price level). Similarly, the supply function of money can be expressed as:

$$Ms. = m\ R. \tag{18.2}$$

where, Ms is the supply of money, R is the stock of reserve money (or, monetary base) and m is the money multiplier. Thus, the supply of money is a function of the stock of reserve money and money multiplier.

In the case of an open economy, the scope of the supply of money is expanded and, in fact, consists of two parts: (a) domestic supply of money and (b) foreign supply of money; so that now we can write the supply function of money as:

$$Ms. = m.\ (R\ d + R\ f) \tag{18.3}$$

where, Rd and Rf are, respectively, domestic reserve money and foreign reserve money.

Monetary equilibrium takes place when total demand for money is equal to the total supply of money in the context of open economy, that is,

$$kPo\ Y. = m\ (R\ d + R\ f) \tag{18.4}$$

Let us suppose, in country A, there has been a consistent rise in its real national income (Y), thus causing a rise in the domestic demand for money. If the nation's monetary authority (central bank) fails to meet this excess demand, for some reason or other, by releasing appropriate amount in its reserve money, that is, *Rd;* the shortfall will be compensated by *Rf,* the foreign reserve portion. This means the country's balance of payments will show up 'surplus'. On the other hand, if there is excess supply of money in the economy, backed by excess reserves, *Rd,* there will be outflow of money from the country, causing a fall in the foreign component of its reserves, *Rf,* which means deficit in the BoP. Clearly, these surpluses and deficits in the balance of payments will be just enough to eliminate the excess in either the demand for money or supply of money in the long run.

The monetary approach, thus, suggests that the country's monetary authority (central bank) has no control over its money supply. It has to abide by the rule of fixed exchange rate system so that the central bank is obliged to release equivalent amount of foreign money in case of excess money supply going out from the domestic country or equivalent amount of domestic reserves in case of excess demand for money being met from outside the country. Thus, the balance of payments disequilibria are automatically eliminated in the long run through inflow or outflow of the country's monetary reserves.

Secondly, it is also clear that, under fixed rate of exchange system, the size of a country's money supply will be one that is consistent with its balance of payments equilibrium in the long run. Of course, there are certain exceptions, a handful of countries, notably the US, regarded as 'reserve currency countries' are able to have control over its money supply and, hence, pursue independent monetary policy.

(b) Flexible rate of exchange and monetary approach

If the rate of exchange is flexible, that is, changing with the changing conditions of demand and supply of foreign exchange, then the monetary approach would predict that any balance of payments disequilibrium is 'automatically' corrected by the *depreciation and appreciation* of currency rather than any movement of international reserves among countries. For instance, if there is excess money supply in the domestic economy, it tends to raise the domestic price level and through it influences the exchange rate. In fact, the higher price level makes the domestic goods costlier relative to foreign goods. So demand for foreign goods rises while that of domestic goods falls. The result is the increased demand for foreign currency and decreased demand for domestic currency in the foreign exchange market. As a consequence, domestic currency depreciates causing a balance of payments deficit. In the long run, the cheap domestic prices (due to currency depreciation) help raise the exports while reducing imports at the same time. The balance of payments deficit is thus automatically corrected. Opposite happens in case there is excess demand for money relative to its supply. The domestic price level lowers, it makes the foreign goods costlier, dampens the demand for foreign exchange and thus exchange rate appreciates which means lesser demand for domestic goods in the international market and hence lower foreign exchange earnings. Thus, balance of payments surplus is automatically eliminated.

Under the flexible exchange rate system, therefore, countries retain their power of controlling the money supply because they would not have to abide by the rule of fixed exchange rate. At the same time, they are able to pursue independent monetary policies.

Determination of equilibrium rate of exchange: It can now be shown that, under monetary approach, the rate of exchange is determined by the rate of relative money supplies of different countries. According to the purchasing power parity theory (*PPP*), the rate of exchange is equal to the ratio of price levels of any two or more countries. For example, in the case of India and US, $R = \frac{Po^*}{Po}$, where, Po^* is the index number of price level in India and Po is the index number of prices in US, R is the rate of exchange. In fact, *PPP* theory is based on the principle of one price and reflects the equilibrium rate of exchange. Now, if we express Ms^* and Ms as the money supply in India and US respectively, and $Md^* = k^* Po^* Y^*$ and $Md = kPo \cdot Y$ as the money demand functions of India and the US respectively, then, assuming monetary equilibrium in both the countries, we can write as follows:

$$Ms^* = k^* Po^* Y^* \text{ and } Ms = k\, Po\, Y \qquad (18.5)$$

In order to obtain our desired ratio, P^* / P, we first get the ratio of the equilibrium equations of both countries so that:

$$Ms^* / Ms = k^* Po^* Y^* / k\, Po\, Y. \qquad (18.6)$$

Now, multiplying both sides of eqn. (18.6) by $k\, Y / k^*\, Y$, we get

$$Po^* / Po = (Ms^* / Ms) \times (k\, Y / k^*\, Y^*) \qquad (18.7)$$

Since we have defined earlier that $R = Po^* / Po$, hence

$$R = (Ms^* / Ms)\ (kY / k^*\, Y^*) \qquad (18.8)$$

Assuming k^* and k as also Y and Y^* remain constant since demand functions of money are relatively stable in the long run, and output, Y and Y^* being the full employment levels of output; rate of exchange will depend on relative rates of change in the money supply of the two countries, India and the US. In other words, if the money supply in India increases by a greater percentage than that in the US, the rate of exchange will increase, i.e., Indian rupee will depreciate in the long run while US dollar will appreciate. Opposite will be the case if money supply in the US increases by a greater percentage than in India, i.e., Indian rupee will appreciate while US dollar will depreciate. Thus, monetary approach emphasises upon relative growth rates of money supply in different countries as an important factor in determining exchange rates of their currencies.

An evaluation of the monetary approach: The monetary approach to balance of payments and exchange rate determination has become less relevant in today's open economy international perspective. In the present globalised and open economy, a number of financial assets, besides money, flow in and out of the country. These assets are influenced by a number of factors. However, monetary disequilibrium is, surely, an important factor in affecting a country's exchange rate determination in the long run. In fact, persistent inflation rate for a fairly long period in a country depreciates its currency. Under fixed exchange rate system, it works well and is a more dependable and stable system. But in 1971, the system was given a goodbye primarily due to the developed countries' search for an alternative system in which independent monetary policies could be adopted. The present system (of flexible exchange rate) allows for this but it unleashes much more uncertainty and instability in the international trade and payments as is presently being seen around the world.

Secondly, the monetary approach ignores the importance of rate of interest as an important determinant of the demand for money (Keynesian version of the demand for money). In fact, the approach is based on the classical monetary theory which lays stress on the long-run determinant of the demand for money, i.e., national income.

18.5.2 Asset Market Approach to Balance of Payments and Exchange Rate

Developed since mid-1970s, the asset market approach views the determination of exchange rate as well as BoP in the perspective of the entire portfolio of assets which include, besides money, bonds (domestic as well as foreign) and securities which are free to be moved by domestic and foreign residents in today's open economy environment. It is an application of portfolio balance theory of demand for money (see chapter 7, sec. 7.3) in international perspective where there are various types of financial assets including foreign bonds and other assets that the asset holder wishes to transact upon. It is in the process of establishing equilibrium in the asset market that the balance of payments position gets disturbed as also readjusted. The rates of exchange for various currencies are also determined in the process.

As we have discussed in chapter 7, an asset holder's decision-making process involves holding money, on the one hand, and various assets with their expected returns and respective risks attached with them on the other. After weighing these returns and risks, the asset holder, if he is a risk averter, arrives at an optimum combination of different assets within his entire portfolio of assets in the risk-return framework.

In the context of an open economy, foreign bonds enter as an independent factor which, in fact, is different in certain respects from domestic bonds. Although, holding both kinds of bonds have similar risks and returns, holding of foreign bonds (which are denominated in foreign currencies) involves an additional risk of currency depreciation. For instance, if a US citizen purchases a certain amount of Indian bonds (either government or private) for ₹ 1 crore to be redeemable on some future date at a certain rate of interest (yield), and after some time, the rupee depreciates, then the bondholder, upon selling his bond, will receive lesser amount in terms of US dollar. From this point of view, it can be said that domestic bonds and foreign bonds are not perfect substitutes. Besides, there can be additional risks of default in their repayment of annuities as also other country-related risks. The bonds carry, on the other hand, a return in terms of expected rise in their market values, appreciation of their prices, which, however, is uncertain since, their market values may have the equal chance of falling in future.

Given the above-mentioned perception of financial wealth, the asset holders (individuals and firms) generally maintain a certain combination of domestic money, domestic bonds and foreign bonds with a view to diversify their asset portfolio and also to maximise their returns or expected utility. In addition, in the case of foreign bondholders, they would further diversify them by spreading among bonds of different countries. Holding different country bonds have certain specific advantages. For instance, in case of any disturbance in the international financial market like ups and downs of interest rates (causing bond prices to change in the opposite direction), diversification would ensure that such disturbance would not affect all the markets simultaneously.

The actual choice on aggregate asset holding depends, finally, upon the asset holder's individual preferences and attitudes towards risk, his own wealth level, the different rates of return offered on different categories of assets, relative inflation rates of different countries and his or her expectations and judgments about the future outcome.

Once an equilibrium is reached in terms of demand for and supply of each financial wealth (total demand = total supply), any change in any of the above-mentioned variables would trigger an immediate and quick reshuffling of his portfolio of assets with a view to arriving at a new desired level of equilibrium. These actions across the global financial markets cause financial flows and, in the process, determine the exchange rates of different currencies of the world. The balance of payments are also affected at the same time. This, precisely, is the asset market approach to BoP and exchange rate determination.

We now restate the above facts more formally and precisely, in mathematical terms.

The exchange rate is a function of (a) domestic interest rate, (b) foreign interest rate, (c) level of wealth of the investors and (d) demand for foreign bonds. Specifically, the exchange rate is a direct function of domestic interest rate and the level of wealth while it is inversely related to foreign interest rate and the demand for foreign bonds. In symbolic terms, we can write :

$$R = f(r, rf, W, fb) \tag{18.9}$$

such that,

$$R. = r,\ W\ /\ rf,\ fb \qquad (18.10)$$

where,

R = rate of exchange (e.g., amount of rupees per US dollar),

r = rate of interest applicable to domestic bonds,

rf = rate of interest applicable to foreign bonds,

W = level of wealth of the asset holder,

fb = amount of foreign bonds on demand.

Equation (5) can be interpreted as follows:

If the domestic interest rate (r) rises, asset holders would like to hold more domestic bonds in place of money (Indian rupee) and foreign bonds. If foreign interest rate (rf) rises, they would prefer to hold more foreign bonds to domestic bonds and money. Purchasing more foreign bonds means demand for dollars would rise (price of dollar would rise) which means the exchange rate would rise; that is, more rupees per unit of US dollar will be required or rupee will depreciate. Thus, as the stock of foreign bonds increases in the asset holder's portfolio, the exchange rate would rise.

However, if the total wealth of the asset holder increases, he will have a tendency to hold more of all assets (positive wealth effect or positive income effect) provided other things are equal.

Other factors affecting portfolio balance

(1) Expected appreciation/depreciation of foreign currency

Holders of foreign bonds might have a perception of appreciation or depreciation of foreign currencies in the future in which such bonds are denominated. If foreign currency appreciates in the future, there is financial gain for bond holders while in the case of depreciation, there is a financial loss for them. Thus, in case of expected appreciation, the demand for foreign bonds will rise while that of money will decline. Opposite will be the case if there is expected depreciation. This is an additional risk for foreign bond holders so that foreign and domestic bonds are said to be imperfect substitutes.

The question is, how would the bond holders discount this risk element? At best, the interest rate differential between foreign and domestic bonds must take care of this risk in terms of certain 'risk premium'. In other words, if the risk premium attached with interest rate differential is low, asset holders will prefer more of foreign bonds and if the risk premium is high, they will be inclined to hold more domestic bonds. Precisely, the same thing is suggested by the theory of uncovered interest rate parity. For instance, if the interest rates in US and India are, respectively, 2% and 5%, and the expected appreciation rate of Indian currency is, approximately, 1% per annum, then the effective interest rate differential will be 5 – 2 + 1 = 4% instead of 3%. Opposite will be the case if there is expected depreciation of foreign currency. In the above example, if the expected depreciation of Indian currency is 2%, then the effective interest rate differential will be 5 – 2 – 2 = 1%.

The equilibrium in the international financial markets is said to be established when the returns in real terms, from them are equalised. Thus, if there are differences in interest rates between domestic and foreign bonds, these must account for (1) expected appreciation rate of foreign currency as also (2) certain risk premium attached with holding such bonds. In symbolic terms, we can write:

$$rd - rf = EA - RP,$$

which leads to $rd = rf + EA - RP$ (18.11)

where,

rd = domestic interest rate applicable to domestic bonds

rf = foreign interest rate applicable to foreign bonds

EA = expected appreciation rate

RP = risk premium.

Now, when will there be disequilibrium in the international financial market? The disequilibrium will take place only when the above condition does not hold. In other words, if the risk premium (*RP*) is lower or expected appreciation rate of foreign currency is higher or foreign interest rate (nominal) is still higher, there will be higher demand for foreign bonds leading to higher demand for foreign exchange and the rise in exchange rate. A reshuffling of entire asset portfolio will take place, preference will shift from domestic money and domestic bonds to foreign bonds. In the opposite case, reshuffling of portfolio will be in favour of domestic money and domestic bonds, lesser demand for foreign exchange and appreciation of domestic currency.

To summarise the asset market model, we can specify at least three demand functions: (1) demand function for money, (2) demand function for domestic bonds and (3) demand function for foreign bonds.

(1) Demand function for domestic money: The demand for money which competes with returns on different other alternative assets, depends on domestic country interest rate (*rd*), foreign country interest rate (*rf*), expected appreciation of foreign currency (*EA*), risk premium of holding foreign bonds (*RP*) along with domestic level of real national income (*Y*), price level (*P*) and level of wealth (*W*) of the domestic country. The last three variables, particularly, real national income and price level determine the transaction demand for domestic money, while the rest four variables determine the asset demand for money which include foreign assets as well. More specifically, the demand for money is inversely related to the domestic country interest rate (*rd*), foreign country interest rate (*rf*) as also expected appreciation rate of the foreign currency (*EA*), while it is positively related to real *GNP (Y)*, price level (*P*) and wealth level (*W*) of the domestic country.

(2) Demand for domestic bonds (*Bd*): The domestic bonds are positively related to domestic interest rate (*rd*) or, fall in bond price but inversely related to interest on foreign bonds (*rf*), expected appreciation (*EA*) while real GNP and price level have positive impacts both on domestic bonds and foreign bonds. Similarly, risk premium (*RP*) and wealth level (*W*) have positive impacts on the demand for domestic bonds.

(3) Demand for foreign bonds (*Bf*): Demand for foreign bonds are positively related to foreign interest rate (*rf*), expected appreciation (*EA*) and the level of domestic wealth (*W*), while it is inversely related to domestic interest rate (*rd*), risk premium (*RP*), level of GNP (*Y*) and domestic price level (*P*).

Let us now recapitulate how equilibrium in the asset market takes place. Clearly, (a) when the total demand for money balance is equal to the total supply of money, (b) total demand for domestic bonds is equal to the total supply of domestic bonds, (c) total demand for foreign bonds is equal to the total supply of foreign bonds and (d) total demand for foreign exchanges is equal to the total supply of foreign exchanges. The supplies of different assets including money are assumed to be exogenously given. Thus, setting these respective demands equal to their given supplies, we obtain the equilibrium values of domestic as well as foreign interest rates as also equilibrium values of exchange rates of the currencies of the nations. These equilibrium values are to be solved simultaneously and, therefore, requires sophisticated econometric tool of simultaneous equation system to be solved. Once these equilibrium values are obtained, any change in any one or several variables causes immediate reshuffling of different assets mentioned above and a new set of equilibrium values are obtained. Accordingly, new set of exchange rates are also reestablished.

Portfolio adjustment in the assets market: It will now be interesting to examine the process of portfolio adjustment of the investors in response to any change in the value of any of the variables mentioned above. Assuming all the three segments of asset market (domestic money, domestic bonds and foreign bonds) are initially in equilibrium. Now, if the domestic interest rate rises, demand for money in the domestic market will go down in favour of domestic bonds. The foreign investors might increase their holdings of domestic bonds, provided other conditions are also fulfilled. The demand for domestic currency will rise while that of foreign exchange will fall so that exchange rate will fall, i.e., domestic currency will appreciate. Opposite will be the effect when foreign interest rate goes up (given the risk perception of exchange rate and expected appreciation rate). In this case, domestic investors would be tempted to buy more foreign bonds, demand for foreign exchange will rise and so also the exchange rate (i.e., domestic currency will depreciate and foreign currency will appreciate). But what would be the combined effect of change in the foreign interest rate as well as the riskiness of holding foreign bonds? For instance, if foreign interest rate rises along with rise in its riskiness, then the effect on the asset holder's portfolio balance cannot be easily predicted unless the levels of both these factors are examined in a suitable simultaneous equations model. However, if the level of riskiness falls while the interest rate rises abroad, there will clearly be rise in the demand for foreign bonds and the result will be a rise in the exchange rate.

If the level of real *GNP* along with domestic price level rises overtime, the demand for money (transaction demand) will rise along with a fall in the asset demand for money, i.e., less demand for bonds (domestic as well as foreign). But if the wealth level of domestic residents rises, may be associated with rise in their savings rate over time, it will have a positive effect on all kinds of financial assets including domestic and foreign bonds.

Clearly, the asset market approach to exchange rate determination is much more complicated. It explains the fluctuations in the asset market and hence the exchange rates in the present-day practice of flexible exchange rate system. From this point of view, the approach is more realistic than the monetary approach. But at the same time, it helps explain the short-run fluctuations in the exchange rates rather than their long-run behaviour. In fact, from a policy point of view, nominal exchange rates of currencies do not count as much their real exchange rates or, real effective exchange rates (REER) which takes account of the relative inflation rates of the respective countries as well. (see appendix 18.A).

APPENDIX 18.A

Purchasing Power Parity theory: The idea that the long-run equilibrium rate of exchange toward which currencies should move is suggested by purchasing power parity (PPP) theory, invented by Gustav Cassel, a Swedish economist in the early 20th century. The theory argues that the exchange rates between different currencies should be determined in a manner that their purchasing powers must be the same. For instance, if a certain bundle of goods in the two countries, India and the US, are purchased for ₹ 1000 and $20, respectively, the theory suggests that the exchange rate of the two currencies, Indian rupee and US dollar, must be ₹ 50 per US $. This is in keeping with the principle of one price. If in practice, this does not hold, then commodity arbitrage will take place to equalise the prices in the two countries. For example, if the price of the same bundle of goods changes to ₹ 800 in India with no change in the US, then traders will purchase at lower price in India and resell them in the US and thereby earn profit. Ultimately, the price level in India will rise due to higher demand and that in the US will fall due to greater supply to equalise prices in the two countries. Thus, commodity arbitrage will operate between the two countries to prevent exchange rates from departing from the principle of one price.

Absolute vs. relative PPPs: There are two versions of the purchasing power parity theory: absolute PPP and relative PPP.

Absolute PPP: The absolute version of PPP simply argues that the exchange rate of currencies should reflect the ratio of price levels prevailing in the two countries. For instance, if *Pd* and *Pf* represent the price levels in the domestic country and foreign country respectively, then the rate of exchange should be: $R = Pd / Pf$, when expressed in terms of the single country's currency.

However, the absolute version of the PPP has certain drawbacks:

(a) It fails to take account of the relative changes in the levels of prices over time in the two countries. (b) The absolute PPP generally considers the transactions that take place within the ' balance of trade' or 'merchandise trade' and ignores the 'capital account transaction' such as capital inflows and capital outflows which affect the rate of exchange to a significant extent.

There are some other drawbacks of PPP theory (which are present in both versions) that include the use of *general price levels* in the two countries. General price levels include both traded as well as non-traded goods (such as bricks, cement, marbles as also certain categories of services doctors, barbers, maids) and the prices of non-traded goods are not equalised by international trade due to various reasons. Still, the relative version of PPP is considered more realistic. The relative PPP is defined as:

$$RE1. = (Pdo/Pd1)/(Pfo/Pf1) \times REo \tag{18.12}$$

where, *REo and RE1* are the exchange rates at periods 0 and 1, *Pdo* and *Pd1* are price levels of the domestic country at periods 0 and 1 and *Pfo and Pf1 are* the price levels of foreign countries at periods 0 and 1 respectively. Clearly, the relative version of PPP takes into account the changes in the price levels or relative inflation rates between the countries over a given time period. For example, if between the two years, 2005 and 2010, India's price indices rise by 25% while those in the US remain unchanged, then the above formula suggests that the rate of exchange of Indian rupee should depreciate by 25% between 2005 and 2010 since, the numerator value goes down by 25% while the denominator value remains the same.

Empirically, it has been more or less established that the actual rate of exchange has a tendency to approach the one predicted by the PPP theory only in the long run. But exactly how long the time period would be, is uncertain.

Nominal vs. Real Exchange Rate: Nominal exchange rate or, nominal effective exchange rate (NEER) refers to the exchange rate in nominal terms such as so much of Indian rupee per unit of US dollar or so much of US dollars per unit of British pound and so on. Clearly, nominal values are subject to change due to unequal price level changes in different countries. The real exchange rate or real effective exchange rate (REER), on the other hand, indicates the exchange rate in real terms when impacts of relative changes in price levels are suitably adjusted.

The formula for relative PPP given above represents the real effective exchange rate or simply real exchange rate. It may be mentioned here that while evaluating the volatility of exchange rates over a period of time of a certain country, attention needs to be focused more on the 'real' rather than nominal exchange rate. From the formula for real PPP given above, it can be concluded that if and when the purchasing powers of the two different currencies are equalised, the value of the real exchange rate (RE) will be equal to one. In other words, if Pi and Pu represent two prices in India and the US, respectively, then

$RE. = e\ (Pu/Pi) = 1$, where e = rupee price of a unit of US dollar and RE is the real exchange rate (PPP rate).

Let us take a concrete example. The price of a readymade shirt in India is ₹ 200 and that in the US is $ 5, and the rupee price of a US dollar (nominal exchange rate) is ₹ 60, then,

PPP = RE = (5/200) 60 = 3/2.

In this case, the value of PPP is greater than one and so it can be concluded that the price of a piece of shirt in the US is higher than that in India. In fact, for PPP to be equal to one, the price of the shirt in the US should have been $ 3.34 or that in India ₹ 300. In other words, so long as the value of RE is greater than one, price in the US is greater than that in India and so the exchange rate will not reflect the PPPs of the two currencies, US $ and Indian rupee.

18.6 INTERNAL VERSUS EXTERNAL EQUILIBRIUM IN AN OPEN ECONOMY

In an open economy model, while internal equilibrium or internal balance is attained when both the commodity market and money market (or, real and monetary sectors) are simultaneously in equilibrium, the external equilibrium or external balance is attained when the balance of trade ($X - M$) or, more generally the balance of payments (BoP) is zero. But, internal and external equilibria are not independent now in the sense that internal equilibrium cannot be attained without the attainment of external equilibrium. For instance, if there is deficit in the balance of trade ($X - M < 0$) the domestic country needs to make payments in terms of foreign exchange (the current account deficit). This requires to be compensated for by way of more exports, [or other channels in the capital account balance]. In any case, in case of deficit in the current account the demand for foreign exchange goes up leading to its higher price of goods in the trading account, or other items in the "invisibles" (the services) or other alternative channels in the capital account balance. If none of these happens and the deficit persists for longer period, the increased demand for foreign exchange leads to its higher price — i.e., actual rate of exchange goes down in the market. But if the country follows a fixed rate of exchange, the extra demand is generally met by illegal market (or, black market, often referred to "hawala" market) or outflow of existing foreign currency assets lying with the central bank. Ultimately, this situation leads to "devaluation" of the currency (the official/de-jure decision). Opposite will be the case when $(X - M > 0)$.

Since most countries have switched over to the "flexible" or "floating" rate of exchange in the modern international payment system, the implications for deficit/surplus in the BoP or, components thereof, needs closer examination in the context of attainment of internal as well as external equilibrium.

In a flexible exchange rate system, as we have noted elsewhere, the exchange rate is subject to regular fluctuation depending upon the relative strength/weakness of a country's currency. In case of persistent "deficit" in the current account, for instance, the domestic currency "depreciates" — more domestic currency in exchange for a unit of other international currency. On the other hand, in case of persistent "surplus" in the current account, the domestic currency "appreciates" — less domestic currency in exchange for a unit of other international currency/currencies. The implication of currency depreciation is that it cheapens exports but makes imports costlier. So, on the one hand, the country is likely to benefit in terms of raising their exports and export-earnings and therefore, is able to partly compensate the deficit. On the other hand, the costlier imports drain away valuable foreign exchange. To what extent the country gains by depreciation, then, depends upon the net increase/decrease in foreign exchange earnings. In case of currency appreciation, on the other hand, export becomes costlier but imports cheaper. Hence, the country's capacity to import rises but hampers export earnings although the foreign exchange position strengthens.

Thus, the surplus or deficit in the current account has a tendency to level off generally through exchange rate mechanism. This is how, under flexible exchange rate system, external balance is maintained. However, in the process, the internal balance does not remain unaffected. For instance, rising exports as a result of currency depreciation raise domestic GDP via export sector. Thus, the level of internal equilibrium income rises. Opposite effect takes place when there is currency appreciation besides the risk of domestic inflation and rising interest rate. Therefore, maintaining both the internal as well as external balance is difficult and often not possible without policy intervention.

18.7 MACROECONOMIC POLICY IN AN OPEN ECONOMY

We have seen earlier (Chapter 4) how, in a closed economy, macroeconomic policies (monetary and fiscal policies) can be usefully applied to achieve internal equilibrium within the framework of IS-LM system — an equilibrium of attaining the right combination of rate of interest and national income. In the case of an open economy, where there are two goals to achieve, viz., zero BoP and striking the correct combination of interest rate and national income (or, full employment level of national income — the potential GNP), the policy frame certainly becomes complicated. Often, the two stated goals may come in conflict with each other. However, within the tool box, we have now an additional policy option — the adjustment in the exchange rate which, however, comes largely under monetary policy tool of the central bank.

We shall first consider the case where transactions take place only in the current account. So, capital flows are assumed to be absent for the time being. We can represent the two balances — internal and external — along vertical and horizontal lines as shown in Fig. 18.6. The internal balance is taken to be achieved when $S = I$ (or, $S - I = 0$) at full employment output (Y_f). Let us assume that full employment level of GNP is achieved at point Z. Along the vertical line through Z, therefore, internal balances are presumed to have been achieved but not necessarily the external balances which are achieved only along the horizontal line. Thus, all points along the horizontal line represent the external balance (current A/C Balance = 0) but not necessarily the internal balance. It is only at the point of intersection of the vertical and horizontal lines (point Z) that both internal and external balances are achieved simultaneously. We should remember that these are ideal situations. The actual situation for a country or economy is generally away from these goals such that economies normally suffer from internal or external imbalances. Now we can draw the actual internal balance ($S - I$) and external balance ($X - M$) curves which are both related to GNP levels at a particular point in time. The ($S - I$) curve is generally rising from left to right — showing that the gap between S and I is gradually narrowing with rise in actual GNP and approaching towards the full employment GNP. On the other hand, ($X - M$) curve is generally falling from left to right to show that with rise in GNP, the external balance gap is narrowing down. Different sets of such curves can be drawn which would pass through different levels of GNP. Here in Fig. 18.6, we have drawn only three sets of such curves — one set passing through the point Z – the full employment GNP level — and the other two through points away from Z – to the left and right of Z (shown here by dashed lines). Let us consider point N first. Here, the external balance has been achieved (since $X - M = 0$) but internal balance has not been achieved since it is lying to the left of Z.

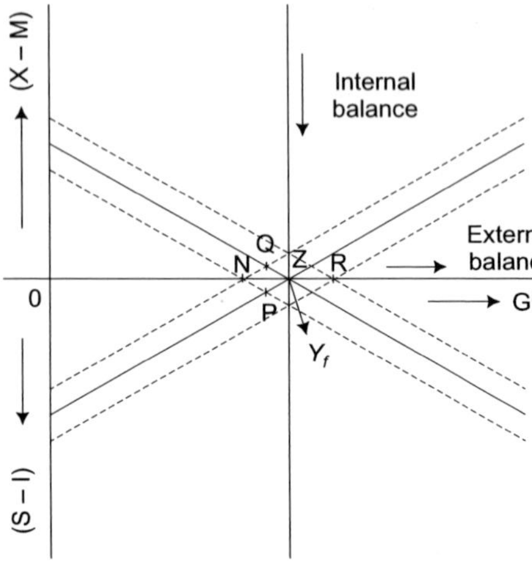

Figure 18.6 *Internal vs. external balance.*

Q is another point to the left of Z (internal imbalance). But Q is equally a point indicating external imbalance as well ($X - M > 0$). This is a situation of surplus in the current account. Another point is observed at P which suggests internal as well as external imbalance but here not only the economy is operating at less than full employment but also experiencing a deficit in the current account ($X - M < 0$). Now, under every such situation macroeconomic policies are applied in a manner so that the actual point moves closer to point Z. What precisely will be appropriate policy or policy-mix depends upon other factors which we further discuss below.

18.7.1 Capital Flows and Internal/External Balance

As we have seen, besides the current account, there is also the capital account as an important component in the balance of payments. There are inflows and outflows of capital within and out of the country in various forms as shown in Table 18.1. These capital inflows (e.g., FDI and FII and other forms of foreign fund flows) are largely determined by the relative rate of interest of the receiving country. No doubt, there are other factors like general business environment, growth prospects, investors' confidence as also political stability of the receiving country, but the real rate of interest is one of the main determining factors of capital inflows. Assuming these other factors as parameters, we can say that capital flows are sensitive to the rate of interest such that higher domestic rate of interest encourages more capital inflows so that interest rate and capital inflows are positively related.

Now, it can be understood that BoP or total external balance is a rising function of the level of income (since, imports are rising function of the level of income) and net inflows of capital is a rising function of the rate of interest. Thus, BoP as a whole is a rising function of both the level of income and the rate of interest. Therefore, BoP – curve can be represented in the $Y - r$ plane. Since our external balance goal is BoP = 0 (neither surplus nor deficit), different combinations of Y and r can show BoP = 0. Such a locus of combinations is a rising (BoP = 0) curve as shown in Fig. 18.7. Now, as far as our

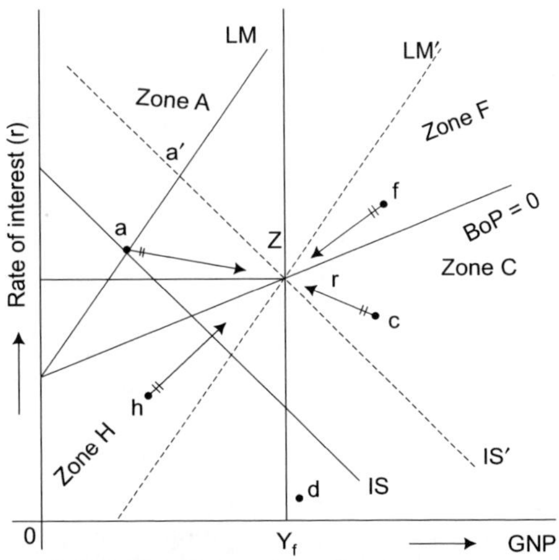

Figure 18.7 *Internal versus external balance and monetary-fiscal policies.*

internal balance is concerned, that remains the same, i.e., achievement of full employment level of income, Y_f. This can be represented, as earlier, by a vertical straight line (Y_f). In Fig. 18.7, two straight lines Y_f and BoP = 0 (this curve shows all such points where BoP = 0) divide the whole quadrant into four zones or regions.

Together with our internal and external balance goals (represented by Y_f and BoP = 0) we have also drawn two sets of IS and LM curves to represent different macroeconomic policy alternatives. The four zones are, zone *A*, lying to the left of both curves Y_f and (BoP = 0); zone *F* lying to the left of (BoP = 0) but to the right of Y_f; zone *C* lying to the right of both curves (BoP = 0) and Y_f and zone *H* lying to the right of (BoP = 0) but to the left of Y_f. All the points of these four zones show imbalance or disequilibrium situations — either in the domestic sector or in the external sector or both.

Now, let us analyse each of these zones by selecting four respective points like *a*, *c*, *d*, *f* and *h*. Point *a* falls in zone *A* which represents less than full employment level of equilibrium. Hence, internal balance is far from being achieved. On the other hand, it is lying to the left of (BoP = 0) curve showing a situation of BoP surplus. Our available policy tools suggest, aggregate demand curve (IS curve) needs to the shifted to the right to reach point *Z*. If this is achieved through expansionary fiscal policy — by enhancing government expenditures, this is likely to increase aggregate demand to equate with the full employment AD, but, as we have seen in Chapter 4 (IS-LM model) this is also likely to raise the rate of interest which will have a dampening effect on investment demand (a component of AD).

However, if the expansionary fiscal policy is combined with expansionary monetary policy (by increasing money supply) so that the LM curve also shifts rightward to LM′, this will ultimately reduce the rate of interest and the economy will achieve both internal as well as external equilibrium at a time. This may occur with certain amount of capital outflow from the economy, since the rate of interest has been forced to come down. Now we examine point *c* in the zone *C*. This point represents BoP deficit but more than full employment level of income. This is just the opposite situation as compared to *a*. This is an inflationary situation combined with BoP deficit. According to our policy alternatives, a contractionary policy (both fiscal and monetary) is required here. Point *f*, lying in zone *F* is similarly placed as point *c* as far as internal balance is concerned. In other words, it suggests over full employment/ inflationary situation. But, it is in the BoP surplus zone. What is required here is to move point *f* towards *Z*. This suggests massive expenditure cut (contractionary fiscal policy) by the government. At the same time, the monetary authority needs to pursue a contractionary monetary policy — reducing money supply. But reducing money supply is likely to raise the rate of interest. However, if the fiscal policy is first vigorously pursued thereby reducing aggregate demand and then, mild doze of monetary policy is applied, the desired goal may be achieved. The fourth case is that of point *h* lying in zone *H*. This indicates a situation of less than full employment income and BoP deficit. Here, expansionary monetary as well as expansionary fiscal policies are required to move IS-LM curves towards *Z*. Here, relatively higher doze of expansionary fiscal policy is required combined with a moderate doze of monetary expansion. But the question still remains whether BoP deficit problem will be solved. In the process of fiscal expansion, GNP will certainly increase and the interest rate will rise too. But the rise in interest rate will be to a greater extent. This will, most probably, encourage capital inflow but will raise domestic import as well. Both of these act as conflicting signals towards BoP problem. Thus, BoP deficit may not be solved to any satisfactory level depending upon the extent of capital inflow as compared to the rise in imports.

In fact, a similar conflicting situation was observed at point *a* in zone *A* where our policy combination was both expansionary — fiscal expansion combined with monetary expansion. We should notice here that if only fiscal policy (expansionary) was adopted, it should have enhanced interest rate which would have encouraged more capital inflow. This would have further increased the size of BoP surplus. However, a larger influence of monetary policy led to a substantial fall in the rate of interest and increased money supply to such an extent that both objectives are attained. The conflict in policy is evident from their impact on interest rate — if one is expansionary, the other should not be expansionary in nature.

The task of fulfilling the twin objectives of attaining internal and external balance simultaneously is very difficult indeed. The policy alternatives that we have discussed above have also their limitations. For instance, monetary policy and fiscal policy are managed and pursued by two different authorities. The monetary policy is conducted by the country's central bank while the fiscal policy is determined by the government of the country which is largely influenced by political factors. Therefore, unless there is satisfactory coordination between the two organizations and unless the goals before them are clearly spelt out, the macroeconomic policies cannot be adequately implemented.

18.8 MUNDELL-FLEMING MODEL

In the later half of 1960s, two economists, Robert Mundell, currently Columbia University Professor and Nobel laureate, and late Marcus Fleming, then a researcher at IMF, developed a model relating to the working of the fixed exchange rate system under perfect capital mobility. It is worth noting here that during the 1960s and earlier, the fixed exchange rate system was in vogue in the international transactions. It was in 1973, the system was replaced by a flexible (or floating) exchange rate. Under a fixed exchange rate system, the foreign exchange rates were used to be determined by a certain fixed value of major currencies of the world against a unit of US dollar as also a certain measure of gold. All international transactions were used to be suitably converted by this fixed rate and every central bank was obliged to honour this commitment. It ought to be mentioned here that the model is equally applicable to a flexible exchange rate regime also in which case the conclusions will be different.

Mundell-Fleming model tried to explain how, in an open economy, under perfect capital mobility, i.e., when capital assets (mainly the financial capital) would move freely across national boundaries without any restrictions, the fixed exchange rate system would lead to the equalisation of the domestic and international rates of interest. Besides, the other two important conclusions of the model are:

1. The countries' central banks would not be able to follow any independent monetary policy, either expansionary or contractionary. In other words, the pursuance of any such policy would prove to be completely ineffective.
2. However, although monetary policy would be completely ineffective, fiscal policy would be fully effective and would work fairly well.

The Mundell-Fleming model was developed in the context of a small open economy which is practically unable to influence either the foreign incomes or the global interest rates. The model tries to extend the *IS-LM* framework to be applied to the open economy, where, now an additional variable of exchange rate (RE) is added to the list of variables (income and the interest rate) as in the case of a closed economy. However, the exchange rate as a variable does not assume significance in the context of the fixed exchange rate because it is exogenously given and the central banks are obliged to maintain this exchange rate. We can assume then that the country's BoP line is a straight line showing zero BoP at all levels (neither surplus nor deficit) at the point of equality between domestic and international interest rates. The above-mentioned conclusions of the model can be illustrated with the help of Figs. 18.8 and 18.9.

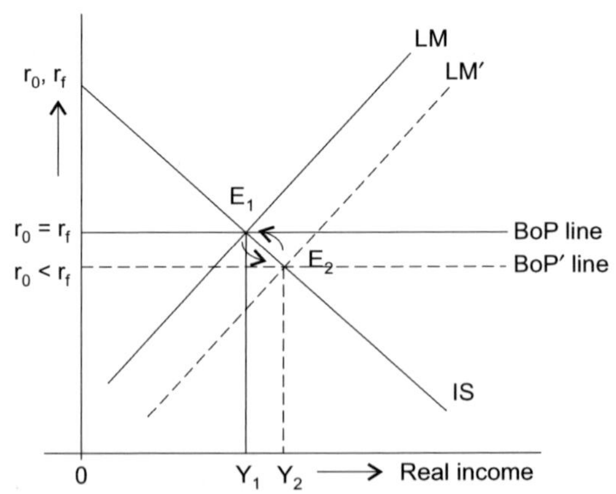

Figure 18.8 *Effects of expansionary monetary policy.*

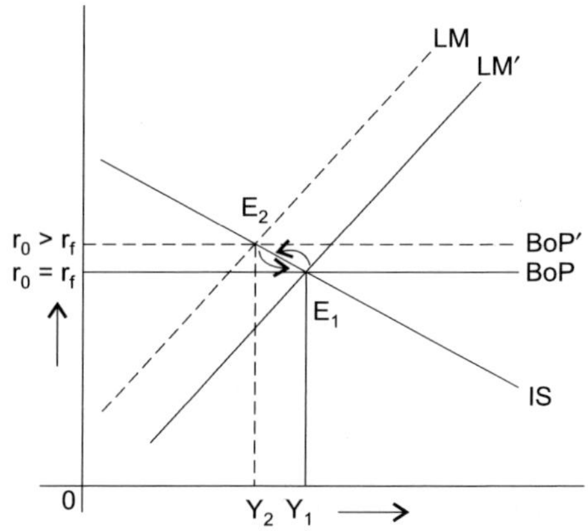

Figure 18.9 *Effects of contractionary monetary policy.*

The central bank's expansionary/contractionary monetary policy becomes ineffective. This is exhibited in the above figures. Let us suppose the initial position of the economy is at the equilibrium point at E_1. Now, if the central bank expands money supply and thereby reduces interest rate, the *LM* curve shifts to the right downwards. This makes the domestic interest rate lower than the international interest rate which results in immediate capital flight from the country in search of better returns to capital. The foreigners demand foreign exchange (dollars, for example) from the central bank, so it sells dollars and purchases domestic money as it is obligated to do so under a fixed exchange rate system. Thus, the expansionary monetary policy is thwarted because the country's money supply is reduced as also its foreign exchange reserves resulting in a BoP deficit. Since the domestic money supply is reduced, the *LM* curve shifts back to its position. It is in this sense said that the money supply is "endogenous because the central bank is bound by rule under the fixed exchange rate system to expand or contract money supply as the situation demands.

In the opposite case, there will be huge capital inflows, the foreigners demanding more domestic money, the central bank obliges, it buys dollars and sells domestic money, money supply increases as also foreign exchange reserves, the country's BoP is in surplus. But the increased money supply reduces the interest rate and again it is equal to the international interest rate. The BoP surplus is also eliminated. Again the monetary policy becomes ineffective.

Fiscal policy effect: The Figs. 18.10 (a) and 18.10 (b) clearly show that the government's fiscal policy is quite effective: For instance, a rise in government expenditures results in a rightward shift of the *IS* curve and there is a rise in national income along with some rise in interest rate. Further, in order to remove the interest rate differential, the central bank will have to increase money supply which means the *LM* curve will shift to the right thus further raising the level

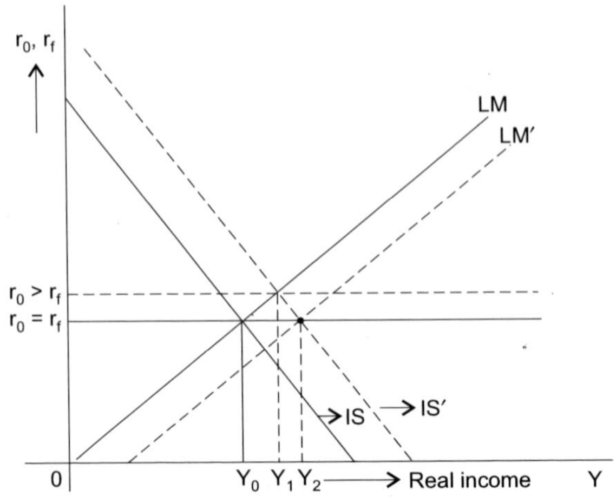

Figure 18.10 (a) *Effects of expansionary fiscal policy.*

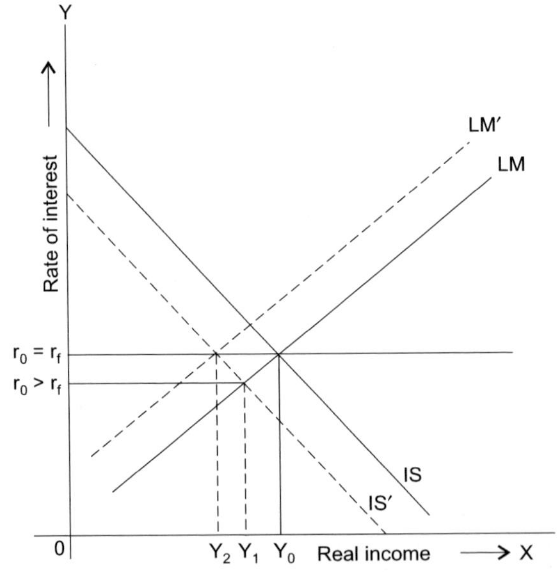

Figure 18.10(b) *Effects of contractionary fiscal policy.*

of national income. Similarly, a fall in government expenditures (leftward shift of the *IS* curve) results in a fall in national income and some fall in interest rate also. The central bank will have to reduce the money supply and thereby raise the interest rate. This further reduces the level of national income. Thus, fiscal policy works effectively in both ways.

Mundell-Fleming model and flexible exchange rate: In a flexible exchange regime, i.e., when the exchange rate is left to be determined by the market forces of demand and supply, the Mundell-Fleming model is equally applicable but the chain of causation is different. It works through the depreciation and appreciation of currency instead of the central bank obliging to maintain the exogenously given exchange rate. Under the flexible exchange rate regime, as we shall examine below, the central bank's monetary policy works effectively but the government's fiscal policy does not work in the desired direction. Thus, the central banks can pursue their independent monetary policy.

The monetary policy effect: Let us suppose, the monetary authority (the central bank), increases the money supply whereby the *LM* curve is shifted to the right resulting in lowering of the interest rate. This triggers capital flight from the country since the international interest rate is now higher. The supply of domestic currency relative to the foreign currency in the foreign exchange market is higher so that the domestic currency depreciates. Country's exports become cheaper but imports are dearer. The BoP position improves and the disequilibrium is automatically corrected. The country's national income rises and the *IS* curve shifts to the right so much that the two interest rates (domestic and international) are equal again. In the opposite case, i.e., if the central bank decreases the money supply and raises the interest rate, the sudden capital inflow will appreciate the domestic currency, the domestic goods will be costly in the international markets and the country's BoP position will worsen by falling exports and rising imports. The country's national income falls and the *IS* curve shifts to the left unless the two interest rates are once again equal (Figs. 18.11 (a) and 18.11 (b) illustrate these cases.

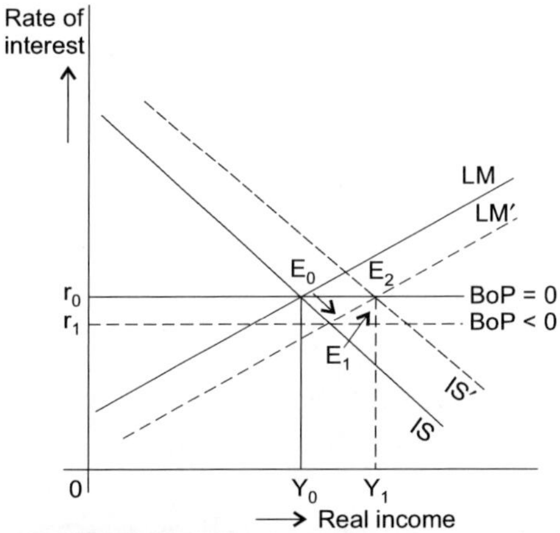

Figure 18.11(a) *Monetary policy (expansionary) effect under flexible exchange rate: Causation is through depreciation of domestic currency.*

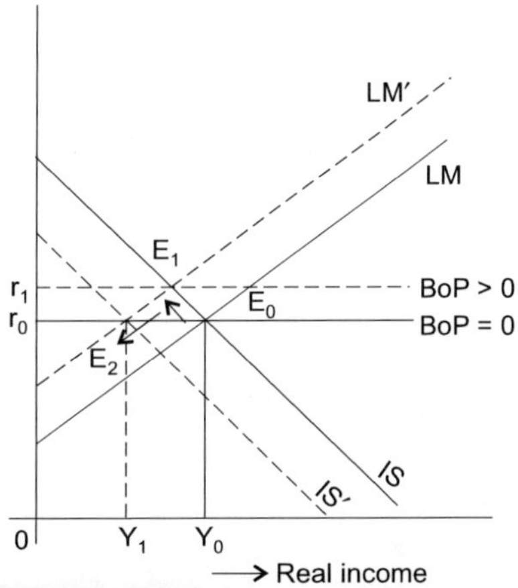

Figure 18.11(b) *Monetary policy (contractionary) effect under flexible exchange rate causation is through appreciation of domestic currency.*

Fiscal policy effect: As far as the fiscal policy is concerned, we can examine its effect by assuming first that there has been a rise in government expenditures. This shifts the *IS* curve to the right which results in a rise in national income as shown in Fig. 18.12 (a). However, this is accompanied by a rise in interest rate which attracts the foreign capital into the economy. This appreciates the domestic currency that makes the exports costly and imports cheap. The net exports component falls and the national income too falls. The *IS* curve shifts to the left resulting in reduction in national income. The gain in national income realised earlier is nullified and thus the fiscal policy action is of no avail.

If there is a fall in government expenditures initially, the *IS* curve shifts to the left. The equilibrium national income falls along with a fall in interest rate. This time, lower interest rate at home causes capital flight which, in turn, depreciates the currency and makes our exports cheaper thus encouraging them. This way, the net exports component rises causing the national income to.go up which means the *IS* curve will be shifting to the right. The purpose of the fiscal policy is defeated Fig. 18.12 (b) illustrates.

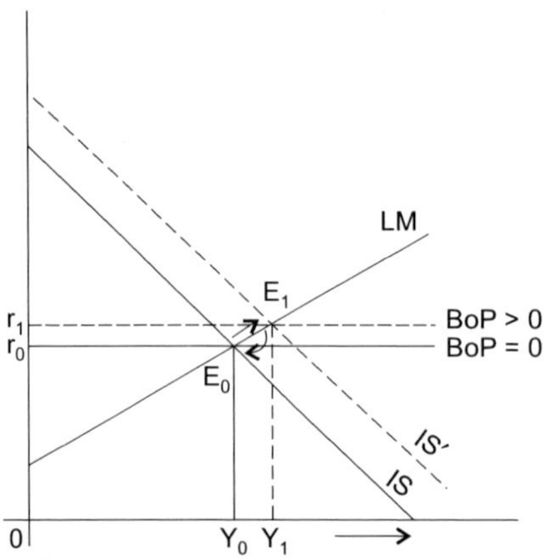

Figure 18.12(a) *Fiscal policy effect (expansionary) under flexible exchange rate: Causation is through appreciation of currency.*

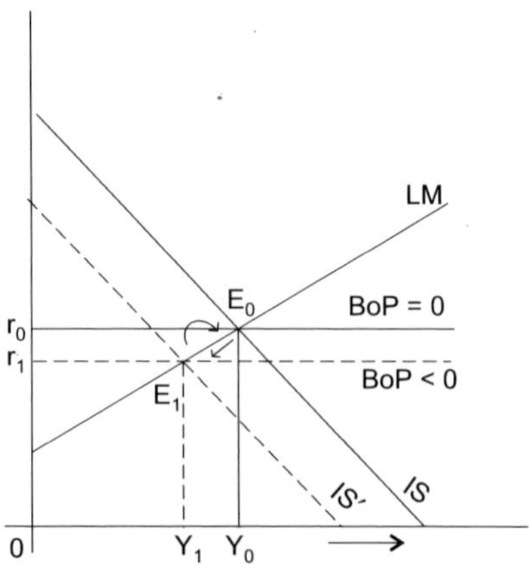

Figure 18.12(b) *Fiscal policy effect (contractionary) causation is through depreciation of currency.*

Mundell's impossible trinity: The above discussion on Mundell-Fleming model leads us to conclude what is popularly known as "impossible trinity" of Prof. Mundell. The so-called trinity unfolds into three possible alternatives or options before the policy makers. These are as follows:

1. Perfect capital mobility.
2. Independent monetary policy of the central bank.
3. Fixed exchange rate system.

Of the above-mentioned three options, a country cannot adopt all of them simultaneously. At best, a country can adopt any two of them while sacrificing the third one. Specifically, any country can have perfect capital mobility and a fixed exchange rate system but cannot pursue independent monetary policy.

Alternatively, it can adopt independent monetary policy and perfect capital mobility but has to do away with a fixed exchange rate system (or, adopt a flexible exchange rate system). The third or final option is to have a fixed exchange rate system along with the central bank's independent monetary policy but has to be content with imperfect capital mobility.

It may be mentioned here that in the aftermath of the post-1973 era of global flexible (or floating) exchange rate regime, most countries pursued the twin policies of independent monetary policy of the central bank along with the perfect capital mobility. However, in actual practice, countries have sometimes faltered and often diluted the 'trinity' rule only to end up with a crisis of some sort or the other. The majority of the countries, at some point of time or other, even in the age of flexible exchange rate, have been seen intervening in the exchange market by their central banks (in order to avoid excessive volatility in the exchange rate).

Exchange rate overshooting: The concept of exchange rate overshooting was introduced by economist R. Dornbusch around the 1970s and which found mention in his book, *Macroeconomics*, coauthored by S. Fischer and R. Startz. The idea of exchange rate overshooting suggests that the exchange rate has a tendency to shoot up initially above its normal trend in response to the monetary policy favouring expansion of money supply. As has been discussed earlier in the context of 'monetary approach to the balance of payments and exchange rate', any disequilibrium in the domestic money market causes disequilibrium in the exchange market also. For example, if there is an increase in the domestic money supply, it causes the exchange rate also to increase which means the domestic currency depreciates. But this happens along with the rise in the domestic price level (due to the rise in the money supply). However, at the initial stage, the exchange rate overshoots the price level, i.e., the rise in exchange rate precedes the rise in the price level. In fact, the rise in the price level is rather slow while the exchange rate, after overshooting, gradually tries to get its level by 'correction' (currency gradually appreciating). Finally, a gradual rise in price level and a gradual fall in the exchange rate (appreciation) peter out at a certain rate of exchange which is consistent with its long-run behaviour. This is illustrated in Fig. 18.13.

The exchange rate is shown on the vertical axis while the time periods are shown on the horizontal axis of Fig. 18.13. The price level can be imagined to be operating from the third dimension. Let us suppose, now, that there has been an increase in the money supply due to the central bank's adopting an expansionary monetary policy. Initially, there will be a rise in the price level at

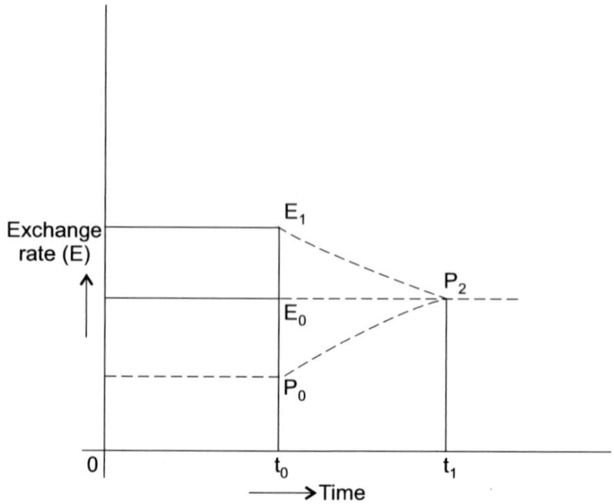

Figure 18.13 *Exchange rate overshooting.*

time, t_0. This is accompanied by an abrupt rise in the exchange rate (domestic currency depreciates) from E_0 *to* E_1. The price rise, however, follows a gradual path to reach P_2 from P_0 as shown by the dashed curve P_0P_2 *in the imaginary third dimension.* As time passes, the initial shoot-up of the exchange rate begins to taper off when the effects of exchange rate depreciation starts producing positive results on the domestic export front and ultimately on the balance of payments. Finally, the equilibrium rate of exchange is established in the long run at E_0 level at time t_1.

SUMMARY

1. Fluctuations in the balance of payments and the rate of exchange of currencies have been a big worry for economists. There are mainly two views or two approaches to deal with these issues: (1) monetary approach and (2) asset market approach. Monetary approach was developed during the 1970s by nobel laureate Robert Mundell and Harry G. Johnson in line with the argument that money supply plays an important role in causing fluctuations in a country's balance of payments as well as in the determination of rate of exchange. This is also an extension of Milton Friedman's 'monetarism' to the international economy. The asset market approach, on the other hand, takes a broader view of the entire portfolio of financial assets that are traded internationally among countries.
2. In the domestic economy, monetary equilibrium is said to be established when total demand for money is equal to total supply of money. In the same vein, monetary disequilibrium is caused either by supply of money

exceeding the demand for it or demand for money exceeding its supply. When the economy becomes open, the scope of the supply of money is expanded so that there are now two sources of it, domestic source and foreign source.

3. When there is monetary disequilibrium in the domestic economy in either form, this is taken care of by the foreign sector. In the case of excess demand for money, for instance, (may be arising out of rising national income over time), there is an inflow of foreign money through 'foreign exchange reserves'. This is reflected in the balance of payments being surplus. On the other hand, if there is an excess supply of money, the excess goes out of the country so that its foreign reserve component is reduced and the balance of payments shows a deficit. However, such monetary movements are just enough to restore equilibrium in the balance of payments in the long run.
4. The rate of exchange is determined by the relative rates of money supplies in the two or more countries engaged in international trade. Thus, if the money supply in country *A* is at a greater rate than in country *B*, *A*'s currency will be depreciating while *B*'s currency will be appreciated in the long run.
5. A critical appraisal of monetary approach shows that it fails to provide a complete explanation of the real-world situation of fluctuations of BoP or the determination of exchange rate. It ignores the role of rate of interest in the demand for money. Secondly, it fails to consider that there are different kinds of financial assets other than money which are currently transacted upon.
6. The asset market approach provides a better explanation of fluctuations in BoP as well as exchange rate determination since it encompasses all categories of financial assets such as money, domestic bonds, foreign bonds and other securities which enter into international transactions. These assets are responsive to different rates of returns and risks. The asset holders, either domestic or foreign, consider all these respective rates of returns along with their associated risks before buying or selling these assets.
7. Initially, the asset holders reach a certain level of equilibrium in the asset market where aggregate demand for each asset is equal to its aggregate supply. But in case there is a change in the rate or rates of returns and/or risk components, there is immediate reshuffling of stocks of different assets which cause BoP disequilibrium, and in the process, the exchange rate fluctuations only to settle down to a new equilibrium position with different rates of exchange.

EXERCISE

1. Explain how the aggregate demand model changes in an open economy as against a closed economy.
2. What are the internal and external balance goals of an open economy. How these goals appear in conflict with one another?
3. What are the main components of BoP? Explain each one of them.
4. Explain the main features of Mundell-Fleming model. Illustrate with examples.
5. What is Mundell's impossible trinity?
6. Distinguish between current account and capital account transactions in the balance of payments. Also, explain the difference between the balance of trade and balance of payments.
7. Explain the interconnection between monetary disequilibrium and balance of payments disequilibrium of a domestic economy.
8. Given the following figures:
   Domestic reserve money = ₹ 1 thousand crore,
   Money multiplier = 4,
   Find the domestic stock of money supply.
   If there is an addition of ₹ 500 crore of foreign reserves, what will be the total money supply in the economy?
9. Explain how the rate of exchange is determined according to monetary approach.
10. Why is the asset market approach considered better compared to monetary approach? What are the main financial assets that a global investor takes into account while making an investment decision across different nations and why?
11. What is risk premium? Explain its role in the investor's decision-making process.
12. How is disequilibrium in the BoP caused according to asset market approach? How is equilibrium restored?
13. Distinguish between absolute PPP and relative PPP theories of long-run exchange rate determination. Explain which version of the theory is better and why?

REFERENCES

1. R. Dornbusch, Stanley Fischer and R Startz, Macroeconomics, 9th Edition, McGraw Hill, USA, 2009.
2. Dominick Salvatore, International Economics, John Wiley & Sons, Seventh Edition, 2001.
3. N. Gregory Mankiw, Macroeconomics, Sixth Edition, Worth Publishers, 2006.
4. R.B.I., www.rbi.org.in.

PART-10

Macroeconomic Policies

19

Modern Macroeconomic Policy: Monetary Policy

Monetary policy is conventionally understood to represent policies, objectives and instruments which are directed towards regulating money supply and cost and availability of credit in the economy.[1] Two key elements emerge from this concept of monetary policy: regulating money supply in the economy in terms of (a) cost of credit (i.e., rate of interest) and (b) availability of adequate credit through banking and financial system. A country's central bank is in charge of accomplishing this task. To this end, however, the monetary authority (the central bank) ought to have a clear idea of the objective/objectives before initiating appropriate actions to influence the interest rate and money/credit supply. Also, it should have, in its control, the necessary instruments to effect the desired result.

The present chapter is intended to discuss the following aspects of monetary policy:

1. Monetary policy: the transmission mechanism
2. Lags in monetary policy
3. Objectives of monetary policy
4. Monetary policy instruments
5. Rules vs. discretion debate
6. Monetary policy in India

19.1 THE TRANSMISSION MECHANISM

Monetary policy operates through the monetary sector. The monetary sector consists of the entire banking sector (including the apex bank, i.e., central bank), other non-banking financial sectors, the stock exchanges and the short-term money market dealing with purchase and sale of various financial instruments. Clearly, monetary policies have to be transmitted to the real economy where

[1] Kanagasabapathy, K. "Monetary Policy Underpinnings: A Perspective", *Economic and Political Weekly*, June 27, 2001.

goods and services are produced creating real GDP. But how this transmission from monetary sector to real sector takes place is very important. There are disagreements, however, on whether the transmission mechanism is more direct or more indirect.

19.1.1 Keynesian Transmission Mechanism

Economists belonging to Keynesian tradition believe that monetary policy transmission is essentially indirect and acts with sufficient time-lag. But those of the monetarist school (followers of Milton Friedman or Chicago School) think that the transmission mechanism is more direct and that monetary policy changes impact the real economy, i.e., output, employment and price-level directly. These views are illustrated in the following figures:

Figure 19.1(a) shows the familiar relationship between the rate of interest and liquidity preference (demand for money), while MS curves show the supply of money. The Keynesian L-curve, as we know, is relatively more elastic suggesting

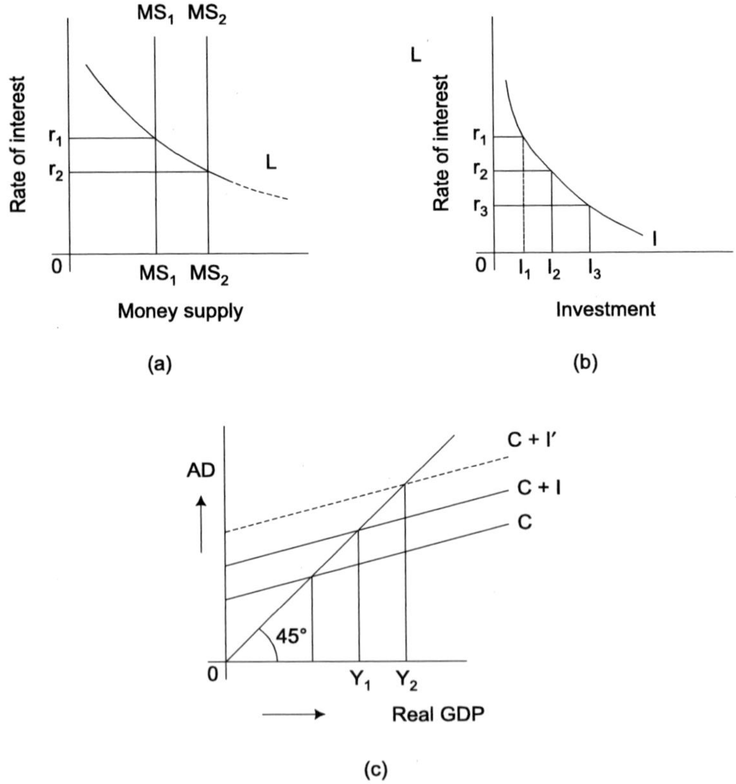

Figure 19.1 *The Keynesian transmission mechanism.*

that a small fall in the rate of interest brings about relatively larger demand for money (or, a small rise in interest rate brings relatively greater fall in money demand). The supply of money is assumed to be exogenously determined by the monetary authority (the central bank). Now, if the central bank increases the supply of money from MS_1 to MS_2, the rate of interest falls from Or_1 to Or_2. In other words, the cost of money borrowing becomes lower. This is reflected on the investment function such that the volume of real investment increases from OI_1 to OI_2 (19.1(b)). Since, investment demand happens to be a component part of the aggregate demand, the whole aggregate demand shifts upward (Fig. 19.1(c)) from $C + I$ to $C + I'$. This results in higher real output (or, real GDP) from OY_1 to OY_2. In the opposite direction, i.e., if supply of money decreases, rate of interest rises, investment demand falls, aggregate demand (and hence real GDP) falls. Schematically, we can, therefore, put the relationships as follows:

$$\text{MS} \uparrow r \downarrow \rightarrow \text{I} \uparrow \rightarrow \text{AD} \uparrow \rightarrow \uparrow \text{GDPr(Y)}$$

and

$$\text{MS} \downarrow r \uparrow \rightarrow \text{I} \downarrow \rightarrow \text{AD} \downarrow \rightarrow \downarrow \text{GDPr(Y)}$$

In the Keynesian approach, therefore, two steps in the transmission mechanism are involved: (1) money-interest rate link and (2) interest-rate-investment link. Now, whether the monetary policy (via, money supply route) will ultimately affect aggregate demand (by affecting investment demand) depends on (a) to what extent any change in money supply brings about change in the interest rate and (b) to what extent a change in the interest rate brings about change in the volume of real investment.

Keynesians are, however, pessimistic about monetary policy influencing significantly the aggregate demand due to weak linkages in both (1) and (2) mentioned above. Firstly, the speculative demand for money (L-function) is, relatively more elastic with a 'liquidity trap' range at very low rate of interest – reflecting the situation of recession or depression. In normal situation, also, as argued by the Keynesians, small changes in interest rate bring about relatively larger changes in the demand for money. This is because, the people, firms and businesses have a perception about the 'expectation' of the normal rate of interest. Keeping this expected rate of interest in relation to the current rate of interest in mind, the community reacts to the demand for money (or, its alternative asset – the 'bonds'). For instance, if rate of interest is lowered, and if the community thinks that the 'expected interest rate' is higher, they will go for more money and wait for interest rate to go up when they would buy more bonds. Similarly, if the current rate of interest is raised, and is higher than the expected normal rate of interest, they will reduce demand for money by converting their cash holding into bonds. Thus, it is not only the current rate of interest (and change in it) but its relationship with expected future rate of interest which is more important. Given this perception, Keynesians feel, the demand for money curve is more elastic. In other words, in case of lowering of interest rate, money is most likely to move from active balance (bonds) to idle balance (cash). (The link between interest rate and demand for money is, therefore, weak and unpredictable.) Given the elastic demand for money (L) curve, a monetary policy initiative either through increase or decrease in money supply will be able to influence interest rate only to a small extent (Fig. 19.1a). A rise in money supply from MS_1 to MS_2, for instance, has resulted in relatively smaller fall in the rate of interest.

In the second stage, the fall in interest rate, no doubt, has an influence on investment curve. But Keynesian transmission mechanism, here, postulates a relatively inelastic investment curve (or, which is not very sensitive to interest rate (Fig. 19.1b). In such a situation, if volume of real investment has to be increased, it will require relatively large decreases in rate of interest for which large volumes of money supply will have to be increased by the Central Bank. Secondly, the Keynesians argue that investment function is influenced not only by the rate of interest but by a variety of other factors including the expectation about future profit and confidence in the future market (see Chapter 4 on 'Investment Function' p. 86-87). To be sure, the investment function during severe recession becomes highly inelastic as has been borne out by evidence during the recent 'Great Recession' of 2008-09 in US and other European capitalist countries. (In the US, despite persistent monetary policy easing since the onset of Great Recession the rate of interest – the Fed rate – was brought to virtually zero) the investment climate did not improve and unemployment persisted, around 9 per cent (till late 2010). However, in more normal situations, the investment function will not necessarily be inelastic. This has now been agreed upon by most Keynesians. This is because, besides real investment in plant and machinery, there are other channels like credit-financed consumer demand, investment in houses, stocks, etc. which are likely to be sensitive to interest rate.

The Keynesian transmission mechanism of monetary policy has yet another channel – that of exchange rate mechanism – to influence aggregate demand. This channel is also indirect. The exchange rate mechanism is operative in an open economy where there is easy capital flow across the national boundaries and where exchange rate regime is flexible, determined by relative demand and supply of foreign exchange.

Let us suppose the central bank follows a policy of lowering interest rate by increasing the supply of money. A lower rate of interest encourages capital flight from the home country – reducing the volume of foreign exchange reserves and thus results in depreciating the value of domestic currency. This means (in the Indian context) that currency ₹ is cheaper in relation to $ or £ currencies. This has the effect of cheapening Indian exports abroad. Export demand may thus be boosted and through more exports (and of course, less imports) the aggregate demand will increase. Opposite will be the effect in case of rise in domestic interest rate. This route of monetary policy effect has several limitations, though. Among others, the success of the policy depends upon the foreign countries' degree of response to domestic country's exports – the so-called elasticity of exports. Also, it depends upon the relative international competitiveness in the global market in real terms.

19.1.2 The Monetarist Transmission Mechanism

Milton Friedman and his associates credited with the development of the school of monetarism which attempted to revive the old Quantity Theory of Money, argued that the relationship between supply of money and real variables like output, employment and real GDP is direct. Therefore, by maintaining money supply in judicious way real variables can be easily impacted. The monetarist approach can be summed up as follows:

$$MS \uparrow \rightarrow AE \uparrow \rightarrow AD \uparrow \rightarrow GDPr(Y) \uparrow \rightarrow P \uparrow$$

MS = Money supply, AE = Aggregate expenditure, AD = Aggregate demand, GDPr = Real GDP and P = Price level.

The detailed mechanism of monetary policy works as follows:

When money supply increases the extra money comes in the hands of the individuals and businesses who find that they have more money than required. So they are tempted to spend this excess money on goods and services as also on purchase of assets. This leads to rise in aggregate demand. This, in turn, leads to more production of goods and services and the level of real GDP, particularly in the short run. Employment, too, increases. However, in the short run, price level also goes up because output in short run increases but to a lesser extent than the rise in aggregate demand. In diagram, the monetarist transmission mechanism can be expressed as follows:

Figure 19.2(a) shows that an increase in money supply (by monetary authorities) from MS_1 to MS_2 simply raises the level of aggregate demand

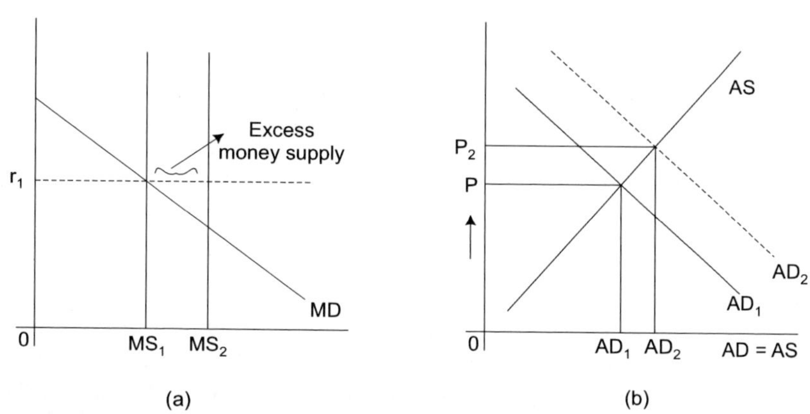

Figure 19.2 *The monetarist transmission mechanism.*

through expenditure increases by the community, but leaving the rate of interest unchanged. Since rise in aggregate demand is associated with rise in real GDP and employment, these are also raised but the price level too increases.

Keynesians, however, do not agree with this line of argument of the monetarists. In particular, they disagree with the direct linkage existing in the first stage, i.e., from supply of money to the aggregate demand. The exact process of transmission, here, Keynesians argue, is vague. For instance, if the supply of money is injected through the central bank lending to government and creating extra money for government expenditure the effect on aggregate demand is more due to fiscal policy operation rather than monetary policy.

Alternatively, if the central bank increases supply of money via the increase in 'reserve money' of the banking sector and/or allow banks to avail of the cheap credit from the central bank to tempt credit advancement, to some extent this results in the increase in aggregate demand. But, certainly not all sectors of the economy can have easy credit money and if they can, this may, ultimately result in inflation. If money supply is injected through 'open-market operation' (buying securities by the central bank) the community's portfolio balance simply changes. The ratio of money to other securities with the public increases – people have more money relative to other securities, but the total portfolio remains unchanged. The point is whether this will lead to increase in aggregate demand. The Keynesians maintain that buying securities by the central bank drives up their prices which implies that their 'yield' (interest rate on bonds, e.g.) falls. People, therefore, will better wait for lower price of bonds and securities and will be reluctant to spend money on goods and services.

The Keynesians, therefore, assert that the linkage is unclear and uncertain.

19.1.3 Indirect Mechanism of the Monetarists

In spite of the controversy over the exact transmission mechanism, economists have, by and large, agreed that monetary policy acts in an indirect rather than direct manner. Secondly, while western capitalist economies like the US, major European countries and Japan (among Asian countries) rely on monetarist, new classical type of monetary policy as a more effective macroeconomic policy, most underdeveloped countries including India still have more allegiance to Keynesian line of monetary policy with 'lags' at several stages of its working.

19.1.4 The Transmission Mechanism of Monetary Policy In India

The transmission mechanism of the monetary policy is crucial in view of the effectiveness of any change in the policy rate of the central bank. In particular, when a central bank decides to lower its policy rate with a view to revive aggregate demand through increased flow of credit to the real economy, the actual transmission mechanism of the monetary policy needs to be understood properly.

In fact, there are various channels through which any reduction (or raising) of interest rate of the central bank gets transmitted to make a combined overall effect on the economy. These channels are as follows: (1) interest rate channel, (2) credit channel, (3) exchange rate channel, and (4) asset price channel. Below we explain each of these channels.

(1) **Interest rate channel:** When the central bank announces a change in its policy rate (repo rate), the immediate impact is generally felt on the various short-term rates such as money market rates or the inter-bank call money rates, rates on certificates of deposits, commercial papers, yield rate on treasury bills, and other financial market rates (exchange rates and equity prices). Also, it influences the medium- and long-term rates like those applicable to government securities/bonds as also corporate bonds which influences the supply and demand for loanable funds in the market. If, for example, the commercial banks have surplus funds, part or whole of which is parked with the central bank on which the latter gives a certain rate of interest, known as reverse repo rate, the commercial banks generally compare this rate with the inter-bank rate. Only in the event of equal or higher inter-bank rate, will the commercial banks be willing to allocate their funds to the other banks in times of emergency.

(2) **Credit channel:** This channel affects the cost of funds for the commercial banks and other financial institutions which are credit providers. When the central bank reduces or raises the policy interest rate, it is generally believed that the cost of funds with the banks (interest costs) goes down or rises and so they will, most likely, advance various kinds of loans (or credit) to their customers at cheaper terms (in case of fall in interest rate). However, this channel may or may not be smooth enough, as it is often thought, depending on other considerations like the credit worthiness of customers, and the banks' own financial positions. Also, it depends on the investment sentiments of the borrowers who are willing to take up investment projects.

For instance, in the case of India in recent years, banks have been suffering from NPA (non-performing assets) or bad loan problems for which they have become hesitant in freely advancing loans to their borrowers. Secondly, the economy itself has been witnessing a slowdown for sometime past which has depressed the investment sentiments of the entrepreneurs. Apart from this, the banks have not come up with the full extent of rate cuts to the customers in line with the central bank's announcement.

(3) **Exchange rate channel:** Interest rate change by the central bank influences the exchange rate also, the price of foreign currency in terms

of domestic currency. In case of fall in policy rate, the price of domestic currency also falls, that is, the domestic currency depreciates making the exports cheaper and imports costlier. This is likely to boost the domestic exports and, via raising the net exports, also raises the level of national income. This way, lowering the central bank's policy rate helps the economic growth process.

(4) Asset price channel: A fall in interest rate raises the price level of many assets like bonds/securities and real estate like houses and thus boosts the value of household or corporate wealth. A house property, for example, can be sold for a higher price in a scenario of falling interest rate since the purchaser can get it at a lower borrowing cost. For the corporates, a lower interest rate can improve their cash flows and thereby raises the demand. We have earlier noted that interest rate and bond prices move in opposite directions. Similarly, the lower interest rate raises the real value of wealth in the economy. Higher asset prices can enhance the value of the collateral or net worth of the borrowers who can now borrow more at competitive prices. This will help raise the aggregate demand in the economy.

The above-mentioned monetary policy channels often work in tandem and sometimes in a fashion that one channel interacts with another.

(Source: Viral Acharya, "Monetary Policy Transmission in India: Why is it important and why has not it worked well", November 16, 2017, Inaugural Aveek Guha Memorial Lecture, Tata Institute of Fundamental Research, Mumbai)

19.2 LAGS IN MONETARY POLICY

We have mentioned earlier that there are time lags in the transmission of the monetary policy. Generally, these lags are as follows: (1) inside lag, (2) intermediate lag and (3) outside lag.

1. **Inside Lag** This type of time lag exists within the organization of the monetary authority, i.e., central bank. This is the lag between the recognition lag and administrative lag; in other words, the lapse of time between the recognition of a problem and taking the action for the problem. For instance, the central bank feels that there is a persistent inflation in the economy and there is need to take some action (raising interest rate) to tame the inflation. After the central bank recognises this problem, it proposes appropriate action within the system of its own administration. Then, finally it announces such action for implementation. But, in between, certain time elapses. This is, precisely, the 'inside lag'.
2. **Intermediate Lag** There is, again, some time consumed between the action taken (for example, change in interest rate upward) and its

effect on the monetary and financial sector (banks and other financial institutions) as to how they react to the rate change – whether they restrict their lending and financing and to what extent. Then the impact on general expenditure decisions by the individuals and businesses also forms another stage involving time-lag.

3. **Outside Lag** Finally, the real economy – real output and price level is affected. The latter two stages are the outside lags.

Schematically, the various lags in monetary policy transmission are illustrated as follows:

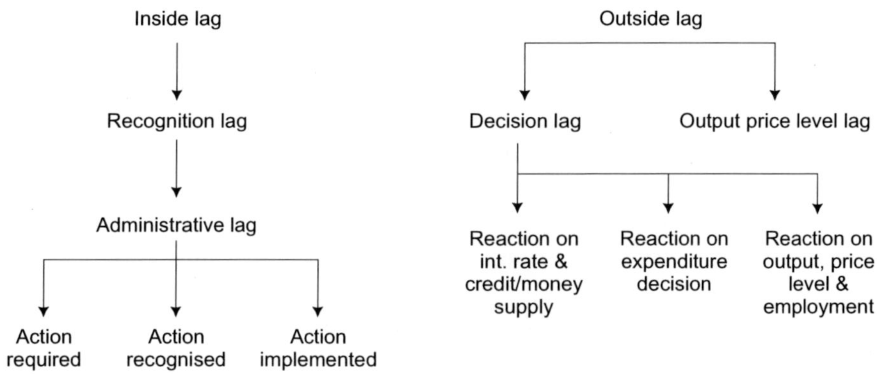

It is pertinent to mention here that these lags, particularly the period of time involved in them, depend on several factors like structure of the economy, level of technology used in dissemination of information and expectations of the people. For example, if the economy is well advanced in terms of industries, commerce, trade and other sectors, the lags will be relatively short. Similarly, if the level of information technology is high, the lags will also be relatively of short duration. People's expectations about the likely impact of the policy change will make these lags either of longer or shorter duration.

19.3 OBJECTIVES OF MONETARY POLICY

19.3.1 Price Stability

Price stability is the key objective of monetary policy. However, the meaning of price stability needs to be properly understood. Price stability means that general price level should be maintained at reasonably low level and there should not be excessive fluctuations of the level of prices in the economy. Price stability in no way means that prices of goods and services should remain constant; instead, it means that the rate of rise in prices (or, the inflation rate) is reasonably low and tolerable for the economy. What exactly this rate should be depends on several factors. Among others, it depends on the stage of development of the economy and the extant internal as well as external conditions of the economy. For instance, in developed industrial countries, the goal of price stability is, by and large, set at 2% rate of inflation on an annual basis while in a country like India most economists believe that 4-5% is the tolerable rate of inflation.

There are basically two arguments in favour of price stability: (1) it helps generate "reasonably" positive real rate of interest in the economy. Real rate of interest is the difference between the nominal rate of interest and the rate of inflation. Now, if the rate of inflation is higher than the nominal rate of interest, the real rate of interest will be negative. A negative real rate of interest will have an adverse impact on savings of the economy. People, in general, will have no incentive to save. This, in turn, will discourage investment activities since, less saving means less supply of loanable funds for investment purposes. (2) secondly, price stability ensures better economic management and raises investors' expectations and hence promotes growth potential of the economy.

However, economists have differed if price stability is the sole objective of monetary policy making. Some have argued that price stability is the only objective of the policy making exercise of the central banking authority. This view is advocated by economists of the western developed countries, particularly, after their bitter experience of the 'stagflation' of 1970s and high inflation of 1980s. They believe, therefore, that once the goal of price stability is satisfactorily achieved, other goals, if they exist, are easily achievable. Other groups of scholars are of the opinion that, in developing countries, 'economic growth' is an equally important goal. This, naturally begs the question whether objectives of price stability and economic growth are in conflict. The much discussed 'Phillips curve' suggests a "trade-off" between inflation rate and unemployment rate. Since, unemployment is invariably associated with low rate of economic growth, it is argued that the rate of growth of the economy will likely be hampered if price stability goal is given the primacy neglecting economic growth. Even though modern views on Phillips curve assert that there is no long-run trade-off between inflation and unemployment, they do agree that such trade-off may well be present in the short run. Thus, in most situations, policy makers will have to address both price stability and economic growth. In fact, there can be multiplicity of goals of monetary policy. But, if one has to choose among these, or, prioritise these, price stability would, arguably, come first.

Price stability and inflation targeting: Sometimes, to ensure price stability, targeting a certain rate of inflation is recommended as a right strategy. Inflation targeting may ensure price stability no doubt. But, as argued above, such policy measures should not be adopted at the cost of other considerations, notably growth of the economy. In a country like India, recent evidence of persisting inflation at a higher level particularly during 2013-14 and 2014-15 compelled the then central bank (RBI) governor, Dr. Raghuram Rajan to adopt a tough stand on inflation front and gear the monetary policy suitably towards that goal which ultimately resulted in inflation targeting strategy. The strategy was successful and soon India's inflation rate softened to a comfortable level although other favourable factors too were responsible for this. It may be mentioned here that subsequently, inflation targeting has formally been announced as the main plank of monetary policy in India.

It can, therefore, be concluded from the above discussion that maintaining price stability is, no doubt, the chief objective of monetary policy but it has to be carefully crafted and interpreted in the right context and, accordingly, suitable policy tools need to be applied. In fact, price stability ought to be a means to achieve sustained growth of the economy.

19.3.2 Supporting Growth of the Economy

As discussed above, the second important objective of monetary policy is to ensure sustainable growth of the economy. Growth is relatively a long-run concern for almost all economies of the world but it needs to be supported in the short run also. As discussed above, even though it is argued sometimes that there is a trade-off between growth and inflation/price stability, the argument is no longer tenable. But the fact that in the short run, such trade-off does appear, policy makers need to take account of this so that economic growth does not hamper. The central bank, therefore, has to keep a constant watch on the trends of growth of GDP along with employment growth. It has to analyse the growth rates of the economy along with its sectoral growth rates. Trends in job growth and unemployment rates are important indicators for economic growth. In this sense, objectives of economic policy and monetary policy virtually coincide.

In order to ensure growth of the economy, adequate flow of credit to the real sector of the economy has to be ensured which lies in the domain of the monetary policy of the central bank. Thus, the central bank needs to monitor the supply of money and credit, through its entire banking and financial system, in a manner that both the above-mentioned objectives of price stability and growth are fulfilled.

It is possible, though, that in the short run, the situation may occur when these two goals may appear to be in conflict. For instance, price level might be rising continuously requiring reining in aggregate demand by raising policy interest rate by the central bank while there is discouraging signals of subdued market sentiment requiring favourable support by easing (lowering) policy rate. These are testing times for the central banks. It has to carefully read the situation and weigh the different pros and cons of what is most likely to happen in the future and, accordingly, choose the right course of action ahead.

Two such instances can be cited in this regard. In the US, during the late 1970s and early 1980s, stagflation (inflation attended with stagnation/recession) occurred as a peculiar problem. The US policy makers, relying heavily on monetary policy, appointed Paul Volcker as chairman of the Federal Reserve who preferred to control inflation rather than reviving the economy from stagnation. Subsequently, the inflation rate, which was running above 10%, gradually softened and came down to a manageable level of 4%. This way, Volcker also succeeded in controlling inflation expectations.

Another instance, although not quite similar, is India's case in a relatively recent period (later half of 2010). Headline inflation was running above 10% while food inflation was above 18% for some time. At the same time, industrial output indicators did not show encouraging trends. There was evidence of credit crunch in the banking sector as well. Amid this conflicting situation, India's central bank chose to target inflation by raising policy interest rate.

19.3.3 Maintaining Exchange Stability

Monetary policy of the central bank also has another objective, that of maintaining the stability of the rate of exchange of the domestic currency vis-a-vis foreign currency. In the present system of flexible/floating exchange rate, the rate of exchange is subject to change continuously depending on the relative pressures of demand and supply of foreign exchanges. In today's globalised economy, there are constant movements of short-term and long-term capital across the countries besides other forms of financial flows. These cause balance of payments of a country as also the rate of exchange of its currency to fluctuate, sometimes to dangerous levels. In such situations, the central bank has to intervene in the foreign exchange market, by either selling or buying foreign currency, in order to stabilise the external value of the currency. Thus, monetary policy has to keep a watchful eye on the balance of payments position and, specifically, the movements along current account as well as capital account transactions. There are occasions when sudden inflows or outflows of capital assets take place between countries due to dynamic changes in the international trade and investment regime. Thus, when there is sudden inflow of such capital, the country's currency appreciates making it stronger in relation to other currencies. Apparently, this may seem to be a good sign, but, beyond a point, this is likely to hurt our exports causing long-term harm. Similarly, when there is sudden outflow of capital from the country, it causes depreciation of the currency thus reducing the foreign exchange reserves. In situations like these, central bank's limited intervention helps save the situation from further deterioration and restore stability in the exchange rate.

Instances of such intervention by the central banks are many in recent history. In the later half of 2010, there was sudden inflow of capital due to rise in foreign institutional investments (FII) arising out of unconventional monetary policy adopted by US Fed Reserve (quantitative easing) programme of bond buying and releasing US dollar most of which sneaked into India and other emerging economies of Asia to their capital markets. This not only led to significant build-up of foreign exchange but also strengthened Indian rupee (rupee appreciated). Money supply in India also proportionately increased causing inflationary conditions. Under such a situation, the RBI had to intervene in the forex market which started buying US dollars until rupee regained its expected level. Indian rupee again remained unstable for some time during 2012-13 and 2013-14. This time, rupee began depreciating reaching nearly ₹ 68 per US dollar due mainly to sudden flight of FII capital from India's stock market on expectations of Fed Reserve's stopping of bond buying programme (taper tantrum) and expectation of a rise in US interest rate. At this juncture, the RBI governor's monetary policy measures subsequently led the rupee to stabilize to find its level at around ₹ 66 per US dollar. More recently, during mid-2018, a challenging situation developed within Indian economy when it suffered from deteriorating current account deficit of 2.4% (against 1.8% in the earlier year) in the face of rising crude oil prices and depreciating Indian rupee (rupee deprecated by more than 14% between January and November, 2018 thus crossing ₹ 74 mark against a US dollar). Most economists and the market, at this juncture, expected the Indian central bank to take steps to stabilise the currency. Adding to the concern was the instability in the financial market, particularly in the banking as well as non-banking financial sector facing the liquidity crisis (one of the biggest infrastructure leasing companies, viz., Infrastructure Leasing and Financial Services (IL & FS) defaulted on interest payments to its investors giving signals to its failure). The rate of interest in the market, particularly the 10-year government bonds, was continuing to soar for some time past. Together, these situations demanded some corrective action from the central bank. Surprisingly, however, the RBI did not raise the policy rate except expressing concern about future inflation risk though it changed its opinion (stance) from "neutral" to "calibrated tightening". Indian central bank here clearly preferred to target inflation and inflation expectations, ignoring exchange stability or other considerations. Subsequently, however, the situation improved and the rupee stopped depreciating, stabilising around 69 per $.

However, even if it is not a case of inflation targeting, there is a limit to the extent of central bank's intervention for exchange stability. It cannot continue buying foreign exchange for a long period since in that case the foreign reserves would deplete. It may then resort to some other measure like capital control 1– putting a ceiling on capital inflows – which largely falls under the government's overall economic policy.

One important consideration that central banks keep in mind before intervention in the forex market is to estimate the 'real' level of appreciation/ depreciation of the domestic currency as against nominal level. In fact, there are two indicators to guide, nominal effective exchange rate (NEER) and real effective exchange rate (REER)[1], that the central banks have at their disposal. Whether the relative exchange rate goes down or up depends on REER rather than NEER.

19.3.4 To Ensure a Smooth and Efficient Financial System

A stable and well regulated financial system can lead to stable and consistent growth of the economy. The responsibility for this rests on the central bank as a regulator of the entire financial system and monetary policy is certainly an important plank of such regulatory mechanism.

A country's financial system consists of the whole set of banking and non-banking financial companies, insurance companies, mutual funds, stock exchanges and the entire money and capital markets as well as the environment in which they function. While safeguarding the financial stability, the central bank uses appropriate monetary policy to ensure adequate supply of loanable funds to the system, on the one hand, and act as a watchdog over the functioning of the system. This is because an oversupply of credit and excessive growth of financial institutions may lead to financial crisis and the central bank has to put brakes on such excessive growth. At the same time, it has to encourage institutions to grow in sufficient numbers at appropriate times to help smooth functioning of the financial system.

It may be mentioned here that in spite of this goal of monetary policy the financial system in most economies of the world are prone to instability due to some reason or other. The great recession that originated in the US in 2008-09 and later spread to EU countries was due to the financial crisis in the housing market. Some economists have argued that such financial crisis and instability in the financial market is the result of wrong economic policies pursued over the last thirty years before the crisis. The central banks' working under extremely liberalised environment often fail to contain the financial instability in the system, and end up incurring excessive risks. Some such situations appeared to be developing in the non-banking finance segment of Indian economy as mentioned above in the case of IL & FS.

19.4 MONETARY POLICY INSTRUMENTS

19.4.1 Bank Rate Policy

Bank rate refers to the rate of interest at which the central bank lends funds to the commercial banks against first-class securities of the commercial banks.

1 REER is an inflation-adjusted risk-weighted cross country rate of exchange. Cross-country rates are the nominal values of different currencies—particularly the principal currencies. The RBI calculates the REER for six country currencies and also for 30 country currencies. REER is arrived at calculating the weighted average of a country's currency value relative to a basket of currencies. The weights for different currencies are determined by comparing the relative trade balances in terms of one country's currency with each other's within the index.

Changing the bank rate means changing the cost of funds made available to the banking system. A rise in bank rate, for instance, means the cost of borrowing increases and similarly a fall in bank rate implies lower borrowing cost. In today's liberalised environment of banking deregulation the concept of bank rate has undergone change. Today, bank rate refers to the 'reference rate', 'signaling rate' or 'targeted rate' which the central bank intends to be prevailing in the market in the medium or long term. In US, bank rate refers to Federal Fund Rate (or, Fed. rate) which is, in fact, the 'targeted rate' or 'suggested rate' which the Federal Reserve of US expects to prevail in the market for ' loanable funds'. In most other countries also bank rate has similar meaning.

(a) Repo Rate Repo (or, repurchase) rate refers to the interest rate at which the central bank advances loans to the commercial banks strictly for short period – ranging from overnight to not exceeding a month. In doing so, the central bank makes advances against short-term securities to be repurchased by the borrowing bank at a later date. How does it influence the money supply or liquidity in the system? If the central bank intends to increase the supply of money with the banking system, it lowers the repo rate and thus enables the banks to borrow at lower cost. The banks can have larger volume of money to meet their liquidity shortage (See Chapter 7 on Banking System and Credit Creation). Alternatively, if the purpose of the central bank is to reduce the supply of money and credit or, suck excess liquidity, it raises the repo rate which makes the credit costlier, such that banks are less empowered to utilize excess liquidity in creating credit to the same extent as earlier. The expansionary process of credit money is restrained in the second case while in the first case this process is encouraged. Thus, the repo rate as a short-term rate of interest influences, initially, the cost of credit and ultimately the entire money supply of the banking system.

This process, of course, is based on the underlying assumption that the banking institutions will be sufficiently responsive to the signal given by the central bank. In other words, if repo rate rises, banks are supposed to pass on this higher cost of credit to their consumers and similarly if repo rate falls, lower cost of credit is expected to be passed on to the customers. Normally, banks respond positively even though they are not under compulsion to do so in the present environment of banking deregulation.

(b) Reverse Repo Rate[1] It is the rate of interest allowed to the surplus of the commercial banks deposited to the central bank. Again, this is

[1] In India, the terms, repo and reverse repo are in vogue in keeping with international usage since October 29, 2004. Before this, RBI used these terms just in opposite senses, i.e., repo in place of reverse repo and reverse repo in place of repo.

related to short period fund transfer and is the reverse process of repo operation. In fact, reverse repo rate is generally lower than the repo rate. The difference between these two rates is known as 'corridor'. If the banking system experiences excess funds which they intend to park with the central bank, the central bank allows the reverse repo rate to these deposits. Any change in reverse repo rate means either lower or higher return to the banks' 'surplus' deposits (with central bank). Normally, when repo is raised, reverse repo is also raised although not necessarily to the same extent. It depends upon the actual market condition for loanable funds, particularly the market rate of interest and the assessment of the central bank regarding the necessity of raising or lowering both these rates.

These two short-term rates, to a large extent, influence the market expectations about interest rates. There are, of course, other rates equally influential, e.g., inter-bank call money rate for overnight loans among the different banks and marginal standing facility (MSF) recently introduced by India's RBI. Both repo and reverse repo rates are called 'policy rates' depending upon which one becomes the principal mode during a particular period of time. For instance, if there is shortage of liquidity in the system and the most banks are seeking short-term funds from the central bank through the repo window, then repo rate becomes the policy rate. On the other hand, when there is excess liquidity in the banking and financial system and the central bank is in a mood to withdraw the excess, the reverse repo rate becomes the policy rate. However, giving incentive to banks in terms of higher reverse repo rate in such situation may not be enough if other rates in the market (e.g., inter-bank call rate) is higher than reverse repo rate.

19.4.2 Open Market Operations (OMO)

Open market operations have, in recent times, become the most popular monetary policy instrument to target the interest rate movement and ultimately the supply of money in the economy. The open market operations refer to the outright purchase and sale of government securities such as treasury bills, government bonds and other corporate bonds lying in the disposal of central bank. It ought to be remembered that central bank initially purchases these securities against which it advances loans to central government as well as other provincial governments. Different countries where provincial governments do not exist, the central bank purchases the Federal Govt. (Union Government) securities. In India, RBI purchases both the Union Govt. securities as well as State Govt. securities.

The central bank can utilize these securities as means of either controlling the supply of money and credit or releasing more of them to the economy. Let us suppose, the central bank feels there is need to suck out excess liquidity from the system. It sells securities and thereby takes away excess money supply. This way, the banking system is left with less reserve money and is restrained to create credit. On the other hand, if the central bank intends to inject more liquidity in the system (since it feels the banking and financial system are short of funds), it purchases securities from the market and thereby releases additional funds. By altering the supply of money through open market operations, the central bank also influences the rate of interest in the market and does not allow the rate to fluctuate too much.

These open market operations can also be carried out through 'repo' and 'reverse repo' windows of the central bank.

The instruments discussed above are all indirect methods of influencing the money supply and credit creation and ultimately the liquidity situation in the economy.

19.4.3 Variable Reserve Ratios (Cash Reserve Ratio and Statutory Reserve Ratio)

Commercial banks, all over the world, have to keep a certain percentage of their deposits (generally, demand and time liabilities) with the central banks. This is known as Cash Reserve Ratio. In some countries, besides the Cash Reserve Ratio (CRR), they have to set apart a certain percentage of deposits with themselves in the form of cash, gold or government securities. This is known as Statutory Liquidity Ratio (SLR). Obviously, these reserve requirements put limitations on the reserve money with banking system and hence also on the process of credit creation and the total supply of money.

Changes in these reserve requirements (increase/decrease in the percentage), changes the process of money supply. For instance, if CRR is lowered, say from 10 per cent to 8 per cent of the banks' deposits, there is net increase in banks' reserves since they have now to part with lesser proportion of their deposits with the central bank. They are, thus, able to translate these extra deposits into credit and hence the money supply. Similarly, if CRR is raised just the opposite effect on money supply takes place. It may be mentioned here that CRR is the *minimum* necessary (percentage) that all commercial banks are required to deposit with the central bank. If they wish, they can keep even higher percentage as well.

It is obligatory on the part of all banks to keep additional deposits in the form of government securities, gold or cash with themselves. This varies from country to country depending upon the extent of government's control over the central bank. In other words, the extent of autonomy enjoyed by the central banks as well as the overall flexibility in the government's economic policy determines these obligatory deposits by the banking sector. Again, raising SLR puts restraints on the banking system on credit creation and money supply. But lowering it releases larger reserve money for banks to use in the process of credit money. Again, it is possible that in certain situations banks may overinvest in government securities – over and above the SLR limit under situations when banks find that credit advancement or, other investment is less rewarding than SLR investments. In that case, part of monetary policy actions take the route of fiscal policy – government borrowing and government expenditure.

Other Instruments Besides the above policy instruments which either influence the rate of interest or the base money (reserve money) to effect the total money supply, the central bank sometimes adopts certain short-term temporary measures like Special Liquidity Adjustment Facility (LAF). This facility is allowed to banks to avail special lending facility by pledging a small percentage of their SLR to the central bank in order to avoid a situation of liquidity crunch. This is over and above the existing repo and reverse repo facilities under LAF.

In the Indian context, Chakravarty Committee Report (1985), which is considered the first important document of monetary policy in India underlining the policy direction in subsequent period, recommended, among other things, 'monetary targeting' as a means to achieve price stability. Specifically, the Committee advocated a 'flexible' as against 'fixed' rate of growth of money supply which implied *monetary targeting with feedback* and so to be modified in the light of information available on expected output performance.

But, targeting a certain rate of money supply and targeting a certain rate of inflation are not exactly the same. In subsequent periods, particularly, following high inflation era of 2013-14 and 2014-15, inflation targeting emerged as a new policy objective.

Broadly, the instruments of monetary policy can be put under two heads: (1) conventional monetary policy and (2) unconventional monetary policy. The conventional monetary policy tools include those which are normally used by the central banks such as (a) bank rate policy, (b) open market operation, (c) variable reserve ratio and other instruments which largely influence the cost of credit of the banking sector or change the volume of reserve money with the banks.

19.5 THE UNCONVENTIONAL MONETARY POLICY INSTRUMENTS

These refer to those instruments which are used under abnormal economic situations like long recessions or depressions. Ever since 2008-09 global recession, the advanced economies like US, UK, European Union and Japan have been using the unconventional monetary policy weapons by their respective central banks. The following are the main unconventional policy instruments.

(a) Quantitative Easing: The US was the first to try this policy tool in the form of large scale purchases of financial assets like sovereign bonds and thereby releasing dollars. The intention of the Federal Reserve was to stimulate the recession-hit economy by pumping money into the market to raise aggregate demand and thereby revive the economy. At the same time, the interest rate in the US (Fed rate) was reduced to near zero (0.00 to 0.25%) thus using ultraloose monetary policy. It may be mentioned here that these unconventional monetary policy tools continued to be applied for a pretty long period, from 2008 to 2015-16. Since December, 2015, the Fed reversed its course on policy rate by raising interest rate by 0.25% to fix it between 0.25% and 0.50%. Another rate hike was announced by the Fed Reserve in March, 2017 by 0.25%, thus raising it to 0.50 to 0.75%. The US monetary policy makers were still very cautious in raising further interest rates since the inflation rate there was still very low (well below 2%, their target rate) and the economy was undergoing slow recovery. However, since then there have been several rate hikes by US Fed alongside inflation pick up as well as employment and economic growth.

Similar situation prevailed in most countries under European Union where recessionary conditions are still continuing till date and the European Central Bank (ECB) has been trying hard to revive its economies by adopting the same type of unconventional monetary policy, i.e., large scale asset purchases (bonds). At the same time, ECB, during late 2015 and early 2016, adopted another unconventional measure as stated below.

(b) Negative rate of interest: Normally, individuals and businesses keep their deposits with the banks which, in turn, pay the depositors some interest on their deposits. This is a positive interest paid by the banks. If, instead, the banks charge interest amounts from the depositors for keeping their deposits or for dissuading them from keeping deposits, then that is the negative rate of interest. In recent years, the ECB as also the Bank of Japan in Asia, have adopted the practice of charging interest from commercial banks against their deposits, thereby discouraging their deposits to the ECB/BoJ. Of late many other countries' central banks like Sweden, Denmark, Switzerland are also adopting the negative interest rates. In the US, the Federal Reserve has further slashed the interest rate to near zero though not negative at present, after the Covid-19 pandemic. However, the purpose of negative rate of interest by the central banks is to discourage hoarding cash by individuals and companies in a desperate attempt to stimulate growth by getting corporations to invest and the individuals to spend. The recent example of negative interest rate policy adopted by the ECB was announced in March, 2016 when the rate was further hiked from –0.3% to –0.4%. In fact, these unconventional monetary policy measures are aimed at propping up the economy through using the extremely cheap money for real investment purposes and discouraging any idle deposit with the banks.

In Japan also, where low growth prevailed over the whole of 1990s and most of the 2000s decade, unconventional monetary policy has been adopted. The Bank of Japan reduced its interest rate not only to the lowest level, but even to the negative level besides asset purchase programme. The recent policy of the Bank of Japan is being dubbed as the Quantitative and Qualitative Easing Policy (QQE).

A recent report in *Times Business*, dated 11 July, 2016, says that in Denmark, homeowners are receiving cheques from their banks because their banks have negative rates of interest. In Japan, citizens are buying ' safes' as it is now cheaper to keep money in safes than in bank accounts. Retired people depending on annuities have seen their incomes drop.

However, the negative rate of interest as a monetary policy tool has not yet shown any prospect as far as emerging economies are concerned. The emerging and developing economies are still suffering from capital shortage although in recent years the bank interest rates have come down, particularly the deposit interest rates as evident in India. But they are not so much market-driven as advanced countries. For instance, certain kinds of deposits are protected (senior citizens and retirees' accounts are generally protected). The lending rates are also higher in emerging economies. Secondly, there are risks for these economies in case they adopt measures like negative interest rate. The foreign portfolio investments will be hindered while bank deposits for lending will get a hit and both these are extremely important for emerging and developing economies (Ajay Chibber, 2020).

(c) Helicopter drop of money: The idea of helicopter drop of money was mooted by economists Milton Friedman, Willem Buiter and others who were staunch believers of the monetarist approach of continued money supply under recessionary or depressionary conditions until the economy rebounds. The idea is to provide money directly into the hands of the public as if money has been dropped by helicopters. This way, the public are induced to expend money so that demand is propped up and, subsequently, real investment takes place. In fact, after the 2008 financial crisis, trillions of dollars were pumped into the financial sector of the economy but growth or low inflation could not be revived. Hence, this extreme form of monetary policy instrument was suggested. However, till date it has not been put to use since there were some signs of pick-up of the economy in early 2017. Secondly, as reported by Catherine Bosiey (*Economic Times*, October 14, 2016), the helicopter drop of money may not have much of an impact as revealed by a study by ING thus: "if people were to receive 200 euros ($ 220) in their bank accounts each month for a year, with no string attached, respondents (some 12,000 consumers) in 12 European countries said they would be more likely to save the cash than spend it. Only 26% said they would spend most of the money, while 52% said they would save it, invest it or leave the bulk untouched while 15% said they would pay back debt." The effectiveness of this new idea is thus questioned as concluded by a senior economist at ING.

However, it may be suggested in the case of Indian economy which is currently (of 2019-20) suffering from slowdown with GDP growth plummeting to 5%, 5.1% (revised) and 4.7% (revised), during the first three quarters of 2019-20, direct transfer of money to the lower income groups of people would, hopefully, raise the aggregate demand and improve the growth rate of the economy through higher consumption expenditures

19.6 RULES VERSUS DISCRETION DEBATE

A subject of long-standing debate in the field of economic policy making has been whether economic policy/policies should be based on certain rules or it should be largely left to the discretion of the policy makers. Economists belonging to the classical/neoclassical school, by and large, believe that policies, monetary or fiscal, should be guided by rules, if there are any; while those having allegiance to the Keynesian school are of the view that policy/policies should be left to the discretion of the policy makers, either the central bank or the fiscal authority (the government). In fact, there are arguments both in favour and against the rule based as well as discretionary policies which we examine below.

Arguments in favour of rule based policies

1. Economic events are largely uncertain and unpredictable. Policy makers are unable to know exactly the outcomes of any policy change since knowledge is imperfect. In such circumstances, it is better to leave the policy/policies to be determined by certain rules available in the policy domain and patiently to wait for the outcome of the policy/policies. This way, the public in general, are left with a better position to predict the outcome of the policy change and thus they can plan their actions in advance. In fact, eminent economists have devised, from time to time, various policy rules to help policy makers implement them for better economic results. Some of these rules are rigid while some are flexible. We shall discuss later in this section, some of these rules and examine how they are put into operation.
2. Some economists tend to believe that historically, whenever the rule based policies have been given a goodbye, economies have suffered serious problems of worst economic performance such as long recessions, high inflation, stagflation, etc. History of advanced developed economies provides adequate evidence of such occurrences. The advent of Keynesian economic policies after the Great Depression of 1929 and adoption of discretionary economic policies, both in the monetary and fiscal policy spheres till 1970s, was associated with periods of relatively high fiscal deficit, inflation, accumulation of high levels of public debt

and stagflation. On the contrary, when rule based policies were followed during the late 1980s and 1990s, better economic performance and lesser occurrences of inflation or recession were witnessed. Again, the reappearance of discretionary policies during the later half of the 2000s was accompanied by booms and bubbles and consequent bust turning into the worst financial crisis of 2008 in the US with its tentacles spread to other countries of the world. Ironically, again, in order to fight long recession, discretionary monetary policies of US Fed Reserve as also other central banks of advanced countries were adopted which remained ineffective for a pretty long period of time.

However, such an association between rule based policies and good economic performance can be contested since, it is hard to establish whether following rule based policies caused better economic performance or better economic performance prompted the use of rule based policies. In fact, the debate ultimately boils down to the controversy between short-run Keynesian and long-run classical/new classical solution of the problems. It cannot be denied that short-run fluctuations within the economy need to be addressed seriously and they are as much important as the long-run ones.

3. Those who argue for rule based policy, simultaneously argue against discretionary policies. One of the disadvantages of discretionary policies is that policy maker is most likely to favour the particular political party in power with a view to patronising it. For instance, if the government is in favour of easy monetary policy to be pursued by the central bank, the latter may oblige the government even though such actions might not be in the best interest of the economy in the long run. This might result in cyclical ups and downs. Such a phenomenon is often known as 'political business cycle', business cycle that results from political dictates of the government in power.
4. If decisions are entirely left to the discretion of policy makers, it might also result in enormous time-gap between the intentions of the authority announced at a certain point in time and actual action taken. Such policies are characterised as 'time inconsistent'. In such situations, the public and the market fail to predict the outcome of the appropriate policy/ policies. One such example in recent history was the US Fed's dilemma to withdraw from quantitative easing (QE) programme which was formally announced sometime in end-2013. However, after several announcements of tentative dates and subsequent postponements, it finally ended the zero-interest rate regime in December, 2015. Thus, the Fed not only unleashed a period of uncertainty, but also, kept the policy makers elsewhere guessing about its action.

Arguments against rule-based policies: Policies based on strict rules fail to solve problems arising from shocks to the economy as well as temporary upheavals.

Economies, whether in the advanced or underdeveloped world, very often encounter problems like temporary shocks such as 'oil shocks' arising from sudden rise in crude oil prices which form a significant portion of import bills of most countries. Secondly, long recessions, high inflation, sudden inflow or outflow of foreign capital as well as volatility of foreign exchange rates, etc., also cause considerable damage to the economy demanding immediate attention of the policy makers. In such circumstances, rule based policies either prove to be inadequate or ineffective. This is all the more important in the present-day world of uncertainties unleashed by globalisation of trade and financial services resulting in competitiveness among nations. Use of discretions by policy makers in such cases is extremely necessary. Public policies are required to address political, economic as well as social concerns of the people such as high unemployment and low growth of the economy and society. Policies, therefore, need to be flexible and dynamic in nature which the strict rule based ones fail to fulfil. For instance, during the post-2008 financial crisis, discretionary (and unconventional) monetary as well as fiscal policies (quantitative easing or bond buying programmes) along with zero interest rate by the US Fed and European Central Bank as also liberal healthcare expenditures were implemented. Even though there are differences of opinion, economists generally credit the policy makers in US for being successful in preventing the US economy from slipping into 1929-30 like depression.

Rules vs. discretion debate can be taken to international macroeconomy, particularly, the exchange rate system. It is well known, that following the "Bretton Woods" arrangement, fixed exchange rate system was adopted thus putting all currencies to be convertible to US $ at a fixed rate as well as at par with gold. This system of fixed exchange rate continued until 1973 when it was abandoned and replaced by "flexible" or "floating" exchange rate system. It is argued by some economists that the earlier system of fixed exchange rate was a system of monetary "cooperation" and hence witnessed an era of economic and financial stability in the world economy. On the other hand, the new arrangement of flexibility in the exchange rate has given rise to excessive instability, currency disorder and exchange rate competitiveness as are currently being witnessed over the world economy. Robert Mundell, along with Marcus Fleming, long back in the 1960s, argued that under a fixed exchange rate system and with perfect capital mobility, the monetary authorities of nations cannot pursue independent monetary policy, such as expanding or contracting money supply at will. Mundell's "impossible trinity", in particular,suggests that, of the three options, viz., perfect capital mobility, fixed exchange rate and independent monetary policy, a nation can adopt any two of these three forgoing at least one option. That is a binding condition and a 'rule' that ensures monetary stability and cooperation among nations. But, a flexible exchange rate system allowed central banks to adopt monetary policies suiting their own economies without much concern for others. In recent years, for instance, the US economy was seen pursuing 'unconventional' (and of course, independent) monetary policy such as 'quantitative easing' (QE), thereby releasing cheap money against bonds along with near zero rate of interest. This practice has later been followed by other economies such as European Union, Japan, etc. Further, to prop up their low growth economies, they resorted to 'currency depreciation' one by one. Economists have termed these exercises equivalent to "beggar thy neighbour" policy amounting to competitive currency depreciation and not currency cooperation. The current situation demands a framework of currency cooperation which would be somewhat mandatory (or rule) for all trading nations.

Below we illustrate some of the macroeconomic rules followed implicitly or explicitly by many economies of the world.

1. Tinbergen's Rule

Jan Tinbergen, the famous Dutch economist and nobel laureate, formulated this rule. The rule is more general and suggests under what conditions a certain economic policy will likely be successful. Distinguishing between policy targets (or, objectives) and policy tools (or, instruments), Tinbergen's rule prescribes that for each and every policy target, there should be at least one policy tool. In his work on macroeconomic modelling, Tinbergen classified some economic quantities as 'targets 'and others as' 'instruments'. Targets are those macroeconomic variables the policy maker wishes to influence (such as inflation rate, exchange rate), whereas instruments are the variables that the policy maker can control directly (such as, central bank's policy interest rate). Clearly, if there are fewer tools than targets, then some policy goals will not be achieved. As an example, we can say that if there are two policy goals like obtaining a certain inflation rate as also a certain growth rate of the economy or an employment target, then one of these goals will not be achieved with just one policy tool of short-term interest rate of the central bank.

2. Taylor's Rule

Taylor's rule happens to be one of the important rules relating to the determination of policy interest rate by the central bank. The rule was formulated by Prof. Bob J. Taylor of Stanford University, USA. This rule tries to establish an empirical relationship between interest rates, inflation rate and the GDP gap,–the gap between actual GDP and potential GDP. The rule provides a fairly good guide to the central bank as to how it ought to fix its policy interest rate keeping in view the difference between the actual and target inflation rates as also between actual and potential GDP growth, the GDP gap. The formula suggested by Taylor is as follows:

$$it. = 2 + \pi t + 0.5 (\pi t - \pi^*) + 0.5 \{(Y t - Y t^*)/Yt^* \times 100\} \qquad (19.1)$$

where, *it* is the policy interest rate (such as Fed rate in US, repo rate in India, etc.), to be set by the central bank; πt is the actual rate of inflation; π * is the target rate of inflation; *Yt* is the actual GDP and *Yt** is the potential GDP of the country; the number 2 is the long-term real rate of interest which is the target (or, reference) rate of interest of the central bank.

Taylor's rule specifically suggests that the central bank ought to set its policy interest rate at a level depending on (a) the difference between actual and target inflation rates, discounted by 50 per cent (0.5), (b) the percentage difference between actual GDP and potential GDP discounted by fifty percentage point and (c) its own target long-term real interest rate (nominal interest rate minus inflation rate). Thus, the central bank's actual policy rate must be set above its target real interest rate plus (a) and (b).

A few examples will illustrate the rule:

(a) If the actual inflation rate in the economy is 3% and there is full employment in the economy (actual GDP = potential GDP), the central bank's policy interest rate will be set at 5.5% = {2 + 3 + 0.5 × (3 – 2)}.

(b) If the actual inflation rate is 5% and there is GDP gap of 2%, then the policy interest rate will be set at 7.5% {2 + 5 + 0.5 × 3 + 0.5 × (–2)}.

(c) If the actual inflation rate is equal to its target inflation rate and there is GDP gap of 1%, then the policy interest rate will be 3.5% {2 + 2 + 0 – 0.5}.

Application of Taylor's rule to different economies depends on their actual economic conditions and the specific targets their policy makers set. However, Taylor's rule is most appropriate for economies pursuing inflation targeting policy. There is no doubt that Taylor's rule is a good guide to monetary policy making particularly in setting the central bank's policy interest rate. In the US economy, it is generally believed that the Fed, by and large, follows Taylor's rule although in other economies of the world where inflation targeting has not found favour as a policy goal, the rule is not strictly followed. It may be mentioned here that India's central bank (RBI) recently adopted inflation targeting policy since 2013 when Indian economy was experiencing a high level of inflation. However, to what extent it will follow Taylor's rule is not yet evidenced. Even within the Taylor's rule, there is ample scope of manoeuvrability with the central bank which only an able, farsighted and experienced administrator of the central bank can properly judge.

3. Money supply rule

Expanding money supply at a certain constant rate is yet another monetary policy rule originating from the school of 'monetarism'. Since monetarists (followers of monetarism) argued that money supply directly influences price level in the long run and hence the level of inflation, expanding money supply at a certain constant rate by the central bank commensurate with the growth of GDP and the demand for money, inflationary problem will be minimised in the economy. It may be mentioned that this monetary rule originated much before the inflation targeting rule like Taylor's rule. Specifically, it is suggested that if GDP grows by an annual average rate of 5%, and the demand for money grows by 1%, money supply should be increased by 6% per annum.

However, this rule too proved less fruitful when it was discovered that demand function for money is not stable and hence unpredictable particularly in developing economies.

Instead of correlating money supply with GDP growth rate, another variant of it has been devised in terms of unemployment rate being correlated with money supply growth. The rule is given in eqn. (19.2).

$$\Delta M/M = 5 + 2(u - 3) \tag{19.2}$$

where, $\Delta M/M$ is the annual percentage growth rate of money supply, u is the actual unemployment rate (an indicator of cyclical fluctuation of business activities), 3 is the natural rate of unemployment (annual), and 5 is the growth rate of money supply in the absence of any divergence between actual and natural unemployment rates. The rule, therefore states that the annual money supply growth should be 5 + twice the difference between actual and natural unemployment rates of the economy. For instance, if u is 4%, which is 1% above the natural unemployment rate, the growth of money supply should be $5 + 2 \times 1 = 7\%$ per annum.

4. Okun's law

Okun's* law is an empirical law which seeks to establish a relationship between the change in the rate of unemployment and the change in the rate of growth in the GDP/ GNP of an economy. This can be represented by a downward sloping curve from left to the right where the X-ordinate denotes the change in the rate of unemployment while the Y-ordinate denotes the change in the rate of growth in GDP/ GNP. The law is named after Professor Arther Melvin Okun who first proposed the relationship in 1962. Clearly, the law is based on observational data on the two variables – change in unemployment rate and change in the GDP rate. The observational data, according to the author, suggest a negative relationship such that a country's fall in the GDP rate leads to a rise in the unemployment rate and vice versa. Okun's law has, basically, two versions— the gap version and the difference version. The gap version of Okun's law states that for every one percent increase in the unemployment rate (moving rightward on the horizontal line on a suggested graph), a country's actual GDP will be roughly 2% lower than its potential GDP. The 'difference' version of Okun's law states the relationship in terms of quarterly changes in unemployment and quarterly changes in real GDP, that is, percentage change in quarterly unemployment and percentage change in quarterly GDP.

Okun's law may, more accurately be called 'Okun's rule of thumb', because it is an approximation based on empirical observation rather than a result derived from theory. Secondly, the law is approximate because factors other than employments such as productivity affect output In fact, in Okun's original statement of his law, a 2% increase in output corresponds to a 1% decline "in the rate of cyclical unemployment; a 0.5% increase in labour force participation; a 0.5% increase in hours worked per employee and a 1% increase in output per hour worked (labour productivity), (Okun, 1962: "Potential GNP: It's Measurement and Significance", American Statistical Association, Proceedings of the Business and Economics Statistics Section, 1962, reprinted with slight changes in Arthur M. Okun, The Political Economy of Prosperity (Washington D.C. Brookings Institution, 1070).

Some economists have empirically estimated the Okun's relationship by regressing GNP on the unemployment rate and found that a 3% decrease in output results in every 1% increase in unemployment rate. (Panchowny, Martin F.J., 1963: Okun's Law: Theoretical Foundations and Revised Estimates in The Review of Economics and Statistics, 75(2) 331-336). However, if some other factors like (a) fresh entrants to the labour force, (b) rise in labour productivity and (c) rise in labour hour per week put in by each labourer, the decrease in the output will be still lower to 2% instead of 3%. Thus, the original estimate holds only when these other factors are assumed to remain unchanged.

*www.wikipedia.org, the free encyclopaedia

Conclusion

There are no precise policy rules which can be applied in increasingly difficult and complex situations of modern-day economic conditions. Even if certain rules are available which have been advocated by eminent economists from time to time, their application in different economies in different times involves good amount of manoeuvrability wherein human ingenuity, foresight and judgement play major roles. It is precisely for this reason that efficient and qualified people with proven track records should be given the sole responsibility to handle the monetary as well as fiscal policy decisions. There are instances in economic history when persons with extraordinary calibre and expertise have been able to solve extremely challenging problems. Paul Volcker's example as a successful Fed Chairman in the US in the 1980s and Raghuram Rajan's as Governor of RBI in India during 2013-16 in controlling inflation are worth remembering. Thus, neither rigid rules (like those applied under gold standard) are appropriate nor total discretion with respect to objectives and instruments are desirable. Hence, the phrase," constrained discretion" is appropriately suggested.

19.7 MONETARY POLICY IN INDIA

The monetary policy in independent India particularly during the first four decades (pre-reform period till 1980s) of planned development era can be broadly described as follows:

1. The principal objectives of monetary policy being focused on price stability with economic growth.
2. Dominance of fiscal policy considerations over monetary policy.
3. Controlled expansion of money supply.
4. Dependence of direct instruments of monetary policy rather than indirect instruments like interest rates and open market operations.
5. Monetary and financial environment being characterized by relatively underdeveloped money and financial markets.
6. Existence of multiple interest rates and administered (govt. determined) concessional rates of interest for priority sector lending by the banking sector.

As is well known, independent India got the legacy of underdevelopment, high population growth and high proportion of poverty. Primary concern of the government was, therefore, economic and social development. Economic development process initiated through Five Year Plans required public expenditures on a large scale. This, in turn, necessitated the government to resort to deficit financing in the annual budgets. To meet the budgetary deficits, the government resorted to borrowing from Reserve Bank of India which could only be possible through monetization. In the short run, however, output growth was not possible. Hence, inflation was inevitable. But the government, was guided by the belief that while growth for the economy was necessary, certain amount of inflationary pressure will also be inevitable. Hence, the monetary policy had to address both these concerns with primary focus being laid on economic growth.

In a sense, the central bank of India, acted more in favour of government's fiscal policy. The RBI, then did not enjoy any antonomy insofar as the conduct of monetary policy was concerned. Neither was the financial system developed enough to respond to RBI policies. The dominance of fiscal policy considerations – meeting the needs of government resources – over monetary policy was evident from high level of statutory liquidity ratios (SLR) that commercial banks required to maintain. In fact, high-level of investment in government securities by banks enabled the government to secure financial resources for meeting budget deficits.

Since the growth rate of the economy was very low during the early periods and the fear of inflation was uppermost, a controlled supply of money by the RBI was resorted to within the existing framework. As instruments of monetary policy direct methods such as changes in reserve ratios (CRR and SLR) and certain selective credit control measures were mostly in operation. Other indirect methods like bank rate and open market operations were not effectively used.

However, it has to be admitted that in spite of such implicit guidelines, in most cases, the expansion of money supply had to yield to the pressures of financing of the on-going government projects and resulted in uncontrolled money supply growth.

The Indian money market lacked depth and was characterized by imperfections and rigidity. Also, several interest rates were applicable to different sectors and different sets of population for advancement of loans from government, semi-government organizations and commercial banking sector. A significant part of credit consisted of concessional categories such as lending to priority sector, like agriculture, small and cottage industries, small businesses and exports. People belonging to ST and SC categories of population enjoyed special concessional loans for various purposes (some of these preferential rates of interest are continuing even today in some form or the other). These concessional rates of interest were used to be determined by the government. Further, government intended to borrow from the market at low rate of interest; hence yields on government securities were kept low. Thus, after independence, as part of planned development, economic policy in India moved from fiscal neutrality to fiscal activism.[1]

A definitive shape to monetary policy framework during the pre-reform period was based on the recommendations made by the Committee to Review the Working of the Monetary System (Chakravarty Committee, 1985). The Committee considered maintaining price stability and provision of adequate credit to the productive sectors of the economy, as the two core objectives of monetary policy and provided a systematic framework for targeting of broad money supply (M_3) corresponding with year to year increases in the acceptable rate of inflation and the expected growth in output. The Committee underlined that the demand for money is, understandtably, not found to be very sensitive to interest rates in India in the context of a system of administered interest rates.[2]

19.7.1 Monetary Policy in the Post-Reform Period

Monetary policy framework underwent significant changes during the post-reform period – particularly during the 1990s. With economic reforms initiated since 1991 major structural reforms were also started in the banking and financial sectors.

Two important reports, viz., Narasimham Committee Report-I and Narasimham Committee Report-II in 1991 and 1997, respectively, provided the platform for far-reaching changes in the monetary, banking and financial systems

[1] YV Reddy, "Government Budgets, Banking and Auditors: What is New? RBI Bulletin, December, 2000.

[2] Chakravarty Committee Report, 1985

of the country in the coming years. For instance, market forces were gradually allowed to play in the financial market. The banking sector was subjected to certain prudential norms to be followed although sufficient deregulation measures were also implemented simultaneously. In the monetary policy front, while Reserve Bank of India was largely released from the clutches of the government control to pursue relatively independent monetary policy, other commercial banks were granted autonomy in terms of taking individual decisions regarding their deposit and lending rates, The RBI, in turn, gradually reduced the statutory requirements of reserve deposits of banks such as SLR and CRR. Also, more and more reliance was placed on indirect instruments of monetary policy such as bank rate (particularly the short term rates of interest) and open market operations.

In a broader framework, although the objectives of monetary policy remained centred around price stability and economic growth these objectives were now tailored to meet the goal of exchange rate stability as well so that the external value of rupee is, by and large, maintained at satisfactory level.

A significant step towards reducing fiscal dominance of monetary policy was taken with the agreement reached between RBI and the Govt. of India in 1997 to discontinue the system of Adhoc Treasury Bills by which the government could borrow from the RBI leading to the monetization of budget deficits. (It came into effect since April, 1997.) The system was replaced by 'Ways and Means Advances' (WAM) to the government within a certain prescribed limits. Henceforth, while the extent of fiscal deficit was significantly reduced in subsequent years, the monetized deficit was almost eliminated from the budget. In case the government exceeded the limit of WAM Advances it was allowed for a few days only at a higher rate. This measure allowed the RBI to do better and more effective co-ordination of the monetary policy.

The two key measures, viz., SLR and CRR were gradually reduced. The SLR which was as high as 38.5 per cent in 1992 was first reduced to 31.5 per cent in 1994 and later to 25 per cent in 1997. Since then SLR is kept more or less at this level. The CRR was also brought down from 15 per cent in 1991 to 8.5 per cent in 2000. Subsequently, it has been revised – generally downwards. (See Table 19.1).

The interest rates on government securities (bonds, treasury bills and other government securities) were made more and more market related in subsequent years particularly during the later years of 1990s and the following decade of 2001-10. At present, most government papers are sold on auction basis which means that government can fetch market based price to them rather than that indicated in them depending on the strength of the demand for such papers in the financial market. Secondly, the maturity period of such papers was reduced generally to the maximum of ten-year period. For instance, the 10-year government bond has now become (benchmark 10 year G-sec.) more popular and widely transacted upon. In recent years, however, the maturity period has again been longer at least in case of some of these papers. Since these government securities are traded through the RBI, the role of open market operations has increased in recent years as dominant form of monetary policy.

During recent years, monetary policy is being more frequently reviewed. While earlier, there used to be six-monthly review of the RBI's is monetary and Credit Policy (in April and October each year) this has been substituted by 'quarterly' review.

Since April, 2010, the monetary and credit policy is being reviewed every six weeks. The organizational structure of the RBI was also suitably changed to include a number of committee/inter-departmental groups in order to better co-ordinate the monetary and credit requirements of the economy as also to continuously monitor money, capital, foreign exchange and securities markets. These committees are the following:

1. **Inter-Departmental Financial Markets Committee** This committee monitors developments in financial markets on a daily basis. It reviews market developments with regard to call money rates, foreign exchange, spot and forward rates, movements in volume of funds both in money and foreign exchange markets, yield rates and volumes in government securities markets and banking as well as other market indicators. The committee makes quick assessments of liquidity conditions and recommends strategies for interventions in money and securities markets.
2. **The Monetary Policy Department** of RBI holds discussions with regard to resource management with the banks which focus, upon reviewing and obtaining a projection of banks' major sources and uses of funds, collecting qualitative information on the goals perceived and strategies proposed to be adopted by the banks in achieving these objectives/goals, obtaining feedbacks on the policy announcements made and suggestions on future policy course and seeks banks' perception on liquidity and market conditions in the immediate context.
3. **The Technical Advisory Committee** on money and government securities market headed by a deputy governor of RBI and members from financial and banking community and academics which advises the RBI, on an ongoing basis, on developments of money and government securities markets.[1]
4. **Monetary Policy Committee (MPC):** Set up and operative since 2016 (separately discussed at page 544).

19.7.2 Monetary Policy in India in Recent Years

In recent times, particularly, since 2013, monetary policy in India has witnessed a significant shift in the policy stance. Around this time, inflation rate was

[1] K. Kanagasabapathy, "Monetary Policy Underpinnings: A Perpective", EPW, Jan. 27, 2001.

alarmingly high with rising inflation expectations. There was a feeling among a section of the public that high levels of inflation had come to stay as a 'new norm'. At this juncture, Dr. Raghuram Rajan was appointed new RBI governor. Within a couple of months, the new governor indicated his stance on inflation front as his first and foremost policy priority. Meanwhile, the Central Statistical Organisation (CSO) also started publishing CPI based inflation data which helped to anchor inflation in a better way. Initially, the RBI took a hawkish view on inflation and started raising the policy rates–repo and reverse repo rates. This way, by taming the inflation expectations, the actual inflation rate was also brought down within a few months.

Of late, inflation targeting in India was clearly spelt out by the RBI governor when, towards the end of 2014, CPI inflation target was fixed at 6% by January, 2016 and at 4% thereafter with a band of (+/–) 2%. Hence, inflation rate in future (beyond 2016) could hover between 6% on the upper side and 2% on the lower side. Thus, it is a "flexible inflation targeting" strategy in place.

In December, 2014, however, the inflation rate in India fell to 5.5% (CPI), while WPI inflation reached near zero which further fell to the negative zone (–2.4%).

Inspired by this trend, the RBI reduced the repo rate by 0.25% (25 bsp) from 8% to 7.75% in mid-December, 2014 and, further, by 0.25% in early March, 2015. Another rate cut was announced on 2 June, 2015 thus fixing the repo rate at 7.25% while the CRR and SLR rates were left at 4% and 21.5% respectively.

Also, on 2nd March, 2015, both the Government of India and the RBI entered into an agreement to formalise the inflation targeting objective so much so that if, in the future, the target is missed, either upside or downside, the RBI would be responsible for explaining the reasons for such breaching of targets.

The monetary policy framework agreement is seen as the landmark shift in the monetary policy in India. With this, India has now joined the group of 55 other countries of the world such as New Zealand, UK, US, Brazil, Indonesia, South Africa and others which have already adopted the goal of inflation targeting. In fact, New Zealand was the first country to adopt inflation targeting and has since become a model for other countries to follow.

Monetary Policy Committee: In July, 2015, the Government of India (Ministry of Finance) released a revised draft of Indian Financial Code (IFC), with the purpose of reducing certain powers of the RBI, particularly, the 'veto' power of the governor, hitherto enjoyed, in case of disagreement among the members of the technical advisory committee of the RBI regarding the interest rate policy decision.

With the approval of this bill and subsequent amendment of the RBI Act, the Monetary Policy Committee was set up in September, 2016. The Committee consists of six members, three each representing the government and the RBI. The

RBI representatives include the governor who is the chairman of the Committee. However, the chairman has no veto power over the majority decision of the committee. He has, instead, a casting vote in case of a tie among the members.

Two things are clear from this change. One is that now the monetary policy is the responsibility of a six-member committee where the government will have an equal say, through its representatives, in the matter of monetary policy making exercises. Second, the autonomy of the central bank is now reduced to some extent in so far as the members representing the government side are expected to exert some influence over policy decisions. However, that a new institutional framework in the shape of Monetary Policy Committee has come up in India is itself a revolutionary step. It may be mentioned that this institutional change took place while Dr. Raghuram Rajan was the governor of RBI who left, after the expiry of his three-year term on the 4th August, 2016 to take up his old teaching assignment at Chicago's Booth School as Professor of Finance. Dr. Urjit Patel was the next governor who chaired the first MPC meeting on 2 October, 2016. Since then, twenty meetings have been held till 6th February, 2020 and it is significant to note that most decisions have been unanimously taken with regard to interest rate fixation keeping in view the prevailing macroeconomic conditions as well as the information on inflation front.

However, according to recent reports, the three government representatives were asked to meet the finance ministry officials before the meeting of the MPC.

Interestingly, however, on the eve of the fifth MPC meeting held on 7th and 8th of June, 2017, all the members ignored the government's advice to meet the finance ministry officials days before the meeting. This has signalled the RBI's insistence of maintaining its autonomy while, at the same time, it has clearly brought to the fore the simmering conflict between the government and the central bank regarding the government interference in the functioning of central bank.

It is time to examine the main prints of the fifth MPC decision. The inflation rate has fallen from 3.89% in March to 2.99% in April, 2017 suggesting well below the central bank's target range. At the same time, while the RBI had earlier forecast the inflation rates for the first and second halves of 2017-18 at 4.5% and 5%, respectively, it has revised its forecast to 2 to 3.5% and 3.5 to 4.5%, respectively. This indicates a wide range of margins in the inflation forecasts within a period of two months which points towards some doubt on the credibility of the inflation forecasting model of the RBI. Secondly, according to some economists (including the one dissenting member of MPC, Dr. Ravindra Dholakia), this time there was scope for interest rate cut to support growth which did not happen. Some economists believe that RBI could not have cut policy rate this time given the government's attempt to influence its decision. The central bank has always considered its independence as sacrosanct and it is important to assert itself if the demands of the government are unwarranted. Whatever might have been the reason behind the MPC decision, one has to think patiently and impartially and should not doubt the credibility of the decision merely based on transient data or without factoring in the impending risk factors such as impact of implementation of the 7th pay Commission and GST.

Let us now examine the policy rate changes during the recent period. Since the beginning of 2015, the RBI has changed its policy stance from being "hawkish" to "accommodative" in view of falling trend of inflation rate and has been reducing repo rate from 8% to 7.25% to 6.75% to 6.25% on 4th October, 2016 which continued until August, 2017 when it was cut to 6%. Since then, RBI has kept the repo rate on hold, thus maintaining a "neutral" stance citing mainly the inflation risks in near future arising out of certain structural reforms carried out by the Government of India as also external factors like rising tendency of imported crude oil prices. On December 6, 2017, in its fifth bimonthly policy statement also, the MPC of RBI, left the repo rate unchanged at 6% along with other rates, again maintaining its "neutral" stance while citing inflation risks ahead as also improved growth prospects for the economy.

In its 7 February, 2018 meeting, the sixth in the current year, the MPC made a reasoned decision to once again leave the policy rate unchanged at 6%.This time the CPI inflation rate had risen to 5.2% in December, 2017. Further, as forecast by RBI, the inflation number was likely to be in the range of 5.1% to 5.6% during 2018-19 in view of the revised fiscal deficit number of 3.5% as estimated in the Union Budget, 2018-19 which is higher than its earlier estimate of 3.3%. The following MPC meeting held in April 6, 2018 also saw no change in the policy rate. The next two MPC meetings, held in June and August, 2018 decided in favour of a rise in policy repo rate by 0.25% each, thus resulting in repo rate standing at 6.5%.

In its next bimonthly MPC meeting held in October, 2018, the RBI went in favour of leaving the policy rate unchanged at 6.5% while all evidence suggested a definite rate hike at least to the extent of 0.25%. This time around, Indian rupee had been depreciating more than 14% since July, 2018 sending it above ₹ 74 per US $, while crude oil prices had been rising too, crossing $85 per barrel thus making the task of managing Current Account Deficit (CAD) still more difficult. This had happened in the background of interest rate in the US gradually rising giving a signal to the rest of the world that the US economy was gradually getting robust and thus attracting foreign capital hitherto invested in emerging markets including India. Foreign portfolio investment of a sizable amount had taken flight in recent times thus making the CAD problem still more difficult. Most economists as also the market players were expecting a rate hike at this juncture, but RBI did not take any serious note of this problem and simply changed its policy stance from "neutral" to "calibrated tightening" implying no chance of a rate cut in the current cycle. In fact, the MPC meeting also made it clear that it was not willing to target any particular level of exchange rate but would instead prefer its "mandated" inflation target. Subsequent developments, however, ended in softening of oil prices around ₹ 50 /US $ per barrel and the rupee ended around 70 per dollar giving a comfortable CAD position. Thus, RBI's position was vindicated in this regard. However, the larger question of addressing the financial instability that developed in the Indian economy and involved a kind of a confrontation between the RBI and the Government ensued a long debate until the RBI board meeting which was held on 19 November 2018.

The following graph (Fig. 19.3) shows trends of two curves, inflation rates and policy interest rates during the period Aug. 2016-Nov. 2019.

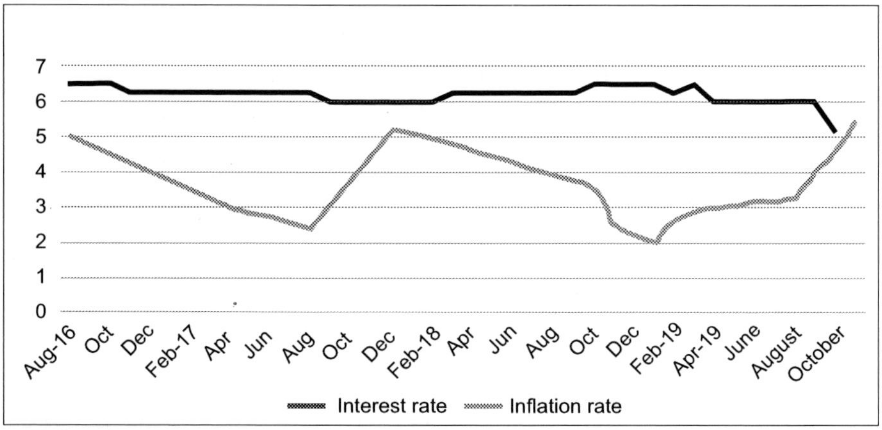

Figure 19.3 *Trends of policy interest rate and inflation rate.*

Figure 19.3 suggests that while the inflation rate had been falling consistently between August, 2016 and August, 2017, policy interest rate was reduced from 6.5% to 6.25% in October, 2016, just once in the whole of 2016. This was followed by another rate cut in August, 2017 by 0.25% (or, 25 basis point). Interestingly, however, just after August, 2017, inflation rate began to rise till December, 2017 thereafter it began to gradually decline over the next twelve months or so. Meanwhile, in February, 2018, the RBI changed its policy stance to "calibrated tightening" having cited the inflation risks ahead and raised the interest rate by 0.25% to 6.25%. This was followed by another rate increase to 6.5% in October, 2018. However, since then, the inflation rate, again, began falling and the RBI, this time, responded with quick two rate cuts (of 0.25% each) in February and April 2019 thus leaving the repo rate at 6% and the corresponding reverse repo rate at 5.75% under its new governor, Sri Shaktikanta Das. It further reduced the repo rate to 5.15% till October, 2019 thus providing enough scope of monetary easing.

The figure further reveals that the "real" rate of interest (policy interest rate minus inflation rate) continued to rise between August 2016 and August 2017 and was the highest in August, 2017 reaching nearly 3.5%. The high real interest rate was one of the arguments advanced by the market for credit clamouring for cuts in policy rate. Of course, although high real interest rate goes well with the "savers", it doesn't favour the "borrowing class", since their borrowing cost becomes much higher in real terms. It may be mentioned here, that most policy makers would advise the real rate of interest to prevail around 2% which would be favourable for both saving and investment in the economy (Chakravarty Committee Report, 1985).

The basic question to examine here is how well the RBI is tracking the inflation ever since its inflation targeting mandate it has received from the government. Figure 19.3, however, does not suggest that the central bank is quite doing it. At times, its inflation forecast is missed even though, by and large, target range of inflation has not been breached. The monetary policy of the central bank, in terms of interest rate fixation, appears to be somewhat sticky in nature, maybe the rate cannot and should not be frequently manipulated.

Table 19.1 *Major monetary policy rates and reserve requirements–Bank Rate, LAF (Repo, Reverse Repo and MSF) rates, CRR & SLR-(Contd.)*

Effective date	*Bank rate*	*Rix range LAF rates*		*Marginal standing facility*	*-Cash reserve ratio*	*Statutory liquidity ratio*
		Repo	*Reverse*			
1	2	3	4	5	6	7
26-07-2011	-	8.00	7.00	9.00	-	-
16-09-2011	-	8.25	7.25	9.25	-	-
25-10-2011	-	8.50	7.50	9.50	-	-
28-01-2012	-	-	-	-	5.50	-
13-02-2012	9.50	-	-	-	-	-
10-03-2012	-	-	-	-	4.75	-
17-04-2012	9.00	8.00	7.00	9.00	-	-
11-08-2012	-	-	-	-	-	23.00
22-09-2012	-	-	-	-	4.50	-
03-11-2012	-	-	-	-	4.25	-
29-01-2013	8.75	7.75	6.75	8.75	-	-
09-02-2013	-	-	-	-	4.00	-
19-03-2013	8.50	7.50	6.50	8.50	-	-
03-05-2013	8.25	7.25	6.25	8.25	-	-
15-07-2013	10.25	-	-	10.25	-	-

20-09-2013	9.50	7.50	6.50	9.50	-	-
07-10-2013	9.00	-	-	9.00	-	-
29-10-2013	8.75	7.75	6.75	8.75	-	-
28-01-2014	9.00	8.00	7.00	9.00	-	-
14-06-2014	-	-	-	-	-	22.50
09-08-2014	-	-	-	-	-	22.00
15-01-2015	8.75	7.75	6.75	8.75	-	-
07-02-2015	-	-	-	-	-	21.50
04-03-2015	8.50	7.50	6.50	8.50	-	-
02-06-2015	8.25	7.25	6.25	8.25	-	-
29-09-2015	7.75	6.75	5.75	7.75	-	-
02-04-2016	-	-	-	-	-	21.25
05-04-2016	7.00	6.50	6.00	7.00	-	-
09-07-2016	-	-	-	-	-	21.00
01-10-2016	-	-	-	-	-	20.75
04-10-2016	6.75	6.25	5.75	6.75	-	-
07-01-2017	-	-	-	-	-	20.50
06-04-2017	6.50	-	6.00	6.50	-	-
24-06-2017	-	-	-	-	-	20.00
02-08-2017	6.25	6.00	5.75	6.25	-	-
14-10-2017	-	-	-	-	-	19.50
06-06-2018	6.50	6.25	6.00	6.50	-	-
01-08-2018	6.75	6.50	6.25	6.75	-	-
05-01-2018	-	-	-	-	-	19.25
07-02-2019	6.50	6.25	6.00	6.50	-	-
04-04-2019	6.25	6.00	5.75	6.25	-	-
13-04-2019	-	-	-	-	-	19.00
06-06-2019	6.00	5.75	5.50	6.00	-	-
06-07-2019	-	-	-	-	-	18.75
07-08-2019	5.65	5.40	5.15	5.65	-	-

Source: RBI.

Note:

1. Indicates no change.
2. Cash reserve ratio is as prescribed under Section 42(1) of the RBI Act, 1934. Statutory Liquidity Ratio is as prescribed under Section 24 of the Banking Regulation Act, 1949.
3. The Liquidity Adjustment Facility (LAF) system was operating on 'suction-based variable rate' during the period from Aprial 27, 2001 to March 28, 2004, and moved to 'fixed rate' mode from March 29, 2004.
4. Till October 28, 2004, nomenclature of repo indicated absorption of liquidity and reverse repo meant injection of liquidity by the Reserve Bank. However, with effect from October

It is worthwhile to mention at this stage that the RBI is now thinking in terms of experimenting with a new tool, that of asset purchase programme (like the western countries of the US and Europe) and releasing money to the economy instead of further interest rate reduction (reported in *Economic Times*, dated 28 December, 2019) in view of the recessionary/slowdown conditions of the economy (the growth rate of the economy has fallen to 4.5% (5.1% revised) in the second quarter from 5% in first quarter and further to 4.7% in the third quarter of 2019-20. It is expected that the average growth rate for the whole financial year of 2019-20 will remain below 5%.

More recently, the RBI has taken several small steps to counter the slowdown and better financial transmission of the monetary policy, that is, flow of credit to the real sector from the banking sector.

While this book was about to be finished, an unprecedented natural calamity in the form of coronavirus (COVID-19) had already gripped the world infecting about 10 million people and killing about 1 million people by the last week of June, 2020 and triggering the world economy, including India's, into further recession. The RBI, in order to fight the COVID induced recession, further tweaked the monetary policy by reducing interest rate (repo rate) to 4% from the existing 4.4% (by 40 basis points) besides other monetary easing measures amounting to ₹ 5.2 lakh crores in the months of March-April, 2020.

Operation twist: The RBI, in the last week of December, resorted to this measure twice, on December 23 and December 30, 2019 and the third time on January 6, 2020 with a view to influence the long-term interest rate in the economy through the yield rates of the government securities (G-Sec). The RBI, in fact, bought and sold the G-Secs. worth ₹ 10000 crore simultaneously in the operation twists. However, unlike other open market operations, operation twists would not affect the RBI's balance sheet. The RBI purchased the long-term

---

29, 2004 nomenclature of repo and reverse repo has been interchanged as per international usage. The current nomenclature is followed in this Table.

5. Since May 3, 2011 the repo rate is the single independently varying policy rate. The reverse repo rate is linked to the repo rate and was pegged at a 100 basis points below the repor rate. The peg was brought down to 50 basis points w.e.f. April 5, 2017 the rate is pegged at a 25 basis points below the repo rate.

6. The Marginal Standing Facility (MSF) was introduced from the fortnight beginning May 7, 2011. Under the MSF, scheduled commercial banks could borrow overnight up to one per cent of their respective NDTL below the prescribed SLR, at a rate determined with a spread of 100 basis points above the repo rate. The borrowing limit was raised to up to two per cent below the prescribed SLR on April 17, 2012. The spread of the MSF above the repo rate was increased to 300 basis points on July 15, 2013. The spread was narrowed to 200 basis points on September 20, 2013 and further to 150 basis points on October 7, 2013 before being restored to 100 basis points on October 29, 2013. The spread was reduced further to 50 basis points on April 5, 2016. The present spread w.e.f. April 6, 2017 is 25 basis points above the repo rate.

government bonds while it sold short-term bonds. This way, the RBI created a shortage of long-term bonds in the market raising their demand and making them costly. This would lower the interest rate (price of bonds and interest rates are inversely related). On the other hand, the RBI sold the short-term bonds thereby reducing the liquidity from the market thus raising short-term interest rate. Lower long-term interest rate would thus help the banks to advance loans to the long-term borrowers and help the economy to fight the low demand situation. In fact, the main problem before the commercial banks is that they are reluctant to lend more in spite of the repo rate being lower in recent years

Private Placement of Government Securities

As mentioned earlier, government securities are generally traded among the select dealers, viz., banks and approved financial institutions. However, this may put pressure on interest rate so that interest rate may go up in case there is shortage of loanable funds in the market. To prevent such undue occurrence, the RBI sometimes decides to put government securities on private placement particularly when market's bid is much higher. The government, then, has a chance of fetching better price for securities while allowing the interest rate to settle at reasonable level.

New Methods of Measurement of Money Supply and Liquidity: Multiple Indicator Approach

New Methods of Measurement of Money Supply and Liquidity has been discussed earlier (see Chapter 6 on Money Supply and Credit Creation). It has now been realized that it is necessary to adopt a multiple indicator approach where interest rates or rates of return in different markets, viz., money, capital and government securities markets along with such data as on currency, credit extended by banks and financial institutions, fiscal position, trade, capital flows, inflation rate, refinancing and transactions in foreign exchange available on high frequency basis are juxtaposed with output data for drawing policy perspectives. In the recent past, conflicting considerations such as need to reduce monetary expansion while at the same time nurturing real sector growth have required the RBI to take studied and well thought out policy decisions.

In more recent times, in the wake of long recessions prevailing in most western countries, and Japan, a new monetary policy, better known as Modern Monetary Theory is gaining currency which would advocate limitless money supply by printing money by the central bank without caring for fiscal deficit or public borrowing or public debt. The modern monetary theory (MMT) has received support from economists like Stanley Fischer, former deputy chairman of the US Fed and several left wing economists of Britain. In fact, the economists observed that when the economy suffers from long period of low inflation and low growth and stagnation with no sign of inflationary pressures ahead, the policy makers would do well to tackle the situation by even monetising the government's fiscal deficit through the central bank. Economists like Nuriel Nubini, Professor of Economics at Stern School of Business, New York University also, in a recent article, has cautioned that if the current situation of low inflation, low growth and longer slowdown continues in the western developed countries, policy makers may find merit in the new idea (which is a new avatar of the helicopter drop of money) in spite of several limitations of the new theory.

SUMMARY

1. Monetary policy refers to the central bank's policies, objectives and instruments aimed at regulating the supply of money as well as cost and availability of credit in the country and economy.
2. The important thing, in this regard, is to understand the 'transmission mechanism' of the monetary policy—how and in what manner, the monetary policy is transmitted to the 'real economy'. There are, however, differences of opinion among economists in this regard.
3. While the classical/monetarist group of economists think that the transmission mechanism is more direct—a change in the supply of money/rate of interest effects the real GDP and price level directly, the Keynesian group of economists are of the opinion that the transmission mechanism is more indirect. It works via two channels—money supplyinterest rate channel, depending on the elasticity of money demand function and the interest rate-investment channel.
4. Keynesians think that the demand for money is more elastic with respect to interest rate, so that a small change in the rate of interest brings about relatively large change in the demand for money. But the second linkage between the rate of interest and the investment demand is weak and in fact, the investment demand is relatively inelastic, so that the change in the monetary policy has uncertain and unclear effect on the real economy.
5. There are time-lags involved in the whole execution of monetary policy. First, there are inside lags—those inside the organisation, from taking the decision with regard to a certain policy to its final form of execution. Then there are intermediate lags—the post-implementation effects among consumers, businesses and other stakeholders which take further time-lags. Finally, there are outside lags taking further time involvement.
6. The main objective of the monetary policy is stated to be the price-stability—price-stability meaning that price-level should be maintained at reasonably low level but it need not remain constant.
7. There are, of course, other objectives of monetary policy, to support the growth of the economy, particularly for underdeveloped countries where concerns for growth of the economy are equally important.

8. However, conflicts between the above two goals, viz., price stability (low inflation) and maintaining 'growth' often do arise when fixing priority on these goals becomes necessary. If the economy experiences relatively high inflation, beyond the monetary authority's expectations, the price stability goal ought to get first priority even though the economy shows signs of slow down recession. However, much depends on the monetary authority's judgement arrived at after proper discussion among the members concerned. A balanced decision, in this regard, is required.
9. Among other objectives, exchange stability or maintaining the external value of the domestic currency is also important. In times when the currency value slides too much due to pressures in the market for foreign exchange, the central bank intervenes and tries to halt the slide by selling the foreign exchange in appropriate quantity and similarly in case of excessive firming up (appreciation) of the domestic currency.
10. In fact, the monetary authority has multiple goals to strike a proper balance among, so that the understanding of the economic situation of the country is essential in its entirety.
11. There are two categories of instruments of monetary policy: conventional and unconventional. Conventional policy tools are those which are used by the central bank under normal situation. These are, bank rate open market operation, variable reserve ratios, etc. which have been conventionally used by the central banks over the world. Bank rate policy, in the present days, refers to the target or reference rate of interest that the central bank wishes it should prevail in the long run. For the short run, the rates are, mainly, repo rate and reverse repo rates. The repo rate is the very short run rate of interest at which the central bank advances loans to commercial banks while the reverse repo rate is the rate at which the central bank accepts deposits from the commercial banks (which have surplus funds to park with)
12. The central bank uses the variable reserve ratios like Cash Reserve Ratios (CRR) and Statutory Liquidity Ratios (SLR) to effect the volume of reserves with the commercial banks. Lowering/raising these ratios imply raising/lowering of the capacity of commercial banks to create credit and advance loans to the commercial sector.
13. Open market operations are resorted to when the liquidity in the financial system is required to be effected. Through purchase and sale of 'securities' (government securities mainly) the central bank either releases or sucks surplus liquidity to or from the system and thereby regulates the liquidity in the economy.
14. 'Rules versus discretion' is a longstanding debate in the context of monetary and other policy domains. Economists are divided on whether policies should be guided by curtain rules (where they exist) or be left to the discretion of the policy makers. There are arguments for and against

both 'rules' and discretion. Sometimes 'rules' do help while in some other situation 'discretion' of the policy markers worked wonderfully. In fact, a judicious use of both in trying situations is required for optimum outcome.

15. Monetary policy in India since independence has been evolving gradually but not progressively until late eighties when Chakravarty Committee Report (1985) was published. Following the implementation of the New Economic Policy in 1991, monetary policy has undergone see changes in terms of liberalisation and globalisation allowing latent forces to come out open and gradually playing dominant roles.
16. In more recent period, India's monetary policy underwent significant institutional reforms in terms of formation of Monetary Policy Committee (MPC) which was entrusted with the entire rate setting exercises along with other tasks of monitoring the Indian economy and making appropriate suggestions. At times, though, conflicting suggestions have been coming from MPC and the RBI, but in most occasions, RBI has come forward with appreciably good policy decisions.

EXERCISE

1. What do you understand by 'transmission mechanism' of the monetary policy? discuss the various channels of monetary policy transmission.
2. What are the main objectives of monetary policy? Discuss the 'trae-off' issue of growth versus inflation in this regard.
3. Point out and explain the various 'lags' in the execution process of the monetary policy.
4. Define 'repo' and 'reverse repo' rates of the central bank's monetary instruments and explain their working in the banking and financial system.
5. How does the central bank regulate the 'liquidity' in the economic system? Explain fully.
6. Summarise the 'rule versus discretion' debate with suitable examples.
7. "Tailor's rule is a good approximation of the application of monetary policy", Discuss.
8. What is inflation-targeting? Examine its role in Indian central bank's inflation-fighting.

REFERENCES

1. John Slowman, Economies, Prentice Hall, London, 1991.
2. R. Dornbusch, S. Fischer and Richard Startz, Macroeconomics 9th Edition, McGrw Hill.
3. C. Rangarajan, Evolving Contours of Monetary Policy" Economic and Political Weekly, Vol. 56, No. 20, May 15, 2021.

4. Y.V. Reddy, "Monetary Policy in India: Objectives, Instruments, Operating Procedures and Dilemmas", in Monetary and Financial Sector Reforms in India, A Central Bankers' Perspective, UBS Publishers, 2000(b).
5. K. Kanagasabapathy, "Monetary Policy Underpinnings: A Perspective," Economic and Political Weekly, January 27, 2001.
6. N. Gregory Mankiw, Principles of Macroeconomics, 5th Edition, South Western Cengage Learning, 2008.
7. www.rbi.org.in.

20

Fiscal Policy

20.1 MEANING AND CONCEPT

Fiscal policy is another important macroeconomic policy tool of the government. Generally, fiscal policy refers to the government expenditures and taxation policies. Almost by all governments over the world, fiscal policy is pursued in different degrees on various types of government or public expenditures as well as taxation functions in order to run the government and its different functionaries. These functions, therefore, include the government's intended policy actions regarding taxation, public expenditures as also public debt management carried out through the annual budgets as authorised by the states' legislatures.

Fiscal policy may be long term as also short term. If the government announces, well in advance, after careful thought and detailed discussions and debates at various stages, as the government's functional protocol demands, it is known as long-term fiscal policy to be achieved over a longer period – 10 or 20 years ahead. Then, all short-term policies that follow, form, by and large, parts of the same broad long-term policy. However, short-term policies may deviate, to a certain extent, due to special circumstances and problems of the economy and are reflected in the annual budget documents.

Fiscal policy space is basically a combination of public administration, political priorities and economic management. For instance, economic management sets the tone of the main economic policies and the associated fiscal policy. These are, then, translated into budgetary policies in such a manner as to practically fulfil these policies bounded and influenced by political priorities. When the policies are implemented, public administrative machinery becomes largely responsible for carrying them out.

Fiscal policies of governments all over the world have to keep up with changing times. In this context, two types of fiscal policies are generally distinguished: (a) expansionary fiscal policy and (b) contractionary fiscal policy. In periods of prosperity and high growth, particularly when tendencies of inflation are evident, a contractionary fiscal policy in terms of reduced public expenditure is advisable. On the other hand, during periods of recession, low growth and unemployment, the expansionary fiscal policy ought to be followed. In relatively normal period of time, a wise use of expenditure and taxation policies needs to be made and possibly combined with appropriate monetary policy.

20.2 FISCAL POLICY AND DIFFERENT SCHOOLS OF THOUGHT

In this section we will examine how the relative importance attached to fiscal policy has been changing with different schools of thought.

1. Classical Economists and Fiscal Policy: Classical economists (Adam Smith, Ricardo, Pigou, Mill and others) were of the opinion that the economic system based on capitalist principles, should be, as far as possible, free from government intervention. The government has, therefore, little role to play in the functioning of the economy. It should be based on 'laissez faire' economic principle. This implies that in matters of taxation, the govt. should impose taxes such that the citizens should feel the minimum tax burden or minimum sacrifice from tax payments. Public expenditure should also be restricted to the essential functions of the government such as maintenance of law and order, defence and providing certain other important public goods and infrastructure. Thus, public expenditure and taxation ought to be carried out in a manner that government budget be, 'balanced'. Also, public debt should be kept at the minimum.

   Achieving full employment or attaining certain rate of growth of the economy by using fiscal policy was never the concern of the classical economists since they believed that the capitalist economy could achieve full employment through automatic forces and unemployment would never exist permanently. Neo-classical economists, who were responsible for expanding the classical ideas and further refining them, also advocated similar views on fiscal policy.
2. Fiscal policy assumed significant role in the Keynesian economic thought. The Great Depression of 1929, as we are aware, resulted in large-scale unemployment of worst kind in the capitalist countries of the world. Lord Keynes, in his 'General Theory' and elsewhere came out with prescriptions to fight Depression which largely relied upon 'fiscal policy' – large scale public expenditure policy to create additional employment and income. In the post-Keynesian era, fiscal policy proved to be an important tool of economic development as well. Hence, in the post-Keynesian literature, fiscal policy played a dominant role and budget deficits, instead of being an unwelcome sign, proved to

be an opportunity for economic development. In fact, budget deficit was thought to be a part and parcel of the fiscal policy and was considered to be a positive contributor to the economic growth.

Both aspects of fiscal policy, viz., public expenditure – either direct purchases of goods and services by the government or transfer payments – and taxation do influence the economic activities by creating additional income and employment. Similarly, they can help create suitable atmosphere for private investment as well. Also, fiscal policy can prove to be an anti-inflationary tool as well. These arguments were meticulously worked out by post-Keynesian economists and applied to various economic situations through budgetary policies.

3. In the post-1970s, again, fiscal policy was rather unseated from its dominant position first, by the emergence of Monetarism and later, by the rise of New-classical economic philosophy. The scope of fiscal policy, according to new thinking, was limited in running the economic system. Monetarists (followers of Milton Friedman) put great reliance on the role of monetary policy since they believed money supply directly influences the real economy. The authors of Supply Side Economics, in particular stressed that low rate of taxation would result in higher tax collections for the government. The main source of inspiration of such thinking was provided by economist Arther Laffer in terms of Laffer curve. Laffer offered the thesis that for an economy like the U.S., tax proceeds fall both when the rate of taxation is very high and also when it is very low. There is, therefore, an optimal rate of taxation at which the tax proceeds are at a maximum level. Laffer curve suggests to moderate the rate of taxation so that tax-payers' incentives to work may increase leading ultimately to higher GDP and higher tax proceeds for the government.

   On public expenditure side, the new classical thinking does not support the idea of excessive government interference in the management of the economy. Thus, reviving and refining the old classical idea of budget management, the new classicals attach greater importance to sound fiscal policy in terms of negligible budget deficit and a relatively low level of public debt.

This, does not, however, minimize the role of public expenditure in capitalist countries (like US, UK and other western countries). In fact, they should be directed to provide essential **public goods**, (law and order, justice, clean environment and creating enough infrastructural facilities for the market as well as general public). Besides, it must be able to meet contingent situations like economic recessions.

20.3 MAIN OBJECTIVES OF FISCAL POLICY

In spite of ideological differences among different schools of thought, the major objectives of fiscal policy in modern times can be listed as follows.

20.3.1 To Bring About Equitable Distribution of Wealth and Income in the Society

Fiscal policy has proved to be an instrument to effect distribution of wealth and income in the society. Through the twin weapons of expenditure and taxation policies, the government can reduce the inequality in wealth and income distribution and thus promote economic and social welfare. Although income distribution as such may not find figure explicitly in the fiscal policy structure of western capitalist economies. Most underdeveloped economies where income distributions are already in very bad shape require fiscal policies geared to this aspect of distributional effects. In India, for instance, most public expenditure programmes are designed to improve the income and wealth distribution. It is a different matter though that due to faulty implementation of those programmes, they have not yielded desired results. In recent years particularly since 1990s, the focus seems to have shifted towards 'growth' of the economy and the concern of distribution appears to have occupied the second position. It is argued that without adequate growth the problem of equitable distribution will not be solved in any meaningful way. In any case, the objective of achieving a fair distribution of wealth and income remains in the agenda of government's fiscal policy framework.

20.3.2 To Ensure Proper Allocation of Resources Among Different Sectors of the Economy

For purposes of 'inclusive growth', fiscal policy aims at the proper allocation of economic resources among different sectors of the economy such as agriculture, industry, commerce and business, social sectors like education and health. Also, through appropriate expenditure and taxation policies the government attempts to bring all sections of society—poor, middle-income earners and other deprived sections of the society onto the path of development. This can be achieved only through higher proportions of public expenditure, as also through equitable tax system. For instance, the shape of a nation's industrial policy, international trade policy or social sector growth policy and how and to what extent economic and human resources are to be allocated are largely determined by the public expenditure policy of the government. In a country like India where there are State Governments, and union territories besides the Central (Union) Government and where regional inequalities persist in terms of socio-economic and cultural differences, an equitable allocation of resources is all the more important. In fact, Indian Government appoints, for every five years, a constitutional body like

'Finance Commission' to decide the allocation of economic resources among the States and union territories, besides other functions. Also, there is the Planning Commission (now revamped as NITI Ayog) which approves development plans for different State governments for transfer of resources.

20.3.3 Achieving Fiscal Consolidation in Government Finances

Even though opinions have differed among public finance experts, achieving a fair measure of fiscal consolidation is one of the major objectives of fiscal policy. Fiscal consolidation is a policy aimed at reducing different components of deficits in government budget as well as public debt accumulation. It may be mentioned that, of the various budgetary deficits, fiscal deficit and revenue deficit are more important. Fiscal deficit is the deficit or excess of total expenditures over total receipts net of borrowings and other liabilities of the government. We have tried, in the next section, to illustrate the concept of fiscal deficit with Indian budget data. The implication of higher level of fiscal deficit is that government's liabilities to pay off the debt increases. Persistence of such a situation may put the government finances in unmanageable condition. In the end, other effects like rise in interest rate, rise in inflation rate, etc., may harm the fiscal health of the economy. Therefore, reducing fiscal deficit to manageable level is the prime aim of the sound fiscal policy.

In the same vein, reducing revenue deficit to as low as possible – in fact, achieving a revenue surplus (i.e., excess of revenue receipts over revenue expenditures) is often advised as a wise measure of fiscal consolidation. The implication of revenue deficit is that the government is incurring more of current expenditure on day-to-day running of government functions than it raises revenues (i.e., tax and non-tax revenues) for such purposes. This happens partly due to lower level of revenues raised by the government and partly due to rise in unproductive and sometimes politically committed expenditures. Secondly, persistence of such phenomenon deteriorates and complicates matters. Therefore, the objective of fiscal consolidation is to turn this part of deficit into 'surplus'. The test of such exercises is that the tax – GDP ratio must be rising consistently. This implies, with rise in GDP, taxes must form larger and larger proportions ever.

Another aspect of fiscal consolidation is that public debt must not rise above a certain proportion of GDP. Public debts, i.e., debts of the government are mainly of two kinds: internal debt and external debt. In whatever manner debts may be measured, they are constant drag on resources of the government and sizeable amounts are regularly paid for repayment of principal and interest. Of course, there is no worry if debts are well managed, i.e., used in a manner that they help strengthen the economy in terms of raising, at a relatively faster rate, the GDP. Thus, along with rise in tax – GDP ratio, fall in debt – GDP ratio is also the desired objective of fiscal consolidation.

In spite of the aim of fiscal consolidation, it is often not possible for all governments and for all situations to pursue this goal. There are political compulsions, external environmental changes (affecting exchange rate etc.) and business cycles which force nations to deter from fiscal consolidation objective. Much depends upon the efficiency of the government, particularly those who are in charge of handling the delicate issues involving formulation and execution of different aspects of fiscal policy. In a country like India, attempts towards fiscal consolidation are seriously being made since 2003 when the Government enacted the Fiscal Responsibility and Budget Management Act with specific medium-term goals of reduction of different deficits being made 'mandatory'.

20.3.4 Raising Adequate Tax Revenues for the Government

Government functions cannot be carried out without revenues. In fact, revenue raising for the government in the form of taxes is one of the most important duties. Historical records show that the governments in all times and under all types of government – kingship, democracy or totalitarian dictatorship – necessarily impose taxes on the subjects or citizens. These taxes vary in terms of the sources they are imposed upon.

In democratic nations of the world today, taxes are mainly of two varieties: direct taxes and indirect taxes. Direct taxes are levied on the citizens' income and wealth and are known as 'personal income tax' or 'personal wealth tax'. Similarly, private business corporations are also taxed on their incomes and are known as 'corporate income tax'. Wealth taxes are also similarly imposed on individuals and corporate bodies. If governments have local bodies such as municipal corporations, local governments or any such body/bodies, different types of local taxes are also imposed on citizens which enjoy different types of services provided by these bodies. State governments may also levy certain taxes/ duties directly on the citizens of the State concerned. These are also included in the 'direct tax' category like the income taxes which are liable to be paid to the Central Government.

Besides the income taxes, there is a large variety of indirect taxes which are imposed on goods and services purchased by the citizens. These are indirect taxes because they are primarily collected by the producers and sellers of goods and services. However, they are subsequently passed on to consumers or customers when they buy or avail of these goods and services.

One of the prime objectives of fiscal policy is to raise adequate revenues for the government from various tax and non-tax sources. The government needs to frame appropriate laws relating to income, wealth and commodity taxes as also the appropriate punishments for infringement of these laws. Secondly, these laws need revision from time to time in keeping with changing times. In a democratic country like India, care needs to be taken to see that the ultimate burden of any tax (incidence of tax) must not fall on the poor and low income citizens who have lesser ability to pay taxes. In fact, the entire tax structure has to be designed very carefully based upon expert opinions and research studies.

In line with the Central Government, the State Governments also have the similar objective of raising revenues from various sources. In fact, commodity taxes (or, emerging 'goods and service' taxes) fall within the jurisdiction of State governments in India. Besides, there are a large variety of fees, duties etc. collected by State governments. State governments also share a certain portion of central taxes with them. Certain professional taxes are subject of State governments.

Thus, tax collection and raising adequate resources from this head is one of the key objectives of fiscal policy. The government has the ability and expertise to explore various innovative methods for improving the collection of tax revenue.

20.3.5 Achieving Overall Socio-Economic Development of the Economy

By suitably using fiscal policy tools, an overall socio-economic development of the nation-state can be achieved and in fact, this is the ultimate goal of all fiscal policy measures. More growth of the economy in terms of raising the rate of growth of GDP or GNP is not enough. This goal is achievable by appropriate public expenditure programmes. There are conflicting views on this objective, though. The economists belonging to Keynesian school firmly believe that fiscal policy is the appropriate vehicle for economic growth as also for overall development of the economy. Those owing their allegiance to 'welfare economics' are also of the opinion that without sizeable public expenditure of the kind geared specifically to the social welfare programmes, overall economic development will remain far from being achieved. This is particularly true for a country like India as also other underdeveloped countries where adequate social and infrastructural developmental expenditures are wanting. The new classical economists, however, advocate a relatively secondary role of fiscal policy except during abnormal situations like economic slowdown (recession, depression) and wars.

In spite of ideological differences, fiscal policy is being increasingly directed towards 'development' of the economy. An underdeveloped economy like India represents a case where fiscal policy tool has been instrumental (particularly during early phase of post-independence period) in bringing about growth and development. It would be appropriate to state that Indian fiscal policy played a more proactive role during the earlier phase in laying down the 'base' of the economic structure. Even during post-1990 period (the post-economic reforms period) when the earlier economic policy was gradually replaced by a more liberal and private sector dominated policy, fiscal policy has not lost shine rather the fiscal responsibility has increased in several directions.

20.4 FISCAL POLICY: THE TRANSMISSION MECHANISM

The transmission mechanism – the way the policy (or, change in it) works through and transmits to the economy – is direct in case of fiscal policy. This is because it affects the real/commodity sector by affecting directly the aggregate demand and hence the real *GDP* and employment. For instance, if there is increase in public expenditure or cut in tax-rate, it raises aggregate demand by shifting the *AD* curve to the right. The real output (at least, in the short-run, increases. Conversely, if there is decrease in public expenditure or rise in tax-rates, the *AD* curve shifts to the left resulting in lower *GDP* and employment. Figure 8.1 illustrates these situations.

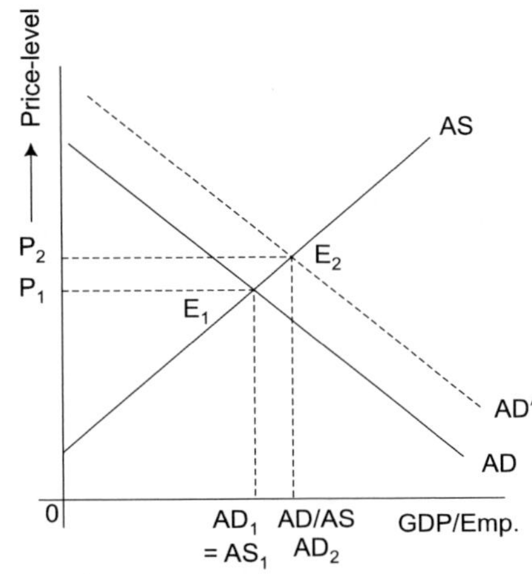

Figure 20.1

The initial situation is represented by *AD* and *AS* curves. Their intersection results in equilibrium at point E_1 with *AD* of aggregate demand and *AS* of aggregate supply. A rise in public expenditure/or cut in tax-rate raises *AD* to *AD′*. In fact, extra expenditure/cut in taxes leaves with the consumers a higher level of disposable income which they are induced to spend. In the short-run, the aggregate supply curve moves along its normal path. A new equilibrium results at E_2 with higher *AD* (= *AS*) and higher real *GDP* which is associated with higher employment. However, in the short-run, some increase in price-level will also be noticed which, in fact, acts as inducement to producers to increase output.

A fall in expenditure level or rise in tax-rates will have the opposite effect. It is easy to work out this effect diagrammatically and readers are advised to do so. Hence, we can write in symbols as:

Public Expenditure	$\uparrow \rightarrow$ AD $\uparrow \rightarrow$ AS $\uparrow \rightarrow$ GDPr $\uparrow \rightarrow$ E $\uparrow \rightarrow$ P $\uparrow$
P.E.	$\downarrow \rightarrow$ AD $\downarrow \rightarrow$ AS $\downarrow \rightarrow$ GDPr $\downarrow \rightarrow$ E $\downarrow \rightarrow$ P $\downarrow$
Tax Rate/Level	$\uparrow \rightarrow$ AD $\downarrow \rightarrow$ AS $\downarrow \rightarrow$ GDPr $\downarrow \rightarrow$ E $\downarrow \rightarrow$ P $\uparrow$
Tax Rate/Level	$\downarrow \rightarrow$ AD $\uparrow \rightarrow$ AS $\uparrow \rightarrow$ GDPr $\uparrow \rightarrow$ E $\uparrow \rightarrow$ P $\downarrow$

E = Employment; P = Price level.

The transmission mechanism, even though more direct in case of fiscal policy does not mean that there are no time-lags at all. In fact, the entire process of policy changes goes through the government machinery which, in most countries takes certain minimum period of time to clear. Most public expenditures, for instance, are not properly phased out throughout the year of the fiscal year. Expenditure budget sanctioned by the parliament goes through the different departments of the government which involve a certain time-lags. It also involves the financial process of government transactions via treasury and banks. Similarly, taxation policy changes also involve certain time-lags. In certain kinds of indirect taxes (excise duties*, commodity taxes, customs-duties) it takes time to work through and pass on to ultimate consumers who bear the burden of such taxes. In case of direct taxes (income taxes, for example, the time-lag is less since most direct taxes are mandatory and collected at source on regular basis.

20.5 FISCAL POLICY TYPES: EXPANSIONARY vs. CONTRACTIONARY FISCAL POLICY

The governments, all over the world, have to keep in mind the changing situations in and around the world economy. While within the economy, there may arise situations marked by economic recession – falling *GDP* falling *AD*, rising unemployment, falling prices; there may also be impacts of external economic disturbances particularly in an environment where economies are integrated through trade and investment channels. Recessions or depressions are not normal situations, but fiscal policy generally is of expansionary type so as to revive the economy. Public expenditures are stepped up to enhance aggregate demand. However, even when the economy needs expansion in terms of basic infrastructure and lifting it from low level of development and also when the economy is in boom period, fiscal policy is of expansionary nature. At the same time, if the period of boom gives signs of 'bubbles' in terms of excessive growth either through monetary and financial expansion or excessive expenditures (either public and private) so that inflationary situation develops, the fiscal policy (as also monetary policy) is, generally, of contractionary type. The public expenditures are cut so that excess aggregate demand generated in the economy is reduced. Even though certain committed expenditures are difficult to cut, most unproductive expenditures can be cut with strong government commitment.

It is worth mentioning here that most developed countries of the west would choose to prefer monetary policy rather than fiscal policy to contain aggregate demand resulting in inflationary situation and inflationary expectations. But in most other less developed economies, a combination of monetary and fiscal policy actions are pursued.

Evidence of expansionary fiscal policy following the great recession of 2008-09 and 2009-10 in most developed as well as affected emerging economies was found. For instance, US resorted to heavy tax cut measures to help boost the individual disposable incomes along with raising government expenditures

* Excise duties in India (e.g., on petrol & diesel) become effective immediately on announcement. In production sector, its final impact on consumers takes time.

on healthcare and education. Similarly, European countries committed heavy public debt due to higher public expenditure and incurring fiscal deficit. In India also, during 2009-10, expansionary fiscal policy was very much evident in government's three consecutive budgets (2008-09, 2009-10 and 2010-11) with fiscal deficits reaching 6.0 per cent, 6.7 per cent and 5.5 per cent as compared to 3.3 per cent and 2.6 per cent in two previous periods (2006-07 and 2007-08).

20.6 FISCAL POLICY AND THE BUDGET

Budget[1] is a vehicle through which the government carries out its fiscal programmes. If there is a long-term fiscal policy that the government aims, this is suitably phased out into annual targets and incorporated in the annual budgets. Of course, each annual budget might have some of its own features marked by special commitment of the government. But by and large, annual budgets reflect the avowed policies of the government.

In India, regular budgets are, sometimes, followed by supplementary budgets which become necessary for certain additional expenditures to be sanctioned by the Parliament. These expenditures, generally arise out of special circumstances occurring during the period.

20.6.1 Various Concepts of Deficits in Budget

In order to explain various concepts of deficits associated with government budget, it is preferable to illustrate these with reference to a particular year's budget. Table 20.1 gives informations on Indian budget for the year 2011-12 at a glance.

Table 20.1 *Budget at a glance: 2011-12: India*

(₹ in crore)

	2009-10 (Actuals)	2010-11 (B.E.)	2010-11 (R.E.)	2011-12 (B.E.)
1. **Revenue Receipts**	572811	682212	783833	789892
2. Tax Revenue (Net to centre)	456536	534094	563685	6644567
3. Non-tax Revenue	116275	148118	220148	125435
4. **Capital Receipts** (5 + 6 + 7)	451676	426537	432743	467837
5. Recoveries of Loans	8613	5129	9001	15020
6. Other Receipts	24581	40000	22744	40000
7. Borrowings & Other Liabilities	418482	381408	400998	412817
8. **Total Receipts** (1 + 4)	1024487	1108749	1216576	1257729

[1] Budget is an annual statement of government's proposed Receipts and Expenditures for the next fiscal year which is tabled in the parliament for getting its approval. After the parliament passes the budget by majority votes, the govt. is authorized to raise revenues and incur expenditures.

9. **Non-plan Expenditures**	721096	735657	821552	816182
10. On Revenue A/c of which	6579525	643599	726749	733558
11. Interest Payments	213073	248664	240757	767986
12. On capital A/c	63171	92048	94803	82624
13. **Plan Expenditure**	303391	373092	395024	441547
14. On Revenue A/c	253884	315125	326928	363604
15. On Capital A/c	49507	57967	68096	77943
16. **Total expenditure** (9 + 13)	1024487	1108749	1216576	1257729
17. **Revenue Expenditure** (10 + 14)	911809	958724	1053677	1097162
18. **Capital Expenditure** (12 + 15)	112678	150025	102899	160567
19. **Revenue Deficit**	338998	276512	269844	307270
(17 – 1)	(5.2)	(4.0)	(3.4)	(3.4)
20. **Fiscal Deficit**	418482	381408	400998	412817
(16 – (1 + 5 + 6))	(6.4)	(5.5)	(5.1)	(4.6)
21. **Primary Deficit**	2.5389	132744	160241	144831
(20 – 11)	(3.1)	(1.9)	(2.0)	(1.6)

Note: Actuals for 2008-09 are provisional; figures in brackets are percentage of GDP.

Source: Union Budget, 2011-12, http/www.indiabudget.nic.in

B.E. = Budget Estimates, R.E. = Revised Estimates.

	2019-2020 Actuals	*2020-2021 Budgets estimates*	*2020-2021 Revised estimates*	*2021-2022 Budget estimates*
1. Revenue receipts	1684059	2020926	1555153	1788424
2. Tax revenue (net to centre)	1356902	1635909	1344501	1545396
3. Non tax revenue	327157	385017	210652	243028
4. Capital receipts	1002271	1021304	1895152	1694812
5. Recovery of loans	18316	14967	14497	13000
6. Other receipts	50304	210000	32000	175000
7. Borrowings and other liabilities[1]	933651	796337	1848655	1506812
8. Total receipts (1+4)	2686330	3042230	3450305	3483236
9. Total expenditure (10+13)	2686330	3042230	3450305	3483236
10. On revenue account of which	2350604	2630145	3011142	2929000
11. Interest payments	612070	708203	622900	809701
12. Grants in aid for creation of capital assets	185641	206500	230376	219112
13. On capital account	335726	412085	439163	554336
14. Revenue deficit (10-1)	666545 (3.3)	609219 (2.7)	1455989 (7.5)	1140576 (5.1)
15. Effective revenue deficit (14-12)	480904 (2.4)	402719 (1.9)	1225613 (6.3)	921464 (4.1)
16. Fiscal deficit [9-(1+5+6)]	933651 (4.6)	796337 (3.5)	1848655 (9.5)	1506812 (6.8)
17. Primary deficit (16-11)	321581 (1.6)	88134 (0.4)	1155755 (5.9)	697111 (3.1)

[1]Includes drawdown of cash balance

Notes:

1. GDP for BE 2021-2022 has been projected at Rs. 22287379 crore assuming 14.4% growth over the estimated GDP of Rs. 19481975 crore for 2020-2021 (RE).
2. Individual terms in this document may not sum up to the totals due to rounding off.
3. Figures in parenthesis are as a percentage of GDP.

Note: A comparison with the 2011-12 budget (given at the previous page) shows at least two changes: The division between 'plan' and 'non-plan' expenditures has been abolished in the new budget document. Secondly, a new item titled "effective revenue deficit" has been added in the new budget, which in effect, reduces the amount of deficit by the 'grants in aid' for creation of capital assets.

1. **Budget Deficit** Budget deficit is the excess of total expenditures over total receipts of the government shown as projected for the coming fiscal year. Referring to Table 20.1, this will be the difference between items 16 and 8. However, looking at the figures in the table we find the difference is zero. In fact, since the budget proposals of 1999-2000, the Indian budgets have given up the practice of showing total budgetary deficit. Therefore, in the present context, budget deficit is irrelevant.
2. **Fiscal Deficit** Fiscal deficit is the most important concept of deficit that has assumed significance in recent years. It is the difference between the total expenditures and the total receipts, except the receipts shown as 'borrowings and other liabilities'. Referring to Table 20.1 fiscal deficit is equal to items 16 – 1 – 5 – 6 = 16 – (1 + 5 + 6). Alternatively, this difference is equal to 16 – 8 – 7 as well. Clearly, while calculating fiscal deficit, government's borrowings and other liabilities' shown in item 7 is left out.

   It needs to be mentioned here, that since 1999-2000, following an agreement between RBI and the Govt. of India, the practice of borrowing by the Central Government through ad hoc Treasury Bills to make up the budget deficit has been discontinued and replaced by a new method, 'Ways and Means Advances' by the RBI with a maximum limit. These advances, granted temporarily, are repaid by the government. Therefore, this part is now treated outside the budget. Thus, whatever shortfall (expenditures – receipts) is shown in the budget is assumed to be compensated by the borrowing programmes of the government. Thus, fiscal deficit is also equivalent to the size of 'borrowings and other liabilities' shown in item 7 in our example (Table 8.1). This can easily be verified by respective figures as well. Fiscal deficit, therefore, gives the signal to the government about the total borrowing requirements from all sources.
3. **Revenue Deficit** It refers to the excess of revenue expenditures over revenue receipts. There are two major heads of government budget: revenue head or revenue account and capital head or capital account. All

major receipts and expenditures are suitably classified, for accounting purposes, and put either under revenue account or capital account. Obviously, if we look at the revenue side only, there are receipts as well as expenditures. The government incurs expenditures for running day-to-day activities of its own departments. It receives/collects tax and non-tax revenues primarily for carrying out these activities. When there is excess of expenditures over revenue on this account, it is called revenue deficit. In the table, this is equal to items 17 – 1.

4. **Primary Deficit** From the fiscal deficit, when we exclude the interest payments (on borrowed fund by the government), the deficit we are left with is defined as primary deficit. Item no. 11 in our table is 'interest payments' to be paid during 2011-12 (budgeted). Obviously, the amount of deficit (as well as percentage) is reduced. When compared to the size of fiscal deficit, primary deficit indicates the extent of interest burden for the government exchequer.
5. **Monetized Deficit** Monetized deficit is that part of the deficit which is met by obtaining credit from the central bank. As a result, central bank's net credit to the government increases. For instance, if the Government of India fails to successfully complete its borrowing programmes, proposed in the budget; it borrows from the Reserve Bank of India against government treasury bills. This results in increase in RBI's net holding of government-treasury bills. The RBI, in turn, would print additional money to meet the requirements of the government. Thus, net money supply increases. Needless to say that this increased money supply, when released out of monetized deficit creates inflationary pressure.

20.6.2 Automatic Stabilizer/Built-in Stabilizer

Let us take an example of an electrical device called voltage stabilizer. How does it function? When the voltage in the main device is more than required, the excess is absorbed by the stabilizer. Similarly, when the voltage is inadequate, it compensates from its own storage. In the field of fiscal policy, if this concept is applied, it would lead to a system of controlling the fluctuations of economic activities that occur during periods of business cycles. Thus, the changes that automatically occur in the fiscal structure (taxation and public expenditure system) and do not form part of the government's conscious or discretionary actions, are called built-in or automatic stabilizers.

Automatic stabilizers are an important feature of the fiscal policy which has twin sides of taxation and expenditure of the government budget. We know that during economic recessions (or, slowdowns) there is a general fall in aggregate demand resulting in fall in national income, employment and output. The opposite happens when there is a boom (or, upswing) in the economy. Automatic stabilizers act as moderators in such circumstances by lessening these fluctuations and helping raise the aggregate demand. We now examine in somewhat greater detail, how automatic stabilizers act.

Under conditions of recessions government's tax collections fall because national income falls. Due to increase in unemployment, individual incomes of employees as also those of the corporates fall. There are mainly three sources of tax resources of the government. Personal income tax, corporate income tax and sales tax / goods and services tax. Given that personal income tax is generally progressive in nature, higher rate of taxes accompanying rise in tax base, when income falls, the tax base also falls so that the tax rate also slips back to lower tax brackets. This means, during a recession, not only total tax collections go down but they go down by a greater percentage than the fall in incomes. This itself has an inherent moderating effect on aggregate demand. For instance, if incomes are falling by 20 per cent, tax collection falls by an even greater percentage, say, 30% or so.

Secondly, corporate income taxes are levied on corporate profits and not on revenues which also have the same characteristics as personal income tax. In other words, during a recession, corporate profits fall by a greater extent than the revenues so that the corporates have to pay relatively less taxes to the government.

In case of sales taxes, or any kind of goods or services taxes, these have a direct relationship with sales volumes of transactions; when sales volumes fall sales taxes fall. Thus, fall in tax amounts effectively means rise in disposable incomes which have a favourable impact on aggregate demand.

Transfer payments: Transfer payments are various kinds of welfare as well as gratuitous payments made by the governments to various sections of society. These include unemployment benefits and subsidies of various kinds. During periods of recession, these transfer payments increase in amounts. Since, unemployment rises during recessions, amounts of unemployment benefits also increase. To the very low income earners, with further fall in their incomes, other welfare benefits are also transferred. These payments and the resultant increase in government expenditures, in turn, raise the level of aggregate demand and thus reduce fluctuations in aggregate income to some extent.

On the other hand, during booms, transfer payments fall in amount since unemployment falls while the level of income rises. Because, aggregate output falls during recessions and rises during booms, it can be said that government expenditures as a proportion of national income rises during recessions and falls during booms. These changes in budgetary position are automatic and do not form part of any conscious and deliberate policy actions of the government. Hence, these are called automatic stabilizers or built-in stabilizers.

Automatic stabilizers also have their multiplier effects. To recall, multiplier refers to the total increase or decrease in income that occurs due to multiplied effect of initial increase or decrease in income. When incomes increase or decrease during boom or recession at the initial stage, they have their multiplied effect on total increase or decrease in income. But the presence of automatic stabilizers lessens the impact of multipliers. This can be verified with the help of Keynesian multiplier formula with tax and transfer functions as reproduced below:

Multiplier $(u) = 1/\{1 - b(1 - t)\}$; where, b = marginal propensity to consume, t = marginal rate of tax. Here, it represents the automatic stabilizer. It should be noted that t in the above formula is obtained from the net tax function which is the combination of tax and transfer functions. So, transfer payment coefficient is also implied in this formulation.

Now, let us initially assume that there are no tax or transfer functions so that $t = 0$. Assuming that the value of $b = 0.8$, then the value of the multiplier becomes 5. This simply means that in the absence of an automatic stabilizer the multiplier is 5. Now, introducing the value of $t = 0.3$, the value of the multiplier becomes 2.27. This shows that the multiplier effect during recessions is smaller as compared to normal times. Similarly, during booms also, the multiplied effects of income increases are smaller compared to normal periods (absence of automatic stabilizers).

The multiplier effect may still be lower if we introduce another automatic stabilizer in terms of import function and import coefficient. The modified formula for multiplier in this case is:

$$(u) = 1/\{1 - b(1 - t) + m\};$$

where, m = marginal propensity to import. Now, taking an assumed value of m = 0.2, and recalculating, the value of the multiplier is still lower at 1.56. (in fact, during recessions imports also decline thus further reducing the fluctuations in aggregate demand).

However, it has to be conceded that, whatever may be the impact of automatic stabilizers the overall effect is not large enough to significantly lessen the fluctuations in aggregate demand during business cycles. Hence, governments in most cases, have to introduce special counter cyclical measures in terms of stimulus packages during recessions while imposing curbs on aggregate demand during booms. The global recession of 2008 bears enough testimony of such stimulus packages by the monetary and fiscal authorities of the US and other advanced economies.

The role of automatic stabilizers has received attention in the treatment of fiscal policy by the classical, monetarists and new classical economists. These economists tend to believe that any fluctuation in aggregate demand and consequent budget imbalances should better be left to be corrected by the automatic stabilizers rather than adopting any type of discretionary policies (fiscal or monetary).

20.7 FISCAL POLICY IN INDIA

In India, there is union government at the centre and several state governments and union territories besides the local governments (municipal corporations and other local bodies within each state). Each government carries out its own expenditure and taxation programmes on annual basis which become applicable to citizens of the country. We shall, however, examine here the fiscal policy actions of Union Government only.

Depending upon the political priorities of the government the expenditure programmes range widely among principal expenditure heads. Public expenditures are broadly classified as Revenue and Capital Expenditures, Plan and Non-Plan Expenditures and sometimes Development and Non-Development Expenditures. There can be long-term fiscal policy as also short-term/medium term fiscal policy depending upon the current conditions of the economy and polity and the long-term goal of achieving broad targets of economic and social development. In India also the government sets long-term fiscal policy and tries to adjust short-term policy to it in subsequent budgets.

It ought to be kept in mind at the beginning that government expenditures are diverse in character and vary from country to country. In developed countries, developmental public expenditures may be small in size relative to their GDPs than those of the underdeveloped ones. However, social expenditures such as maintaining law and order, defence, research and development, providing and maintaining basic infrastructural facilities (roads, communications, schools, hospitals, parks, playgrounds, etc.) form a significant proportion of the public expenditures equally in developed as well as underdeveloped countries.

As far as taxation policy is concerned, taxes form the main source of revenue for the government and virtually all governments are concerned about raising as much revenue as possible so that the size of the deficits in the government budget is kept at the minimum. Higher level of deficit leads to higher public debt which itself is a tricky area of public finance management. In spite of all this, it is not often possible for governments, particularly of India's size and diversity, to pursue the goal of fiscal discipline. In fact, the central point in this regard is the 'efficiency' and 'rationality' of carrying out different types of public expenditures and raising tax as well as non-tax revenues for the government which, in turn, depend on the growth of GDP.

Fiscal policy pursued in India in the early post-independence period was largely driven by Keynesian philosophy. The country started the planning era with five-year plans which stressed on heavy public investment programmes for industrialization as well as agricultural development. Lack of basic infrastructure in almost all important sectors of the economy required large public expenditure programmes. Since public sector industries played the key role in industrial development, public expenditure policy occupied the centre-stage in fiscal policy structure. At the same time, the contribution of public revenue – particularly the tax and non-tax revenue shares were low enough to support large public expenditure programmes. Hence, the natural outcome in the budgetary operations was 'deficit'. So, budgetary deficit happened to be an integral part of almost all post-independent government budgets. Not only this, the size of budget deficits continued to swell. The financing of these budget deficits was carried out often by taking loans from Reserve Bank of India which led to the creation of money by printing notes.

For instance, in the first five-year plan, the size of deficit financing was ₹ 330 crore, while that of the second five year plan, it was ₹ 950 crore. During the third plan, the actual deficit financing was of the order of ₹ 1330 crore. During the next two plan, the deficits were, respectively, of ₹ 2960 crore and ₹ 2820 crore. Since then, deficit financing had been continuously increasing reaching the size of ₹ 11,350 crore in 1990-91. Although the actual size of fiscal deficit used to be still higher, it was not generally shown separately in the budgets, since all borrowings used to be shown as part of capital receipts and therefore, part of the total receipts of the Central Government. This limited concept of deficit financing was modified and corrected following the Chakravarty Committee Report on the working of Monetary System. Thereafter, a broader concept of deficit, the fiscal deficit was adopted and published in subsequent budgets of central government.

As far as revenues are concerned, in the early years, taxes formed a small proportion of GDP. For instance, in 1950-51, total taxes formed just 6 per cent of GDP which increased to 10 per cent in 1960-61 and subsequently to 14 per cent in 1970-71.[1]

Similarly, public debt, in early years of independence, was mainly incurred for development purposes. As far as internal debt is concerned, it formed 98.5 per cent while the share of external debt was only 1.5 per cent of the total debt in 1950-51. In subsequent years, however, the share of external debt increased gradually and reached about 34 per cent of total debt in 1970-71.

20.8 FISCAL POLICY IN THE POST-REFORM ERA (POST-1990-91)

At the fag end of 1980s and beginning of 1990s India's public finance was passing through a crisis, arising out of the enormous external debt. At one stage, India's foreign exchange reserves fell to such a level that the country had to part with sizeable amount of gold reserves to pay off her external debt.

Economic reforms in the country began with 'paradigm shift' in the basic economic policy. The structural adjustment and stabilization policies – the twin

[1] Currency and finance, RBI, various years

set of policies formed the base of the new economic policy. These policies gradually unfolded into liberalization, privatization and globalization.

The implication for structural adjustment policy for the fiscal policy structure was to implement substantial reforms for sound fiscal policy. These reforms included almost all areas of fiscal operations, viz., taxation, expenditure, deficit and debt management.

In the following pages we have tried to capture these developments in broad terms.

Table 20.2 *Trends in deficits of the central government (1990-91 – 2011-12)*

	(as percentage of GDP)			
Year	*Revenue deficit*	*Primary deficit*	*Fiscal deficit*	*Revenue deficit as percentage of fiscal deficit (RD/FD) × 100*
1990-91	3.3	2.8	6.6	49.4
1991-92	2.5	0.7	4.7	52.7
1992-93	2.5	0.6	4.8	51.7
1993-94	3.8	2.2	6.4	59.2
1994-95	3.1	0.4	4.7	64.6
1995-96	2.5	0.0	4.2	59.2
1996-97	2.4	–0.2	4.1	58.2
1997-98	3.1	0.5	4.8	63.5
1998-99	3.8	0.7	5.1	74.8
1999-00	3.5	0.7	5.4	64.6
2000-01	4.1	0.9	5.7	71.7
2001-02	4.4	1.5	6.2	71.1
2002-03	4.4	0.5	5.3	82.2
2003-04	3.6	0.0	4.5	79.7
2004-05	2.4	0.0	3.9	62.3
2005-06	2.5	0.4	4.0	63.0
2006-07	1.9	–0.2	3.3	56.3
2007-08	1.1	–0.9	2.6	41.4
2008-09	4.5	2.6	6.0	75.2
2009-10	5.2	3.2	6.5	81.0
2010-11	3.2	1.8	4.8	66.3
2011-12	3.4	1.6	4.6	74.4

Source: Economic Survey, 2004-05 and 2009-10 & 2011-12.

Table 20.2 shows that fiscal deficit in the post-1990's was rather at moderate levels (with a couple of years registering more than 6.0 per cent). The average level of fiscal deficit for the first ten years was 4.08 per cent of GDP. During the next eight years, the average fiscal deficit was higher at 4.44 per cent. The next two years, i.e., 2008-09 and 2009-10 reported relatively higher levels of fiscal deficit with 6.0 per cent and 6.5 per cent, respectively. In next two years

(2010-11 amd 2011-12) the fiscal deficit shows lower levels of 4.8 per cent and 4.6 (BE), respectlively. However, as frequently reported the actrual deficit levels are likely to be higher than budgeted due to actual expenditures exceeding the budgeted ones. However, these two years can be treated as exceptional years affected by 'global recession' and forcing the government to announce fiscal stimulus packages in the form of increased public expenditure as well as tax concessions. The fiscal deficit levels were thus pushed up arising out of this abnormal situation in spite of the mandate given by the FRBM Act, 2003. What is more worrying is the revenue deficit trend. Revenue deficit averaged around 3.05 per cent during the first decade but rose to 3.5 per cent during the next eight years. Again, we omit, from our analysis the next two years for the same reasons mentioned above. The trend in revenue deficit naturally impacts the percentage of revenue deficit in total fiscal deficit shown in the last column. Thus, this percentage is observed to be rising almost continuously. In some years it has exceeded 70 per cent and also 80 per cent in some other years (2002-03) and 2009-10. Revenue deficit was lowest in the year 2007-08 with 1.1 per cent of GDP but has never become zero as mandated under FRBM Act, 2003. On the other hand, in 2008-09 and 2009-10, it has increased substantially to 4.5 and 5.2 per cent respectively, but fell subsequently to 3.2 and 3.4 per cent in next two years.

As far as primary deficit (fiscal deficit excluding interest payments) is concerned, during the early years, it has been recorded on the higher side although in some years, it has reached the level of zero and even negative (suggesting surplus on this account) levels; for instance, in 1995-96 and 1996-97. In the later years, it remained at the modest level, reached zero during two years and negative levels in another two years, but recording increases in two-three years.

The above observation clearly suggests that interest payments, which is an important component of revenue expenditure, influences, to a large extent, the total fiscal deficit and revenue deficit in particular (see Table 20.4).

20.8.1 Trends in Public Expenditures

Expenditure budget of the Central Government consists of: (a) Revenue Budget and (b) Capital Budget. Each of these two budgets (or, accounts) has two sides viz., receipts and expenditures. Thus, together there are four sub-heads:

(i) Revenue Receipts

(ii) Revenue Expenditure

(iii) Capital Receipts

(iv) Capital Expenditure

In this section, we shall focus on the expenditure side only, i.e., revenue expenditure and capital expenditure (ii & iv).

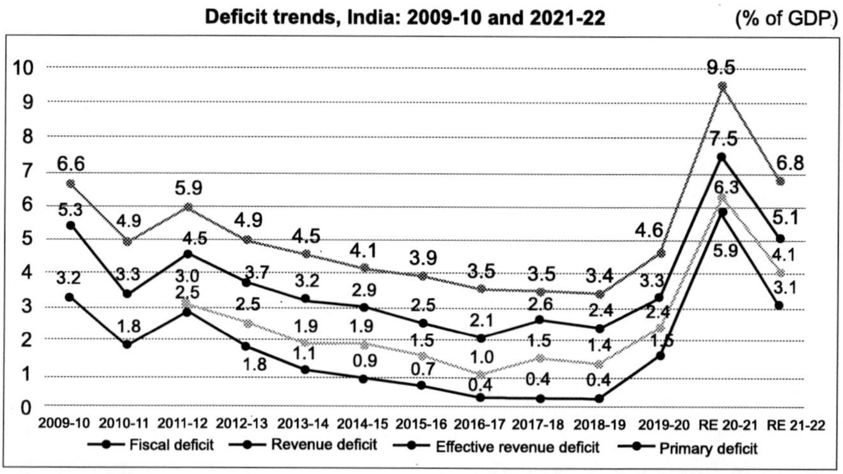

Figure 20.2 *Trends of different categories of deficits of the central government: 2009-10–2021-22 (BE).*

Source: www.indiabudget.gov.in

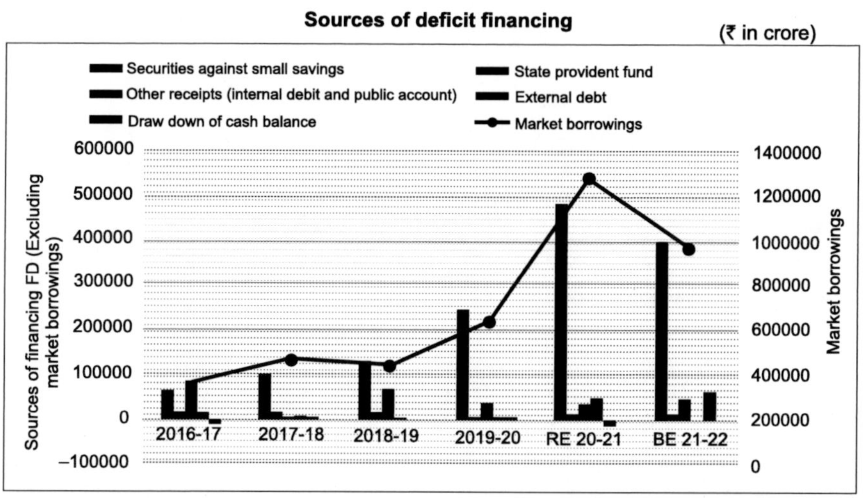

Figure 20.3 *Sources of deficit financing: 2016-17–2021-22 (BE).*

Table 20.3 *Deficit statistics: 2019-20–2021-22*

(in ₹ crore)

	2019-2020 Actuals	*2020-2021 Budget estimates*	*2020-2021 Revised estimates*	*2021-2022 Budget estimates*
1. Fiscal deficit	933651	796337	1848655	1506812
	(4.6)	(3.5)	(9.5)	(6.8)
2. Revenue deficit	666545	609219	1455989	1140576
	(3.3)	(2.7)	(7.5)	(5.1)
3. Effective revenue deficit	480904	402719	1225613	921464
	(2.4)	(1.8)	(6.3)	(4.1)
4. Primary deficit	321581	88134	1155755	697111
	(1.6)	(0.4)	(5.9)	(3.1)

Sources of financing fiscal deficit

1. Debt receipts (net)				
2. Market borrowings (G-sec + T bills)	624089	535870	1273788	967708
3. Securities against small savings	240000	24000	480574	391927
4. State provident funds	11635	18000	18000	20000
5. Other receipts (internal debts and public account	44273	50848	39129	54280
6. External debt	8682	4622	54522	1514
7. Draw down of cash balance	4971	(–)53003	(–)17358	71383
8. Grand total	933651	796337	1848655	1506812

Source: www.indiabudget.com: Budget 2021-22.

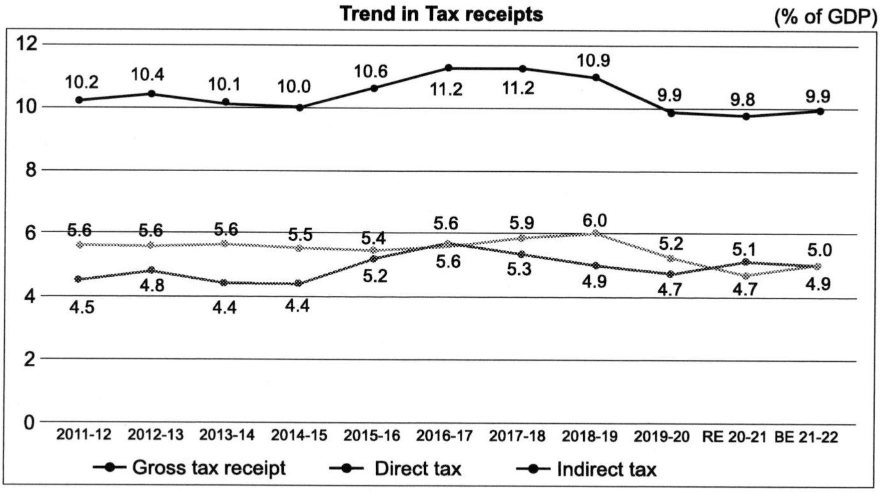

Note: GDP is as per the latest estimates published by CSO.

Figure 20.4 *Trends of tax receipts: 2011-12–2021-22.*

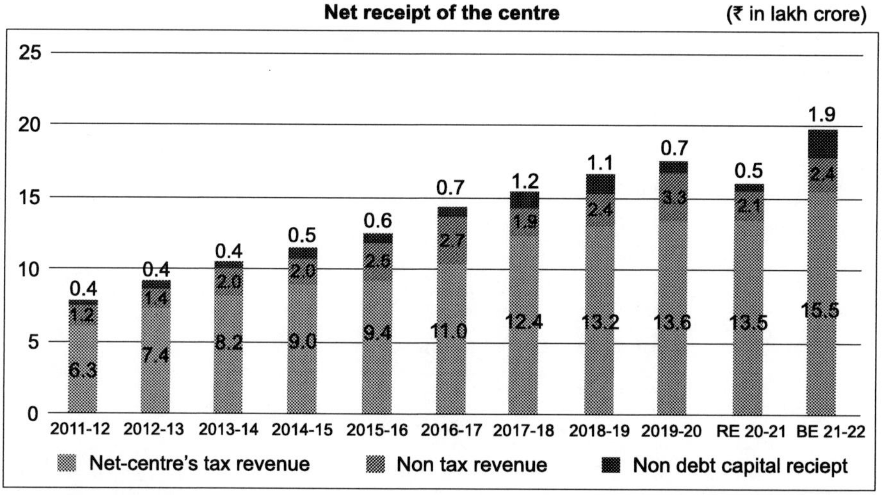

Figure 20.5 *Net receipt of the central government: 2011-12–2021-22 (BE).*

Source: www.indiabudget.gov.in (Budget 2021-22)

Revenue Expenditure As we have already mentioned, revenue expenditures are made for the normal running of the government departments and various services, interest payments on debts, subsidies of various kinds, etc. Broadly, the expenditures which do not result in creation of assets for the government are treated as revenue expenditures. All grants given to State Government and Union Territory and other parties are also treated as revenue expenditures even though some of these grants may be used for creation of asset.[1] Revenue expenditure remained around 13 per cent of GDP since 1990-91 till 2001-02, increased to 13.8 per cent in 2002-03, but again came down to 13.3 and 13.1 per cent in next two years[2]. Since 2004-05 till 2008-09, the revenue expenditure hovered around 12 per cent. During 2009-10 and 2010-11, revenue expenditure increased to 14.2 and 14.8 per cent respectively (Table 20.4).

Table 20.4 *Composition of revenue expenditure*

Years	*Interest Payments*	*Major Subsidies*	*Grants to States & UTs*	*Defence*	*Others*
1997-98	36.4	9.9	12.7	14.5	26.5
1998-99	36.0	9.6	11.9	13.8	28.7
1999-00	36.2	9.1	12.0	14.1	28.5
200 0-01	35.7	9.3	13.6	13.4	28.0
2001-02 (Prov.)	35.1	10.1	13.4	12.7	28.7
2002-03 (BE)	34.5	11.4	14.0	12.8	27.2
2003-04	NA	NA	NA	NA	
2004-05	33.0	11.6	14.0	11.4	29.9
2005-06	30.2	10.1	16.8	11.0	31.9
2006-07	29.2	10.4	16.5	10.0	33.9
2007-08	28.8	11.4	18.2	9.1	32.5
2008-09	24.2	15.6	15.7	9.2	35.4
2009-10	23.4	14.9	15.5	9.9	36.4
2010-11	22.6	12.6	15.1	8.9	40.8

Source: Economic Survey, 2002-03, '03-04 & 2011-12.

An analysis of Table 20.4 shows that as far as interest payments are concerned, these form the highest percentage of total revenue expenditure. Only since 2005-06, interest payments have been overtaken by expenditures on 'Other' categories which, of course, consist of several items including 'salaries' to central government staff. Grants to States and union territories form the next highest category. Between the next two expenditure items in order, viz.,

[1] Union Government Budget Document, 2010-11 Chapter 3.

2 Economic Survey, 2002-03, p. 24

subsidies and defence, it is evident that while the share of subsidies has been rising over time – from 9 per cent in the closing years of 1990s to 11-12 per cent (with highest being nearly 16% in 2008-09) in the late 2000s, that of defence expenditure, it has been on the decline generally.

Among major subsidies are: (a) subsidies for domestic LPG, kerosene supplied through public distribution system (PDS) and freight subsidy for remote areas, fertilizer subsidy for BPL households and subsidies for other petroleum products (petrol and diesel).

20.8.2 Trends in Taxation and Tax-GDP Ratios

Table 20.6 (p. 581) gives data on different sources of tax revenues in India during the period 1990-91 – 2010-11. Direct taxes have been shown under two categories, viz., personal income tax and corporate income tax, while indirect taxes have been broadly classified as customs duties, excise duties and service taxes. All the taxes have been expressed as (a) the proportion of total tax revenues and (b) proportion of gross domestic product in percentage terms. The data indicate that direct taxes, as proportion of total gross tax revenues over the period have been consistently rising – from only 19 per cent in 1990-91 to 36 per cent in 2002-03 to more than 56 per cent in 2010-11. This is evident in both categories of income taxes. Indirect taxes, on the other hand, show declining trend as percentage of total tax revenue. Thus, from more than 78 per cent in 1990-91 indirect taxes declined to about 63 per cent in 2000-01 and further to 44 per cent in 2008-09. One of the important contributions has been made by service taxes in recent years which, in 1990-91 did not exist. Presently, its contribution in total taxes is about 10 per cent. As for customs duty, it shows falling tendency over the period, particularly during the 1990s, although in the later period, it seems to have stabilized at around 17-18 per cent. Excise duty, on the other hand, has remained, by and large, around 37-38 per cent during 1990s, but has come down significantly during the later period. These results seem to be the outcome of various tax reforms measures – from simplification of tax structure to rationalization of tax rates – during the post-reforms period.

As proportion of GDP (or, tax GDP ratio), the percentage of total tax revenue to GDP, however, has not shown any marked change. While it was slightly above 10 per cent in 1990-91, it has been fluctuating between 8 and 9 per cent during most of 1990s period. Since 2004-05, tax-GDP ratio shows signs of improvement – from 9.4 per cent to 12 per cent in 2007-08. However, against the budget estimate of 10.8 per cent in 2010-11, the actual realization (though provisional) was only 10.4 per cent.

Direct taxes, as percentage of GDP have been rising by and large, almost consistently over the whole period of observation – from just 1.9 per cent in 1990-91 to 3.2 per cent in 2000-01 to 6 per cent in the closing years of 2007-08

Table 20.5 *Central government expenditures: 2019-20–2021-22*

(in ₹ crore)

	2019-2020 Actuals	2020-2021 Budget estimates	2020-2021 Revised estimates	2021-2022 Budget estimates
A. Centre's expenditure				
I. Establishment expenditure	570244	609585	598672	609014
II. Central sector schemes/ projects	757091	831825	1263690	1051703
III. Other central sector expenditure of which	727025	887574	826536	1011887
interest payment	612070	708203	692900	809701
B. Transfers				
IV. Centrally sponsored schemes	309553	339895	387900	381305
V. Finance commission grants	123710	149925	182352	220843
VI. Other grants/loans/transfers	198707	223427	191155	208484
Grand total	**2686330**	**3042230**	**3450305**	**3483236**

Capital expenditure of the government

	2019-2020 Actuals	2020-2021 Budget estimates	2020-2021 Revised estimates	2021-2022 Budget estimates
Gross budgetary support	335726	412085	439163	554236
Ministry of railways (IEBR)	80166	90792	132442	107758
IEBR (excluding ministry of railways)	561388	581871	513046	475073
Total	977280	1084748	1084651	1137067

Source: www.indiabudget.gov.in

and 2008-09. The indirect tax share in GDP, however, does not show any pattern. It can be said to have been fluctuating around 5 per cent and 6 per cent over the period except those in 2008-09 and 2009-10 followed by 4.5 per cent in 2010-11. The last few years' outcome might be due to some relaxation given in the budgets keeping in view the Great Recession of 2008-09.

India's Tax-GDP ratio in recent years: The tax to GDP ratio in India during the last four financial years (2017-18–2020-21) has been declining. From 11.2% in 2017-18, It has declined to 11% in 2018-19. But in 2019-20, it has further declined to 9.9% before improving to 10.2% of GDP in 2020-21. The fall in tax GDP ratio was due to the fall in the central government's gross tax revenue collection (3.4% fall) in the financial year 2019-20 against its revised budget target (*Business Standard*, June 24, 2020). It has been envisaged that in the financial year 2021-22 the tax GDP ratio would be 10.8% of GDP.

Table 20.6 *Sources of tax revenue in India: 1990-91 – 2010-11*

Tax revenue as percentage of gross tax revenue								
	1990-91	'96-97	'97-98	'98-99	'99-00	'00-01	'01-02	'02-03
Direct (a)	19.1	30.2	34.7	32.4	33.7	36.2	36.9	38.8
PIT	9.3	14.2	12.3	14.1	14.9	16.8	17.1	18.0
CIT	9.3	14.4	14.4	17.1	17.9	18.9	19.5	20.6
Indirect (b)	78.4	69.1	64.5	66.7	65.5	62.9	62.2	60.5
Customs	35.9	33.3	28.9	28.3	28.2	225.2	21.6	19.2
Excise	42.6	35.0	34.5	37.0	36.0	36.3	38.8	38.8
Tax revenue as percentage of GDP (at current prices)								
Direct (a)	1.9	2.8	3.2	2.7	3.0	3.2	3.0	3.7
PIT	0.9	1.3	1.1	1.2	1.3	1.5	1.4	1.7
Indirect (b)	7.9	6.5	5.9	5.5	5.8	5.6	5.1	5.8
Customs	3.6	3.1	2.6	2.3	2.5	2.3	1.8	1.8
Excise	4.3	3.3	3.2	3.1	3.2	3.3	3.2	3.7
Total#	1.0	9.4	9.1	8.3	8.9	9.0	8.1	9.6

Note: PIT = Personal Income Tax; CIT = Corporate Income Tax.

Includes taxes referred in (a) & (b) and taxes of Union Territories and 'other' taxes.

	2006-07	*'07-08*	*'08-09*	*'09-10*	*'10-11(B.E.)*	*'10-11-(P)*
1. Direct (a)	46.4	49.9	52.8	58.9	56.6	55.2
PIT	15.9	17.3	17.5	19.6	16.1	17.5
CIT	30.5	32.5	35.3	39.2	40.4	37.7
2. Indirect (b)	51.0	47.0	44.5	39.2	42.2	43.5
Customs	18.2	17.6	16.5	13.6	15.4	17.1
Excise	24.8	20.8	17.9	16.5	17.7	17.1
Service Tax	7.9	8.6	10.1	9.4	9.1	9.0
3. Tax Revenue as percentage of GDP						
Direct (a)	5.1	5.9	5.7	5.7	601	5.7
PIT	1.7	2.1	1.9	1.9	1.7	1.8
CIT	3.4	3.9	3.8	3.8	4.3	3.9
Indirect (b)	5.6	5.6	4.8	3.8	4.5	4.5
Customs	2.0	2.1	1.8	1.3	1.7	1.8
Excise	2.7	2.5	1.9	1.6	1.9	1.8
Service Tax	0.9	1.0	1.1	0.9	1.0	0.9
Total	11.0	11.9	10.8	9.7	10.8	10.4

Source: Economic Survey, 2002-03, & 2011-12, Govt. of India.

Segregating further, the *Business Standard* has observed that the direct tax GDP ratio fell to its lowest in 14 years at 5.1% while the indirect tax GDP ratio was at a 5 year low in FY 2019-20.

20.8.3 Public Debt, Debt – GDP Ratio and Debt Sustainability in India

Public debt is one of the prime concerns of public finance. Fiscal policy needs to focus on this aspect because, in recent years, there is a growing tendency of public debt not only in India but also in most western capitalist countries to surpass limits.

Public debts are of two kinds: internal debt and external debt. Internal debt is the debt incurred by the Government from internal sources, i.e., citizens of the country (individuals, companies or institutions). The external debt is the debt from various external sources such as foreign governments, various international lending agencies and foreign private companies/institutions.

The budgetary practice in India distinguishes three kinds of public debt liabilities:

1. Internal debt liability
2. External debt liability
3. Other liabilities

These liabilities are shown as outstanding liabilities of the Central Government.

It may be mentioned here that the Consolidated Fund of India (the Account of the Govt. of India) secures both categories of public debt – internal and external subject to a limit but not the 'Other liabilities' as provided under Article 292 of Indian Constitution. Another provision of Indian Constitution (Article 293) relates to borrowings by the State Government Budget to limits placed by the State Legislatures upon security of the Consolidated Fund of the respective States. However, a State's power to borrow is limited to internal debt only. Besides, a State has to obtain prior permission of the Union Government so long as it owes any outstanding debt to the Govt. of India.

India's internal debt includes market borrowings through securities and bonds, treasury bills issued to RBI, other special securities to RBI, state governments, commercial banks and other financial institutions. Broadly, these have been classified as (a) market borrowings (b) other borrowings (others) and (c) other internal liabilities and presented as Outstanding Internal Liabilities of the Central Government.

External debt of the government of India consists of a variety of sources but have been broadly classified as:

1. Multilateral External Debt
2. Bilateral External Debt

Table 20.7 gives figures of total stock of Central Government Liabilities during the period 2004-05 – 2010-11.

A look at Table 20.7 provides evidence on the trends of Central Government's total liabilities (outstanding) during the last eight years. The total liability is composed of the internal and external debt burdens of the government. While the total internal liabilities have decreased from about 60 per cent in 2004-05 to 52.4 per cent in 2009-10, the market borrowing component of the internal debt has increased from 23.4 per cent to 27.0 per cent between 2004-05 and 2009-10. However, it ought to be remembered that the fiscal year 2009-10 can be considered to be exceptional year since the impact of global economic recession (2008-09) necessitated stepping up fiscal stimulus resulting in higher than stipulated fiscal deficit. This, in turn, was reflected in higher percentage of market borrowing. During 2010-11, the revised estimate of total internal liabilities have decreased to 49.2 per cent while the budget estimate of these liabilities were about 27 per cent. The market borrowing component, however, remained almost at the same level of 27 per cent during 2010-11 and 2011-12 as per revised and budget estimates respectively.

External debt, on the other hand, has remained almost stagnant or decreased marginally during this period (around 2.2 to 2.3%) of GDP, except during 2005-06 and 2006-07 when the debt increased to 2.5 and 2.4 per cent respectively.

Public Debt and Debt-GDP Ratio

Public debt in India as reflected in total outstanding liabilities of the central government (Table 20.7), i.e., both internal as well as external liabilities combined, shows a falling tendency – from 61.6 per cent in 2004-05 to 51.2 per cent in 2010-11. During 2004-05 – 2008-09, the debt-GDP ratio remained around 61.0 per cent during first two years of observation, although thereafter it came down to 56-57 per cent followed by further decrease to 51 per cent in 2010-11.

Looking at adjusted figures, however, the debt-GDP ratios are higher in most years. For instance, in 2004-05, the adjusted debt-GDP ratio was 65.6 per cent, falling gradually to 63.7, 61.6, 59.3, 58.8 and 56 per cent, during subsequent period ending 2008-09 and falling further to 53 per cent in 2010-11.

The difference between the unadjusted and adjusted figures lies in the fact that whereas the internal liabilities make no difference, the external debt part was converted at historical exchange rate (pre-determined or fixed exchange rate) in case of unadjusted figures while the adjusted figures have been arrived at on the basis of prevailing rate of exchange of the year end (end-March, each year).

It is obvious from the table that most of India's public debt is of internal debt/obligation category and the share of external debt is not much, even if adjusted figures are taken into account.

Thus, as percentages of GDP, internal liabilities contributed to 49.8 per cent in 1990-91, but subsequently went up to 52.8 per cent in 2000-01, 56.7 per cent in 2001-02, 60.7 per cent in 2002-03, 60.9 per cent in 2003-04 (Economic Survey, 2003-04). From 2004-05 onwards, there is a declining tendency observed in internal liabilities. Thus, from 59.7 per cent in 2004-05, the ratio decreased to

Table 20.7 *Outstanding liabilities of the central government*

	2004-05	2005-06	2006-07	2007-08	2008-09	2009-10	2010-11 (RE) (₹ crore)	2011-12 (BE) (End march)
1. Internal liabilities	1933544	2165902	2435880	2725394	3036132	338376	3774758	4181842
	(59.7)	(58.4)	(56.7)	(54.6)	(53.9)	(52.4)	(49.2)	(46.9)
(a) Internal Debt	1275971	1389758	1544975	1808359	2028549	2349148	2703844	3110618
	(39.4)	(37.5)	(36.0)	(36.3)	(36.0)	(36.4)	(35.2)	(34.9)
(i) Market borrowings	758995	862370	972801	1092468	1326094	1746623	2882036	2425036
	(23.4)	(23.3)	(22.7)	(21.9)	(23.6)	(27.0)	(27.1)	(27.2)
(ii) Other	516976	527388	572174	715891	702455	602525	621808	685582
	(16.0)	(14.2)	(13.3)	(14.4)	(12.5)	(9.3)	(8.1)	(7.7)
(b) Other Int. Liab.	657573	776144	890905	917035	1007583	1034613	1070914	1071224
	(20.3)	(20.9)	(20.8)	(18.4)	(17.9)	(16.0)	(14.0)	(12.0)
2. External Debt	60878	94243	102716	112031	123046	134083	156347	170847
(outstanding)	(1.9)	(2.5)	(2.4)	(2.2)	(2.2)	(2.1)	(2.0)	(1.9)
3. Total outstanding	19994422	2260145	2538596	2837425	3158818	3517544	3931105	4352689
Liabilities (1 + 2)	(61.6)	(61.0)	(59.1)	(56.9)	(56.1)	(54.5)	(51.2)	(48.8)
4. Amt. due from Pakistan & share of Prepartition Debt	300	300	300	300	300	300	300	300
5. Net liabilities (3-4)	1994122	2259845	2538296	2837125	3158878	3517544	3930805	4352389
Memorandum items	191182	194078	201204	210083	264076	249322	278885	304146
(a) Ext. Debt	(5.9)	(5.2)	(4.7)	(4.2)	(4.7)	(3.9)	(3.6)	(3.4)
(b) Total outstanding liabilities (adjusted)	(65.6)	(63.7)	(61.4)	(58.9)	(58.6)	(56.3)	(52.8)	(50.3)
(Figures in brackets indicate percentages of GDP)								
(c) Internal Liab. Non-RBI	(54.7)	63.1	51.6	49.6	47.7	47.3	44.8	42.9
(d) Outstanding Liab. Non-RBI	60.6	58.4	56.3	53.8	52.4	51.2	48.4	46.4

Source: Economic Survey, 2009-10, Chapter 3 & 2011-12, Chapter 3.

56.7 per cent in 2006-07, 53.9 per cent in 2008-09 and 49.2 per cent in 2010-11 as per revised estimate. The budget estimate for 2011-12 was put at 47 per cent.

The external debt portion (as percentage of GDP) (adjusted) formed 11.7 per cent in 1990-91 and has shown consistent decrease over time. It reached the level of 7.9 per cent in 2002-03, 6.7 per cent in 2003-04 (R.E), 5.9 per cent in 2004-05, and 4.7 per cent in 2006-07. For 2008-09, the estimated (as per budget) debt was 4.5 per cent.

One point needs clarification at this point including fiscal transfer. The government's total internal liabilities are composed of two parts, viz., internal debt and other internal liabilities. Within the first category, market borrowings form the main component while the 'others', though not fully detailed, is no less significant. The second category, i.e., 'other liabilities' includes a variety of government's obligations to pay to various individuals and institutions/bodies.

In absolute figures (or, nominal terms), however, the internal (as also external) liabilities have been rising consistently but since GDP too is growing by and large, it neutralizes, to some extent, the nominal growth in debt.

Some experts are of the opinion that apart from 'within budget' items, there are a significant number of 'off-budget' items which add to the total debt obligation of Central and State governments taken together. Although both the central and state governments have built up a sizeable proportion of contingent liabilities (about 10 per cent), some of the 'off-budget' items are debt of State Electricity Boards, oil subsidies and special purpose vehicles for investment in infrastructure created by the government.

According to a Finance Ministry Report titled 'India's External Debt – A Status Report', … India's external debt rose to 16.5%, from $ 224.5 bn in FY 09 to $ 261.5 bn in FY 10, which puts India among the top 10 debtor nations in the world. However, the share of external debt in total public debt was 10.7% end March 2010 according to official external debt figures. Bulk of India's external public debt is from multilateral and bilateral creditors with foreign institutional investment in govt. securities accounting for less than 1% of total public debt.

The composition of central government public debt shows that the bulk of sovereign debt is from domestic sources (about 89%) and external debt accounts for about 11% most of which is from multilateral/bilateral sources. Out of this, 13.7% is in the non-marketable debt like securities issued to National Small Savings Fund, 14-day State Govt. treasury bills etc. These cannot be traded in the secondary markets, the way govt. bonds can. Such bonds comprising long-term and short-term bonds are marketable or are traded by eligible market participants including foreign institutional investors. About 50% of the domestic debt is cornered through their investments in dated securities while insurance companies account for 22%.

Since India does not access international capital market as a sovereign entity, the refinancing risk due to foreign commercial investors is, at best, minimal for the country. The low-refinancing risk and the ability to meet debt commitments from forex reserves (which now stands at $ 285 bn.) is no cause of concern. India's foreign exchange reserves provide a cover of 106.7% to the external debt stock as at end March 2010, while the share of short-term debt in total external debt was 20.1% at end-March 2010. Thus, both are not alarming by popular bench marks.

India Debt to GDP ratio: India's total debt (as a ratio of GDP) in recent years, (2010-2020) has been rising consistently particularly from 2015 to the latest year for which the data is available from 68.77% 74% in 2020 (www.tradingeconomics.com). Further the debt GDP ratio has risen due to the government's increased borrowings to deal with Covid-19 pandemic in 2021 and 2022, as shown in the following table:

Years	2010	2012	2013	2014	2015	2016	2017	2018	2019	2020
Debt-GDP%	67.36	66.65	67.06	66.58	68.53	68.77	69.8	70.78	73.72	70.0

However, India's external debt to GDP ratio during the 2013-2021 period, as shown in the following table, has improved from 22.4% in 2013 to 21.1% in 2021. In 2017 and 2019, the ratio showed even still some improvement at 19.8% and 19.9% respectively.

Years	2013	2014	2015	2016	2017	2018	2019	2020	2021
External Debt/GDP US$ (end March).	22.4	23.9	23.8	23.4	19.8	20.1	19.9	20.6	21.2

Source: RBI.

Long-Term Debt Components

1. Multilateral
2. Bilateral
3. IMF Loans
4. Export Credit
5. Commercial Borrowings
6. NRI Deposits (above one year maturity)
7. Rupee Debt (Rupee Denominated Debt owed to Russia and Payable through Exports)

All the above sources compose the total long-term debt.

Besides the above, there are short-term debt consisting of (a) NRI deposits (upto one year maturity), (b) foreign currency (B&O) deposits (upto one year maturity) and (c) others (trade related) of which, short term debt over six months.

Table 20.8 *India's external debt at a glance*

	End March		
	2002R	*2003R*	*2004R*
	(US $ million)		
Long term debt	96,098	100,344	107,060
Short term debt	2745	5009	4770
Total ext. debt	98,843	105,353	111830
	(₹ crore)		
Long term debt	468932	4,77,093	471154
Short term debt	13,396	23,793	20,725
Total ex. Debt	4,82,328	500886	4,91,879
	Ratio as per cent		
1. Ext. debt to GDP	21.2	20.3	17.8
2. Short term debt to total ext. debt	2.8	4.8	4.3
3. Short term debt to foreign currency assets	5.4	7.0	4.4
4. Debt service to current receipts	13.4	15.8	18.3
5. Concessional debt to total debt	35.9	36.6	36.0

Note: R = Revised.

Source: E.S. 2004-05/website: http:indiabudget.nic.in

	Ratio as per cent		
	1991	1995	2000
1. External debt to GDP	28.7	30.8	22.1
2. Short term total ext. debt	10.2	4.3	4.0
3. Short term debt to foreign currency assets	38.2	20.5	11.2
4. Debt service ratio	35.3	25.9	17.1

Table 20.9 *Compositional share and key indicators of India's external debt*

	(End March) Share in total debt (%)			
Components	*1991*	*1995*	*2000*	*2004 (Sept)*
A. Long-term debt	89.8	95.7	96.0	94.3
(i) Multilateral	25.0	28.8	32.0	26.6
(ii) Bilateral	16.9	20.5	18.5	14.6
(iii) IMF	3.1	4.4	0.0	0.0
(iv) Export credit & comm. borrowings	17.3	19.8	27.2	24.2
(v) NRI deposits	12.2	12.5	13.8	26.9
(vi) Rupee debt	15.3	9.7	4.5	2.0
B. Short-term debt	10.2	4.3	4.0	5.7
C. Total debt (A + B)	100.0	100.0	100.0	100.0
Memo items				
1. Govt. debt	59.6	60.1	47.7	38.9
2. Non-govt. debt	40.4	39.9	52.3	61.1
3. Total	100.0	100.0	100.0	100.0

Source: E.S. 2004-05/website: http:indiabudget.nic.in

According to the Global Development Finance, 2004, World Bank, India ranks eight among the top fifteen debtor countries of the world. India's debt indicators compare well with those of other countries as revealed by Table 20.10.

Table 20.10 *International comparison of external debt-2002*

Country	Total ext. debt	Debt sustainability indicators			
		Debt to GNP	Debt service	Short term debt to total exp debt	Concessional debt to total debt
	US $ billion	Ratio as per cent			
1. Brazil	227.9	52.5	68.9	10.3	1.4
2. China	168.3	13.4	8.2	28.5	17.8
3. Russian Federation	147.5	43.3	11.3	11.1	0.4
4. Mexico	141.3	22.6	23.2	7.0	0.9
5. Argentina	132.3	138.4	18.3	11.2	0.9
6. Indonesia	132.2	80.3	25.0	17.6	24.0
7. Turkey	131.6	72.7	46.8	11.5	3.5
8. India	104.4	20.7	14.9	4.4	38.4
9. Poland	69.5	37.2	22.5	12.8	9.5
10. Philippines	59.3	71.4	20.2	9.4	21.1
11. Thailand	59.2	47.6	23.1	20.1	16.6
12. Malaysia	48.6	54.9	7.3	17.2	6.6
13. Chile	41.9	68.1	32.8	9.0	0.7
14. Hungary	35.0	54.4	33.9	16.2	0.3
15. Colombia	33.9	43.3	40.2	11.2	2.7

Source: Global Development Finance 2004, the World Bank, quoted in E.S. 2004-05.

Table 20.11 *International comparison 2008*

Ratio of S.T. debt to total debt		Ext. debt of GNI (%)	Short term debt to ext. debt	FE res. to ext. debt	Concessional debt to total ext. debt
	Argentina	49.7	29.8	36.1	1.3
	Brazil	**18.7**	16.5	75.9	1.0
10.2	Chile	40.3	22.7	28.7	0.4
5.4	China	**11.6**	54.5	413.9	10.1
2.8	Columbia	22.5	11.9	46.6	2.1
3.9	Croatia	97.7	10.5	28.1	2.1
13.2	India	**18.9**	19.8	125.2	21.7
14.1	Indonesia	33.9	24.8	40.4	26.2
16.3	Kazakhstan	107.7	12.2	18.4	1.0
20.4	Malaysia	29.4	28.4	189.9	6.1
19.3	Mexico	**17.3**	5.1	49.0	0.6
	Philippines	41.9	10.8	51.2	20.0

Contd..

Contd..

18.3	Poland	47.7	30.9	33.6	0.4
	Romania	51.5	35.7	46.8	1.6
	Russiant Fed.	29.4	21.4	129.1	0.4
	South Africa	**15.8**	38.2	75.9	-
	Thailand	26.5	34.3	138.7	9.6
	Turkey	38.8	16.6	30.4	2.1
	Ukraine	52.9	31.1	44.1	2.2
20.	Venezuela	**18.7**	27.1	78.2	0.5
All Developing Countries:			24.5		

Source: Global Development Finance, 2009, World Bank; quoted in ES, 2009-10.

Note: F.E. = Foreign Exchange.

Note: PR = Partially Revised.

Table 20.12 *India's key external debt indicators (%)*

Yrs	*Ext. debt (US $ bn)*	*Ratio of total ext. debt to GDP*	*Debt service ratio*	*Ratio of FE reserves to total ex. Debt*	*Ratio of concessional debt to total ext. debt*	*Ratio of short term debt to FE reserves*
1990-91	83.8	28.7	35.3	7.0	45.9	46.5
1995-96	93.7	27.0	26.2	23.1	44.7	23.2
2001-02	98.8	21.1	13.7	54.7	35.9	5.1
03-04 R	112.7	18.0	16.1**	100.3	35.8	3.9
04-05 R	134.0	18.1	5.9^	105.6	30.7	12.5
05-06 R	139.1	16.7	10.1#	109.0	28.4	12.9
06-07 R	172.4	17.5	4.7	115.6	23.0	14.1
07-08 R	224.4	18.1	4.8	138.0	19.7	14.8
08-09 PR	224.6	20.5	4.4	112.1	18.7	17.2
End June '09 PR	229.8			115.4	18.9	15.9

Debt service ratio is the proportion of gross debt service payments to external current receipts (net of official transfers)

** Work out to 8.2% with the exclusion of prepayment of US $ 3.797 mm. and redemption of Resurgent India Bonds (RIBs) of US $ 5.547 mm.

^ Work out to 5.7% with the exclusion of prepayment of US $ 381 million.

Work out to 6.3% with the exclusion of IMDs repayment of US $ 7.1 billion and prepayment of US $ 23.5 million.

A compositional analysis of India's external debt reveals that long-term debt constitutes the bulk of total external debt while short-term debt forms a small proportion. In 1991, the long term debt formed about 90 per cent while the share of short term debt was only 10 per cent (Table 20.9). Overtime, the share of long-term debt has further increased with corresponding decrease in the short term debt. In 2004, these respective shares stood at 94 per cent and 6 per cent. Further, within the long-term debt category, multilateral debt occupied the largest percentage share with 25 per cent in 1990 which gradually increased to 32 per cent in 2000 although in 2004 it stood at 26.6 per cent.

Bilateral debt, on the other hand, formed about 17 per cent, increasing gradually to 18.5 per cent in 2000, but decreased to 15 per cent in 2004.

Between government and non-government external debt, there has been a growing tendency in recent years for private external debt to increase. Thus, while the share of government external debt is gradually declining that of private debt is increasing. In 1991, the ratio between government and non-government debt stood at about 60 : 40, which, in 2000 changed to about 48 : 52 and further to 40 : 60 in 2004.

External Debt-GDP Ratio and Other Key Indicators of External Debt in India

Table 20.12 provides useful information about India's sustainability of external debt. The external debt-GDP ratio is the first indicator to suggest to what extent the country's GDP bears its relationship with its external debt. Thus, this ratio which was 28.7 per cent in 1990-91 has been consistently falling and reached 16.7 per cent in 2005-06, although in a next three years it has slightly gone up to 20.5 per cent in 2008-09 (although figure represents partially revised one).

The debt service ratio, which is defined as the proportion of gross debt service payments (interest and principal component) to external current receipts (on current account in the BOP) over the period 1990-91 – 2008-09 shows a consistently falling ratio – from 35.3 per cent in 1990-91 to just 4.4 per cent in 2008-09. This implies that India's debt sustainability (external) has substantially improved over the period. Similarly, India has exhibited a remarkable performance in terms of backing of foreign exchange reserves to total external debt. The ratio of foreign exchange to total external debt was just 7 per cent in 1990-91 which improved to about 55 per cent in 2001-02 and by 2003-04 it reached the level of 100 per cent which means foreign exchange reserves were just equal to the total external debt. By the end of 2007-08, this ratio reached 138 per cent although in the next year, it fell to 112.0 per cent – possibly due to global recession. Thus, by and large, all indicators suggest quite favourable debt sustainability of India.

Lastly, an international comparison of external debt (Table 20.10 and 20.11) suggests that India's position among the list of 20 most indebted countries of the developing world is number seven in 2008 which was eight in 2002 (Table 20.10). From this point of view also India compares favourably well in terms of indebtedness.

Fiscal policy in India: developments in recent years

On fiscal consolidation: The National Democratic Alliance (NDA) government formed at the centre in 2014 attempted several initiatives to strengthen the fiscal position of the government of India. The first such initiative was to prepare a fiscal consolidation roadmap over a medium term. It set fiscal deficit targets for the next few years by: (a) improving the revenue position of the central government, on the one hand, and (b) compressing/revamping government expenditures in several ways on the other. The fiscal deficit targets for the years 2014-15, 2015-16, 2016-17, 2017-18 and 2018-19 were set at 4%, 3.9%, 3.5%, 3.2% and 3% of GDP, respectively. Further, a committee headed by Sri N. K. Singh, the former revenue secretary of the Union Government, was formed to review the Fiscal Responsibility and Budget Management (FRBM) Act of 2003. The Committee has recommended, among other things, reduction of the fiscal deficit to 2.5% of GDP by 2022-23. For first three years, the government successfully stuck to the fiscal deficit targets, in fact, in the first year (2014-15), it improved upon the earlier position by reducing the fiscal deficit from 4.5% to 4.1% to 3.5% as revised subsequently. However, it needs to be mentioned here that there has been fiscal slippage in the fiscal 2017-18 since, now the fiscal deficit numbers stand at 3.5 of GDP instead of 3.2% as shown in the budget for 2018-19. Similarly, for the next fiscal (2018-19) also, while the fiscal target was set at 3%, the estimate in the budget is 3.3%. Thus, in both these years, the fiscal slippage has been to the extent of 0.3 percentage points.

The main reasons cited by the government for not being able to meet the fiscal deficit targets are both: (a) an increased expenditure beyond original budget estimates, and (b) a reduced revenue collections (tax and non-tax revenue) on taxation front. For instance, new development in terms of expenditure in agriculture such as increased minimum support prices (MSP) for more than a dozen agricultural products, health and education and enhanced HRA allowances for central government employees in the budget for 2018-19 are responsible for increase in expenditures. There is no doubt that these expenditures are welcome since our agriculture sector is faced with farmers' distress as much as health and education and hence require focused attention. But the outcome of these expenditures depend on the efficiency and governance quality of these programmes. Secondly, there is a big political compulsion before the government because general election as well as some State elections were due in the year end of 2018 and early 2019.

The central government's revenue collections also sometimes pose problems like shortfall in collections against expected lines. As is well known, the government at the Centre has already rolled out Goods and Service tax (GST) in July, 2017 replacing "Vat "and a number of other indirect taxes. GST is one of the ambitious long awaited fiscal reforms introduced in the country which represents a one nation one tax regime. In spite of initial hiccups of the new tax regime, GST is now reported to be gradually stabilised. However, as reported by government sources, growth targets of GST have remained deficient in majority of State governments. Thus, while the overall deficit for states is reported to be at 13%,some are falling short of targets in the range of 26% to 42% (TOI, Sept. 29, 2018). However, one optimistic note has been expressed in the recent report of the government reducing its public borrowing programme by ₹ 70,000 crore, during the second half of the fiscal 2018-19. However, this is as per government's expectations of additional financial resources from raising the interest rates of several small savings schemes from October 1, 2018. If the trend goes on according to government expectations, one may be hopeful that the government may well be on course to fiscal consolidation path and fiscal deficit target may well be within reach in 2018-19. However, fiscal 2019- 20 has thrown up certain challenges on the fiscal front. The economy has shown signs of "slowdown", growth rate of the economy has gone down to 5% and 4.5% during the first two quarters of fiscal 2019-20. While public expenditures have increased due to tax concessions given to corporate sector in order to prop up demand to fight the slowdown in the economy, government's tax collections have also remained below expectations. The slowing economy may very well be putting pressure on the government to exceed its fiscal deficit target of 3.4% of the GDP.

Any amount of fiscal slippage indicates that the government's borrowing programme will have to be enhanced which means that the market rate of interest will go up thus crowding out the private borrowing for investment. In fact, in recent times, there is evidence of rising yield rates of government securities (September end and early October, 2018) thus signalling that the market is going to bear with higher rate of interest.

Perhaps for this reason, a section of academia in India argues for "flexible" fiscal policy target for the Indian economy (like 3% to 3.5% or 3.5%to 4%) instead of "fixed" targets. This is because, in a country like India, a number of political factors (for instance, expenditure promises in the forthcoming election year), often compel the government to resort to excess expenditures over the budget estimates or, for certain contingent situations, government's actual revenue collections may fall short of expectations. Another instance of such contingent situation is the growth slowdown of the economy as is being experienced by Indian economy (growth rate of the economy has plummeted from 7.5% in 2018 to 5% in 2019-20 on average). Under such unforeseen circumstances, it is prudent on the part of fiscal authority (the government) to set a range of targets so that there is scope for certain flexibility which is practical as well as attainable within the government's resources. Apart from this, in emergent situation like Covid-19, triggering a health emergency around the world, fiscal deficit would, naturally, go up as has happened in India too. Accordingly, as the budget document 2021-22 shows, India's fiscal deficit is estimated to have increased to 9.5% to GDP during 2020-21 fiscal year and is estimated to remain at 6.8% of GDP in 2021-22.

APPENDIX: A. 20

The Salient Features of the FRBM Act (2003)

1. Central Govt. will be taking appropriate measures to reduce the fiscal deficit and revenue deficit so as to eliminate revenue deficit by March 31, 2008 and thereafter build up adequate revenue surplus.
2. Rules will be made under the Act to specify the annual targets for reduction of fiscal deficit and revenue deficit, contingent liabilities and total liabilities.
3. The revenue deficit and fiscal deficit may exceed the targets specified in the rules only on grounds of national security or national calamity or such other exceptional grounds as the Central Government may specify.
4. The Central Government shall not borrow from the Reserve Bank of India except by way of advances to meet temporary excess of cash disbursement over cash receipts.
5. Reserve Bank of India will not subscribe to the primary issues of the Central Government securities from the year 2006-07.
6. Central Government will be taking suitable measures to ensure greater transparency in its fiscal operations.
7. Central Government is to lay in each financial year before both Houses of Parliament three statements, viz., Medium Term Fiscal Policy Statement, Fiscal Policy Strategy Statement and Macroeconomic Framework Statement and Demands for Grants.
8. The Finance Minister is to make a quarterly review of trends in receipts and expenditure in relation to the budget and place the review before both Houses of Parliament.

Source: Economic Survey, 2003-04 page 36 and Economic Survey 2011-12. www.indiabudget.com (Budget 2021-22).

SUMMARY

1. Fiscal policy refers to a set of government policies relating to government expenditure, taxation, and management of public debt.
2. Fiscal policy objectives are various – raising adequate resources for the government finance (tax and non-tax revenues), carrying out various types of expenditures-revenue and capital expenditures, developmental and non-developmental expenditure for meeting the various short-term and long-term objectives of the government programmes and for overall development of the economy.
3. While fiscal policy might necessitate incurring public debt – both internal and external – it aims at formulating and adopting such concurrent policies to manage them.

4. Fiscal policy has the direct impact on the aggregate demand of the economy. It can raise aggregate demand if public expenditures are increased and/or taxes are lowered. Similarly, it can reduce aggregate demand in case public expenditures are reduced and/or taxes are raised. Thus, the transmission mechanism in case of fiscal policy is more direct than that of monetary policy.
5. Different schools of thought, however, have differed with regard to the role of fiscal policy on the economy. While classical economists believed that role of fiscal policy is limited and taxes should, therefore, be raised in a manner that their burdens on citizens are minimum, the Keynesian economists have emphasized the more active role of the fiscal policy. In fact, in Keynes' view, fiscal policy can be used as an instrument of economic development. The monetarists and more recent new-classical thinking (revivalists of old classicals) again do not attach much importance to fiscal policy. To them, monetary policy is a much more effective tool in the management of the economy.
6. Fiscal policy may be long-term or short-term. Often the long-term goals of fiscal policy are suitably phased out and incorporated in the short-term policy which is mainly reflected through annual budgets of the government.
7. There are different concepts of deficits: budget deficit, fiscal deficit, revenue deficit and primary deficit. These concepts carry useful meanings and importance from practical points of view. Of these, the most important concept is the 'fiscal deficit' which truly captures the overall deficit in the government budget. A rising deficit indicates government's increasing burden of managing the economy by incurring borrowing and debt.

   Revenue deficit is the indication of excess expenditures on government's normal functions over the revenues collected by taxes and other sources. Primary deficit is the fiscal deficit minus interest payments.
8. A prudent fiscal policy is the one with minimum fiscal deficit – generally not above 4-5 per cent of GDP and revenue deficit being either zero or surplus in place of deficit.
9. In underdeveloped countries, it is often not possible to achieve fiscal consolidation due to a variety of reasons. Some of the public expenditure items are pressing and committed on political grounds for which deficits become unavoidable.
10. Fiscal policy in India followed in the immediately post-independence years was marked by high budgetary deficits, low level of taxation and high borrowings by the government with high level of external debt. Deficit financing – financing budget deficit by taking loans from

Reserve Bank of India and consequent monetization of deficit ruled the first few decades of public finance policy in India.

11. Structural reforms policy started in India in early 1990s ushered in paradigm shift in economic policy regime with liberalized policy in major areas including management of public finance. Reforms in taxation and public expenditure policy with focus on reduction of fiscal and other deficits were initiated. During 1990s, while the structure of tax-rates was rationalized, public expenditures were aimed more and more towards efficiency lines.
12. In early 2000, a new regime in fiscal policy management started with the enactment of Fiscal Responsibility and Budget Management Act, 2003 which required, mandatorily, on the part of the government to reduce fiscal deficit to manageable level and gradually reducing revenue deficit to zero and turn into revenue surplus by 2008. The government have been trying hard to achieve these targets and have substantially succeeded. But recession in the global economy with certain impacts on Indian economy necessitated fiscal stimulus to be taken by the government resulting in higher level of public expenditures and reduction of tax revenues, particularly during last phase of 2000-2010.
13. Public debt management is another area of fiscal policy. In India, as in other countries, public debt consists of internal and external debt. Internal debt consists of government's internal borrowings and other liabilities while external debts are of various kinds and from various sources mainly multilateral and bilateral sources and of long-term and short-term category. During the 1990s, as the evidence suggests, the proportion of internal debt (in terms of total internal liabilities) has been varying around 90 per cent and is gradually on the increase. Thus, most of the public debt in India is of internal category. As far as external debt is concerned, the share of long- term debt is more than 80 per cent while that of the short-term debt is correspondingly lower. There is comparatively less risk of India's sovereign debt. A good proportion of external debt is of concessional debt. Besides, certain debt sustainability indicators suggest that debt-GDP ratio is comparatively low and not alarming. Similarly, debt-service ratio has been consistently falling and stands presently at satisfactorily low level (4.4 per cent). India, presently is the seventh most indebted country in a list of twenty most indebted countries.

EXERCISE

1. Examine the role of fiscal policy in the present-day economic administration of the government.

2. Distinguish between 'expansionary' and 'contractionary' fiscal policies and examine their relative importance in upswing and downswing of business cycles.
3. During which period of time in recent history, did fiscal policy assume significance?
4. Examine the main objectives of fiscal policy.
5. What do you understand by 'public good'. Enumerate the main categories of public goods provided by the governments of different countries. Examine also their relative importance in the public expenditure policy of the government.
6. Distinguish between the following concepts with examples from the Indian budget:
   (a) Fiscal deficit and revenue deficit,
   (b) Fiscal deficit and primary deficit,
   (c) Revenue expenditure and capital expenditure,
   (d) Revenue deficit and effective revenue deficit,
   (e) Revenue receipts and capital receipts.
7. On the basis of Table 20.2, examine the trends of different types of deficits of Indian economy.
8. Examine the trend of tax-GDP ratio of India in recent years.
9. What do you understand by 'public debt'? What are the different categories of public debt?
10. Explain the concept of 'automatic stabiliser' and point out the views of different schools of thought on the importance of automatic stabiliser.

REFERENCES

1. G. Ackley, Macroeconomics: Theory and Policy, Macmillan, New York, USA, 1978.
2. G.N. Mankiw, Macroeconomics, 6th Edition, Worth Publishers, 2006.
3. G.N. Mankiw, Principles of Macroeconomics, 5th Edition, South Western Cengage Learning, 2008.
4. Government of India, Union Budget and Economic Surveys, 2011-12 and subsequent years available in ww.irdiabudget.gov.in
5. John Slowman, Economics, Prentice Hall, London, 1991.
6. Government Budget of India, 2021-22 of India.
7. RBI, www.rbi.org.in

References

1. Abheek Barua (2020), Broken Into Chain Stores, The Economic Times, March 13.
2. Ackley, Gardner, Macroeconomics: Theory and Policy, Macmillan, New York, 1978.
3. Asian Development Bank (ADB), "Global Food Price Inflation and Developing Asia", reported in The Economic Times, April 27, 2011.
4. Basu, Kaushik (2020), Economic policy must account for varied effects of epidemics, Mint, March 12.
5. Baumol, W.J., Economic Theory and Operations Analysis, Prentice Hall, 1971.
6. Baumol, W.J. and Alan Blinder, Principles of Macreconomy, Cengage Learning USA, 2009.
7. Bhaduri, A., Macroeconomics, Macmillan, India, 1990.
8. Bloomberg Report, (2020), Recession Risk is Real ...., Mint, March 18, 2020.
9. Buiter, Williem H. (2020), Abolish cash to get a large economy expanding swiftly, Mint February 26.
10. Chetan Ahya (2019), We are moving from globalisation to slowbalisation, The Economic Times, June 12.
11. Chhibber, Ajay (2020), Don't Shoot from the Hip, The Economic Times, March, 3.
12. Crouch, R.L., Macroeconomics, Harcourt Brace Jovanovitch, 1972.
13. Deepak Nayyar (2020), Failing health of globalisation: Covid-19 blow to a stressed order, Mint, March 13.
14. Dehejia, Vivek, (2020), The convergence of rich nations with the rest has gone off the track, Mint, 27 January.
15. Duesenberry, J., Income, Saving and the Theory of Consumer Behaviour, Cambridge, Mass., 1949.
16. Dutta, LN. (2014), A Textbook of Modern Macroeconomics, IK International Publishing House, New Delhi.
17. Ferber, R., "Household Behaviour", in Surveys of Economic Theory, Vol. III, MacMillan, 1967.

18. Gang, Fan, "Chinese Economy's Secret Recipe", Mint, Delhi, July 8, 2010.
19. Giradi, Daniel (2017), Old and New Formulations of the Neoclassical Theory of Aggregate Investment: A Critical Review, Working Paper 2017-03, February. Department of Economics, University of Massachusetts, Amherst.
20. Government of India, Union Budget and Economic Surveys 2002-03 and subsequent years till 2011-12 available in http.//www.indiabudget.nic.in.
21. Hoover, Kevin D., "New Classical Macroeconomics", http.//www.econlib.org/library/Enc/NewClassicalmacroeconomics.html.
22. Jorgenson, D. W. (1963/1967), Capital Theory and Investment Behaviour, nber.org (PDF).
23. Klein, LR (1969), An Introduction to Econometrics, Prentice Hall, India.
24. Krugman, Paul., "Third Drepression is Looking Real", The Economic Times, June 29, 2010.
25. Leijonhufvud, A., "Preventing Financial Instability", Mint, Delhi, July 16, 2009.
26. Lipsey, R., An Introduction to Positive Economics, ELBS, Edition, 1969.
27. Mankiw, G.N., "Macroeconomics, 6th Edition, Worth Publishers, 2006.
28. Mankiw, Gregory, N., "Are we all Keynesians again", Mint Delhi, September 23, 2009.
29. Mankiw, N. Gregory, Principles of Macroeconomics, 5th Edition, South Western Cengage Learning, 2008.
30. Meier, G.M. and R.E. Baldwin, Economic Development: Theory, History, Policy, Asia Publishing House, Bombay, 1964.
31. Moorthy, Vivek., "The Neglected part of Fisher", Mint Delhi, March 3, 2009.
32. Nassim Nicholas Taleb (2007), The Black Swan: The Impact of the Highly Improbable, Random House, USA, Allen Lane, UK.
33. Pankaj Mishra (2020), The Covid pandemic will revive the idea of an all powerful state, Mint, March 23.
34. Parker, Jeffrey (2010), Theories of Investment Expenditures, www.reed.edu.
35. R. Dornbush, Stanley Fischer and R. Startz, Macroeconomics, 9th Edition, McGraw Hill, USA, 2009.
36. Rajadhyaksha, Niranjan, (2020), Covid-19, O-rings and the worry over supply chain disruptions, Mint, February, 26:

37. __________ (2020), The potential impact of Covid-19 on the cost of capital up ahead, May 13.
38. __________ (2020), Time for the orchestrated use of three different economic levers, Mint, December 4, 2019.
39. Rajrishi Singhal (2020), A Revolution is due but don't hold your breath just yet, Mint, July 19, 2020.
40. Rakshit M., "Inflation and Relative Prices in 2006-10: Some Analytical and Policy Issues:, Economic and Political Weekly, April 16-22, 2011.
41. Reserve Bank of India, Different publications, available at http.//www.rbi/scripts/publications.
42. Rodrick, Dani (2020), The Choices we make will shape the post-pandemic world, Mint, May, 14.
43. ______ and Stefani Stantcheva (2020). A redesigned social contract for altered post-pandemic realities, Mint, June, 16.
44. Roubini, Nouriel (2020a), The white swans that could set off the next major global crisis, Mint, February 24.
45. Roubini, Nuriel., "A Global Perfect Storm", Mint Delhi, June 18, 2012.
46. Roubini, Nuriel., "How to Prevent a Great Depression", Mint Delhi, October 3, 2011.
47. Roubini, Nuriel and Stephen Mihm, Crisis Economics, Allen Lane, Penguine Group, USA, 2010(a).
48. _______ (2020b), The Great Depression that we might be staring at this decade, Mint, April 30.
49. Ruchir Sharma (2020), The Pandemic Isn't Changing Everything ..., The Times of India, May 5.
50. Salvatore, D., International Economics, John Wiley & Sons, 7th Edition, 2001.
51. Schwab, Klaus (2020), Let us prepare for the Great Reset of modern capitalism, Mint, June 5,.
52. Shapiro, E., Macroeconomic Analysis, Second Edition, Harcourt Brace Johanovitch, 1970.
53. Sharma, Ruchir (2016), The New Population Bomb, The Times of India, March 14.
54. Sharma, Ruchir (2020), Can Coronavirus Cause a Recession? The Times of India, March 2.
55. Slowman J.; Economics, Prentice Hall, London, 1991.
56. Stiglitz Joseph., "Developing Countries and Global Crisis", The Economic Times, New Delhi, April 20, 2009.
57. Stiglitz Joseph., "The End of Neo-Liberalism", The Economic Times, New Delhi, July 14, 2008.

58. Swaminathan S. Anklesaria Aiyar (2020), Recession to Get Viral, The Economic Times, March 13.
59. The Economist, "A Special Report on Future of Food", February 26-March 4, 2011.
60. The Economist, "Europe's Rescue Plan" (A Report), October 29, 2011.
61. The Economist, "Greece's Debt Crisis: Bail-out 2.0", June 11, 2011.
62. Varsha S. Kulkarni and Raghav Gauhar (2020), Inequality is an Economic Drag, The Economic Times, 21 January.
63. Weintraub, A., Eli Schwartz, J.R. Aronson (eds.), The Economic Growth Controversy, Macmillan, USA, 1973.
64. Yahya, Chetan, "The Origin of India's Inflation Problem:, The Economic Times, February 10, 2011.

Index

O

P

Q

R

S

T

U

V

W

Y